COUDERT
BROTHERS

COUDERT
BROTHERS
A LEGACY IN LAW

*The History of America's First
International Law Firm
1853–1993*

VIRGINIA KAYS VEENSWIJK

WITH AN INTRODUCTION BY
LOUIS AUCHINCLOSS

TRUMAN TALLEY BOOKS/DUTTON
NEW YORK

TRUMAN TALLEY BOOKS/DUTTON
Published by the Penguin Group
Penguin Books USA Inc., 375 Hudson Street,
New York, New York 10014, U.S.A.
Penguin Books Ltd, 27 Wrights Lane, London W8 5TZ, England
Penguin Books Australia Ltd, Ringwood, Victoria, Australia
Penguin Books Canada Ltd, 10 Alcorn Avenue,
Toronto, Ontario, Canada M4V 3B2
Penguin Books (N.Z.) Ltd, 182-190 Wairau Road,
Auckland 10, New Zealand

Penguin Books Ltd, Registered Offices:
Harmondsworth, Middlesex, England

First published by Truman Talley Books/Dutton an imprint of Dutton Signet,
a division of Penguin Books USA Inc.
Distributed in Canada by McClelland & Stewart Inc.

First Printing, April, 1994
10 9 8 7 6 5 4 3 2 1

LIBRARY OF CONGRESS CATALOGING-IN-PUBLICATION DATA:
Veenswijk, Virginia Kays.
   Coudert Brothers : A Legacy in Law: the history of America's first international
   law firm 1853–1993
   / Virginia Kays Veenswijk : with an introduction by Louis Auchincloss.
      p. cm.
   Includes bibliographical reference and index.
   ISBN 0-525-93585-1 : $30.00
   1. Coudert Brothers—History.   2. Law firms—New York (N.Y.)—
History.   3.Lawyers—New York (N.Y.)—Biography.   I. Title.
KF355.N4V43   1993
340'.06'07471—dc20   92-38682
                                                                        CIP

Printed in the United States of America
Set in Baskerville
Designed by Eve L. Kirch

CONTENTS

INTRODUCTION

by Louis Auchincloss

Because I once contemplated writing a novel in the form of one of those privately written histories, compiled by a revered and retired partner, of a great New York law firm, I made it my business to read all such as were available. I'm afraid that I found poring through them a sufficiently tedious business. That, of course, was not the fault of their authors. They were not written for outsiders. They were written for those more intimately concerned with the litigations and corporate reorganizations involved and who would presumably not be put off by the hagiographic treatment of deceased partners. But my project for a novel did not survive my research.

The story of Coudert Brothers, however, is something like the book I intended to write. It reads like a rich, adventure-filled, multigenerational novel.

Of course, the author started with two decided advantages over the historian of less exotic firms. She had the fascinating factor of a continuing family control, the remarkable survival of great legal talent through several generations. The firm was started in 1857 by three brothers, Frederic René, Charles, and Louis Leonce Coudert, continued after Frederic René's death in 1903 under the aegis of his son Frederic and his nephew Paul Fuller, Jr., and after Frederic's death in 1955 under that of his three sons "Fritz," Alexis, and Ferdinand, until 1966 when executive control was transferred from the family to a five-man committee (on which sat two Couderts). The story of such a family intertwined with the hundred-year story of the firm that dominated their lives provides a centralizing interest not available to the annalists of other partnerships.

The second advantage for the Coudert historian is the international nature of the firm's practice, from its representation of the French consulate in New York during the Second Empire to today, when it has offices abroad in Paris, London, Brussels, Moscow, Tokyo, Hong Kong, Singapore, Sydney, Beijing, Shanghai, and São Paulo. Charles Coudert, father of Frederic René, was an ardent Bonapartist who had been condemned to death in 1824 in the "White Terror" of Louis XVIII, but who had managed to escape to America where he later befriended the exiled Louis Napoleon, future emperor, thus establishing a transatlantic connection never to be broken.

The history of the firm is inextricably intertwined with that of U.S. foreign relations. The post–Spanish War expropriation cases involving the seizure of assets of Spanish nationals in Cuba, largely lost by Coudert representing the latter, became precedents for victories when Coudert acted for the British government in the First World War. We find Frederic René battling in 1893 to extend the concept of the three-mile limit to save the seals in the Bering Sea from extinction and, three years later, again in London, using all his diplomatic as well as legal skills to arbitrate the dangerously explosive border dispute between Venezuela and British Guiana. We learn of his son Frederic's long and successful fight to establish the civil rights of the "nationals" (not yet citizens) in the islands taken over from Spain and of the essential role he played in pushing the manufacture and transport of aircraft to Britain in 1940. And this book clears up the tangled tale of Coudert's representation of the Banque de France in the German seizure of Belgian gold stored in the bank, which rumormongers claimed smacked of "Vichyism." A cited letter dated December 30, 1944, from General de Gaulle to Coudert Brothers, congratulating the firm for its skillful handling of the matter, should put an end to such talk. If the general was a Vichyite, then we all are.

In time, the firm—to survive in the competitive post–World War II era of enormously burgeoning law firms—had to expand its practice from international matters, litigation, and estates (the "big three" of the early years) to represent major corporations and had to double and redouble the number of its lawyers. But a distinct individuality, a public spirit, and a high ethical tone were always preserved, and the flavor of these is aptly caught in this history.

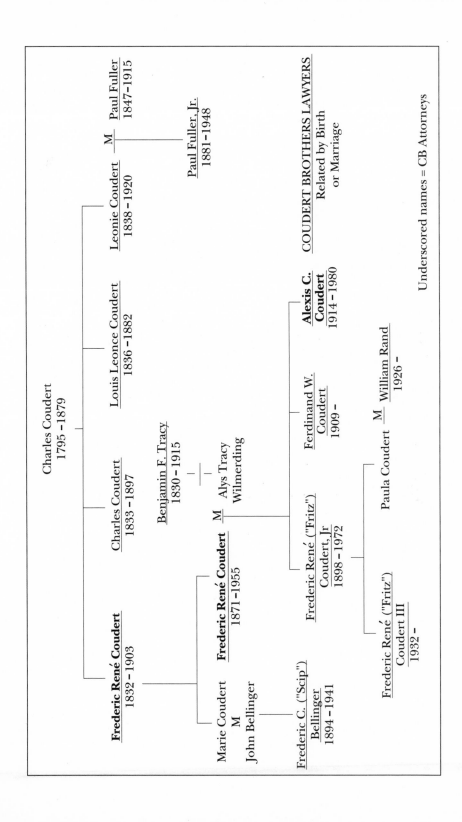

Charles Coudert
1795 –1879

Frederic René Coudert
1832 –1903

Charles Coudert
1833 – 1897

Louis Leonce Coudert
1836 – 1882

Leonie Coudert
1838 – 1920

M

Paul Fuller
1847–1915

Paul Fuller, Jr.
1881–1948

Benjamin F. Tracy
1830 –1915

M Alys Tracy
Wilmerding

Frederic René Coudert
1871–1955

Marie Coudert
M
John Bellinger

Frederic René ("Fritz")
Coudert, Jr
1898 –1972

Ferdinand W.
Coudert
1909 –

Alexis C.
Coudert
1914 –1980

Frederic C. ("Scip")
Bellinger
1894 –1941

Paula Coudert

M

William Rand
1926 –

Frederic René ("Fritz")
Coudert III
1932 –

COUDERT BROTHERS LAWYERS
Related by Birth
or Marriage

Underscored names = CB Attorneys

COUDERT
BROTHERS

Chapter One

PÈRE ET FILS

O n September 6, 1876, Union Square, then one of the most fashionable areas in New York City, was *en fête*. Thousands of people had crowded into the park to witness the unveiling of a statue of the Marquis de Lafayette, the hero of both the American and the French revolutions. The French tricolor and Old Glory waved in the bright sunshine, and the rooftops and windows around the square were filled with New Yorkers of all ranks and distinctions. They had a long wait ahead of them, for because of confusion among the event's organizers, the ceremonies began two hours late.

Even then, the proceedings went anything but smoothly. First, the French consul general, Edmund de Breteuil, presented the statue as a gift from France to the citizens of New York. But unfortunately, or so the newspapers reported the next day, M. de Breteuil's voice was inaudible just a few feet away from the speakers stand. Next the mayor of New York, an undistinguished Tammany Hall politician, came forward to accept France's gift. His speech was to follow the playing of "La Marseillaise" by the military bands. Apparently not familiar with that noble anthem, the mayor plunged into his remarks just as some of the bands roused themselves for a last chorus. Drowned out by the music, his words, too, had to be accepted on faith by his audience.

The French sculptor Auguste Bartholdi, who had been in a state of panic for months over the slapdash American attitude toward the installation of his statue, must have felt something akin to despair at this point. *Lafayette* was important to him not only in itself but as the opening salvo in his campaign to win New York City's support for the colossal statue he hoped to erect in its harbor—the *Statue of Liberty*. In France, the fund-raising campaign for this visionary project had already begun, and Bartholdi had been counting on the dedication of *Lafayette* to reveal his artistic genius to the populace of New York and enlist mass support for his *Liberty*. As the belated *Lafayette* ceremonies limped on, however, the strain on the crowd's patience boded poorly for Bartholdi's public relations campaign.

Nonetheless, the raising of the gigantic American flag that had covered *Lafayette* was met with prolonged cheers. And the crowd settled down good-humoredly enough for the speaker whom they had really come to hear—Frederic René Coudert.

The senior partner in the New York law firm of Coudert Brothers, Coudert was a forty-four-year-old lawyer whose professional eloquence had already earned him considerable public fame. "To listen to him was to be charmed," said one contemporary, and his clear, musical voice could reach without apparent strain even the farthest ranks of a massive open-air gathering such as that at Union Square in 1876.

Having delivered his first public address at the age of eighteen, Coudert had by 1876 been charming New York audiences for years, and no one knew better than he how to capture and hold their attention. As a lawyer he excelled in the orderly exposition of facts, mustering them into a strong line of argument, but as a public speaker he was too experienced to serve up that kind of fare on Lafayette's birthday to the vast throng standing, jammed elbow to elbow, in Union Square. No text of his speech survives, but the newspaper reports show that Coudert went immediately and swiftly to the hearts of his audience, giving them sentiment, unabashed patriotic sentiment.

He gained his first applause with a glowing review of America's progress in the century since it had won its independence. Then, gesturing toward a nearby statue of George Washington, Coudert conjured up Lafayette from his grave and, with more than a touch of Victorian pathos, imagined him choosing to face through eternity his mentor and friend. This being New York City in 1876, the majority of Coudert's audience were probably Irish and German immigrants holding only the vaguest notion of who Lafayette had been; but most everyone had at least heard of Washington, and that name drew, as Coudert must have expected, automatic applause. Coudert then envisioned Lafayette and Washington receiving Abraham Lincoln into heaven with open arms, and the crowd—with vivid memories of the president martyred scarcely more than a decade previously—responded warmly. It only remained for Coudert to add that Lafayette, looking at America that day, would have felt with Lincoln "charity for all and malice toward none"—a thinly veiled jibe at the Republican policies of Reconstruction, which were anathema in the overwhelmingly Democratic city of New York—and he had won his audience completely.

From then on, to the punctuation of frequent applause, Coudert felt free to elaborate on his theme of why Lafayette should be remembered—as one who had "served the cause of freedom"—and he concluded with a stirring tribute to France. One newspaper quoted him as exclaiming at his climax, "Generous, chivalrous—if you will, quixotic—France"; another reporter took down the phrase as "loving, cheerful—impetuous, if you please—characteristic France!" But everyone agreed it had been a terrific speech. Despite the ceremony's floundering start, the *New York Herald* declared that it had ended up "an event in the history of New York long to be remembered."

After all his months of nervousness and worry, Bartholdi could relax and enjoy the rest of his visit to New York, for "the spectacular inauguration of *Lafayette* commanded serious recognition of his project for the harbor." From that date forward, partly through Coudert's continuing help, the French artist's vision of the *Statue of Liberty* would move closer and closer to reality.

If the peak of Bartholdi's career was yet ahead of him in 1876, so, too, was the high point of Coudert's. Although already successful, Coudert was well known in 1876 only in his native New York. It was over the next two and a half decades that his name would emerge on the national scene as the representative of the United States in a number of important international arbitrations, as the friend and counselor of a U.S. president, as a frequent contributor to the serious national periodicals, and, of course, as a speaker popular far outside the precincts of Manhattan. His admirers would try, unavailingly, to persuade him to run for the U.S. Senate and to accept a major diplomatic post, and he would turn down several offers of nomination to the U.S. Supreme Court. In fact, to borrow a tribute once paid to the British statesman Lord Esher, Coudert's ability was ultimately to be measured not by the offices he held but by those he refused.

The excuse Coudert invariably gave whenever he declined a public office was the demands of his legal practice. This reason was not the whole truth, but it was certainly part of the truth, for as

Coudert personally went from strength to strength during the next twenty-five years, so did the firm of Coudert Brothers. In 1876 it conducted a busy enough practice, serviced by three partners—Coudert and his younger brothers Charles junior and Louis Leonce—and at least three associates. By Frederic René Coudert's death in 1903, the number of lawyers in the firm had more than doubled, making Coudert Brothers one of the largest law firms in America. What is more important, it had developed from a New York law office that happened to have an extensive list of foreign clients into a truly international law firm, the first of its kind. Operating on an international scale and emphasizing the practice of private and public international law, Coudert Brothers had by then five offices, three of them overseas.

In 1876 Coudert Brothers was just on the verge of this expansion, it being not quite three years later that the partners opened their first foreign office, the Paris branch known as Coudert Frères. The most successful of all the firm's early branches, the Paris office would prosper to such an extent that Coudert Brothers would be identified thereafter, until quite recently, as a predominantly French-American law firm.

It is this close association with France that renders Frederic René Coudert's remarks on September 6, 1876, particularly interesting, for they represent his first public address on the subject of France—or the first, at any rate, of which we have a record. Moreover, it seems peculiarly fitting that the specific topic of his speech was Lafayette, not merely because the Revolutionary War general endures as a powerful symbol of French-American amity but because Lafayette had a real influence on the fortunes of the Coudert family. In his youth Charles Coudert, the father of the Coudert brothers, fell under the spell of the revolutionary nobleman with results that dramatically altered the family's history. Frederic René Coudert did not refer to this in his speech; no doubt he judged it not the time or place. But if we could conjure Frederic René Coudert up from his grave and ask him where the history of Coudert Brothers properly begins, it is not unlikely that he would respond, "With Lafayette."

The place where the paths of the Marquis de Lafayette and Charles Coudert crossed was France. The time was 1821, the sixth year of the Bourbon Restoration and a bad year for liberals like Lafayette. Louis XVIII was ruling France as a constitutional monarch, but the Ultraroyalist faction—so-called because they were more conservative than the king—dominated the Chamber of Deputies. Their control of the government had already allowed the

Ultraroyalists to increase the electoral power of landed noble families and to impose restrictions on the press. A full agenda of laws restoring special privileges to the nobility and clergy, at the expense of the middle class, was expected.

Lafayette, who had been only nineteen when he volunteered his sword to the American rebels, was now sixty-three years old, but he had not lost—and never would—the revolutionary fervor kindled in his youth. The role he had played in the American and French revolutions had earned him enormous prestige among his countrymen, and this prestige he deployed against the Ultraroyalists. Openly, from his seat in the Chamber of Deputies, Lafayette opposed the reactionary group. In secret, the former general did more: he encouraged and joined in the plots of the *carbonari*—the underground conspirators pledged to achieve constitutional government and the rights of man through agitation and, if possible, revolution.

One of the men swayed by Lafayette's influence into joining a *carbonari* conspiracy in 1821 was Charles Coudert, a headstrong twenty-five-year-old cavalry officer of high ideals. Despite his relatively young age, Coudert was a battle-experienced veteran of the Napoleonic Wars. And while it was the marquis who drew him into the plot, it appears that Coudert was willing to be recruited principally because the plotters aimed at replacing Louis XVIII with Napoleon's son, known as the king of Rome. For young Coudert was neither a republican nor an anticleric like Lafayette, but an ardent Bonapartist.

Born in Bordeaux, France, on December 27, 1795, Charles Coudert grew up in those exciting times when Napoleon was conferring glory upon France, extending its power far across Europe. His parents were Jean and Anne Laffe Coudert, prosperous members of the middle class. At one time the editor of a news sheet, the *Bulletin General de Bordeaux et du Dep. de la Gironde,* his father eventually became a professor at a secondary school in Bordeaux, and his mother was also evidently highly educated, for Charles often spoke of her as a *maîtresse femme.* This couple provided Charles and his brothers with a good education and apparently encouraged their patriotic fervor, not only allowing Charles and his brother Victor to volunteer for Napoleon's cavalry, but furnishing both boys with the horses, uniforms, and equipment needed for service in the Guard of Honor, the so-called "Young Guard." Thus, at age seventeen, "fired with enthusiasm" for the emperor and eager to share in France's glory, Charles reported for duty on July 3, 1813, to the guard's Third Regiment.

Yet in 1813 Napoleon's years of glory were all but finished.

Coudert was just in time to miss the triumphs and to participate instead in the tragedies of the 1813–14 campaign with its inconclusive engagements and mounting losses and desertion. Among the major battles in which Coudert fought, for example, was the Battle of Leipzig, a three-day struggle in October 1813 so bloody that the Germans called it the *Völkerschlacht*—the Slaughter of the Nations. Fired upon by their own allies, fighting without ammunition, blown up and drowned in their retreat, the French army of 115,000 men suffered 55,000 losses. Charles's brother Victor left a leg behind on the battlefield, and Charles himself took an Austrian lancehead in his right arm. Still, the Coudert brothers were among the ragged typhus-infested survivors who reached France weeks later. The typhus apparently bypassed Charles, his wound healed after a fashion, and in February 1814 he fought again at Montereau and Montmiral as the Allies advanced on Paris. In April, Napoleon abdicated, and Coudert, refusing a lieutenant's commission offered by the new Bourbon king, was discharged in July 1814. He was eighteen years old, the holder of the Grand Cross of the Legion of Honor awarded for his bravery at Leipzig.

For the rest of his life Coudert had some disability in that wounded arm, but he bore his scars proudly, and he also treasured another memento—a portrait of the emperor on horseback that he had received from Napoleon's own hands. The futility of bloodshed he had seen, which he was more than intelligent enough to recognize, made no difference to his loyalties. If anything, the crucible through which he had passed only increased their strength. Like so many other veterans of Napoleon's Guard of Honor, he would hold fast to his enthusiasm for Bonaparte for the rest of his days.

Indeed, upon Napoleon's return from exile in 1815, Coudert petitioned for a rank in a light cavalry regiment, stating that "my sole ambition is a glorious death for the Emperor and my country." Perhaps fortunately for him, however, the sought-after commission did not materialize quickly enough for him to participate in the Waterloo campaign and Napoleon's final defeat the next month. A year later, by no means reconciled to the Bourbon restoration but apparently missing the military life, Coudert enlisted as a private in a cavalry regiment. He was promoted rapidly to corporal and then sergeant, despite his Bonapartist convictions, and in January 1821 he was sent to study at the elite cavalry school at Saumur. Coudert later said that when he returned to Saumur as a cavalry veteran, he had thought he was a good rider, but he had to unlearn there all he knew and start again. Meanwhile, the years of peace slipped past, apparently without incident. But Coudert was obviously following the course of political events, disturbed by what he saw. Then he was recruited into the *carbonari,* and his life turned upside down.

There were at least half a dozen conspiracies afoot in the last months of 1821, as the opposition, deprived by the new election law of any hope of gaining power by legal means, resorted to revolution. By the standards of our terrorist-ridden age, however, both the *carbonari* and the *Chevaliers de la Liberté,* with which they were linked in the west of France, were hopelessly amateurish in their planning. Far too many people were involved in their plots, dooming them all to betrayal, whether deliberate or accidental. In the case of the *coup d'état* on behalf of the king of Rome in which Coudert was involved, betrayal came in both forms.

The date of the uprising organized by the cell in Saumur was set for December 26, 1821. On the eighteenth of that month, two noncommissioned officers informed General Gentil-Saint-Alphonse that some kind of conspiracy seemed to be afoot among the students at Saumur; the general did not take this revelation too seriously, but did pass the report on to his superior officer. Then on the twenty-fourth of December, the home of a merchant in Saumur caught fire, and the students from the military school turned out to fight the blaze. One of these was killed when a burning wall collapsed, and on his corpse were found documents confirming the details of the plot.

By Christmas morning, thirty-five to forty junior officers and noncommissioned officers had been arrested. A Lieutenant Delon managed to escape, but ten others—seven students from Saumur, including Coudert, and three officers from the Tours garrison—were turned over to the military tribunal in Tours. For two months they were held in the Tours dungeons while the authorities conducted their interrogations, trying to discover the names of the leaders organizing the *carbonari.* Suspicion floated freely around Lafayette, but his young accomplices did not betray him, and he remained safe behind the redoubt of his impregnable name and position.

Finally, on February 20, 1822, the court-martial convened. The trial of the ten prisoners and of the fugitive Delon, who was tried in absentia, lasted over six days, but the judges took only forty-five minutes on February 28 to determine their verdict. Two men were acquitted, six given prison sentences, and three—Delon, a young officer named Sirejean, and the twenty-six-year-old Coudert—were condemned to die. It was expected that Sirejean and Coudert would be executed on or shortly after March 8, the day a review board would meet and seal their death sentences.

There followed a race against time to save Coudert's life, some details of which might seem implausibly romantic if they were not documented by a number of sources, the liveliest of which are the memoirs of Laure Junot, the Duchesse d'Abrantès. One of *"les grandes amoureuses romantiques"* of the Napoleonic era, d'Abrantès had lost her fortune in the ruins of the empire—but she kept her friends and played a leading role in Restoration society. She knew everybody and everything, and, though she was not averse to a bit of embroidery where it would help her story and was innocent of any hint of objectivity, her memoirs remain among the most illuminating of the period.

As she tells the story, then, Charles Coudert was visited very shortly after his sentencing by his elder brother, Eugene, who had become head of the family upon their father's death. Eugene Coudert wept and railed against the judges, but Charles had no time to waste on emotion. Under the spur of death, he remained coolheaded and he saw a chance—a slim chance—of reprieve. "Go find Madame Récamier," the prisoner urged his brother. Récamier, the perennial leader of the Paris salons, was at this time in about the same position as her friend d'Abrantès—middle-aged but still fascinating to men, impoverished but rich in connections to those in power. Although she remained a liberal at heart, her current lover was the conservative politician and author René de Chateaubriand and one of the habitués of her salon was Mathieu de Montmorency, a leading Ultraroyalist cabinet member.

Revealing either that he had received good advice from some unknown interested party or that he had remarkable knowledge of the political currents in the Paris salons, Coudert pinned his hopes on Récamier's friendship with Montmorency. *"Il est premier ministre . . . il est tout puissant!"* Charles is alleged to have told his brother. "He is first minister . . . he is all powerful. . . . she can see to everything through him."

Eugene needed no further urging. He hastened away from Saumur toward Paris and the convent of Abbaye-au-Bois. Récamier was then living in one of the rooms on the convent's upper floor, which the nuns rented out to indigent ladies of good character, but she received her guests on the second floor in a spacious uncarpeted salon lined with an assortment of chairs and *bergères*. It was here that Eugene found Récamier on March 1 or 2. He was accompanied by the wife of General Donadieu, an Ultraroyalist deputy from Bouches-du-Rhône. She went along not to perform the introductions—Madame Donadieu was a complete stranger to Madame Récamier—but to support Eugene, who was close to total collapse.

According to d'Abrantès, Eugene staggered into Récamier's presence, so distraught that he immediately fell on his knees, weeping and sobbing, "Save him! Save my brother!" Récamier had him lie upon her chaise longue and attempted to restore him to his senses. But he would not be calmed, and his contribution to the interview consisted mostly of the repetition of these same phrases.

Fortunately, there was also present at this encounter Pierre-Simon Ballanche, who was at the time perhaps better known for his adoration of Récamier than for his literary talents. A conservative in his political views, Ballanche was also a devout Christian with strong convictions about the universal brotherhood of man. This charitable man announced that he was acquainted with Charles Coudert and that, although they differed politically, he would do his utmost to save the younger man's life. Récamier then affirmed her willingness to help, too, but noted regretfully that Montmorency, who normally arrived at her salon at 4:30 in the afternoon, was not expected on this particular day. "But you can trust me to do everything I can to save your brother," she said with emotion, and Eugene was sent away somewhat reassured. Still, Montmorency did not appear the next day either, and so, two days later, on March 3 or 4, Récamier completed an artful toilette and set off, escorted by Ballanche, to pay some calls herself. First, the couple stopped to meet with the review board official who would sign the death warrant, but he proved impervious to her charms, and they ordered their carriage on to the home of Montmorency. To her shock and distress, here Récamier again found that her entreaties were in vain. Her great friend Montmorency, on whom every hope depended, was not only disobliging but inflexible. "Madame Récamier," he told the Comte de Castellane irritably, when that peer showed up a short time later on the same errand, "is very wrong to try to make me see the brother. It's very disagreeable; why should his case be more interesting than any other?"

Why indeed? Before the week was out, many notable figures in Paris would be working on Coudert's behalf, yet it was quite clear that, aside from Ballanche, none of these were personally acquainted with Charles Coudert or his brother Eugene. Although the Coudert family from provincial Bordeaux did have a few friends in military circles, most notably the Marquis du Chambon, a former artillery captain whose eldest son had married one of the Couderts' sisters, its own influence was negligible. Moreover, the majority of those among the Parisian elite who tried to help Charles Coudert had no sympathy for the *carbonari*—not that Eugene was admitting the slightest culpability on his brother's part.

What excited interest in young Coudert seems rather to have been simply the pathos of Coudert's situation—a young, brave soldier beloved by his family and that family in despair—coupled with indignation at the thought of his being condemned to execution for a mere political crime. Whether conservative or liberal, Récamier and her generation had seen the political wheel of fortune turn innumerable times since 1789 and had little faith left in the stability of any regime. The theme that runs through their correspondence and memoirs is the folly and insolence of judges who would pass a death sentence on Coudert for political acts, when the judges themselves might be in the dock for the same reason at the next change of government.

One person to whom Eugene and Récamier did not turn for help, of course, was Lafayette. That hero had narrowly escaped arrest himself in January in connection with another abortive uprising, and to be linked with him could only hurt Charles Coudert's cause while adding fuel to the suspicions of the police that Lafayette was indeed one of the heads of the *carbonari*. Nonetheless, during his first few days in Paris, Eugene did approach the great liberal deputy Benjamin Constant. One historian has described Lafayette as the figurehead of the opposition party, Constant as its brain. He was a logical person for Eugene to turn to for sympathy and advice, but he had no influence with the authorities himself, and all Eugene's appeal to him seems to have accomplished is the alienation of the far more powerful Chateaubriand. As Récamier's lover, Chateaubriand may have initially been willing to help her, but upon hearing that Eugene had approached Constant, he washed his hands of the matter. "The brother of that young man has completely tainted our efforts," he said with considerable annoyance. "He is an admitted liberal; he has addressed himself to Benjamin Constant."

Constant, in turn, however, may have brought into the reprieve effort the Duc de Broglie, an Orleanist who occupied at this time the middle ground between the Ultraroyalists and the liberal opposition. He called upon Récamier and wrote several letters on Coudert's behalf, but, predictably, none of them bore fruit. It is through one of de Broglie's letters, though, that we know that by March 4, in addition to Récamier, Montmorency had been petitioned by "many members of the party in favor." Others, such as the Duc de Laval, attempted to reach the king directly, but Louis XVIII responded stonily to all demands, and the Duchesse de Duras reported that he had forbidden anyone to mention the name Coudert in his presence.

In fact, on March 7, the day before Charles Coudert was to be executed, all the efforts of this glittering array of some of the greatest names in France had come to nothing. That night, still composed but without hope, Charles took up a quill pen in his prison cell and wrote a farewell to his mother, sending his love but expressing no regret for the course he had taken.

Constant, though, was still trying to save him. With only twelve hours left in which to obtain clemency from either the king or the ministry, he wrote to Récamier, outlining one final argument she might use with Montmorency. Remind him, Constant urged, of that revolutionary year of 1792, when he, too, was in danger of being executed by the state. Remind him of how men of completely different political views from his own came to his rescue and helped him to escape France and the guillotine. The tone of Constant's letter to Récamier is urgent, imploring, and heartrending. It seems certain she would have acted on it.

Perhaps it was this last-minute appeal that succeeded; perhaps not. Coudert was not led out to be shot on March 8, yet, curiously, despite all the memoirs and correspondence published by the principal actors in this small drama, it is not at all clear whose influence proved finally effective. One biographer of Madame Récamier believes it might have been through the Comtesse du Cayla, who was then the favorite of Louis XVIII, that Récamier was able to obtain a reprieve.

All that is certain, though, is that the executions of Coudert and Sirejean were stayed. By March 14, 1822, Charles knew that the verdict had been overturned and a new trial ordered, for he wrote to Récamier expressing his undying thanks, and on April 20 he and Sirejean appeared before their new judges. The proceedings were brief, with the verdict handed down on April 21. The unfortunate Sirejean was again condemned to death; he went before the firing squad ten days later, facing his executioners with composure and giving the order for the fatal volley himself. Coudert, however, this time was found guilty not of participating in the plot but only of having been aware of it and failing to reveal it to the authorities. His sentence: five years' imprisonment.

But merely saving Coudert's life was not enough for Récamier. She promptly started plotting his escape from prison as well and made the initial delicate approaches to an official of the prison where Coudert was held. However, being a great lady—and also being still hard up for funds herself—she delegated much of the actual planning and finance of the escape to Ballanche. By the results, the writer rose admirably to the task. The prison guards were bribed, and, piece by piece, Eugene smuggled in to his brother the clothes in which he would escape. On the appointed day, July 30, 1822, Charles walked out of the military prison. It is said that he coolly stopped to put some of the guards in the prison yard through a practice drill before leaving.

In New York newspaper profiles of Charles Coudert published after his death, two different accounts of his flight from France are offered. In the *Evening Post*'s version, Récamier arranges for him to go into hiding in France while his brother Eugene, using Charles's name, travels to England, thus throwing the pursuit off the scent. Later, after the uproar of his escape has died away, Charles crosses the Channel at leisure using a borrowed passport. In the other version, which appears to be the one his children accepted, Charles goes directly to Calais, bluffs his way past the French inspectors, and sets sail for England. Meanwhile, the story handed down in the du Chambon family is that Coudert arrived on horseback at their home in Vigière and hid there for some time before embarking for London.

All accounts agree, though, that after nearly eighteen months' stay in England, Charles decided to emigrate to America. Before taking this step that, in the days of slow ocean travel, would separate him perhaps forever from his family, Charles determined to return to Bordeaux to say farewell. The story is told that he borrowed the passport of a fellow countryman named Langlois and sailed for Calais in the company of a friend, a Colonel LeClerc. "Coudert's memory for names was woefully uncertain," the story continues, and going through customs at Calais, he forgot what his name was supposed to be. Quick-wittedly, even as the inspector began to ask him to identify himself, he came up with a ruse: "he stared blankly at his interlocutor with an affectation of deafness that would have made his fortune on the stage." This gave LeClerc the cue he needed to lean over and yell in Coudert's ear: "Langlois, the officer wants to know your name!" Thus, he was admitted to France and, after visiting his family, slipped away again, sailing for America.

As Coudert's ship passed through the Narrows into New York Harbor in 1824, he would have seen on either side wooded shores broken by farmland and directly ahead at the tip of Manhattan Island clustered buildings of two, three, or at the most, four stories. Visitors were enchanted with the beauty of the natural setting, especially as viewed from the elegant promenade of the battery at the foot of the island. Even so captious a critic as the English author Frances Trollope, who turned her well-bred nose up at most of America's sights on a visit in the 1820s, called New York "a lovely and a noble city."

The city was also developing rapidly. In fact, with the first section of the Erie Canal just opened, New York was about to take off on the rocketing course of growth that would leave the mercantile pretensions of its rivals, Boston and Philadelphia, far behind. Thanks to its "big ditch," which made it the chief entrepôt for goods moving in or out of the Ohio and Mississippi valleys, New York would dominate the nation's internal commerce within a few years. In the meantime, it already was the preeminent port for America's transatlantic trade with Europe. Onto its docks flowed European goods of all kinds, thence to move into the warehouses and stores owned by the merchants, who, as a class, gave the city its aura of cosmopolitanism and fashion.

At the time Coudert arrived, to his good fortune, the fashion in New York was for all things French. The wealthiest ladies would wear only French dresses and undergarments; they furnished their homes with French gilt mirrors, porcelains, and ormolus; and they aspired to speak French in polite company. Trollope ascribed the city's preference for French fashions and culture to a lingering resentment against England in the aftermath of the War of 1812. But a more positive factor causing an upsurge of interest in France in 1824 was Lafayette's triumphal tour of America, which touched off displays of wild popular enthusiasm.

The old hero's last visit to the republic that he had helped to found began in August 1824, and he brought in his entourage a number of former Bonapartist soldiers interested in settling in the New World. By then, Coudert had already been in America for five months, having arrived on March 1, 1824, on a small sailing vessel that had left Bordeaux in January. Shortly after his arrival, he met the French consul at a French bookstore on Cortlandt Street, and that Bourbon official said to him, "Ah, Mr. Coudert, I have been waiting six weeks for you." Protected from extradition by American law, Coudert was unalarmed. The former soldier had more pressing problems: finding lodgings and, with only two hundred francs to his name, earning a living.

While in America, Lafayette wrote to *"mon cher Coudert"* in the most cordial terms and presumably would have been willing to assist Coudert with introductions. His help was not needed, however, for Coudert had brought with him other letters of introduction from France, and by summer he had already determined upon an occupation. Knowing little English, and preferring an occupation of the sort that Frenchmen of his class and time deemed suitable for a gentleman and military hero, Coudert had settled upon the expedient of offering lessons in French and in horsemanship.

The next several years of Coudert's life are, as one might expect, obscure. Still, New York was apparently ready to support yet another French teacher, and he did obviously succeed in securing pupils. By 1826, at any rate, he felt himself sufficiently well-established to provide for another, for in October of that year, he married a seventeen-year-old French girl, nearly thirteen years younger than himself. His bride was Jeanne Clarisse du Champ, the daughter of "a prominent French citizen." It is believed that her father, Jean Baptiste du Champ, may have been a planter in Martinique before moving to the Carolinas and then to New York, but otherwise we know little about Jeanne Clarisse, except that between 1828 and 1842 she produced seven children—including the founders of Coudert Brothers—and then died of consumption at the age of thirty-five, after which her sister Virginie du Champ took over the care of the household. Because Jeanne Clarisse's children never knew her as adults, she remains a shadowy figure.

One cannot help wondering, however, if Jeanne Clarisse did not bring a dowry with her, for it appears to be in the late 1820s, not long after his marriage, that Charles opened an academy—what today we would call a private high school—offering instruction in French in a full range of courses to the sons of the well-to-do. Or perhaps he found backing for this project elsewhere, but start the New York Lyceum he did, and this school was the means by which he provided for his growing family for the next quarter century.

It was a famous school in its time, for in the New World Charles Coudert had stumbled, quite by chance, upon his true métier. He certainly had been an excellent soldier—a Grand Cross of the Legion of Honor permits no argument on that score—but as a teacher he was superb. One of his former pupils, in a tribute to the schoolmaster, referred to his "personal magnetism and eloquence," making it clear that Coudert was one of those teachers blessed with the knack of capturing youngsters' attention and imagination. One can picture him, with the erect military bearing he kept all his life and his cavalryman's panache, winning the hero worship of his students. But he also brought to his new profession, we are told, "a conscientious assiduity, an uncalculating devotion, a discriminating observation."

Throughout the life of Coudert's academy, it seems to have functioned as both a boarding school and a day school. Two partial lists of pupils survive, one from around 1834 and one from 1850, and both show a heavy proportion of French and Spanish surnames. Nonetheless, the pupil lists also contain names such as Livingston and Dillon, drawn from New York's own countinghouse aristocracy, and in later years, it was said that the graduates of

Coudert's academy were largely "Old New Yorkers"—that is, those who could trace their ancestry back to the city's earliest Dutch and English settlers.

In the 1830s the school was located at fashionable addresses, first on Cortlandt Street and later on a large semirural tract on Eighteenth Street near Seventh Avenue. That it flourished initially is attested to by the fact that Coudert was able to buy out and merge into his own two other academies founded by Bonapartist émigrés. A still more telling indication of the New York Lyceum's success is the fact that, although many other Bonapartist refugees returned permanently to France in 1830 upon the accession of Louis-Philippe, Coudert did not. He could afford to visit his family in the early 1830s and did so, but he remained settled in the United States.

Nonetheless, as successful a teacher as Coudert was, money was always a problem. Coudert's abilities "made him a force in the field he had chosen," his son-in-law remarked gracefully many years later. "But the remuneration accorded to the teacher in those days was small—smaller even than the still inadequate compensation of today." In 1839 Coudert's slim financial resources were depleted by a disastrous decision to move the lyceum to an estate in New Jersey. The enrollment plummeted, partly because epidemics of chills and fevers ran through the student body. In 1843 Coudert returned to Manhattan, buying a house and erecting a schoolhouse, on St. Mark's Place in newly developed Greenwich Village. But very few students returned with him, and the parents of many of those who were left were unable to pay their tuition, so that times continued hard for the Coudert family. A profile of Coudert's son Frederic René, published during the younger man's lifetime, stated bluntly: "Mr. Coudert started life about as poor as anybody possibly could be."

Nonetheless, Charles Coudert and Jeanne Clarisse while she lived provided their children with an excellent home life; certainly as adults their children indicated in every way possible that they had received the best of upbringings. In fact, no one seems to have felt the force of Coudert's "personal magnetism" more deeply than his own children, or to have loved him more dearly. There were seven children in all, but Maria Coralie seems not to have survived infancy, Anne Coralie died at the age of eighteen and Claire at thirteen. The four survivors—Frederic René, Charles junior, Louis Leonce, and their sister, Leonie—are all of interest to us, for their life stories are intimately connected to the history of Coudert Brothers.

The oldest was Frederic René, born on March 1, 1832. The

family prodigy, he had all of his father's quick wits, his mind moving at the kind of high speed that tends to win the label of *brilliance*. As a youth, he not only raced through his lessons with ease, but also observed people intently. In time, he would become as quick at reading others as he would his books, anticipating their comments and reactions through mental processes so fast they appeared to be intuition. Sensitive and sometimes hot-tempered, he schooled himself to an appearance of impassive dignity in public, but, when surprised into a smile, his dark eyes would light up—and it became clear that he had inherited a good share of his father's charm.

The second oldest boy, Charles junior, born December 30, 1833, had an entirely different temperament. Where his brother was quick and agile, Charles was solid and methodical. Where Frederic René enjoyed the play of words and ideas, Charles respected facts. He was neat in all things, precise, and of unshakable integrity. Yet while Charles's reserve was formidable and his manner somewhat cold, his family found him the most tenderhearted of men. With their opposing character traits, Frederic René and Charles complemented each other on many levels, and the bonds of affection between the two were strong and durable.

Not far behind Frederic René and Charles came their brother Louis Leonce, born on April 26, 1836. A surviving photograph shows that Louis's eyes were even larger and more soulful than Frederic René's and that as a young man he had a darkly romantic look. But, in fact, his personality was pure sunshine. Warm, friendly, and outgoing, he, even more than Frederic René, was distinguished for his tact and charm. A nephew recalls him as having had a "peculiarly pleasant and conciliatory disposition," and the number of his friends was legion.

The only surviving daughter was Leonie, born February 23, 1838. A thoroughly good girl, she grew up into a model of Victorian womanhood. With apparent devotion, she nursed whatever family members were ill, interested herself in the neighborhood poor, and took great comfort from her religion. Like her brothers she was kindhearted and, even more than they, deeply charitable.

Charles and Jeanne Clarisse raised this brood in various homes, usually located close by the lyceum. Wherever they kept their household, it was always French in tone. The children learned French in their cradle, invariably used that language in speaking with their parents, and received their schooling in French as well, for they did not attend public schools but were tutored by their father. In later years others would marvel at the Couderts' command of French. The real wonder, though, is that their

English—which was truly their second language—was as good as it was. Yet, although they spoke English neither at home nor at school, they seemingly picked it up easily from the very atmosphere of the city, becoming perfectly bilingual. Just the faintest accent shadowed Frederic René's English; it was his exquisite diction and careful enunciation in English that made the greater impression on his listeners.

As immigrants do, Coudert senior clung not only to his native tongue but also initially to his fellow countrymen. Until his children were adults, his associations and friendships were primarily limited to New York's small community of French exiles, but within that circle he rapidly became a "leading and influential member." The boys would have been only infants when Louis and Joseph Bonaparte visited New York in 1836 and were lionized by society hostesses, but they must surely have heard many times how their parents were among those who entertained the future Napoleon III and his uncle and were entertained by them, in turn. As the children were growing up, too, they must have heard their father and his friends discuss French politics by the hour, for Coudert senior remained a staunch Bonapartist and, always hoping for a Bonapartist revival, he followed French affairs closely through the columns of the French newspapers and the *Courier des Etats-Unis,* New York's own French newspaper established in 1828. A friend of the senior Coudert once related that he was walking with the schoolteacher in 1848 when, hearing a newsboy cry, "Extra! News from France," Coudert turned to him and said, "There is Louis Napoleon come into power, sure"—and so it proved.

More formally, in their lessons with their father, the children also learned to appreciate the history and culture of France. The eldest son, Frederic René—about whom we know the most because he lived in the public eye to a far greater degree than his brothers and sister—drew constantly on this store of knowledge in his speeches and writings. But the young Couderts—at least, the boys—also imbibed the full range of a liberal education, especially a familiarity with the classics. Their father created about him an atmosphere of "culture and refinement"—the Victorian stock phrase denoting a love of literature and the arts. In fact, Coudert senior was said to "devour books." Reading was one of his great pleasures even in his advanced old age: at eighty-three, bedridden and weak, he would be asking his sons to bring him more volumes, or "I will have to read my old ones over again." Judging by the attention his sons would give to their libraries, he passed this trait on to them as well.

Perhaps the most decisive impact Charles Coudert, Sr., had on his sons, though, lay in the fact that, as a "French gentleman of the old school," he raised them to be gentlemen in the same mold as himself. This meant not only that the boys learned such arts as horsemanship and fencing, but also that they acquired the manners of gentlemen. In later life, for example, Frederic René was famed for the exquisite courtesy he demonstrated in court: "The prominent feature of Mr. Coudert . . . was his unfailing courtesy, in which he made no discrimination between individuals, and was as punctilious in politeness toward the humble amanuensis as to the learned referee. He was indeed the able lawyer and polished gentleman."

The sons of Charles Coudert, Sr., however, were gentlemen in more than manners. Throughout their lives they observed a strict integrity, and different as Frederic René, Charles, and Louis Leonce were in personalities, in this characteristic they showed clearly their common upbringing. The standard adhered to by their father—who would not betray another even to save his own life—was a high one, and for the sons it would not be enough merely to be honest, moral, and well-meaning. Rather, as Frederic René would express it, integrity would consist in those qualities displayed—and the example is a telling one—by the chevalier Bayard, *sans peur et sans reprôche.*

Thus, despite the family's straitened circumstances, the Coudert children received an upbringing that was by the standards of New York City in that period more patrician than not. Through their education and the formation of their characters, Charles Coudert, Sr., clearly was equipping his sons to take a place among the elite of their community. Yet, from the point of view of that elite, the young Couderts were being raised with a crippling disadvantage: they were being brought up to be devout Catholics like their father, who was a "constant attendant" at the Church of the Nativity. And Catholicism in the eyes of the "better element" of New York City—or the entire United States, for that matter—was quite simply the wrong religion.

Indeed, the Coudert boys' childhood coincided precisely with the two decades when anti-Catholic prejudices in New York were most outspoken and unrestrained. These were the decades of the great Irish exodus, when the native-born Protestant residents felt themselves, their traditions, and their values in danger of being submerged by one of the largest tidal waves of immigration in the history of the world. The statistics tell the story: when Charles Coudert, Sr., arrived in 1825, New York City was receiving about 4,000 immigrants a year; when his oldest two children were still toddlers, in 1835, the number had risen to 60,000 per year; and the average between 1840 and 1856 was about 200,000 per year—far more immigrants per year than the entire population of New York City when Coudert senior first knew it. By 1845 block after block of the "lovely and noble" city had turned into squalid Irish slums, and two-thirds of the inmates of the city's poorhouse, lunatic asylum, and penitentiary were Irish Catholics.

Of overwhelmingly Dutch and English Protestant stock, the native-born found some three hundred years of ancestral anti-Catholic prejudices stirring vigorously to life under the impact of the Irish migration, and during the Coudert children's youth, the antipathy between Catholics and Protestants was open and virulent, with Archbishop John Hughes encouraging his priests to abuse Protestantism from their altars and the Protestant clergy printing rabid tracts warning of the Vatican's mission to subvert democracy in America. These were the years when fictional works such as Maria Monk's *Awful Disclosures* . . . of seduction and infanticide among the Catholic clergy stirred riots and mob attacks on convents, and Hughes, overreacting, preached on the inevitable conversion to Catholicism of all inhabitants of the United States, "the people of the cities, the people of the country . . . the Senate, the Cabinet, the President, and all!" Live and let live was not the order of the day.

Although the crudest forms of anti-Catholicism all but disappeared by the end of the Civil War, behind drawing-room doors a quiet prejudice remained, reinforced by a view of history that assumed the future belonged to the Protestant Anglo-Saxon "race" by virtue of its innate superiority to the Catholic Latin "race"—a view that took a deep hold on American thought in the 1840s and lasted out the century.

Thus, while some elements of the young Couderts' French heritage made them gentlemen fitted by breeding to move into the most influential circles in New York City, the element of their religion made them, nonetheless, outsiders by birth. Under these circumstances it would not have been surprising if the young Couderts had chosen to embrace some parts of their heritage more ardently than others, but, in fact, they lived with the contradictions and remained loyal to the whole—although their Catholicism was, indeed, more than just a matter of loyalty to them. All four children grew into adults of simple, deep piety, while Frederic René, in particular, was a public champion—a *chevalier,* one might say—of their father's faith.

Catholic and Protestant tensions in New York City during their formative years helped shape the later careers of the Coudert sons, but their native city offered them during those years not only the challenge of overcoming others' prejudices but also great opportunities. In addition to foreigners, young Americans from innumerable backwater towns and farms swelled New York City's population in the 1830s and 1840s, because the city had what young men wanted: the thrill of varied forms of entertainment—theaters, concerts, horse races, lectures, ice-cream parlors, and gymnasiums; the stimulation of ideas expressed in dozens of newspapers, some selling for as little as a penny; the sense of living in the most up-to-date, bustling city in the nation, the starting point for every fad and fancy; and, above all, the promise of prosperity. New York was a place where a young white male could feel that, if he could just get the right toehold, he had a chance of bettering himself and fulfilling his dreams. It was in this atmosphere in the late 1840s, that the Coudert boys, one by one, reached their early teens and set out to make their mark on the world.

Chapter Two

BROTHERS IN LAW

T he first of the Coudert brothers to leave their father's
schoolroom was the eldest, Frederic René, who displayed an
early and unusual aptitude for the classics. At the New York Lyceum, Latin was taught by Dr. T. Olcott Porter, whom the Coudert
boys regarded as one of their family. "A prince among men" is the
way Frederic René once described him: "Tall, handsome, intellectual, courteous, with a heart as tender as a woman's." This admiration for his teacher was paralleled by an enthusiasm for Porter's
subject, and Frederic René mastered his Caesar, Cicero, and Sallust
so readily that he passed Columbia College's entrance examinations when he was only fourteen, some three years earlier than normal.

Frederic René's academic accomplishments were not uniform.
He never learned much mathematics, for example, perhaps in part
because he was always "thoroughly" frightened of the lyceum's
math instructor, Le Père Simone. A one-eyed former Napoleonic
soldier, "Old Sims" had what Frederic René described as a "real
and dangerous" temper, and he was eventually fired for his inability to control it in the classroom. "In justice to him," Frederic René
later said gallantly, "the small amount of mathematics I got would
have been very much larger if my capacity to learn had equaled his
capacity to teach." But the fact remained that Frederic René's
knowledge of this useful subject was decidedly limited.

At Columbia College, however, the classics were all that really mattered. As late as 1846, when Frederic René entered, Columbia showed no interest in educating young men for engineering, commerce, or other pursuits in which mathematics might be an asset. It existed solely to prepare its students for the gentlemanly professions—that is, law, medicine, and religion—and, accordingly, it offered in its columned building in lower Manhattan a course of study that heavily emphasized Latin and Greek.

The only other college in New York City at this time, the institution that later became New York University, had the same narrowly defined mission of cultivating a professional elite. Just how exclusive in spirit the two colleges were is indicated by the fact that in 1846, when the city had a population of around 500,000 people, they enrolled between them only 287 students. Yet both colleges had ostensibly democratic admission policies. Even Columbia, which had strong ties to the Episcopal church, had no religious test for admission, and both set their tuition low in a deliberate effort to attract a broad student body. Nonetheless, the enrollment lists of the two colleges read like a roll of the city's most patrician families, for few others could afford a college preparatory education for their sons. In an era when families were large and only paupers had access to free schooling, one had to be exceptionally fortunate to attend high school, much less college.

Recognizing this fact, the professions emphasized apprenticeships rather than classroom study. Until 1846 the basic requirement for admission to legal practice in New York State was simply the completion of a seven-year clerkship in a law office, begun not earlier than the age of fourteen. In 1846 even this standard was relaxed, with applicants to the bar thereafter having only to demonstrate to a judge of the state's Supreme Court that they possessed "the requisite learning and ability," however obtained.

The looseness of the formal rules for bar admission notwithstanding, during the Couderts' youth no one was in any doubt that some credentials for the practice of law were superior to others. What counted was the reputation of the attorney with whom the young man had privately studied law and the amount of Latin and Greek he had mastered before that, for the medieval tradition of scholarship was alive and well in pre–Civil War America, and the study of the learned languages was still considered the true test of intellectual capacity and fitness to practice the profession of law at its highest level. Since those who studied the classics, whether in high school or college, came for the most part from a background of wealth and privilege, not surprisingly they did, in fact, constitute the bulk of the profession's elite. One directory limited to prominent New York attorneys, for example, shows that about 60 percent of those listed from Frederic René's generation had attended college and another 17 percent had completed high school. Less than a quarter had apparently achieved success without the benefit of classroom grounding in Latin and Greek.

When Frederic René entered Columbia, therefore, he was taking a major step toward amassing as distinguished a set of professional credentials as his time and place had to offer. It was his family's support that enabled him to do so. By living at home, Frederic René avoided the expense of the college's commons, and, although the New York Lyceum was woefully short of students in 1846 and the family's finances were at low ebb, Papa Coudert found a way for his young son to earn his own tuition by setting him up in business as a private teacher of languages. Every afternoon throughout his college years, Frederic René took over a lyceum classroom to give lessons "to a large class of boys in Spanish and French."

In addition, Frederic René did some private tutoring of adults. When he was fifteen or sixteen, for instance, his father was approached by a "man of means from New Orleans by name of Tiblier," who wanted to learn French before traveling to Europe. The schoolmaster referred this assignment to his son, who "joyfully accepted" and gave the desired lessons in the evenings in the deserted schoolhouse. "It was a family trait" to be industrious, Frederic René said in his old age, "and the three boys, of whom I now alone am left, were always ready and happy to make contribution to the common treasury."

Working his way through college did Frederic René's studies no harm. Despite his youth he won several academic prizes in his undergraduate years, and he relished his lessons, particularly, of course, those in the classics. Professor Charles Anthon, who taught both Latin and Greek, impressed young Frederic René "immensely." Nearly four decades later, Frederic René would still be able to recall Anthon's comments on specific passages, and he regaled his own son with stories of how Anthon used to expel students from the classroom for mispronouncing their vowels, dismissing them with the words "Boy, get out of here!" Professor Henry Drisler, then a young instructor in Greek, was also a favorite, and Drisler and Frederic René would keep up a correspondence based on their mutual interest in the classics for more than forty years.

Frederic René did not enjoy such a pleasant relationship with all his teachers, however. There was at least one unhappy encounter, when in 1848 a professor used the revolutionary events then taking place in France as the occasion for some derogatory remarks about French achievements. Young Coudert, who would always fire up easily at any insult to his heritage, "was stung into a retort," which revealed that his knowledge of history was better than his teacher's. Thrown on the defensive, the professor saved his dignity by cutting the teenager short with "an admonition that no discussion of 'politics' was allowable."

That episode rankled, but Frederic René still always spoke with respect of Columbia's faculty during his student days and credited his "excellent teachers" with the fact that he graduated in 1850 with the highest grades in his class. For his valedictory address, Coudert reviewed the political "isms" of the day, and he apparently handled this controversial subject with tact, for his speech and its delivery were well received by his audience and favorably commented upon by the press. Immediately following this triumph, Frederic René, now eighteen years old, began the study of law itself.

The U.S. Census of 1850 records Frederic René Coudert's occupation at age eighteen as lawyer, but, in fact, he was then nearly three years shy of the minimum age at which he could apply for admission to the bar. He spent those years "reading law" under the direction of Edward Sanford, one of the most respected practitioners in the city. A schoolteacher himself before studying law, Sanford was well equipped to train others. Forty-one years old in 1850, he had already served as a criminal court judge and state senator, and as a lawyer, he had a reputation for being "very eminent, powerful and successful in enforcing the rights of his clients."

Because a law clerkship was a form of training, it was unpaid, so Frederic René had to combine his studies with paying jobs. Turning to writing and translating, he parlayed his fluency in French into regular free-lance work for the *New York Herald,* translating the French newspapers from which the *Herald* was accustomed to lift, more or less wholesale, much of its European news. In addition, he contributed articles to the *Spirit of the Times,* the leading sporting journal of its day, which under the editorship of William T. Porter raised reports of horse races to a literary art form. Again, working posed no interference to Frederic René's course of reading in Blackstone, Kent, and other legal authorities. "Always a great reader and a close student, his preparation for the Bar was thorough," a later partner assures us.

In any event, Frederic René wasted no time beginning practice. His twenty-first birthday, the first date on which he could appear for examination before a state Supreme Court judge, fell on March 1, 1853. By May 1853, when the canvassers gathered names for the annual city street directories, Frederic René was to be found at 38 Broadway, sharing offices with Frank Ferris, another young attorney, and his name is duly recorded in Rode's 1853 street directory as "Coudert, Frederic R., lawyer."

Meanwhile, Frederic René's brothers had been acquiring an entirely different set of experiences. Not as academically brilliant as their older brother, both Charles junior and Louis Leonce progressed through elementary school at the normal rate and left the lyceum in their early teens to go to work. Money was definitely a motive in this interruption of their formal schooling, but the younger boys were not so much abandoning their education as branching out to pick up a background in commercial subjects in the only way in which it could then be obtained—through practical training. A junior clerkship in an established mercantile house was deemed more valuable for boys who intended to pursue a business career than classroom study—or at least enough parents felt that way that competition for such positions among middle-class boys was intense.

Thus, when some "excellent gentlemen" who were Spanish nationals offered Charles junior the chance to leave school and work for their commercial house, the opportunity was seized upon as one too good to pass up. "Although he was but thirteen years of age," his older brother later noted with a touch of fraternal pride, "he could read and write English, French, and Spanish and could make himself extremely useful" to his Spanish employers. When it came Louis Leonce's turn to start working full-time, he plunged in with characteristic good humor. There survives a rollicking letter that he wrote to his family sometime before 1855. The rest of the family had apparently gone off on vacation, but Louis Leonce had been unable to leave his job and was left on his own at 95 St. Mark's Place. The whole letter resonates with the teenage thrill of being alone, unsupervised, in the city and grown up enough to be employed.

Nonetheless, the younger boys—or more likely, Papa Coudert—decided that a business career was not for them. In 1850, when Frederic René had finished college and the lyceum, flourishing again, was "overflowing with pupils," Charles junior left the Spaniards and at the age of sixteen began his high school studies. He also inherited Frederic René's afternoon Spanish and French classes and over the next several years combined teaching and studying, finishing the lyceum's courses in 1853 or 1854. With a respectable amount of Latin and Greek at his command, Charles junior was now ready to start "reading law."

From the sequence of what followed, it seems clear that the

brothers had by then definitely resolved upon going into practice together—if, indeed, they had not laid plans to that effect much earlier—for roughly simultaneous with the start of Charles's legal studies came the dissolution of Frederic René's short-lived association with Frank Ferris, with whom he had been sharing offices at 38 Broadway. Although Coudert and Ferris both stayed in the same building for several years, the former practiced alone while Charles junior spent a year or so preparing himself for the bar—and presumably helping his brother at the same time. Early in 1855, shortly after turning twenty-one, Charles junior was admitted to the New York State bar, and the two brothers immediately went into practice together, moving to 157 Broadway.

Meanwhile, Louis Leonce was wrapping up his classical studies at the lyceum. By May 1856, Louis Leonce, then twenty years old, was finished with high school and had joined his brothers at 157 Broadway. He was not yet a lawyer, merely starting his own crash course of law reading, but the older two had his name listed with theirs in Trow's City Directory of 1856, regardless. Plainly, it was just a matter of time until Louis Leonce "joined" the firm, which, following family tradition, he did at the earliest possible moment, passing the bar in April 1857, the same month that he turned twenty-one. It is the 1857 city directory, therefore, that for the first time lists not only all three brothers as lawyers (now practicing at 39 Ann Street), but also the name they chose for their partnership: Coudert Brothers. Thus, the modern firm of Coudert Brothers has a choice of starting dates: its origins clearly go back to 1853, when Frederic René hung out his shingle, but purists, if they wish, may hold by either 1855, when two Coudert brothers first practiced law together, or 1857, when the brothers seemed to have turned their fledgling enterprise into a legal partnership.

The partnership the Coudert brothers founded was evidently an equal one, in which they divided the profits share and share alike. The work of the office, however, was allocated from the beginning in accordance with the partners' different training and talents. With his oratorical ability and his greater fund of legal scholarship, Frederic René was the partner who handled the firm's trial work. He was the partner most frequently in the public eye—and he did his best to keep himself and his firm conspicuous. He spoke at political rallies, he gave public lectures, and he used the experience he had gained as a journalist to cultivate friendly relations with the press. It would be some years, of course, before he would find his engagement book crowded with invitations to speak and the press began to turn to him for a reliably quotable statement on just about any subject, but even as a young man Frederic René worked hard at promoting Coudert Brothers in every legitimate way he could.

Charles junior and Louis Leonce, on the other hand, took their business training and applied it to the work of an office practice. Charles junior's forte was the preparation of wills, estate and trust accountings, contracts, collection letters, real estate mortgages, surety bonds, and similar documentation where his understanding of business practices and bookkeeping was a major asset to the firm. He was a quiet man. "Loquacity," he once said, "has, if I know myself, not been my foible," and he stayed at his desk and out of court.

Louis Leonce also kept mostly to his office, although he assisted Frederic René in certain kinds of trial work and occasionally appeared in the lower courts. His overriding strength, however, was his attractive personality, which, as the firm grew, eventually resulted in his being saddled with supervising the staff. And the tradition that comes down in the family is that he had "a wonderful touch with the clients."

A friend of the Couderts once described the firm's division of labor as similar to that found in France between the *avocat* and the *notaire,* but, in fact, there was nothing foreign or exotic in the way the Couderts organized their office. Until well after the Civil War most American lawyers were solo practitioners, but where partnerships were formed, they usually were two-man firms, bringing together a courtroom specialist with someone who preferred the behind-the-scenes drafting and accounting work. Lincoln and Herndon, Stanton and Dewey, Edmonds and Field—the list of such partnerships is long. Coudert Brothers was only one of many, but one that survived.

There may have been moments, of course, after 1857 when the brothers worried about the firm's survival, but the leanest days seem actually to have been those when Frederic René practiced law alone, for, by a quirk of fate, his chief asset—his outstanding preparation for the law—did not draw in as much business from other attorneys as it should have. One of the benefits of the nineteenth-century system of "reading law" was the flow of patronage it facilitated between established practitioners and young men just beginning their careers. Successful lawyers before the 1870s seldom hired young lawyers as associates when they had more work than they could handle; instead, they farmed out the overflow to the more trustworthy of their former law students—men whom they had trained themselves and knew to be able and loyal. Thus, the leaders of the bar avoided increasing their overhead, while the younger men could count on a fairly steady flow of business while they tried to develop a clientele and reputation of their own.

Having completed a prestigious clerkship, Frederic René might reasonably have expected to have his way smoothed, too, by such referrals. But his mentor, Edward Sanford, died unexpectedly in September 1854 at the age of forty-four, one of the hundreds who perished in the sinking of the transatlantic passenger ship *Arctic*, and Frederic René was left, just as he was being joined by Charles junior, without a connection to a well-established lawyer and in no easier starting position—from a short-term point of view, at least—than if he had not spent seven years earning honor upon honor.

Talking years later about the tribulations of starting a practice, Frederic René said wryly, "You may have an office, which is a great deal of itself, and you may rejoice in a sign board, gold and black, and you may take great comfort in the possession of a degree from Columbia College, but until you have felt the quickening influence of your client's presence, until his coming has aroused your dormant possibilities . . . you cannot flatter yourselves that you have attained the dignity of a real lawyer." And he was surely remembering the elation he felt whenever a client appeared in his doorway in the 1850s when he added that "obscurity and despondency" are the young attorney's companions until the arrival of a client brings "sunshine into the desolate office."

Nonetheless, some lawyers may have given a few cases to Frederic René. The former congressman Edward Curtis—who may well have been the father of Edward Curtis who was a lyceum boarding student in 1850—seems to have sent some business from his Washington, D.C., office. More importantly, Charles O'Conor, a strange, solitary man whom his generation believed to be the greatest courtroom lawyer of the day, also gave work to young Frederic René. The latter served as a junior to O'Conor in *Lahens v. Fielding*, which involved a question of commercial law, and he spent so much time in O'Conor's company working on legal matters that he became as much a friend as O'Conor ever allowed anybody to be. But this relationship was a two-way street, for custom dictated that younger men should not appear in appellate court, and, consequently, Frederic René had to refer his appellate work to others, of whom O'Conor surely was one.

On the whole, however, in the earliest years of their practice the Couderts had no choice but to find their clients from among their own circle of acquaintances—which, in view of their extreme youth, really meant from among their father's acquaintances. Indeed, it was later said of the old schoolteacher that it was "through his influence" that his sons' "law business steadily increased." Since Papa Coudert's connections lay largely in New York City's French and Spanish populations, this means that from the start Coudert Brothers' clientele was heavily composed of foreign nationals.

The first Coudert Brothers client of which there is any record, for example, was Dr. Theodore Gaillardet, a French physician accused in 1858 of criminal assault upon the proprietor of his lodging house, one Hiram Cranston. In the initial affidavits made May 27, 1858, witnesses alleged that the doctor had been caring for a patient in his rooms at the New York Hotel, a not uncommon practice of the time. The witnesses also stated that, upon learning on Wednesday, May 26, that the patient had smallpox, Cranston had ordered Gaillardet to pack up and leave the boardinghouse, whereupon the Frenchman violently and wantonly attacked his landlord. Bail was denied on the twenty-seventh until Cranston might be pronounced out of danger.

The defense, however, presented another side of the story. It alleged that Dr. Gaillardet had been treating Mr. Armentero, a merchant from Havana, for the measles, not the deadly smallpox. On Tuesday evening Cranston had callously told the physician that his patient must leave by 8:00 the next morning. First protesting, Gaillardet had eventually agreed to find other lodgings for Armentero once the weather improved and the Cuban could be moved without further endangering his health. Nonetheless, after Gaillardet had set out on his rounds on Wednesday morning, Cranston had unilaterally arranged to send Armentero to a hospital—a move almost equivalent to executing the Cuban, since New York's hospitals were little more than death traps. Fearing for Armentero's life, Mrs. Gaillardet ran out of the boardinghouse to find her husband and report what was going on. Thus alerted, the physician hastily secured decent lodgings for Armentero and returned to the New York Hotel, where he found himself served with an eviction notice and his wife upstairs in tears, having been insulted by Cranston and ordered not to appear at the supper table. Gaillardet then ran to the dining room and hit Cranston over the head with the nearest object—a bottle of champagne.

The *New York Times* solemnly concluded that the act of violence was "not entirely without cause nor entirely without excuse." What the court concluded we don't know: there are no surviving reports of New York criminal court proceedings in 1858. Yet we may fairly suppose that Coudert Brothers was successful in defending the French physician from the worst consequences of his temper, for more than forty years later a New York judge mentioned this case as one that helped to establish Frederic René's reputation as a skilled courtroom advocate.

Other clients whose relationship with the firm seems to date at least to the 1860s, if not the 1850s, include the Moras, a Cuban family whose head established in 1855 the New York banking firm of Mora, de Navarro & Co. The partner in this firm was José de Navarro, the Spanish consul general in New York, who had made his initial fortune in the warehouse and shipping business in Cuba and who organized in the 1850s the first steamship line between Brazil and the United States. The Moras, too, were engaged in shipping and warehousing, and it may have been on their legal business that Charles junior made the trips to South America and Cuba that he is said to have taken "very early in his career." The firm seems also to have represented quite early on the French steamship line, the Compagnie Generale Transatlantique, known to New Yorkers as the General Transatlantic. Its longtime agent, Louis de Bebian, attended the Couderts' weddings and funerals for years, and he may well have known the father before meeting the sons.

The most important of Coudert Brothers' early clients, however, was the French government, which gave the firm the legal business of its consulate in New York City. Much of this work seems to have consisted of criminal extraditions, and it is doubtful that the cases could have been particularly remunerative. But the connection was almost priceless in terms of prestige and of contacts with persons who might need a French-speaking attorney in New York. In particular, the French consulate administered the estates of French nationals who had died in the United States and also assisted heirs to estates with U.S. assets to secure U.S. legal representation. The connection with the consulate, therefore, was to prove extremely useful to the brothers as they developed a thriving estates and trusts practice.

The exact date that Coudert Brothers began representing the consulate is not known, but this aspect of their practice was well established before 1870, which means that the relationship began while Napoleon III ruled France. Given Papa Coudert's lifelong and outspoken Bonapartist sympathies, his personal acquaintance with the future emperor (whom he had entertained in New York in 1836), and his still lively network of contacts in France, the conclusion is irresistible that the former soldier had much to do with his sons being chosen as the consulate's attorneys.

Thus, with their father's constant support, the brothers built up a practice distinguished by its foreign clientele. Such a practice was not a novelty in a city so dependent on trade and foreign investment as New York had always been. In the early 1830s, for example, R. M. Blatchford had prospered by handling loan transactions on real estate mortgages for overseas clients, occasional admiralty and marine insurance cases sent by the same clients, collections for local merchants and foreign exporters, and primitive forms of investment trusts designed to attract foreign capital to the United States.

As far as can be determined, the Couderts' practice after it matured differed in hardly any essential from what Blatchford's had been in the 1830s, except that Coudert Brothers could offer a special expertise in consular law and that, drawing on the ability of its senior partner, it handled a relatively greater volume of litigation. But whereas Blatchford's foreign clients were mainly British, Coudert Brothers' were French, Spanish, and Latin American— and that was a new development for the city's bar. Just ten years earlier it is doubtful that a law firm depending on French- and Spanish-speaking clients could have supported even one, much less three attorneys, but in the 1850s America's trade boomed with both France and Latin America, and investments flowed from France, in particular, to the United States. The right people in the right place at the right time, the Couderts were busy by the early 1860s creating for themselves a virtual monopoly on the legal business of merchants and other wealthy individuals who spoke French or Spanish.

They built their success partly on plain hard work, the virtues of which they were not ones to underestimate. In the New York courthouses nearly every day, Frederic René watched carefully the leaders of the bar and singled out three whom he thought especially talented—Ogden Hoffman, James T. Brady, and Charles O'Conor—but he deplored the work habits of two of these. Hoffman, who could hypnotize a jury "so modestly and gently and courteously that really it was not fair to the other side," had unfortunately, Coudert observed, been endowed "at his birth with a splendid fund of unconquerable laziness." Brady left the impression on his young colleague "that he could do anything—if he only cared to try . . . if he had settled down doggedly to work," but his genius, Frederic René concluded, was not matched by his industry.

Frederic René, on the other hand, made no claim to genius, but he had the willpower and drive to work long hours, and he did so. Thus, Christmas Eve 1861 found him at the office dashing off a note explaining that he could not get home in time for the Christmas tree-trimming "without leaving divers matters in an unsatisfactory condition—I shall not therefore imperil my (already

tottering) reputation for attention to business by an early departure." In fact, he missed the tree-trimming altogether, and December 26 found him right back at the office again at the customary
early hour. At times, his system rebelled: one night, also in 1861,
he confided on paper that "that worst of all trouble, *je ne sais quoi,*
had made me most wretchedly indigo." Wanting to go home, still
he had to remain "addling my brain over stupid paper until my
head splits, my eyes ache, and the late train threatens departure."
But the mere act of releasing his discontent on paper cheered him
up, and he went back to work "feeling better than when I began."

The third member of the triumvirate of lawyers admired by
young Frederic René was one nobody could accuse of lacking energy, Charles O'Conor. The sheer law learning exuded by
O'Conor, the numberless legal tomes he had digested, and his
careful preparation of each case awed even Coudert. O'Conor was
a model to Frederic René in other ways, too, for he was a Catholic
who had overcome the weight of prejudice against his religion to
reach the very top of his profession. His achievements, however,
were apparently gained at a high emotional cost, for O'Conor gave
the impression of being an absolutely cold man who would bend
not an inch to gain friendship or goodwill from either client or
colleague.

Frederic René's son years later was told the story of how one
afternoon his father and O'Conor had been traveling together on
one of the Fourth Avenue horsecars: "There entered the car a
rather unpleasant looking individual, who greeted Mr. O'Conor;
the latter never replied in the slightest way to the greeting, and
upon my father whispering to him: 'That is the man who paid you
Five Thousand Dollars last week,' he replied: 'Young man, I do not
have to greet any damn scoundrel who happened to have paid me
Five Thousand Dollars, or any other sum of money!' "

Such independence may have suited O'Conor—but it was not
for the Couderts. Courtesy was too far ingrained in them, for one
thing, and they also had a strong streak of practicality that kept
them aware of who was paying the bills. When told by a client "not
to lose an hour" in commencing a case in Washington, D.C., in
1862, Frederic René left on the 7:30 P.M. train from New York, not
even bothering to go home to pack or make his farewells. When he
and Louis Leonce went to a dinner where they would inevitably
run into clients—and prospective clients—they were shrewd
enough to go "arrayed in a style of Oriental magnificence." The
words are Frederic René's, poking fun at himself, but his instructions on which clothes should be sent down to the office for him

to wear to this dinner—"my best suit of black"—are detailed and exact.

In short, the brothers were good businessmen, and it was well they were, for they had others than themselves to support. As soon as Louis Leonce, the youngest boy, had graduated from the lyceum in 1856, Papa Coudert had shut down his school and, at age sixty, retired from teaching. In the same year the whole family—father, three sons, Leonie, and Tante Virginie—moved together to the town of Pelham in Westchester County. Thereafter, the Coudert boys were increasingly responsible for paying the household expenses and for providing their father with a comfortable old age. And his retirement was very comfortable. In Pelham, Papa Coudert could ride daily, as he delighted to do, keep his dogs, go hunting in season, and live the life of a country gentleman. Indeed, he styled himself on deeds henceforth as "Charles Coudert of Pelham, Westchester County, gentleman."

After thirty years of teaching, however, perhaps it was not so easy for the senior Coudert to give up the pleasure of training a bright young mind. Perhaps the house simply seemed empty—the boys were at their office all day; his youngest child, Claire, had died in 1855 of consumption; Leonie was a young lady of nineteen. In any event, Papa Coudert in 1857 brought home a ten-year-old orphan, Paul ("Francisco") Fuller, who became, in all but name, the fourth Coudert brother.

Fuller's story rivals in romance that of the senior Coudert himself. His parents were "New Englanders of straight English stock," originally from a small town in Vermont. William Fuller volunteered to serve in the army at the outset of the Mexican War, and, when he was posted to the San Francisco garrison, he took his pregnant wife with him. Thus, Paul entered the world on January 26, 1847, on board the clipper ship *Thomas E. Perkins* shortly after it had rounded the Cape Horn headed for California.

Paul's mother, Mary Shuffleton Fuller, died on the troop ship fifteen days after giving birth to him, and, there being no room for a baby at an army post, his father arranged for a Mexican family to nurse and care for him. After his discharge from the army, William Fuller returned briefly to Vermont, taking his three-year-old son with him, but went back to California with his son, apparently to take up a claim for bounty land there and to seek his fortune in the gold rush. On his return to California in 1853, William Fuller again entrusted his six-year-old son to the care of a poor Mexican family and set off into the California wilderness. He was never seen or heard from again. Meanwhile, young Paul "Francisco" Fuller continued to live with the Mexican family, speaking Spanish and apparently raised in the Catholic faith. At the age of nine, perhaps giving up hope of his father's return, Paul decided to leave his foster family. Somehow he made his way on foot across the entire United States in 1856 in search of his real family. None of the details of this incredible journey are known; Fuller did not care to talk about this chapter of his life. By some means, however, he did reach Vermont, but an aunt there proved less than welcoming and young Fuller kept on moving. By the age of ten he was one of the great horde of homeless boys living on the New York City streets.

It was the anomaly of a waif speaking Spanish with a perfect accent that first caught Charles Coudert, Sr.'s attention as he walked through the city one day. He stopped, questioned the boy—and ended by bringing Fuller into his home and taking his education in hand himself. For the next two years, Fuller studied under Coudert full-time, and the lessons continued after the boy, at twelve, was considered old enough to ride the train daily to downtown Manhattan with the Coudert sons and make himself useful to them. In Fuller's development over these years lies one of the proofs of Papa Coudert's genius as a teacher, for the orphan grew up recognizably a product of the Coudert mold—in his acute sense of honor, in his command of French and Spanish, in his love of literature, and in his devout faith. He was never formally adopted. But the love and trust flowing between him and the family were as strong as if he had been born into it.

Although Fuller eventually became a Coudert partner and one of the most famous international lawyers of his day, he started with the firm as the office boy. If he had the typical duties of an office boy in 1859, he commenced the day by laying the fires in the stoves and doing some perfunctory cleaning. A few years before this cleaning would have been an uphill effort, for the first Coudert offices—at 38 Broadway, 157 Broadway, and 39 Ann Street—were in dark, dingy buildings that had retail shops on the ground floor and narrow stairs leading to offices where the rents got cheaper at each successive flight. "The young fellows" just starting out in the law perched up in the fourth and fifth floor stories where the rents were very low indeed and the landings notoriously filthy.

While this kind of building remained the standard premises for law offices until well past the Civil War, New York City acquired in the 1850s its first modern buildings constructed exclusively for offices, which provided good light and air, internal spaces specifically designed for office use, and more impressive entrances and façades. It was to one of the earliest and most handsome of these, the Merchants Exchange at 38 William Street, that Coudert Brothers moved around 1858. Its elegant columned frontage occupied a whole city block and made a public statement concerning the prosperity of its tenants.

This was the Coudert Brothers office to which Paul Fuller first reported to work and from which for several years he ran all the multitude of errands that had to be run before the telephone's invention. Frederic René referred to him jokingly as the "Fuller Express," as he carried the brothers' messages about the city, home to Pelham, and often, by 1861, to the houses of the Westchester girls they were wooing.

The fact that all three brothers were courting is probably the best evidence there could be that the firm was firmly established by the early 1860s, for none of the Couderts was the sort to raise expectations before he could afford to support a wife. But having all three partners lovelorn and distracted at the same time posed a definite challenge to the practice. One afternoon in 1861 found Frederic René complaining about Louis Leonce's inability to make up his mind whether to attend a dinner where his love might or might not be present. He "oscillated, vibrated, gyrated and exasperated me," Frederic René reported. *"Imprimis.* If you ever have a brother who is in love and you wish to be master of your time, your temper, and your convenience, make no engagements, lay out no plans. . . ." But Frederic René was really in no position to cast stones, for he was spending quite a lot of time during office hours writing notes to his own *"chère amie"*—a Miss Lizzie McCredy—and self-admittedly having trouble at times keeping his mind on his work.

But in a short period, all three courtships were successfully concluded and life stabilized again. The kinds of families the brothers married into reveal much about the circles in which the Couderts were moving by the early 1860s. Charles junior was the first to wed, marrying in January 1861 Margaret Elizabeth ("Marie") Guion, a member of a large Westchester clan of French Huguenot descent. An uncle, Stephen B. Guion, had established the Black Star line of packets running between New York and Liverpool, which by 1853 had metamorphosed into the Williams & Guion line; and another uncle, William H. Guion, was a wealthy cotton commission merchant and shipper who also served as manager of the Williams & Guion agency in New York. Marie's father was said to have been one of the founders of Williams & Guion as well, but he died relatively young, leaving his widow and children without an adequate income. They lived as dependents in the household of a very elderly maternal uncle, where their mother served as a cross between housekeeper and companion.

Next, Frederic René married in February 1862 into another Westchester family with mercantile connections in the city. His bride, Elizabeth ("Lizzie") McCredy, was the daughter of Dennis McCredy, a second-generation Irish Catholic who had built up a prosperous business in the Wall Street district as a bill broker, an occupation combining elements of modern-day factoring, banking, and foreign-exchange trading. Many of his clients were probably engaged in the cotton and sugar trade, for he sent Lizzie—after she had finished her schooldays at the Convent of the Sacred Heart in Manhattanville, N.Y.—on a trip in 1859 to visit family friends in Nassau, the West Indies, Havana, and Charleston, South Carolina.

Then, sometime before October 1862, Louis Leonce wed his beloved Nora Edmonds, no doubt to his oldest brother's relief. Her father, Judge John Worth Edmonds, had been a power in the state's Democratic party from the early 1830s until 1853. "A tall, shaggy man, with bushy brows," he had radical leanings, winning an early fame by defending labor unions against charges of criminal conspiracy and introducing, as inspector of prisons, a system of rewards at the Elmira Reformatory as a substitute for corporal punishment. Elected to the bench in 1845, Edmonds gained an enduring reputation as one of the state's finest judges, but in 1853 he felt impelled by conscience to announce publicly his belief in spiritualism and, anticipating the uproar that announcement would provoke, he resigned his seat on the New York Court of Appeals. Thereafter, he practiced law privately in New York City, ridiculed by some for his religious beliefs but respected by the professional colleagues who knew him best, such as his former law student Samuel Tilden.

What the Couderts' new relatives by marriage had in common was that they all belonged to that group of New Yorkers who embraced, almost as an article of faith, the principles of free trade. The livelihood of New York export/import merchants, bankers, shippers, and commodity brokers like the Guions and McCredys obviously depended on an unimpeded flow of transatlantic and Caribbean commerce, and for over thirty years families like these had found their voice in the Democratic party, which was the stronghold of sound money, low tariffs, and laissez-faire economics. Edmonds, for example, as a labor attorney had rested his argument in the Hudson shoemaker case in 1836 on the principle that a restraint on unions interfered with the unrestricted competition vital to trade.

The Couderts were also Democrats, one and all. This was almost inevitable since the Democrats were the only party to welcome Catholics, and, years later, when Frederic René had become one of its most influential members, it was said of him that he had been born into the Democratic fold. But the Couderts were not Democrats merely by default, but convinced adherents of its free trade, antiprotectionist, low-tariff platform. And like others in the predominantly Democratic port city of New York, whose trade depended heavily on the South's cotton, they would have preferred to have the conciliatory Stephen A. Douglas elected president in 1860—in the hope that his election would prevent a civil war. In fact, Frederic René campaigned for Douglas, this being the first of the numerous presidential campaigns in which he took an active role.

But it was Lincoln who was inaugurated in March 1861, and the South seceded, provoking the Civil War. In the first flush of patriotic fervor, thousands of New Yorkers answered Lincoln's call for volunteers in April 1861. It was probably around this time—when Frederic René was still single—that he considered the idea of raising a regiment composed of French exiles. But nothing, in fact, came of the scheme. As the year progressed, the war became increasingly unpopular in New York City as its mercantile houses were indeed thrown into a temporary depression by the loss of the cotton trade, and it is likely that Coudert was unable to find enough volunteers. By 1862 the military fever had definitely passed, and the brothers married, continued their practice, and remained civilians throughout the war.

In the 1864 elections, Charles junior, at least, relented and voted for Lincoln. But Frederic René campaigned and voted for the Democratic candidate, George McClellan. The oldest Coudert brother had thought the war a folly to begin with; now he believed "that the war could be brought to an end—that it should be brought to an end."

Nevertheless, the Civil War brought Frederic René an important professional opportunity: the chance to work with Reverdy Johnson on the Blockading cases, a set of U.S. Supreme Court cases that turned on the legality of capture of ships engaged in running the Gulf blockade and the confiscation of their cargos. A Democrat from Maryland, Johnson had started in practice in 1816 and ever since Daniel Webster's death had been acknowledged the greatest lawyer in America. Lincoln thought highly of Johnson, consulted him on legal matters and sent him in 1862—shortly after Johnson had been elected to the U.S. Senate—on a special mission to New Orleans to investigate foreign consuls' complaints that the occupying federal army had been seizing neutrals' property.

Of the three Blockading cases that Johnson argued before the

U.S. Supreme Court in 1864, two, *The Venice* and *The Baigarry*, arose in the District Court for the Eastern District of Louisiana, and the third, *The Andromeda*, involved a Louisiana shipowner. Presumably, then, Johnson's representation developed from his visit to Louisiana as a special agent in 1862. By 1864, however, although he was still a U.S. senator and still conducting a very sizeable private practice, Johnson was virtually blind and needed younger men's assistance. There is no record of exactly what Frederic René contributed to the preparation of these cases, but the rights of neutrals in wartime were a significant issue in each of them. From his familiarity with consular law, Frederic René may have been of help on this point. Moreover, the *Andromeda* was nominally owned by Caro & Co., whose principals were French citizens resident in Cuba, and both the *Baigarry* and the *Andromeda* were captured off Cuba, so that at a more mundane level there may have been depositions in French and Spanish requiring translation.

Argued in wartime, the cases for the captees met with a marked lack of sympathy from the bench, as it upheld the legality of the U.S. Navy's actions in *The Baigarry* and *The Andromeda*. But in *The Venice*, where the ship was at anchor in Union-occupied territory, where "it was not asserted that any breach of blockade was ever thought of," and where the ship was seized after the publication of a military order assuring all rights of property to persons within the territory who had not engaged in active hostilities, the Court decided for Johnson—reluctantly. It ruled that the foreign shipowner, by remaining in Louisiana after the outbreak of war, had forfeited a neutral's ordinary right to protection of his property, and the property could have been seized had it not been for the military's own order to the contrary. It was not a very satisfying victory for those interested in protecting neutrals' rights, but to get any ruling by the Court against the government while the Civil War still raged was a triumph in and of itself.

The Civil War blockade also brought Coudert Brothers at least one case of its own—one that was to become the occasion of Frederic René's first argument before the U.S. Supreme Court. This was *United States v. Mora*, in which Coudert represented the Cuban merchant and banker Fausto Mora—called Foster Mora in the report of the case. Mora had stood surety for a bond that the New York collector of customs had demanded in 1863 before he would grant a clearance for the *Sarah Marsh* to sail for Matamoras, Mexico. A town on the Rio Grande directly opposite the Confederate state of Texas, Matamoras was a favorite port for shippers who planned to sell their goods in Texas in contravention of the blockade. In view of the destination, therefore, the collector demanded a bond at double the value of the cargo—which was a rather modest sum, given that blockade-run goods could often fetch in Texas at least ten times their value in New York. The bond, secured by real estate in New York, was to be collected upon if the shipper failed to present within seven months a consular certificate establishing that the goods had been actually landed and consumed in Mexico.

The *Sarah Marsh* reached Mexico in March or April 1863, but the proof of where the goods were consumed was never forthcoming, and the government sought collection on the bond. In the Circuit Court for the Southern District of New York, the defense rested on the ground that the collector had no authority to demand a bond double the value of the cargo in question. When the government offered to present proof that part of the cargo had been "sold to the military authorities of the so-called Confederate States in Brownsville, Texas," the court sustained the defense's objection and, upon the defendant's motion, directed a verdict for Mora, which the jury duly returned.

It took until October 1878—more than fifteen years after the *Sarah Marsh* sailed for the Gulf—for the appeal to reach the U.S. Supreme Court. Here the defense's arguments in the lower court were reiterated, with Frederic René maintaining that the Treasury Department regulations under which the bond was collected were broader than the provisions in the underlying congressional act from which the Treasury's authority was derived. The statute must be strictly construed, he said, especially since the bond in this case was not a voluntary one and was "highly penal."

The Court was not persuaded on this point, finding in the act language giving the Treasury broad discretionary powers and determining that the lower court had erred in rejecting the government's evidence that the condition of the bond was breached. The verdict was overturned, and the case remanded for retrial.

The loss disturbed not in the least the Couderts' cordial relations with the Moras, who remained clients of the firm. Given the size of the investments that the firm was managing for them a few years after *United States v. Mora,* it would seem that twenty thousand dollars was probably considerably less than one year of Mora's usual income by 1878. In other words, this legal battle—like several later Coudert cases before the Supreme Court—was probably fought out mostly as a matter of principle.

As a result of his upbringing, Frederic René was always sensitive to questions of honor. Nevertheless, despite his one outburst of military fever at the start of the Civil War, he never could see in the spectacle of Americans killing Americans, amidst the break-down of their political and legal system, much occasion for pride. In hindsight, he consistently spoke of the Civil War as a tragedy—not a source of honor and glory but a rather senseless slaughter.

He felt differently about the two struggles the reform wing of the Democratic party undertook in the aftermath of the Civil War—its local fight against municipal corruption in New York City and its national effort to end the army's occupation of the South and restore that region to the rule of law. In these wars, fought through the courts and the ballot box, Frederic René enlisted with wholehearted enthusiasm, in no doubt about what the honorable course might be.

The leader of the Reform Democrats in New York State was Samuel J. Tilden, who had started in politics as the protégé of Martin Van Buren and Judge Edmonds. By 1869 he had worked his way up to chairmanship of the state Democratic party, which position he used to launch the crusade that toppled New York City's corrupt Democratic boss, William Tweed. As soon as he made his first moves against Tweed, Coudert began to support him and quickly became known as a "Tilden man."

One of the lasting outcomes of the Tweed fight was the founding of the Association of the Bar of the City of New York, which represented an effort to bring together the "decent part of the profession" to stand up to Tweed's corrupted judiciary. To this end, the "call to organization" was circulated quietly—almost secretly—to those considered the leaders of the bar in December 1869. Some two hundred signed, and high up on the list were the three Couderts, who doubtless also attended the January 1870 organizational meeting at which Tilden gave the most memorable address.

Frederic René's contemporaries who, like him, were original founders and later presidents of the bar association included William M. Evarts, James C. Carter, Joseph H. Choate, and Wheeler Peckham. Each of these four talented younger lawyers worked under Charles O'Conor, the prosecutor of the Tweed ring, in the courtroom battle against Boss Tweed and his subordinates. Coudert, though, played his most memorable role not as a prosecutor but as a campaigner, working vigorously for the slate of Tilden candidates that swept Tweed's out of the state assembly and, thereby, made possible the actual prosecutions.

Frederic René also stumped for the Democrats and a platform calling for an end to military rule in the South in the 1868, 1872, and 1876 presidential campaigns. The later campaign, which pitted Tilden against Rutherford B. Hayes, was the election that was stolen—in the opinion of the Democrats of the time and of later historians—by Republican manipulation of the vote count in three southern states, one of which was Louisiana. By November 9, when it became obvious that the Republican returning board in Louisiana was likely to throw out enough Democratic votes to swing Louisiana back into the Hayes camp, the Tilden forces decided to ask eminent citizens from throughout the nation to go to Louisiana and supervise the board's count. From New York, as one of its two "visiting statesmen," went Frederic René, accompanied by his wife, Lizzie. The Republicans sent their own "statesmen"—who proved much cleverer and far less scrupulous—and the result was that an electoral vote count achieved by bribery and certified by two forged signatures was sent to the electoral college, leading ultimately after a great deal more maneuvering to Hayes's inauguration.

"My father always felt Mr. Tilden had been defrauded of the election," said Frederic René's son, who could remember being taken as a small child to visit Tilden. "The old gentleman was palsied, I think, at that time, and I can see him now. He was very trembly, and my father called him 'Mr. President' and had a nice talk with him." While at Tilden's home—this visit would have been in the early 1880s—Frederic René may also have discussed some business with Miss Anna Gould, who was a relative of Tilden's by marriage and who came to live with him and read aloud to him by the hour when his eyesight failed. Coudert Brothers looked after Miss Gould's investments for her—a fact that takes on some significance when one realizes that Tilden knew intimately every attorney of any note in New York. He relied on Charles O'Conor and James C. Carter for advice about his will in these declining years, but for the honest and conservative handling of the affairs of a maiden lady who could easily be taken advantage of, he apparently thought Coudert Brothers unsurpassed.

Through the political activities of its senior member, linking it to the reforming wing of the Democratic party, Coudert Brothers reinforced its reputation for integrity and also acquired a few clients such as Miss Gould. But the brothers gained a much more important infusion of clients from the simple event of moving their households in 1866 from Westchester County to South Orange, New Jersey, a fashionable semirural village of some three thousand inhabitants.

This was a joint move, for the Couderts never resided more than a few miles from each other while Papa Coudert lived. Family tradition has it that the senior Coudert, as a good French patriarch, took it for granted that his sons would bring their brides home, all to reside together under his roof, and that the younger Couderts did accede to his wishes initially. Tradition also says that conflicts among the wives proved the scheme impracticable, but even if the wives had not had trouble with the arrangement, it is difficult to see how it could have been sustained in view of their fertility rate: the three couples produced twenty-five children all together, of which sixteen survived to adulthood. As this brood outgrew the Pelham house, Charles junior, and Louis Leonce and their families moved to New Rochelle, a different town but only a few minutes from Pelham on the railroad line.

In South Orange, the families settled down into the same arrangement. With Papa Coudert lived Tante Virginie, Leonie and Paul Fuller as well as Frederic René, Lizzie, and their children, while the Charles junior and Louis Leonce families took separate residences nearby. Charles's wife, Marie, held herself a bit aloof, but the others seem to have been more or less constantly running in and out of each other's households, and whenever one brother was traveling, the other two made a point of visiting the absent member's family to check up on their needs. As Frederic René was to say, "We were members of a united and affectionate family, sharing each other's burdens."

The choice of South Orange was, no doubt, prompted by two factors: the presence of a sizeable French community and the location there of Seton Hall College, a Catholic institution. The two were, in fact, not unrelated, for the French community—which included such families as the Theobauds, Boisabins, Barrils, and Reynauds—were strong supporters of the college and active in its affairs. Papa Coudert's house was less than a mile south of the college, and soon he and his household had become admirers of Father Michael A. Corrigan, its twenty-seven-year-old vice president.

Educated abroad, Corrigan was an urbane and intelligent man who seems to have appreciated the Couderts as much as they appreciated him. To him, Papa Coudert could make his confession in French, a fact that was of tremendous comfort to the old man. Leonie, the Couderts' still unmarried sister, confided in him her troubles, and Lizzie found him a source of strength as four of her eight children died in infancy. Charles junior and Louis Leonce considered him a friend, and Frederic René trusted his judgment and allowed Corrigan to draw him into active service to the church.

In 1868 Corrigan became president of Seton Hall, and at the next annual meeting Frederic René was elected to the board of trustees, where he would serve for nearly twenty years, being awarded an honorary LL.D. in 1880 for his efforts. It was probably also due to Corrigan that Frederic René became active in the Catholic businessmen's associations—the Catholic Union and the Xavier Union—and in 1873 undertook a course of public lectures at the Cooper Union under the sponsorship of the Catholic Union.

Coudert's lectures had various subjects—"Manners and Morals," "The Fine Art of Lying," and "The Church and the Bar"—but only one unifying theme: the need for mutual tolerance and respect between Protestants and Catholics. This was a topic on which Coudert felt deeply, and he labored hard over the research and polishing of his addresses. But what emerged were talks that were immensely entertaining—witty, tongue-in-cheek, rendering absurd the excesses that both religions had displayed in past persecutions. Coudert was using a weapon that he had honed in the courtroom: his ability to evoke laughter. He had a deadpan style far removed from the rhetorical bombast of most nineteenth-century speakers, a quiet voice, an almost total lack of mannerisms—and a wicked relish for picking out inconsistencies, illogic, and unwitting hypocrisies. As was said of him on another occasion: "He was as mild and sarcastic as might be expected from the opportunity offered, but always so smilingly polite that even the men he was cutting into ribbons could not help joining in the general merriment at their expense." It was perhaps the perfect style for an attack on intolerance—and Coudert did so well in this debut performance that the church would call upon him again and again as its spokesman.

Thus, the move to South Orange resulted in Frederic René's securing the Catholic church as a more or less lifetime client of his advocate's skills, albeit a nonpaying one; but it also produced far more lucrative contacts. One of these was the Hoguet family, Frenchmen active in the Xavier Union; Henry Hoguet was the president of Emigrant Industrial Savings Bank, of which Frederic René became a director. Coudert Brothers also represented businessmen George V. Hecker and J. J. Barrill, who were also Seton Hall trustees. The most important contact, though, was probably Eugene Kelly, an Irish immigrant who made a fortune in the dry goods business during the California gold rush. Kelly returned to New York in 1857, married the niece of the archbishop of New York, John Hughes, purchased an extensive estate immediately east of the Seton Hall campus, and started a banking business. The Kelly and Coudert families became close friends, and Eugene Kelly & Company provided Coudert Brothers with the finance for its real estate ventures, both those representing the brothers' personal investments and those undertaken on clients' behalf. For, as its list of clients resident overseas grew, the firm became increasingly involved in investing client funds in the United States—not in corporate stocks or bonds, almost all of which were highly speculative commodities in the post–Civil War era, but in New York and New Jersey mortgages. From the firm's 1883–84 ledger, it appears that Coudert Brothers made it a practice to deposit with Eugene Kelly & Company all such client funds while waiting for deals to close and to work closely with Kelly in these ventures.

As their business agents in France, on the other hand, Coudert Brothers used Cazade, Crooks & Reynaud—the Reynaud being Albert Reynaud, an old friend of the family. (It was whether or not to attend Reynaud's dinner that had set Louis Leonce to "oscillating" back in 1861.) Reynaud manned the New York office and appears to have lived in or near South Orange and to have been put to work by Corrigan, after he became bishop of Newark in 1873, on some of the business affairs of the diocese.

This Kelly-Coudert-Reynaud connection was of major importance to the history of Coudert Brothers, for out of it grew in 1879 the venture that made Coudert Brothers an international firm— the Paris branch office of the firm that was known in France as Coudert Frères.

Chapter Three

À PARIS

F or all their fluency in French and their knowledge of French culture, the Coudert brothers and their sister never had the chance to visit France itself until they were adults. Ever family-minded, Papa Coudert had kept up a correspondence with his relatives through the years, and his brother Eugene had visited him in New York when the boys were young. But the return visit was apparently not paid until 1870, when not only could the Couderts afford a vacation in Europe but also regular steamship service had reduced the hazardous ocean passage to a week or two.

This 1870 trip was followed by others in short order, and by 1879 all of the second generation had visited France at least once, and most of them several times. In these first encounters with their *"belle patrie,"* the younger Couderts displayed reactions not much different from those of other American tourists of their day. For example, the attention given to cooking and the richness of the food were delightful but more than digestive systems used to plain American fare could sometimes handle. Louis Leonce shipped artichoke plants back to the States for his kitchen garden but complained about "ceremonious dinners which produce crapulousness" and bemoaned that "no Frenchman can be induced to spend less than two hours at his breakfast. I dread being asked to breakfast and would like to avoid dinner . . . as I am tired of eating." Paul Fuller was struck by the novelty of being in a predominantly Catholic country where all business stopped on a religious holiday: such things didn't happen in America!

And Frederic René evidently went home and confided his shock at the boldness of the French streetwalkers to his friend Edward Patterson, for when the latter finally got to France himself, he reported: "Paris is all you claim for it except in the point of morality. I have not found it as immoral as you did." With tongue in cheek, he added, "No blandishments have been showered upon me by the French ladies, which considering my great personal attractions must astonish you and me. . . ."

After enough trips, the Couderts lost their sense of surprise and discovery at France's "foreignness" and became quite comfortable there. By the time of an 1882 visit, Lizzie was writing home to the children that "Papa looks as serenely happy as usual while in Paris." But this adjustment took several years. And if in New York City, the Couderts sometimes felt more than a little French, in Paris they always knew themselves to be Americans.

Still, family was family, wherever found, and the first trip in 1870, which was primarily a visit to meet the French branch of the Couderts, was a great success. Papa Coudert, Tante Virginie, Leonie, Frederic René, Lizzie, Charles, Marie, and assorted children descended upon the Château Lambert as the guests of Papa Coudert's fifty-year-old nephew, Marquis du Pont du Chambon, an attorney himself. The du Chambons and Couderts were soon on intimate terms, but the highlight of their stay was the reunion of Papa Coudert with his brother Victor after nearly forty years. Whereas seventy-four-year-old Papa Coudert was "a splendid specimen of vigorous and manly old age," Victor was almost eighty years old, had been partially paralyzed by a stroke, and could only walk with crutches. Frederic René described their meeting as follows:

"The Franco-Prussian War had just broken out at that time, and I recall that my father said laughingly to his brother immediately after the first greetings had been exchanged, *'Eh bien Victor, pourquoi ne vas tu pas te battre contre les Prussians?* [Eh, Victor, why don't you go to fight the Prussians?]' To which the invalid answered looking with admiration on his younger and more vigorous relative: *'Ah j'irais a bien si j'etais comme toi* [Ah, I certainly would, if I were in your condition],' and I really believe that the old gentleman meant it."

From Lambert the Coudert entourage went to Paris, where they heard the crowd sending off France's soldiers with the cry "To Berlin! To Berlin!" Instead, it was the German troops that swept into France and began a siege of Paris in September 1870, only weeks after the Couderts' return to America. In New York the

French consul general Victor Place was by September engaged in purchasing U.S. weapons from Remington & Sons for use by the French forces still fighting in the provinces—and thereby setting the stage for a scandal that would rock both the French and American governments and involve Frederic René in an effort to see justice done.

The scandal from the American side of the Atlantic arose from the fact that U.S. Neutrality Laws prohibited the U.S. government from selling arms to either France or Germany during the Franco-Prussian War. Accordingly, the War Department had duly banned Remington & Sons, which the French government had retained as its agent, from entering a bid when a large quantity of "surplus" army weapons was auctioned off in October 1870. Yet virtually all the successful bidders, it was later proved, were simply dummies for Remington & Sons, and the attempt to disguise the connection was not even halfhearted: one buyer was a Remington attorney, and another was a Remington son-in-law. Moreover, the War Department sold at this auction not only useless surplus, as it was authorized to do, but at least 190,000 brand-new Springfield rifles, ammunition recently manufactured at U.S. arsenals, and a long list of other nonsurplus munitions. It later seemed to certain observers that the sale was explicable only if someone fairly high up in President Grant's administration had been induced to look the other way.

Meanwhile, on the other side of the Atlantic, the French government did its accounts once the war was over and realized that it had entrusted $6.8 million to Victor Place, its consul in New York City, for payments to Remington & Sons but had received in return weapons for which the U.S. government had been paid only about $4 million. Where did the missing millions go? On the premise presumably that the best defense is a good offense, Sam Remington laid charges in Paris in June 1871 that Consul Place had pocketed it. Place, on the other hand, maintained that he understood that Remington had used the missing funds to "grease people's hands" in order to secure the armaments that France had so urgently needed.

In an illicit arms deal, of course, anything is possible, but given that the Grant administration today is remembered principally for its unbridled corruption, it seems probable that Place was telling the truth and Remington covering for the War Department officials he had bribed. Coudert Brothers, the attorneys for the consulate in New York, believed in Place's innocence in any event, as did the first French court to hear his case, which acquitted him of charges of wrongdoing in the fall of 1871.

But if Place was innocent, it followed that Remington & Sons must be guilty of bribery in the United States, and so Sam Remington could not let the matter drop. He appealed the decision, renewing the charges against Place in France. At this point the acting consul general in New York, Bellaigne de Burghas, and Frederic René, accompanied by Paul Fuller, departed in a great hurry for Paris, sailing on November 18, 1871, in hopes of reaching France before Place's retrial would begin on December 13.

"Frederic leaves very unexpectedly for Europe the day after tomorrow upon important business," Lizzie wrote to Father Corrigan, somewhat distraught at the speed of events. "It is quite a trial to all of us as you may well know." Because Coudert Brothers' nineteenth-century files were disposed of during the 1950s, it cannot be said with certainty what de Burghas, Coudert, and Fuller hoped to contribute to Place's defense, but it seems likely that they were carrying with them an affidavit signed by Remington's head bookkeeper alleging that the company had made out backdated invoices, deliberately inflated other invoices, and generally "cooked" its books in order to defraud the French government ("*pour mieux tromper le gouvernement français*"). Certified on September 16, 1871, by notary public George H. Young, who was a member of Coudert Brothers' staff, this affidavit had apparently been prepared for the first trial, but not used. When the Coudert attorneys sailed for France in November, their objective was perhaps to see that this document was introduced, but most definitely to help Place's defense in some way.

As they crossed the Atlantic in one direction, however, Sam Remington was crossing in the other, headed for Washington, D.C., where he obtained official-looking letters attesting to his probity from the same administration officials who had sold the U.S. arms to his dummies. At the retrial, which was postponed to January to allow Remington time to return from the United States, the defense was not allowed to introduce the bookkeeper's affidavit, which was the strongest evidence available that the missing millions of dollars had disappeared after being turned over to Remington. The best Place's attorneys could do was to leak this document to the French press. On the other hand, the court accepted as evidence the endorsements presented by Remington from the U.S. secretary of war and others and gave them full credit as representing the official view of the U.S. government on the subject. The weight given to these letters made the verdict almost inevitable, and on January 26, 1872, the French court—to the outrage of members of France's diplomatic corps who had packed the courtroom to support Place—sentenced the former consul general to two years' imprisonment for defrauding the French government.

A footnote to the Place affair appears in the Coudert correspondence in May 1873 when Paul Fuller ran into de Burghas in Paris and learned from him that Place was still in prison and hope for a pardon was fading. Fuller was in Paris at this time, however, to try to help yet another unhappy prisoner, Baron Gauldreé Boileau. Boileau, who had served as first secretary of the French Legation in Washington, D.C., under Napoleon III and minister plenipotentiary to Peru, was married to Susy Benton, a daughter of former U.S. senator Thomas Hart Benton. In the late 1860s the Boileaus' eldest son had attended Seton Hall College in South Orange, and the Boileau and Coudert families had become quite friendly.

Through his marriage to Susy, Boileau acquired as a brother-in-law General John C. Frémont, the western explorer and former presidential candidate who, after the Civil War, became president of the Memphis, El Paso and Pacific Railroad. Boileau's legal misfortunes began when the Memphis and El Paso fell into financial difficulties in 1869, and it decided to sell bonds for construction finance in Paris. The baron was one of the French promoters, and it was eventually alleged that he and others had misrepresented the company's situation, giving investors the impression that the railroad was already a functioning transcontinental line and that the U.S. government had guaranteed the interest on the bonds. In fact, several French newspapers had quickly branded the bond issue a fraud, and the U.S. ambassador had urged the U.S. government to investigate. Still, some $6 million of bonds were sold, and Boileau was said to have collected $150,000 for his services.

For a number of years the threat of a French prosecution shadowed the Boileaus' life without quite materializing. The blow finally fell in March 1873 when the criminal tribunal in Paris arraigned Frémont, Boileau, and six others on charges of swindling and named a date just a few weeks later for the start of the trial. On such short notice none of the Couderts could apparently travel to France, but Paul Fuller, then twenty-six years old, represented the firm and provided assistance to the Boileaus and their French attorney, Victor LeFranc. Susy later told the Couderts that, during the trial, "Dear Paul Fuller grew to be much to me . . . and your names were always in our talk. We looked to you so much for advice, and sympathy—all of which you have given in full measure."

It was a point in Boileau's favor that, although he had been out of the country at the time of the indictment, he had returned to France to defend himself. And at his trial he was able to prove that he had taken his commission in railroad bonds, not cash, and that once he realized the railroad was failing, he had sold the bonds for what he could get and turned all the proceeds over to Mr. Grey for the benefit of the other French investors. Moreover, others testified that Boileau had never misrepresented the railroad's situation and that he had tried to restrain one of the promoters who did. All this testimony produced a very favorable impression on both the Parisian and the New York newspapers—but not on the judge. Not only was Boileau found guilty, but an immediate appeal failed and the baron entered prison.

Susy Boileau and her French advisors then tried to obtain a pardon, while in the United States Frederic René and Bishop Corrigan circulated a petition for clemency among the Catholic bishops of their acquaintance. Susy was grateful for Frederic René's "never tiring efforts," but neither approach won a release.

Victor Place in prison, Baron Boileau in prison—the failure rate must have been disheartening. Yet the impression the Couderts were making in French legal circles was clearly a good one: it was in 1875 that France conferred upon Frederic René the order of Chevalier of the Legion of Honor. Moreover, Frederic René was becoming known in the United States as a person with a useful understanding of foreign legal systems. This reputation was further enhanced by his report on the York and Antwerp Rules of General Average, which were adopted by an international conference in Antwerp in August 1877. General average is the principle under which losses are adjusted when cargo or freight must be jettisoned to preserve the ship and the safety of its passengers, and the 1877 conference of the Association for the Reform and Codification of the Laws of Nations represented a private voluntary effort by shipowners, adjusters, insurers, and jurists from every Western nation to arrive at a few uniform rules.

Frederic René attended the Antwerp conference, whose proceedings were conducted in French, as the delegate of the Chamber of Commerce of New York, the Board of Marine Underwriters of New York, and the Board of Marine Underwriters of New Orleans. There he contributed to the debates, first joining with the Continental delegates to fend off an attempt by Lloyd's of London to scuttle the entire conference and subsequently working to ensure that the Antwerp revisions reflected American practices as much as possible. In this, owing in large part to his fluency and persuasiveness in French—which set him off noticeably from the other American delegates—he was almost wholly successful. As New York insurer Walter R. T. Jones noted, of the twelve rules adopted, "eight rules virtually conform to our practices, two modify in a small degree average allowances, one modifies slightly, but makes universal allowances already recognized. One changes our practice." Sending Frederic René to Antwerp had entailed "heavy expenses," Jones wrote, but no person "can have doubt of the ability with which the mission was fulfilled."

What made the greatest impact in New York mercantile circles, however, was Coudert's published report, which was widely circulated in the city. The thirty-nine-page pamphlet not only summarized the conference proceedings—somewhat inaccurately, as Frederic René modestly made no reference to his own contributions—but also provided a masterful discussion of the liability of shipowners, disposing of the idea that British and American law coincided on this point. Presenting an overview of the subject from an international perspective that encompassed French, British, and American commentaries, statutes, and case law, it constituted something of a tour de force, both for its readability and for the legal scholarship displayed.

At the 1878 Conference of the Law of Nations held in Frankfurt, Frederic René's name appeared prominently in the report of progress toward adoption of the York-Antwerp Rules in the United States, and he attended the 1879 session in London and was a delegate again at Berne in 1880, by which time incorporation of the rules was a standard feature of bills of lading worldwide and even Lloyd's was including them in insurance policies.

Although Frederic René had advanced an American point of view at Antwerp, he argued as vigorously—and far more bluntly—in New York against a faction of diehards in the Chamber of Commerce who wanted to accept no modification of American practices. "If we thought it beneath our dignity to yield on any point of our practice and of our law; if we thought it wiser and better to build up around us a Chinese wall of national prejudice," he told the chamber on February 6, 1879, "then our course could be consistent with nothing but a refusal to participate in these international councils." The chamber must divest itself of any prejudice "created against these rules, by the fact that they were made abroad and mostly by foreigners," he said—no doubt in that tone of bland, deadpan sarcasm that he did so well.

The truth is Frederic René was sometimes impatient with American parochialism. He had genuinely liked and been impressed by the men he met at the Law of Nations conferences, and he had greatly enjoyed the spectacle of private citizens from various countries meeting and conclusively settling their differences without any reference to their respective governments. It appealed to the same democratic instinct that made him always inclined to go through the press to the people when other channels were blocked—the instinct that the people are the basis of whatever authority the law may have.

Frederic René used public opinion again as a lever in obtaining governmental support for two notable Franco-American projects during the 1870s. One was the American fund-raising campaign for Bartholdi's *Statue of Liberty*, which Frederic René launched on October 8, 1876—one month after *Lafayette*'s dedication—by granting the press an interview in which he expressed his shock at learning that Philadelphia was angling to steal the *Liberty* project from New York City. In reality, Philadelphia was no less apathetic about the *Statue of Liberty* than was New York. But the cities were traditional rivals, and, moreover, New York was writhing with jealousy in the fall of 1876 at the success of Philadelphia's Centennial Exhibition. So while there surely must have been some broad winks exchanged at Frederic René's press conference, the New York reporters and editors recognized that they were being handed a good story, and they played along with him wholeheartedly, in the process creating a degree of popular interest where almost none had existed before.

It was only a week later that Frederic René organized the actual fund-raising committee for *Liberty*, which took the name L'Union Franco-Americaine de New York and duly elected him its president. Using the need to thwart Philadelphia's allegedly larcenous intent, this group secured the city's official endorsement of Bartholdi's dream and even won a modest subsidy from the municipal public works department to install *Liberty*'s arm and torch in Madison Square in 1877. L'Union gave everyone who subscribed to *Liberty* a free ticket to ascend the torch and also collected the profits from the sale of photographs at the site. It was a small beginning, but the committee Frederic René established saw the project through to its completion in 1886, and Frederic René continued as its president for five or six years and as an influential member thereafter. Thus, it was under his leadership that the first American steps were taken toward realizing the hopes of Bartholdi and his French sponsors.

Not long after the start of the *Liberty* campaign, Frederic René turned to the problem of ensuring American participation in the Paris Exposition of 1878. The difficulty here was that the Grant and then the Hayes administrations had refused to provide for a general display of American products or to introduce the necessary sponsoring bill into Congress—thus frustrating the handful of American businessmen who wanted to put up displays at the expo. One of these was Robert A. Chesebrough, the inventor of Vaseline and founder of the company that became Chesebrough-Ponds, who was anxious to develop the European market for his products. Chesebrough's wife and Frederic René's were sisters, so Chesebrough turned naturally to his brother-in-law for help.

On Frederic René's advice, Chesebrough organized a committee of like-minded businessmen and had them send Coudert to Paris as their representative. Frederic René returned with a protocol-defying permission from the Duke Descazes for a display of products by Americans on their private account. Nudged by Frederic René, Secretary of State William Evarts considered the embarrassing position in which the Hayes administration might find itself—and had the congressional bill introduced, whereupon Chesebrough's committee of businessmen lobbied it through.

"I know well my dear friend," Chesebrough wrote to Coudert once his display was drawing admiring comments at the expo, "that your services were and are at the foundation of the whole matter and that without you, neither I nor anyone else could have done anything at all. . . ." Chesebrough was convinced that Frederic René was a heavy gun—"a perfect 100 pounder"—when it came to this kind of diplomatic and political maneuvering.

Because of Frederic René's skills as an advocate and his civic-mindedness, Coudert Brothers had numerous connections in France by 1879, the year in which the firm acted on the adventuresome and, in the climate of American law practice of the age, quite unprecedented idea of establishing a branch office in Paris. If Frederic René had been a sole practitioner, however, it is doubtful that the firm would have opened a Paris office then, for the *"Succursale à Paris"* seems to have been established in the summer of 1879 primarily in response to the needs—and hopes—of the "notarial" side of the practice.

The American lawyer whom Coudert Brothers chose to head the Paris branch was twenty-eight-year-old Edmond Kelly, who had joined Coudert Brothers in 1877 as a law student. Born near Toulouse, France, to American parents in 1851, Kelly attended a British public school before earning a B.A. from Columbia College in 1870, a second B.A. in science from St. John's College, Cambridge University, in 1875, and his LL.B. from Columbia in 1877. Said to have wit and magnetism, he impressed the Coudert partners with his efforts in a most complicated litigation involving remote genealogical researches in Hesse-Cassel, local customs and legislation, and the survival of treaty relations after the extinction of the local autonomy of the duchy. Kelly's display of "knowledge, acumen and persistency" in that case led directly to his selection as head of the Paris office.

The work of actually organizing the Paris office and seeing that Kelly got off to a good start, however, fell to Louis Leonce Coudert, who was the logical choice for the job as the firm's administrative partner. By July 21, 1879, Louis Leonce had virtually finished setting up the office at 3 rue Scribe, the same building in which the firm's business agents in France, Cazade, Crooks & Reynaud, already had their offices. The firm's space was not yet fully furnished, but the bank account had been opened, stationery had been printed, and Louis Leonce was able to advise his brothers that they could start sending their cables directly to Coudert Frères.

Edmond Kelly was also already at work by July 1879. In fact, Louis Leonce reported that Kelly had taken care of a client matter and handled the business "faithfully and intelligently"—but a problem had developed with the fee. Kelly had been willing to set-tle for two thousand French francs (about four hundred dollars), but Louis Leonce had intervened and collected twenty-five hun-dred francs, although he thought that was still too little for the work done. Having collected the fee in francs, Louis Leonce planned to deposit it to Coudert Frères' account and use it to buy office furniture—so it is perhaps fair to describe this sum as the first fee earned by the Paris office.

Despite the progress already made, Louis Leonce was, none-theless, moving through the closing weeks of July 1879 at a hectic pace, for he was in Paris not just to oversee the opening of Coudert Frères but also evidently to drum up business for the New York office. To this end he had prepared a form letter, and Cazade was taking him around, introducing him to useful contacts such as a director of the Credit Lyonnais. Louis Leonce was also making contacts on his own, and on July 23, 1879, he wrote his brothers:

> I have returned from an interview with Danielle Co. They have given me a list of 39 of their friends and correspondents to whom I am to send my circular letter referring to them. They are to get 1/4 of one per cent on capital and 1/8 on payment of interest paid thru them. I objected to this 1/8 but it amounts to but little & they were very anxious to get it. . . . I then called on Vernes Co., Banker friends of Crulon Co., who thinks something may be done—but nothing decided yet. . . . Fausto Mora has called here; he thinks this agency a 'big thing.'

What Louis Leonce was apparently doing was locating French capital for investment in the United States in private bonds backed by mortgages. These mortgage bonds were an instrument particularly suited for foreign investors, since restrictions by certain states on alien ownership of real estate—and the perpetual threat of such restrictions being imposed by other states—made it difficult or undesirable for foreigners to own U.S. real property or mortgages directly. The instrument itself was not new, but Coudert Brothers put an unusual twist on it by putting its own reputation behind the mortgage bonds purchased on the firm's recommendation: "Although no guaranty was given of these mortgages, such as mortgage companies later furnished," Frederic René's son later recalled, "I think that in all cases where a client lost money through foreclosure sales the office made good the principal."

Approaching the business in this frame of mind, the Couderts were, of course, cautious about their recommendations. As a result, the firm's clients were steered primarily toward bonds issued by Eugene Kelly & Company, the investment bank headed by Eugene Kelly (who was no relation to Edmond Kelly), which was one of the major financiers of the burgeoning residential developments in New Jersey's Essex, Hudson, and Bergen counties immediately opposite Manhattan. But the Couderts also favored mortgage bonds on the brownstones rising along Fifth Avenue between Washington Square and Central Park, and the issuer of these was often Frederic René's brother-in-law Robert A. Chesebrough or their former neighbor in South Orange, John T. Lord, who was the trustee for the Boileaus—again, men whom the Couderts knew well and trusted implicitly.

The firm apparently made its money in the mortgage-bond business strictly from performing title searches, drawing up loan papers, drafting assignments, and providing other related legal services to their French clients who were purchasers of the bonds. In such of the firm's accounts as survive from this period, at any rate, there is no trace of fees or commissions received from Kelly, Chesebrough, or other bond issuers. As for the finder's fees, it is interesting to note that five years after the Paris branch opened, Coudert Brothers was paying the "1/4 of one per cent on capital" to only one French firm, if that. Apparently their mortgage-bond practice developed not through solicitation so much as word of mouth.

But it grew very rapidly. By 1883–84 legal services rendered in connection with the mortgage-bond business amounted to roughly twelve thousand dollars after expenses, or about 10 percent of the firm's gross profit. By contrast, the more conventional legal services that Edmond Kelly was rendering in Paris brought about twenty-five hundred dollars into the firm's profit column for 1883.

The partners were satisfied with this profit and with Kelly's work, but the Paris branch was still something of a headache for the New York partners during its first years because of Kelly's independence. Louis Leonce was in Paris during this period almost more than he was in New York. His visit in the summer of 1879 was followed by another one covering most of November and December 1879, and he spent nearly a whole year, from at least June 1881 until May 1882, in Paris, during which time he was trying to recover from an illness but also visiting the office at 3 rue Scribe frequently. And he was back again in July 1882.

It was during this last visit that Frederic René wrote to his youngest brother in Paris:

> We sent you a despatch on Saturday, calling attention to Kelly's stamping our papers with his individual stamp. The particular paper was [illeg.] Durand's will. I do not understand that as intelligent a man as K. should opine that we can accept such a situation. The difficulty seems to be that he does not understand our theory, at heart, viz: that the office is C.B.'s. He is a very excellent fellow & I like him much so that I hope no misunderstanding will arise—If it must come however, better now than later. One of us can take the helm for a few months, if K. is not satisfied to remain on the basis of C.B.'s proprietorship, until we get a *remplaçant*—We are considering the question of an aid for K. It is not an easy problem to solve. . . .

Kelly, in fact, was preparing to start his own practice in France. Having become deeply interested in civil law, he was studying French law and would receive his *Licence en Droit* in 1883. In August 1883 Frederic René himself visited Kelly, but the misunderstandings were not cleared away, and Kelly left Coudert Brothers in 1884 to set up his own office—taking with him, according to Frederic René's son, "a number of our clients."

By then, however, Coudert Brothers was ready for the change. Waiting in the wings, so to speak, at the New York office was Henry Cachard, a young lawyer of French descent who came to the firm in 1883 to complete his legal studies. Sent to Paris to manage the branch office, he made it "quite successful" within a few years and would serve as its head until World War I.

Papa Coudert lived to see his sons reach back across the Atlantic and establish their branch office in his native France. By then he was a venerable eighty-three years old, but alert and still deeply interested in French politics. He read the newspapers every day, and much younger men such as Eugene Kelly and Bishop Corrigan found him entertaining company.

Nonetheless, Papa Coudert suffered badly from rheumatism in his last years, and he needed fairly constant attendance. Moreover, he became despondent whenever his surviving offspring were not actually under his eye, and he fretted about their safety—not unreasonably, given that nine of his grandchildren died in childhood between 1863 and 1878. For that matter, none of his sons liked to be separated from their families either. Frederic René and Louis Leonce seldom traveled any distance without taking at least one of their children along for company, and even so they lived for the mail from home, detailing the activities of the rest of what Louis Leonce called the "little folks" and Frederic René his "chicks." Charles junior, on the other hand, spared himself this kind of worry in his middle age by rarely traveling at all if he could help it. But Papa Coudert, with his advancing years and declining mobility, took the occasional separations particularly hard.

The responsibility for keeping Papa cheerful and satisfied was felt by all his children, but it fell most heavily on his daughter, Leonie. She was the one who had to care for him day in, day out, and she did so uncomplainingly for years, while her youth slipped away and her chances for marriage all but disappeared. Indeed, loath to lose her devoted attentions, her father actively discouraged Leonie's potential suitors.

A series of Lizzie's letters, written when Leonie was already thirty-three years old, goes far toward illustrating why the beautiful Coudert daughter was then still unwed:

> November 21, [1871], 5:30 p.m.... Yesterday, Mr. Walton (Leonie's steamer friend) called and made a regular visitation. Papa got into fits & gave Leonie ditto....

> 9 p.m.... [Leonie] is now in the parlor with Nora [Louis Leonce's wife] entertaining a young gentleman by the name of Dorrance whose mother & sister came with them on the steamer. Nora's voice quite drowns Leonie's as heard from the distance....

> Dec. 4th ... Tomorrow is the night for the Voss party.... I am very sorry that poor Leonie can not go, but she fears that Papa will be displeased & indeed as he is full of cranks that is not unlikely.

When Tante Virginie, who had stood as a mother to the younger Couderts, died of bronchitis in 1872, Leonie became even more her father's "mainstay at home where she remained to care for him and smooth as far as possible the rough paths of old age. . . ." It appeared that Leonie would die a spinster, but there was at least one man who wished otherwise: Paul Fuller.

Fuller was nine years younger than Leonie, and his feelings for her must have been strictly fraternal for years. But there are indications of a special bond between the two once Paul had grown up. When Leonie visited France in 1872, it appears that she sent Paul letters not meant for the family's eyes, and in 1873 when he was in France for the Boileau trial, Paul wrote to her every day without fail. They had much in common: they were both intensely religious, sensitive to suffering, and given to doing good works in an unobtrusive way. As Frederic René's wife, Lizzie, was to say, they both had "lovely souls."

If Leonie was self-sacrificing and dutiful to a fault, Paul was distinguished for his "quality of self-effacement." He could never be induced to put his interests ahead of anyone else's—least of all those of Papa Coudert, the man who had rescued him from the streets. The result was a rather unhappy period for Paul in the early 1870s when it seemed he could bear to live neither with the Couderts nor without them. He left his position as a salaried associate at Coudert Brothers in 1874 to practice on his own, but returned within a year. He rented a room for himself in the city—but Leonie and Papa Coudert seem to have kept a room ready for him at their home as well.

Apparently it took a strong push from Lizzie—possibly aided by Bishop Corrigan—first to get this gentle pair together and then to win over Papa. But in March 1877, Paul Fuller, age thirty, and Leonie Coudert, age thirty-nine, were finally wed. On the second day of their honeymoon, Lizzie reported to them that Papa Coudert was being "brave and splendid" about Leonie's absence. In fact, Papa did not have his courage tried for very long, for the couple returned in a few weeks, Leonie to resume caring for her father and Paul to report back to work—although no longer as an associate. Papa Coudert had not lost a daughter; rather Coudert Brothers had gained a new partner, its first in twenty years.

Papa Coudert also lived to see the Fullers' first child, a boy who was, inevitably, named Charles. Not long thereafter, on December 31, 1879, just after his eighty-fourth birthday, the Coudert patriarch died as he would have wished—surrounded by all his children. Louis Leonce had been in Paris, but summoned home when his father began to decline, had arrived in time. With the usual Victorian relish for a good deathbed scene, one New York newspaper reported that "at last [Louis Leonce] came and joined the circle by the bedside. Then Frederick [*sic*] said: 'Father, bless us, that we may know you recognize us all.' And the old man raised his hand feebly, in token that he knew them all, and peacefully passed away."

At the funeral, the three sons and Fuller were the pallbearers, while Bishop Michael Corrigan took the theme of his funeral sermon from the text "Honor thy father." His voice often breaking from emotion, he used the occasion to expound on the "devoted manner in which the family of the dead man had obeyed the Scriptural injunction."

The New York newspapers printed not only paragraph after paragraph on the funeral service but also separate lengthy profiles of Coudert senior's life. From the intimate nature of much of the information that was published, it seems indisputable that the family had provided the press not with a conventional death notice but with a full-blown biographical sketch. The Couderts were certain that their father had been a most remarkable person, and they spared no effort to ensure that the passing of this man who had so shaped them—and their practice—should not go unnoticed.

One immediate effect of Papa Coudert's death was a loosening of the Couderts' ties to South Orange. For several years before his death, father and sons had been accustomed to rent Manhattan brownstones off Fifth Avenue during the worst of the winter months. After his death, the brothers started to live a larger portion of the year in Manhattan, while the Fullers took up year-round residence in Washington Square. At the same time, the brothers' country residences became more scattered, with Charles's family spending the summers at a farm in Middletown in the far northwestern corner of New Jersey, Frederic René's at a gentleman's farm in Metuchen, and only Louis Leonce's staying in Orange Valley.

Finding it increasingly difficult to attend board meetings in South Orange, Frederic René resigned as a Seton Hall trustee but became more active instead in Columbia College's affairs. Similarly, he and Paul Fuller shifted their attention from the orphanage attached to Seton Hall to the St. Vincent de Paul orphan asylum in New York City; Fuller became involved in the management of New York's French church, St. Paul's; and both began to take an interest in Fordham College—all, no doubt, at the instigation of Michael Corrigan, who was elevated from bishop of Newark to archbishop of New York in November 1880.

Not long after Papa Coudert's death, however, Corrigan had to comfort the family in yet another loss—that of Louis Leonce. The youngest of the Coudert brothers began to ail soon after his father's funeral. Initially, the doctors diagnosed his problem as dyspepsia arising from the general effects of overwork and advised him to go abroad. Accordingly, Louis Leonce spent a long period in Paris, but he returned in 1882, feeling better, and assured his brothers that he could handle the New York office while they took their usual summer vacations. Believing him, Frederic René and Charles departed for Europe in August—only to be recalled by a cable informing them of their brother's collapse. It was now clear that he had stomach cancer, and he declined rapidly, dying at home in South Orange on September 15, 1882, with his brothers by his bed. He was only forty-six years old and left, besides his widow, Nora, five children, the youngest of them still a toddler.

"Mr. Coudert was looked upon as one of the leading French lawyers in this city," said one of the obituary notices. "He was counsel for the French, Belgian and Italian governments. . . . Mr. Coudert was well known as a man of strict integrity; and his attentiveness to business gained him a large patronage. His genial way and amiable manners won him a host of friends. . . ." Louis Leonce had not been a powerful courtroom advocate or a great legal scholar. But he was hardworking and diligent: when he showed up at 8:00 one night in 1871 to do some research in Frederic René's lawbooks, Lizzie had not been at all surprised. He provided an able reinforcement to Frederic René in the consular business of the firm, especially the extradition work. Most importantly, he had performed well in the relatively thankless role of firm administrator, and as such, had set up and watched over the first of Coudert Brothers' overseas offices.

It was Paul Fuller who as junior partner inherited Louis Leonce's administrative mantle, and in this role, it was said, "his kindly friendship toward all members of the office and his complete lack of vanity or selfishness created an atmosphere of kindliness and cooperation." The firm that Fuller had to manage in the early 1880s, however, was not the small, intimate office suggested by the wording of this encomium, but one of the largest legal practices in the country. Analyzing the legal directories in major American cities, Wayne K. Hobson has determined that in 1882 there were only fourteen law firms with five or more attorneys and none with more than eight. As he himself notes, his figures are unfortunately less than reliable, for some firms listed associates in the directories and others did not. Still, Coudert Brothers, which had at least eight lawyers in 1883, must be counted as one of the giant firms of the period.

Moreover, Coudert Brothers differed from most of its contemporaries not only in size but also in the way its work force was organized. Whereas most large firms had perhaps five or six partners supported by a few unpaid law students, Coudert Brothers was organized in a pyramidal style similar to that used by successful businesses of the time. At the top of the pyramid were the three partners, and immediately below them no fewer than five associates. Furthermore, although two of the Coudert associates—Henry Cachard and Edward K. Jones—appear to have been law students, all five drew a regular salary, which was one that they could afford to live on. Below the associates came a small army of clerks, scriveners, and nonlegal personnel. Among these was George Guion, a relative by marriage of Charles Coudert, Jr., who performed property appraisals for the firm; Joseph Collin, a French notary who had left Alsace after the German occupation in 1870; and another Frenchman, Mr. Bené, who served as cashier. The total payroll for the nonlegal staff in 1883 was about six hundred dollars a week—at a time when a young clerk's average wage was eight dollars a week and an income of thirty dollars a week could support a family respectably—indicating that Coudert Brothers probably had not fewer than twenty people on its support staff in 1883.

Coudert Brothers' employees worked in New York at 68–70 William Street in what was outwardly an old-fashioned atmosphere. The furniture was upholstered in oilcloth, a fabric that had gone out of favor at the time of the Civil War; the chairs were "uncompromisingly upright"; the floors were bare; and the only decorations were trunks of estate records, some photographs in cheap frames, and "ranks upon ranks" of calfbound books. The musty, staid setting, however, was misleading in some respects. Although Coudert Brothers saw no reason to update its office furnishings, it was quick to adopt any novelty that might improve efficiency. Thus, by 1883, Coudert Brothers already had a telephone—despite the fact that the exchange could connect the firm only to the courts and a few other law offices—and it was using "typowriters" and carbon paper to make copies of correspondence.

The three partners also continued their businesslike practice of personally maintaining the firm's central ledger, transferring into that volume on an almost daily basis the entries from individual client accounts. The system they used was an archaic one of balance-sheet bookkeeping—they had probably learned it back in the 1840s—but for them it served its purpose. In an average week, approximately thirty thousand dollars, most of which was client funds, flowed through the firm's hands, and every penny of it was recorded and accounted for by a partner.

Coudert Brothers was equally efficient in dispatching of its clients' business and its billing, as attested to by at least one satisfied party, who had referred an insurance suit to Frederic Coudert. He wrote:

> Mrs. H. requests me to say to you and your House, that your success in the litigation—your fidelity to her interests, the promptness with which you have made your remittances and the reasonableness of your charges, have been to her very gratifying . . . and allow me to add if you knew the lady you would attach double value to her commendations.

The scale on which Coudert Brothers was operating in 1883 had long since required it to departmentalize, also in imitation of the methods of successful business establishments, and here again Coudert Brothers seems to have been a pioneer among American law firms. By 1883 it had apparently three major departments: Real Estate, Estates and Trusts, and Litigation. The first two were supervised by Charles Coudert and accounted for the bulk of the firm's employees; the last was Frederic René's domain.

The Real Estate Department specialized in managing rental properties for owners, especially clients resident abroad and women and minor children. In addition, the department handled the legal aspects of purchases, mortgages, estate appraisals, and mortgage-bonds. It was headed by James Richards, Jr., an 1858 graduate of Princeton, who held degrees from both the Law School of the University of the City of New York and Columbia Law School, where he had been chosen alumni orator in 1864. Richards joined Coudert Brothers in 1875, when he was already thirty-six years old and an experienced practitioner. In time he would become a partner, but in 1883 he was a salaried associate, paid $125.83 every half month.

The Estates and Trusts Department was headed by Daniel J. Holden, who graduated from Yale in 1864 and Columbia Law School in 1866. Holden worked for another attorney for a time before starting his own practice, and by 1874 Coudert Brothers was subcontracting to him some of its estate accountings. In 1880 Holden gave up his practice to join Coudert Brothers as an associate, not only receiving a salary but also apparently being allowed to collect fees for his services to clients he had brought to the firm. A deeply religious man, Holden had "exhaustless patience with the intricacies and inconsistencies of his clients' and his opponents' statements" as well as a gentle manner that stripped his tenacity of any irritation. He, too, would after many years become a partner; from the beginning of his association with the firm, he was an "honored and beloved friend."

While these two experienced associates anchored the busy Real Estate and Estates departments under Charles Coudert's general supervision, the junior associates were clustered in the Litigation Department. Frederic René seems to have liked to have at least one associate in training in admiralty law: in 1883 this was Edward K. Jones, who went on to establish an admiralty practice of his own. The other Litigation associates in 1883 were Henry Cachard, who was being groomed to take over the Paris office, and J. N. Lewis, who continued to work with the Couderts on some cases after establishing his own practice.

The Litigation associates were essentially law students in training who seldom stayed for any length of time, but there was no need for them to stay since Frederic René always had Paul Fuller to back him up. Fuller preferred plotting strategy and writing briefs to arguing in court, yet, despite his self-effacing tendencies, he was actually a "graceful and incisive speaker" and an effective litigator. In addition, Litigation had George Young as a managing clerk, and whatever Frederic René or Fuller might miss with respect to procedure and forms, Young could be relied upon to catch.

Various historians of American law have perceived a connection between the rise of the large law firm and the development of corporate law practices. Hobson, for example, has concluded that the "trend toward large law firms was . . . particularly a response to the needs of corporations, which were increasing in both number and size." Not all large firms specialized only in corporation law, he adds, but "they all had corporations among their most important clients." These corporations were generally the railroads, whose voracious need for fresh capital and whose inability to withstand competition kept them shuffling through a constant round of stock offerings, bond issues, bankruptcies, mergers, acquisitions, reorganizations, and takeover wars that not infrequently involved real bloodshed. Thus, Sherman & Sterling grew from providing advice on takeover techniques to Jay Gould; Sullivan & Cromwell achieved prominence from its reorganizations on behalf of the Northern Pacific; and Bangs, Stetson, Tracy & MacVeagh expanded on the railroad underwriting business of J. P. Morgan. But Coudert Brothers in the nineteenth century represented neither the railroads nor their underwriting banks.

In fact, Coudert Brothers presents an exception to Hobson's theory, for it grew even as the overwhelming majority of its fees continued to come from individuals. In 1883, for example, Coudert Brothers received approximately a third of its income from handling investments for the well-to-do, most of whom were either foreigners or Americans resident abroad. This aspect encompassed virtually all the work of the Real Estate Department, including the embryonic "mortgage-bond" business. Approximately another third came from estates and trusts, including not only the fees for their administration but whatever litigation they provoked, which alone provided Frederic René with nearly half his caseload. The final third consisted of other litigation of various kinds, but mostly involving commercial, patent, and admiralty disputes or the representation of foreign consulates.

To this last category belong such corporate clients as Coudert Brothers had in 1883–84, and they included some famous names and provided some interesting cases. In the field of patent law, for example, Coudert Brothers was just collecting the last of the fees due it for advising the U.S. Electric Light Company in connection with an action for infringement of patents started in the French courts in 1881 by the Edison Company. U.S. Electric Light held the patent for the incandescent lamp with carbon burner invented by Hiram Maxim, who had earlier invented the Maxim gun, and its patent was ultimately ruled in the U.S. courts to precede Thomas Edison's. However, Edison had access to Drexel, Morgan money, and Maxim did not, so that the French patent suit disappeared when, U.S. Electric Light having reached the end of its capital, the Edison Company neatly removed its competition by buying out its assets.

In the area of admiralty law, Coudert Brothers was representing W. R. Grace & Co. in a dispute concerning the German bark *Herzogen America.* They were also handling numerous minor matters for the Compagnie General Transatlantique—and billing the latter a regular five hundred dollars each quarter with no apparent regard for the value of the work performed. In 1884 Coudert Brothers also began steering the Williams and Guion Steamship Line through the liquidation necessitated by the personal bankruptcy of William H. Guion, the uncle of Charles Coudert's wife.

In the area of general commercial law, Coudert Brothers was defending the Belgian Glass Company against claims for commissions by a U.S. sales agent, a case that Frederic René would win both in the lower courts and in the New York Court of Appeals in 1886, and also representing Crédit Général de Flandres in a matter involving the protest of some bills of exchange. Eugene Kelly & Company retained the firm to represent it in a suit, as did one of Kelly's former partners in California. Some very old clients, Banque de France and Coty, however, had no major litigation in

1883–84 and generated only $250 and $25 respectively in fees. Finally, there were three companies to be incorporated, one of which—U.S. Equitable Gas Light Co.—would eventually turn into a fairly important client.

As the record shows, Coudert Brothers was receiving the bulk of its "corporate" fees in the early 1880s for providing help with litigation, rather than from practicing corporate law as the twentieth century understands that term. And the fees it collected were relatively modest. The "notarial" side of the practice billed quite small fees for its services—$25 for drawing up a will, $10 for an eviction, $125 for a foreclosure—but handled so many different matters that the total mounted up to about $60,000 in 1883. On the other hand, the Litigation Department handled fewer cases but billed from $1,300 to $13,700 per case in 1883–84, producing about the same amount of income. Frederic René's fees were neither particularly high nor low for his sort of trial work. Yet, by contrast, a corporate lawyer like David Dudley Field could pick up $48,000 for a few weeks' effort during a railroad takeover war, while William Nelson Cromwell became an instant legend when he coolly collected $200,000 for one night's work for the Northern Pacific.

Nonetheless, even if Coudert Brothers was not tapping into the treasuries of the railroad magnates, the firm was making a quite satisfactory amount of money. In 1883 Frederic René and Charles each cleared $33,580.90 profit from the firm, while their junior partner, Paul Fuller, received $8,140.26, and another $6,322.13 in fees was credited to Louis Leonce's estate. The senior partners' shares, in particular, were handsome sums, worth in purchasing power about ten times that amount, after tax, today. This income provided them and their families with a life-style in which they moved from their brownstone city houses off Fifth Avenue in the winter to their spacious country homes in New Jersey in the summer. The children went to private schools, their wives bought the latest fashions at Lord & Taylor and fancy foods from Louis Sherry, and when their numerous daughters grew older, the family trips to Europe, Bar Harbor, Maine, and the watering places in the South became more frequent as the girls whirled through the social season.

Moreover, while maintaining this very comfortable standard of living, both the brothers and Fuller were actually underspending their incomes. Instead of each drawing out his share of the profits at the end of the year, the partners let their surpluses ride and invested them together in the partnership name—mostly in real estate. Aside from their father's house in South Orange and three particularly valuable residences that had been allocated to Louis Leonce's estate, the firm owned eighteen properties in 1883–84. These included three farms in New Jersey, four brownstones in Manhattan, one in Brooklyn Heights, an office building in the Wall Street area, six rental residences in various New Jersey cities, and some lots in undeveloped sections of Brooklyn and Queens. The firm also owned a modest number of stocks and bonds, but the only shares it did not sell off during the period covered by the 1883–84 firm ledger were Chesebrough-Ponds and another Chesebrough venture, the Real Estate Exchange Ltd. The turnaround on the other shares was so rapid that it is obvious that the Couderts regarded corporate stocks and bonds as more suitable for small speculations than long-term investment.

When Louis Leonce died, one newspaper guessed that his estate might be worth $250,000. In terms of his share of the partnership surplus, Louis Leonce's estate was actually worth closer to $60,000, whereas Charles's share by 1883 was about $44,000 and Frederic René's about $73,000. Given their large families and the office's high overheads, these were not negligible figures, and all three had probably accumulated savings and investments aside from the partnership surplus as well. Still, the Couderts were not as wealthy as the press apparently thought they should be. Other New York attorneys of their stature, such as William Whitney, Samuel Tilden, and William Evarts, were millionaires or close to it: Why not the Couderts?

In fact, had the Couderts wished to be extremely rich, the opportunity to be so was always before them from the early 1880s on. This was a pivotal period in which the Democrats began to rise to power again, and there were any number of corporations looking for a lawyer like Frederic René Coudert who had solid Democratic political connections and the subtlety of mind to know how to use them. The railroads and utilities, in particular, were hostages to the political process in the nineteenth century, in constant need of a municipal franchise here, a legislative subsidy there, a loosening of a restrictive charter, or a revision of the many state laws that were written for an eighteenth-century rural economy. These were the companies that would pay enormous fees for advice that would help them to evade the legal restrictions on them and allow them to expand.

This was, also, however, a type of business that Frederic René and his partners would not touch. It was said of Frederic René in 1890 that "he would have gained probably the largest practice of any lawyer in New York had he consented to aid corporations in doing things which were perverse in such a way that they might keep well within the letter of the law." But Frederic René, and Charles, and Paul Fuller had all been raised by Papa Coudert to consider honor of the first importance and wealth a poor second.

This does not mean that the Coudert partners scorned the making of money. On the contrary, as Frederic René told a group of Columbia law students, "even attorneys are human. They desire to live out of their labor, to provide for their families, to lay aside some provision for old age. They will, as a rule, prefer wealthy clients to poor ones and will not consider themselves criminals because they do not always attach a sacerdotal character to their profession." Yet Frederic René indeed believed that the law "is a profession and not a trade." The rules of commerce do not apply, he said, and the lawyer is not free in conscience to try to maximize his rewards "if it involves the slightest sacrifice of professional or personal honor. His self-respect cannot be measured in money."

That Charles and Paul Fuller felt the same is beyond doubt. Charles, for example, had eight children and a wife whom the rest of the family thought extravagant, yet he chronically undercharged the wealthy widows and orphans whose estates and trusts he managed, billing them about 2½ percent of income when the going rate was twice that much. Moreover, it was not unusual for Charles's Real Estate Department to arrange all the repairs on a building, advertise it for rent, lease it—and collect a dollar or two for the service. Paul Fuller was, in his way, even more incorrigible, for he "was always at the disposition of those who had worthy cases but were without means to compensate an attorney for the necessary advice." His partners were not so tactless as ever to ask Paul exactly how much *pro bono* work he did, but one later partner was convinced that "the greater part of his time was actually spent in aiding those who, he knew, could not possibly repay him."

With these attitudes toward their profession, not surprisingly the Coudert partners made no real attempt to expand their practice between 1883 and 1893 and showed no signs of wanting to tinker with its already successful formula. Apparently the practice was as large as they wanted it to be, and they were all making just about as much money as they wanted to make. Indeed, after some thirty years of hard work, the two surviving Coudert brothers began to relax a bit in their middle age. Perhaps Louis Leonce's death had warned them that life is fleeting, but in the 1880s their attention turned outward more and more from the family and the firm. Already a recognizable public figure, Frederic René spent an increasing amount of time on speakers' platforms and civic and charitable boards. And Charles—while no speaker himself—began to indulge his own interest in politics, lending his name and silent sponsorship to some of the same reform movements in which Frederic René was so deeply involved.

Chapter Four

CHAMPIONSHIP
OF THE RIGHT

Among the causes that Frederic René Coudert could not resist was women's rights. As a husband and brother, as the father of three daughters, and as a partner in a law practice that derived much of its business from women clients, Coudert had no doubts about women's intellectual abilities. Accordingly, when preliminary planning began in the mid-1880s for Barnard College, a woman's college to be associated with Columbia, Coudert threw his influence as president of Columbia's Alumni Association behind the proposal and proved himself "friendly and active" in winning the support of Columbia's trustees.

Believing that discrimination based on sex "is as stupid as it is unjustifiable," Coudert also rejoiced in women's acquisition of property rights, spoke out unequivocally in favor of female suffrage, and welcomed the opening of job opportunities for women. The gallantry toward the opposite sex that was a part of his French heritage caused him some pangs when confronted with the idea of women serving in the military or the police but, even so, he resolutely praised the contributions of the female nurses who had served in the Civil War and of the women detectives he knew in the New York City police force. Women's activities, he said, should not be limited by his or any other man's sensibilities.

As for the admission to practice of New York State's first women lawyers in 1894, Coudert thought it a step long overdue. Interviewed by the press on that occasion, he remarked:

[Women] are quite competent to perform the duties of a lawyer. The truth is that intellectually they are, at least, if experience demonstrates anything, the equals of man, as they are upon the whole his superiors from a moral standpoint. . . . If they are fit to be stenographers, typewriters, and law clerks, that is, to serve men, they must be permitted to rise in the scale and to make men serve them. . . . It seems to me that it is gross injustice for men, because they have the power of a despot to use it despotically by arbitrarily selecting certain roads upon which women shall be allowed to travel, and reserving all others exclusively to themselves.

Coudert did not simply speak in favor of equality, but did his best to promote it on the only occasion that he held a public office. As a member of New York City's Board of Education in 1881–83, he took up the cause of the primary-school teachers, who were all women, and labored to raise their salaries to the level of those received by the all-male body of secondary-school teachers. The Primary Teachers Association was almost embarrassingly thankful for his "championship of the right" and presented him years after he left office with an award for his efforts to help "the unconsidered and unfriended" women teachers.

Coudert also tried to ensure that the appointment of all the teachers in the city system was based on merit rather than political patronage. But he accepted the position of education commissioner, in the first place, primarily to assist another group much discriminated against in the nineteenth century—his fellow Catholics. Their problem was not a lack of civil rights—no law impeded any Catholic's advancement—but, rather, an overwhelming social prejudice and the feeling on the part of many Protestants that Catholicism was somehow antidemocratic and, therefore, unAmerican. Since the 1840s, the issue of the nonsectarian public schools—which the church urged its children not to attend—had been the usual lightning rod around which Catholic versus Protestant tensions crackled, and when the Democratic party in 1880 for the first time nominated a Catholic, William R. Grace, for mayor, a storm broke over the prospect of a Catholic administration steering the city schools.

As heavily Democratic as New York City was, Grace scraped into office by a bare thirty-three hundred votes and faced the immediate task of demonstrating that his critics were wrong and Catholics were not bent on subverting the public school system. With this end in view, Grace asked Coudert—who was his attorney as well as one of the few reform Democrats who had been willing to campaign for him—to accept an appointment to the Board of Education. Although reluctant to serve, Coudert had not the heart to desert Grace and, thus, let himself become the test of a Catholic's fitness to direct a nonsectarian educational system. He refused any salary, but worked with "unusual zeal," giving the position more attention than political appointees normally did. And apparently he succeeded in fulfilling Grace's hopes, for when Grace ran again for mayor in 1884, the schools were not an issue and Grace won by a comfortable margin.

As a Catholic who had grown up in the days when the "Know-Nothing" movement was at its height, Coudert was always sensitive to what he called the "contempt" and "cheap mockery" directed against his faith. In private, he himself was not always respectful of the church's hierarchy—which he once described as the "quasi-petrified body of Old Rome"—but he did believe firmly in his religion's tenets and loved it for the beckoning light he felt it held out toward a greater humaneness and charity. As president for two terms of the United States Catholic Historical Society, as president of the Catholic Club, as a trustee of St. Patrick's Cathedral, and in numerous addresses and debates, Coudert sought consistently to dispel the prejudices separating Catholics and Protestants and to create an atmosphere of better understanding and respect.

Coudert was particularly proud of his contribution to the defusing of tensions surrounding the issue of Catholic institutions by his appearance in 1886 as counsel in *People, ex. rel. v. N.Y. Catholic Protectory,* a suit testing whether a child of one religious background could be committed by the state to an orphan asylum run by a different denomination. The child in question was a Protestant who had been sent to the Catholic Protectory asylum, and Coudert, as attorney for the indigent child, sought the boy's discharge from the Catholic asylum and his transfer to a Protestant orphanage. Therefore, Coudert ostensibly appeared before the New York Supreme Court in opposition to the Catholic church. In fact, however, the court's decision in Coudert's favor was also a victory for the Catholic church, for it provided the interpretation of the law that the church wanted: that Protestants and Catholics should be allowed to look after their own, and the state should respect the charters of religious charitable institutions. In selecting this test case, Coudert had taken a carefully calculated backhanded approach, which permitted the church to make its point without stirring up the anti-Catholic feelings that might have manifested themselves had Coudert been trying to transfer a Catholic child out of a Protestant asylum.

In the same dual role of easing Protestant fears and defending the church, Coudert came to the fore again as a chief spokesman for the Catholic church between 1894 and 1896 when the American Protective Association took up the old Know-Nothing platform and unleashed a torrent of anti-Catholic propaganda. Impatiently and with an undisguised contempt for the American Protective Association, he gave out press interviews countering its accusations of orgies in nunneries and helped to muster notable Protestants to do the same. He also, in a related action, testified on the church's behalf in 1894 when the subject of sectarian aid was under consideration at the New York State Constitutional Convention. The American Protective Association had deluged the convention members with anti-Catholic literature and testimony, and some Republican party leaders had decided to appease the organization, which seemed to have demonstrated real grass-roots support. Coudert, however, played a major role in turning the convention around by his address. His brief was an eminently reasonable one, disclaiming public aid for the Catholic schools but seeking to secure its continuation for Catholic charitable work among the poor, and it roused all his eloquence. The *New York Times* called his address the "most brilliant speech of the day, in fact the best speech delivered before the committee. . . . It was brilliant and incisive, humorous and exhaustive."

Praise such as this, however, was almost the norm wherever and whenever Coudert delivered a public address, and his speaking ability was a major reason why civic and charitable causes valued his services. He was not only unafraid to present an unpalatable or unorthodox viewpoint, but his calm, relentless logic, allied to a strong sense of humor, was difficult to resist. He had a knack for turning hostile or skeptical audiences into friends.

One of Coudert's best-known triumphs came in 1879 at a political rally in Madison Square Garden, which was crashed by the opposition Tammany forces who proceeded to stage a counterdemonstration in the aisles. With fistfights breaking out on the floor, Coudert became the one speaker who could catch the attention of the crowd amidst the "noise and tumult" and quiet them enough so that his every word reached "the furthest corner of the building." On another occasion, addressing a group of businessmen, he "caused his hearers to applaud so loudly that hundreds passing by in the street tried to get in to hear, but could not find room."

These were political meetings, but Coudert was equally effective before large audiences when working with less emotional subjects, and he was, in fact, honored several times for his "occasional addresses." Venezuela presented him with its Order of Bolívar for his dedication in 1884 of a statue of the South American liberator, and Columbia College not only selected him, from among all her alumni, to deliver the oration at the college's centennial celebration in 1887, but awarded him an honorary LL.D. for his efforts as well. Coudert certainly earned this doctorate, for the undergraduates in his audience were in a boisterous mood at the start of the centennial ceremonies. Seated in the upper galleries of the Metropolitan Opera House, they continued talking and laughing among themselves as Coudert began to speak, stamped their feet in rhythm and sailed pieces of folded paper toward every pretty girl in the orchestra seats below. Moreover, Coudert's talk was in no way designed to ingratiate himself with the boys; among other things, he argued that they should not be relieved from the mandatory study of Latin and Greek and that intercollegiate sports, while admirable in concept, should be kept well subordinate to academic studies. But before his two-hour address was finished, Coudert had caught "the lords of the upper gallery" and "he received such an ovation from the audience and the boys that his usually dark and impassive face gleamed light with pleasure and surprise."

To his contemporaries, however, Coudert seemed to excel above all in the genre of the after-dinner speech, delivered in the more intimate surroundings of a club or private banquet hall. Coudert belonged to over a dozen clubs—professional ones such as the Law Club, athletic ones such as the Fencers, literary and scholarly clubs such as the Century Association and the American Geographic Society, and social ones such as the Metropolitan and University clubs. He often lunched at the Downtown Association, but his "hang-out," to use the slang term current in his own day, was the Manhattan Club, the stronghold of the reform Democrats. It was to the Manhattan Club that Coudert customarily repaired after work to play billiards with Edward Patterson throughout the 1880s and 1890s.

Coudert fitted happily into club life, and he was in much demand not only at club dinners but at annual gatherings of fraternal organizations for his mastery of that nineteenth-century ritual—the response to a toast. "On occasions of fraternity," Patterson later reminisced, "there were few who approached him in the happiness of his impromptu speeches; none who equaled him in originality, or surpassed him in the grace or exquisite finish of his style."

The *New York World* singled Coudert out as the "most popular post-prandial talker" in New York City, and Coudert, in turn, confided his belief that "the less formal preparation a man makes, and the more he lets the occasion prompt his words, the happier his remarks will be." Still, Coudert's surviving notes from a Sons of St. Patrick's annual dinner show that, while his introductory comments were jotted down at the banquet itself, the bulk of his remarks were thought out in advance. To prepare for these smaller gatherings, where men of influence came together, Coudert evidently worked almost as hard as for his major addresses, yet the effect produced was one of effortlessness: "There was a blithesome spirit and a delicate mental touch about him," said one commentator, "that made it a distinct pleasure to hear the words that fell from his lips."

A major strength that Coudert brought to civic life, in fact, was that the personality revealed by his speeches was so essentially good-humored and almost irresistibly likeable. Aside from his family, Coudert had only two intimate friends—Archbishop Corrigan and Judge Patterson, both of whom were cultured, public-spirited men much of his own stamp. His acquaintances, though, extended to every social level, and "he was a personal favorite wherever he was known." In New York City by the early 1890s, Coudert could scarcely appear on a public platform without being almost submerged in applause. For instance, in 1893 the newspapers reported that "Cheer after cheer was given when Frederic R. Coudert came on the platform, and again the applause was deafening every time his name was mentioned."

"For one who has never been accused of being magnetic," the *Times* wrote another time, "Mr. Coudert has a remarkable popularity and following. But those who know him and know his unfailing courtesy and kindness, his ready sympathy and aid, should have no difficulty understanding why it should be so." In a similar vein, the *Albany Law Journal* recalled after his death that "Socially Mr. Coudert was a most charming man. Gifted with many graces, the most notable was his invariable courtesy, a quality that is said to be an attribute of true greatness. Mr. Coudert possessed it to an extraordinary degree."

Coudert's courtesy was not simply a matter of manners but, according to Paul Fuller, the outgrowth of his interest in other people, his willingness to listen to and learn from them, and his "quick sympathy which showed an instant comprehension of [another's] attitude, whether or not he shared it." These traits made him particularly useful in committee and board positions that required the services of a peacemaker or conciliator among factions. His chief contribution during his ten years as president of the French Benevolent Society, for example, was said to be his quieting of dissensions and enmities that had previously impaired the members' charitable work, and one of his most significant services to the Association of the Bar of the City of New York arose from his ability to find and hold a middle ground in the running dogfight between the association's own leaders and the brilliant maverick lawyer David Dudley Field.

One of the finest legal minds of the nineteenth century, Field had an outsized talent for antagonizing his professional brethren. He had represented the railroad magnate James Fisk in the litigation that had produced an example of judicial corruption so flagrant it prompted the founding of the bar association in 1870; however, when called to the witness stand in the subsequent prosecutions led by the association's founders, Field had taken an arrogant, high-handed line, defending himself with the manner of a genius brushing off gnats. He survived two attempts by the association to censure him during which the association, to its frustration, was unable to turn up any actual evidence of wrongdoing, and Field then retaliated by publishing a list of actions that he alleged demonstrated his accusers' incompetence as lawyers. Professional and personal jealousy, he said, was causing the association to attempt to injure him.

Field, however, was far more than a lawyer with some dubious clients. In the 1840s, he had single-handedly drafted New York's code of civil procedure, which had served as the prototype for codes adopted by twenty-seven other states and three territories, and he had an international reputation as the preeminent exponent of the codification of laws. It was Field's very fame that made his refusal to join the association's campaign against Tweed so infuriating to that group's leadership. On the other hand, Field was profoundly angered by the association's opposition to the civil code that he was attempting to lobby through the state legislature during the 1870s, and he grew even more bitter when, the legislature having finally adopted his code in 1879, the association persuaded Governor Lucius Robinson, a Democrat, to veto it. Field's response was to persuade his Tammany contacts to withdraw their support from Robinson, which resulted in Robinson's defeat in the 1879 fall election.

Coudert was no friend of Tammany. As he once stated, "I have never been a member of Tammany Hall, but have rather been connected with organizations, always Democratic, that have been opposed to it." Nor was he any admirer of Field, whom he believed to be dangerous in his zealotry for codification and altogether too willing to bypass the democratic process in order to get his code enacted. Moreover, Coudert had done his utmost to oppose Field during the 1879 gubernatorial campaign. Together with Wheeler Peckham and William Whitney, Coudert engineered the rally that was the immediate response to Tammany's defection from the Robinson ticket and valiantly, if futilely, tried to keep Robinson's reelection chances alive.

Yet Coudert had assiduously avoided any personal attack on Field even in the heat of the campaign, a self-restraint that few of Robinson's other supporters had demonstrated. Thus, when the struggle over the passage of the civil code was rejoined in Albany in 1881 and Field's friends began claiming that the bar association's continued opposition was based only on a dislike of Field, not on the merits of the code, the association selected Coudert to be its spokesman in the legislative hearings. His appointment was noted "as a mark of his fairness, courtesy and popularity," which is to say that it was believed that Coudert's arguments could not credibly be attacked on the grounds of a personal bias he himself had never shown—neither toward Field nor toward any other opponent. And so it turned out. In his remarks, Coudert straightforwardly and gracefully addressed and defused the issue of personal ill-feeling between Field and the association's leaders, and his performance undoubtedly contributed to the civil code's failure to pass in 1881.

Coudert's objectivity regarding codification was, however, quite genuine, as the association learned two years later when Coudert chaired an association committee that was explicitly charged with producing arguments against Field's penal code. To the surprise of the general membership, Coudert's committee issued a report endorsing that code on the grounds that, unlike the civil code, it was well-drafted, fairly stated the state's existing laws, and was backed by public demand. As a result, the association found itself, for once, supporting one of Field's reforms. Although Coudert's dislike of Field continued unabated, the following year he also served amicably enough with him in an effort to devise a method to unclog the court calendars.

Regarding the entire controversy over Field and his codes, which dominated the first twenty years of the bar association's existence, a modern history of the association concludes that "On the whole, the debate was kept to a high level. There were some tart remarks about Field but, considering the extent to which his reputation made it safe to abuse him, not many." Coudert was one of the most prominent of the cooler heads working to preserve the association's dignity and reputation for fairness, which in the long run was probably more important to the profession than whether the state laws were codified or not.

How the association itself felt about Coudert's role in this bitter controversy is demonstrated by his election as president of the association in 1890 and 1891. Coudert's terms as president were not distinguished by any major initiatives, but he performed an important service to the association immediately after retiring from the office. This was his leadership of the movement to remove Judge Isaac Maynard from the New York Court of Appeals. A former state prosecutor, Maynard had received an interim appointment to the court in 1891 as a reward from the regular Democratic organization for his tampering with the election returns in Dutchess County. As the outgoing president of the bar association, Coudert chaired an association committee that promptly protested Maynard's appointment and called for his removal from the bench. The association's report being ignored by the regular Democrats, the lawyers' organization began a campaign to defeat Maynard when he had to stand for election in the fall of 1893. Coudert organized this campaign as well, and to him belongs much of the credit for the success of the crusade, which he described as one to defend "the honor and purity of the bench."

It should be recorded that standing up to defend the purity of the bench took a certain amount of bravery for a New York City lawyer in the second half of the nineteenth century. Although some judges, such as Coudert's friend Edward Patterson, were notably incorruptible, the majority had purchased their nominations from the bosses and acted under political orders. Thus, a lawyer who defied the system was in danger of seeing his practice destroyed by judges ordered to rule against his clients. Even the bar association, that group of elite lawyers, only twice found the courage to take action against the machine's control of the judiciary—in its anti-Tweed crusade of 1870 and, after a gap of more than twenty years, its anti-Maynard campaign of 1891–93. By volunteering to head the movement against Maynard, therefore, Coudert was potentially jeopardizing his firm's future, but he did so with his partners' full support. Charles Coudert's was the first name, in fact, on the list of persons opposed to Maynard's election that the *New York Times* printed on October 26, 1893, with Paul Fuller's appearing further down the column. Moreover, both Charles Coudert and Fuller served as vice presidents of the Cooper Union mass meeting that launched the election campaign against Maynard, which meant that they sat conspicuously on the dignitaries' platform, lending visible approval to their senior partner as he delivered the main address of the evening.

In fact, Fuller thought Frederic René might have gone farther in his attack on Maynard. Invincibly courteous, the latter held back even at the Cooper Union meeting from a personal attack on the judge. While listing his misdeeds and calling firmly for his removal from the bench, Coudert still spoke of him that evening with some kindness: "Notwithstanding the grave offense which Judge Maynard has unquestionably committed, I cannot but feel a real and deep sympathy for him in his distressed and humiliating situation," Coudert confessed. It was this "reluctance to hurt the individual," Fuller concluded, that "hampered" his partner as a reformer; "untiring and merciless as were his assaults upon the wrongs he sought to right," Coudert's anger at wrongdoers came and went quickly. He did not have it in him to nurse a grievance or sustain a grudge.

Coudert demonstrated this characteristic yet again in 1894, when he prosecuted the Board of Managers of the Elmira Reformatory, who had permitted corporal punishment and other brutalizing measures to be reintroduced in contravention of the state law that Judge Edmonds had worked so hard to enact back in the 1840s. Whereas a more conventional prosecutor might have portrayed these trustees as villains, Coudert could not bring himself to describe them as anything other than honorable men who "have not given their duties the attention they should."

Despite Fuller's judgment that Coudert's innate courtesy and sympathy "hampered" him, he was still remarkably effective in whatever civic or professional responsibilities he shouldered. He did indeed treat Field, Maynard, and the Elmira trustees with respect rather than the scorn that certain others felt they deserved. Nonetheless, the record shows that, through Coudert's efforts, Field's civil code, for better or for worse, was vetoed once again in 1881, Maynard was thrown out of office by an aroused electorate, and the Elmira prison gained a new and more conscientious management, which for a time, at least, kept a tighter rein on the warden and guards.

As a New Yorker, Coudert could hardly escape the evidence of the corruption of the democratic process, and no other subject, not even the need for religious toleration, bulks so large in his writings and addresses as the importance of eliminating graft, machine politics, and the influence of special interests. In this, Coudert represented the best thinking of his times; it was his generation—not the later Progressives—that first proposed as solutions to these problems such measures as the creation of a civil service, direct election of U.S. senators, female suffrage, and the initiative, referendum, and recall. Coudert placed his faith, though, less in specific reforms than in good schools and newspapers—which he thought would destroy the bosses' hold on the electorate—and the nomination of honest, intelligent candidates.

As a result, Coudert threw most of his political energies not into fighting for specific legislation—not even for the lowering of the tariff, dear as that was to his heart—but into working for the election of "decent men" to public office. This was almost a second full-time job for him, for he was not only an enthusiastic campaigner, but one of the architects and leaders of the reform Democratic organization in New York City. In time, he headed two of the more important units within that organization: the broad-based Young Men's Democratic Club (later just the Democratic Club), which elected him president sometime before 1888, and the more exclusive Manhattan Club, where he progressed from a seat on the Board of Managers in the late 1870s to the first vice presidency from 1880 to 1889, and finally to the presidency from 1889 to 1899. With its steep entrance dues of two hundred dollars, the Manhattan Club served as the gathering place for the leadership of the anti-Tammany forces, and in its clubrooms reform candidates were chosen and strategy planned.

Riddled by factions, each headed by a strong and ambitious personality, the reform Democrats had no single leader. While Coudert headed the Manhattan Club, however, they had a more than competent steward who was able, by virtue of his own popularity and tact, to keep the various factions running in the same harness and the same general direction at election time. Since the reform Democrats could not win an election at any level without first gaining an endorsement of their candidates from either the regular Democratic bosses or the reform Republicans, known as Mugwumps, Coudert's personal popularity and social skills also had to stretch to forging external alliances and truces of various kinds. The reform Democrats' candidates sometimes won, sometimes lost, but while Coudert presided over the Manhattan Club, it was always a potent political force.

Given that he had this kind of power base, in addition to his exceptional qualities as an orator and his general ability, Coudert was naturally often asked to run for elective office himself, and he invariably declined, citing the demands of his practice. In the case of the nomination that he refused to the New York Supreme Court and the appointment that he turned down to fill a vacancy on the state's highest court, the Court of Appeals, reluctance to abandon his practice doubtless was his prime motive. His friend Patterson did make this sacrifice, giving up a substantial income for the much smaller salary of a state judge, but Coudert, although tempted, did not.

Coudert's name, however, was also mentioned in connection with other offices whose incumbents normally combined active practice with their public duties. One of these was mayor of New York City, a position that a combined group of reform Democratic and reform Republicans asked him to run for in July 1890. "He was formally asked if he would consent, and was told that the nomination would come to him with such cordial expressions from men of all parties that it would seem to be tendered to him on a silver platter. He asked for a week to consider the matter," and then declined, because, regardless of custom, he would have wanted, if elected, to give his whole time to the position and "in justice to others associated with him in business affairs," he could not do so.

Coudert also drew back from another joint movement of Mugwumps and reform Democrats to nominate him for U.S. senator in 1892. In fact, he simply refused to take it seriously. Writing to Lizzie on December 28, he commented, "The papers of yesterday evening . . . are full of the senatorial subject. You will be amused but do not screw up your expectations to the glittering prize. This talk in advance normally means nothing but the advent of a dark horse at the last moment. I think too that I am particularly offensive to some of the great and good men who sacrifice themselves in the public good at Albany. They will not forgive me my action in the Maynard case. . . . So enjoy the pictures while they last but do not advertise for a palace in Washington for the present."

Others, however, felt that if Coudert had been willing to encourage some of his would-be supporters, prizes such as these would have been well within his grasp. "The trouble with Coudert," wrote the *Philadelphia Press* in 1890, "has been always, so far as a political career is concerned, that he has been too self-respecting, too proud in the best sense of the word, ever to hint that he desired political preferment. Had he possessed more assurance, been better capable of swallowing his pride, he could easily have gained high political honors. He has the mannerism which captivates men . . . and his integrity is something which is perhaps his chief honor."

Pride did indeed hold him back, for he was determined not to participate in that unlovely spectacle of politics in the Gilded Age—the scramble by professional politicians for office. Early on Coudert had formed the opinion that the trade-offs involved in office seeking were not for him nor for any person "ambitious of honest and self-respecting independence." To seek office—to put one's own interests forward—was to him an action that would taint his reputation for integrity, which he cherished both for its own sake and as the source, he felt, of whatever political influence he had acquired. How, after all, could he keep the trust of the various factions in the reform movement if he were thought to be person-ally ambitious himself?

Beyond pride, however, was a realism that told him that his re-ligion would constitute a crippling political disability outside the precincts of New York City. He might have a chance of being nom-inated for senator or governor—but never could he actually be elected to offices like these. His pessimism in this regard showed it-self most clearly in some remarks he let slip in 1894 when address-ing the New York State Constitutional Convention on behalf of Catholic charities. "At the close of his speech," the *New York Times* reported, "Mr. Coudert, in his suavest tones, said that he realized that neither he nor any of his family for generations could aspire to any of the big public elective offices in the gift of the people. He never had, as many other idiots, the Presidential bee. Nor had he any hope of ever being mentioned as a candidate for Governor." In another version of these same remarks, Coudert was quoted as say-ing, "I know that if I were the Archangel Michael under my insig-nificant form, unless I gave up my faith, I could never enter the White House except as a visitor."

However smoothly delivered, these words in cold print seem to carry a distinct undertone of pain. Yet the words themselves pro-vide the key to understanding why Coudert so rarely expressed this hurt, at least in public: if he believed that he and the next several generations of his family could not be elected to a major public of-fice because of their religion, he also had faith that, given suffi-cient time, religious differences would cease to matter in the United States. Like most of the best-educated men of his genera-tion, Coudert felt that history was a record of moral progress and, however slowly and despite whatever setbacks, "Reason must tri-umph in the end. Blind men in broad daylight may insist that all is darkness; but that is the result of their infirmity. The light is there nonetheless." Coudert expected a better future for his coun-try and for the world, an attitude that made it possible for him to bear somewhat philosophically, and often even to laugh at, the im-perfections of the present.

In the meantime, although he grumbled fairly often at the time politics took from his practice, Coudert derived considerable satisfaction from his position high in the counsels of the reform Democrats—particularly during Grover Cleveland's sudden rush to national prominence in the early 1880s, which resulted in the Democrats occupying the White House in 1884 for the first time in twenty-four years. Cleveland was, as far as Coudert was concerned, almost everything he could ask for in a candidate: aggressively hon-est, opposed to machine politics and the spoils system, favorably disposed toward tariff reform, a friend of the economic interests of the middle class, and no friend at all of religious bigotry. Coudert gave his wholehearted support to Cleveland in his 1882 campaign for the governorship of New York and the 1884 presidential race, and he was credited—by New York Democrats, in any event—with having swung into Cleveland's camp the crucial independent votes that provided the narrow margin of victory in both cases.

Coudert's friends in the Manhattan Club immediately decided that the appropriate reward for his contribution to Cleveland's election in 1884 would be the ambassadorship to France, but the president disappointed their hopes. In fact, the president shocked the Democratic party by proving stubbornly determined not to make any appointment to any office that might be interpreted as a reward for campaign services. Coudert had no problem with this; indeed, there is no evidence that he wanted a diplomatic position that would not only force him to give up his practice but require him to deplete his own savings to meet the expenses of representing his country. Moreover, he, too, was opposed on principle to handing out offices on the basis of political loyalties. Thus, while other Democrats chafed irritably at Cleveland's seeming ingratitude toward his party, Cleveland and Coudert remained what the press described as "warm personal friends."

It was a friendship based on a commonality of interest rather than true compatibility. In fact, in some ways, Coudert and Cleveland were a study in contrasts. Physically imposing, Cleveland was ponderous in build, weighing some three hundred pounds, whereas Coudert had a fencer's wiry frame. And their appearances accurately reflected their temperaments, with Cleveland being blunt, bull-headed, and strong-willed, while Coudert was quick-witted, sensitive, and considerate of others' feelings. Coudert had "a mind like a Toledo blade, skillful, neat, so deft, so effective both in parry and defense"; the president, on the other hand, wielded his considerable intelligence with all the finesse of a battle mace.

As a result, their friendship was a limited one. In their correspondence during Cleveland's first term, for example, there is no sign of the informality that either displayed toward his true intimates. There is, however, every indication of mutual cordiality and esteem, and Cleveland did serve Coudert two good turns during these years, which the New York lawyer appreciated. The first was Coudert's appointment as a government director of the Union Pacific Railroad, a position much more to his taste than an ambassadorship because he looked upon it as a recognition of his ability as a lawyer rather than as a political campaigner. Indeed, Coudert leapt upon the job with the same alacrity as he would respond to a retainer from any reputable (and wealthy) client. On April 4, 1885, the very day that he received Cleveland's offer, Coudert wired back his acceptance, following that with a letter stating that "Although my engagements and natural inclinations have disinclined me to accept any public office, I am anxious to contribute by every means at my command to the prosperity and success of your administration. . . . I shall accept the position named, without stopping to inquire how far you are actuated by a too partial estimate of my capacity in that direction."

As the Union Pacific's major creditor, the federal government controlled three seats on its board, and the principal challenge facing Coudert and his two fellow government directors was to determine what position the government should take in the aftermath of the Crédit Mobilier scandal that had brought the railroad to near bankruptcy under Jay Gould. Many of the farmers and others victimized by the Union Pacific's previous management wanted the government both to prosecute the Gould "railroad ring" and to take over the railroad's operation. Its new president, Charles Francis Adams, however, advocated refunding at a lower rate of the railroad's debt and improving the security held by the government.

As a director from 1885 to 1889, Coudert decided that, more important than vengeance on the railroad's previous management, was keeping the Union Pacific solvent so that it could meet its obligations to the government and, hence, to the taxpayers at large. And the best hope of saving the Pacific from bankruptcy, he concluded, lay in the "intelligent and faithful supervision of Mr. Adams." Thus, Coudert threw his support behind the debt-refunding plan that Adams wanted and which his fellow director E. Ellery Anderson drafted. Enactment of the plan, however, was blocked by the midwestern and western Democrats in Congress, and after Cleveland left office, the railroad indeed slid into bankruptcy.

The relationship between Cleveland and Coudert was also brightened by the events surrounding the unveiling of the *Statue of Liberty*. Initially, this had promised to be a source of conflict, for the French confidently expected that the invitations to the inauguration in 1886 would be issued by the United States government, while the president rightly pointed out that it was impossible for him to use his public office to send out invitations to a private function. Still, after long negotiations with the French, who did not understand the niceties of the U.S. Constitution, and with Cleveland, who was determined not to overstep his constitutional limits, L'Union Franco-Americaine de New York worked out a compromise under which the U.S. ambassador to France would be permit-

ted to hand out L'Union's private invitations to the members of
the French delegation.

At the last moment, though, Bartholdi announced that he
could not attend without some official recognition from the president, and Coudert was thrust forward by the other members of
L'Union to see what he could do with Cleveland. Demonstrating
his understanding of the president's character, Coudert wrote him
a letter as tactful as it was diffident in requesting Cleveland's aid;
and demonstrating, in turn, his essential goodwill toward Coudert
and the entire *Liberty* project, Cleveland responded by return post
with a letter, to be shown to Bartholdi, unequivocally stating that
his administration indeed appreciated Bartholdi's work and he
himself "earnestly" hoped that Bartholdi would be present. Accordingly, when Coudert presided over the reception greeting the
French delegates only four weeks later, he had the satisfaction of
welcoming Bartholdi, and the unveiling itself took place in the atmosphere of utmost cordiality as Bartholdi, Cleveland, and
Coudert took their seats on the platform.

If there were anything needed to increase Coudert's estimation of Cleveland, it was supplied in January 1888 when the president devoted his entire State of the Union address to the need to
lower the tariff, setting that as the main issue of his reelection campaign the following autumn. Thus, Coudert looked forward ea-
gerly to chairing New York State's Democratic Convention in May
and leading the state's delegates to the national convention, safely
lined up for Cleveland. Then the chief justice of the Supreme
Court, Morrison Waite, died on March 23, 1888, and the relationship between Coudert and Cleveland underwent a sudden revolution as Coudert's friends began to pressure the president to
appoint the New York lawyer to the nation's highest judicial position.

For reasons now obscure, New Yorkers were convinced in
March 1888 that Waite's successor would be chosen from among
their own ranks, and the two most likely candidates appeared to be
E. J. Phelps, then ambassador to Great Britain, and Frederic René
Coudert. Coudert had the support of the Manhattan Club and its
allies and of the Association of the Bar of the City of New York,
which signaled its preference by selecting Coudert to deliver the
traditional memorial address on the late chief justice. Although at
this date Coudert had argued relatively few cases before the Supreme Court, his reputation as a legal scholar among his peers was
impeccable. As one newspaper commented, "The suggestion was
made to Cleveland that there was no lawyer at the New York bar,
perhaps none in the country, of the Democratic party who was bet-

ter qualified to serve as Chief Justice . . . and this was no extravagant statement. Coudert is a better jurist than he is an advocate, and he is great in the latter capacity."

Nonetheless, Cleveland indicated within a few weeks that he was leaning toward Phelps, who also had an excellent professional reputation, but this preference, according to one newspaper, "caused violent opposition from Irish-Americans, for Mr. Phelps' course while Minister had been such as to give great offense to this influential element in the Democratic party." Pressure was brought to bear upon the president to abandon Phelps and nominate Coudert. Coudert's closest friends did not make the mistake of trying to overpersuade Cleveland; Archbishop Corrigan, for example, confined himself to a short, gentle note stressing the "purity of Coudert's private life" and avoiding any reference to Phelps, the Irish, or the church. But others were more ham-fisted.

Finally, convinced that he would lose the election if he appointed Phelps, Cleveland gave in—but, resenting having his hand forced, he took his revenge by nominating, not Coudert, but Melville W. Fuller, an Illinois lawyer who had not particularly distinguished himself either in practice or in public service. The president made the nomination, moreover, with no advance warning to his New York supporters to cushion the blow to their expectations. "It was certainly with a sense of mortification that Coudert's friends learned that the President had appointed a comparatively obscure lawyer of the West for this high office," reported the *Philadelphia Press*. "Coudert himself must have been chagrined a little, although he never manifested it."

Coudert may not have let his feelings show in public, but he was not only chagrined, but deeply hurt. Phelps's nomination he could have accepted, but to be passed over in favor of someone who, from the initial information available to him, seemed far his inferior in accomplishment and ability stung Coudert in his most vulnerable spot, his pride. Nor did it help matters that rumor ran freely that Coudert had been snubbed because he was a Catholic. "His religious connection . . . is understood to have been one reason," the *New York Times* printed in an 1895 profile of Coudert, "why he does not now occupy a very high, if not the very highest, judicial position in the United States, although the precedent of the Catholic Chief Justice Taney was in this case very much in point." Coudert's religion, however, seems to have been a factor only to the extent that the president was in no mood to accommodate the Irish vote: backing away from Phelps was concession enough, and more than the New York politicians deserved, was apparently Cleveland's attitude.

Yet the expectation that Coudert would be asked to accept the nomination had been so widespread that Coudert had the feeling that he had been made a fool of, and his hurt lasted a long time. More than four years later, for instance, while working to return Cleveland to office, Coudert broke suddenly into French to vent the old grievance in the middle of a letter to Lizzie: *"Et tout cela pour l'homme qui n'a pas vouler me faire Chief Justice—Frederic, mon ami, tu n'es qu'un imbecile"* [And all this for the man who didn't want to make me Chief Justice—Frederic, my friend, you are nothing but a fool].

But the point is that, although he nearly choked at times on his wounded pride, Coudert continued to work for Cleveland. He did chair the state convention in May 1888, he led New York's delegates to the national convention, and he remained a Cleveland loyalist. In his first anger, Coudert announced that he would not campaign in the fall, but he even reversed himself on this by the summer of 1888. Reversing himself was an awkward maneuver, too, for Coudert was apparently not willing to present himself as eager to help the man who had, he felt, insulted him, but a pretext was found when the Clevelands invited the Couderts to dinner in the White House. Within a few days of this dinner, the press began to print stories of how Coudert had been so captivated by Cleveland's young bride that he had decided to stump for her husband after all. The excuse begged for facetious treatment, and it received it— but Coudert seems to have felt less silly saying that Mrs. Cleveland "is just the lady whom we all want as the mistress of the White House" than forcing out any kind of personal praise for President Cleveland.

The strain of the situation took its toll on Coudert, and by late August, in an uncharacteristically irritable mood, he was shipped off to France by Lizzie under instructions to rest and try to gain some weight. Accompanied by his son, Fred, and joining in France his eldest daughter, Virginia, Coudert not only began to relax but seems to have come to terms with his resentment. At any rate, the *Times* reporter who met Coudert's boat on his return in September described a man feeling younger than his fifty-six years, with seemingly not a care in the world: One of the first to run down the gangplank, where a host of friends and relatives were waiting to greet him, "he was fairly lifted from his feet and carried out of the throng by his enthusiastic friends. And his first words, after the usual greetings, were 'How's President Cleveland getting along?' " The reporter than added what the New York Democrats most wanted to know: "He intends to take his coat off and go to work for the national Democratic ticket."

* * *

Despite his good intentions, though, Coudert and the other reform Democrats were unable to repeat their 1884 success in persuading independents and Mugwumps to vote for the Democratic ticket. Defeated for a second term, Cleveland retired to private practice in New York City, making it clear that he was relieved to be rid of the cares of the presidency and had no desire to return to active political life.

Having been first a staunch Tilden man and then a Cleveland supporter, Coudert thus found himself in 1889 uncommitted to any party leader for the first time in nearly twenty years. His own stature had never been higher; he was respected for having done his duty by Cleveland, putting the welfare of the party ahead of his personal feelings. Yet it was an open question in what direction he would wield his influence as president of the Manhattan and Democratic clubs. Indeed, with Cleveland in retirement, party leaders throughout the country were, like Coudert, examining their options for 1892; Coudert, however, was one of the first of the former Cleveland men to make up his mind. In the spring of 1890, well in advance of the next presidential election, Coudert announced his choice—which was, of all people, Grover Cleveland. His endorsement, which was first published in *The Epoch* and rapidly reprinted in the major Eastern newspapers, sent out shock waves of surprise, partly because the *cognoscenti* knew of the coolness between Coudert and Cleveland but mostly because the ex-president was the one man who didn't seem to want the office. The political commentators were, on the whole, astounded.

Yet Coudert seems to have known what he was doing. He wished, for one thing, to block the presidential aspirations of New York's Democratic governor David B. Hill. Popular with the regular Democrats in his state, Hill was beginning to position himself for a run at the White House—but the reform wing thought him not of high enough character even to be governor, a position that he had gained over the opposition of Coudert, among others. Hill was not, in fact, personally dishonest, but some of his friends and appointees were, and winning votes was said to be more important to him than any set of principles. *Slippery* is the adjective that has stuck to his name in the history books.

Looking for an alternative to Hill, particularly one who was potentially more appealing to independent voters, Coudert confessed that he could see no one with a better chance of winning than Cleveland. The latter's famous tactlessness, which had so bruised Coudert's own feelings, had alienated enough congressmen to doom most elements of the Democrats' legislative agenda, but, as Coudert pointed out, his "open and honest" administration had been widely respected. In fact, Cleveland had lost the 1888 election in the electoral college, not in the popular vote count.

Coudert, moreover, had been struck afresh by Cleveland's fundamental decency when he learned that the ex-president, settling in New York City, was unable to join the Manhattan Club because he could not afford the admittance fee. Coudert's son, then in his late teens, recalled being shown Cleveland's letter "saying that he would like to join the Manhattan Club, and that he might do it later, but that at the present time he didn't have any funds to pay the initiation dues, and that he wouldn't come into any club under conditions! He was actually too poor to join the Manhattan Club, although he had been President of the United States and Governor." Between Cleveland with his rigid honesty and Hill, who seemed to be doing quite well for himself out of politics, Coudert found the choice easy to make.

There is no evidence as to whom Coudert consulted before making his endorsement, although he almost certainly discussed it with at least a few close friends, such as ex-mayor Grace, his brother Charles, and Judge Patterson. But after April 1890, it seems clear that he was working in concert with other Cleveland men. The business of securing the presidential nomination was a complex one: some had to persuade Cleveland himself that he should run, some had to rebuild his old support base in the South and West, and some—and this is the task for which Coudert took prime responsibility—had to neutralize Hill. There is no point in detailing all the Byzantine maneuvers that this entailed. It is sufficient to say that Coudert initially tried, through gentle words, to induce Hill to withdraw from the race in favor of Cleveland, and for a time he actually seemed to be succeeding. But the Coudert-Hill courtship ended abruptly when Hill arranged Maynard's appointment to the bench, and open warfare thereupon developed between New York's reform and regular Democrats, resulting in both groups sending their own delegates to the 1892 convention. With Coudert talking himself hoarse, the tide of support at the national convention turned to Cleveland, who went on to capture the presidency again in the fall.

During the four years he had been out of office, the personal ties between Cleveland and the Couderts had been re-strengthened. For one thing, since both the former president and the Coudert Brothers partners lunched regularly at the Downtown Association, they simply saw each other more often. Cleveland, who usually dodged every private social function he could, attended the wedding of Charles Coudert's daughter Aimee to

McKenzie Semple, an assistant state attorney general, in November 1890, lifting that affair into a major society event. And Frederic René's daughter Virginia became engaged during this period to the son of Cleveland's closest friend, E. C. Benedict, a fabulously wealthy investment banker and noted yachtsman. At any rate, it was the recollection of Coudert's son that his father and Cleveland were "on very good terms."

Nonetheless, Cleveland had barely taken the oath of office again when he "grievously disappointed the Independents in New York by failing to select Frederick [*sic*] R. Coudert as minister to France" and nominating instead a former Louisiana senator, James B. Eustis, "whose chief qualification was that he needed the job." Fred Benedict was bitterly indignant on his father-in-law's behalf. "I am as unable now to explain the reason for Mr. Cleveland's disappointing us, as I was in Paris," Benedict wrote to Coudert on April 25, 1893. "On every turn the greatest disappointment is expressed and generally in 'variations' that are unfit for publication." Benedict reported that Cleveland's private secretary, Dan Lamont, had probably worked against Coudert's appointment. William Whitney, he added, had said that he would have "nothing more to do with Cleveland," while "the Judge [probably Judge Patterson] and myself have decided we will not speak to the 'Buffalo Bummer' as Eustice [Eustis] called him in a Washington club three days before he was appointed." Referring to Coudert's amateur status in politics, Benedict also wrote, "My conclusion is, that politics and horseracing are equally honorable ventures, and a gentleman rider has no show with the professional jockey."

By the summer of 1893, though, Coudert knew that he would once again become involved in the affairs of the Union Pacific. The railroad had gone bankrupt, and Coudert's letters to Lizzie show that he was aware that he would be appointed a government receiver later in the year. Moreover, in July 1893, another Supreme Court justice, Samuel Blatchford, had died, and Coudert's name had already been mentioned in the press as a likely successor. An article appearing on July 22, 1893, for example, related that:

> New Yorkers generally feel that the new Supreme Court judge ought to be, and will be, chosen from their State. A name which is used more than any other in connection with this gossip is Frederic C. [*sic*] Coudert. . . . If he should be selected it is generally prophesied that he will cast a large sized glimmer in the path of Washington society. He is a close personal friend of Mr. Cleveland, and is rich. In fact, he has about all the law busi-

ness of the French population in New York. And added to these qualifications he has a handsome wife, who would not fail to make the Coudert home in Washington one of the most popular of the Supreme Court circle.

Unbeknownst to the press, however, the "rich" Mr. Coudert and his wife were worrying at this point about money, for the first time in many years. The country was entering into the grip of the Panic of 1893, and the practice was slow. In this context, Coudert wrote to Lizzie on August 24, 1893, "I have thought much more of the Judgeship lately than heretofore. For some reasons I think it would be a good thing. I am a little tired of the banging and knocking and anxieties of the profession. But no man knows what is best for himself, so I do not propose to set my heart upon it, especially as there are serious *cons* to balance the *pros.*"

Cleveland, who was recovering from a secret operation for cancer, took his time about choosing a successor to Blatchford, and meanwhile the Couderts' law practice began to be seriously affected by the depression. In particular, as factories and businesses closed down, an increasing number of people were thrown out of work and became unable to meet their mortgage payments. Prices plummeted steeply in the New Jersey real estate market, and many of the Coudert Brothers clients who held bonds backed by New Jersey mortgages found their bonds becoming worthless or much reduced in value. True to their word, the firm's partners started dipping into their private capital to buy out their clients' holdings and protect them from loss.

In the fall of 1893 Cleveland nominated a New York lawyer to the vacant Supreme Court seat, his choice being not Coudert but William B. Hornblower. A younger man than Coudert, Hornblower was still an old friend; he and Coudert had worked together on many a common bar association and reform Democratic cause, including the anti-Maynard campaign. Maynard's patron, David B. Hill, however, was now in the U.S. Senate, and, taking Hornblower's nomination as a personal insult, he invoked the custom of senatorial courtesy—the tradition that the Senate would not confirm a man to office over the objections of a senator from the nominee's home state. By a margin of six votes Hornblower's appointment was defeated in January 1894.

Next, Cleveland sent before the Senate the name of another distinguished member of the New York bar, Wheeler Peckham. Peckham was even more objectionable to Senator Hill, for as president of the bar association, he had appointed the Maynard investigating committee, on which Hornblower had served, and he had actively combated Hill's nomination as governor in 1888. After a brief and nasty fight, in which Hill freely libeled Peckham's character, the New Yorker was defeated on February 16 by a vote of forty-one to thirty-two.

Then, Cleveland turned immediately to Coudert, which was, in effect, an escalation of the war, for Coudert had not merely served on but chaired the Maynard investigatory committee, had organized and led the campaign resulting in Maynard's defeat at the polls, had opposed Hill in 1888, and had snatched away from Hill the presidential nomination in 1892. Coudert may have had a fair idea that Cleveland would be approaching him, for on January 24 he and Lizzie had attended a White House dinner whose guest list was composed mostly of Supreme Court justices and the New York lawyers most prominent in the reform wing of the party. At that point Peckam's name was before the Senate and already seemed doomed, so that the president may have used the occasion for a few private words with Coudert. Whether he knew the offer was coming or not, however, Coudert took virtually no time at all to decline it. Peckham was defeated on February 16, and by February 18 Coudert had refused to allow his name to be placed in nomination.

According to Cleveland's biographer, Coudert declined "for business reasons," which given the state of the economy and the firm's finances might very well have been his entire reason for refusing. He may also, of course, have not wished to have his name dragged through the mud by Hill, particularly if he thought his chances of confirmation were nonexistent. The Republican Mugwump senator Carl Schurz believed that Cleveland had only to persist in order to win, for public opinion seemed to be rallying to the president in his battle with Hill—but Schurz had an interest in fostering a civil war within the Democratic party, which Coudert did not. In any event, Coudert said no, and Cleveland gave up the struggle, nominating Senator Edward D. White of Louisiana, a choice that Hill promptly and ostentatiously endorsed.

In June 1894 Cleveland offered Coudert an appointment as the new minister to Russia. Although admitting to Cleveland that the ambassadorial post presented a "strong temptation," Coudert again declined. "Any indefinite absence would be accompanied with so many disturbing results," he wrote, "that I must perforce remain at home."

That was not to be the end of Coudert's chances for public office, however, for another Supreme Court seat opened up in the summer of 1895, and once again Coudert's friends proposed his name. Justice Howell Edmunds Jackson's death in August found Coudert in Paris and Lizzie in Bar Harbor, Maine, where the

Pattersons and Whitneys were also vacationing. Apparently, Patterson and Whitney asked Lizzie to find out whether her husband would be interested in the Supreme Court nomination, for she cabled him asking if he would accept the judgeship, if offered. He cabled back, "I leave it to you am satisfied either way," and followed up on August 12 with a letter elaborating that brief response:

> Your dispatch inquiring whether I would accept the Supreme Court is received. I answered leaving it to you to determine as, after all, it concerns you quite as much as, if not more than, it does me. As you would not ordinarily address abstract questions to me—or anyone else—through the channel of the Transatlantic cable, I assume that you have some material motive in desiring to secure my opinion. I wish that your dispatch had been somewhat more explicit but perhaps you had not the data for that purpose. The pros and cons seem very nearly balanced, so very near that I am indifferent on the subject. . . . The Herald of to-day announces that the appointment has been tendered me and I have had various congratulatory manifestations. Depew [Chauncey Depew, New York Central president and U.S. senator] whom I met this a.m. at the Continental was very pleasant and says "We shall all be delighted in New York" if it is true.

Without waiting for her husband's letter, however, Lizzie had already given Judge Patterson the green light, and he, in turn, had passed the word on to William Whitney. Making it clear that the nomination was far from secured, Whitney wrote to Patterson on August 13 that "I cannot approach Mr. Cleveland directly on the subject but Col. Lamont is at Sorrento and I will do what I think w[ould] be the best for Mr. Coudert."

While the word from the Coudert camp was that Coudert was interested, Hornblower was sending out discouraging messages. The result was that in November 1895, Cleveland formally offered the nomination first to Coudert. Circumstances this time were different in one material respect than they had been two years earlier: Hill and Coudert had effected something of a truce. Persuaded by the interests of party loyalty, Coudert had actually endorsed Hill's candidacy for governor in 1894. Although when it came time to campaign, Coudert found himself conveniently out West on a tour of the Union Pacific system, he had chided Paul Fuller and his own son, Fred, for campaigning for Hill's opponent, Everett P. Wheeler. "This is the first time I hear from home," he wrote in reply to a letter from Lizzie shortly before Election Day. "I am not pleased with Paul nor with Fred for neglecting me so completely, but no doubt their anxiety to help Wheeler to destroy the Democratic Party forbade other and less important work."

But if there was good reason to believe that this time Coudert could win automatic confirmation, there were also, as Coudert had noted in August, several reasons to decline the nomination. The most important of these was that Charles Coudert was not at all well, while James Richards was also not in the best physical condition. No doubt the collapse of the mortgage-bond business in the wake of the 1893 depression had played its part in destroying the health of the partners heading the Real Estate Department, but the firm was understaffed and the partners' capital was continuing to diminish. At the same time, Fred was now a partner of the firm, and should his father go off to Washington, D.C., he would become at age twenty-four, the only partner with the Coudert name active in the firm. Moreover, the other two partners—mild-mannered Paul Fuller and the even milder Daniel Holden—could scarcely be expected to control and guide headstrong young Fred the way his father could. "The question of the big Boy," Coudert confessed to his wife, "is the one that troubles me most."

There is no way of knowing what weight all these factors played in Coudert's decision—and perhaps all along he had never wanted anything more than the gratification of being asked—but in November 1895, Coudert again formally declined the nomination to the Supreme Court. Cleveland then turned to Rufus W. Peckham, brother of Wheeler Peckham, who was duly confirmed. Three times Coudert had come close to serving on the Supreme Court, but it was not to be. Had he been less ambivalent about the position, he probably could have secured it, at least on the last offering in 1895, but he *was* ambivalent and let it go by. He had once told Lizzie, "I am very glad to say that I am quite content with my private estate and will not grieve if I remain there," and that is where the matter rested.

Chapter Five

IN THE CAUSE
OF PEACE

I t was in 1890, as the Coudert brothers approached their sixties, that the firm received an infusion of new energy in the person of Frederic René Coudert's son and namesake. Only nineteen when he first "went downtown" to start his law apprenticeship, young Fred was to spend sixty-five years altogether at Coudert Brothers, most of that time as the dominant force in its affairs.

Today the Coudert Brothers lawyers who joined the firm just before or after World War II still have firsthand memories of Fred Coudert. To them, he was the "Old Man," a figure of great dignity and presence of whom they stood in not a little awe. The recurring word they use to describe him is "brilliant," and throughout his life, the characteristic that made the most immediate impression on those who knew this Coudert was always the power of his intellect.

That Fred junior, who was born on February 4, 1871, was going to take after his father in this respect was almost immediately apparent to his family. His mother, Lizzie, was already convinced that "there was never a finer or more intelligent boy," when Fred, at nine months of age, began prattling French baby talk to his grandfather, and both parents watched over the boy's development carefully. As dissimilar to the stereotype of the remote Victorian *pater familias* as he could be, Frederic René was exceptionally tender-hearted toward all his "chicks" and deeply involved in their upbringing. There are frequent glimpses in the family letters of

Frederic René personally attending to his son: getting the little boy ready for school in the morning, helping him with his homework, trying to amuse him during a convalescence from illness, and coaxing him out of a youthful tantrum. This was not a household where the children were left to the care of servants or relegated to a nursery.

Indeed, the one occasion when Frederic René and Lizzie took a trip by themselves—the 1876 visit to New Orleans for the Tilden/Hayes vote count—left the children feeling so lonely, despite the presence of their grandfather and all the nearby aunts, uncles, and cousins, that the experiment was not repeated. What this meant was that in the 1880s, when Lizzie was chaperoning the older girls through the social season at various watering places, Frederic René stayed home to look after the boy. Alone together, father and son spent long summer days riding, fencing, fishing, joking, talking, and building a relationship that his son later described as "the closest and dearest that I have had with any man."

The intimacy of this relationship was particularly remarkable because Frederic René and his son had very different personalities, with young Fred displaying a strong will and passionate spirit that he may have inherited—if such things can be inherited—from the ardent French cavalryman who was his paternal grandfather. Fred was a cheerful boy who kept his father vastly amused with his pranks and antics, but when he wanted something, he wanted it with his whole heart and soul. Fred's baby pictures, in which his strong determined chin and jutting lower lip are as pronounced as in all his later photographs, give an idea of what Frederic René was up against in trying to guide his son. "As fierce as ever" was Frederic René's casual comment on Fred at age thirteen. On another occasion, he reported to Lizzie that "Fred was very jolly & thus far we have had no rows. I am almost sorry I said that lest the usual result follow that accompanies these imprudent speeches." And, indeed, the very next day Frederic René recounted a noisy scene in which Fred, "wild with spirits," gave a fair imitation of "a wild gorilla."

In dealing with Fred, however, Frederic René proceeded gently, never raising a hand to the boy, for he strongly disapproved of corporal punishment for children. No more than he could tolerate the idea of the Elmira prisoners being beaten could he spank a child. Frederic René relied instead on the power of reason or, if that failed, reason's close ally, sarcasm. Given Frederic René's mastery of words, his occasional caustic comment might still have withered a more sensitive child, but Fred, whose soul was definitely on the sturdy side, was not daunted. In fact, the boy seems to have been far more in awe of his mother and older sisters, who took a sterner line with him. They were his usual authority figures, whereas his father was mentor, confidant, and ally.

In any event, Fred as a child so thoroughly absorbed all his father's main principles and ideals that there was not much room intellectually for them to clash as adults. They both took for granted the importance of integrity and gentlemanly conduct, the dangers of fanaticism, the need to bend to social usage, the superiority of the present day over the past, and a host of other values, so that, reasoning from these shared assumptions, Frederic René and Fred never differed very much on any conclusion. A comparison of their published addresses shows that the father's are subtle, humorous, and designed to play upon the reader's emotions, while the son's are direct, argumentative, and intended to convince the reader intellectually. But, with respect to the views presented, either could have written the other's essays without any difficulty. Despite the gulf between their styles, they thought alike.

Like his father, Fred was a precocious scholar. His parents sent him to private day schools in New York and New Jersey to learn his Latin, and by the age of fifteen—one year older than his father had been, but still very young—he was deemed ready to enter Frederic René's alma mater, Columbia College. There he promptly started to win academic awards, most notably the Prize Scholarship in History in his sophomore year.

Although Columbia had moved to what is now midtown Manhattan and expanded somewhat by the 1880s, it was still a small college. Fred later recalled that, when he entered in 1886, a janitor wearing a high hat closed the college gates at 1:00 P.M. each day "so that nobody could go in or out. At one o'clock the school was over." The college library, moreover, was open only one and a half hours a day. Yet Columbia was just beginning to reshape itself after the model of the German universities, at the urging of a German-trained professor, John W. Burgess, who had been brought to Columbia to start a School of Political Science in 1880.

Burgess's vision was of a faculty encouraging independent research in politics to prepare young men for public office. Theodore Roosevelt had studied under Burgess during the school's first year and had been strongly influenced by him, and Fred Coudert also felt his impact. "Burgess, when he came to Columbia, was soaked in all the German learning," Fred later wrote, ". . . and he had his theory of the Teutonic government of the world, which he taught us boys. I thought it seemed sound. I used to tell my father about it, and he used to laugh, because his sympathies were largely French."

Frederic René Coudert, Sr., "thought Burgess had gone much too far—that the Teutons had not absorbed all the wisdom and knowledge of the world." But another reason he had to be doubtful of Burgess's influence on his son was the very premise of the School of Political Science: that young men should, after proper graduate training, go directly into politics. The elder Coudert did not wish his only surviving son to become a politician; as any man who has built a flourishing business might, he wanted young Fred to come into the family firm.

It was in February 1890, when Fred was about to complete his B.A. degree and announcing his desire to do graduate work under Burgess, that Frederic René published "Young Men in Politics," an essay that surely arose from long discussions between father and son. In it, while acknowledging the lure and fascination of politics, Coudert cautions:

> . . . the young man who starts upon life with the idea of making politics—or call it statesmanship—a profession and to earn his daily bread by public service, unfits himself for all other occupations, gambles away his independence, and runs the risk of finding himself in the end with the alternative of losing his living or forfeiting his self-respect. First, let him be his own master—that is to say, able to work his way through life by his unaided exertions; then let him serve the public. The public can wait. He may not think so, but some one will do the needful until he has fitted himself to take his trick at the helm and sail the ship of state. . . .

It appears that the lines of communication between father and son were strong: Fred not only heeded his father, but Frederic René yielded to his son. The result was that Fred did attend the School of Political Science, but he simultaneously began working at Coudert Brothers. A law clerk in the mornings, Fred rode uptown in the afternoons to attend Burgess's graduate-level lectures, which were delivered at 3:00 P.M. to the dismay of the college janitor. Fred received his M.A. in political science in 1891, en route to his Ph.D., which he would collect in 1894.

Fred never attended law school or received a law degree. Instead, his Coudert Brothers clerkship and private course of reading constituted Fred's sole preparation for the bar, and they were more than sufficient, even though the standards for admission had been considerably tightened since his father's time. Sitting for the bar shortly after turning twenty-one in 1892, he "passed such a brilliant written examination that the commissioners dispensed with the usual oral one," according to a contemporary newspaper account.

Writing a brilliant examination in the law, however, is no guarantee of interest in the routine details of the profession. Even after he had been admitted to practice and was practicing as a Coudert Brothers attorney, Fred clung to the pursuit of his doctoral studies, which were much more congenial to him. All his life Fred had the type of mind that enjoys dealing, not with detail, but with broad concepts, major ideas, subjects of general importance. In short, he liked arguing theory, and, as the historian Allan Nevins was to point out, his interest was "in the substance of law, as distinguished from its technicalities." Since the beginning lawyer seldom encounters anything but technicalities, it seems that much of what Fred was exposed to at Coudert Brothers simply bored him. Initially, his powerful mind did not find there the scope it wanted.

Certainly, it is clear that during his late teens and early twenties, the family business was competing for Fred's attention with a number of more exciting activities. Aside from graduate school, for example, Fred also had a major commitment from 1890 onward to Squadron A of the New York state cavalry, whose maneuvers often necessitated his absence from the offices at 68-70 William Street. In addition, as with other members of his generation, to whom Teddy Roosevelt was then preaching the virtues of physical fitness, sports and exercise had an important place in Fred's daily life. While still a schoolboy he had begun working out regularly in private gymnasiums, and by early adulthood he was an expert rider, fencer, duck hunter, and sailor, and when the bicycling craze hit, he became a passionate cyclist. To read Fred's joyous account, written when he was twenty-three, of racing an Englishman through Paris from the arc to the place de la Concorde—"shooting in and out among the [horse]cabs is half the spark"—is to understand why at this period his father was referring to him as "the big Boy."

Still, Frederic René, although nearly forty years older than his son, was not unsympathetic. When Fred was in the running for promotion within Squadron A, Frederic René confessed to his wife his hope that "before I return Fred will have his shoulder straps. I do not believe that he takes it more to heart than I do." And he recognized that the quality in Fred that one family member has described as an "élan vital"—a zest for life—needed some such outlet as competitive sports.

But even an indulgent parent's patience may snap, and on at least one occasion—it was in the spring of 1894—Frederic René gave his son a sharp dressing-down to the effect that twenty-three-year-old Fred did not know as much as he thought he did and had better attend seriously to business. This confrontation came just before Frederic René left on a trip to Texas, where he shortly received a letter in Fred's characteristically bold, flourishing hand that began, "As regards your attempted sarcasm as regards my ability, intelligence, legal tact, etc. they are [in] very poor taste and show a remarkably jealous disposition." Waving a red flag of defiance at his father, Fred then recounted, amongst some office and family news, how he had taken the morning off from work to go riding with a friend and that he expected "a grand blowout" that night at one of his clubs to leave him sleepy for a week, although he had other social engagements lined up for every other night in the week as well. The letter finishes with a cheeky postscript in which Fred notes that he has decided to take over his father's office: "When you return, I am going to put you in Adams' room and have had all your things removed as this room would be crowded otherwise."

Fred's tone is very much in the rough joshing style that nineteenth-century clubmen used to one another, but behind the joking is visible Fred's wish to have something important to do, some work that matched his own estimate—and it was no low estimate—of his abilities. On the other hand, Frederic René's scolding may have done some good by stirring Fred's competitive instincts. By telling Fred that he was not good enough, the senior partner of the firm was challenging him—and Fred could not resist a challenge.

Only a few months later Fred was crowing to his father, "I secured a reversal in the Hecker Case on the spot. My main joy is that it is such a grind on you who have said I was incompetent and should only go to the police court. You might as well retire, I can attend to the cases of the General Term or anywhere else." The news must have come as a joy to his father, too, for he proceeded to transfer to Fred more of the important clients and important cases, and on these the latter never disappointed. Within about a year, Fred was carrying his weight sufficiently to be made a partner, and given great responsibility, Fred's enthusiasm for the practice of law grew proportionately. He was to come close to running for political office several times before the decade was out, but when the nominations did not come his way, his disappointment was evanescent. He was discovering that politics was not the only way in which a man might leave his mark on the world.

In April 1893 Frederic René and his son sailed for France, where the senior Coudert was scheduled to participate in an international arbitration as one of the three advocates representing the government of the United States in its efforts to protect the Bering Sea seal herd. As it turned out, this Bering Sea arbitration was to prove a significant event in the careers of both Coudert lawyers. For them both, it was one of those golden moments that occur so rarely in anyone's life, a time that Frederic René was to refer to afterward affectionately as "our summer of the seals."

The seals in question were those that bred on the American-owned Pribilof Islands near Alaska, but otherwise spent their lives swimming in the international waters of the Bering Sea and Northern Pacific. Slaughtering the seals indiscriminately, Canadian and British commercial sealing vessels had so reduced their numbers by 1886 that the extinction of the species seemed near. Alarmed, the Cleveland administration in that year began seizing sealing schooners in the open waters and bringing them into U.S. ports for confiscation proceedings. Great Britain responded by sending a warship of its own to the Bering Sea, and for a time—unlikely as it may seem in retrospect—a war between Britain and America was a distinct possibility.

Cooler heads prevailing, the two countries signed a treaty agreeing to submit the dispute to arbitration. Although Great Britain and the United States had arbitrated previous disagreements, most notably the *Alabama* claims arising from the Civil War raids of British-built Confederate ships, there was no standing mechanism for international arbitration, and diplomatic negotiation was required to reach agreement that the tribunal would meet in Paris and would be composed of two "jurists of distinguished reputation" from Great Britain, two from the United States, and three from neutral European countries.

It fell to the Republican administration of Benjamin Harrison to prepare the United States' case and select its advocates. As a Democrat, Coudert was not among the three lawyers originally selected but was called in when one had to resign only two months before the tribunal was to meet. According to Judge Patterson, John W. Foster, then secretary of state, "objected to his being retained, declaring that it was impossible for any man at such a late day to familiarize himself with the great mass of testimony which it was necessary to understand in detail." But later Foster said, "In less than six weeks after Mr. Coudert's retainer, I had occasion to go over the matter with him and I have not yet recovered from my amazement at the thorough mastery of that complicated case, which he had been able to acquire in that incredibly short time."

At age sixty-one, Coudert was at the peak of his powers. Moreover, the case appealed greatly to his sense of chivalry, as the essence of it was the defense of the gentle, harmless seals against the cruel and bloody practices of the pelagic sealers. In fact, to a degree that would warm the heart of any environmentalist today, the entire American team had a strong consciousness that they were fighting on the side of justice and simple decency. Unfortunately, they had some difficulty finding a legal argument that would support the United States' well-intentioned actions. The State Department's assertion that America had territorial rights in the waters of the Bering Sea foundered when, at the very last minute, it was discovered that some key Russian documents had been mistranslated. The department then switched to preparing its case on the basis of a neatly conceived argument drawn up by the secretary of the navy, Benjamin F. Tracy—who would later join Coudert Brothers—which asserted the United States' property rights in the migrating herds on precedents drawn from English common law treating the right of a landowner to wild animals frequenting his land.

No one, however, was in clear control of the case. Former ambassador to Great Britain E. J. Phelps was the nominal leader of the team of advocates, but James C. Carter never doubted for a moment that *he* was the leading counsel. The heir to Charles O'Conor's mantle as the intellectual leader of the American bar, Carter was simply oblivious to the possibility that he might not have been intended to head the Bering Sea team, and, his personality being not unlike O'Conor's, no one seems to have quite had the nerve to disabuse him of this notion. Furthermore, Carter, like O'Conor, was a loner, and he gave no warning of the line he intended to pursue.

Thus, when Carter made the opening presentation of the United States' case at Paris, his fellow counsel found themselves listening to an exposition of a sweeping theory of natural law that maintained that there was no absolute right of ownership: under the laws of nature, property was held only for the benefit of mankind as a whole. "His theories of property," as Fred was to note, "were highly socialistic," and, as arguments placed before a panel of successful professional men in 1893, highly disastrous. "They caused great anxiety to my father," Fred wrote, "and to Mr. Phelps, who was a much more practical lawyer than was Mr. Carter." Still worse, Carter, who was not a particularly effective public speaker, droned on for eight days, delving in metaphysics and philosophy to a degree self-indulgent enough to try the tribunal's patience.

Speaking immediately after Carter, Coudert had to repair the damage. As previously agreed, he was to lay out the facts of seal life and sealing practices and the details of the dispute. At the same time, it was clearly incumbent upon him to try to win back the tribunal's goodwill and to construct some sort of bridge between

Carter's idiosyncratic theories and the Tracy argument with which Phelps was scheduled to conclude. He spoke for four days, presenting an array of facts in a style that held the courtroom entranced. The published text of his address still today—even without the benefit of Coudert's musical voice and charming manner—has the capacity to involve the reader in the plight of the seals and in the argument for their protection. The 275 pages wind their way through such details as the range of the firearms used by the sealers and the distinctive skin coloring of the Pribilof seals, but not a word is wasted. As the Baron de Courcel, the president of the tribunal, commented when Coudert had finished his oral argument:

> You have captivated our attention by a remarkable display of talent. We have to thank you for the great ability, liveliness and humor with which you have carried us over what would otherwise have been a rather dreary field of questions of fact. Allow me to add that, as a Frenchman, I have been happy to see shine in your manner some of the best characteristics of the French nation.

The American press and public, meanwhile, had been following the proceedings in Paris as if they were a kind of grand sporting event, looking to the American lawyers to do them proud and uphold the national honor. Since the baron's remarks constituted the first "score" for the American side from the press's point of view, they were quickly reprinted throughout the country under such triumphant headlines as PRAISE FOR MR. COUDERT and MR. COUDERT ASTONISHES THE BERING SEA COURT BY HIS FLUENCY. In its lead editorial of May 10, 1893, the *New York Times* noted:

> Although it is a dictum of a court much older than the Tribunal of Arbitration now sitting at Paris that "fine words butter no parsnips," yet the American people will appreciate the graceful compliment paid to MR. COUDERT. . . . Should the American government need consolation when the great "case" is settled, this much of it, at least, will not be denied to it.

With four more lawyers yet to speak—all at length—the hearings continued into July, and the false start provided by Carter proved impossible to overcome. By a 5–2 vote, the tribunal ruled that the United States had no right to protect the seals outside the three-mile limit and that the regulations on sealing to be adopted by international agreement should be formulated not in the absolute interest of the species, but taking into account the interest of the sealers. The panel agreed at least that some regulation was needed, but, on the whole, the United States clearly lost.

Fred Coudert, however, seems to have gained in Paris in the spring and summer of 1893 a lasting interest in international law. Throughout the hot, wearing days of argument, the young lawyer sat as a fascinated observer of the public sessions and the American team's conferences behind the scenes. The caliber of the people involved, the attendant social life ("very agreeable" was his comment), the loftiness of the issues, but, most of all, the importance of the proceedings as an alternative to war impressed him greatly. Indeed, the older he grew and the more wars he lived through, the more certain Fred became that at Paris in 1893 he had witnessed something remarkable, and as an old man, he did his best to ensure that it should not be forgotten, prevailing upon one of the junior counsel in the matter to write his reminiscences of the arbitration, publishing himself a recollection of James C. Carter, and placing his memories of the arbitration in the firm's and Columbia's archives.

During most of Fred Coudert's long association with Coudert Brothers, he was the firm's clear and unquestioned leader, and he could have taken it into specialization in any field he chose. Yet, under his direction, Coudert Brothers remained an international law firm, largely because cases involving the law of nations remained those that interested him the most. The Bering Sea arbitration came just when Fred was mature and trained enough to appreciate keenly all the legal issues involved, yet young enough to be impressionable, and it is almost certainly the time when his commitment to international law became fixed.

For his father, on the other hand, the arbitration opened the taps on a last, exceptionally strong surge of professional activity. Vaulted into national prominence for the first time as an international lawyer—as opposed to a leading Democratic orator— Frederic René returned to New York to find himself sought after as a speaker and writer on international affairs. It is after 1893 that the usual appellation following his name in the press switches from "the well-known advocate" to "the distinguished international lawyer."

To a considerable extent, Frederic René had already made his most important contributions to international law. If he had died in 1892, he would still deserve remembrance for his thirty-some years of consular law practice, in the course of which he prosecuted so many extradition cases that he had done "more than any other man to settle the law relating to the construction of treaties with foreign powers, affecting such cases."

He was also one of the small handful of American attorneys responsible for the development in his era of admiralty law, with its important implications for international relations and trade. Case by case, he, Carter, Joseph Choate, Robert Benedict, and a few others hammered out the interpretation of the international rules of general average, salvage, navigation, and other points affecting international shipping. Coudert's departure for the Bering Sea arbitration, for example, had been slightly delayed by his having to appear in the district court representing the foreign owners of the *Venezuela* in a salvage dispute, while one of the first matters of business he had to attend to on his return from Paris was the preparation of the appeal to the Circuit Court of Appeals in the collision case, *The Umbria.*

Moreover, in the field of private international law, Coudert Brothers continued to hold a virtual lock on matters with a French or Latin American connection. For example, when an American contractor failed to fulfill his contract to construct waterworks for the city of Havana, Cuba *(Runkle et al. v. Burnham),* and when another American who had built and was operating the waterworks in Venezuela had his property seized *(Underhill v. Hernandez),* the ensuing legal tangles almost inevitably seemed to find their way to the Coudert offices. The senior Coudert also litigated such interesting questions as whether a private telegraph cable could be laid between Haiti and the United States without governmental consent *(United States v. La Compagnie Française des Cables Telegraphiques et al.);* what should happen when a New Orleans bank found that its interpretation of a common French banking term differed from that used in France *(Reynes v. Dumont);* whether a French company could sell its business and goodwill in New York and then establish a new branch in New York using the same trade name *(Knoedler et al. v. Boussod et al.);* and what rights private citizens have in claims against foreign governments *(United States v. Bayard, Bogardus v. Grace).*

But these contributions by Frederic René Coudert to the development of international law were the kind that could be appreciated only by specialists. His personal success before the Bering Sea tribunal, on the other hand, provided him with the opportunity to reach the general public, which he was not slow to take advantage of. Throughout his career he had repeatedly sought to rouse public opinion for one good cause or another, from the *Statue of Liberty* to domestic political reform to religious toleration. Now he added international arbitration to that list of causes, producing between 1893 and 1897 four major addresses or essays on the subject.

Its economy in a depression, America was in a particularly chauvinistic mood during these years, with Teddy Roosevelt and others trumpeting that arbitration was an intolerable abrogation of American independence—and that the United States could never get a fair break from the European powers anyway. Accordingly, in these major writings, Coudert spends considerable time countering this type of view and calming fears. In addition, obviously stimulated by his exposure to Carter's ideas on natural law, he repeatedly argues that the underpinnings of international law cannot be either natural law or morality. A Burkean conservative, Coudert points out that man in a natural state is prone to violence and that law, the alternative to violence, is, rather, a product of civilization. As a student of history, he also notes drily that men have never had difficulty arriving at repugnant results while asserting their interpretation of "morality."

As a counterpoise to the theorizing of Carter and others, Coudert insists on international law being viewed as a product of history, brought into being to serve the self-interest of individual nations and gaining wider acceptance in his era simply because technological advances had driven up the cost of war, democracy had made it more difficult to justify with respect to trivial causes, and the current European balance of power lowered the chances of any one power being able to conduct a quick, limited war. International law, Coudert says, is a convenience, not a system of law at all. But it could, given public acceptance over a sufficient number of years, become a custom between nations such as Great Britain and the United States, and as a custom, in time, gain something of the force of law.

Accordingly, in addition to laying out his views on international law, these writings are also an impassioned argument for public acceptance of arbitration as a tool for the settlement of disputes between nations. Coudert's abhorrence of war, based on his hatred of what happened to the United States during its Civil War and to France during the Franco-Prussian War, is particularly close to the surface in the article he wrote for *Harper's Magazine,* "International Arbitration," and it is clearly the impelling force—as opposed to a dry intellectual interest—in his advocacy of arbitration.

Perhaps the most impressive feature of "International Arbitration," however, is its eerily prophetic delineation of what the next major European war would be like. "We are thus rapidly approaching the hitherto unknown condition where huge armies will destroy each other before either is visible to the other save through a telescope," he wrote, adding "a new vista of horrors may teach the world, at any moment, that the wars of the past have been as the games of children."

It was because of his hatred of war—at least, of unnecessary war—that Coudert accepted in 1896 Cleveland's appointment of him to the Venezuela Commission and viewed it as one of the most important assignments of his life. This commission was a group of five prominent Americans asked by the president to ascertain where the disputed boundary between Venezuela and British Guiana ought to lie, and it constituted Cleveland's response to both Venezuela's request for help and Great Britain's refusal to arbitrate the matter. Standing foursquare on the Monroe Doctrine, Cleveland took the position that if Britain, secure in its overwhelming military and economic superiority to Venezuela, would not submit the matter to a proper international tribunal, the United States would determine whether it thought Venezuela's claim was just and, if so, would support its sister republic to the utmost. The president wished partly to shame, partly to force Great Britain into arbitration, but should his ploy fail, war was the obvious alternative.

The names of the Venezuela commissioners were announced on January 1, 1896, and the very same day, the London *Times*—which must have received advance notice from the British government—heaped scorn on Cleveland's five appointees, reserving the bulk of its sarcasm for Coudert, whom it described as "a New York lawyer and Tammany politician." Coudert, of course, was not a Tammany politician. Neither had he given out offensive "prejudgments of the matters in controversy" to the press in which he denounced England as "the bully of the world," as the *Times* accused him of doing. The *Times*' denunciation was so far off the mark, in fact, as to be almost ludicrous and to suggest that a very curious set of files must have existed on Coudert somewhere in the British Foreign Office—perhaps because of his friendship with such Irish-American leaders as Eugene Kelly and William Grace.

In any event, in due course the misapprehension was corrected through private channels: the *New York Times,* for example, under a Washington dateline printed lengthy excerpts on January 3 from "International Arbitration," while the New York Republican leader Hamilton Fish arranged for his son-in-law, Sir Stafford Northcote, M.P., to meet with Coudert at a dinner party in Washington. Meanwhile, Coudert immediately got down to work. On January 18, his old friend, the New York lawyer Joseph H. Choate, wrote from Washington that "Everybody here is still wild" about the Venezuela matter and feeling "decidedly jingo" and that Coudert was still in town "in search of the Venezuela boundary."

The true boundary line, of course, was not to be found in

Washington, but through research into the historical documents concerning the settlement of Guiana. The members of the commission were not expected to perform the actual research; for that, a young Cornell historian, George Nelson Burr, was hired. But Frederic René exerted every effort he could to locate possible evidence and assist Burr. He prevailed upon Archbishop Corrigan, for example, to contact the Office of Propaganda at the Vatican to find out what records might be available concerning the activities of the early church missionaries in Guiana. "I make no apology, my dear Archbishop, for bothering you," Coudert wrote to Corrigan, "for, after all, we are both serving the powers that be, and although it is sometimes hard to believe that they originate from above, still we may be assured that in this instance at least, they are working in the cause of humanity and peace."

Frederic René and Fred also went to Holland in the summer of 1896, so that the former could see for himself the original Dutch records that Burr was investigating. Coudert spent three months on the Continent in all, and, when the reporters learned of his return and came knocking on his door at 13 East Forty-fifth Street in October, he spoke warmly of Burr, saying that he expected his report to be "clear, thorough, intelligent, and judicial."

Just before the commission was to report, however, the British relented and agreed to arbitrate. At Cleveland's suggestion, Venezuela asked Frederic René to represent it in the actual arbitration, but Coudert, who was experiencing some health problems, refused the retainer. Instead, Benjamin F. Tracy, retired from public office, and former president Benjamin Harrison became Venezuela's counsel and won a judgment that, as Fred was to say, drew "very much the same boundary line which the American commission had determined. It was more or less a compromise, as decisions of fact often are where there is great conflict."

On February 28, 1897, during the closing days of the Cleveland administration, Coudert was summoned to the White House on yet another foreign policy matter. The president's handwritten note, delivered to Coudert at the Arlington Hotel in Washington, D.C., read simply, "Can you call on me—anytime 8 p.m. to 2 a.m.," prompting Fred to write to his mother: "President has just summoned Pa to come see him this eve. Can't be an office!" Yet it was, of a sort. An American dentist, arrested by the Spanish authorities in Cuba, had recently died in prison to the outrage of the American public. Congress was on the verge of passing a resolution recognizing the independence of Cuba from Spain, and Cleveland wanted to send Coudert to Cuba on a diplomatic mission to avert war. This Coudert declined to do, but he, Cleveland, and Secretary of State Olney conferred as the lights burned in the White House on Sunday, February 28, and again the night of March 1.

We have a good idea of what advice Coudert provided, because on his return to New York City, he gave several press interviews—obviously with the administration's blessing—intended to send Spain two reassuring messages: that Congress's resolution was not binding on the executive branch and that Cleveland would surely veto it anyway. The *New York Times,* for example, began its seven-paragraph summary of Coudert's views, as follows:

> Frederic R. Coudert, recognized as one of the greatest authorities in international law, reached this city last night from Washington, where he had been engaged in conference with President Cleveland and Secretary Olney.
>
> "I do not believe," he said, "that the declaration of Congress recognizing the independence of Cuba could be regarded as a technical violation of the neutral laws or the laws governing the comity of nations. At the present stage no European power would be likely to look upon it in that light.
>
> "It must be understood that only the executive head of the United States is invested with the power of officially recognizing the independence of any country. The resolutions of Congress can only be regarded as the resolutions of any body, having no effect in international law. These resolutions therefore cannot be regarded as a casus belli by Spain.
>
> "I have not the slightest expectation that President Cleveland will support the action of Congress. . . ."

With Cleveland and Olney determined not to let the United States plunge into a war with Spain and with the incoming McKinley administration giving the Congress no encouragement either, this crisis passed by, although a war with Spain would come a year later after the sinking of the *Maine*—a war in which Fred would nearly lose his life.

Early April 1897 found both Frederic René and Fred in Washington again, where each was scheduled to argue a case before the U.S. Supreme Court—probably the only time in the history of the Court that a father and son appeared on the same day for different clients. Fred's case was a consular law problem that had arisen suddenly just a few weeks before when Joseph A. Iasigi, the Turkish consul in Boston, had been arrested as a fugitive from justice on a warrant issued by a New York City magistrate. In the U.S. District Court Frederic René had argued for his release on the grounds that only the federal courts had jurisdiction over foreign consuls, and upon the district court upholding the arrest on March 12, an appeal was allowed to the U.S. Supreme Court—for a date conflicting with a previously scheduled case that Frederic René was committed to argue. Thus, Fred was handed the brief on *Iasagi v. Van de Carr* and accompanied his father to Washington, D.C., prepared to make his debut before the nation's highest court. He had celebrated his twenty-sixth birthday less than a month before.

Entrusting Fred at twenty-six with a Supreme Court case, however, was not as rash a move as it might seem. This was a case in which Fred could do no actual harm, for the Turkish government had dismissed Iasagi as its representative even before the district court had ruled, and, on a practical level, the whole matter was moot. Indeed, Iasagi's discharge gave the Supreme Court sufficient reason to rule that the petition for the writ of habeas corpus had been properly denied, since Iasagi was no longer a consul at the time of its denial. Fred, however, accredited himself well before the Court. In fact, he was said to have made a "brilliant" presentation of the argument for federal jurisdiction over consuls.

When Fred told the story in later years of his debut before the Supreme Court, however, he preferred to emphasize the comic aspects. Although time was short, Fred had prepared carefully—so carefully that he was able to make his oral argument without reference to even so much as a note. He had also rehearsed how he would employ the gestures, the pacing, and other rhetorical arts that he had learned from his father. Therefore, he found it rather disconcerting that "all the justices were apparently paying no attention to me except Mr. Field." Justice Stephen Johnson Field, eighty-one years old, gave Fred's presentation a close attention that reassured Fred that he was making an impression on at least one member of the distinguished court. "It encouraged me a great deal," Fred told the clerk of the Court after the ordeal was over. "Yes," said the clerk. "Justice Field always listens. He can't hear a word though, because he's so deaf!"

Given Iasagi's dismissal, however, Coudert Brothers had not had much hope of success in this appeal. Frederic René, on the other hand, did expect to win his admiralty case, *The Umbria*, which he was handling for the Cunard Line, a most important client. Back in 1888 the *Umbria*, under the command of a Captain MacMicken, had collided in the fog off Long Island with a French steamship, the *Iberia*, cutting the latter in two, and the question of whether there had been negligence on both sides and the damages should, therefore, be divided had been moving through the court system for years. According to his son, Frederic René's argument in this final appeal ran along these lines: "There have been eleven judges engaged in this case for the last four years. Captain MacMicken had just the 37th of a minute to decide what course to pursue. It is a little hard to charge him with negligence in that brief time."

The decision, however, went unanimously against Coudert, and Fred later happened to discover why—a story he recounted years later to illustrate "the uncertainty of litigation." As Fred told the tale:

> Many years afterward Mr. Justice Brown, who had written the opinion, retired from the court. At lunch at his house I spoke of the *Umbria* and how that was decided.
>
> "Well, I'll tell you," he said. "It's a curious enough thing. I wrote the opinion for dividing the damages, and it seemed to be the opinion of the court at the last consultation in June. I was to have published the opinion, and it would have been in your father's favor. But," he said, "Justice White said to me, 'Now, Brown, won't you wait until after vacation? I have some doubts about that case, and I would like to discuss more fully with the Court questions of fact. I doubt if there was negligence on both sides.' "
>
> Brown said, "Of course I yielded . . . as it was a question of fact. When we got back into the autumn, Justice White raised the question again, and at that time he had another judge with him. I think that it must have been McKenna, because McKenna nearly always went with Justice White. That made two judges, and then a third said that he was very doubtful, and we ordered a re-argument.
>
> "You know White is a very persuasive and a very insistent man, and the first thing I knew he had five judges with him, and that was a majority. So they said, 'You'll have to change your opinion on the question.' So I had to rewrite my opinion, and that is how it came about!"

The Umbria, though, was but one of the many major cases Frederic René was handling in the mid-1890s. According to Fred, his father was arguing cases "almost daily," while at the same time, in quick succession, he had the Bering Sea arbitration, the work generated by the Union Pacific's bankruptcy, and the Venezuela Commission. "Finally he overworked so that it strained his heart and he didn't live very long," Fred said. "I always thought that he would have lived for a long time after that if he hadn't been so pressed by these things all coming together. They were all things that would strain the nerves."

Fred did not mention it, but there was another strictly personal matter that seriously affected his father's health from 1897 on—the death of Charles Coudert and a subsequent lawsuit brought against the firm by Charles's widow, Marie.

Charles Coudert's death on July 13, 1897, followed a prolonged illness, which was reported to be a pulmonary infirmity complicated by nervous exhaustion. The second oldest of the Coudert brothers had always been a hard worker—the type to stick to his post "like the boy on the burning deck," as Frederic René once described him. As early as 1891, however, there were signs that he was exhausting himself. "He needs rest and must have it or break completely down," Frederic René wrote in May of that year when Charles was "quite sick." But only four days later, the senior partner reported that Charles was at the office again "working as hard as ever and seems like himself again, altho' that is not saying a great deal."

By April 1894 Charles was clearly headed for a complete breakdown. "Uncle Charles is not well," a family member wrote to one of his nieces. "Madam Charles said he never says anything at the table: 'He is so gloomy.' " In August of the same year, Charles went up to the Adirondacks, seeking to throw off his persistent cough and fatigue, but although he visited numerous other spas over the next three years, his weakness grew more pronounced, and he seldom came into the office.

The onset of Charles's breakdown coincided with the worst depression in American history before the 1930s, a time when Eugene Kelly was shutting down his bank, all the markets were at a standstill, and Frederic René was writing glumly that "Business is a memory." Not only did the firm need to dip into its capital to bail out clients who had invested on the partners' advice in real estate that had now plummeted in value, but Charles was heavily invested himself in the same type of properties and burdened with a large number of mortgages.

Frederic René was in something of the same case, but he and Lizzie were able to effect economies that Charles evidently could not. Charles had a wife who had grown up as the poor relative in a relatively wealthy family and for whom, as an adult, the best of everything was none too good. Her spending habits had been raising eyebrows in the family for years. Moreover, Charles had seven surviving children to Frederic René's four—one son, whose education was entering its most expensive stage when the depression struck, and no fewer than six daughters who had to be suitably married and dowered. Two of these had already married by 1893, but

Aimee, whose wedding Grover Cleveland had attended, had the misfortune to have her young husband die from an unsuccessful stomach operation—which was conducted at their home, as hospitals were still not to be trusted—and she had returned, as a dependent, to her father's roof, with an infant son besides.

The other married daughter, Claire, had wed a French nobleman, in one of those alliances of American money and European titles that were so common at the end of the nineteenth century. Claire Coudert's marriage to the Marquis de Choiseul was a classic case, particularly in that it was engineered by her mother, Marie—or "the General in Green Velvet," as the Frederic René Couderts referred to her—and it was preceded by the settlement upon the bridegroom and his mother of a considerable amount of property by the bride's father.

In addition, there soon followed two more society weddings: Constance's to William R. Garrison, a grandson of her father's clubmate Commodore Garrison, who had once owned the Missouri Pacific; and Daisy's to Frank Glaenzer, the son of an American merchant resident in Paris who had contributed significantly to the *Statue of Liberty*. All together, Charles had drains on his savings in the mid-1890s that it would have taken a good many years to restore, at best. But, dying in 1897, he was not given the chance to rebuild his fortune.

Even though it had been so long foreseeable, Frederic René was still prostrated by Charles's death, which left him, the eldest, the last survivor of the original three brothers. He and Charles had lived together under the same roof until they were well into their thirties; they had practiced law together for a full forty years; both their personal and professional lives had been almost inseparably intertwined. No sooner had his brother expired than Frederic René collapsed, and—as if life without his brother were unimaginable—he thought himself to be dying, too. Although the newspapers reported that Frederic René had been present at the funeral service in St. Patrick's Cathedral, he was, in fact, in bed at his country home in Metuchen, New Jersey, at the time of the service, his face metaphorically turned to the wall.

Probably because Frederic René—who had always been the firm's spokesman—was struggling with what Lizzie called "the heavy affliction he has been called upon to bear," no one seems to have prepared a proper obituary notice for Charles. Large headlines and a fair amount of space were given July 14 to his passing on, but the newspapers were at a loss for much to say. After stating that Charles had been Frederic René's brother, one of the firm's original partners, and had never held political office, they mostly resorted to generalities. By July 15, however, the *New York Tribune* had apparently inquired around sufficiently to produce this assessment: "Charles Coudert did not become a brilliant lawyer, and the success of the firm has been chiefly due to his brother's personality, but he was a painstaking and methodical worker, and had a capacity for managing the firm's business affairs, which were in his charge for many years."

In the context of the period, however, "a brilliant lawyer" would still mean simply an outstanding pleader in court. It is entirely possible that Charles Coudert was exceptional, perhaps "brilliant," as a legal advisor and counsellor, as a draftsman of contracts and wills, even as a negotiator or deal-maker—but between the loss of the firm's nineteenth-century files and Charles's quiet, retiring life-style, we can never know this for certain. In his own day, the style of practice Charles developed, as Paul Fuller remarked, "makes no public annals." Fuller himself was more concerned with character than anything else, and, therefore, the memorial of Charles that he undertook for the Bar Association of the City of New York, which Charles had helped to found, stressed his brother-in-law's "stainless integrity and loyalty":

> His personal character was the basis of his success. All who knew him—the clients whom he assisted, his brethren at the bar with whom he advised or with whom he contended, as well as the social friends who enjoyed his companionship; all who had intercourse with him—recognized the strict and stern uprightness which allowed no swerving to the right or to the left for the easier attainment of an end; the mental and moral rectitude which blinked no fact, however untoward, and which disdained every advantage to be had at the cost of truth; the love of right; the courage which, in the words of the poet, could always "bear to look into the swarthiest face of things for God's sake who so made them."

For want of any other enlightening comment, this is how Charles Coudert will have to be remembered—as an honorable man who never failed at any trust; there have certainly been many lawyers, more famous, who accomplished less.

In any event, Charles's estate seems to have been long on depreciated real estate and short on cash, and it was clear that, without the income he earned, someone in his family was going to have to forgo the Tiffany jewels and transatlantic trips to which they had all become accustomed. His widow was determined that it would not be she. Exactly one week after Charles's death, Marie fired the opening shot in a campaign to overthrow his will, which left the bulk of the estate to their children, and have accepted for probate an earlier will, which left most of the estate to her.

In Metuchen, Frederic René rallied sufficiently to tell reporters that he "did not believe there was any possibility of a [will] contest, as no matter how the will was drawn the money would go to his brother's family, and there was no bitterness between the wife and children of the dead man." Frederic René, however, was telling a flat lie, for he well knew that Marie was completely estranged from three of her daughters—Grace, Clarisse, and Aimee. He had, in fact, been present when Marie had refused a reconciliation with these girls "at the very death bed" of her husband. He also knew that relations between Marie and her daughter Daisy Glaenzer were far from ideal: a few years earlier Marie had profoundly shocked her son-in-law by spending a whole month in Paris, almost on the Glaenzers' doorstep, without letting her daughter know she was in town.

By August the will contest that Frederic René had said would not materialize was in full swing, with Marie alleging that Charles's final will was the result of "undue influence" exerted upon him by "someone"; by September the scandal sheets were insinuating that that "someone" was her brother-in-law Frederic René and that he had long attempted to break up her marriage to Charles. Although Marie's attorney denied that his client would allege any such thing, the yellow press milked the story so hard that it even began to leak into the respectable newspapers.

Long before September, however, Frederic René had collapsed again and had been removed to Bar Harbor, Maine. His family put the word out that he was ill and suffering from overwork, but, in fact, his chief ailment seems to have been depression. Apart from mourning his brother's death, he was grieving at the loss of the family unity, which he had so much taken for granted. To have the Coudert name spread over the columns of the gossip sheets and his own reputation for integrity attacked was bad enough; that the attack should come from within the family itself was almost more than he could endure. Week by week, throughout August, September, and October, Frederic René's departure from Maine was postponed. He was heartsick to such an extent that, for once in his life, he could not attend to business.

The two people left to manage the office in Frederic René's absence were Fred and Paul Fuller. It was they who had to face down whatever whisperings were running through the business district and answer the questions of well-meaning acquaintances. ("People think Mrs. C. an unnatural mother and those who do not know ask if she is a step-mother," Fred reported.) Furthermore, they had to dissolve the old partnership, a task made herculean by the need to collect on fifteen thousand dollars of outstanding fees, while the office had to be moved from 68–70 William Street to a new location at 100 Broadway. Moreover, both Fred and Paul were desperately worried about Frederic René, with Fred dispatching bracing notes to Bar Harbor almost daily.

In the family letters of this period, we can see Fred and his uncle Paul working smoothly together. Aware that Paul in this crisis had been unable to take a vacation of any kind, Fred is touchingly solicitous about his uncle's health, whereas Paul writes to Fred without any evident consciousness of a difference between them in age and experience. The tone and content of his letters are as from one partner to another, rather than uncle to nephew. The financial worries, Paul's opinions on the staff's capabilities, and the steps he thinks should be taken are presented to Fred, mulled over with him, as an equal.

"A lovable man" is how Fred would describe his uncle Paul some twenty years later, and as an example of the kind of relationship they enjoyed, Fred recounted the story of how he came to make his second appearance before the U.S. Supreme Court, in November 1897. The case was actually Frederic René's, one involving the defense of a leader of a revolutionary army in Venezuela who had forced a U.S. citizen, who had the contract to supply water to the city of Bolivar, to continue to operate the waterworks during the insurrection *(Underhill v. Hernandez)*. This was not a cut-and-dried matter like *Iasagi v. Van de Carr;* the issues were complicated ones touching the sovereignty of nations, recognition of states and governments, and the legal status of de facto governments. Careful judgment was required in the selection and presentation of the arguments. Frederic René was to have prepared the brief, but as the court date drew nearer and the brief remained still unwritten, Paul finally sat down and, in a burst of concentrated down-to-the-wire effort, drafted the firm's argument, which he then insisted that young Fred go to Washington to present. Knowing that this meant that his name rather than Paul's would go down in the record as the counsel in the case, Fred demurred. But Paul would hear of nothing else and had his way.

Although both were overworked, Paul and Fred were united in their insistence that Frederic René must not return to the office while the will contest raged. "I know [how] difficult it is to make him look with indifference upon all the mortifying and annoying occurrences that have supervened," Paul wrote to his nephew in August. "If he could possibly wash his hands of that, or let us meet whatever is disagreeable concerning it, I feel satisfied that he would mend."

Have "Pops" engage in some literary effort, Fred wrote to his mother, or ship him off to Europe: do anything but don't allow him near the office. "I absolutely dread Pa's coming here. Two days of the fretting and worrying over [Charles's will] will undo all the good work. . . . He must keep aloof from the whole matter and leave it to outsiders as a pure business matter."

The outside counsel engaged by Coudert Brothers, as representatives of Charles's children, did finally reach an out-of-court settlement with Marie in late December 1897. A month earlier, despite his partners' misgivings, Frederic René had returned to the office and sat for a press interview, announcing himself in perfect health and "ready and willing" to accept retainers. Since the firm's revenues had fallen off during Frederic René's four-month absence, this was good for the firm—but, as Paul and Fred had feared, it was perhaps too early a return with respect to their senior partner's health.

He was still not himself over the winter of 1897–98, but rallied to meet the crisis in 1898 when Fred was called off to war. Yet he could not keep up his old hectic pace long. In 1899 he retired as president of the Manhattan Club and began necessarily to cut back his caseload.

Until his death in 1903, despite increasing health problems, Frederic René would continue to practice law and would be looked to for the final decision in all important firm matters, but the effective day-to-day control of Coudert Brothers passed in 1899 to Paul and Fred. It would be they who would guide the partnership into the twentieth century, Paul providing the wisdom and Fred a dynamic energy that soon made its impact on the firm.

Chapter Six

THE TORCH PASSES

A t the turn of the century, Coudert Brothers was a giant among law firms, with seven partners and about nine associates in its New York office and at least three attorneys in its Paris office. Moreover, it was still the only firm with an overseas branch office. The trend in the legal profession, however, was now clearly set toward growth—more firms were approaching Coudert Brothers in size, a few Boston and Philadelphia firms had opened small outposts in New York City—and anxious articles were beginning to appear, wondering whether these developments would not introduce into the profession the impersonal atmosphere of the factory.

Several photographs taken in 1899 show that Coudert Brothers' offices were as businesslike as they had ever been. The solid but unpretentious furniture, the venetian blinds and plastered walls, and the up-to-date modern conveniences, including steam heat, electric light, and desk telephones, made the firm's premises indistinguishable from those of any prosperous commercial enterprise of the period. Yet, after two decades of experience as a large-scale organization, Coudert Brothers still retained a gentlemanly ambience.

This is not surprising, for the Coudert founders had been careful to staff their enterprise, at every level, with gentlemen. "My father," Fred would recall with specific reference to the firm's hiring practices, "had ever believed that the so-called minor virtues of po-

117

liteness and consideration were not merely the result of training and an outward veneer, but that they really sprang from those innate qualities of heart and head that characterize the best type of men." Thus, a law student in the early 1890s was remembered years later with considerable respect for "his cheerful, kindly, smiling face, and his ever pleasant and polite reception of clients." The firm wanted intellect, but it definitely valued manners too.

Coudert Brothers evidently did not believe that these qualities were confined to any one particular kind of background, for the associates at the turn of the century included Protestants and Catholics, graduates of obscure colleges and Ivy League degree-holders, Democrats, of course, but also a Republican and even one Socialist. All they had in common was that they were gentlemen, and the firm treated them as such. Coudert Brothers paid good salaries, even to law students, whom other firms expected to work for free. Moreover, the partners' letters clearly show a concern that their employees not work such long hours as to endanger their health or cause them to slight family commitments. Behind the grave Victorian courtesy with which all the attorneys and clerks addressed each other, a simple kindness pervaded the firm, and the result was a marked degree of stability among the salaried associates and clerks.

In assessing the condition of the firm as it was left by its founding members, its size and stability at the subpartner level should not be overlooked. From 1897 to 1903 Coudert Brothers went through considerable turmoil in its upper ranks, primarily because of illness and death. This was a six-year run of bad luck that might have broken up or, at least, markedly weakened any other firm, but with its large body of well-trained associates and clerks who steadily went about their business, Coudert Brothers weathered this turbulent period without major upset.

The very size of the firm, too, meant that there was a depth of talent available. As already noted, Charles Coudert had been understudied for years by James Richards in real estate law and Daniel J. Holden in estates and trusts, while Frederic René Coudert had trained Paul Fuller as a litigator and, more recently, his own son, Fred. But beyond these first-string and second-string players, there was another layer of up-and-coming men by the late 1890s, young contemporaries of Fred's who would be ready for increased responsibility when the older partners died or retired. Coudert Brothers, as its founding partners had created it, was like a well-organized team with players in training down to the sandlot level, and in this respect, it contrasted sharply with the loosely organized—and ultimately less durable—partnerships that were more typical of the times.

Another chief legacy of the founding brothers was undoubtedly the prestige embedded in the name Coudert Brothers, which had as its main locus the firm's expertise in international law. The first generation of Couderts had consciously created this prestige and had selected and trained their successors so well that the firm's reputation not only survived them but continued to grow. Even before Frederic René began to suffer from his mortal heart ailment, for example, Paul Fuller was already recognized by the profession for his erudition in international law. The orphan taken in by Charles Coudert, Sr., had grown into a "bibliophile of rare discernment and fanatic attachment, an omnivorous reader, a scholar of wide attainment," who maintained a private library of some twenty-five thousand volumes.

Not every field of law requires cultivated scholarship of the kind that Fuller possessed, but consular law was one in which Fuller's learning was decidedly useful. In one of his most celebrated U.S. Supreme Court cases, *Tucker v. Alexandroff* (1901), for example, Fuller's discussion ranged from the marine ordinances of Louis XIV to the Columbian Exposition of 1893 as he argued, on behalf of the Russian government, for the return of a deserter from the Russian Navy. Moreover, in the nineteenth century, Latin nations had the agreeable custom of appointing scholars and men of letters to foreign diplomatic positions, and Paul Fuller's love of learning made him most welcome personally to these men. In fact, Paul Fuller's scholarship is probably the chief reason that Coudert Brothers' consular practice was not affected by Frederic René's illness and death. And the fact that the firm did represent a large number of foreign governments, in turn, enhanced its prestige. Few references to Coudert Brothers at this time fail to mention—sometimes in rather awed tones—that its clients included the governments of France, Belgium, Italy, Venezuela, Russia, Turkey, et al.

The firm's prestige grew not only from its scholarly expertise, however, but also from its more than forty years of practical experience in transnational problems. No law firm knew better what pitfalls awaited Jersey City attorney Robert O. Babbitt when he wanted to engage in some speculative investments in Mexico; or how to draw up a marriage settlement when Jay Gould's daughter, Anna, decided to marry the impecunious Count Boni de Castellane; or what procedure should be followed by a Newark doctor with a claim to the estate of a Spanish nobleman, the Marquis de Sesto, who had died without leaving a will. By the late 1890s

Coudert Brothers had been handling these kinds of matters for years.

The type of work the firm dealt with routinely is suggested by the estate of John Daniel Brez, a Swiss multimillionaire who died in 1899. His will, which Coudert Brothers had drafted, was probated in Brooklyn, and it left to Elizabeth Gillet, a Swiss citizen, all the income from thousands of large bonds in over twenty-five American railroads, several utilities, and a few gold mines. Coudert Brothers administered the estate, which entailed coordinating the efforts of one executor, a Frenchman with a brokerage business in New York who bought and sold the bonds for the trust, and of a second executor, a Morgan, Hartjes banker in Paris who transferred the funds to Mrs. Gillet in Switzerland. In correspondence with its Paris office, Coudert Brothers also arranged the foreign taxes and prepared the various declarations and statements of income.

The Brez estate was not one of the more complicated ones handled by Coudert Brothers, but obviously its administration required a command of the French language, expertise in jurisdictional questions, familiarity with foreign income and estate tax provisions, and knowledge of American and foreign business practices. Coudert Brothers had these skills at its command and used them, not on rare occasions, but daily. Unlike other American law firms, it was staffed to meet the needs of foreign clients and Americans with foreign investments, for not only the senior partners in the New York office but many of the clerks were entirely fluent in French and Spanish as well as English, while correspondence in German and Italian was also taken in stride.

Furthermore, in the Paris office, the two senior attorneys—Henry Cachard and Henry Peartree—offered between them expertise in American, French, and British law. Cachard had been admitted to the New York bar while working as an associate at the New York office, and after his transfer to Coudert Frères in 1884, he had studied for and received his *Licence en Droit* to practice in French courts. Cachard's interest in French law was such that he published in 1895 the first English translation of the French civil code. A monumental undertaking, the translation had its imperfections. In fact, there are wags who maintain that Frederic René Coudert, who never qualified to practice in France, knew more about French law than Cachard did, for Coudert always insisted that France's civil code could not be adequately rendered in English while Cachard had the folly to attempt the task. Whatever its deficiencies, however, Cachard's translation was the authority for several generations of lawyers. "We all complained about it," one

American lawyer who practiced in France before World War II has commented, "but we all used it. Everyone had his copy of Cachard."

Peartree, on the other hand, was originally an English barrister. Moving to New York and qualifying as a U.S. attorney, he also worked for Coudert Brothers for several years before being transferred to Coudert Frères. Remembered, like so many of his Coudert contemporaries, as "a great gentleman," Peartree made it possible for Coudert Frères to provide advice to the large number of English-speaking expatriates in France who had investments in Great Britain as well as the United States.

Both Cachard and Peartree, moreover, were founders in 1894 of the American Chamber of Commerce in France, which met until 1899 in Coudert Frères's offices on rue Scribe. Peartree, as the Chamber's second president (1898–1900), led an energetic effort to insure strong American participation in the Paris Expo of 1900 and to gain permission for the Stars and Stripes to be flown from the Eiffel Tower during a chamber banquet, while Cachard's presidency in 1903–1904 was marked by lobbying efforts for a treaty of reciprocity and lower French duties on "talking machines."

Although no complete, or even partial, list of clients has survived from the turn of the century, it is clear that the firm's peculiar expertise attracted a considerable number of individuals who moved in the highest society. Anna Gould, who eventually divorced her Italian count and married the Marquis de Talleyrand, was probably the most colorful of these. Perhaps the most distinguished was the Marquis Henri de Breteuil, whom Marcel Proust used as the model for the aristocratic "M. de Bréauté" in *Remembrance of Things Past*. But far and away the most generous was Madame D'Olivera, a wealthy Florentine, who expressed "her gratitude to the firm" by giving Frederic René several hundred Byzantine and Renaissance works of art and religious relics. In effect refusing the gift, Frederic René donated the relics to Archbishop Corrigan and presented the young Metropolitan Museum (of which Eugene Kelly was a founder) with the tapestries, enamels, and objets d'art as well as eleven paintings from the fourteenth to the sixteenth centuries that became the nucleus of the museum's Renaissance collection.

Many of the more dazzling names on the client list were secured by the Paris office, for "Birdy" Cachard—as Fred Coudert called him when both were young—had "a faculty for obtaining clients, especially those of social prominence, as he was very fond of the social life." America's love affair with foreign titles was then at its peak, and such clients lent glamour and additional éclat to the firm.

Another class of individuals who began to capture the public's imagination in the late 1890s were the great "money men," such as J. P. Morgan, who were then raising unprecedented sums to create the "trusts" and other large-scale enterprises on both sides of the Atlantic. While Coudert Brothers apparently had no role in the creation of any of the purely domestic trusts, if a Wall Street deal had an international twist, the firm was often to the fore.

In 1899, for example, we find the underwriters of the Kern Incandescent Gas Light Company—including investment banker E. C. Benedict, Boston financier Thomas W. Lawson, and one of the Havemeyers of the "Sugar Trust" family—gathering in the offices of Coudert Brothers to decide whether to meet the call for an additional assessment to raise capital for this company, which was utilizing foreign patents to build streetlights in competition with the Edison patents. In the same year Paul Fuller, on a visit to Paris, was being wined, dined, and treated to his first automobile ride by one of Edmond Rothschild's associates while they waited for the head of the French Rothschilds to return from a Mediterranean yacht cruise. Fuller's business, which was connected with the Société Electrique, required Rothschild's personal attention, and the courtesies shown to Fuller were by way of apology for the delay.

On the same Paris visit, moreover, Fuller was also engaged in negotiations on behalf of a syndicate of American investors organized by the Baron Robert Oppenheim, an investment banker with offices in Paris and London. The Oppenheim syndicate, which seemingly had some assurances of interest from J. P. Morgan, was seeking nothing less than to purchase the rights to dig the Panama Canal. Those rights—which had been granted by Colombia to the French engineer Ferdinand de Lesseps, whose effort to build the canal had ended in bitter failure in the 1880s—now belonged to a successor to de Lesseps' venture, the Compagnie Nouvelle de Panama, and Fuller seems to have spent considerable time in 1899 in the ultimately fruitless attempt to secure them for his group of private American investors.

The loss of virtually all the nineteenth-century records of both the New York and the Paris offices makes it difficult to be certain, but Coudert Frères appears to have worked for or with the Morgan interests on a number of other international ventures, particularly after the House of Morgan acquired the Drexel, Hartjes Bank in Paris in the mid-1890s. In any event, the fragmentary records that have survived are dotted with names—Rothschild, Benedict, Morgan—that ring of gold.

This, then, was the firm as it was left by the original Coudert brothers to their partners and successors: respected for its expertise in international law; prestigious, even somewhat glamorous, in reputation; large and stable; and staffed by men who, although naturally interested in making money, had been advised by Frederic René Coudert to "Remember that you may be both a lawyer and a gentleman; but if you have to choose between the two, take the latter."

For all of Coudert Brothers' strengths, the firm still had some significant weaknesses in 1899, the most important of which was probably the lack of an active strong litigator at the partner level. Frederic René Coudert, sixty-seven years old in this year, had entered the "long twilight" of his struggles with heart disease. There were days he could come down to the office, but he would never appear in court again.

The next litigating partner in order of seniority was Paul Fuller, a lawyer who was superb at preparing a brief but who was not a courtroom attorney in the fullest sense. Slim, bespectacled, already white-bearded at age fifty-two, Fuller had the somewhat retiring disposition of a scholar. Although he was a fascinating conversationalist and excellent at quiet negotiations with small groups of people, he was an intensely private person, and speaking in front of a crowded courtroom in the blaze of publicity was far from being his favorite activity. Fuller probably wrote virtually all of the firm's major briefs in 1899, yet as far as can be determined, he did not make even a single court appearance in that year.

Moreover, in 1899 Fuller was heavily engaged in other duties related to the general management of the firm. When the partnership had re-formed in 1897 after Charles Coudert's death, Fuller had expressed hopes of passing on some of his responsibilities as managing partner to James Richards, the head of the Real Estate Department. "I should like Richards to take a more general supervision of all the financial matters," Fuller had written to Fred in the fall of 1897. "He is cautious & conservative & will help to run the office on an economical basis, both as to expenses, & advances for clients. . . ."

Unfortunately for Fuller's plans, Richards began to suffer a breakdown in his health not long thereafter, following his wife's death. Hospitalized for a considerable period, Richards resigned from the firm in 1899, when he was sixty years old. He would eventually recover, start a new career as a solo practitioner in the slower-paced environment of Long Island, and practice law well into his eighties—but he never returned to Coudert Brothers.

So Fuller in 1899 was still carrying the management load alone. As he had a delicate constitution, which was perhaps a legacy from his childhood deprivations, it was not wise for him to push himself too hard. Yet in the difficult years after Charles Coudert's death, it was impossible for Fuller to rest properly. In 1899 alone, for example, he had to oversee two office moves, as the New York office took over new premises at 71 Broadway and the Paris office, after twenty years on rue Scribe, relocated to 35, boulevard Hausmann. He also made an extended business trip to Paris, took charge of reorganizing the Real Estate Department, and, as we shall see, arranged for the opening of a new branch office in Washington, D.C. It is no wonder that Fuller ran a chronic fever much of the year and that, on top of the briefs that he had to research and write, he had no strength to spare for the court appearances, which were, even at the best of times, something of a tribulation for him.

The most senior litigation partner after Fuller was Fred Coudert, who at the age of twenty-eight had already showed considerable talent for advocacy. Fred had a poise, polish, and confidence beyond his years, and he might have been able to take over a large share of the litigation load in 1899—except that he, too, was ill during most of the year, still recovering from the various tropical diseases he had picked up during his service in the Spanish-American War. This was the "glorious little war" in which a few hundred American soldiers were killed by the Spaniards and over five thousand by the U.S. Army and the War Department, whose ignorance of the basic elements of sanitation allowed typhoid, yellow fever, and malaria to run unchecked through the army camps. As the acting captain of a volunteer unit of cavalry, Fred had had a busy time in the summer of 1898 trying to protect his men from the lethal bungling of their superiors, and it is much to his credit that, although he was on active service for only five months, Fred twice found himself threatened with court-martial—once for refusing to place the troop mess next to the latrines and another time for giving some fever victims "leave" so that they could escape from the camp hospital where disease-carrying flies were so thick they coated the tongues of unconscious men.

The responsibilities of his situation—the fine line he was constantly treading between obeying army regulations, which he earnestly wanted to do, and keeping his men fit and alive—gave Fred many a sleepless night. In fact, it was in the army that Fred began what was to become a lifelong struggle with insomnia, but he and his men developed considerable ingenuity at circumventing the elderly generals who snorted at talk of microbes. With the help of money sent to them by their parents, Fred and his men bought their own food so that they would not have to eat the army's contaminated tins of beef, and, once they had landed in Puerto Rico, they rented, whitewashed, and fumigated a house. This became Troop A's private hospital, which the army knew nothing about, staffed by its own nurse. "Whenever I had anybody sick, I sent them to that hospital, and I didn't make any report of it," Fred later said. "By that time I had gotten to taking things into my own hands."

The armistice came before Troop A was sent into action, and, thanks largely to the initiative and common sense of their acting captain, every member of the troop survived the war. But Fred himself succumbed in September 1898, after the armistice, to a combination of typhoid fever and malaria. Shipped delirious to a camp back in the States, he was rescued, almost on the verge of death, by his family. Although Fred gradually recovered, the lingering effects, he recalled, "crippled me up for a year or so." This meant that, from the spring of 1898 to the fall of 1899, he could not be counted one of the assets of the firm.

The fourth litigation partner was Joseph Kling, who had been made a partner upon Charles Coudert's death in 1897. An associate in the Litigation Department, he was the first choice of both Fred Coudert and Paul Fuller for promotion to partner and Fuller had had designs on Kling's administrative abilities as well, noting in 1897 that "if he takes a position as partner I think he can supervise the work of all the subordinates, & see that each earns his pay." In this hope Fuller was again disappointed, for Kling spent barely two years as a Coudert Brothers partner. Since there is neither an obituary nor a directory listing for him in New York City after 1899, presumably he moved away. In any event, whatever strength he brought to the partnership was fleeting at best.

Coudert Brothers had a number of able associates who could handle the work in the lower courts, but the remunerative appellate work would not come to the firm while clients felt that it lacked an outstanding litigator. This was especially true of the shipping lines that had provided Coudert Brothers with an extensive admiralty practice. For example, General Transatlantic, the French passenger line, which was one of the firm's oldest clients, gave its business after 1898 to Edward K. Jones, an independent practitioner whom Frederic René had trained. Another admiralty client of equally long standing, W. R. Grace & Co., also sought other counsel beginning around 1897. Coudert Brothers lost essentially its entire admiralty practice in the late 1890s, undoubtedly because of Frederic René Coudert's ill health.

This was painful because the appellate cases brought in good fees, even though Coudert Brothers did not perhaps charge as much as certain other firms. For instance, William Nelson Cromwell, acting as the general counsel for the Panama Railroad, had chided Coudert Brothers in 1894 for submitting a bill to the railroad that was, in his estimation, too small. Cromwell suggested that the railroad should pay $10,000 for the work in question, which was the third round of appeals in an admiralty case, with the fee being divided 60/40 between Coudert Brothers and himself. At that rate, by the time the case reached the U.S. Supreme Court in 1897—where Frederic René, incidentally, won the decision—the legal fees and court expenses paid by the railroad might well have exceeded the sum in dispute, which was only $38,861.86. Nonetheless, if Coudert Brothers seemed modest in its billing practices to Cromwell, who was, after all, famous for the audacity of his bills, the appellate work was still a major source of revenue that the firm could not afford to lose.

In addition, appellate work brought with it valuable publicity, which in turn generated new business for the firm. And Coudert Brothers did, in fact, need new business. At the same time as the work from the shipping lines was disappearing, that cluster of clients who might best be described as the South Orange crowd—Eugene Kelly, Albert Reynaud, John Lord, and others—were reaching old age and dying or retiring. These were men who had conducted personal businesses, and their enterprises generally did not survive them, so that the gaps they left in the ranks of regular clients would have to be filled by new and different businesses.

The firm was not at all in desperate straits. The consular work came in steadily, and the "notarial" side of the practice was flourishing. It was said that when Charles Coudert died in 1897, the firm had nearly two hundred wills actively in probate, and the trunks and boxes in the Estates and Trusts Department were loaded with hundreds more, guaranteeing a flow of business for many years to come. Moreover, interest in real estate investment was actually starting to revive, and, although Coudert Brothers would never again become involved in guaranteeing property investments for its clients, real estate would remain an important segment of the practice for another decade or two. But even the "notarial" practice could be expected to wither after a time without new clients, and there was no partner on that side of the practice who was a generator of business in 1899. Daniel J. Holden, the head of Estates and Trusts, who had been made a partner in 1893, was an excellent man, who ran his department well. He was active on bar association committees and prominent in the lay affairs of the Protestant "mission church" movement, yet he does not seem to have had the dynamic character or reputation that attracts new clients.

The other estates and trusts partner in 1899 was thirty-seven-year-old Lorenzo E. Semple, who came from a well-known Alabama family. His father, Henry Churchill Semple, was a Harvard Law School graduate who, after distinguished service in the Confederate Army, had established his practice in Montgomery, Alabama, and become a power in that state's Democratic party. His mother was from a Louisiana Catholic family, and one of Lorenzo Semple's brothers would become a Jesuit priest and college president, while a sister headed a convent in Mexico City. Lorenzo Semple himself came to the law late. An Annapolis graduate, he served ten years as a naval officer before resigning his commission to attend the University of Virginia Law School.

When Semple finally arrived in New York City around 1893 to begin practicing law, he would have met the Couderts immediately, for it was his brother McKenzie Semple who had married Charles Coudert's daughter Aimee and subsequently died on the parlor operating table. Paul Fuller and Fred Coudert saw a great deal of Semple after Charles Coudert's death, when Semple was appointed guardian of one of Charles's minor daughters, and they conceived considerable respect for his conduct during the painful months of the will contest. It was this respect and liking that probably prompted Coudert Brothers to invite Semple into partnership in 1897. Semple began proving his worth quite quickly, but in 1899 he was still a relatively inexperienced lawyer.

Not even Paul Fuller could fill in for Frederic René as a business getter, for Fuller had a "dread of publicity," according to one newspaper account, "that is all the more impressive because it is genuine and without the slightest affectation." His avoidance of the limelight was so extreme that he refused to let his name be listed in any kind of "Who's Who," he would not grant interviews to the press, and he declined all public honors. This trait was apparently the byproduct of Fuller's very deep religious faith, which inclined him to do good unobserved. Fuller's family and friends respected this side of his character, and his selflessness was a tremendous asset in his management of the firm. But it made him essentially a "lawyer's lawyer"—the expert to whom others come for advice, but whose name is scarcely known to the public at large.

Accordingly, if Frederic René was missed as a litigator, his absence was also felt as the visible head of the firm. Although much more understated than most other great advocates of his generation, he still had had that touch of showmanship that makes "good copy," and his youthful experience as a journalist had made him adept at press relations. In court or out, win or lose, Coudert had almost always received warm and sympathetic treatment from reporters. Fuller was most definitely a leader of the bar, but Coudert had been a *famous* leader of the bar—a distinction of little significance to the day-to-day work of the firm but of considerable importance to its prospects for growth.

With all the advantages of hindsight, therefore, it is clear that the firm had three pressing needs in 1899. First, the Litigation Department required immediate reinforcements at the top, preferably mature men who could bring new clients to the firm. Second, for the health of the firm over the long run, the young men in every department had to be brought along as quickly as possible. And third, someone was needed to deal with the press, serve as the firm's spokesman, and, in general, generate, as Frederic René had done, news coverage that would keep the Coudert Brothers name before the public and enhance its reputation.

In late 1898 or early 1899—we are not certain which— Coudert Brothers moved boldly to address the first of these needs when it opened a branch office in Washington, D.C. The setting up of this office was an entirely different proposition from the founding of the Paris office twenty years earlier, for which, it will be recalled, a young associate had been sent out from New York. Instead, for this venture Coudert Brothers allied itself with two lawyers already in Washington. One of these, Crammond Kennedy, had an established practice specializing in international law, while the other, Edward I. Renick, possessed an extensive network of contacts as the result of a thirteen-year career with the U.S. State Department.

Born in Scotland in 1843, Kennedy emigrated to New York City at fourteen, took up evangelical work, and by the age of fifteen was being acclaimed as "the boy preacher." His name was kept in the public eye by his subsequent services as a chaplain during the Civil War, fund-raiser for the Freedman's Commission, which provided schools and other assistance to former slaves in the South, and editor of the *Christian Union*, an influential religious journal connected with Henry Ward Beecher's ministry. In the 1870s, while continuing his evangelical work, Kennedy earned his living as a real estate broker and attended lectures in law at Columbia. He was admitted to the bar in 1878 and practiced in New York before moving to Washington, D.C.

As might be expected of a former "boy preacher," Kennedy was a courtroom lawyer, and much of his practice seems to have arisen from matters before the Court of Claims, the federal court in Washington, D.C., with original jurisdiction over claims against the U.S. government arising from contracts, constitutional issues, and all non-tort issues. We do not know whether Coudert Brothers approached him with regard to the Washington office or he laid the idea before Coudert Brothers, but he was not simply hired by the firm. He had an active practice that was merged into Coudert Brothers', or, as Kennedy would express it in his "Who's Who" entry: "His law business has been consolidated with that of Coudert Bros. . . . And he is now in charge of Washington office of that firm."

The other original member of the Washington, D.C., office, Edward I. Renick, was a forty-three-year-old lawyer from Georgia who had graduated from the University of Virginia Law School in 1881. In 1886 Renick was the first appointee from Georgia to enter the newly founded U.S. civil service and subsequently became the first person in the whole of the United States to pass the civil service examination for a legal position. He began in the State Department in a twelve-hundred-dollar-per-year clerkship and advanced through the grades to chief of the Bureau of Statistics, in which capacity he made substantial improvements in the consular reports, and in 1894 he was promoted to chief clerk of the State Department. As chief clerk, Renick probably helped to organize the work of the Venezuela Commission on which Frederic René had served in 1896, and he was doubtless familiar with all the foreign claims in which the State Department was involved.

Kennedy and Renick established Coudert Brothers' office at 609 Fourteenth Street by 1899, and one of the first cases they worked on together was a major U.S. Supreme Court case, *La Abra Silver Mining Co. v. United States,* involving what the Court deemed to be a fraudulent claim presented by an American-owned mining company to a Mexico–U.S. claims commission. Given Kennedy's and Renick's backgrounds, it seems likely that, in opening the Washington, D.C., office, Coudert Brothers was hoping for an increase in foreign claims work as a result of the Spanish-American War, but the firm may also have had an eye to the possibility of acquiring as clients some of the foreign embassies in Washington to add to its substantial New York consular practice.

The Washington office proved useful as well at times as an observation post for political currents. In 1902, for example, Paul Fuller and Fred were eager to present to the Roosevelt administration, which was about to purchase the Panama Canal, the case for retaining Coudert Frères to provide a legal opinion on the validity of the title held by the Compagnie Nouvelle de Panama. It was obvious to the Coudert Brothers attorneys, of course, that no other American law firm could give a more expert opinion on the French title or provide it more expeditiously. (Fuller and Cachard had already examined the title closely in 1899 when Fuller was counsel for the syndicate then trying to obtain the Panama concession.) Therefore, Fuller wrote to Crammond Kennedy, delicately inquiring whether the State Department ("that already knows and is somewhat familiar with the international reputation of C.B.") or the Department of Justice would be entrusted with retaining a firm to provide an opinion on the title. Kennedy admitted he did not know the answer to Fuller's "grave and important question" but promised, "On this point I shall be on the outlook for light and more light will doubtless come."

The final decision, it eventually became apparent, would rest with Attorney General Philander Chase Knox, and Fuller and Fred decided to make a two-pronged approach to Knox in July 1902. On the one hand, Frederic René consulted with Senator Frank Pavey, who offered to seek Senator Mark Hanna's intercession with Attorney General Knox. At the same time, Fred instructed associate Henry Weston Van Dyke in the Washington, D.C., office to try to obtain an interview directly with Knox or Assistant Attorney General Charles Russell, who was about to sail for Paris. Keeping in touch with Fred several times a day by telegram, telephone, and letter, Van Dyke pursued Knox and Russell to Atlantic City and had two cordial conferences with the latter. As a result of these meetings, Van Dyke felt fairly confident that "we have the inside track." But Coudert Brothers did not have the inside track with the Roosevelt administration on Panama Canal matters. It was William Nelson Cromwell who held that position, and he was careful to ensure that Russell never went near the Coudert Frères office during his trip to Paris. Nonetheless, Fred was "more than pleased" at Van Dyke's initiative in chasing all the way to Atlantic City to see the two officials and complimented him on taking the matter up "with such vigor." Fred also endorsed Van Dyke's proposal to take an extra day to enjoy the surf at Atlantic City before returning to the oppressive heat of Washington in July.

Not long after opening its Washington office, Coudert Brothers took a further step toward shoring up the Litigation Department when General Benjamin F. Tracy joined the firm in "of counsel" status. A contemporary of Frederic René's, Tracy rose to prominence as a Civil War general and subsequently achieved renown in New York City as the prosecutor of the "whisky ring," composed of illegal distillers who had been bribing internal revenue agents. Appointed secretary of the navy under President Benjamin

Harrison in 1889, Tracy brought to fruition William Whitney's plans for the modernization of the fleet, earning lasting fame as the "Father of the American Fighting Navy." He returned to private practice in 1893, ran unsuccessfully for mayor of New York City on the Republican ticket in 1897, and then spent the next two years representing Venezuela in the arbitration of its boundary claims, for which he received a fee of fifty thousand dollars. His decision to join Coudert Brothers seems to have been made shortly after his return from the Paris arbitration in late 1899.

Although sixty-nine years old, Tracy was in vigorous health and his shrewd, analytical mind was as sharp as ever; indeed, he would remain active professionally for another ten years and continue "spry and sprightly" right up to his death in an automobile accident in 1915. Tracy's reputation as an advocate was outstanding, and because he had held national office, his name may have been even better known across the country than Frederic René's. Naturally, his old firm of Tracy, Boardman and Platt wanted him back in 1899, and Tracy did not sever his ties with it entirely, but from 1900 on he seems to have given more attention to his affiliation with Coudert Brothers.

There was the best of reasons for this staunch lifelong Republican to join forces with the Couderts in preference to his old partners: his beloved granddaughter, Alys Tracy Wilmerding, had married Fred Coudert in May 1897. Her father having died when she was small and her mother never having remarried, Alys had grown up in General Tracy's household. He was more father than grandfather to her, and she was particularly dear to him, so that the general had a deep interest in promoting the success of the promising young lawyer she had married.

Coudert Brothers was proud to have General Tracy associated with it, and on the firm letterhead from 1900 through 1915 his name was always placed more prominently than the names of the partners themselves. His biographer suggests that Tracy specialized in estate contests, and a letter written by Fred Coudert in 1904 indicates that the formidable skills the general had developed as a prosecutor remained intact. Fred wrote glowingly of a "most admirable cross-examination" during a will contest that had made the witness "very uncomfortable and put him in the position of contradicting himself over and over again." Yet Tracy also seems to have done a good bit of work for insurance companies. He was a director of the Metropolitan Life and United States Casualty companies, as well as of an unidentifiable company that Fred Coudert referred to as "Mutual Life." Insurance work was not new to Coudert Brothers. As far back as the 1870s, Louis Leonce Coudert had been a di-

rector of several insurance companies, and one of the director-
ships Frederic René kept until his death was that of the Washington Life Insurance Company, but it appears that Tracy's affiliation
with Coudert Brothers may have given a fresh impetus to this kind
of trial work and may be one reason why the firm received retainers from numerous insurance companies to defend claims arising
from the San Francisco earthquake and fire of 1906.

Having Tracy affiliated with the firm, yet not a partner, seems
to have been an excellent arrangement, for it strengthened the
firm at the top during a few critical years without diluting its identity. The situation was made all the more ideal by the fact that the
general was soon, like Paul Fuller, engaged in an effort to broaden
young Fred Coudert's experience. In 1901, for example, the city of
Santa Cruz, California, hired the general to represent it in a U.S.
Supreme Court case involving the redemption of some municipal
bonds, *Albert H. Waite v. City of Santa Cruz*. Tracy, however, handed
the responsibility for the case over to Fred. Conscious of his relative inexperience at age thirty, Fred expressed some nervousness
about this. Writing to his father, Fred said, "Gen. Tracy wants me
to argue against Dillon [John F. Dillon, the opposition attorney] so
I go to Washington without him. The California attys. are here and
have made no objection. One was in Congress six years and was a
Judge in Cal. When he finds me out he may cut up rough but so
far he seems satisfied." Fred worked hard—the Court referred to
the "elaborate brief of counsel for the city"—but he lost the case.
Still, as Tracy knew, being thrown up against formidable opponents
was the best way Fred could learn.

Fred was not the only young lawyer in the firm who was being
helped along and encouraged in these years. In 1900, Coudert
Brothers printed a new batch of stationery, listing not only the
partners and Tracy, but two associates. In the past the names of
Fuller, Richards, and Holden had appeared on the firm's letterhead a few years before each became partner, so presumably this
step signaled to John P. Murray and Charles B. Samuels that they
could expect to rise to partnership level in due course. Murray had
been an associate since 1893, working on the litigation side, primarily on extradition cases. Samuels was an "office lawyer" who
had come up through the Real Estate Department. They did not
have the longest service with the firm; at least one associate,
Charles Frederic Adams, had been with Coudert Brothers for
twenty years, and there were probably others who had joined before Murray and Samuels. It seems that it was on the basis of their
ability rather than sheer seniority that these two men were designated what one might call "partners apparent" in 1900.

Also in 1900 Coudert Brothers brought back to the firm as a senior associate Howard Thayer Kingsbury, a nephew of partner Daniel Holden who had clerked for the firm while preparing for the bar in 1893 and who had been practicing law meanwhile with the New York firm of Lee & Lee. Kingsbury would see his name appear on the Coudert Brothers letterhead in 1903 and would become a partner along with Murray and Samuels in 1904. We know little about Samuels, except that he was a native Virginian and grandson of Judge Green Berry Samuels of the Virginia Supreme Court. Murray and Kingsbury were northerners but came from very different backgrounds. Murray, born in 1870, was a member of an Irish Catholic family from Jersey City, who earned his B.A. and M.A. degrees from St. Peter's College in New Jersey, while Kingsbury, born in 1872, was a blue-blooded descendant of a Puritan governor of Massachusetts, the son of a New England clergyman, and a graduate of Yale University. Yet both had outstanding academic records—Murray had graduated *summa cum laude* from St. Peter's, and Kingsbury had been elected to Phi Beta Kappa—and both were to make important contributions to the firm as partners.

In the long run, however, perhaps the partners' most important decision concerning an associate was the transfer in 1899 of John B. Robinson to the Paris office. An 1894 honors graduate of St. John's College in Fordham, New York, Robinson had been working as a trusts and estates associate under Daniel Holden since 1895. He was neither the first nor the last associate to be sent over to help Cachard and Peartree—but he was the one who would stay, succeed, and ultimately head Coudert Frères from World War I straight through World War II and beyond. His length of service and effect on the firm's fortunes would be equaled in his generation only by Fred Coudert's.

As for the firm's third need—the need for someone to keep Coudert Brothers' reputation glowing in the light of publicity, as Frederic René had done—that was soon taken care of as well. As early as 1900 Fred Coudert had begun to prepare the first of what would become a long line of U.S. Supreme Court cases, known as the Insular cases, which would not only stand as milestones in the history of constitutional law and affect millions of lives, but would also establish Fred, at the age of thirty, as one of America's most eminent lawyers.

The Insular cases concerned the fate of the various islands in the Caribbean and Pacific—most notably, Puerto Rico, the Philippines, Hawaii, and Guam—which the United States had acquired in the burst of expansionist fever that accompanied the Spanish-American War. When the first military victories had been announced, anti-imperialists like Frederic René Coudert had hoped that the United States would not keep these territories after the war. "It would be exceedingly unfortunate," Frederic René had said in an interview in May 1898, "if the outcome of this war should result in fostering an appetite for foreign conquest among our people. Such an appetite, if developed, might result in the breaking down of the fundamental principles of our free, republican form of Government, upon the maintenance of which the future prosperity and happiness of our people depend."

The tide of public opinion, however, ran against sentiments such as these. There was no question by the end of the war that the United States would keep all its prizes, except Cuba. What was not decided was how they would be governed. Would they be treated like colonies or like potential states, and would their residents be viewed as foreign subjects or as new Americans protected like other Americans by the Constitution? The issue, as popularly expressed at the time, was: Does the Constitution follow the flag?

Coudert Brothers' involvement with this issue began in late 1899 when a Mr. Elias DeLima, who had an importing firm in New York City, visited the firm's offices and was ushered in to see young Mr. Coudert. DeLima imported sugar from Puerto Rico, and he had paid, under protest, $13,145.26 in U.S. customs duties on three cargoes of sugar since the date the United States had assumed sovereignty over Puerto Rico. What he wanted to know was: since the tariff applied to foreign countries and Puerto Rico was now owned by the United States, could he get his money back?

Fred Coudert later indicated that he had been flummoxed by Mr. DeLima's "apparently simple question." Speaking of himself humorously in the third person, Coudert described how he handled his first meeting with this client:

> The practitioner looks wise, wiser probably than he feels, and tries to conjure up some phrase of his college days, speaks of the law of *postlimium,* or of belligerent rights, or uses some other phrase which is equally unintelligible to his client. He racks his brain in vain to remember what he never knew, allows his client to depart, wiser, perhaps, but not quite certain as to his rights.
>
> The lawyer then sets to work to learn something about the problem. He soon learns that he has entered upon a field where no torchbearer leads the way: where there is little or no precedent, or if there is any precedent, it is so conflicting and

so difficult of application as to be of little or no value. Still, after much study and reflection, he is able to propose that which he believes to be sound and to be entitled to the consideration and study of the Court.

What Coudert quickly realized was that DeLima's complaint encapsulated the entire issue of whether the United States government could treat Puerto Rico differently from, for example, what was then the territory of Arizona. It was unthinkable that goods shipped from Arizona should pay customs duties when they entered into one of the states of the Union. Why, then, should Puerto Rican sugar be taxed at the port of New York? At stake was nothing less than whether the United States was going to remain a republic, or become an empire with its mainland citizens enjoying constitutional rights denied to the residents of the insular possessions.

There were several other attorneys at this time with tariff cases similar to *DeLima,* which were proceeding through the customs courts—a choice of forum that conceded in advance that the products of Puerto Rico were imported merchandise. Fred, however, was anxious to reach deeper to the fundamental constitutional questions, and, accordingly, he conceived the strategy of bringing a common-law suit against the collector, George R. Bidwell, on the grounds that Puerto Rico was part of the United States and its merchandise could not be considered "imported" at all.

In 1900, as *DeLima* was winding its way through the lower courts, clearly headed for the U.S. Supreme Court, Congress enacted the Foraker Act, which acknowledged that Puerto Rico was not a foreign country subject to the general tariff but which set up a separate tariff applicable to Puerto Rico alone. Fred saw that if he could bring a suit under the Foraker Act, he would have an even stronger basis to test whether the constitutional provision that "all duties, imports, and excises shall be uniform throughout the United States"—and, by extension, the Constitution itself—applied to the new possessions. Without such a case, he feared that the Supreme Court, in deciding *DeLima,* would avoid the constitutional question altogether.

"So I went to Mr. DeLima again," Fred later explained, "and said, 'You have got to find me some case that came subsequent to the act called the Foraker Act. . . . Then we will have the Constitutional question of the power of Congress squarely before us.'"

DeLima could find only "a little case," involving $659.23 in duties paid on oranges by another importing firm, S. B. Downes & Co., but that was good enough for Fred. With some help from his Uncle Paul, Fred worked "like a dog" preparing the briefs for

DeLima v. Bidwell and *Downes v. Bidwell.* It appears that he wrote both voluminous briefs during a few weeks at the end of December 1900, tackling them with that ability to become intensely absorbed in an idea that was so much a part of his nature. He was aware that what he was doing was important, and he stinted nothing as he put the final polish on his arguments.

When Fred rose to begin his oral argument before the Supreme Court on January 8, 1901, the galleries were packed with dignitaries and reporters, for the "Insular tariff cases" had already attracted considerable publicity. A few weeks earlier the Court had heard two cases that had raised rather narrow, technical issues, but the cases Fred was now bringing before the Court were expected to confront the judges for the first time with those questions that the public found most exciting. Businessmen wanted to know whether the Court would uphold protectionism to the extent even of allowing a Republican Congress to tax goods passing from one part of United States territory to another. Persons with an interest in foreign policy hoped for an indication from the Court as to whether the government could operate with as free a hand in the "American colonies" as the European powers did in their overseas colonies—that is, untrammeled by any constitutional considerations. Others simply wanted to know what the likelihood was of all these "alien races, many of them savage and all speaking languages other than our own" being eventually admitted to citizenship, for that was one of the clear implications of a ruling that the Constitution did indeed follow the flag.

Fred's briefs were far-ranging, touching on all these issues. He drew his central argument, however, from a thesis he had heard Professor Burgess propound in the Columbia classroom not so many years earlier, to the effect that there may be a difference between the government of a country and the state, which embodies the sovereign power. In most European countries, Fred argued, the government and state are indistinguishable: the government is sovereign. But in the United States the state is the American people: they created their government and are sovereign over it. Accordingly, since the people are sovereign and they intended the Constitution of the United States to "be a limitation upon the government which was its creature and not its creator," the U.S. government, wherever in the world it may be acting, is always subject to the Constitution.

This was the argument to which Fred kept returning over the four days that he and the attorney general presented their cases. For example, Fred cited the situation in the old Northwest Territory—the current Midwest—at its settlement by the veterans of the Revolution. Would his opponents claim that these settlers were not subject to the Constitution and "might have been crucified or subject to all the horrors" that the Bill of Rights was intended to outlaw? "I rubbed that into the Court on the first day," Fred said. "I thought I could win out on that."

But although Fred adhered for three days to development of his constitutional argument, he did not disappoint the gallery. On the fourth day he moved boldly into the underlying issues of public policy, attacking the concept of protectionism head-on, decrying the claim of the imperialists that a government subject to the Constitution would be an "impotent" government in the international realm, and pointing out that the United States had incorporated tens of thousands of Spanish-speaking and French-speaking peoples in its expansion to the Pacific, with no ill effect on the commonweal and, indeed, with considerable benefit.

Fred Coudert's willingness to cross the dividing line between law and politics in his Supreme Court argument is reminiscent of Frederic René Coudert's approach to the law, for the senior Coudert was always aware that the two are inextricably linked in American life. It is even possible that Frederic René may have encouraged his son to address the policy issues, but, given Fred's own natural inclination to dig to the heart of a matter and his general fearlessness when convinced he was in the right, he probably reached this decision on his own. On the other hand, Fred had spent too much time around his father and his father's friends to be in any doubt that judges are human and that their decisions often reflect public opinion. Since public opinion in 1901 was divided on "the Constitution and the flag," it was doubtless no surprise to Fred that the Supreme Court justices found themselves unable to issue a clear opinion in these initial Insular cases.

As Fred had expected, the Court decided 5–4 in *DeLima v. Bidwell* that Puerto Rico was not a foreign country within the meaning of the general tariff act. Thus, DeLima was entitled to recover his $13,145.36 of illegally extracted customs duties. This was gratifying, but the verdict in *Downes*—which one suspects was rather more important to Fred, despite the small sum involved— was quite muddled.

Justices Fuller, Harlan, Brewer, and Peckham, in dissent, came down solidly endorsing Fred's argument that wherever the U.S. government acts, it is always subject to the Constitution. The other judges, though, were in complete disarray. Justice Brown took the line that the United States refers only to the states in the Union and the government is not subject to the Constitution in the territories and other possessions except to the extent it chooses to be.

Justices White, Shiras, and McKenna, on the other hand, admitted that the Constitution is always operative over the government but found that some clauses of the Constitution are meant to apply only to the states, some only to the states and "incorporated territories," and some to all states and territories, whether "incorporated" or not. These justices did not attempt to define what an "incorporated territory" might be or to clarify which clauses were which; they went straight from the general distinction to the decision that Puerto Rico was "unincorporated territory" and the uniform tariff clause did not apply to it. What the ninth judge, Justice Grey, had to say was "pretty hazy," in Fred's words, but he, too, was certain that Congress could enact a special tariff for Puerto Rico. "Thus," as historian Samuel Eliot Morison drily concluded, "the Republican party was able to eat its cake and have it: to indulge in territorial expansion, yet maintain the tariff wall against such insular products as sugar and tobacco, as foreign." Satirizing the Court's decision, Finley Peter Dunne had his fictional Mr. Dooley conclude, "No matter whether th' constitution follows th' flag or not, th' supreme court follows th' iliction returns."

Fred personally had some reasons to be content, for all the justices, with the exception of Brown, had accepted his contention that the government is born of and is limited by the Constitution. They had also conferred upon him the honor of ordering his *DeLima* brief to be printed in its entirety in the official Supreme Court reports. This was a rare distinction, particularly for a young man, and Fred found himself somewhat lionized, with offers pouring into the office for him to speak and write on the Supreme Court's decision.

But Fred was not content, for the Court's divided opinion had raised more questions than it settled. Out of intellectual curiosity—or perhaps it might be more accurate to say, intellectual frustration—Fred wanted to press on and discover which constitutional clauses, in the Supreme Court's opinion, did pertain to the insular possessions. Therefore, when he was asked to appeal to the Supreme Court the conviction for manslaughter of a Japanese resident of Hawaii named Mankichi, he seized upon the case, for Mankichi had not been tried in accordance with the "trial by jury" provisions of the Constitution and his case offered an opportunity to test whether that particular clause applied to "unincorporated territory." Coudert took the case without fee and paid the court expenses out of his own pocket, simply because he was so absorbed in the issue. Again, Paul Fuller was on the brief, as well as three other associates at Coudert Brothers, but Fred wrote most of the brief for *Hawaii v. Mankichi* and presented the oral argument on March 4 and 5, 1903.

The decision was once more a divided one. The same four dissenters agreed that Mankichi was entitled to the protection of the Bill of Rights, with Justice Harlan writing a particularly eloquent opinion. The other five judges, though, had no intention of extending the Bill of Rights to a Japanese resident of an island inhabited by "uncivilized" natives. As Justice Brown later told Fred, "You know, in that Hawaiian case we had to strain the timbers of the law until they groaned, but we couldn't allow a jail delivery in Hawaii!" Justice White—the Louisiana lawyer who had been appointed to the Supreme Court after Frederic René declined the nomination— was even franker. Some years later, he told Fred, "Why we couldn't incorporate ten million black skinned people like that in the United States! Think what the consequences would be!"

To arrive at the decision they wanted, the majority of the Court resorted to distinguishing between the various rights embodied in the Constitution. Some, they wrote, were natural rights, and some—such as trial by jury—merely procedural rights. Inhabitants of "unincorporated territories," they ruled, were not entitled to procedural rights. Thus, the Court opened up another wide area for judicial discretion. The *Mankichi* decision left the Court the sole arbiter not only of what were incorporated or unincorporated territories and of which clauses of the Constitution applied in which particular territories, but also of which constitutional rights were procedural and which were "natural." In effect, the Court "reserved the right to decide on each topic as it might come up without laying down any general principles."

No commentator on *Mankichi* has ever pretended that there was any coherent intellectual basis for the Court's decision. The results simply reflected "the judges' own feelings about the territory in question: all constitutional rights were to be extended to those in which the people were sufficiently advanced to deserve them, while in more backward areas only limited rights were considered possible." Moreover, the Court's views were stated with a notable lack of clarity. What was happening, as Morison has pointed out, was that the United States was creating an empire while refusing to admit the existence of that empire. The logic of the Court's decisions had to be far from clear, James Truslow Adams noted, for the situation was not logical.

The Court itself, however, seems to have been pleased with its distinction between natural rights and procedural rights, for such distinctions became a regular feature of Supreme Court decisions in subsequent Insular suits, and it is a concept that still looms large in civil rights law today. To Fred Coudert, though, the *Mankichi* decision appeared fundamentally wrongheaded. It disturbed him partly because it seemed to collapse the "elaborate structure built up from . . . Marshall's day down to our own." Although presentiments of *Mankichi* can be found in the 1884 case of *Hurtado v. California,* it seemed to him a departure—rather a radical departure—in constitutional law, and Coudert, like his father before him, was a legal conservative, preferring to see changes in interpretation gradually introduced to prevent shock to the system.

But even more deeply, Coudert was disturbed by the prospect of the Court periodically examining "natural rights" and deciding what rights and liberties citizens should have at any particular moment in light of the Court's own conception at the time of what is fundamental and what is not. The lack of abiding protection implicit in such an arrangement and the lack of certainty as to the results in any individual suit were objectionable to him. He acknowledged that the law must change to suit the times, but he was convinced that in *Mankichi* the Court had gotten the scales weighing change and certainty completely out of balance. What should be the correct balance was an issue that would exercise him for a number of years, resulting in a series of articles that were published in book form under the title *Certainty and Justice* in 1913. And he would return to this issue again and again in later years, for it never quite lost its fascination for him.

As lawyers know, however, a lack of certainty in how the courts will rule—a "gray area" in the law—is a wonderful generator of litigation. As a legal theorist, Fred Coudert had philosophical problems with the Court's early Insular decisions. As a senior partner in Coudert Brothers, on the other hand, he soon found that these decisions were splendid for business.

Chapter Seven

OF ALIENS
AND AUTOMOBILES

F rederic René Coudert suffered several heart attacks between 1899 and 1903, but each time his "splendid constitution pulled him through." Perhaps because Papa Coudert had lived to such a venerable old age, Fred remained optimistic about his father's chances for a return to full activity, and in the fall of 1903 this positive attitude seemed justified, for Frederic René was making an excellent recovery from his most recent heart attack. After a pleasant, relaxing visit to France, he and Lizzie had decided to spend the winter in Washington, D.C. But the senior Couderts had no sooner finished fitting up the "handsome home" they had rented on S Street than Frederic René suffered another severe attack. After several days of pain, he lapsed into unconsciousness and died on Sunday morning, December 20, 1903, at the age of seventy-one.

Fred had just visited his parents in Washington en route to the isolated Outer Banks of North Carolina for a few days of duck hunting. A wire bearing word of his father's heart attack was sent to Kitty Hawk, where the U.S. Weather Service maintained a telegraph station, and was hand-carried by boat to Fred's hunting camp. Fred left the camp immediately, but all the trains from the South were delayed that weekend by winter storms and, even as he waited for a train, unaware of his father's death, the arrangements were being made for the funeral service at St. Patrick's Cathedral

141

and the newspapers began to set the type for his father's obituaries.

The papers were lavish in their coverage of Frederic René's death. THE FAMOUS LAWYER PASSES AWAY, the *New York Times* headlined on its front page, and the *Herald* proclaimed in a series of decks, EMINENT INTERNATIONAL JURIST A VICTIM OF HEART DISEASE IN WASHINGTON / HAD A DISTINGUISHED CAREER / RECOGNIZED AS A LEADER OF THE AMERICAN BAR. The metropolitan weeklies and law journals followed in due course with their own tributes, but these provided little immediate comfort to Fred Coudert. Frederic René had lived a full life, not only earning fame himself but enjoying in his final years the acclaim his son received for the first Insular cases. Still, Fred would insist to the end of his own long life that his father had died too young, too soon. Fred had been so focused on his father's getting well that Frederic René's death seems to have caught him emotionally unprepared.

Fred's grief, however, was of the sort that turns inward. He had little to say at the time, but a small incident on January 1, 1904, less than two weeks after Frederic René's death, may provide a glimpse of his feelings. On that holiday morning, after breakfasting with Alys and his own two little sons, Fred walked over to the stately elegant reading room of the bar association, on West Forth-fourth Street. "I like this place," Fred wrote reflectively on that New Year's Day. "It is absolutely quiet, nothing but books and mute men." Touchingly, from all the places to sit in the large, mostly empty room, Fred chose one from which he could see the painting of his father, which graced the premises because of Frederic René's former presidency of the bar association.

"Right in front of my desk is the French portrait of Pa," Fred wrote. "It is wonderfully like him in some ways." So, sitting by choice under the benign gaze of his father, he scratched out a short, stoical letter to his mother, reflecting on the year past, which "has not ended very cheerfully for ourselves and our friends." And, no doubt glancing up from time to time at Frederic René's countenance, he worked away the rest of the morning on one of the firm's briefs—in solitude, but, perhaps, not quite alone.

The probability is high that the brief Fred was working on that New Year's Day was connected with an Insular case, for Coudert Brothers was then arguing dozens of such cases in many forums. There were appeals being prepared to the territorial courts for the return of property confiscated during the U.S. occupation, requests for compensation being laid before the U.S. War Department in Washington, D.C., Philippine tariff cases being readied for hearings in the Court of Claims and U.S. district courts, and cases in territorial and lower federal courts testing the effect on land titles of the change from Spanish to American sovereignty. Eventually some of these cases would find their way to the U.S. Supreme Court. In fact, of the twenty major Insular cases ultimately decided by the Supreme Court, no fewer than seventeen would be argued by Coudert Brothers—a statistic indicating the preeminence the firm enjoyed in this special field.

One of the larger groups of Insular cases handled by Coudert Brothers involved property expropriated by the U.S. Army in Cuba during the few years when Cuba lay under U.S. military rule. Among the items ordered seized by the military governor of Cuba, General John R. Brooke, were a waterworks and a dock, which became of particular concern to Coudert Brothers. As Fred Coudert related the story in 1901:

> He [Brooke] saw the waterworks and the dock—excellent things for municipal purposes—and was told on inquiry that they belonged to individuals, and that the source of their ownership was concessions granted by the dying Spanish government. "Why," he argued, "that will never do. These gentlemen are Spaniards; moribund, beaten and at the point of leaving the island forever. Spain wanted to favor her own citizens; it is a fraud on the rights of the United States"; and as guardian of Cuba's rights he sent his troops to take possession of this dock and his engineers to take possession of the waterworks, and if my recollection serves me rightly, he omitted the formality of notifying the concessionaires. However, they found it out in a very short time, and being accustomed to the old Spanish custom and the ancient and obsolete methods of the Spanish law which compel payment for property taken for public use and do not expropriate a man until he has had his day in Court, they were very much surprised.

Taking counsel in Havana, the property owners were advised to go to New York and consult Coudert Brothers, which arranged for its Washington office to apply to the U.S. War Department for the return of the property. The War Department's initial reply, however, was that the franchises were monopolies, and "monopolies were odious." Coudert Brothers responded that even in the United States there were government-sanctioned monopolies, such as the street railways and utilities, whereupon the War Department dropped the monopoly defense but argued that the Spanish government had had no right to grant the franchises for the waterworks and dock. Coudert Brothers found it simple enough to demolish this argument, too, for Spain had been the legitimate ruler of Cuba at the time the franchises were granted and under international law had remained such until the signing of the peace treaty.

> The Administration [Fred wrote] finally adopted a peculiar attitude. . . . You would assume that either the wharf and the waterworks franchises were both illegal or that they were both valid. . . . But this is what they did. They said, "You can have the waterworks; they are in the nature of a private concession; but a dock—United States ships go to a dock; a dock is a very important thing; we think we will keep the dock," and so in fact they did. On what principle, on what theory? it was asked. "It is not a question of theory; it is a practical question, and we have concluded to keep this dock. Go to the Cuban Government when we are out and begin some suit against them."

Since the Platt Amendment prescribed that all acts of the U.S. military government in Cuba should be *res adjudicata* and forever unquestioned in Cuban courts, this was of no comfort to Fred Coudert and his clients. And thus began a long quest for justice on behalf of the dock owner, as well as several other clients whose property had been similarly confiscated. In some instances Coudert Brothers found loopholes it could use to get the suits before U.S. or Cuban courts, but in one notable case, involving a slaughterhouse owned by a Spanish countess, Doña María Francisca O'Reilly de Camara, the firm found itself blocked from every reasonable avenue of redress. Finally, in frustration, Fred Coudert brought suit against General Brooke personally for "trespass" against his client's property rights. Suing a U.S. Army officer as an individual troubled Coudert's conscience, especially since his sister Marie was married to a regular army officer, John Bellinger, and Bellinger and many of his West Point classmates were Coudert's own friends. Fred had no wish to alienate his friends nor did he think the expedient fair to Brooke, but he also felt that, in order to obtain justice for his client, he had no choice but to pursue all possible paths. And, painful as it was, this mechanism did succeed in getting the countess a day in court, after seven years of more conventional attempts had failed.

Many of the Cuban expropriation cases had strong parallels to the Blockading cases on which Frederic René had worked during the Civil War. In fact, in several of them, Coudert Brothers liberally cited the old Blockading cases, including *The Venice* and *The*

Baigarry. As with the Blockading cases, however, the U.S. courts proved reluctant to second-guess decisions made by U.S. Army or Navy officers in territory under military control, and the firm lost most of these Cuban cases, despite the effort and ingenuity put into them.

Coudert Brothers initially fared much better with a group of Philippine customs cases, winning a hard-fought victory in the U.S. Supreme Court—only to have success snatched away from it by the former Philippines governor and U.S. secretary of war, William Howard Taft. The Philippine customs in question were paid by various merchants in Manila on goods imported from the mainland United States. At the time the United States owned the Philippines, having purchased the archipelago from Spain for $20 million at the close of the Spanish-American War, but its ownership was being hotly disputed by Filipino revolutionaries who sought their country's independence. It cost the United States some $600 million between 1898 and 1903 to put down this so-called insurgency, and the army financed its operations partly by seizing arriving ships and, in effect, holding their cargoes ransom. For authority the army pointed to an executive order, which had expired in 1898 at the end of the Spanish-American War.

Coudert Brothers' clients had paid millions in such illegally extracted duties, and, as some of them had been financially ruined in the process, the firm had agreed to handle the suits on a contingency basis. By 1904 the suits were ready to be argued in the Court of Claims in Washington, D.C., where Secretary Taft interposed a long brief opposing the claims and attempting to show that some of the claimants had aided the insurgents. As Coudert was to write, "This defense utterly broke down"—Taft was unable to prove his allegations—but the Court did decide against the firm's clients on other grounds.

At this stage, to save all parties expense and trouble, Fred Coudert and the U.S. attorney general's office together selected the claim of Warner, Barnes & Company as a test case for an appeal to the U.S. Supreme Court. This meant that Coudert agreed not to put all his other related cases on the Supreme Court docket for argument, and the attorney general agreed, if the Warner, Barnes decision went against the government, not to contest the other cases but to let the claimants take the expedited route of simply requesting an entry for judgment—a court order that their claims be paid. This was an oral stipulation—a gentleman's agreement, in effect—and it proved disastrous for Coudert Brothers and its clients, for, as Fred Coudert was to learn much later, Taft, although he had worked closely with the attorney general on the litigation up to that point, did not consider himself or his department bound by it.

The Supreme Court decided *Warner, Barnes and Company, Limited v. United States* in April 1905 in favor of Coudert's clients, whereupon the attorney general, much chagrined, hastened to move for a rehearing. After extensive delays on the government's part, the case was duly reargued, and the Court again, in May 1906, decided by a solid 7–2 majority in favor of the claims. The firm's celebration, however, was short-lived, for Taft immediately went in person to Congress and obtained passage of an act "ratifying all duties collected by former officers in the Philippine Islands." This law could not prevent Warner, Barnes & Company from getting paid, but it cut the ground out from under the other Coudert Brothers' clients whose claims were then being readied for entry of judgment. By Act of Congress, the illegally extracted duties instantaneously became legal, leaving all the other claimants without redress.

The firm, of course, challenged the validity of the congressional act, which looked to it exactly like the kind of retroactive law forbidden under the Constitution's due process clause, but the Supreme Court upheld the act in *United States v. Heinszen & Company* in 1907. Justice White, writing the majority opinion, found that "although the duties were illegally exacted the illegality was not the result of an inherent want of power in the United States to have authorized the imposition of the duties" and that, therefore, the act was not "retrospective legislation enacting a tariff . . . but an exercise of the conceded power dependent upon the law of agency to ratify an act done on behalf of the United States which the United States could have originally authorized." Less tortuously, and perhaps more sensibly, Justice Harlan's concurring opinion simply stated that the act should be construed as withdrawing the consent of the United States to be sued in the matter.

Distressing was the word Fred Coudert used to describe this outcome years later. "We only received for our clients a comparatively small amount of money involved in the test case; our other cases in the Court of Claims being dismissed on the ground of this statute." Fred's recollection was that these dismissals deprived his clients of "some Three Million Dollars, and ourselves of liberal contingent fees."

Like a terrier, however, Coudert did not quite give up. Some five years later, when Great Britain and the United States were negotiating schedules of claims to be submitted to an international tribunal for arbitration, he saw to it that the British government requested the inclusion of the Philippine customs claims. But Taft, by then president of the United States, refused to allow these claims to be arbitrated. Virtually every other claim pressed by Great Britain was accepted by the president as a proper subject for arbitration, but not these. In response to the British embassy's request for an explanation, Taft blandly replied, "It is not the policy of the Administration to arbitrate them."

The arbitration treaty with Great Britain had been high on Taft's agenda as president, and Fred Coudert, although a Democrat, had been one of those who had played a prominent role in mustering public opinion in Taft's support on this issue. Taking advantage of this fact, Coudert wrote personally to the president in January 1913, asking him what the justification was for excluding the customs claims. Two days later, on January 10, 1913, Taft penned an astonishingly rude and hostile letter, informing Coudert bluntly that he would not allow them to go to arbitration because he felt they lacked merit. To appreciate the tone of Taft's reply fully, however, it is necessary to remember that Taft had been governor of the Philippines during the insurgency and was still convinced that some of Coudert's clients had favored the rebels, even though he had been unable later to prove that they had given the rebels active assistance. Moreover, some of Coudert's British clients apparently were Jews—Jews and Chinese dominated the islands' mercantile trade—and Taft believed both groups to be altogether too expert as businessmen. Many Filipinos resented these foreigners who prospered in their midst, and Taft during his sojourn in the islands had picked up their attitudes. (As governor, he had once told a congressional committee that Congress should forbid Chinese immigration to the Philippines, giving as his chief reason "that neither an American nor a Filipino could compete with a Chinese in any species of business.") Thus, without explicitly referring either to the claimants' politics or to their religion, the president's January 10, 1913, letter to Coudert fairly bristles with disdain:

> Your clients got the benefit of the added price that the duties which were imposed gave them in the markets of the Philippines, and what you have been trying to do is collect that money twice. You got it once in the price of the goods, and now you want it again out of the treasury of the United States.
>
> You will excuse me if it does not arouse in me the slightest sense of injustice in favor of your clients, or awaken any desire to help them mulct the government of something they never lost.

> I do not even refer this to the State Department ... because I understand the character of your claims completely and fully.

In a profound but controlled rage, Coudert answered at length in a tone of voice only barely more civil than the president's. Fred was angered by the insult to his clients' integrity, by the reflection on his own integrity, by the statement that his clients' claims—which, after all, had been upheld in the nation's highest court—lacked merit, but, first and foremost, by the illogic of the president's position. "You have answered me that the American case was so strong you would not arbitrate," he wrote with heavy sarcasm. "Pardon me, however, if my mind wholly fails to follow your logic. If, as you have publicly stated, fear of defeat should not be a national deterrent to arbitrate adverse claims, surely confidence of complete victory should scarcely justify the United States in refusing such submission at the continued instance of a foreign nation." Taft declined to answer this missive, and the Philippine customs claims never were arbitrated.

In fairness to Taft, it should be mentioned that during his governorship of the Philippines he had developed a great affection for the Filipino people, which was generally reciprocated. He had refused to countenance any demonstration of racial prejudice against the Filipinos, introduced notable reforms, and conceived it as his duty, his mission, to protect the islanders from exploitation. Indeed, it is hard to resist the suspicion that had Coudert's clients been Filipinos, Taft would have supported rather than blocked their claims. But admirable as Taft's attitude was in its time and place, it sat at odds with Coudert's more abstract humanitarianism, which demanded that the rules not be bent or broken for anyone. And Coudert felt that Taft had definitely bent the rules when he had refused to accept the Supreme Court's verdict. When Taft told Coudert, "I am sorry to say so but your letter of January 8th does not seem to call from me the slightest feeling in favor of your claimants," Coudert snapped back angrily, "It is not a question of sympathy for the claims or against them" but of his clients being deprived of any forum in which to present their case—through an action by Congress that amounted to a "violation of international good faith." It was this poor sportsmanship that rankled: "Great Britain allows Americans to have recourse to her Courts and honors the judgments obtained against her Sovereignty," Coudert wrote. "Were not the rules of international law violated in ousting the Court of Claims of jurisdiction and thus preventing the entry of judgment after our claims had been held to be good by the highest tribunal?"

As maddening as the Philippines customs and Cuban expropriation cases were, however, Coudert Brothers handled others that were as deeply satisfying. One such suit was *Municipality of Ponce v. Roman Catholic Church in Puerto Rico,* which provided Fred with an opportunity, following in his father's footsteps, to defend the Catholic church. This 1908 case arose from the refusal of the city government of Ponce, Puerto Rico, to allow the Catholic church to register its ownership of the local cathedral, the city arguing that the church was not a "legal personality" entitled to hold property and that the edifice had been built in part with municipal funds and, therefore, belonged to the people. The underlying problem, of course, was that under Spanish rule the Catholic church had been the state church of Puerto Rico. Under American rule, the church would no longer be government-supported, but could it retain the property that it had acquired from the state, through taxes, for example, or through colonial labor levies?

It was Bishop W. T. Jones of Puerto Rico who went up to New York to consult with Fred Coudert on this issue. "I suppose," Fred said, "because I had been in the Insular Cases he came to me and asked if I wouldn't take up the case in the Supreme Court." Coudert, Howard Thayer Kingsbury, and Paul Fuller worked on the brief together, but it was Coudert who dug up the law published by Emperor Constantine in A.D. 321 recognizing the church's capacity to take and acquire property. To Coudert's delight, Chief Justice Fuller appreciated this rather unusual citation and stated in his majority opinion that "Counsel for appellee well argues that the Roman Catholic Church has been recognized as possessing a legal personality . . . since the time of the Emperor Constantine. . . . Such recognition has also been accorded the church by all systems of European law from the fourth century of the Christian era." Justice Fuller also concluded that the funds used to build and repair the cathedral had been irrevocably donated and the source of the funds could not affect the church's title.

In 1908 when *Ponce* was being argued, the position of the Catholic church was a source of controversy in numerous Latin countries, including France, and while anti-Catholicism had abated in the United States, good Catholics were mindful that it could recrudesce. The disestablishment of the church in the former Spanish territories held the potential for stirring up enmities both in the new territories and on the mainland. Fred Coudert always felt that the *Ponce* decision helped to defuse this potentially explosive situation, and he was proud to have played a part in it. "By a decision of the Supreme Court," he said nearly fifty years later, "we avoided all the civil dissension that came from conflicts between church and state in Latin countries. That's never passed into history, and so far as I know, no one except a few lawyers has ever paid any attention to that decision . . . but it illustrates the value of our Constitutional system."

Another satisfying case was *Gonzales v. Williams*, which Coudert and Fuller argued in 1903, representing a Puerto Rican woman, Isabella Gonzales, who had been deemed an alien by U.S. immigration inspectors and denied entry to the mainland United States. Coudert Brothers successfully maintained that, since Puerto Rico was a possession of the United States, Puerto Ricans were Americans, not aliens; and, as a result, Puerto Ricans have traveled freely to and from the mainland ever since. The case was also significant, however, because it was in the course of preparing for this Supreme Court appeal that Fred Coudert devised a novel theory of nationality that was eventually to become written into U.S. law.

Prior to 1903 the United States recognized only two classes of persons: citizens and aliens. Puerto Ricans and other inhabitants of the new U.S. possessions, Fred pointed out, belonged to neither group. They were not citizens, since Congress was unwilling to grant them political power, but neither was it logical to treat them as foreigners or aliens—for to what country could they belong, if not to the United States? Moreover, Coudert insisted, it was not fitting that the islanders be subject to American rule, owe America allegiance, and receive none of the benefits of being Americans. "He who is called to bear the burden should derive some benefit or compensation therefrom," Coudert wrote. "What 'commodium' or advantage does the Señorita [Gonzales] reap from her situation?"

That question, in fact, encapsulated Coudert's underlying concern with the entire issue of America's new insular possessions. While not enthusiastic about the acquisition of the new territories, Fred repeatedly stated that he was not opposed to expansion per se. As a soldier in Puerto Rico, he had seen what passed there in 1898 for a sanitation system, for a road network, for medical care, and he believed that the islanders were almost certain to benefit materially from American rule. Yet the greatest asset the United States had to offer, Fred thought, was the protection of civil rights embedded in its Constitution. If the Constitution was not extended to the new territories, America's growth would not be expansion, but the rawest and most immoral form of imperialism.

In July 1901 Fred had gotten into quite an excited discussion on this point with Theodore Roosevelt, who was then vice president of the United States. For the past several years, the Couderts had been summering at Oyster Bay on Long Island's North Shore, near Roosevelt's home, Sagamore Hill. Roosevelt was an unbridled apostle of imperialism, and after dinner one night at Sagamore Hill, he and young Coudert had had an enjoyable and lively debate during which Roosevelt, in his inimitable style, had bashed Coudert's opinions right and left. Perhaps because he had had some trouble getting a word in edgewise that night, Fred sat down the next day and reiterated in a letter to Roosevelt his own view that "Our expansion should be a better and different kind of expansion from any that has yet preceded us." The United States should not be blindly imitating England and the other great European powers, but improving on their moral record. "We should carry with us . . . at least, certain applicable provisions of the Constitution which are the results of centuries of struggles on the part of English speaking men," he wrote.

Because of its implications for her civil rights as well as its obvious absurdity, Coudert could not accept the proposition that Señorita Gonzales was an alien. Therefore, he proposed the term *national* to encompass both citizens and the inhabitants of the new American possessions—one group possessing political rights and one not, but both enjoying civil rights. This would make the basic distinction in nationality and immigration law between nationals and aliens, rather than between citizens and aliens. The Supreme Court accepted Coudert's terminology, although it did not accept in 1903 the contention that noncitizen nationals had all ordinary civil rights. But Coudert was merely ahead of his times in his thinking. In the decades to come, at varying speeds when dealing with various locales, Congress was gradually to extend to the insular possessions every constitutional protection that Coudert had ever argued they should have, and more besides. And, at the age of eighty-three, Coudert was to see Congress enact the Immigration and Nationality Law of 1954, which incorporated into statutory language the entire theory of nationality that he had worked out over fifty years before.

When the first Insular cases came into the office, Coudert Brothers had moved fast and aggressively to support and develop this new area of practice. In the spring of 1901, with three or four Cuban expropriation cases already in hand, the partners had opened a branch office in Havana, and two years later they set up another office in Manila, as a direct consequence, Fred Coudert said, of the first retainers received in Philippines customs matters.

Moreover, the Washington, D.C., office expanded on the flood of Insular claims work, from two lawyers in 1899, to three in 1900, and four by 1902. By the time Frederic René Coudert died in 1903, Coudert Brothers had three offices—Washington, Havana, and Manila—concentrating on the firm's Insular business.

Precisely because of this concentration, however, all three offices proved short-lived. The volume of Insular cases handled by Coudert Brothers was large—but not large enough to carry all the overheads of three separate offices. As this fact became apparent, Coudert Brothers began closing down the branches as fast as they had been set up—Havana in 1905, Washington by 1906, and Manila in 1907.

Of the three ventures, Havana was probably the most disappointing, for its prospects for success must have seemed very bright indeed in 1901. In opening the office, Coudert Brothers hoped to attract additional claims work, but there was also definitely legal business to be secured in connection with Cuban-American trade and investment. Even before the Spanish-American War, American business interests had invested some $50 million in the island, and U.S.–Cuban trade before the war was valued at $100 million—facts of which the firm was well aware because for more than forty years it had had clients engaged in this trade. Cuba, lying so close to the United States, was familiar territory to the Couderts: Fred's mother, Lizzie, had visited family friends there when she was a girl, and his uncle Charles and probably also his father had traveled to Cuba on business for clients before they had ever visited France.

With these long-standing ties, Coudert Brothers was able in 1901 to set up its Havana representative in the offices at No. 2, calle de Tacón, of "Mr. Mendoza, son of the Chief Justice of Cuba, and one of the leading lawyers there," and it seems fair to assume that the firm had visions of a fruitful relationship with Mendoza, involving referrals of business back and forth. But the hoped-for business simply never materialized. Coudert Brothers not only did not pick up new clients from among the American businesses that were scouting the prospects for increased trade with Cuba, but the volume of claims work sent north by the Havana office never amounted to more than a thin trickle.

The problem, according to Fred Coudert, was not a lack of assistance from the Mendozas, who remained friends of the firm, but "the inadequacy of our representative there." In criticizing this American attorney years after the fact, Coudert tactfully refrained from mentioning his name, and it has not been possible to discover his identity from any other source. Still, given the initial advantages enjoyed by the Havana office, it seems that Coudert was

correct to ascribe its disappointing results to the firm having selected the wrong man for the job.

On the other hand, the Manila office, in retrospect, turned
out better than one might expect. The fifth Coudert Brothers office to be established, the third in a period of only four years, it
was by far the boldest venture the firm had yet undertaken. The
Philippines were halfway around the globe from New York City, in
a part of the world with which Coudert Brothers had had no previous experience. And, despite four years of U.S. occupation, communications with the islands were not much better than they had
been in 1898, when it had taken a full week for word of Admiral
Dewey's victory at Manila Bay to reach the White House.

Still, American businessmen had sanguine hopes for the Philippines. In the process of justifying the cost of purchasing the archipelago, American imperialists had dwelt long and loudly on the
richness of the islands' natural resources. Exports of tin, coal, ag-
ricultural products, and precious metals were confidently predicted to reach $200 million a year under U.S. rule. It was against
the backdrop of these roseate predictions that two Coudert Brothers lawyers started the long journey to the Pacific to open the Manila office in 1903.

One of these travelers was sixty-year-old Crammond Kennedy
from the Washington, D.C., office, who had been taking an interest
in events in the Philippines and who had recently published a
pamphlet on the capture of the revolutionary leader Emilio Agui-
naldo. The other was Paul Fuller, Jr., the second oldest of Paul and
Leonie Coudert Fuller's three sons. Only twenty-two years old,
young Paul was a tall, slim, good-looking young man who already
displayed the quiet kindness and literary tastes that marked his father. After attending St. Francis Xavier College and Columbia University, he had received his bachelor of law degree from New York
Law School in 1901. Paul junior, however, had had to wait until he
turned twenty-one in 1902 before he could take the bar exam and
be admitted to practice, and meanwhile he had been clerking for
the New York firm of Gould & Wilkie. At the close of 1902 the
young lawyer joined Coudert Brothers as an associate, and shortly
thereafter he was packing his bags, having been tapped for the adventure of accompanying Kennedy to Manila.

The office Kennedy and Fuller junior set up was located at
86 calle Rosario, and the men they hired to serve as Coudert
Brothers' resident representatives were Charles C. Cohn and a
Mr. Hausserman. We know nothing about Messrs. Cohn and
Hausserman, but their performance on their own, after Kennedy
and Fuller had departed in the summer of 1903, was certainly

more than satisfactory to the New York partners. Their efforts, Fred wrote, produced "considerable business and numerous claims from the Islands." But the predicted trade between the United States and the Philippines never materialized, and American investors displayed a vast indifference to the islands, so that when the Philippines customs cases foundered in the wake of the *Heinzen* decision in 1907, Coudert Brothers decided to close its first Far Eastern office.

Similarly, "as the returns were found not to justify further retention," Coudert Brothers shuttered its Washington, D.C., office in 1906. One of the problems with the Washington office was that Edward Renick, the former State Department man, had died unexpectedly around 1901. Visiting Paris to help the firm settle the affairs of Anna Gould de Castellane, he had contracted a fever and died at age forty-five. Fred's opinion was that Renick "probably would have made a success of the [Washington] office," but Kennedy on his own could not make it profitable. It seems that Coudert Brothers was generating more business for Kennedy than the other way around.

The three "Insular" branches—Washington, Havana, and Manila—were all given time to prove themselves: none was shut down in less than four years. But when they did not become profitable, apparently neither Paul Fuller nor Fred Coudert—who together were then running the firm—had trouble reaching the decision to cut the losses. Both Fuller and Coudert were intellectually caught up in the constitutional law issues raised by the Insular cases. They enjoyed this work and had no hesitation about indulging themselves by occasionally taking some cases without fee. *Gonzales v. Williams,* for instance, was a *pro bono* case, for Señorita Gonzales was an indigent; and Coudert Brothers certainly did not charge Bishop Jones for its efforts in the *Ponce* suit. But Fuller and Coudert were both careful about the firm's expenses and, having survived the depression of 1893, not inclined to let the partnership get overextended on any front.

The shutting down of these offices was handled adeptly and amiably. The Washington, D.C., associates did not lose their jobs: they were apparently offered positions at the New York office, which Harry Weston Van Dyke, at least, accepted. And Coudert Brothers evidently remained on good terms with Kennedy in Washington and Cohn in Manila, for the firm worked on cases with each almost up to World War I.

In fact, the closing of the three offices seems to have made relatively little difference to the volume of Insular work conducted by the firm. Without having the expenses of the branch offices,

Coudert Brothers still continued to dominate this field. Howard Thayer Kingsbury was the "junior" on much of this Insular litigation, and the autobiographical sketch he wrote in 1911 for the twentieth reunion of his Yale class gives an idea of the variety of Insular matters then passing through the firm's hands:

> I still practice law as a member of the firm of Coudert Brothers, and I have found both the interest and the emoluments of the profession increasing—the former much more rapidly and extensively than the latter. I have been engaged in some cases in the United States Supreme Court of rather exceptional interest; among them one which established the property rights of the Roman Catholic Church in the territories acquired from Spain; one which vindicated the validity of native land titles in the Philippine Islands; and another which determined that the cession of the Philippines and the re-organization and new charter of the City of Manila did not relieve that city of its outstanding municipal debts.

Although the short life-spans of the Washington, Havana, and Manila offices suggest that the Insular cases were a brief, rather marginal episode in the history of Coudert Brothers, they actually played a vital role in the firm's fortunes for nearly fifteen years. Arising at the moment that Frederic René Coudert's health was failing, bringing Fred Coudert an almost instant fame and recognition, satisfying Fred's desire to contribute to the political life of his times in a way that strengthened, rather than weakened, his ties with the firm, and keeping many of the firm's other young litigators busily—and happily—employed from the turn of the century to World War I, they appeared on the scene as if delivered to order by a benign fate.

In 1903 Coudert Brothers lost not only Frederic René Coudert but also Daniel J. Holden, who died unexpectedly in June of that year, also of heart disease. When the partnership was reorganized in January 1904 and Kingsbury, Murray, and Samuels were made members of the firm, Coudert Brothers suddenly became a very young firm, with the average age of the partners dropping from fifty-two years to thirty-five.

At the head of the firm as senior partner was Paul Fuller, who, although he had been associated with Coudert Brothers for forty-five years, was still only fifty-seven years old. Next oldest at forty-one was Lorenzo Semple, who followed Holden as head of Estates and Trusts, which this new generation now started calling the Surrogate's Department. Then came the litigators Howard Thayer Kingsbury, thirty-three, Fred Coudert, thirty-two, and John Murray, thirty-one. The head of the Real Estate Department, who also helped Fuller with some of the administrative work, was Charles B. Samuels, who belonged to the same age group as Kingsbury, Coudert, and Murray. And a few years later, around 1906, Paul Fuller, Jr., would also become a partner while still in his early twenties.

The venerable Benjamin Franklin Tracy remained "of counsel," but it fell to Paul Fuller, as senior member of the firm, to provide guidance to his young partners, and there could have been no role more congenial to him. Fuller had a singular rapport with youth, perhaps because he was both tolerant and nondirective. In fact, because of his interest in helping young men, Fuller was at this time helping to found Fordham Law School, and he was named the law school's first dean in 1905, a position he would hold until 1913.

As Judge William Hughes Mulligan, a later dean of Fordham Law, was to write, "Although this man had never spent a day in a classroom, Fordham was indeed fortunate in obtaining his services as the first Dean of its Law School," and the official historian of Fordham University called Fuller, simply, "a happy selection." As dean, Fuller distinguished himself by recruiting an exceptionally able faculty, including Judge Alton B. Parker, who had just been defeated as the Democratic candidate for president, running against Teddy Roosevelt. Sympathetic to labor as a judge, Parker would represent the American Federation of Labor and Samuel Gompers in some notable cases over the next few years.

In line with his own interests, Fuller saw to it that the Fordham curriculum contained courses on civil and Roman law, as well as the more standard offerings on common and U.S. statute laws. Dean Fuller and his faculty also devised a program that took longer to complete and exceeded the minimum requirements for passage of the bar examination "in the interests of higher standards." Often regretting that he himself had not had any academic preparation for the law, Fuller believed "it was better to begin life late and well prepared than early and unfit." At the same time, however, Fuller insisted that the law school offer its classes in lower Manhattan and that lectures be conducted six days a week, starting at 4:30 P.M., "to afford a better opportunity for those employed as law clerks in downtown New York to attend its sessions." To obtain the brightest students, Fuller believed that the law school had to draw from the working classes, not just the well-to-do. Fuller never forgot his own beginnings, and his interest in poor boys who showed "pluck and determination" along with ability was always especially high.

The qualities that made him a beloved dean, of course, also informed his dealings with his own young partners. "One of the gentlest of men," he was never impatient, and the litigation partners were constantly seeking him out for critiques of their briefs. Utilizing his "very extraordinary erudition," Fuller seems to have run, in effect, one-on-one seminars that constituted an extraordinary postgraduate education for his colleagues. And he was constantly nudging them all into the foreground. "I have frequently known him," Fred said, "to write briefs in interesting cases in the highest Courts of this State or in the United States Supreme Court, and then to sign those briefs with the names of juniors who had done little more than assist him in collecting authorities."

The period between 1903 and World War I, at any event, seems to have been a happy one for the partnership. They were a congenial group; and, given the deaths, illnesses, and financial setbacks that had marked the previous decade, this era in the firm's history has the appearance of a calm following a storm. In fact, however, the pace of change in American life was accelerating in the early years of this century, and the firm, in ways both minor and major, was adjusting itself to new developments.

One of these developments was the advent of the title search company, which removed the need for law firms to employ their own clerks to research and record titles. Another was a streamlining in court procedures, which simplified the form in which documents had to be presented and which made typewritten documents acceptable. As a result, lawyers no longer had to employ scriveners, who were experts in such arcanery as how many spaces of indentation the second paragraph of a pleading required and in what color ink the third copy of a will should be prepared. It is probably these two developments that lay behind a reduction in the number of support personnel employed by Coudert Brothers in the early 1900s.

At the same time, respectable women were appearing in numbers in Manhattan's business district. In the nineteenth century, according to Elihu Root, only two types of women were ever seen below Canal Street—streetwalkers and women so rich they simply didn't have to care about their reputations. The generation that came of age in the 1890s, though, was impatient with such Victorian shibboleths, and women began coming downtown to visit their lawyers in person. It is probably no coincidence that simultaneously spittoons started disappearing from downtown offices, carpets began appearing, and law firms began to feel the pressure not only to be prosperous but to look prosperous. This was a pressure that Coudert Brothers, by and large, resisted. In 1907 the firm moved to 2 Rector Street, one of the new skyscrapers made possible by the widespread introduction of the electric elevator, but its decor remained the same utilitarian fare. Spittoons it had never had, but it did not now acquire carpeting, paneling, or elegant artwork either.

The firm was more receptive to another innovation of the new century—the female secretary. We do not know when Coudert Brothers hired its first woman staff member, but it almost certainly had some women secretaries by 1909, which is the year that eighteen-year-old Florence A. Bainbridge came to work for Coudert Brothers. She would begin as a secretary, would be promoted to cashier, and would retire some sixty years later as one of the most important, respected, and loved personages in the firm.

The changing times were also reflected in the firm's clientele, as Coudert Brothers acquired clients in industries that had not even existed ten years earlier. From the motion picture industry came the Pathé Exchange, Inc., French producers and distributors of the silent "flickers." And the new automobile industry contributed Michelin Tires, which established a factory in Milltown, New Jersey, in 1907 with Coudert Brothers' help, as well as the French automobile manufacturers Renault, André Massenat, and Panhard & Levassor, which the firm represented in connection with the export to the United States of their luxury motorcars.

It was through its representation of these foreign firms that Coudert Brothers was drawn into one of the most famous legal battles of the day—the Selden patent case. The story of the Selden case begins with an upstate New York lawyer, George Selden, who carefully crafted and filed a patent in the 1890s based on work being done in Europe on the internal-combustion engine. Selden did not invent the internal-combustion engine and did not claim to, but his artfully worded patent describing how other men's discoveries might be combined to create a workable automobile gave him the sole right to license and collect royalties on future automobile development in America. As one of Henry Ford's biographers, Robert Lacey, succinctly described the next steps leading up to the Selden patent case:

In 1899 Selden had gone into partnership with a group of Wall Street investors who saw the chance to cut themselves in on the profits of the growing American car industry, and when the syndicate tried to enforce Selden's patent against the five largest U.S. carmakers of the day, they met with surprising success. Rather than fight Selden, the carmakers ... decided to join him, since an alliance would save them a costly legal case and also offer them the chance to license or control their commercial rivals in the future. Thus was born, in March 1903, a few weeks before the formal incorporation of the Ford Motor Company, the Association of Licensed Automobile Manufacturers.

The first step the ALAM took was to sue the leading mavericks outside its ranks, which consisted of the Ford organization and the group of French firms represented by Coudert Brothers, which included Panhard & Levassor, André Massenat, and Henry and A. C. Neubauer, two Dutch importers headquartered in Paris who sold Panhard and Renault automobiles in the United States. There were more than thirty other independent car manufacturers who stood outside the ALAM, but Ford and the French companies faced the first assault. Ford, in particular, had been vocal in decrying the Selden patent, while the French companies had been highly successful in the American market; their defeat, the ALAM reckoned, would set an example for the others. The stakes were large. "A judicial upholding of this patent," *Automobile* told its readers, "would entitle those who control it to have every unlicensed gas motor vehicle in the land battered to pieces by officers of the law and destroyed, whether found in the possession of manufacturers or innocent purchasers."

In face of the complaints that rained down upon them in 1903 and 1904, Ford and the foreign firms joined forces, with Ford's attorney Ralzemond A. Parker and the Coudert Brothers litigation team consulting each other freely. Eventually all five suits were merged for purposes of judicial decision, although the ALAM insisted that separate testimony be taken in the case of the French firms—which increased the costs for the defendants. What no one realized in 1904, however, was that the first round of litigation would last nearly six years.

Most of this six years was consumed in taking depositions, which took an unusually long time because of the technical engineering evidence involved. Moreover, the then-prevailing federal rules of procedure for suits in equity left the deposition process virtually uncontrolled. Allan Nevins has described the first years of the Selden suit as follows:

> Evidence was taken in many different cities—New York, Providence, Boston, Lansing, Ithaca, Rochester, Pittsburgh, Detroit, Philadelphia—where witnesses residing more than a hun-

dred miles from the court were asked to appear for examination. Sometimes they testified before notaries public, but usually before examiners approved by the court. Counsel for both sides were present. The examiner kept order, saw that a proper record was made, and granted delays; but he had no authority to rule on objections, which were frequent, or to compel a witness to be "responsive." In the absence of a court official with full powers, attorneys naturally put in all the evidence they thought might be effective, while their opponents objected with frequency and vigor to impugn as much of the case as they could. An objection having been made, the witness answered, and the judge was supposed to make his own decision as to the character of such testimony.

The result was a Himalaya of evidence, amounting with the exhibits and briefs to more than 14,000 pages and 5,000,000 words. The exhibits alone—photographs, printed articles, patents and attendant charts and drawings, catalogues, leaflets—filled five volumes when the record was later printed for appeal. The mass and character of the material accumulated was to be influential in changing the procedure in future patent suits, most of which today are tried in open court, with a judge ruling on objections and excluding irrelevant material. Meanwhile the Selden suit [with its appeal] dragged its way through eight long years.

John P. Murray was the Coudert Brothers attorney on this case, the one who conducted the examination and cross-examination of witnesses in these far-flung locales, attended to the voluminous research, dealt with the technical experts on the firm's defense team, and mastered all the details of the case. Very much an Irish American in appearance, with fair skin, curly hair, and an uptilted nose, Murray had "an infinite capacity for taking pains." Yet he was "a lively man" who had a way of setting people at ease. One young lawyer, new to Coudert Brothers, would never forget being taken around to be introduced to Murray. Some of the other partners had been rushed, rather dismissing, so the young man, a Canadian named John Dubé, had begun by apologizing for disturbing Murray, to which Murray replied, "Don't apologize; it is to our advantage to meet you and have you with us." The warmth of his manner sent the young man away feeling as if he were someone truly important to the firm, not a nuisance but an asset. He was "very human," Dubé recalled, "so nice, never on his high horse."

Murray was also an excellent lawyer, who had considerable courtroom experience, having served as the firm's chief trial representative defending the Globe & Rutgers Fire Insurance Company, Pennsylvania Insurance Company, Pacific Insurance Company, and American Insurance Company in litigation arising from the San Francisco earthquake and fire of 1906. Murray did not, however, have a great deal of experience with patent cases, but, then, no one at Coudert Brothers did. Frederic René Coudert had handled quite a few patent appeals in his heyday, and Paul Fuller may (or may not) have assisted him on them. Still, Fuller was not actually a patent lawyer, and the patent experience of the new generation at Coudert Brothers really amounted to only one case. This was a suit contesting Goodrich's contention that it held a pioneer tire patent, which Fred Coudert had argued on behalf of Michelin. Coudert Brothers had won that case, but the partners' collective experience did not begin to approach that of Ford's attorney, Parker. An elderly man, who was one of the leading patent lawyers in the country, Parker was dedicated to winning the Selden case, so that Coudert Brothers was well content to have the cases merged and to lean on this lawyer who, Fred Coudert later said, "knew more than anybody about the Selden Patent Case."

Fred Coudert's role was less time-consuming than Murray's—but vital. With his fluent French and his understanding of the French legal and business climate, he maintained close relations with the clients, keeping them informed of the progress of this interminable—and, to them, no doubt, rather mystifying—suit. He also organized and edited Murray's final briefs and made an appearance during the oral presentations, which finally began on May 28, 1909, in the New York District Court of Judge Charles Merrill Hough.

A curious feature of the trial was the fact that, in the midst of the arguments, a transcontinental auto race from New York to Seattle was launched from a starting line in City Hall Park right under the courthouse windows. The court went briefly into recess as the attorneys, judge, and witnesses crowded around the windows to watch the preparations for the race. Coudert—described by Nevins as "youngest and most outspoken of the counsel"—took advantage of the situation to point up one of the weaknesses of Selden's case. "Your Honor," he said, with feigned surprise, "there is something that puzzles me. I see a Ford car, two Ford cars, but I see no Selden car!" Judge Hough is reported to have laughed.

But Hough was not a patent specialist, and the opinion he finally issued in September 1909 was favorable to Selden. The defense briefs, especially Parker's, were described by those familiar with the case as "impressive," but they were long and technical and Judge Hough gave little evidence of having understood them. Accepting assumptions that even the plaintiff's counsel had agreed were untenable and dismissing most of the history of the development of the internal combustion engine as irrelevant, Hough's opinion "drove the defense lawyers berserk." Ford and the defense lawyers could hardly believe their eyes as they read through the opinion, and they were burning to get started on the appeal.

Alarmingly, though, the French firms wrote Coudert that they wanted to withdraw. The suit had been long and costly for them; they thought it best to ask the ALAM for a license and end the struggle. About to leave for France, Coudert cabled, "Wait until I come over." In Paris he gathered the Neubauer and Panhard officials and urged them to let him continue. His clients were not convinced. Coudert then, in Nevins's words, "produced his trump card." Speaking in his fluent French, he told them, "Gentlemen, I have said that we can win; I will now prove to you how much I believe it. If you will join in the appeal, which will involve your paying the costs of printing the record—I cannot legally do that myself—I will charge you nothing for my services if I lose." The cost of printing that record of five million words would not be a small expense, but the clients agreed, and on November 22, 1910, Coudert and Murray were back in court for the appeal.

At the appellate level, written briefs are far more important than oral arguments, and the combined defense team was allowed only four and a half hours for its oral presentation. Of this four and a half hours, Fred Coudert took forty minutes at most—but he made them count, demolishing the reliability of the ALAM's chief expert witness, Dugald Clerk, who was an authority on gasoline engines. A few weeks earlier Coudert had been sitting in the waiting room at Betts, Betts, Sheffield & Betts, waiting to see Samuel R. Betts, one of the ALAM's counsels, when he noticed a large table piled up with books and magazines. A compulsive reader, Coudert wandered over to the table and began looking through the items there, one of which turned out to be a set of proofs of the new edition of Clerk's standard work. Flipping through the pages, Coudert to his surprise found Clerk stating in print that Selden was not entitled to a pioneer patent, the basic work on the gasoline engine having been done by Otto, Daimler, and Benz.

Coudert obtained his own copy of the British expert's book, and before the oral arguments began, but in the presence of the appellate judges, he asked the ALAM's counsel if they based their case primarily on Clerk's testimony. "They conferred a moment, then replied that they did." Coudert then produced the book, and Betts, sensing what was coming, protested that the book was not in evidence. Judge Noyes interrupted, advising Betts drily, "I think we can judge well enough if what [Mr. Coudert] has to say is applicable or not." In his oral argument, Coudert then proceeded to ravage Clerk's prior testimony, using his own published words against him.

Coudert also did what some trial lawyers spend a lifetime learning to do: he didn't use up all his allotted time. When he had said enough, with an exquisite sense of timing, he sat down. One of the ALAM's lawyers later congratulated Coudert on "a very fine piece of work, excellently organized, very well delivered." As the appellate judges, unlike Hough, were patent experts and the defense briefs were again outstanding, in January 1911 Ford and the French firms received an overwhelmingly favorable decision. The ALAM did not contest it; instead, the would-be monopoly dissolved itself, and the American automobile industry proceeded on its way unshackled.

One of Henry Ford's biographers has stated that it was Ford's David against Goliath victory in the Selden patent case that turned him into an "American folk hero," and it certainly did the reputations of John P. Murray and Fred Coudert no harm. One effect of the Selden case, however, was that it made Fred Coudert an advocate for stringent regulation of automobile drivers. In June 1909, during the first trial, Coudert's client André Massenat had driven Coudert in from his summer home in Oyster Bay to the courthouse in Manhattan in a big European luxury car. "The machine cut a swath through the Long Island traffic, scattering chickens and livestock and frightening horses, cyclists, and people afoot." Coudert, the descendant of expert horsemen and no mean rider himself, arrived at the courthouse, much shaken, and found himself sitting next to Ford.

> "Mr. Ford," he remarked as he wiped his brow, "I came in from Oyster Bay by car. We didn't kill anyone, but everybody on the road hated us, and it was probably sheer luck that we didn't have a collision. I think you are creating a social problem with your car." Ford replied calmly, "No, my friend, you are mistaken. I'm not creating a social problem at all. I am going to democratize the automobile. When I'm through everybody will be able to afford one, and about everyone will have one. The horse will have disappeared from our highways, the automobile will be taken for granted, and there won't be any problem."

"By God, he was right!" Coudert exclaimed in 1953, recounting this incident. In 1909, however, Coudert was deeply disturbed by his own vision of the future, wherein the wealthy man swept through the countryside in his expensive machine leaving death, destruction, and class hatred in his wake. In 1912, as soon as he was free of the Selden case, Coudert formed the National Highways Protective Society "to protect the public who use our highways," and over the next several years, his lobbying in New York State was responsible for the introduction of some of its basic highway safety laws, including the licensing of drivers and the introduction of speed limits and traffic signals. He also worked with the State's district attorney on the *Rosenheimer* appeal in 1913, which established the constitutionality of the act instituting penalties against hit-and-run drivers. Murray, a New Jersey resident, was similarly concerned, and it was he who drafted the Frelinghuysen automobile laws enacted by his home state. The two Coudert attorneys might have continued this work for some years, but both were caught up in 1914 in a larger matter—aiding the Allies in World War I.

Chapter Eight

WAR FOR DEMOCRACY

"I am a believer, perhaps temperamentally, that it is worthwhile trying to do things," Fred Coudert once said, by which he meant that he thought that the individual could help to make the world a better place. Like his father, he also believed that, in the United States, lawyers had a peculiar chance—and duty—to contribute to the betterment of mankind. The Couderts were scarcely alone in these beliefs. Indeed, this outlook was so common among the elite members of the bar in the nineteenth century that historians have a phrase for it—the Websterian ideal.

In the early years of the twentieth century, however, the Websterian tradition was undergoing a subtle decline, for men like William Nelson Cromwell at Sullivan & Cromwell and Francis Lynde Stetson at Stetson, Jennings & Russell were acknowledged as leaders of the bar, yet seemed to have little time to spare for public interest activities. Still, the expectation remained that a "name" partner in a major New York law firm would apply his abilities in a civic-spirited manner, and Fred Coudert accepted this tradition wholeheartedly.

A major difference between other "name" partners and Coudert, however, was that he was considerably younger than most and had to earn his way daily. He had inherited only opportunity, not money or leisure with it: his father had left an estate of less than half a million dollars, all of it to be held in trust for Fred's mother during her lifetime and then to be divided, in the French fashion, equally among Fred and his sisters. As Fred would be fifty-four years old before his mother died and he received his share, the law was no mere avocation to him; it was his livelihood.

Moreover, Coudert seems to have been the chief business-getter of the firm—in today's slang, its "rainmaker." Like Michelin and Renault, such clients as Coty and Moen expected Coudert to give his personal attention to their affairs. It was Coudert who was appointed the counsel to the French bondholders of the St. Louis & San Francisco Railroad Company when the railroad faced reorganization in 1914, although it was Lorenzo Semple who set off for New Orleans to travel the line and investigate its actual condition. The contribution Coudert made to the firm's overall prosperity is suggested by the fact that in 1914, when he wanted to accept an appointment as New York City's corporation counsel—a politically powerful post that would have placed him in charge of all the city's civil litigation—his partners opposed the idea. Equally as imbued with the Websterian ethos, they, nonetheless, pointed out that the firm could not do without his full-time attention to the practice even temporarily, and he accordingly declined the post.

Thus, whatever Coudert did without pay, he had to do within the interstices of a busy practice that he could not afford to neglect. The *pro bono* Insular cases were "extras" on top of an already heavy workload. So was his representation of the small depositors—mostly poor immigrant laborers—who lost their savings in the failure of Henry Siegal & Co., a private bank, which Coudert thought had shown a "scandalous" indifference to the welfare of its least sophisticated depositors. For that matter, Coudert clearly looked upon his retainer as a special assistant attorney general by the federal government in 1913–14 as a form of *pro bono* work, for, although he was paid one thousand dollars a month, he spoke of that as a negligible sum. He took the assignment not for the money but for the challenge of seeing whether he could salvage anything from the government's previous failed efforts to prosecute the so-called "Hard Coal Trust," a group of railroads that controlled the Pennsylvania coal mines in alleged violation of the Sherman Antitrust Act. Coudert believed in the antitrust laws: "Our whole industrial structure," he wrote, "depends upon these great remedial Statutes which maintain the existence of liberty and equality by keeping open the door of opportunity." But he was ultimately no more successful than his predecessors had been in persuading a conservative U.S. circuit court on this point.

In addition to his *pro bono* work, Coudert's belief in "doing things" led him to accept appointments to several nonprofit boards. He served a term, for example, as a member of New York

City's Board of Education, using the position to promote such progressive causes as adult night schools; technical high schools; nutrition programs for immigrant children; the introduction of modern languages, the social sciences, and laboratory sciences into the high school curriculum; and the professionalization of the faculty and administration. An advocate of suffrage and equal rights, he was elected to Barnard College's board of trustees around 1913, and he was a director of the American Embassy Association, a group lobbying for salaries for U.S. ambassadors to prevent these posts from becoming, in Coudert's words, "the perquisite of the plutocracy." He served on several committees of the Bar Association of the City of New York and was active in any number of single-issue pressure groups, advocating causes ranging from the arbitration treaties to defeating a city charter revision that he thought would politicize the educational system.

The heaviest demands on Coudert's time, however, came generally not from his one or two charitable cases a year or the monthly meetings of nonprofit organizations and committees, but from his writings in the field of jurisprudence. Believing that the real battle for reform lay in the realm of ideas, Coudert read and wrote extensively on topics relating to legal theory and philosophy from 1901 onward, producing each year two or three major law review articles or contributions to the proceedings of various learned societies, in addition to a flood of book reviews, speeches to clubs and organizations, and writings for the popular press. In sheer number of words—not counting his briefs—he was turning out the equivalent of a full-length book every two years, accomplishing this output by ruthlessly sacrificing nights, weekends, and vacations. The time put into study and thinking, however, did not seem like a sacrifice to him. He was living on the edge of—and was very much a part of—a revolution in legal thought, and his intellectual excitement spilled out not only into his practice but also into almost every spare moment he had.

The conventional view of the law in the period before World War I was a static one: the Constitution and statutes were fixed in meaning, and the lawyer's job was simply to ascertain by an examination of precedents what that meaning was and to advise his clients accordingly. The new approach saw the law as the product of dynamic social and economic forces, and the more daring thinkers like Coudert went on to maintain that interpretation of the Constitution and statute law must change to reflect changes in society and that sociological data might often be a better guide than precedent in determining a law's validity. The seminal work in this new kind of legal philosophy had been done by Holmes, Gray, and

Thayer at Harvard Law School in the late nineteenth century, but the philosophy itself had barely begun to influence the nation's law schools, including Harvard, and was almost unknown among the practicing bar and bench when Roscoe Pound gave it the name "sociological jurisprudence" in 1907. Yet, by then, Coudert had for almost six years been advocating this approach in his writings. In fact, he seems to have been the first, and for many years the only, "name" partner in a major firm to understand and accept as a matter of course the fundamental tenets of what is still considered modern jurisprudence.

Coudert stood in the advance guard of legal thought largely because his training was different from most other lawyers. He had learned his theory not in law school but in a doctoral program in political science and economics, and he had received his practical exposure to the law from his father, whose habit of thinking in terms of comparative law and whose highly developed historical consciousness had made him a strong relativist in outlook and philosophy. Thus, everything in Coudert's background urged him to reject as pure fiction the idea that the law consists of a body of fixed principles to be found in previous cases through the exercise of objective logic. Rather, he understood that the law derives its authority not from logic but from public opinion, which, in turn, is shaped by economic and social circumstances. As the time in which he lived was a period in which circumstances were changing rapidly, he argued that major legal questions of interpretation "should not today be determined as a matter of theory or of deduction from general principles, but simply as questions of expediency." By expediency he meant what serves the public good, and that determination, he noted, "belongs to the domain of the social sciences." Although a member himself of the American Social Science Association and the Academy of Political Science, Coudert was not proposing that lawyers cede their special field to the social scientists, but that they should broaden their concerns ("politics, economics, law, cannot be put into watertight compartments"), use the "new knowledge" to understand more scientifically the times in which they were living, and cease to treat "common law rules as fetiches [*sic*]."

Accordingly, a running theme in Coudert's writings before World War I is the folly of blindly following precedent without regard to the circumstances under which it arose or consideration of whether it might still be apt. One of his best essays, "Riparian Rights: A Perversion of *Stare Decisis*," for example, traces the three-hundred-year history of the courts' efforts to uphold a doctrine instituted by the Tudors and having no loftier rationale than royal greed. Its erudition lightened by a vigorous sarcasm, "Riparian Rights" rolls smoothly to its concluding remonstrance against judicial narrowness and hostility to change.

Like many thinking men of his time—but like few other "downtown" lawyers—Coudert believed that judicial conservatism had reached dangerous proportions. He was alarmed by the string of decisions overturning legislation aimed at regulating corporations, decisions that assumed the principles of laissez-faire economics were eternal verities, and in numerous essays he attempted to demonstrate that, while the ideas of Bentham and Mill had been a healthy influence in their time, their time was past. "The regulation movement of recent years," he wrote, "is nothing in the world but a part of the general movement of self-defense on the part of the community, because conditions have changed so that it is necessary to keep the individual, who is running madly in his automobile on the public road or stock-jobbing with hundreds of millions, within bounds, or the community must suffer."

The remedy some proposed at the time for the difficulties thrown by the courts in the path of social reform was the abolition of judicial review, but Coudert argued that it would be preferable to forestall the judges' narrow interpretation of the law through amendment of state and federal constitutions. Judicial review should not be abandoned because of impatience with the current illiberalism of the courts, he wrote, for it constituted the only safeguard in the American political system for the country's minority groups. An unbridled legislative power might work reasonably well in relatively homogeneous societies like England and France, but America needed, in Coudert's opinion, a check like judicial review to delay at times the expression of the majority will and force the modification of ill-considered laws. Thinking specifically of the potential for religious persecution, he wrote, "It is impossible to protect the rights of the minorities unless there be courts to which an appeal may be taken from the doubtful legislation of the moment."

Subsequent history, and the civil rights movement, in particular, have vindicated Coudert's views, although he never anticipated the liberalism of the federal courts in the 1950s. Rather, Coudert expected that the American courts, with their reliance on precedent, would always be innately conservative and American legislatures, elected by universal suffrage, would continue to be innately liberal; from maintaining the interaction between the two, however, he expected there to emerge that best of all possible results— evolutionary change. Deploring both reactionaries and radicals, he criticized the former more frequently in the era before World War I simply because he feared that they were the stronger group: "The history of the law," he told a group of lawyers meeting at the Yale Club in 1911, "indicates that with constant oscillations the general movement has been forward and the danger greater from conservative forces than from radical."

There is no record of how Coudert's brethren at the bar reacted to such sentiments, but his old mentor Professor Burgess looked upon Coudert as one of the most brilliantly satisfactory of his former students. Nearing retirement in 1912, Burgess wanted Coudert to succeed him as Ruggles Professor of Constitutional Law at Columbia, a prestigious, part-time lectureship, and Coudert was minded to accept. In fact, asked a few weeks later by the alumni to stand for election as an alumni trustee of Columbia, Coudert declined, citing the offer from Burgess and explaining that "As a member of the faculty, I couldn't be a trustee." With his enthusiasm for the developments then taking place in constitutional law, Coudert clearly would have enjoyed the opportunity to expound upon them in an academic setting, but he did not, after all, succeed Burgess. "Later on and upon investigation of the matter," Coudert noted, "I found I was unable to accept the invitation to accept the Chair of Constitutional Law." What the laconic statement means is that Coudert got wind of the fact that many of the faculty hoped that the appointment would go to their colleague Professor Frank Johnson Goodnow, and he gracefully withdrew his name from consideration in deference to Goodnow.

Coudert's gesture was wasted, for Goodnow did not get the Ruggles chair, the trustees appointing instead William D. Guthrie, whose views on the constitutional protection of the property rights of corporations were at the very opposite end of the spectrum from Coudert's and Goodnow's. Goodnow departed to become president of Johns Hopkins University, Coudert was elected a charter trustee of Columbia—he assumed, as a sort of consolation prize—and he apparently gave up any further thought of an academic appointment.

It is interesting to note, however, that the chair which Coudert might have filled was one in constitutional law, not international law. Throughout this prewar period Coudert was also writing on topics of international law, sometimes for French journals, and his familiarity with French law flashes in and out of all his articles. A charter member of the American Society of International Law, which was founded in 1907, he contributed some excellent papers to the society's annual proceedings, but Coudert was not thinking as systematically about the law of nations as about the law of corporations—partly because there seemed to be no broad principles in dispute. Rather, there was, as Coudert later said, "a general belief in necessary and axiomatic progress toward the substitution of law for force" in relations among nations. Of course, Coudert was aware that popular opinion lagged somewhat behind the thinking of the bar's leaders: when stumping in favor of the arbitration treaties in 1911, he had, after all, been able to speak in Buffalo only under police escort, and from the speaker's platform he had watched a mob break up a New York rally he was to have addressed. Yet international law and arbitration seemed an area where it was less necessary for an individual to try to "do things," for the march of history had surely made war obsolete as a method of resolving disputes among civilized nations. As Coudert noted ruefully many years later, if the charter members of the American Society of International Law, himself included, had been told in 1907 that world war would erupt in Europe in less than a decade, it "would have seemed to them a grotesque and an impossible happening, a mad dream, 'a tale told by an idiot'!"

Expecting the Balkan crisis to blow over, in late July 1914 Coudert sailed for France on his annual visit to Coudert Frères, and he had only just arrived in Paris on August 3, the day that Germany declared war on France. Together with his friend Jean Cruppi, a former minister of foreign affairs, Coudert rushed to the ministry's office and waited until Cruppi, white-faced, emerged with confirmed news of the hostilities. Having so many well-placed friends like Cruppi in France, Coudert was more aware than most of how ill-prepared France and its allies, England and Russia, were for war, and he spent these initial weeks of the war deeply afraid that he was about to watch the Franco-Prussian War repeat itself, as the Germans captured large amounts of French territory while the French were still struggling to mobilize.

An immediate problem for Coudert Frères was the large number of American tourists stranded in France when the passenger liners cancelled their sailings. There were tens of thousands of American citizens in France that summer—the exact number is unknown since Americans did not use passports then for travel to Europe—and most of them soon ran out of funds, for the banks had immediately stopped cashing checks on U.S. banks and honoring letters of credit. The firm found itself functioning as a sort of unofficial consular outpost of the U.S. embassy, advancing funds to and arranging transportation home for those travelers who were clients, or friends of clients, or even vaguely known to friends of friends. Coudert himself, however, had no intention of leaving France in its moment of peril. On the contrary, he was anxious for something that he, as a citizen of a neutral country, might do to help it.

When Cruppi mentioned to Coudert that there were about eighty refugee children in Belfort, near Alsace, who needed to be withdrawn from what was about to become a battle area, Coudert quickly volunteered his assistance. Finding an automobile and driver, he and Cruppi were soon jolting east behind the French lines, encountering a steady flow of refugees on the roads—thus becoming among the first to witness this now familiar feature of twentieth-century warfare. At Belfort, the Frenchman and the American were confronted not by 80 children, but 205 pathetic little ones. Unprepared for such numbers, they still found transportation for all of them from the French military government and got them safely back to Paris, where American friends of Coudert had already begun to set up a home for the children in an old seminary near Yvetôt.

On a similar rescue mission, Coudert also journeyed to the north of France, where he noted the perilously thin supplies of munitions being dragged by horses to the front, the German army having already overrun the territory in which most of France's munitions factories were located. On this trip, too, he "saw great droves of men, old, haggard and broken, and young children, and babies, some alive and some dead, carried by their wretched mothers, streaming down the roads." These were the first of the Belgian refugees to come stumbling through the French lines, bearing tales of the guerrilla-style resistance being put up by the Belgians against their invaders and of the German High Command's reprisals against the civilian populace.

Back in Paris in early September, in the time he could spare from looking after his orphans and office affairs, Coudert restlessly walked the streets, visiting the cafés, talking with everyone from workingmen to professionals, trying to gauge the public mood and come to grips with what was happening. The German guns could now be heard in the eastern suburbs of Paris, and the French government had evacuated the capital. Coudert stayed until the German advance was turned back at the Battle of Marne and it was clear that Paris would not fall. He remained long enough, in fact, to become completely permeated with the atmosphere prevailing in France at that time. By mid-September 1914 he was convinced that the war was nothing less than a struggle between democracy and military despotism and that, since democracy was the central issue, his own country had a vital interest in its outcome. Coudert returned to America committed heart and soul to the Allied cause with a special intensity, not only because of all his personal ties to

France and his lifelong love of that country, but because he had seen France's sufferings at firsthand. At forty-three, he was past the age of carrying a rifle, but World War I was to become his war, as the ridiculous little Spanish-American War had never been.

In New York City in the late fall of 1914, Coudert continued his work to aid the French children. Having recognized after the Marne that it would be a long struggle, he and a few other Americans in Paris had organized the Franco-American Committee for the Protection of the Children of the Frontier. While August F. Jaccaci and Mildred Bliss remained in France to administer this organization, Coudert took on the office of treasurer and committed himself to finding more donors in the States. He was to pour great energy into this project, and by 1916 the committee would be supporting twelve hundred children in some two dozen homes and running a sanitorium for children arriving injured or ill from the villages in the path of the armies.

The most serious problem facing the Allies in the early days of the war, however, was their shortage of war material. Unlike Germany, they had not stockpiled in anticipation of war, and the British factories and the few remaining French factories could not produce the guns, armaments, uniforms, and other accoutrements needed, while the third major Allied nation, Russia, was scarcely industrialized at all. The Allies had an urgent need to purchase supplies from the United States, the one industrial power not affected by the war, and, to do so, they would also need loans from U.S. banks. Shortly after proclaiming American neutrality in August 1914, President Woodrow Wilson had announced that loans by American bankers to the combatant nations "are inconsistent with the true spirit of neutrality." To overcome this restriction, the French government got together in August a group of important French industrialists to borrow indirectly for the government from certain American banks. One of these was the Guaranty Trust Company, for which Coudert Frères acted. John Robinson worked on this loan, and he would recall later that "A rather amusing incident was the fact that Mr. Coty [a longtime client of Coudert Brothers] was greatly flattered at being chosen as an important French industrialist!"

Later the Wilson administration eased its policy, allowing the Allied governments to borrow directly from private American sources. In September 1915 the Anglo-French Financial Commission arrived in America to arrange a loan of $500 million, which represented the largest single loan ever syndicated in the United States. Coudert Brothers represented the French government in connection with the Anglo-French loan, a retainer it received on the recommendation of Ambassador Jean-Jules Jusserand. Jusserand, a scholar and literary historian, was, said Fred Coudert, "very friendly to Mr. Paul Fuller," but Coudert Brothers was also a logical choice for this retainer because of its long representation of the Banque de France, the French central bank, and the French consulate.

In addition, the New York office was deeply involved in the actual procurement of war supplies. The Russian government, for example, asked John Murray, who had handled extradition cases for Russia for the past twenty years, to serve as the legal advisor to the Imperial Russian embassy on its military purchases. The first problem handed to Murray, on December 2, 1914, involved securing an adequate bank guaranty for the fulfillment by Du Pont of a multimillion dollar gunpowder contract. From that moment on, Murray spent the better part of his days, including Saturdays, reviewing contracts, examining bills of lading, issuing opinion letters, attending closings, and conferring endlessly with bankers, manufacturers, and Russian officials. The following extracts from his desk diary give an idea of the time he devoted to this single client:

> *Thursday, December 10, 1914.* Called at Vanderbilt Hotel in the morning and conferred with Military Attache on the transaction of business with The National City Bank. Thereafter called at National City Bank, interviewed Mr. Gardin, and secured Pass book showing total credits to date of $16,222,525.64. In the afternoon called with the Military Attache and saw J. P. Morgan at his office in reference to the proposed guaranty by J. P. Morgan & Company on the Dupont [sic] contract.
>
> *Friday, December 11, 1914.* Had conference with Colonel Golejewski, Mr. Medzikhovsky, Baron Korff, and one other Russian gentleman at office of Baron Korff in the Locomobile Building, 51st Street, from three to five o'clock. *Friday night* drafted proposed agreement between Military Attache and Dupont.
>
> *Saturday, December 12, 1914.* Drew agreement between Military Attache and Dupont. Looked into cases re Wright-Curtiss Aeroplane litigation in accordance with promise made to Mr. Medzikhovsky of preceding day. Had conference 12:00–1:00 P.M. at Hotel Vanderbilt. . . . Discussed proposed agreement with Dupont and gave to Mr. Medzikhovsky extract from Aeroplane cases and informed that so far as I had been able to learn, no settlement had been reached between the Wrights and Curtiss. P.M. redrew proposed agreement with Dupont and mailed three copies of same to Colonel Golejewsky [sic] at Washington.

Monday, December 14, 1914. Received telegram from Military Attache requesting that I meet him in Wilmington Tuesday morning, December 15.

Tuesday, December 15, 1914. Left home 6:40. Spent day in Wilmington. . . . Left Dupont's office at 5:30 and arrived home at 10:00 P.M.

Over the next three years, there were only occasional weeks when Russian matters did not make comparable demands on Murray's time. Although the firm's records from the World War I period are fragmentary, it appears that Coudert Brothers also assisted France and later Italy, once it joined the Allies, with their purchases. It was probably Lorenzo Semple who principally represented these governments, for it was he who was decorated by both during the war for his services in assisting the flow of munitions and supplies.

As important to the Allies as obtaining supplies was the interruption of American shipments to the Central Powers. The German Army might be undefeatable on the Continent, but the British Navy controlled the high seas and easily intercepted the unarmed, unescorted merchant ships carrying American cargoes bound for Germany and nearby neutral ports in northern Europe. American ship and cargo owners naturally aired their anger to their representatives in Washington, D.C., and the U.S. government, in turn, protested to the British those seizures that violated the American concept of what constituted the rights of neutrals in wartime. Soon there was a storm of charges and countercharges, and Coudert wound up in the center, for he was hired as legal advisor to both the British and French governments on these issues.

Coudert's recollection of how he came to be retained by the British was that he had been in Washington, D.C., on business in November 1914 and, walking past the British embassy, had decided on impulse to leave his card for the new ambassador, Sir Cecil Spring-Rice. Scrawling the message "Best wishes for a British success," he handed his card to the doorman, who knew Coudert by sight and told him, "The Ambassador has been trying to get in touch with you all day." Coudert said, "There must be some mistake. The Ambassador doesn't even know me." But the doorman was not mistaken, for, returning to his club, Coudert was handed a stack of telephone messages from Spring-Rice. Retracing his steps to the embassy, Coudert found the ambassador "in a state of nervous agitation."

[The ambassador] said, "There's a great deal of controversy and many legal problems arising out of the blockade and the contraband list. We need an American adviser, someone who knows American law and what the U.S. had done in the past during war time."

I said, "I would be glad to do whatever I can for you and your people as a piece of war work, just as I would for the United States. But my efforts would be completely useless unless I have first been cleared by the State Department. I will have to talk to Mr. Lansing [the acting secretary of state]."

"Oh, that's all right," said the Ambassador. "Mr. Lansing was the one who suggested we have an American lawyer."

Coudert went over to the State Department to see Robert Lansing, whom he knew very well. Lansing had been a junior counsel at the Bering Sea arbitration, and, since both Coudert and Lansing were international lawyers, their paths had crossed many times since then. Thus, Lansing was comfortable confiding to Coudert the reason he had suggested that the British get an American lawyer to advise them: "The real truth is that the best precedents for a strict British blockade are what we did to the South during the Civil War, but I can't tell him that! But you can."

Lansing was referring to the irony underlying the diplomatic confrontation between the United States and Great Britain: the fact that the two countries had staked out opposing stands on the "freedom of the seas" during the Napoleonic Wars, had reversed themselves a perfect 180 degrees during the Civil War, when the Union had been maintaining a blockade and Great Britain had been the neutral shipper, and had now switched back to their original positions. Thus, the State Department had available to it a number of British precedents to cite, whereas the Foreign Office, with Coudert's help, would rebut with precedents drawn from American law. International law on the subject of neutral trade was far from fixed, and Coudert saw in the situation the same essential conflict as that prevailing in the realm of corporate regulation to which he had been giving so much thought:

> The questions raised [in 1914–17] were of a very real legal complexity, and I believe that the view taken of them by public lawyers would depend largely upon the view entertained of the nature of law in general. As in municipal law, so even more markedly in international law, we find two schools of thought; the one favoring certainty and strict adherence to adjudged and settled precedent, the other advocating the development of legal principles and their extension to meet new needs and

situations. Each nation necessarily pressed the legal view which
was dictated by its own immediate interests.

Coudert himself was intellectually comfortable developing the
British position, arguing for the more expansive view of allowable
belligerent actions. There was certainly irony, though, in the fact
that he would be relying upon the U.S. Supreme Court decisions
in the Civil War Blockading cases, some of which had been recently reaffirmed in the Cuban expropriation cases arising from
the Spanish-American War: his father, after all, had been on the
losing side in the Blockading cases, and he himself had contested
the Blockading decisions in the Cuban cases just a few years back.
But, originating in the U.S. Supreme Court, these were obviously
the hardest precedents for the Wilson administration to argue
against. On December 26, 1914, the U.S. State Department presented the British government with a summary of its complaints,
and the Foreign Office's reply on February 10, 1915, while mild in
tone, was loaded with American precedents that Coudert had supplied, mostly from the Blockading cases. The note contained
American precedents for all the contested British actions: the taking of American ships into British ports for search, the extension
of the law of contraband to include items not used for strictly military purposes, and the "doctrine of continuous voyage," under
which the British seized shipments to neutral Scandinavia, Denmark, and Holland that it feared might be reexported to Germany.
"Of course," Coudert said, "it was difficult for Washington to do
anything then!"
The exchange of notes in the winter of 1914–15, however, was
far from being the end of the matter. There were continuous incidents on the high seas prompting a steady stream of protests from
the State Department, and Coudert was in constant contact with
the Foreign Office's legal advisor, supplying precedents and arguments to suit each specific incident, as well as with the British ambassador. Moreover, once a British reply was delivered, quite
frequently the State Department would call Coudert down to Washington for discussion. The legal questions became so complicated
that in 1915 the State Department hired Frank Polk as its counselor and also set up a board headed by international law expert
James Brown Scott to provide advice on specific blockading incidents. It was usually Polk, however, who haggled over the technical
questions with Coudert. "I would go constantly in to see him,"
Coudert recalled, "and we would talk the matter over. He would
tell me that he thought that the British had gone too far and they
ought to ease up. I would go back and talk with the British. These

were legal matters and legal questions, and we had some very interesting discussions in regard to them."

In all the subtleties, though, Coudert never lost sight of what seemed to him to be his fundamental responsibility to his clients: to reduce the friction between them and the United States. His hope, as he told both Lansing and Polk, was "to be a buffer between the State Department and the Allied Governments and to absorb as much of the shock as possible." The shocks were great indeed, for the issues involved were the same ones that had brought Great Britain and the United States to war in 1812 and the Allies' actions aroused deep indignation in the United States. Nearly every day the newspapers wrote of "Orders of Council" and "prize courts"—terms that were automatically associated in American minds with British tyranny and injustice—and any one of the numerous "search and seizure" incidents could have triggered a breach with Great Britain.

In explaining why the United States and Great Britain did not reach the point of an outright rupture, historians generally credit Britain's policy of providing generous compensation for confiscated cargoes, Germany's ineptness in handling its own conflicts with the United States, and Lansing's pro-British inclinations. Coudert himself gave Lansing and Polk great credit. After the war, he said that having in the State Department these two men, "who were from first to last thoroughly imbued with the justice of the British and French cause," was the chief reason why "we got along so well with Great Britain and turned so many sharp corners when they were holding up American ships. . . ."

Also of importance, though, was the fact that Lansing, Polk, Scott, and Coudert were all international law experts, at a time when the circle of American international lawyers was small and tightly knit. Many a time before the war, they had listened to each other read papers before the American Society of International Law and debated each other in annual meetings. As international lawyers, they all recognized that when dealing with the "law" of blockades, they were in a gray area. While Coudert vigorously made the most of the Civil War precedents and Polk countered with the older case law and raised distinctions, both, as lawyers, knew that, if their clients were private individuals, they would advise them to settle out of court. Thus, by common instinct, they strove to smother the sparks of controversy in what Lansing called lawyers' verbosity and Coudert referred to as lawyers' haggling.

As friends or friendly acquaintances, moreover, they could, within limits, speak frankly with each other. As Polk would caution Coudert when it was time to "ease off," so Lansing upon occasion would warn him, when a strongly worded note was on its way, to "tell your British friends not to answer the note—not to say anything tart or disagreeable, and probably it will blow over." Coudert then would find some way to persuade Spring-Rice at the British embassy or Jusserand at the French embassy to hold their fire.

In Spring-Rice's case, this was not always easy, for the ambassador suffered from the nervous excitability associated with Graves' disease, a disorder of the thyroid. Once, for example, Lansing told Coudert, "Now, Fred, you have got to keep Springy away from me. . . . He came in here and talked war to me the other day, and after all, I'm Secretary of State. I can't have England threatening me with war! Keep him away!" So Coudert rounded up the embassy people, and they kept Spring-Rice away until he had calmed down. Another time Spring-Rice summoned Coudert to the embassy at 7:00 A.M. to inform him that the U.S. Navy was sending a gunboat manned by Germans to the Great Lakes to train its guns on Canada. "The thought went through my mind," Coudert recalled, "that the British Ambassador was losing his mind." Not knowing what else to do, he listened and listened and finally insisted on having a little breakfast. Spring-Rice exclaimed, "Is there nothing that can break your calm and your phlegm? Have you no nerves at all?" But gradually, as Coudert sipped his coffee, the ambassador settled down, until Coudert was able to slip off to the State Department and learn that what had so alarmed Spring-Rice was a planned exercise to raise a sunken boat blocking navigation. The "Germans" in question were nothing but a bunch of naval reservists from Milwaukee.

As counsel to the British and French, Coudert's role, in fact, was about two parts lawyer to one part unofficial diplomat and one part publicist. This is illustrated by the concerns that took him to England and France in the summer of 1915, braving the German submarines. The *New York Times* announced in advance that Coudert was expected to confer with the French government to resolve the issue of the *Dacia,* a German merchant ship transferred to American registry, which had been carrying cotton to Rotterdam when seized by a French cruiser. The case of the *Dacia* raised a host of legal problems, of which the most important from a diplomatic perspective was the Allies' inclusion of cotton on their contraband lists. This practice had deepened a farm depression in the South, and the congressmen from the cotton states were planning retaliatory measures against Great Britain. Unbeknownst to the *New York Times*, the major purpose of Coudert's trip, however, was not to discuss the *Dacia* with the French but to confer, at Spring-

Rice's request, with Sir Edward Grey, the British foreign secretary, on all the ramifications of the cotton controversy.

Coudert met in London not only with Grey, but with Arthur Balfour, Austen Chamberlain, Attorney General Sir Edward Carson, Lord Robert Cecil, and numerous others. Discussing Anglo-American relations with all and explaining the power wielded by the southern congressmen, Coudert must have presented the case well, for before he left, Grey had set into motion a scheme to buy up the southern cotton crop at prices that would rescue the cotton growers from their plight. Coudert, indeed, had a very cordial reception from all these men, most of whom he was meeting for the first time, and subsequent correspondence indicates that many of them, especially Balfour and Chamberlain, recognized in Coudert a source of information on American politics and public opinion well worth developing. Interestingly, although a citizen of a neutral country, he was invited to attend in London a high-level conference between representatives of the French and British foreign offices on the legal issues of contrabanding cotton, and he then went on to Paris to speak privately with the same French officials and the French foreign minister.

In France, Coudert was already a known quantity—recognized as a friend of France and, as one of his friends said, "by what you have personally done for France's afflicted children, peculiarly *persona grata.*" At the Foreign Ministry and at private dinners and luncheons, he and French officials seemed to have discussed at length the prospects for America's entry into the war, which Coudert had to explain were not good. What was said about the *Dacia* is not known, but the French prize court condemned both ship and cargo in August 1915. Whether by accident or design, the decision came down at a time when the news of the British price supports for cotton had already driven the *Dacia* off the front pages.

World War I was not the only foreign policy problem confronting the Wilson administration. On August 9, 1914, while Fred Coudert was caught up in the outbreak of hostilities in Europe, Paul Fuller, Sr., was at the White House, conferring with President Wilson on another difficult issue—U.S. relations with Mexico, where rival generals were contending for the leadership of the Mexican Revolution in the wake of the resignation of the military strongman Victoriano Huerta. Wilson had refused to recognize Huerta and had done his utmost to unseat him, to the extent of first blockading Vera Cruz to prevent arms from reaching him and then sending in the marines to occupy the port. When Huerta fled

Mexico on July 15, 1914, however, he left behind him a country torn by civil strife. Zapata's forces were strong in Morelos and Guerrero, Pancho Villa's in northern Mexico, Carranza and his right-arm Obregón controlled must of the rest of the nation, the U.S. forces were still in Vera Cruz—and no one at all in Washington, D.C., knew what was going to happen next.

President Wilson was not short on information about the various factions in Mexico, but, not sure how much any of it could be trusted, he had decided to ask Fuller to go to Mexico as his personal representative to evaluate the situation. In particular, Wilson was concerned about a report that Pancho Villa seemed to be gearing up his army, possibly for an attack on the forces of Obregón. Fuller was the president's choice for this mission because, Wilson wrote to Secretary of State William Jennings Bryan, "He is a Democrat, is full of sympathy with the purposes of the administration, and is accustomed by long habit to deal with our friends in Latin America." The president had met Fuller just a few months earlier when the lawyer had visited the White House to warn Wilson in confidence that the U.S. ambassador to the Dominican Republic was using his position to extort money from Dominicans, thus giving the administration forewarning of a scandal that was later laid open by the *New York World* and a presidential inquiry. "I formed a most delightful impression of Mr. Fuller," Wilson wrote of that first encounter.

At their White House meeting on August 9, Fuller and the president seem to have come to a quick understanding. Wilson's instructions were verbal, and no notes were kept, but Wilson apparently asked Fuller to ascertain whether Villa would restrain his troops and support an effort to establish a new government through free elections. Fuller accepted the assignment on the spot, waived a salary, and set off for Mexico almost immediately, for by August 12 he had reached El Paso by rail. Met there by a State Department agent, he continued on by train into northern Mexico to Juárez, to Chihuahua, and to Santa Rosalia in search of the general. On August 16 at Santa Rosalia, Fuller and Villa finally met and had the first of several long conversations.

The semiliterate former outlaw and the erudite New York lawyer seem to have taken to each other at once. Ostensibly, they had nothing in common. At sixty-seven, Fuller was thin, storklike in appearance, and in even frailer health than usual; he had been accompanied to Mexico by his physician—no doubt at the insistence of his wife, Leonie. Old-fashioned and somewhat ascetic in his habits, Fuller carried with him only one battered old carpetbag. His white beard and mustache were trimmed in the manner of the Second

Empire, his eyes peered out gently from behind thick glasses, and he spoke with an ornate courtesy and conducted himself with a dignity that already seemed to belong to some bygone age. He was a quixotic figure, particularly by contrast to the robust thirty-six-year-old Villa, who seemed the very incarnation of Mexican *machismo.*

But Fuller, raised by Mexicans, knew and despised the system of peonage as much as Villa did. Having experienced the great contrast between wealth and poverty from the underside, the lawyer had long ago aligned himself on the side of social justice. Fuller's youngest son, Leonce, who had been killed in an amateur hurdle race in 1911, had once been accused, as a young criminal lawyer defending the poor, of having no idea of abstract justice but rather of always being "for the underdog, right or wrong." In a memorial of Leonce written in 1914, Fuller had defended his son's and his own point of view by stating, "Justice is the perfect adjustment of relations . . .; whenever these relations result in there being an 'underdog,' the prescription is one of maladjustment, or in other words, of the failure of justice." A system like peonage, which perpetuated and institutionalized injustice, was to Fuller not an abstract but a burning wrong, crying out for correction.

Thus, Villa found in Fuller a sympathetic audience as they talked of Villa's boyhood as a *peón,* his outlawry for defending his sister from rape by a landowner's son, the course of the revolution in all its aspects. Fuller thought Villa entirely sincere in the hopes he expressed of seeing the current military anarchy replaced by a representative civil government that "will do away with privileges" and raise the people "from the condition of virtual serfdom in which they are kept." When Fuller returned to El Paso on August 19, having been accompanied by Villa for part of the journey, he carried with him the general's written pledge to this effect and his statement of "our controlling desire for a pacific solution of our difficulties. . . ." And, in fact, within a week of Fuller's departure Villa had hospitably received General Obregón and worked out a truce with him, which was the outcome Wilson had most hoped for.

On the train back to New York, Fuller wrote out his report, which included a sensitive character sketch of Villa, much quoted by later historians, which described him as "an unusually quiet man, gentle in manner, low voiced, slow of speech, earnest and occasionally emotional in expression but always subdued with an undercurrent of sadness." Fuller expected to visit his office before turning in his report, but a telegram reached him on board the train, requesting that he go directly to Washington, D.C. At the White House, he made his report in person to Wilson, who asked him now to return to Mexico to meet with Carranza in Mexico

City. Wilson was in a hurry, and, accordingly, only a few days later Fuller set off again, but this time accompanied by Leonie instead of the physician, who presumably could not spare the time for more travels. Leonie was seventy-six years old, too old, one would think, for a journey to a country torn by revolution where transportation was uncertain and often primitive. She and Paul, however, were still as deeply devoted to each other as they had been upon their marriage, and, in his state of health, she would not let him travel alone.

Fuller's second mission, lasting from August 26 to September 18, produced no pledges from Carranza comparable to those offered by Villa, and his meetings with Carranza were formally polite. Fuller expected no less, for Carranza was known to be suspicious and resentful of the least sign of *yanquí* interference in Mexican affairs. Indeed, both Carranza and Obregón stiffened when Fuller merely mentioned Wilson's pleasure at the Obregón-Villa pact. What disturbed Fuller, however, was to find that many of the men around Carranza were filled with "the spirit of proscription and revenge" against all those who had served under Huerta, no matter how inadvertently or in however minor a post. He wrote Wilson, "*Vae Vichio* seems to be the dominant note of the Southern or Mexico City faction, and the continuance by government by military decrees affords every faculty and every temptation for carrying the vengeful rule to the extreme. . . ." He also found conditions in the South far more disorderly than in the North under Villa. Carranza, he concluded, was "a man of good intentions but without any sufficient force to dominate" the worst of his associates.

Fuller had scarcely turned in his report to Wilson when it began to be attacked by Carrancista sympathizers in the United States and Mexico. The Carrancistas did not know exactly what was in Fuller's confidential report, but they seem to have had a fair idea that Fuller had a more favorable impression of Villa than of Carranza, and they asserted that Fuller, a prominent Catholic layman, favored Villa because he believed the northern general could be more readily influenced by the United States to restore the Catholic church to its old position of privilege. This was the contention of the Progressive journalist Lincoln Steffens, for example, who wrote some letters in this vein to his friends in the administration.

Yet Fuller's final recommendations were not at all what Steffens supposed. First, Fuller advised the president that the United States should not offer aid, sympathy, or recognition to any of the factions in Mexico—not Villa, not Carranza, not anyone. Rather, the president should withdraw the marines from Vera Cruz, refrain from intervening in Mexican affairs, and simply let events take their course. When some sort of representative civil government was finally formed, the United States should recognize it, of course, but in the meantime it should not favor one military *caudillo* over another. Sensitive to Mexican nationalism and pride, Fuller made noninterference the first priority.

In particular, Fuller advised that Wilson should not attempt to secure pledges of fair treatment of the church. "The wanton spoliation of church property and the persecution of priests is unquestioned," Fuller wrote, "but those now in power are not in mental condition to give the subject rational treatment, and I believe that present insistence upon any particular line of action would result in turmoil and confusion." When the courts began to function again in Mexico, Fuller expected that the church would take its complaints to the courts; but only "time, tact, patience" would ever "bring justice into this distorted and angry controversy." The entrance of the United States into the dispute would only heat up rather than cool passions, in Fuller's opinion.

Finally, Fuller warned Wilson that, although the Obregón-Villa truce was promising, there might be a long period of anarchy before anything resembling a representative nonmilitary government emerged. If there were to be further bloodshed in Mexico, the United States must accept that and leave the Mexicans to work out their own revolution, for chaos on the United States' southern border was preferable to the tyranny that had previously reigned there:

> . . . even if the triumph of [Huerta's] adversaries should be spoiled by their own dissensions or by their excesses and recognized unfitness to establish the orderly and impartial government for the establishment of which the strife was undergone, and further strife be needed to purge away unworthy ambitions and to bring to the front the saving remnant of fit and worthy men who may make a government of the people and for the people, this new sacrifice had better be borne than permit a relapse into the system which for more than a hundred years has proven inadequate for the advancement of the masses, and has brought the country to its present condition of profound distress.

This was the policy that Wilson did indeed follow, at least for a time. Evacuating the marines in November, he watched the breakdown of the tenuous accord between Villistas and

Carrancistas without taking sides, merely trying to stay informed. In January 1915 he considered asking Fuller to go to Mexico as a State Department agent but, before mentioning it to Fuller, decided the post was not prestigious enough for a man of Fuller's caliber. From time to time, however, he conferred privately with Fuller, who apparently continued to counsel patience.

There was a rising tide of protest in the United States, however, against Wilson's policy of "watchful waiting." Fred Coudert, for one, thought that by standing by and doing nothing about the anarchy in Mexico, Wilson was virtually inviting the Germans to step in and establish bases there; and Coudert was only one of many angry American voices arguing that Wilson was making a shambles of the Monroe Doctrine. Seeking a way out of the impasse, Wilson eventually agreed to Lansing's suggestion that the five ranking Latin American envoys in Washington meet to help the State Department select a faction to recognize, and he appointed Paul Fuller his personal emissary to this Five Power Conference, which convened in August 1915. Before the conference broke up, though, it was apparent that the Carrancistas' military victories had placed them in effective control of most of Mexico. Insofar as a victor was ever going to emerge, it appeared to be Carranza, and, with the somewhat reluctant concurrence of the Latin American envoys, the United States recognized his de facto government in October 1915.

The following month, on the night of November 29, 1915, Paul Fuller died suddenly of a heart attack. He and Coudert had attended a private, formal dinner that night, and "Uncle Paul" had seemed very cheerful and perfectly well when he left the company. But upon arriving at his apartment, Fuller had put his hand to his head, collapsed upon a sofa, still in his evening clothes, and was dead almost instantaneously. "I am sure it was an awful shock to everybody," wrote Fred Bellinger, a young relative who was visiting the Couderts. "Uncle Fred would not believe it at first and said, 'Why he can't be. I just dined with him.' "

Coudert himself said Fuller's death was a particular shock, "for he seemed exceedingly well and active of late." In fact, in the months before his death, Fuller had been more in the public eye than ever before in his life. In addition to his continuing role as an advisor to Wilson on Mexican affairs, he had been active in a bipartisan effort to reform New York State's constitution and had joined with Coudert, publisher George Henry Putnam, Henry L. Stimson, and a few like-minded men to form the American Rights Committee to promote the Allied cause. The very day of his death, on behalf of the American Rights Committee, Fuller had drafted a memorandum to Wilson on German submarine warfare and American neutrality. "You may be sure," Wilson replied to the committee, "that I shall read it with added interest because of the very touching and almost tragical associations connected with it. Mr. Fuller always struck me as a man intently bent upon the promotion of the real interests of the country."

It was a fair statement, but not quite broad enough. The orphan informally adopted by Charles Coudert, Sr., whose "rags to riches" saga had taken him from office boy to senior partner of Coudert Brothers, had been intently bent on promoting the real interest not just of his own country but of humanity. As a friend described Fuller at his death, he was "a scholar, a public citizen, a powerful lawyer, and an open-hearted, clear-minded gentleman, whose life was given to many good causes and whose friendship had in it a peculiar warmth. . . . He always believed that something could be done and never feared consequences." Stretching from the Mexican War to the sinking of the *Lusitania,* Paul ("Francisco") Fuller's life was an American epic.

Among the condolences Fred Coudert received on his uncle's death was a letter from his cousin the Marquis du Pont du Chambon, who wrote of Fuller's *"grand coeur, ses sentiments nobles et éléves et aussi la profonde affection, l'attachement sans bornes qu'il avait pour toute la famille"* [his great heart, his noble and lofty sentiments, and also the profound affection, the limitless attachment that he had for all the family]. Also prompt to pay his tribute was Alexis Carrel, the French biologist and surgeon who had received the Nobel Prize in 1912 for his pioneering work in organ transplants. From a chance shipboard meeting in 1906 there had grown up between Carrel and Coudert what was to prove a lifelong friendship, and Coudert had named the youngest of his four sons after Carrel. From France, Carrel now wrote of Fuller's rare combination of moral and intellectual qualities: *"Mr. Fuller était, dans las plus haute signification du mot, un juste"* [Mr. Fuller was, in the highest sense of the word, a just man].

Both du Chambon and Carrel wrote from the western front, where du Chambon, although well along in middle age, was fighting in uniform for France and Carrel, also in uniform, was operating a surgical unit and developing new methods of treating wounds. Indeed, virtually everyone Coudert knew in France was in the war in some fashion or another, even the women. The daughter of Coudert's cousin Daisy Coudert Glaenzer, for example, had charge of an ambulance corps at the front, and Constance Coudert Garrison's daughters were ambulance drivers. Even Fred's cousin

Claire, the Duchesse de Choiseul, who had resolved her financial problems by the dubious course of becoming the mistress of the sculptor Rodin and had heretofore been best known for dancing an impromptu striptease for Rodin's guests, had shown an unexpected capacity for sacrifice: she was nursing tubercular French soldiers returned from the German prison camps, work for which she would receive several medals from the French government.

Despite the total mobilization of the French people, however, the war was going badly for the Allies. Both the eastern and western fronts had turned into an indescribable slaughter, where thousands died to gain a few feet of ground that might be lost again, at equal expense, the following day. Some of this Coudert saw for himself, for, through the intervention of the minister of foreign affairs, he and his wife, Alys, were given rare, official permission to visit the front lines in the winter of 1915–16 and again in the summer of 1916. The rest of the picture, despite the censors, was sketched in for him by his relatives and friends in France. Increasingly, in 1916 the letters arriving at Coudert Brothers from France were black-bordered, and the word recurring in many of them was *fatigué*. France was staggering from exhaustion and numbness; America's help was needed.

Coudert's response was to intensify his efforts to arouse sympathy for the Allied cause. He was continually being approached by reporters, whose questions he took very seriously, preparing careful and often quite lengthy memoranda on the legal aspects of the war in advance of each interview. In addition, he was engaged in private correspondence with the editors of publications that seemed sympathetic to the Allies, presenting them with arguments that could be advanced in their editorials, and he also conducted a heavy correspondence with other leaders of opinion. He gave enough speeches during this neutrality period to fill two volumes, and he got double duty out of a number of them by having them printed in pamphlet form and sent to whatever "men of affairs" he thought might be receptive to the Allied outlook.

Throughout 1915, Coudert had his friends in France collect for him letters from soldiers at the front, and these, translated by Coudert, were published in book form in 1916, with an introduction by Ambassador Jusserand. Deeply moved by the *War Letters from France*, Coudert's friend, the philosopher Henri Bergson, told him this volume constituted a great service to the Allied cause. Coudert also got hold of some film footage of French troops, probably from the Pathé Exchange, and he showed these brief motion pictures when speaking to various clubs and gatherings. Most of all, however, Coudert was working with certain organizations, trying to rouse enthusiasm for the Allies—particularly the France-America Society, of which he was an officer, the American Rights Committee, which he had helped to found, and the National Security League.

Of these, the National Security League was the most successful. Founded late in 1914 by lawyer Stanwood Menken, the league's purpose was summed up in the word *preparedness;* the idea was to muster popular support and lobby for an increase in America's military strength. Given the widespread aversion to involvement in the European war, the league was careful not to state exactly what America was to be preparing for, but its leaders—which consisted basically of the Roosevelt wing of the Republican party plus a sprinkling of Democrats like Coudert—and most of its members were in no doubt, even in 1914, that the point of "preparedness" was to be able to step in to help the Allies, if they could not win the war on their own.

"A pretty small minority" is the way Coudert described interventionists like himself at the start of the war, but the league did make considerable headway over the next year, particularly on the East Coast. By 1916 it had acquired some five hundred thousand members and was able to stage a gigantic rally in Washington, D.C., at which Coudert was a principal speaker. "Mr. Wilson and the administration were not at all pleased with the meeting, because we went out there right under the nose of the administration," Coudert recalled. "We had a very big and successful meeting, with great applause and a good deal of newspaper notice connected with it. I know that Mr. Wilson didn't like that, because I don't think he was very friendly to me after that."

Coudert had campaigned for Wilson in 1912, had served him as a special assistant attorney general, and would in time, after Wilson's death, come to admire him again. But in 1916 the president's disapproval meant far less to him than the praise he was receiving from people like the philosopher Émile Boutroux, who wrote that his sympathy *"nous est une force en même temps qu'une joie"* [is a strength to us as well as a joy]. Moreover, Coudert was seeing a great deal of Teddy Roosevelt at this time. The ex-president, Coudert said, "was very bitter about Wilson—spoke about him in very bitter terms," and some of Roosevelt's feelings spilled over into Coudert, who thought Wilson was being too "pusillanimous" toward Germany.

If anything, Coudert took Wilson's coolness as a flattering sign that his efforts were having some effect. Similarly, he was immensely gratified when a German-American publication, *Vireck's Weekly,* put out a picture called "The Poisoned Tree," showing the

American citizens who should be hanged in Berlin for their pro-Allied activities, and he found himself dangling prominently on the tree as "Frederic R. Coudert, Counsel for Great Britain and France." Although he never said as much, one suspects he was also rather delighted when, during court proceedings in the U.S. District Court in Norfolk, Virginia, over the ownership of the *Appam*, a British passenger ship captured by the Germans, Hans Berg, the commander of the German prize crew, tried to throw a punch at Coudert, who was acting as the opposition's lead counsel.

Indications like these that his efforts for the Allies were not entirely futile were important to Coudert, for he was increasingly frustrated by the course of events. Despite small signs of widening public sympathy for the Allies, relations between the Allies and the Wilson administration were actually growing worse, not better. In deference to pressure from the United States, Germany had stopped its submarine attacks on neutral shipping, but England not only continued to seize American cargoes but had blacklisted a number of American firms, forbidding British companies to trade with them, British ships to carry their products, and British ports and fueling stations to allow entry to any ships hauling their cargoes. Wilson, asking for an increase in the appropriation for the navy, intended to provide armed escorts for American merchant shipping—a course of action almost certain to lead to war between England and the United States.

Kept busy running down to Washington, D.C., counseling on these matters, Coudert was one of the few who knew how seriously American relations with England were deteriorating. Adding to the tension under which he was living, moreover, was the danger posed by German saboteurs and espionage agents. On the night of July 29, 1916, an explosion at the Black Tom docks of the Lehigh Valley Railroad in Jersey City blew up munitions purchased by the Russian government, causing millions of dollars in damage to surrounding property and claiming several lives. This was the start of the Black Tom case, which was to have a long life in the courts and before the Mixed Claims Commission after the war, with Coudert Brothers representing the Russian interests. Immediately, however, it emphasized how important were the files at Coudert Brothers' offices, crammed with confidential information on Allied war purchases and shipments as well as high-policy matters, and intensified the firm's preoccupation with security.

The heaviest emotional burden Coudert was carrying, however, was his embarrassment at the profits America was making from the war. From his perspective, America was not carrying its share in the war for democracy; worse, it was experiencing an economic boom built on the bodies of French, British, and Russian boys. There was a sordidness about this situation that appalled him and, for a time, shook his faith in the essential decency of his own country. Coudert and his partners back in 1914 had resolved that they themselves would not profit from the agony of the Allied soldiers. Coudert, in fact, had told Spring-Rice at their first meeting that he did not want a fee, and, after Spring-Rice insisted on a retainer, had set it at a thousand dollars a month, since that was the amount he had been paid when representing his own government as a special assistant attorney general. A few weeks later Murray had arranged with the Russian government to serve for the same fee of a thousand dollars a month. There is no record of what Coudert Brothers charged the French, but since all the partners were ardent Francophiles, it is unlikely that France was charged any more than England or Russia.

To sustain a firm the size of Coudert Brothers, a partner would normally have had to generate at least thirty thousand dollars a year in fees. If Coudert, Murray, and probably Semple were spending virtually all their time on clients paying twelve thousand dollars a year, this had to mean diminished incomes all around when the members of the firm divided the profits at the end of the year. Coudert, Murray, and Semple, who held the largest partnership shares, would have suffered the greatest drop in income, but Kingsbury and Paul Fuller, Jr., would not have been unaffected. Kingsbury and Fuller junior, however, were just as committed to the Allied cause as the others. Kingsbury's talents ran to the literary and linguistic, rather than the political, but he was a great admirer of French culture. His translation into verse of Rostand's *Cyrano de Bergerac* had been recognized as the standard English-language version of the play since Richard Mansfield had used it in his 1898 production, and Kingsbury's translations of French poetry from the period of the Great War leave no doubt about where his sympathies lay. As for Fuller, France was his ancestral and spiritual home as much as it was Coudert's.

Coudert, however, was the partner who was in the public eye and who stood the abuse that came to those who advocated intervention. The National Security League leaders were said to be anxious to drag America into war in order to swell the profits of the war industrialists. Not having any war industrialists as clients and not making any money from the war himself, Coudert could shrug off such attacks, but they did not help to relieve his growing anxiety and bitterness over America's neutrality policy.

As 1916 went on its way, the death tolls mounting, Coudert

found himself increasingly on edge. At a dinner party at Lansing's house, Coudert listened to President Wilson say, almost casually, that he expected that the Allies and the Central Powers would both soon be exhausted—as if it made no difference to Wilson which won the war—and Coudert could keep himself from a rude retort only by a strong exercise of will. Thereafter, he stayed away from Wilson entirely. Knowing himself to be in an uncertain temper, he also avoided his old mentor Professor Burgess, who remained sympathetic to Germany, because he did not want to quarrel with him.

In November 1916 Emperor Carl acceded to the Austrian-Hungarian throne and shortly thereafter asked his brother-in-law, Prince Sixtus of Bourbon, who was serving in the Belgian army, to begin secretly to sound out the Allies on whether they would welcome Austria-Hungary making a peace separate from Germany. During the very earliest stages of this secret diplomacy, in December 1916, Fred Coudert was visiting England and France. "Prince Sixtus came to see me in London," Coudert recalled, "because he knew that I had means of communication with Colonel House [Wilson's representative in earlier mediation efforts] over here. Prince Sixtus was very anxious that the President of the United States should tell France and Great Britain that he was willing to back a separate peace with Austria."

Coudert conveyed the message, but his hopes of seeing the German alliance thus weakened were not sanguine, for he had already discussed the idea of a separate peace with Premier Aristide Briand. As all of these discussions were highly confidential, Coudert did not make notes about them, and he did not talk about them later until he was interviewed for the Columbia oral history project in the 1950s. By then, Coudert cautioned his interviewers, his memory was quite possibly faulty, but he recalled that Briand had said that he strongly favored a separate peace himself but that "it was impossible to do anything" with Clemenceau, who was "absolutely adamant" on the principle of unconditional surrender.

Returning to the United States by early January 1917, Coudert resumed his publicity activities on behalf of the Allies. Feverish for activity, he agreed to make an extended speaking tour of the Midwest in the spring of 1917 for the National Security League, and his speeches on this circuit have a stridency, an emotionalism, almost a desperation unlike any other of his writings. But the Germans, also hard-pressed, had resumed their submarine attacks, and it was in St. Paul, Minnesota, on this tour that word reached Coudert that Wilson had asked Congress for a declaration of war against Germany. The era of American neutrality had ended.

Chapter Nine

PROSPERITY IN
THE TWENTIES

I f I may say so," Lord Robert Cecil wrote to Fred Coudert shortly after America declared war on Germany, "I think both our countries owe a great deal of gratitude to men like yourself, who, during the delicate negotiations on the various subjects that have cropped up during the war, have always, while maintaining the rights of their own countries, shown every desire to work for friendship, and not to embitter any controversies that have arisen." Cecil, the cabinet minister responsible for the blockade, added, "I for one am sincerely grateful to you for much friendly advice, and I hope it will not be long before I shall be able to welcome you here again. . . ."

From France's Chamber of Deputies, Jean Cruppi wrote to congratulate Coudert on *"la renomme qui, dans nos deux pays, s'attache si justement a votre nom, a votre talent, a votre oeuvre de solidarité Franco-Americaine"* [the renown that in both our countries attaches itself so deservedly to your name, your talent, your work on behalf of Franco-American solidarity]. And Deputy Georges Louriac said that he thought of Coudert whenever he saw an American soldier. When would Coudert be coming to France, Louriac inquired, to see the fruit of his efforts?

There was nothing Coudert wanted more than to be back in England or France—in uniform. He had already been shelled by the Germans on one of his visits to the trenches. In London, he and Alys had heard the sounds of a zeppelin dropping bombs

192

nearby, and they had rushed to the doorway and craned their necks to see the cigar-shaped object floating in the sky. Characteristically, Coudert had run out into the street and climbed a light post to keep the zeppelin in sight. He wanted quite badly to enlist, but the U.S. Army was not interested in a forty-six-year-old. Even his efforts to wangle an appointment in the Judge Advocate-General Corps were disappointed: the army had more French-speaking lawyers than it could use, he was told kindly but firmly.

In the spring of 1917, Coudert was invited to dinner by Colonel House, and they talked about the situation in Russia, where the czar had abdicated. Elihu Root was about to head a U.S. mission to Russia to report on what could be done to support the provisional government under Kerensky. "I think," said Coudert, that House "had some idea that he might ask me to go, but evidently it would have been unwise for me to go, as people told him, for several reasons." One reason was that Coudert Brothers had represented the old czarist government since at least the 1880s and it was continuing to represent the Kerensky government. Thus, Coudert was not to have the chance to serve his nation in wartime even in a diplomatic capacity.

The Coudert who did end up serving in the American Expeditionary Force was Fred Coudert's eldest son and namesake, who was known in the family as Fritz. An eighteen-year-old sophomore at Columbia University when the United States declared war, Fritz was tall, athletic, and "a vigorous out-of-door man," but he had trouble with the army's eye exam, and it took some string-pulling by neighbor Teddy Roosevelt to get him a second lieutenant's commission. Shortly after his twentieth birthday, Fritz sailed for France as a first lieutenant and company commander, and he saw service in the front line. On his first leave after the Armistice, however, he dashed for Paris, and on December 4, 1918, he reported from the premises of Coudert Frères: "Have had a long chat with dear old Peartree. He is such a good fellow! The office, according to all accounts, is doing remarkably well and is running like clockwork." A week later, in another note home, Fritz wrote, "Mr. Peartree continues in good health and good humor. Business appears to hum; the place is full of clients."

Mr. Peartree's health was of considerable interest, for the other senior partner Henry Cachard had retired the previous year. Charles B. Samuels had gone over to Paris from the New York office in 1915 to help with the workload, but even so the Paris office was understaffed and overburdened. It could not be otherwise, for Coudert Frères, as the leading American law firm in France, was handling legal matters for the U.S. government, the embassy, the American Navy, the American Army in France, and the Red Cross. The military alliance between France and the United States and the presence of the U.S. Army in France raised every conceivable kind of legal difficulty, and Coudert Frères was called upon to advise on many problems.

For example, the American entry into the war meant that the French government could now borrow directly from the United States government and issue bonds against this indebtedness. John B. Robinson, the junior partner at the Paris office, served as the advisor to the United States on the first bond issue. As he recalled:

> I was requested to examine into the validity of these bonds and reported I found them illegal, which created some disturbance in the French Finance Ministry.
>
> I then talked with Mr. Clunet, the well known specialist on international and administrative law, who first thought I was wrong and then that I was right as the French authorities had proceeded in the same manner as they always did when a bond issue was made for the requirements of the annual budget. But the law or decree authorizing them to borrow from the American government merely authorized the borrowing of such amounts necessary for the National Defence, or words to that effect, without stipulating any amount, whereas, in the case of bonds issued under the requirements of the budget, the amount is always specified. There should have been a law, or at least a Government decree, fixing the amount to be borrowed.
>
> Finally, the US Government was satisfied with a simple letter from the Minister of Finance, Mr. Klots (who knew little about finance) stating that the matter was in order (which, of course, it was not!).

The New York office, meanwhile, was similarly overwhelmed with work. Munitions purchases declined after the United States entered the war, because the production of the Allied factories had finally increased sufficiently to meet much of the demand, but there were protracted negotiations for the British, French, Belgian, and Italian governments regarding other war contracts and shipping matters, alien property seizures, loans, and various contracts. This business continued to occupy Coudert, Semple, and Murray full-time throughout 1917 and 1918.

As for the other partners in the New York office, Charles B. Samuels had been in Paris since 1915; Howard Thayer Kingsbury had been commissioned a captain in the New York National Guard artillery and in December 1917 was made a major and judge advocate in the guard; and Paul Fuller, Jr., was in Washington, D.C., simultaneously holding down three interrelated government appointments. Specifically, Fuller junior was serving as director of the Bureau of War Trade Intelligence, which scrutinized applicants for export licenses to ensure that U.S. goods did not reach enemy hands; as acting director of the Bureau of Enemy Trade, which had similar purposes; and as a member of the Censorship Board, representing the War Trade Board.

These were not Fuller's first government appointments. He had spent a few months in the fall of 1915 as U.S. commissioner to Haiti, shortly after President Wilson had sent in the marines to take over that country. The seizure of Haiti represented one of Wilson's experiments in "missionary diplomacy," of which the objective was to prevent U.S. businessmen, working in collusion with local politicians, from robbing the island blind. Fuller's task at that time was to obtain the signature of the new Haitian president, installed by the marines, on a treaty giving control of Haiti's customhouse to the United States and then to set up an honest administration of the customhouse and introduce procedures intended to put Haiti's fiscal affairs in good order. His service as "Envoy Extraordinary" was brief, but apparently sufficient to imbue Wilson with confidence in his abilities, leading to the wartime appointments two years later.

In 1917 Fuller, his wife, and their five small children moved to Washington, D.C., for the duration. The children realized, of course, that the move was connected with their father's government job, but they never knew what exactly that job was. He did not talk about his work, for Fuller was serving, in effect, as head of one of the major U.S. intelligence agencies in World War I. A precursor of sorts of the Central Intelligence Agency, the intelligence bureau that Fuller directed had hundreds of agents, open and undercover, around the world, particularly in neutral countries, gathering information on the enemy, conducting investigations, and trying to penetrate the efforts of enemy firms to disguise themselves. This information was exchanged with the intelligence divisions of the army, navy, and Department of Justice, and Fuller also had access to European intelligence information through his seat on the Censorship Board. His discretion was so complete, however, that he never offered any anecdotes about his job, even to his family, and took its secrets, which must have been many, to his grave.

Having only three active partners put a real strain on Coudert Brothers. "We were quite overwhelmed with [government] work," Fred Coudert would recall, "and were unable to give necessary time and attention to smaller and more insignificant matters, especially as there was a shortage of younger men in the office." Fortunately, there were three senior associates—James Barclay, James Hopkins, and Charles A. Conlon—all of whom were overage for the army. In fact, these three were the same age as the partners and had started working for Coudert Brothers in the 1890s. All three were essentially specialists in estates, trusts, accountings, and investments, and they did most of the work for the firm's individual clients during the war. As a result, Barclay and Hopkins would become partners of the firm in 1919, and Conlon was promoted to a status that gave him a listing on the firm stationery and considerably more money in 1920. Nonetheless, because of their high-minded patriotism, which limited what they were willing to charge for war-related work, never had the Coudert Brothers or Coudert Frères partners worked so hard to earn so little as they did between 1914 and 1918.

By the end of the war, Fred Coudert, in particular, had nearly worked and worried himself into the grave. Fred Bellinger reported to his cousin Fritz that at Christmas 1918, "Uncle Freddy" had had a small tree, but "he looked very tired and very old." Coudert was only forty-seven years old, but he had not exercised regularly since the war began, had dropped virtually all amusements and pleasures, and had been working around the clock for more than four years. The old insomnia was back in full force, and his vision was full of dark and apocalyptic forebodings about the world's future, for he was certain that the decision not to invade and occupy Germany was a major mistake and no lasting peace could arise under the circumstances.

Examining him, Coudert's doctor told him, quite bluntly, that unless he changed his entire life-style, he could expect to be dead within a year or two. Coudert had to relax, take a vacation, get regular exercise, and learn to manage stress better. It would not be the last time that a hard-driving Coudert Brothers litigator was warned about his physical condition—in this century an astonishing proportion have died in early middle age—but Fred Coudert actually took his doctor's advice. Intensity would always be a part of his character, but in 1919 he returned to siphoning off some of that competitiveness into physical activity. In the summer of 1919, with his brother-in-law Thomas Riggs, Jr., who was governor of Alaska Territory, and his son Fritz, Coudert went on a hunting and camping trip in the Alaska wilderness. He took up golf, which turned into a consuming passion; he became highly proficient at figure skating; and he began to fence again. As a fencer, one of his sons would recall, Coudert displayed such concentrated ferocity that he sometimes made his opponents more than a little nervous, but he enjoyed himself; and with his returning good health came a revival of his good spirits and optimistic outlook.

At the same time as Coudert was determinedly restructuring his personal habits, the firm also began to enjoy a revitalization. In both cases, it took several years to throw off the effects of the war, but by the early 1920s the Paris office was booming, and the New York office was more than making up for the financially lean years of World War I.

In a formal sense Coudert Brothers and Coudert Frères were not the same firm in 1919, and, in fact, they had been distinct entities for a good many years. Sometime after Henry Peartree joined the Paris office, probably in the 1890s, a French partnership (*société en nom collectif*) had been formed under the name of Coudert Frères to conduct the business in France. The French regulations of such partnerships proved cumbersome, though, and Coudert Frères was reorganized as an American partnership during or just before World War I. The New York partnership of Coudert Brothers was one of the partners in Coudert Frères, contributing the name and assets and receiving in return a 10 percent distributive share of the profits; the remaining partners were the individual senior attorneys in the Paris office.

On a day-to-day basis, however, the two partnerships presented themselves to the world as if they were simply branch offices of the same firm. The New York and Paris letterheads carried the addresses of both firms, and in correspondence the attorneys on both sides of the Atlantic almost invariably spoke of "our New York office" and "our Paris office." Using systems set up by the original Coudert brothers, the two offices tried to stay coordinated, informing each other of new matters received, for example, and numbering the cables and letters they exchanged. Since dozens of cables and letters went back and forth between the offices each week, the numbering system was forever breaking down—generating a heavy correspondence between staff members in which each politely but vigorously sought to cast all blame upon the other. The method of charging for the cables also prompted proposals by the Paris office for improvements in the system, which were strongly opposed by Florence Bainbridge, the cashier in the New York office, because they would ease the life of her Paris counterpart but produce more work for her. The staffs obviously knew each other's systems intimately and thought of themselves as members of sister entities.

Indeed, Coudert Brothers and Coudert Frères were siblings, for both were ultimately controlled by the same "family" partners, who, after 1915, were Fred Coudert and Paul Fuller, Jr. Even though Coudert and Fuller were not personally partners in Coudert Frères, the two partnership agreements interlocked and were so structured as to give them final say on every important decision on both sides of the Atlantic, and jointly they controlled the names of both firms, their leases, and their assets. Furthermore, the partnership agreements had short terms ranging from two to five years, and upon their expiration Coudert and Fuller could reorganize each firm, inviting into partnership with them whomever they wished at the same or new levels of shares. Thus, the cousins could also make and unmake partners, and they controlled the allocation of profits. In actual practice, they exercised this power only in consultation with and upon the agreement of the other senior attorneys, but they were, in the final sense, the heads of both firms.

The essence of the situation, then, was that, in terms of authority, Coudert Brothers and Coudert Frères were truly branches of the same family firm. Where the legal distinction between the two made a great difference, however, was in the distribution of profits, for each partnership kept its own earnings, aside from the 10 percent paid by Paris to New York. Thus, the fortunes of the Coudert Frères and Coudert Brothers partners could and often did vary widely, and in the postwar years it was Coudert Frères that first experienced a boom in activity.

This might seem an anomaly, given France's exhaustion by the war. In May 1920, Fred and Alys Coudert flew across the English Channel to France, and they noted from the air that the evidence of France's sufferings was still abundant eighteen months after the Armistice. In Paris the talk they heard was mainly of the high taxes, massive unemployment, lack of coke and coal, and declining value of the franc.

Nonetheless, Coudert Frères had plenty of work, partly because the drop in the franc's value against the dollar, to just one-third of what it had been before the war, had turned France into a paradise for Americans. The long-standing expatriate colony of Americans swelled in the 1920s to some fifty thousand residents. According to John Dubé, who worked for Coudert Frères in the 1920s, a retired U.S. Army officer at that time could afford a villa in the south of France, a maid, a cook, a chauffeur, and possibly a pied-à-terre in Paris. "He could never have lived like that in New York," Dubé said. "That's the real reason so many Americans were there." And being there, they made wills, got married, signed contracts, bought property, transferred securities, got into automobile accidents—and generally created business for their lawyers. Most of this business went through the hands either of Coudert Frères or the S. G. Archibald office, which was the successor to the practice Edmond Kelly had set up after he left Coudert Frères in the 1880s. There was a strong sense of rivalry between the two firms, but, according to Dubé, it was Coudert Frères that got the most profitable business. Henry Cachard had established Coudert Frères as the attorneys of "all the important French society people, the wealthiest Americans, the best English families" in France, and John B. Robinson successfully built on this foundation throughout the 1920s and 1930s.

As senior attorney at Coudert Frères after Henry Peartree retired in 1920, Robinson was a towering figure in the firm—not only metaphorically but literally, for he was well over six feet tall. Wearing a mustache, carrying gloves and walking stick, turned out in impeccable tailoring, Robinson made an impressive appearance, and his ability matched this surface distinction. Insofar as he had a specialty, it was wills, estates, and trusts, but his real genius, according to one of Fred Coudert's sons, was that "he knew all the combinations of French and American law and how to make them work together." In this ability, he was "one of the greatest" in the firm's history.

"People had confidence in his integrity," Dubé said, and, to illustrate the point, he recalled an occasion where Robinson had acted for "some California movie people" in negotiations for the purchase of a patent from a French company: "By Friday we had concluded all the details and were ready to sign the contract on Saturday. The Frenchman said no, he'll sign on Monday, Saturday he fishes. The Americans were appalled; they had to be in London on Monday. So the Frenchman, not willing to give up his fishing, shrugged and asked John Robinson to take his power of attorney and sign for him. And that's what happened. They both had Robinson as their attorney. Everyone had such confidence in him, you see."

Robinson always had one or two partners at Coudert Frères, but the partners tended to come and go. In the 1920s, for example, Charles B. Samuels returned to the New York office, Joseph DuVivier left, eventually to start his own practice in Paris, and Hugh A. Baynes retired after four years. Robinson, therefore, was the constant at the upper level, supervising a large staff of younger lawyers. By 1922, in fact, Coudert Frères had ten associates, including Russell I. Hare and Watson C. Emmet, who would later become partners themselves, L. L. Autie, Grier Bartol, Leon Fraser, P. Maillard, Roland S. Palmer, Charles L. Ronsseray, and Maurice Sadron. Cesar Eram, a French attorney, provided advice on matters relating to French law, and a Frenchwoman, Mlle. Drouville, who was a notary, attended to some of the French legal business with Eram.

According to Dubé, everyone in the office loved Robinson, who had an intangible quality of leadership that made people work for him willingly. Still, it appears that Robinson himself was never quite happy with the administrative responsibilities that were his lot. Indeed, he did not much care for the "business" side of the law at all. He never carried a business card, his files were seldom up to date, and he threw correspondence that came into the office into a basket on his desk, where it would sit sometimes for days on end. "He had one critic only, his secretary, Madame Bazin," said Dubé. "She couldn't stand the way he would let letters go unanswered. But he would smile at her and stretch his hand over that basket on his desk, and say, 'Why, I have everything under control. It's all here, right under my hand.' "

Nonetheless, the staff, including the long-suffering Madame Bazin, stayed with Robinson for years—and the clients flocked in. The majority of new clients registered by the Paris office in the 1920s were individuals, including various Whitneys, Drexels, Guggenheims, Vanderbilts, Gulbenkians, Wanamakers, and the like, as well as numerous individuals with less famous names but perfectly respectable assets. Although Coudert Frères was consulted on every kind of issue, from a dispute with a dressmaker to a suit for alienation of affections to the recovery of a loan made to dancer Isadora Duncan, the bulk of the business these individuals brought in related to wills, estates, and trusts. According to the firm's records, well over half of the estate matters originating in the Paris office during this period were also worked on by the New York office, suggesting that many of them probably posed issues in the conflict of laws.

Since the founding of Coudert Frères in 1879, the conflict between French and American laws of succession had generated considerable business for both offices. At the heart of many of the problems they jointly confronted was the doctrine of *renvoi*, which Fred Coudert once summarized as follows:

A is an American domiciled in France, leaving property both there and in the State of New York. His succession is opened in New York either by the appointment of an administrator or the probate of a will. The New York law says that devolution of his property, testate or intestate, is determinable by the law of his domicile, and refers the matter to French law. The French courts hold that it is determinable by the law of his nationality, which is American, and refer the question back to the law of New York, as that of his nationality. The New York court might, of course, refer the matter back to the French law . . . and the legal lawn tennis might go on forever.

In practice, however, the New York courts by 1919 generally attempted to apply French domestic law in such cases. A typical Coudert Brothers case, therefore, might involve the Paris office being retained to write the will for an American resident in France, the New York office in due course submitting the will to probate in New York, the Paris office providing evidence of the testator's domicile, preparing papers, and briefing when necessary on the French law of succession, and the New York attorneys handling the New York court appearances. Almost as often, though, the firm had to deal with the problem in the reverse form of a French national domiciled in New York at the time of his death, in which case New York would claim jurisdiction because of the decedent's domicile and the French courts by virtue of his nationality.

Although a great many of these estate matters were cut and dried, the law in this area was not completely settled. Indeed, Coudert Brothers had helped to unsettle it in 1913 when it won a celebrated case, *United States Trust Co. of New York v. Hart,* in which an American was held to have been domiciled in New York even though he had lived abroad for thirty-two years before his death and had no trace of physical residence in New York, aside from a club membership. Thanks partly to *Hart,* there was continuing uncertainty as to how the courts might rule in any given case. Moreover, Coudert Brothers frequently dealt with cases involving unusual facts that didn't fit what rules had evolved. Writing to his son Fritz, who was then in law school, Coudert described one such case in 1921:

> . . . I have before me the question of whether a man could acquire a new domicile without ever having had a fixed habitat, *i.e.,* a Frenchman who has spent thirty years in the United States, living in various hotels or lodging houses a night or two at a time. Lawyers seem to differ on this, but I incline to believe on general principles that a domicile could be so acquired if intention existed to throw off the old domicile and to remain within the United States *as a whole.*

The firm's principal experts in these matters were John B. Robinson in Paris and Lorenzo Semple and Fred Coudert in New York, for whom the conflict of laws of succession represented an endlessly fascinating jigsaw puzzle. Given large assets, it was a game that could also be enormously lucrative, as demonstrated by the Jacques Lebaudy estate. The son of the French "Sugar King," Lebaudy had headed a private armed expedition to North Africa in 1903 and set himself up there as "Emperor of the Sahara." Ousted by French troops, he removed himself to the United States and took up residence in Long Island. Coudert first met him when Lebaudy visited 2 Rector Street and offered him the chief judgeship of the Sahara. "It was evident," Coudert wrote later, with considerable restraint, "that Mr. Lebaudy was a highly eccentric character," and on his next visit to France, Coudert called on Lebaudy's sister and brother-in-law, the Count and Countess de Fels, to apprise them of the "Emperor's" condition. "They could do little," Coudert wrote, "but asked that they be kept informed regarding him, and the family kept in contact with the Coudert office."

On January 11, 1919, Lebaudy was shot and killed by his wife, and the Countess de Fels asked Coudert to take charge of the estate, which was valued at $7.5 million. Charles B. Samuels, appointed co-administrator, "gave unremitting attention" to the administration of the assets, which were located in France, Chile, England, South Africa and other parts of the British Empire, as well as in the United States. Samuels's administrator's fees eventually brought $118,636.49 into Coudert Brothers' coffers, but the firm made even more from its legal services, which ranged from negotiation of a settlement with Lebaudy's common-law wife and daughter to representing the heirs before the U.S. tax commissioner to the actual surrogate court proceedings. With Coudert Brothers receiving $350,000 and Coudert Frères $50,000 for their services, the firm made over $500,000 all together from the Lebaudy estate.

Hard on the heels of the Lebaudy fee, moreover, came the payment in the Gould estate suit, which began in 1916 as a suit by the younger children of Jay Gould questioning their brother George's management of their father's estate. By the time the litigation ended eleven years later, the Duchess of Talleyrand (neé Anna Gould) and her brother Frank had triumphantly extracted some $16 million extra out of the estate. The lawyers' fees seemed so fantastic at the time that Alexander Schlosser gave them considerable space in *Lawyers Must Eat*, his 1933 recounting of the "most lucrative lawsuits in history." According to Schlosser, Coudert Brothers received $151,999.98 at the final settlement in 1927 for its representation of the duchess. But that was only the final payment.

The firm's records are incomplete, but it appears that over the years it made at least $200,000 and probably more from the suit.

Another area of the Paris practice that took off after World War I was corporate work, for the changing economic conditions attracted American companies as well as individuals. Corporations like General Motors, Western Electric, Frigidaire, Du Pont, 3M, ITT, and others set up European subsidiaries in the 1920s with the help of Coudert Frères. The head of Western Electric's legal department, for example, came to Paris in 1927 to consult Coudert Frères about conforming its distribution contracts to French law, then retained the firm to organize subsidiaries in France and Italy, and ended by "borrowing" John Dubé for a year and a half, during which time the young lawyer set up operations for the company in all of Latin Europe and the Near East.

It is significant that when Western Electric's business had reached the point of threatening to absorb all the time of a Coudert Frères attorney, Robinson suggested that the company take one of his men onto its payroll. In fact, Dubé's recollection is that Robinson offered Western Electric its choice of either Bartol or himself—both quite promising associates. This generosity on Robinson's part meant, of course, a loss of fees for Coudert Frères, and to understand it, one must realize that Robinson came of age in the 1890s, a time when some of the best legal minds were maintaining that a lawyer could not be truly professional while devoting all or almost all his time to one client. The financial dependence on the client, it was felt, would compromise the attorney's independence and place him in a master-servant rather than a professional-client relationship. Robinson, at any rate, kept at arm's length from corporate clients and was proud to state at the end of his life that he had never served on a corporate board of directors, except that of the Guaranty Trust.

There were, however, corporate clients that Robinson enjoyed working with. He had a strong interest in the arts, and he gave considerable personal attention to clients like Durand Ruel, dealers in oil paintings and other artworks, and to the firm's many clients in the motion picture industry. These included such companies as Paramount Studios, United Artists, Société des Grands Cinemas Français, and Permolin Film Corporation, as well as individual producers like Charlie Chaplin. Robinson's objective was not to contain Coudert Frères' surging corporate practice, but to keep the firm from becoming dependent on a few corporate clients.

The third area of the Paris practice that exploded under postwar conditions was that of loans by U.S. banks to European governments and corporations. World War I left the United States a creditor nation for the first time, and the capital flow reversed direction across the Atlantic, bringing considerable business to Coudert Frères. Some of this originated in the New York office, but most of it came directly to Coudert Frères from such investment banking houses as Dillon Read & Company, Chase Securities Corporation, Wood, Gundy & Company, and Marshall, Field, Glore, Ward & Company. Coudert Frères advised on issues to the Czechoslovakian and Polish governments, to Silesia, to the cities of Genoa, Barcelona, Cologne, Milan, Soissons, and Rome, to the Paris subways (Métro and Nord Sud), the Italian State Railways, and such entities as the Italian Public Works Credit Consortium and the Union of Hungarian Mutual Credit Associations. There were bond issues and mortgage loans as well for private French companies such as Cie Parisienne de Distribution d'Électricité and the Compagnie Nationale du Rhône. Even the General Transatlantic shipping line—which had disappeared from Coudert Brothers' client list "in the Silurian Age," as Fred Coudert phrased it— showed up again in connection with a proposed $7.5 million bond issue.

All this activity turned the postwar era into a golden age, quite literally, for the Paris office. In 1922, when its fortunes had not yet reached their height, Coudert Frères made a net profit of $312,748, after all expenses and salaries. After paying 10 percent to the New York office, this left the three partners—Robinson, Baynes, and Samuels—with $281,478.20 to be divided among themselves. Robinson almost certainly made more money each year throughout the 1920s and 1930s than any of the New York partners, including Fred Coudert and Paul Fuller—which seems not to have bothered the latter two in the least. Coudert and Robinson were described by one who knew them both as being "like brothers," and Coudert was only too pleased to have someone in the Paris office whose integrity, ability, and leadership were of the first order.

At any rate, the Paris attorneys lived well in the period between the wars. Eventually Robinson would purchase a château in the countryside and indulge his appreciation of the arts by furnishing each room in antiques from a different period in French history. Even a relatively junior associate, Leon Fraser, could enjoy France to the fullest on his salary, given the exchange rate. In 1922, at age thirty-two Fraser found himself "the confidential adviser of Morgan partners and other international money men. He lived in a fashionable apartment in the Étoile section of Paris and every morning rode in the Bois de Boulogne, on at least one occasion with the Prince of Wales."

Fraser at this time was one of the young men helping Bayne and Robinson work out the terms of American loans to European governments, and his remarkable life story would become the subject of a two-part *New Yorker* profile by Matthew Josephson in 1942. Not the least extraordinary thing about Fraser's life was the fact that he worked for Coudert Frères at all, for in 1917 he had been eased out of a Columbia instructorship in political science by several trustees, including Fred Coudert. At the time, which was immediately after the United States entered World War I, Fraser was one of the campus's most vocal pacifists, and Coudert and a few other trustees had refused to renew his contract because of his very public antiwar sentiments, which they believed to be damaging to Columbia's reputation. The distinguished historian Charles Beard had thereupon resigned in protest, and Fraser became overnight a powerful symbol of martyrdom in the cause of academic freedom. While quantities of ink were spilled on his behalf in Greenwich Village and Morningside Heights, however, Fraser quietly enlisted as a private in the army, saw action in France, and emerged from the war a holder of the Distinguished Service Medal with the rank of major. By 1922 the erstwhile pacifist was acting director of the Bureau of Veterans Affairs in Washington, D.C., and bored with the job, while Coudert, who had kept track of Fraser, was regretting the role he had played in 1917.

Coudert had not had a change of heart with respect to the principles he thought were involved. Indeed, when discussing the "Fraser case" in his eighties, he reaffirmed that the welfare of the university had sometimes to take priority over academic freedom: "We're all for academic freedom, but I don't think you want to go into a university or a school just for the purpose of pulling it down. . . . I think there's a kind of implied contract. You have to do what's best for the University." This was an attitude very typical of nineteenth-century Ivy League college graduates, who tended to be intensely protective of their alma maters and to continue to regard them as small, vulnerable, and easily destroyed by public opinion, long after they had grown into major institutions. For example, Coudert's language almost exactly parallels that used by Justice Oliver Wendell Holmes, Jr., in a private letter written in 1919, counseling young Felix Frankfurter to stay aloof from a controversy over academic freedom then raging at Harvard Law School: "Martyrs I suspect generally are damned fools. . . . Of course, I believe in academic freedom, but on the other hand it is to be remembered that a professor's conduct may affect the good will of the institution to which he belongs."

In any event, while not backing down on the principle,

Coudert clearly felt that it had been misapplied in 1917. Fraser came up to see him, and the next anyone knew Coudert had arranged for Columbia to present him with an alumni medal and Fraser was working for Coudert Frères. It is not clear, however, who approached whom about the job. According to Josephson, "Whenever Coudert was asked how it happened that the firm employed Fraser, he just said, 'Oh, boys will be boys.' " As for Fraser, he went from Coudert Frères to a position as general counsel to the Dawes Plan, then helped to establish the World Bank in 1930, and returned to New York in 1933 to become president of the First National Bank, then one of the giants on Wall Street. At this stage in his life he told some old Columbia friends that one thing he had learned was that "the academic men tended to oversimplify the motives of men of affairs"; it was a statement that might stand as a summary comment on his relationship with Coudert.

While Paris prospered in the 1920s, the New York office also did well financially, although it is difficult to say exactly how well because of the way it kept its books. Seventy years after the founding of the firm, Coudert Brothers was employing the same antiquated "balance sheet" bookkeeping system it always had, but with two important differences. One was that the partners personally did not keep the central ledger; all entries in that volume for the 1920s are in one hand, that of the cashier, Florence Bainbridge. The other is that Miss Bainbridge did not enter all receipts as they came in. Instead, monies received, while recorded promptly in the separate client ledgers, were often transferred to the central ledger only when they were needed to balance a debit, such as a disbursement or a distribution of profits. As a result, the central ledger no longer presented an up-to-date, comprehensive picture of the firm's finances, and a partner who wanted such a picture could either pick his way through all the hundreds of separate client account books—or he could go down the hall and ask Miss Bainbridge. The true running account of how the firm was doing was not in the central ledger but in Miss Bainbridge's head.

Presumably, when Miss Bainbridge was first promoted to cashier, someone must have checked her accounts, but in time she was given complete trust, which, in fact, she amply deserved. In private life, Miss Bainbridge was actually Mrs. John Kinghorn, but she was always Miss Bainbridge at the office, and she reminded some of a Victorian spinster schoolmarm, principally because of her fierce rectitude and her "no nonsense" attitude. If Miss Bainbridge said something was so, it was, and if she said she would do something, it was done. The partner who went over her books after her retirement in 1969 found that her entries were absolutely reliable, even though by then she was well up in her seventies, and throughout her life, Miss Bainbridge apparently never had an "off day" when it came to fulfilling her duties to the firm.

By the late 1920s, Miss Bainbridge was not merely the cashier but, to all intents and purposes, the financial officer of the firm, and the partners relied upon her entirely as both employee and friend. John P. Murray, for instance, had only two children, both of whom were mentally retarded. He loved his daughters dearly—"I thank God every day for those two little girls," he once told a friend—and he made careful arrangements to provide for them after his death. There were trusts to pay for their care, an institution run by nuns had been selected, with much thought, to look after the girls, and a guardian named. But, in his will, Murray asked Miss Bainbridge to visit his daughters frequently, and he empowered her, if dissatisfied with how they were being treated, to make any new arrangements she thought best. Miss Bainbridge was then a relatively young woman, only in her thirties, but that was how deep the partners' trust in her ran.

Since Miss Bainbridge's central ledger from the 1920s does not show the firm's complete income, however, it is impossible to state with certainty how much profit was made. At an educated guess, though, in 1922 when Coudert Frères showed a profit of $282,478.20, Coudert Brothers' profit was probably somewhere around $430,000. But the Coudert Brothers' partners earned less on a per capita basis than the Coudert Frères partners did, because there were so many more of them. During most of the 1920s there were seven partners in New York (or eight, if Samuels was there) compared to three in Paris (or two, if Samuels was in New York). In fact, Coudert Brothers was rather overstocked with partners after Hopkins and Barclay became members of the firm in 1919.

By then these two had each spent a quarter-century of honorable service as associates and had carried the load when the firm was short-staffed during the war; to invite them into the partnership was the obvious and decent thing to do. Coudert Brothers, however, did not add more associates at the same time. During the immediate postwar years, the American economy went through a recession as wartime commodity prices collapsed, and Coudert Brothers, not having made much money during the war, was cautious about restaffing at the associate level. By 1919, therefore, the New York office had lost its "pyramid" shape of a few partners at the top supported by many salaried juniors. This was a change that had actually been evolving for some time, partly because of the fading out of the real estate practice, but it is in 1919 that the ratio—

which seems to have been about one-to-three in the 1880s and approximately one-to-two at the turn of the century—had clearly dropped to nearly one-to-one, where it would stay for many decades.

One other obvious change in the firm's postwar practice was the lessened importance of consular work. This was probably connected with the U.S. Supreme Court's decision in *Rocca v. Thompson* in 1912 that allowed the State of California to refuse to honor the right of consular officers to administer the estates of their deceased nationals, even though that right was embedded in treaties that would ordinarily, under the Constitution, take precedence over state statutes. Coudert Brothers had been on the losing side of this case, and Fred Coudert, for one, was absolutely baffled by the outcome. The decision by the California court he attributed to the xenophobia in California at the time, which was mostly directed at the Japanese. "The present case was in litigation at or about the time when the Japanese school question was of paramount interest in the State of California," he wrote, adding that "the atmosphere of the State of California may have insensibly caused its learned courts to gravitate" toward a view hostile to foreigners' treaty rights. Coudert in 1914 rather presciently described the "attitude adopted, especially by the legislators and people of California as to the Japanese people" as "an attitude so incompatible with their dignity and so insulting to their civilization that, if continued in, it may well result in an attack on us." Coudert thought this attitude "a supreme folly," but it at least offered some explanation of the lower court's decision. That the U.S. Supreme Court upheld the California court's ruling, however, he could not understand at all.

Around the time of the *Rocca v. Thompson* decision, Coudert had been reading intensively the works of his friend Henri Bergson, the philosopher who stressed the importance of the irrational in human affairs. Addressing the American Society of International Law that year, Coudert stated that he could only attribute the Court's decision to a majority having fallen under Bergson's spell. Elaborating this theme, he sent his fellow lawyers into convulsions of laughter, for every lawyer at some point has suffered, or thinks he has, from irrationality on the bench—but the implications of the *Rocca v. Thompson* decision were not funny for Coudert Brothers. If consular officers could no longer administer the estates of their nationals who died in the United States, they would not be hiring Coudert Brothers to help them with these estates or, even more importantly, recommending Coudert Brothers' services to the families of the deceased. In one blow, *Rocca v. Thompson* deprived the firm of what had been, almost since its founding, a very nice source of referred business. Coudert Brothers remained counsel to the British and French consulates in New York until well into the 1930s, but the connection was then definitely more honorary than remunerative.

Nonetheless, the estates and trusts practice continued to provide a steady flow of income, as it always had, as well as such occasional dazzling windfalls as the Lebaudy estate fees. Estates and trusts work permeated the firm, in that virtually every partner was an administrator, trustee, or fiduciary of one or more estates or trusts, while the estates also were a source of work for the litigators. There were four partners, however, who specialized in this area: Semple, Samuels, Hopkins, and Barclay. Although Semple was the head of the Estates and Trusts Department, a considerable portion of his practice actually consisted of providing help with investments to what law firms and banks today like to call "high net-worth individuals." The nature of this service is suggested by a letter the firm received in 1916 from a French client, who at the time he wrote was shivering in a rat-infested trench under shell fire:

> Will you remind me kindly to Mr. Semple. Will you also please tell him . . . that I want to profit of the actual good form of the American market. I want him to make as profitable investments for me as he possibly can. . . . Interesting speculations can be made at present on steel and cotton. Mr. Semple being a Southerner must be well acquainted with everything concerning cotton. I leave it to him to act to the best of my interest, for you understand I am not in a position out here to give any direct orders; you may even wonder that a man who may be shot any day should bother about business matters; *mais bah! on n'y a pense pas* and it is really too bad to let go such good chances as are offered at present by the American market. . . . So please show my letter to Mr. Semple so he may do his best for me.

Samuels also had wealthy clients whom he shepherded through political and domestic upheavals, although after 1919 he seems to have spent most of his time on the Lebaudy estate. But Hopkins, known as "Hoppy," was strictly an estates and trusts man. A "down-to-earth" person, modest and unassuming, he handled mostly the routine affairs. Barclay, too, did only estates and trust work. A Scot by birth, Barclay had a brilliant intellect; he had studied Greek at the University of Edinburgh when its classics department was at its height, and for many years he was the regular reviewer of Italian publications for the *Journal* of the American Society of International Law. A small man, somewhat bent over, he delighted in accountings, which he prepared in a miniscule, spidery handwriting. Peering at the books through his steel-rimmed glasses, he was precise and painstakingly careful, charming to deal with but inclined to shy away from any real responsibility. Also working most of the time on estate matters was a very senior associate, Charles Conlon, and several junior men, including Thomas W. Kelly, a Fordham University graduate, who would turn out to be the future leader of this department.

The bulk of estates handled by the department were modest in size; many must have been between $10,000 and $30,000, for the records are full of fees of just a few hundred dollars. And at least one trust, which produced over $40,000 a year for its beneficiary, brought only $500 a year to the firm for its administration. The firm charged $10 for preparing an individual income tax return in the 1920s, $250 for a complicated estate accounting, and probably did quite a lot of work for its most valued clients for free. The volume of activity, coupled with the big, dazzling fees from estates like Lebaudy's, was presumed to compensate for the firm's low charges. Although Fred Coudert at one point did try to get his partners to set their minimum fee at $25, Coudert Brothers went right on writing wills for only $10 up to World War II. "We did that as a loss leader, to get the business," according to his son Ferdinand, who was an associate in Estates and Trusts in the late 1930s.

The firm's other major specialty in the 1920s remained litigation. The cases argued were diverse, for Coudert's own interests were broad and he had no desire to confine himself to any one corner of the law. Even though his heart was in the field of international law, he joked in 1927 that it alarmed him to hear himself described as an international lawyer: "When another lawyer says that to me in a public place, I feel he is aiming to get away with some of my best domestic clients." Thus, the cases that Coudert, Kingsbury, and Murray argued in the 1920s and the fees they received were extremely varied. They included, for example, $10,000 for representing Louis Comfort Tiffany in a riparian rights suit against the town of Oyster Bay, $29,500 for arbitration of a Costa Rican claim, $11,950 for representing Crucible Steel Corporation in a commercial dispute, $49,500 for patent and trademark work for Botany Worsted Mills, and around $100,000 for representing the Countess Niel in an estate suit.

Multiplying these figures by eight gives a rough idea of their purchasing power in the 1920s, as well as an appreciation of the compliment paid to Fred Coudert when he walked into a congressional hearing room in 1922 and one onlooker turned to another and speculated that Coudert was probably getting paid five to ten thousand dollars for his testimony. "It is always delightful to have some people think you are worth something," replied Coudert.

Most of the firm's litigation was in the lower courts, but Coudert Brothers did have four major U.S. Supreme Court cases in the decade after the war. One of these was a late straggler in the firm's line of Insular cases, *Yu Cong Eng et al. v. Trinidad, Collector* (1926), in which Coudert successfully argued that a Philippine statute prohibiting Chinese merchants from keeping their accounts in their own language was a violation of this minority group's right to equal protection of the laws. In the others, Coudert Brothers represented the British government in various matters arising from the war itself. The *Muir* case (1921) concerned the liability of merchant ships that had been commissioned by the British government to carry supplies during the war. The key question was "how far, if at all, they were subject to the ordinary processes of the court." Coudert successfully maintained that ships, when operated by the government, were "akin to public vessels and not subject to ordinary process." Since governments were increasingly operating businesses, Coudert thought this case had some interesting implications beyond the admiralty aspects. And in *Strathearn Steamship Company, Limited v. Dillon* (1920), the provision of the Seaman's Act of 1915 protecting seamen's rights to draw a portion of their wages before the end of a voyage was held applicable to foreign seamen on foreign vessels visiting U.S. ports.

The most widely publicized of these U.S. Supreme Court cases was the *Disconto-Gesellschaft* case (1925), in which Coudert argued that certificates of stock are not merely documents serving as evidence of the ownership of shares but are themselves property—a fundamental point in commercial law. The case arose when the British public trustee, acting as alien property custodian, had seized from Germans at the beginning of the war endorsed certificates of stock ("street shares") in United States Steel Corporation and had asked the company to transfer ownership to its nominees. U.S. Steel refused, responding to demands by the German owners who contended that their actual shares in the company were intangible and the certificates were simply paper. Judge Learned Hand in a full opinion in the U.S. district court found for Coudert's client, the British public trustee, and his decision was upheld by the Supreme Court in an opinion written by Justice Holmes.

Coudert was particularly pleased at the outcome in this case, which affected the ownership of some $50 million of stock, because the public trustee had not asked any lawyer other than Coudert for an opinion but had relied entirely upon Coudert Brothers and its presentation of the case. The barrister for the public trustee, Chetham Strode, came over to hear the Supreme Court arguments. When they were finished, one of the judges—whom Coudert was too discreet to name—sent a note by page across the courtroom to Coudert. It read, "I congratulate the King in having such a competent advocate in his cause." Coudert, of course, promptly passed the note over to Strode: "I thought that would be very useful to me when I came to settle with the government for the fee."

Coudert Brothers' retainers from the British and Russian governments, adjusted slightly upward to $1,250 a month to account for postwar inflation, continued to around 1923. As Coudert's comment suggests, however, the firm also collected separate fees for the litigation it handled. There is no record of how much Coudert Brothers finally charged the British public trustee, but it billed the Russian government more than $125,000 during the 1920s for its work in the Black Tom explosion cases.

The Russian government in this instance was not the Bolsheviks, who came to power in November 1917, but the Kerensky regime, which had briefly attempted a constitutional rule of Russia between the fall of the czar and the Bolshevik Revolution. The United States recognized the Kerensky government-in-exile as the legitimate government of Russia until 1933, and, as far as the State Department was concerned, the diplomatic representative of Russia was Boris A. Bakhmeteff, the University of Moscow engineering professor whom Kerensky had appointed ambassador to the United States. It was on behalf of this government-in-exile that Coudert Brothers sought to collect damages from the Lehigh Valley Railroad for the Russian-owned munitions and supplies destroyed in the Black Tom dock explosion. Losing on the liability issues, the railroad vigorously contested the legitimacy of Bakhmeteff and his successor through two appeals, for nearly $2 million was at stake. Coudert Brothers, however, defeated its opponents every time, deftly utilizing the distinction between state and government that Coudert had perfected in the Insular cases. Although in a different guise the dispute went on into the late 1930s, the Lehigh Valley paid the full claim in the late 1920s.

In a way, Coudert Brothers was acting in the Lehigh Valley matter on behalf of the U.S. government as well as the Russian government, for Bakhmeteff had agreed that any damages collected would be paid to the U.S. government in partial settlement of the loans that the United State had made to Russia in 1917, which the

An artist's impression of Charles Coudert, Sr., as a French soldier, from an unsigned, undated sketch in the family's collection.

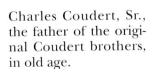

Charles Coudert, Sr., the father of the original Coudert brothers, in old age.

Charles Coudert, Jr., the brother who applied his mercantile training to the law.

Louis Leonce Coudert, the youngest brother, who established the firm's office in Paris.

New York, August 30, 1879

Dear Sir

We have opened a branch office in Paris

Communications relative to European

business may be addressed to

"Coudert frères,

3 Rue Scribe,

Paris,"

as forwarded through us

Yours, etc.,

Coudert Brothers

Counsellors-at-Law,

68 and 70 William St.

N. Y.

Announcement of the opening of the Paris office in 1879.

Frederic René Coudert, the leader of
the firm, in the 1860s.

Frederic René Coudert presenting his argument in a consular
law case in the 1890s.

Leonie Coudert, sister of the firm's founders, in the 1860s.

Illustration from the New York *Evening Post* profile of Paul Fuller at the time of his diplomatic mission to the Mexican revolutionary factions.

Leonie Coudert Fuller and husband Paul Fuller, at a Paris cafe in the 1890s.

Nora Coudert, in mourning for her husband Louis Leonce Coudert.

Elizabeth ("Lizzie") Coudert, in the 1890s, when the newspapers were predicting she would make a stunning Washington society hostess should her husband Frederic René Coudert be appointed to the U.S. Supreme Court.

Robert Chesebrough, founder of Chesebrough-Ponds and inventor of Vaseline, turned to Frederic René for help in securing an invitation to exhibit his products at the Paris Expo. Charles Coudert's wife, Marie, sits immediately to Chesebrough's right.

Frederic René Coudert's only surviving son and namesake, at the time of his graduation from Columbia University at age 19.

Fred Coudert as a young cavalry officer at the outbreak of the Spanish-American War.

RUE DE RIVOLI

Sir Philip Burne-Jones sketched himself as a middle-aged adjunct to one of Fred and Alys Coudert's energetic tours of Paris, for the amusement of Fred's parents back in New York.

Frederic René Coudert poses behind his desk in the late 1890s, flanked by his son, Fred, and a bearded male secretary.

Frederic René ("Fred") Coudert in 1912, already well established as the second-generation leader of the firm.

Benjamin Franklin Tracy, former Secretary of the Navy, served in an "of counsel" capacity and fostered the career of his granddaughter's husband, Fred Coudert.

James Richards, the first Coudert Brothers partner who was not a relative.

Paul Fuller, Jr., a formal portrait from the 1930s.

John B. Robinson took over as head of Coudert Frères after World War I.

MR. COUDERT EXPLAINS NEW ORDER IN COUNCIL

SAYS THERE IS TO BE NO CHANGE IN PRESENT PRACTICE.

Authority on International Law Comments Upon Declaration of London —Says It Is Not Law, and Is Being Used as a Convenient Manual of Maritime Belligerent Law — The Doctrine of Ultimate Destination.

Frederic R. Coudert, an auth ternational law, was asked yes representative of The Journa

Newspaper headlines reflect the various roles Fred Coudert played as legal advisor to the Allied governments during World War I.

NIEUW AMSTERDAM STEAMS.

Mr. and Mrs. F. R. Coudert and Mrs. Bayard Taylor Among Eighty Americans Aboard.

Colonel S. Listoe, the American Consul General at Rotterdam, was a passenger on board the steamship Nieuw Amsterdam, of the Holland-America line, when she steamed from her pier in Hoboken yesterday. Colonel Listoe has been in Washington for several weeks on leave of absence and is returning to his official duties. The Nieuw Amsterdam carried 89 first, 100 second and 200 third cabin passengers. She had a cargo of 12,000 tons and there were 80 Americans aboard.

MUST BE LEAGUE OF NATIONS OF SOME KIND, URGES COUDERT AND OTHER LEADERS TO WORLD

International Lawyer Declares It Is the Result of Logic of Events Rather Than of the Will of Statesmen or of the Theories of Political Philosophers—Julian Street and John Hays Hammond Urge Great Caution in Drawing Terms of Any United States of Nations—Lawrence Abbott Gives Sturdy Support and Mrs. John F. Yawger Opposes.

The second Frederic René Coudert, on the occasion of his fiftieth wedding anniversary in 1947.

Fred Coudert, golf-
ing in the 1920s with
his youngest sons,
Alexis *(center)* and
Ferdinand.

Congressman Frederic
René ("Fritz") Coudert,
Jr., and his son, Frederic
René Coudert III (also
known as "Fritz"), in the
1940s. Direct descen-
dants of the founder, they
were the third and fourth
generation to carry on
his name and practice.

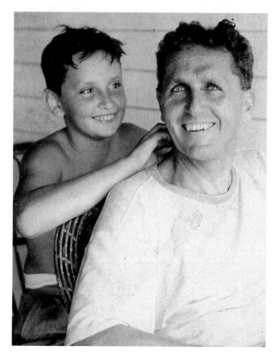

Alexis C. Coudert, who led the firm's international expansion in the 1960s and 1970s.

In a firm of generalists James E. Hughes, Sr., concentrated on a commercial law practice.

Carleton G. Eldridge, Jr., and E. A. ("Mike") Dominianni, on a business trip to Israel.

Allen H. Russell, visiting London on business in the 1970s.

Charles Torem and Alexis Coudert, at the one hundredth anniversary party for Coudert Frères in 1979.

President Jimmy Carter and Ambassador Sol M. Linowitz, at the time of the Panama Canal Treaty negotiations.

James B. Sitrick, Chairman of the firm's Executive Committee, 1982–93.

Inset: 38 Broadway, New York, in the 1850s, housed the first Coudert law office. The Grace Building *(on the left),* which houses Coudert Brothers' New York office today.

Communists refused to recognize. Thus, the certified check from the Lehigh Valley Railroad was endorsed over to the U.S. government, which ended up the main beneficiary.

The "big cases"—the ones involving constitutional issues and public policy matters—remained very near to Coudert's heart, and the firm's strength in this area was a source of pride. Yet while Fred Coudert continued to conduct a practice very similar to what his father's had been, the world was changing around him. Under Fred's leadership, the firm had been tidily profitable; indeed, the partners who retired at the end of the 1920s seem to have done very well from their association with Coudert Brothers. Murray left an estate of over $1 million, for example, and Samuels purchased a gentleman's farm in his native Virginia with his savings. Still, other downtown firms were growing much more rapidly.

Even before World War I a number of law firms had caught up to Coudert Brothers in size, including Sullivan & Cromwell, White & Case, and the Cravath firm. During the 1920s these firms far outstripped Coudert Brothers, particularly in the number of associates employed, which is to say that just as Coudert Brothers was losing its "pyramid" shape, other downtown firms were beginning to bulge at the bottom as Coudert Brothers had once done. In total number of lawyers, Sullivan & Cromwell, White & Case, Cravath, and Davis, Polk, among others, were roughly two or three times the size of Coudert Brothers by the end of the decade.

These were all "Wall Street" firms, in that their important clients consisted of investment banking houses, railroads, utilities, and other large publicly traded American companies. In fact, many of them exemplified the dependence on one client that Robinson so dreaded. Thus, according to Cravath's historian, "much the greater part of its income" came from supervising issues of railroad securities for Kuhn, Loeb & Co. The fortunes of Davis, Polk (formerly Stetson, Jennings & Russell) were intimately tied to J.P. Morgan & Company and its investment banking arm, Morgan Stanley & Co., and White & Case got much of its business from Bankers Trust, to name just a few examples.

What kept these firms expanding in the 1920s was, of course, the great bull market of 1923–29, during which new corporate offerings increased fourfold to $9.9 billion, new state and municipal offerings nearly tripled to $1.5 billion, and the number of foreign issues also tripled to $1.25 billion. By the 1920s corporate law—especially the branch known as securities law—was obviously the field to be in, in terms of profitability. Actually, that much had been obvious for years. Even in 1910 Fred Coudert had observed, somewhat regretfully, that "the prizes of commercial and industrial practice have become, owing to industrial development, much greater than those of the forum." Since, in America, money tends to attract status as a magnet attracts iron filings, by the late 1920s success in litigation was no longer the key to prestige in the profession; the criteria had shifted to a firm's list of corporate clients. As compared to the nineteenth century, it was a sort of borrowed prestige: the more famous the client, the more highly regarded the firm. Lawyers began listing their corporate directorships and the names of their chief corporate clients in the legal directories. In a genteel way, there was a race on, not just for fees but for status.

Whereas Coudert Frères's corporate clients were predominantly American blue chip companies, the corporate client list of the New York office in the 1920s was almost entirely made up of U.S. subsidiaries of French companies. It was Paul Fuller, Jr., whose practice concentrated on servicing these corporations. A charming, urbane man, with a great ease of manner and—not incidentally—a perfect command of French, Fuller junior had the same "wonderful touch" with clients that had distinguished his uncle Louis Leonce, as well as a high degree of competence in general commercial law.

His client list included, for example, Michelin Tire Company, which paid him a regular four-thousand-dollar annual retainer throughout the decade for counsel regarding its New Jersey factory. For Coty perfumes, Fuller set up a U.S. manufacturing subsidiary in 1922, in which the major shareholders were François Coty and his longtime U.S. agent Benjamin Levy. For a final fee of ten thousand dollars, Fuller prepared the shareholders agreement, by-laws, and other corporate papers, hired and supervised outside counsel in the re-registration of the trademarks and patents, edited the new contracts for the sales force, and otherwise did very much the same kinds of things Coudert Brothers would do today in the same situation. One significant difference, though, was that the tax advice provided was directed entirely to estate taxes; even though the United States had an income tax by then, its bite was apparently not sharp enough to be worth worrying about. In its first year of operations, Coty, Inc., produced sales of $1.2 million, showed a good profit, and provided Fuller, its corporate secretary and general counsel, with business for many years thereafter.

Fuller's largest client in the 1920s, however, was the well-known newsreel producer Pathé Exchange, Inc., which, together with its various affiliates, paid him a regular retainer of $3,750 a quarter. When the original French owners sold out to American investors, Fuller was appointed president of the company, with the full approval of his partners, for Pathé generated a tremendous amount of legal business. There were continual lawsuits or threatened lawsuits with distributors, agents, producers, and the motion picture industry's various censorship boards, as well as a good deal of lobbying for lower customs duties on film. The movie industry in these early days was both turbulent and litigious, and Pathé produced nice fees throughout the 1920s, the high point perhaps being 1921, when Coudert Brothers received $42,500 and Coudert Frères $1,750, in addition to Fuller's $15,000 retainer.

Though select, the corporate law component of Coudert Brothers' practice was also small—so small that Fuller had time for a considerable list of individual clients. One of these was Prince Louis of Monaco, who appointed Fuller his consul general in New York City in 1920. After all its decades of consular law practice, the firm greatly enjoyed having one of its own acting as a consul, and one of the first things Fuller did was give a dinner for his fellow diplomats. This was a tremendous success, Fred reported merrily to his son Fritz, with Fuller "lording it over" the firm's old friends and clients, the British and French consuls, on behalf of the little principality.

Between the prince of Monaco and the Pathé Exchange, however, there was no comparison in terms of income to the firm. If Coudert Brothers was not to be increasingly eclipsed by other firms, it would have to expand its corporate business, and one person in the firm who may have seen this, perhaps a little more clearly than his elders, was Fritz Coudert, for it was he who was responsible for introducing into the firm in 1927 two men to expand and reinforce the corporate practice—Thomas K. Finletter and George S. Montgomery, Jr.

After being discharged from the army, Fritz had collected his Columbia B.A. degree by passing special examinations offered to returning servicemen and had entered Harvard Law School. It was at Harvard that he met Montgomery, an editor of the *Law Review.* A native of the Dakotas who had studied at the University of Alberta before coming east to attend Dartmouth, Montgomery was a colorful character—"sort of a swashbuckler," according to one present-day partner—and he had had an adventurous World War I career as a U.S. naval aviator, losing a leg but beating the odds that killed most of his fellow pilots.

Montgomery and young Coudert parted ways when Fritz transferred for his final year of law school to Columbia, which had outstanding courses in international law that were not available at Harvard. But they met up again a year later when both joined Cravath, Henderson and DeGersdorff as associates. A big "factory" firm, Cravath had eight partners, thirty-three associates, and seventy nonlegal staff members in 1923. One of these associates was Thomas K. Finletter, the scion of an old Philadelphia family who had taken both his undergraduate and his law degrees at the University of Pennsylvania, although his studies had been interrupted by service as a field artillery captain in the war. Five years older than Montgomery and Fritz, Finletter was already married, to a daughter of conductor Walter Damrosch. Anything but a swashbuckler, he was a prematurely balding, scholarly man, with a reserved manner; some thought him rather cold on first acquaintance.

Montgomery and Finletter were at Cravath as their entry step toward a career in corporate law. Fritz, however, had pretty much made up his mind as a teenager that he would be a litigator, carrying on the family tradition. In fact, he and his cousin Frederic Coudert ("Scip") Bellinger seem to have made a pact that when they grew up, they would not only become lawyers but join the family firm together. Thus, from France in 1918, Fritz admonished one of his younger brothers to study hard because "Scip and I will be very lonely without you in Coudert Brothers." It was felt, however, that it would be a good idea for the young men to get a portion of their training elsewhere, as Paul Fuller, Jr., had done in his time. Accordingly, Fritz entered Cravath, never meaning to stay.

Cravath had nothing to offer a future litigator. It did not even have a litigating partner, and the associates spent their time mostly drafting securities documents. After a record short stay of exactly three months, having remained just long enough to get the measure of the place, Fritz resigned to begin work at Coudert Brothers. But obviously he kept in touch with Finletter and Montgomery, and in 1927, when a wave of retirements swept through the New York office, he suggested their names as replacements for the outgoing men. As a result, Finletter came into the firm as a partner in 1927, bringing with him several clients, including Consolidated Laundries, Inc., a large commercial New York laundry, and Montgomery became a senior associate, under an arrangement whereby he received a percentage of the firm's profit.

This was an unusual move for Coudert Brothers, for it was the first time that the firm had ever gone outside its own ranks to create a partner—aside from Lorenzo Semple, who was virtually family. In a firm as small as Coudert Brothers, where partners were made only infrequently, the selection of a partner was a grave decision, not undertaken lightly. That Finletter was invited into the firm suggests a serious desire to expand the corporate practice. It would be some years before the corporate clients would outnumber the individual clients—indeed, at times, the rate of change would seem almost glacial—but with the addition of Finletter and Montgomery in 1927, the first deliberate step had been taken in this process of transformation.

Besides Finletter and Montgomery, five other men were made partners between 1927 and 1929 as Murray, Samuels, and Semple retired and Barclay resigned. By the time this grand shuffling was completed in July 1929, the firm had eleven partners, seven of whom were in their thirties. They included Fred Coudert, age fifty-eight, his cousin Paul Fuller, Jr., forty-eight, and Fritz, thirty-one, who together as the "family partners" controlled 52½ percent of the shares and constituted the management of the firm. Howard Thayer Kingsbury, fifty-nine, and James Hopkins, fifty-seven, were the other remaining partners of Fred Coudert's generation, and promoted from associate status were Mahlon Doing, thirty-four, a Cornell Law School graduate with a tough analytical mind who took over Murray's insurance practice; Thomas Kelly, thirty-six, who specialized mostly in estates and trusts; Percy Shay, thirty-five, who Fred Coudert thought was one of the best brief writers in the firm but who spent a good part of his time assisting Fuller on Coty's affairs; and Scip Bellinger, thirty-six, who, with Fritz, handled much of the trial work in the lower courts. The ink was barely dry on the new partnership agreement when the stock market crashed in October 1929, so it was this group of predominantly young men who would see out the Depression together.

Chapter Ten

FAITH DURING
THE THIRTIES

In 1928 at the unveiling of a portrait of his father's friend Judge Edward Patterson, Fred Coudert reminisced about his youth and those evenings, two or three times a week, when the judge and his father used to relax in the Coudert library after dinner and canvass legal questions in light of their knowledge of philosophy, history, and culture. To them, he recalled, the law was "a great department of human activity which possessed the highest interest in itself. It was no commercialized job by which a man earned his living. I hardly ever heard those good men discuss the money side of the law—the side to which we must all give attention to be sure— but which they in those delightful conversations never adverted to. A legal problem was a great living, dignified thing, full of intellectual interest. . . ."

This comment is profoundly revealing of Fred Coudert's own attitude toward money. Like his father, he enjoyed having a substantial income and knew how to live well, but the making of money was simply a duty that a man owed to himself and his family. To him money was a prerequisite: the goal was the leading of a cultured, intelligent life. Coudert was interested in the firm, involved in his cases, but his great joy was discussing ideas with writers, jurists, scholars, and others of an intellectual bent.

For over thirty winters, up to the eve of World War II, for example, there gathered for dinner almost every Tuesday night at the Coudert home at 124 East Fifty-sixth Street a group of close friends whom Justice Benjamin Cardozo, one of the regulars, dubbed "The Philosophers." The central group, aside from Cardozo, included the scientist and natural philosopher Alexis Carrel; Father Cornelius Clifford, a brilliant Oxford-trained priest with a facility for ancient languages; and, after 1917, Boris Bakhmeteff, who eventually became a U.S. citizen and wrote standard works on hydraulic engineering. Joining them from time to time were such notables as Columbia's president Nicholas Murray Butler, Cornell historian George Nelson Burr, the French philosophers Henri Bergson and Émile Boutroux, the poet Alfred Noyes, and various French and German professors and thinkers. The caliber of the group is suggested by the fact that, on the evenings when Carrel, Butler, and Bergson were all present, the Coudert home had three Nobel Prize winners sitting down to dinner at the same time.

After he moved to Washington, D.C., to serve on the U.S. Supreme Court, Cardozo missed these weekly gatherings at the Couderts', and he wrote to Fred, "It makes me swell with pride to think that I was privileged so often to dine with so notable a group of philosophers and savants. Perhaps a few of us—like myself—were philosophers only by brevet, but the trappings and decorations of the title were precious none the less." Cardozo was usually able to return from Washington, D.C., however, for the luncheon that Coudert gave annually at his summer place in Oyster Bay in June, after the Supreme Court had adjourned. This was an occasion for judges and lawyers only, and the guest list varied. Chief Justice Charles Evans Hughes was frequently there, as well as Justice Harlan Fiske Stone, who had previously served as dean of Columbia Law School, Justice Learned Hand from the U.S. Court of Appeals, and such leaders of the New York bar as George Wickersham and former presidential candidate John W. Davis. These June sessions went on until World War II, the judges having, as Hughes said, "a delightful day" meeting with old friends, and their host having a chance to discuss legal ideas and philosophy informally with some of the best legal minds of his generation.

Although Coudert was willing to explore and debate just about any topic, the intellectual area of the law that most concerned him in this interwar period was the development of effective mechanisms to avert a repetition of the horrors of World War I. Was it possible to create a law for humanity? And how could it be developed and supported? These were the questions that preoccupied him, quite apart from the cases that came his way in regular practice. A champion of the concept of the League of Nations even before World War I had ended, Coudert remained for more than fifteen years a persistent and steady advocate of American membership in the league and the Permanent Court of Justice at the Hague, popularly known as the World Court. He was a founder and later the president of the New York branch of the League of Nations Association, and, as chairman of the New York State Bar Association's Committee on International Law, he led in obtaining that body's repeated endorsements of American adherence to the World Court. He expressed the same concerns through such organizations as the International Law Association, the American Society of International Law, and the American Academy of Political Science. All together his writings and speeches between 1919 and 1939 fill seven volumes, and nearly 80 percent of this material concerns the League and international peace.

In a tribute paid to Coudert after his death, it was said that he had been an "influential" spokesman for the League, but, in fact, the shell of American isolationism was so strong between the wars that neither Coudert nor anyone else ever succeeded in putting the slightest dent in it. Although the U.S. presidents and their secretaries of state in this period were usually internationalists, the majority controlling Congress accurately reflected the isolationist sentiments of the electorate and prevented American participation in both the league and the World Court. This was a political problem, and, controlling no bloc of votes himself, about all Coudert could do was to keep trying to shift public opinion through his speeches and to provide his friends in policy-making positions with sympathy and moral support.

Those friends, though, were numerous and very highly placed. From letters written to Coudert by General Henry T. Allen, the commander of the U.S. occupation forces in Germany, for example, it appears that Coudert was being used as a sounding board and source of advice during the reparations crisis of 1921–23 by both Harding's secretary of state Charles Evans Hughes and the French Socialist prime minister Aristide Briand. Coudert's efforts to explain the French point of view on reparations and other postwar problems would eventually result in his being appointed a Commander of the Legion of Honor in 1933. Several notes also survive from the 1920s and 1930s warmly addressed to "My dear Fred" from the British Conservative prime minister Stanley Baldwin, which express such sentiments as "You have saved the sanity of a Prime Minister," "You never fail me in moments of crisis," and "If you are still in London [next Wednesday], what a joy to see you!" During these years Baldwin was settling Britain's war debt with the United States and trying to get the United States to take a more responsible role in Europe, so that it seems quite likely that Coudert was providing Baldwin, at the least, with a sympathetic understanding of his problems in dealing with America's obdurate isolationism.

Coudert also did not hesitate to use his affiliations to help his friends in power. Among the letters from 1931, for example, is one from Coudert's old friend Henry L. Stimson, who was then Hoover's secretary of state. Writing confidentially, shortly after the Japanese invasion of Manchuria, Stimson noted that the State Department had been working with the League in trying to solve the dispute but the "peace machinery which Western nations have hammered out in our various treaties does not fit these three governments [USSR, Japan, China] much better than a stovepipe hat fits a naked African savage." Stimson concluded with the statement "I hope our peace people at home will be reasonable about such a difficult situation. They are not always reasonable." Taking this as a call for help, Coudert immediately organized the passage of a resolution by the League of Nations Association in support of Stimson. He moved rather quickly, for less than three weeks later Stimson wrote to express his appreciation of the resolution, adding, "I should also like to thank you for the personal support you have given to my efforts."

In 1932, before the Manchurian crisis had run its course, Coudert still had hopes that the League could contain belligerents, and, as an early supporter of Franklin Delano Roosevelt's candidacy for president, he tried to persuade Roosevelt to advocate openly the United States' admission to the League. Roosevelt rightly regarded that, however, as a form of political suicide. His intention was apparently to do exactly what he did do after the election: have the United States participate in virtually all the League's activities without actually becoming a formal member. "My method will get us there faster," he told Coudert in 1932. "Think that over and for heaven's sake, maintain your faith. . . ."

By 1935, though, it was evident to Coudert that the democracies in the League had no intention of taking a firm line against Germany, Italy, and Japan. The question seemed to be, he wrote then, not whether there would be a war, but whether it would break out sooner in the East or in the West. As the United States passed the Neutrality Act, denying aid to any belligerent regardless of which party had started the conflict, Coudert stepped up his writing and lecturing, arguing that this neutrality policy not only would prove futile in averting war but was likely to encourage further aggression. He felt that some show of determination and force by the democracies was needed; among the various ideas he played with was an Anglo-American naval agreement, a military alliance among England, France, and the United States, and a collective embargo by the three nations on trade with aggressors only. With regard to the last idea, he wrote, "A policy so outlined will not guarantee certain peace, but it will, at least, not allure us into a false security—that this nation can live and prosper regardless of what is happening in the rest of the world."

Coudert made these statements, probably not coincidentally, at a time when Baldwin was struggling to rearm Britain and, as prime minister, find some backing, whether from France or the United States, for a tougher stance toward Italy and Germany. Indeed, Coudert's thinking was closer to Baldwin's than perhaps to that of any American political figure, but, then, his acquaintance with Baldwin went back a long way. The connection was actually a family affair begun in the early 1890s when Fred's father had struck up a friendship with Sir Philip Burne-Jones, son of the Pre-Raphaelite artist. A kind, delightful man, who embellished his letters to the Couderts with charming sketches, "Sir Phil" took a great liking to young Fred. Fred and Alys visited Burne-Jones on their belated honeymoon, and his London home thereafter served as family headquarters on all trips to England. Burne-Jones and Baldwin were cousins—cousins who were deeply fond of each other—and, thus, Fred Coudert knew Baldwin from those halcyon years of peace before 1914, although it was in the fevered days of the war that their friendship ripened and found a basis apart from their affection for "Sir Phil."

As Baldwin's most recent biographers have pointed out, the prime minister was a very special type of conservative, in that he was sensitive to the moral challenge of socialism and led his party into accepting a certain measure of state control of industry. Coudert was of a same ilk; he thought socialism an impractical idea—he once said that no one familiar with Tammany Hall hacks could possibly want to put control of the economy wholly into politicians' hands—but he also saw, as far back as the turn of the century, the clear need for government regulation to protect the poor and weak. Thus, when many of Coudert's friends were recoiling from Roosevelt as from a viper because of his New Deal economic policies, Coudert was describing him as "our capable and most lovable President." Paul Fuller was also a New Deal Democrat, and one of his sons-in-law can remember Fuller being cut dead at a private club by fellow members who hated Roosevelt for his "betrayal" of capitalism. Both Fuller and Coudert, however, dismissed this sort of attitude as mere class antagonism.

Still, like a true conservative, Coudert resented government encroachment upon the individual. Prohibition, for example, infuriated him, as representing an attempt by the federal government to invade the privacy of the home and regulate every American's dining habits. Exactly how fired up he got is evident in the report of his testimony before the House Judiciary Committee in 1930 as a director of the National Association against the Prohibition Amendment:

> It was a belligerent tone, bristling with defiance of the law, which Frederic R. Coudert, New York lawyer, refused to accept as a law.
>
> Mr. Coudert, who said he appeared before the committee to voice his own convictions, "regarding this miscalled amendment," asserted that it had been "engendered in a war enthusiasm and passed, I believe, unfairly and at the behest of an honest but fanatical, and therefore highly dangerous and organized minority, ecclesiastical and otherwise."
>
> Members of the committee had little success in interrupting the New York attorney, whose close-cropped gray hair almost bristled at times as he argued in an earnest, rasping voice. He was interrupted frequently by the applauding audience, and especially when he contended that the Eighteenth Amendment was "a bloc opinion, a religious opinion—a piece of fanaticism."

Social experiments like Prohibition, Coudert thought, should be confined to the states; to foster such experiments was one of the purposes of the federal system. And when Coudert broke with Roosevelt, the breach came in 1937 over the president's "court packing" scheme, which Coudert believed would have made a shambles of the checks and balances among the executive, legislative, and judicial branches and thus edged the United States closer to the vulnerability to mass hysteria evident in Germany and the USSR.

Like Baldwin, Coudert was most truly the conservative, however, in his values. He was a child of the nineteenth century, and words like *honor, decency,* and *moderation* meant a great deal to him. He developed an intense dislike for ideologues, whether Communists or Nazis, because of their worship of force and the Absolute State, their contempt for individual liberty, and their persecution of others on the basis of race, religion, or class. Most of all, Coudert missed the easy uniform assumption of the prewar world that the traditional values of Western civilization were praiseworthy and correct, and he wanted to see those values conserved and applied to modern circumstances.

For someone of Coudert's outlook, therefore, the entire sweep of events between 1919 and 1939 was almost consistently depressing, for international affairs did nothing but go from bad to worse. Coudert was beset by personal problems as well. For one thing, he had been one of those convinced that the Dawes Plan would stabilize the world economy and that the American stock market's rise was underlaid by a real prosperity. "You can't go wrong on America," he told a British friend, and he invested in common stocks a good portion of his savings and of the inheritance he received after his mother's death in 1925. Like many others, he even bought some stock on margin, and, accordingly, he spent the long Depression years watching his savings shrink as the stock market kept ratcheting farther and farther downward. Also profoundly worrisome was the illness of his second oldest son, Tracy, who suffered a nervous breakdown as a teenager in 1919 and, thereafter, became more and more disoriented and anxiety-ridden until he was finally institutionalized. The initial symptoms were uncannily similar to those a McCredy aunt had suffered in 1879, but medical science, and Fred himself, seemed helpless to check, much less reverse, the problem.

Troubled by all these matters, Coudert refused to let them get him down. He always had faith that someday Tracy might improve, and he certainly held onto his love for his son. One of the lawyers in the firm can remember Coudert radiating a quiet happiness one day in the 1930s as he packed up to leave the office early. "I'm going to see Tracy," Coudert explained, alight with anticipation. As for the stock market, Coudert never quite gave up hope there either. "It is rather shocking to have the Chase Bank at 75 and Steel at 100," he wrote in 1931, "but I believe they will both come back, although the process must be slow." A year later, when things had gotten worse, he wrote, "If something is not done in the way of cooperation with Europe and matters continue as they are, it may be necessary to have a moratorium on debts in the next few months, otherwise everybody whose home is under mortgage or who owes any money will be ruined. However, there is nothing to do but to carry on and remain cheerful. In the meanwhile, I am very hopeful that the good sense of the American people may finally reassert itself and that they will act intelligently. . . ."

"My father," said his son Ferdinand, "was an optimist, really quite an irrepressible optimist. He was, I think, in his way, quite a brave man." Home movies of Coudert from the early 1930s, when he was in his sixties, show him in his prime and they reveal something of the strength of personality that allowed him to dominate any setting, whether a congressional hearing room or the firm's offices. With piercing eyes under shaggy brows, Coudert is magnetic on film; he draws the eye even when surrounded by his much taller, more handsome sons. The personality that attracted so many friends is also obvious, particularly in one sequence where Coudert is walking along the top of a Roman wall in the south of France. The primitiveness of the camera introduces a speeded-up jerkiness to his movement, not unlike that of the early silent movies, but even so the impression is one of authority and dignity. As Coudert draws near the camera, however, he pauses, suddenly grins straight at the lens, and jumps into the air, waving his arms above his head in a bit of unabashed clowning.

That boyishness, which persisted well into old age, must have had much to do with his ability to hold onto a positive outlook and keep trying to improve matters. "I have faith and hope," he said once, as the world lurched toward disaster, "and I cannot believe that ignorance and prejudice, super-nationalism and parochialism can win in the long run. I believe that they can hold their own like bigotry and religious hatred and persecution of race against race for a long time, because the brute inheritance is an old story and it is slow in being shaken off, but it is and must progressively be shaken off."

Coudert's vigorous optimism, his civic and intellectual interests, and his friends in elevated places had a very decided influence on Coudert Brothers in the 1930s, for they were important in helping to create a high internal morale. Whether his younger partners and the staff members shared Coudert's political views—and many did not—they were still enormously proud to be associated with him. There was a solid satisfaction in knowing that whenever their senior partner left for or returned from Europe, reporters would be down at the pier to question him on his view of the European situation. When the newspapers speculated over whether Coudert would be asked to serve as secretary of state in 1933, when he gave a keynote address on Lawyers' Day at the New York World's Fair, or when he lectured at Oxford University on the U.S. Supreme Court's decisions in the New Deal cases, everyone's pride in working for Coudert Brothers went up another notch. And although the firm took it for granted at the time, in retrospect it is quite clear that it made a difference that the mood prevailing at the top of the firm during the Depression was not one of sourness or despair but of confidence—on however thin the evidence—that the world, the republic, and the firm would survive.

In the 1930s, visitors to Coudert Brothers' office at 2 Rector Street took a cage elevator, operated by a girl attendant, to the tenth floor, which the firm shared with a dentist and a smaller law firm. The Coudert Brothers' receptionist sat at a desk in the hallway, and, after identifying themselves, visitors were passed through to the reception room itself. A small space furnished with one hard wooden bench, the room was in keeping with the decor of the offices beyond, which were distinguished mainly by their linoleum floors, plain wooden chairs, and dirty windows.

One client, Dr. René Pierre Lacombe, thought the premises had a certain charm. *Dickensian* was the word he used to describe them, saying that he always had the feeling that around the next corner he would find an elderly clerk perched on a high stool wielding a quill pen. In fact, although the offices were at a different location, they did look much the same as they had in the nineteenth century when Fred Coudert and Paul Fuller, Jr., were boys. No doubt Coudert and Fuller never changed the office decor partly because it was comfortable and familiar and partly because they had not been brought up to waste money on outward frills. But the unchanging appearance of the office serves as a convenient symbol for the fact that Coudert and Fuller not only practiced law all their lives in the same atmosphere their fathers established but ran the firm very much along the same lines.

Coudert and Fuller inherited in the New York office a practice divided between estates and trusts work and general litigation, with a small corporate component. All of its basic characteristics—from the wide client base, mainly composed of wealthy foreigners and Americans resident abroad, to the outstanding reputation for expertise in international law—remained the same from the time they joined the firm until their deaths. There were changes, of course, in clients and in personnel, but the fundamental nature of the practice did not alter. Accordingly, one might deduce that Coudert and Fuller saw themselves as custodians of the firm and brought little of their creativity to bear on its management. One might equally well conclude, though, that the cousins had too much sense to tamper with success, for the old formula laid down by the original Coudert brothers kept on working well for their successors. It worked, in fact, even in the Depression.

The New York office's earnings seem to have dropped at the bottom of the Depression to less than half of what they had been in the peak years of the 1920s, but the salient fact is that Coudert Brothers always did show a profit—a profit adequate to protect the partners' life-styles. The firm's continued profitability, in fact, confounded the expectations of James Barclay, the cautious, meticulous Scot. Bothered by what seemed to be a speculative streak in Fred Coudert's character, Barclay had become deeply concerned in the late 1920s about the risk to his personal savings, should the firm lose money and make a call upon the partners for additional capital. Accordingly, in January 1929 Barclay withdrew as a partner and went back to work as a salaried employee, at a wage of $550 a month. This was a very decent income in 1929, when $400 a month could purchase the upper-middle-class life-style of a Manhattan brownstone or big suburban house staffed by several servants. Nonetheless, as things turned out, Barclay would have done just as well in the short term remaining a partner and much better in the long term, for he continued working for Coudert Brothers into the 1950s.

Moreover, Barclay's apprehensions about the partners' having to make a capital contribution were not fulfilled. As Percy Shay once confided to a younger colleague, at some other major New York law firms "things were so bad in the Depression that the partners had to make contributions to pay the staff and the administrative people," but at Coudert Brothers, "We partners never had to contribute a cent."

Coudert Brothers' salvation lay largely in the fact that the Depression was selective in its effects. Although the prices of common stock collapsed, most blue-chip companies continued to pay their bondholders in full. As a result, the wealthy whose fortunes had been conservatively invested in bonds not only kept their wealth, but were often better off than ever because of the general deflation in prices. The trusts that Coudert Brothers administered generally contained nothing but gilt-edged bonds (because they were the only type of holding considered proper for a trust), and most individual clients of the firm also seem to have invested primarily in fixed-income securities. Thus, from its clientele of wealthy individuals and their estates and trusts, Coudert Brothers continued to derive a steady business throughout the Depression.

In fact, the number of new client matters reported by Coudert Frères in 1931 was nearly double that reported in 1921, and, as in 1921, most of these new matters involved estates that would eventually be worked on by the New York office as well. In addition, Tom Kelly in the New York office's Surrogate's Department turned out to be a good business getter. Personable and well connected in New York social and political circles, he put together a list of VIP clients that seemed to grow longer every year, and, as a result, his partnership share was increased in 1932 from 3 to 5 percent. Gerald Dunworth, who joined Coudert Brothers as a law student in 1935, noticed at the time that the firm was very busy in the surrogate's court, and it was his guess—and apparently a correct one—that estates and trusts were paying the rent and overhead.

The rest of the firm's income came, in true Depression style, by scraping a dollar wherever a dollar was to be found. The Depression increased the number of bankruptcies, of course, and Finletter perforce became an expert in this area. In fact, in 1931 he began teaching a course on bankruptcy at the University of Pennsylvania Law School, and he published three standard works on the subject later in the decade: *Principles of Corporate Reorganization* (1937), *Cases on Corporate Reorganization* (1938), and *The Law of Bankruptcy Reorganization* (1938). Among the major reorganization cases that came his way were the bankruptcy of a major chain of New York lending libraries and the reorganization of the company operating the Vicksburg Bridge in Vicksburg, Mississippi. Late in the decade, Finletter was retained by the Savannah & Atlantic Railroad; he brought it out of Section 77 reorganization, and it became the first railroad to be so discharged.

Coudert Brothers was also fortunate in having some very complex government litigation in the worst years of the Depression. The most important was the Black Tom explosion case, which moved in 1929 before the Mixed Claims Commission at the Hague, as the Lehigh Valley Railroad and Russian government sought compensation for their losses from the German government. The case was heard and reheard for five years, with the Germans putting up a stiff defense; it then moved, on the question of the commission's authority to assess damages, to the U.S. Supreme Court, which decided against Germany, and back again to the Mixed Claims Commission, which after eleven years handed down a final decision against Germany in 1940. Since there were still German assets frozen in the United States from World War I, the claimants and their attorneys all got paid in full. Monaco also provided the firm with some interesting work, including a test of whether a foreign government could sue an individual state without that state's consent, which the U.S. Supreme Court decided in 1933 in the negative in *Monaco v. Mississippi.*

Furthermore, the movie industry flourished in the 1930s as people flocked to theaters to escape their cares, and United Artists, MGM, and other major studios continued to provide Coudert Frères with a brisk amount of business, while the Pathé Exchange remained a profitable client for the New York office. Coudert Brothers also had many individual clients who were engaged in show business, and Scip Bellinger—who was personally at home in the theaters and night spots along Broadway—once distinguished himself by defending comedian W. C. Fields against a charge by a N.Y. Humane Society officer that a canary Fields used in his vaudeville act had, when flying on the stage, struck a piece of scenery and, thus, died by "torture." Bellinger's cross-examination in this 1928 "canary case" hilariously turned the tables on the Humane

Society officer, convincing the judge that the officer in his thirst for publicity, was the party who had callously mistreated the bird, and Bellinger won a triumphant and rapid acquittal of Fields on all charges.

This show business practice that had grown steadily through the 1920s was reinforced when Lewis Innerarity joined the New York office as a senior associate sometime before 1931. A graduate of the University of Maryland Law School, who had originally practiced in Maryland, Innerarity was then in his mid-forties, and he had a client list of his own, which was heavily sprinkled with Broadway stars and performers.

The divorce rate went up in the Depression, and Innerarity's clients, in particular, seem to have been frequently in divorce court. Indeed, one of Dunworth's first assignments at Coudert Brothers was to serve a summons in a divorce action on a Broadway actor, Everett Marshall, whom Dunworth finally located reclining on a float off Jones Beach, surrounded by a bevy of skimpily clad chorus girls. Dunworth did not enjoy the assignment as much as he might have, however, for he came close to being shoved, in his best double-breasted suit and wing tips, into the ocean by the angry Mr. Marshall, and, making a hasty retreat, Dunworth resolved never to serve one of Innerarity's summonses again, if he could help it. But Coudert Brothers went right on doing divorce work, criminal work, claims and collections, and all manner of things that other prestigious firms no longer handled. The founders of Coudert Brothers had been general litigators, taking on any type of case that came along, and Fred Coudert had never seen any reason to break with this tradition. This old-fashioned lack of specialization—which by then was unusual for a New York firm of Coudert Brothers' caliber—seems, on the whole, to have worked to Coudert Brothers' advantage in the 1930s.

The firm even benefited from its own mistakes. At least, practices that would be frowned upon today as poor management turned out to be blessings in disguise, such as the leisureliness with which the firm allowed its clients to pay their bills. In 1929 Coudert Brothers had five or six very substantial fees outstanding for work done earlier in the decade, including the $125,000 from the Lehigh Valley case. The belated payments in these matters came in exactly when most needed, and, even after the appropriate shares were paid to retired partners, they alone could have floated the firm though several Depression years if the firm had not received a penny from any other source. Moreover, Miss Bainbridge's slowness in recording income, while unorthodox, had the definite merit of ensuring a rather high level of cash reserves.

One place where money did not come in the Depression, however, was out of the staff's pockets. According to Rudolph ("Rudy") Reimer, who joined Coudert Brothers in 1927 as a mailroom clerk, there were no layoffs, no cutbacks, and no pay cuts for staff members during the Depression. Reimer even received regular raises, his salary moving from eleven dollars a week in 1927 to eighteen dollars a week in 1933—a sum he remembers well because, small as it was, it was just large enough to enable him to get married. Moreover, although there was no medical insurance or formal pension plan, the staff knew that the firm had always looked out for its own and had no doubt it always would. "It was a wonderful firm, and Mr. Coudert, Senior and Junior, were wonderful men," says Reimer firmly.

The decisions on salaries and hiring—indeed, all financial decisions—were essentially made by the triumvirate of Fred Coudert, Paul Fuller, Jr., and, in a junior role as the heir-in-training, Fritz Coudert. These decisions followed "long confabs" between the senior Coudert and Miss Bainbridge, conducted behind closed doors, so that Miss Bainbridge undoubtedly had considerable influence, but the final decisions were made by the family partners, and, by the results, it seems safe to surmise that they were animated by a deep sense of responsibility to others in the firm. While waiting for business to pick up, as Coudert always believed it would, the firm protected its own. It did not have a lot of money to offer associates and staff—the starting salary for an associate in 1935 was eighteen hundred dollars (about seventeen thousand 1990 dollars)—but it could and did offer security, a pleasant working environment, and the challenge of meeting very high standards.

The pleasantness of the working environment arose, in part, from the harmony prevailing among the partners. "We were a good team," recalls one lawyer who joined the firm in the 1930s. "We all worked pretty well together." This is remarkable, for Coudert Brothers, small as it was, contained a wide diversity of personalities. In Litigation, for example, there was Percy Shay, "one of the politest men in the world," endowed with such scruples that "he would never cross the street unless the light was green, and then only after he had checked and double-checked the color of the light." On the other hand, his fellow litigator Lewis Innerarity was, in Dunworth's opinion, "the meanest, toughest lawyer in New York," an attorney who always wanted to go for the jugular whether it was strictly necessary or not. James Hopkins and Tom Kelly in Estates and Trusts also presented a sharp contrast. Hopkins, who had never attended law school but had prepared for the bar by clerking at Coudert Brothers, was a throwback to a nineteenth-century style of practitioner. Like a country lawyer, he kept a big safe in his office, which protected, among other items, a bottle of medicinal whisky. He wore a full set of long underwear, summer and winter, which was no secret to his colleagues because when "Hoppy" leaned back in his chair and propped his feet on the open bottom drawer of his desk, the long johns peeped out under the bottom cuffs of his trousers. Kelly, younger than Hopkins by a good twenty years, possessed, on the other hand, both polish and a solid academic background. A "dear wonderful man," he showed great patience with the young associates, using a Socratic method of questioning to help them learn how to analyze problems and discover solutions for themselves.

That a group like this got along amicably, with mutual respect, is a tribute to its members, in the first instance. Personality conflicts occur in any organization, and, in Paris, Coudert Frères had a serious rift in the 1930s. In his dislike of administration, Robinson by 1931 had delegated most decisions to his partner Russell I. Hare, and a third partner, Watson C. Emmet, found that whenever he came to Robinson with an idea or a problem, Robinson would wave him off, telling him to go see Hare. This irritated Emmet, who did not work well with Hare. Those who knew them agree that both Emmet and Hare were "good men, very pleasant," but the chemistry between them was wrong, and in 1933 Emmet left Coudert Frères, taking with him a junior partner, Roland Palmer. "I'm sorry to say they left rather angry with the firm," recalls John Dubé.

Managing partners must take the blame for situations like this, and, therefore, some credit for the fact that nothing of the sort occurred at the New York office must go to Paul Fuller, Jr., who became its managing partner in 1927, replacing John Murray, who, in turn, had taken over from the senior Fuller in 1915. Like his predecessors, Fuller junior was—in a highly informal way—responsible for sorting out disputes, bringing to a partner's attention any inadequacies that might exist in his work, seeing that workloads were fairly distributed, and generally managing the human side of the firm. These were tasks that Fuller junior apparently handled with the same combination of tact, consideration, and firmness that made him successful in dealing with the volatile management of Coty, Inc., or the sometimes imperious Prince Louis.

Tall and slim, Fuller was almost alarmingly good-looking, but his elegance was balanced by an endearing absentmindedness. John Hurd, who became Fuller's son-in-law, says that many years after he first started courting his future wife and a mere week before their wedding, Fuller was still having trouble remembering his name. "Mr. Fuller was also clumsy in many ways," Hurd recalled recently. "He could have trouble tying his own shoelaces; but when he was concentrating—when he was tying a fishing lure, for example—his deftness was really something beautiful to see." What the whole family remembers most vividly, however, is Fuller's open tenderness and gentleness, particularly toward women and children. "He had the sort of manners that, if a little three-year-old girl toddled in, he would just automatically stand up," Fuller's grandson has said. "He was a gentleman through and through."

Fuller's secretary for many years was Alice O'Brien, who had started with the firm as its switchboard operator. Miss O'Brien was a "sweet, kind woman," but also working for the firm was a Miss Gould, who was "a real terror." Miss Gould had temper tantrums and, in the grip of these, would sometimes start throwing things. The firm did not want to let Miss Gould go, for she was a hard worker with long years of service. Still, no one quite knew what to do with her. For a time, Miss Gould handled the correspondence with Coudert Frères, but her letters had a nasty tone that surely did interoffice relations no good. Finally, Miss O'Brien was transferred to another partner, and Fuller took on the awful Miss Gould. From his manner, no one, least of all Miss Gould, could ever have suspected to what extent he had martyred himself.

In dealing with his male colleagues, however, Fuller was made of sterner stuff. "What always impressed me about Mr. Fuller," says Hurd, "was how principled he was. He had a very firm idea of right and wrong, and he was in no way a martinet, but he was not one to tolerate what was wrong. He would never do anything wrong himself, you see. He was just the most remarkable man. You could not imagine him doing anything simply because it was to his own advantage." From various scraps of correspondence, it appears that it was invariably Fuller—not Fred Coudert—who took the younger partners aside when a problem arose and pointed out the corrective action needed, and one surviving letter, from Scip Bellinger, suggests that such lectures were not resented, but appreciated for the dispassionate spirit in which they were presented.

Fuller's influence was a quiet one, exercised behind the scenes and evident mostly to his fellow partners. The associates in the firm, in fact, seem to have scarcely been aware of his management role. Rather, their horizons were filled, first, by the partner or partners to whom they immediately reported, and then, more remotely, by the senior partner, Fred Coudert. Jim Hughes, Gerry Dunworth, and Hugh Fitzgerald, all of whom joined the firm in the 1930s, did not have a great deal of contact with the "Old Man," but he did read their briefs and memos—more regularly perhaps than they realized—and from time to time he would invite them into his office to talk about their cases. These associates found the senior Coudert kind and very charming on these occasions. "Mr. Coudert really took an interest in all of us," recalls Fitzgerald. "He couldn't have been nicer."

Around the water cooler, however, the newest associates heard their older counterparts—notably Frank Wells and Walter Barry—recount hair-raising tales of what it was like to work directly under the "Old Man." Wells and Barry were litigators, which meant that they were working usually under deadline pressure. In litigation, the quality of the work is often a function of the time available to do it in; it is not uncommon for a lawyer to write a brilliant brief in one case but on another occasion, pressed for time, to turn out an argument that, on a generous estimate, might just be passable. According to Wells and Barry, though, Coudert insisted that everything going out from the firm be perfect every time. A tough boss, he expected skill in analysis, thoroughness in research, and literary talent in the drafting, whatever the circumstances or the value of the case. Moreover, Coudert had very strong opinions on how to do things and an iron will in enforcing them. He did not brook insubordination or back talk in the office.

Wells, in his way, though, was as much a perfectionist as Coudert, and he had his own ideas on how to do things. "Wells was like a fighting terrier," says Fitzgerald. "He was not afraid to tackle anybody." Wells and the "Old Man" had some monumental clashes, and Fitzgerald, concerned for his friend, asked him one day if he didn't worry about getting fired. "No," said Wells, surprised by the question. "The Old Man may come down hard on me sometimes, but, you know, that's as far as it goes. He's too big a man to hold a grudge." And then, warming to his subject, Wells added, "I tell you, Mr. Coudert is really a great man in my book."

Mr. Coudert also had not been the father of four lively boys for nothing. He knew very well when to turn a blind eye—and with Wells and Barry a blind eye was often a necessary attribute, for the pair of them were incorrigible practical jokers. Their most famous prank, which backfired on them somewhat, was directed at Howard Thayer Kingsbury. Kingsbury was always called Colonel Kingsbury, in recognition of his services as a colonel in the New York National Guard during World War I and a lieutenant colonel in the Officer Reserve Corps of the U. S. Army from 1921 to 1934, in which capacities he had drafted some of the state's and nation's major military laws. Kingsbury, however, was not really a military type at all, but rather a litterateur. Translator, poet, amateur actor, author of scholarly legal articles, and expert in Elizabethan literature, he had those polished manners that distinguished so many Coudert Brothers lawyers of his generation.

At some point in the 1930s, Wells and Barry got hold of a key to Colonel Kingsbury's office, and, whenever he left his desk, they would lock his door and hide the key. This went on and on, the colonel taking the joke like a gentleman, until one day his patience snapped. Returning to find the office door locked again, the colonel doubled up his fist, smashed the glass door, and, with bleeding fingers, reached in, turned the knob, and entered, slamming the door behind him. Apparently nothing was ever said to Wells and Barry, but they did not pull that particular joke again.

The two of them together were also expert at absenting themselves from the premises. If they were not at their desks, the chances were they were down in the lobby shooting the breeze with the shoeshine man or in the building's second-floor coffee shop, either drinking coffee or playing the one-armed bandits that the proprietor kept in a back room. Still, when the pressure was on, both Wells and Barry worked like demons—often they went right around the clock—and Coudert evidently understood their need, when the pressure eased, to blow off steam.

The firm did not turn a blind eye to truly outrageous behavior, however. It did have its standards, and one associate went way over the line when he was discovered in a compromising position with a secretary in the midst of the annual Christmas party sometime before World War II. That put an end not only to the associate's career at Coudert Brothers but, for several decades, to the firm's Christmas party.

On the whole, though, the small number of older lawyers in the firm made no effort to quash the high spirits of their younger colleagues. They did not even work them particularly hard by today's lights: the Litigation Department had its own rhythms, but generally the firm expected everyone to leave the office at five. This was in contrast to some of the "Wall Street" firms, where, it was said, associates were treated with no more consideration than galley slaves. The young men at Coudert Brothers, nonetheless, did have the sense that they had better do their best—not because they were overtly pressured into it, but because the other lawyers in the firm seemed so highly skilled, thorough, and ethical. The example set, Fitzgerald would recall, was a truly formidable one. "I admired those men so much," Dunworth once said. "I don't think I've ever met a group of men I respected more."

* * *

In the spring of 1935 the placement director of Columbia Law School warned members of the graduating class that hiring by the city's law firms seemed to be virtually at a standstill. "He strongly suggested," recalls James E. Hughes, who was a member of that class, "that we consider ourselves on our own and do our best for ourselves." A native Missourian, Hughes was just about to turn twenty-two, having started college young and gone through Columbia's undergraduate college and law school in an accelerated six-year program. Hughes prepared his résumé, which noted that he was in the top 10 percent of his class and had been chairman of the Moot Court Committee, and began doggedly sending it to law firms. Some of his classmates got no jobs at all; some who had good records had to accept positions that provided them with a desk and a telephone, but no salary. In the summer of 1935, however, Hughes got a break: George Montgomery of Coudert Brothers called him in for an interview, and, after a follow-up meeting with Fred Coudert, Hughes began work as an associate at "the very liberal sum of $35 a week."

Hughes quickly learned that he owed his job to the fact that "the firm was then in something of a period of expansion, to a limited degree." It was the very depths of the Depression, yet a number of the firm's corporate clients were becoming increasingly active. Among these was the Banca Commerciale Italiana, which ran both an agency and a general commercial banking operation in New York; Consolidated Laundries, Inc., the client that Finletter had brought to Coudert Brothers; Coty, Inc., and its various subsidiaries; and the Buckley family's oil and gas companies. All four clients continued to grow throughout the late 1930s, and a stash of research memoranda from the early months of 1938 gives an idea of the range of legal questions they posed to the firm. In those few months, for example, Coudert Brothers advised Coty, Inc., on the labeling of perfume products and the validity of a proxy conveyed by telegram, qualified Coty Sales Corporation to do business in various states, prepared a suit for Consolidated Laundries, Inc., against a competitor that had adopted a similar trade name, and counseled Banca Commerciale Italiana on how best to notify depositors that, in view of the continuing chaos of the Spanish Civil War, it intended to close down its Spanish peseta accounts.

These particular memoranda from early 1938 were written not by Hughes, but by Fred Coudert's third oldest son, Ferdinand W. Coudert. As the newest associate in 1938, Ferdinand was apparently at everyone's beck and call, for he wrote memoranda in those months responding to questions from just about every partner and senior associate in the firm. Several of these questions, like the

Banca Commerciale Italiana's closure of its Spanish peseta accounts, provide glimpses of the deteriorating international situation. Paul Fuller, for example, needed to advise a young American born in France whether he might be caught up in the French military draft if he visited France, while Fred Coudert requested an opinion on the remedies available to the owners of an American ship seized by Franco gunboats off Spain.

Experts have long agreed that it was the impending wars in Europe and the Far East that finally lifted the world economy out of the Depression. Given Coudert Brothers' small number of corporate clients at this time, none of which was of the "Smokestack America" variety, the spurt of international trade prompted by rearmament actually had little effect on the firm. What is visible in the firm's records, however, is the nervousness of individuals as they began to reorganize their lives in response to the European situation. This is reflected, for example, in the growing number of U.S. tax queries received from the Paris office. And perhaps the liveliest client either Coudert Brothers or Coudert Frères had in 1938 and 1939 was Durand Ruel, the dealer in fine art, for its business picked up considerably as prudent investors exchanged European stocks and currencies for Old Masters placed in safekeeping in the New World.

If the effect on Coudert Brothers, with its estates-oriented practice, was only indirect, the U.S. economy, nonetheless, was in far stronger shape in 1939 than it had been in 1935, as illustrated by Hugh Fitzgerald's experience in hunting for a job in the former year. A graduate of Notre Dame and Columbia Law School, Fitzgerald had started work in 1937 for a small downtown firm, and he decided to make a change in 1939. Whereas Columbia Law School had been able to provide no help at all to Jim Hughes in 1935, in 1939 it could alert Fitzgerald to a job opportunity at Coudert Brothers, and ultimately, Fitzgerald found himself weighing no fewer than three offers: one from the Manhattan district attorney's office, which had the reputation of being one of the best berths for a young litigator; one from a Wall Street firm; and one from Coudert Brothers, which was looking for an associate to handle the U.S. tax questions that Coudert Frères was sending over in every mail delivery from France.

Uncertain which position to accept, Fitzgerald turned to his father, who said, "Remember, it's important that you like the people you'll be working with." This proved decisive advice, for Fitzgerald already "knew, liked, and respected" Ferdinand Coudert, who had been in his class at law school and had compiled an impressive record there. Fitzgerald was also slightly acquainted with Ferdinand's younger brother, Alexis, who had held the highest grade average in the law-school class behind them and had then clerked in 1938–39 for Justice (later Chief Justice) Harlan F. Stone of the U.S. Supreme Court. Figuring that he couldn't go wrong being associated with men of their caliber, Fitzgerald took the job offer from Coudert Brothers.

In doing so, Fitzgerald became the first in a long line of associates attracted to Coudert Brothers partly by its reputation, but partly by the impression made by these younger Couderts—especially Alexis, who did virtually all of the firm's hiring after 1944. It is axiomatic that family businesses often have trouble securing talented individuals, who understandably may be wary of a setup dominated by family members who might lack the ability of the original founders. In the past, in fact, Coudert Brothers had had upon occasion to face up to the fact that it was employing Coudert relatives whose performance was not entirely satisfactory. In the 1890s, for example, one of Louis Leonce Coudert's sons had been gently eased out of the firm by his uncle, Paul Fuller, Sr., and directed into a sales career, where he proved indeed far more successful. And before World War I, Paul Fuller, Jr.'s older brother Charles had worked briefly for the firm, shown little aptitude for the law, and also had been steered off—apparently with no hard feelings—toward a general business career.

In the case of Fred Coudert's three lawyer sons—Fritz, Ferdinand, and Alexis—there was no question of a lack of legal ability, however. Among the younger associates, gathering around the water cooler, it was agreed that all three were highly intelligent and likable. The only question ever in debate—unbeknownst to Fritz, Ferdinand, and Alexis, of course—was simply which was the most talented of the three. This was not an easy question to settle, because the three brothers were not alike and they had different talents that took them in different directions.

Fritz, the eldest, was the litigator, following in his father's and grandfather's footsteps. Tall, good-looking, and smooth in manner, Fritz made an excellent appearance in the courtroom. Justice James C. McReynolds of the U.S. Supreme Court wrote Fritz's father in 1936, "It was a great satisfaction to me to see the fine way in which your son carried himself during the argument of the recent extradition case. How lovely to have a boy like that to hold up the family prestige." And one of Fritz's former classmates at Columbia Law School once observed that Fritz had been "just head and shoulders above everyone else in the class. He was so highly educated, so intelligent, and with that patrician background, we were all sure that he was going to be one of the great trial lawyers in the country—if he had just stuck to his last."

Fritz, though, was as much, if not more, interested in politics, an interest he shared with his cousin and closest friend, Scip Bellinger. Fred Coudert, moreover, encouraged this interest. Immediately after the Spanish-American War, Fred himself had been briefly "boomed" by the Democratic party for several offices, most notably the State Senate, and had been disappointed when the nominations did not come his way. Later he was to take a wryer view of politics, describing it as "always interesting, exciting and sometimes not wholly useless." Still, he had every sympathy with the fascination politics held for his son and nephew, and he made it easy for Fritz to serve as a special assistant U.S. district attorney in 1924 and for Scip to do the same the following year.

Working for the U.S. district attorney's office, Fritz and Scip directed Prohibition enforcement prosecutions and acquired a good deal of exposure to the corruption in the city's law enforcement offices. In 1929 Fritz made his first bid for elective office, running as the Republican candidate for Manhattan district attorney on the ticket headed by Fiorello La Guardia and promising a cleanup of law enforcement in the city. Although he chose to be a Republican, in the tradition of his mother's side of the family, he had his father's full support, as well as that of many of his father's friends in the legal community, and he put up a vigorous, well-financed campaign. The whole La Guardia ticket went down to defeat, but Fritz did a little better than the top of the ticket, and it appeared that it would just be a matter of time before he ran again.

In the event, Fritz did not stand as a candidate again until 1938, but he and Scip spent those nine years building a solid base within the Republican party. Through a committee of young lawyers that he organized to provide a free defense to persons accused of violating the Prohibition laws and through his appearances in occasional well-publicized criminal trials, Fritz kept his name before the public, and simultaneously he consolidated his position with the party's leadership, serving as a delegate to the annual state Republican conventions. Meanwhile, Scip was becoming well-acquainted with ward bosses and party workers throughout the city. Fritz was the most outgoing of the Couderts, yet, like many politicians, he revealed few of his deepest thoughts and feelings, except to his closest friends. Scip, on the other hand, "had the common touch," and in due course his network of political pals and acquaintances blanketed the city. In 1937 Scip managed the mayoral campaign of former U.S. senator Royal S. Copeland, doing well for the party in a rather hopeless cause, and in 1938 he had the satisfaction of managing Fritz's successful campaign for state senator, representing a Manhattan district.

The one thing marring Fritz's victory was the fact that Scip developed the symptoms of heart disease not long thereafter. In June 1940, after a prolonged period of inactivity, Scip resigned from the firm, and he died in September 1941 at the age of forty-seven. Despite the loss of his friend and confidant from childhood days, Fritz won reelection to the State Senate in 1942. In fact, Fritz would serve in elective office continuously for twenty-two years, in the State Senate until 1946 and then in the U.S. House of Representatives from 1946 to 1960. Thus, after 1938, Fritz practiced law only part-time, when the legislatures were not in session.

It was exactly as Fritz, then forty years old, was cutting back his commitment to the firm and the practice of law that his younger brothers, Ferdinand, age twenty-nine, and Alexis, age twenty-four, were passing the bar. Ferdinand came to the bar late, for he originally planned to become a professor rather than a lawyer. Gifted in languages and particularly interested in the Slavic languages and culture—an interest initially awakened by the Russian émigrés who frequented the Coudert home—Ferdinand took his B.A. at Harvard in 1930 and studied at Berlin University in 1930–31 and the Ecole des Langues Orientales in Paris in 1931–32. He then started doctoral work at Harvard, acquiring his M.A. degree in Slavic studies in 1933. Fred Coudert, who could have been happy in an academic setting himself, encouraged his son's studies, but in 1934 he felt obliged to ask Ferdinand to reconsider his career plans, in light of what salaries and job prospects were for professors in that Depression year and in view of the evaporation of Fred's own savings and, along with them, of his hope of being able to provide his son someday with at least a small independent income. The choice was left to Ferdinand, who, deciding to be realistic, declined a fellowship to the University of Prague and entered Columbia Law School in 1934.

Unlike his litigating older brother, Ferdinand ended up specializing in estates and trusts. According to a now retired Coudert Brothers partner, the "Old Man" once indicated that, among his three lawyer sons, he believed Ferdinand had the strongest intellect. Ferdinand was certainly the best writer of the three, and he had the sort of "puzzle-solving" mind that lent itself to the complexities of international estates as readily as to linguistics. Charles Torem, who as a partner in the Paris office in the 1950s often referred estate matters to Ferdinand Coudert, has said that Ferdinand was "great—*very* great—on international trusts and wills."

Ferdinand himself says that he ended up specializing in estates and trusts partly because "it was thought that I had a good bedside manner when it came to making wills." His quiet *politesse* indeed made him popular with the firm's extensive list of widows, and he was soon taking care of what he describes as "some of the more mature ladies." Sent to Paris shortly before the Munich crisis to become more familiar with Coudert Frères's operations, Ferdinand was charged with looking after trusts that the Moslems' spiritual leader, the Aga Khan, had set up for his grandchildren. For the scholarly young lawyer, one of the most pleasurable parts of that experience was the discussions he used to have with the Guaranty Trust officer on the form of trusts in French and Arabic law.

According to Ferdinand, he grew quite interested in time in property law and enjoyed the advising on investments, but the law was always something of a second choice for him. "It was Alexis who was a brilliant lawyer," he says. "He had a passion for the law, the only one of us who really did. My brother Fritz was a good trial lawyer, but the interest in politics was overriding. Alexis, though, was born for the law, everything to do with it."

Alexis, the youngest of the brothers, would become a specialist in corporate law and the moving force behind the firm's modern expansion, but in the late 1930s all of that was well in the future. In 1941, a little over a year after Alexis joined Coudert Brothers as an associate, a reporter from the *New York World-Telegram* interviewed seventy-year-old Fred Coudert at the Fencers Club on the tenth anniversary of his presidency of the club. Explaining that one of his favorite dueling opponents was his son Alexis, Coudert lightly added, "Fred, Jr. is the politician, Ferdinand is the lawyer and linguist, and Alexis is the fencer." This casual quip, however, could not disguise the fact that their father was proud of them all and delighted to have them with him in the firm, giving the name "Coudert Brothers" an entirely new significance.

Chapter Eleven

WAR AGAIN

After the Munich crisis of September 1938, France and Great Britain began racing to catch up with Germany in military strength. To French military planners the top priority was more fighter planes and bombers, for the French air force was so small and obsolete that, as Prime Minister Édouard Daladier said confidentially in 1938, the "Germans can bomb Paris whenever they choose." It was estimated, however, that the combined manufacturing capacities of the French, British, and Canadian aircraft industries were only enough to bring the air forces of these three countries up to parity with the Luftwaffe. To achieve superiority, additional capacity would have to be found elsewhere.

The obvious solution, as in World War I, was to turn to the United States, and in October 1938 financier Jean Monnet arrived in Washington to begin exploratory talks on behalf of the French Ministry of Defense with the U.S. government. Monnet hired as U.S. counsel the firm of Sullivan & Cromwell, a choice that annoyed Treasury Secretary Henry Morgenthau, Jr., to whom President Roosevelt had assigned the responsibility of dealing with the Monnet mission. Sullivan & Cromwell was then representing the Franco government in a suit against the Treasury Department, and according to historian John Morton Blum, "The Secretary felt the French should hire instead a counselor with a clear record of sympathy for the democracies." To Ambassador William Bullitt,

Morgenthau complained that Monnet with his Wall Street connections "doesn't seem to realize there has been a New Deal over here." Nonetheless, with Morgenthau opening doors, the Monnet mission was able to discover what types of military designs were available, to work out some of the details of finance, and to place orders for six hundred modern aircraft.

These six hundred planes were just a fraction of what was needed, and in the summer of 1939 the French sent over another aircraft purchasing commission that would ultimately negotiate orders for nearly five thousand airplanes and ten thousand aircraft engines. Arriving in August to set up its offices in New York, the commission hired Coudert Brothers as its lawyers. The change in counsel from Sullivan & Cromwell to Coudert Brothers may or may not have been prompted by Morgenthau's complaints, but certainly the commission could not have chosen a law firm with a stronger record of sympathy for the democracies or one—given the nature of Coudert Brothers' practice at this time—with fewer ties to the major Wall Street banks. The last was important to Morgenthau: on his authority the French would be "jumping the line" ahead of the U.S. armed forces on some of their orders, and he was anxious that no one be able to allege later that the French had been given priority because of "Wall Street influence."

In his position, Morgenthau had to think about electoral politics. The Coudert Brothers lawyers assigned to work with the French, however, were interested only in getting on with the work. War was clearly imminent in August 1939, and there was an atmosphere of urgency surrounding the first meetings with the French Aircraft Purchasing Commission. But just a few weeks after its arrival, the commission hit its first major obstacle when, on September 3, 1939, France and Great Britain declared war on Germany following Hitler's invasion of Poland. This put France into the position of a belligerent, and, under the provisions of the American neutrality laws, belligerents were barred from the purchase of armaments and military supplies. Until the Neutrality Act could be repealed or amended, the commission's hands were tied.

In fact, a movement was even then under way and had been under way all summer to repeal the American embargo on arms, one in which Fred Coudert was personally involved. Returning from a visit to England and France in July 1939, Coudert had written to the *New York Herald Tribune*, "I am convinced that Hitler and Company (in which I include the military cliques governing Germany, Italy and Japan) mean to strike in the very near future unless deterred by the fear that the western democracies would be able to obtain supplies from America. . . . The only way that America may be certain to keep out of war is to prevent war. No better method now presents itself than so to amend the act that war supplies may go unfettered to those who are defending themselves." These sentiments were repeated in different words by many concerned citizens that summer, as an informal network of pro-Allied Americans began to coalesce under the leadership of Kansas editor William Allen White. Months later the group would become formally organized as the Committee to Defend America by Aiding the Allies. In September 1939 it was still simply a loose congregation of old friends and acquaintances, with a backbone provided by those New York lawyers who had led the military preparedness and pro-Allied publicity campaigns of 1915 and 1916, such as Charles Burlingham, Grenville Clark, Frederic R. Coudert, William Donovan, Stanwood Menken, and Henry Stimson, to name just a few.

As in 1915, this group was running against the tide of American isolationism, and the bill to amend the Neutrality Act was initially defeated in the House of Representatives in July 1939. But those favoring reintroduction of the amendment had two advantages they had lacked in 1915: a friendly administration in the White House and a much sharper ideological contrast between the European belligerents. Ever since the first Neutrality Act had passed in 1935, Coudert had been predicting that, when war actually came, the American people would never be able to tolerate a policy of evenhanded treatment of democratic France and Britain, on the one hand, and the totalitarian, "racialist" German Reich, on the other. And, indeed, on the wave of revulsion against Germany's and Russia's quick dismemberment of Poland, Congress did repeal the embargo on the sale of arms in the fall of 1939, and President Roosevelt was able to sign the amendment into law on November 4, 1939.

During the two months between the outbreak of war and repeal of the embargo, Germany fortunately did not attack the unprepared Allies. In fact, there would be no military action in Western Europe until the spring of 1940, as both sides scrambled to strengthen their forces. This was the period that came to be known as the "phoney war," or the *"drôle de guerre."* It provided a blessed breathing space for the Allies, but, as no one knew how long it would last, there was tremendous pressure on the commission and its lawyers to get the French aircraft orders moving in late 1939. Thomas Finletter and George Montgomery headed the Coudert Brothers team working with the French, with associates Alexis Coudert and Jim Hughes rounding out the group. "The French told us," says Hughes, "that they *must* have the planes," and the Coudert Brothers team worked through that winter "at a feverish rate." Hitler could attack France at any time, and there was a sense in the office that the fate of a nation was riding on the outcome.

The problems, however, were numerous, beginning with the question of funding. In repealing the embargo, Congress had placed all military purchases on a "cash and carry" basis: the Allies would have to pay cash for their purchases and carry them in their own bottoms. Yet, as France had run an unfavorable trade balance with the United States since 1914, the French Treasury was reluctant to approve large-scale overseas expenditures. Moreover, since France had not fully repaid its World War I debts to the United States, another long-standing U.S. law prohibited it from borrowing from American sources. All of this made for a limited budget, but on that budget France wanted to buy only the most modern, advanced planes, primarily fighters. To get those planes on the schedules it wanted, France would have to pay for the retooling and, in many cases, the expansion of production lines in the American aircraft factories: in effect, it would be paying a premium for new production models and accelerated delivery dates.

With money so short, Hughes recalls, one of the first questions that came up was the cost of the performance bonds: "It was the custom in production industries that the purchaser, especially a government, require producers to put up performance bonds to secure the purchaser against nonperformance, unreasonable delays, and so forth. These bonds were purchased from bonding and insurance companies, but, because of the size of the orders in this case, the bonds would have been terribly expensive. The Commission realized that, added to the cost of the planes, the purchase of bonds was going to cut into the number of planes they could order. There was a lot of discussion and finally, with Coudert Brothers' full approbation, the Commission authorized us to discontinue the practice."

The American aircraft manufacturers—most of them small, young, and still headed by men who had built their first models with their own hands—did not let the French down. Montgomery, the former World War I pilot, later would wax eloquent over the "exceptional ability, vigor, ingenuity, integrity and character" with which the fledgling aircraft companies had met the challenge of the foreign orders. Having been given a green light by the White House, these companies were, in fact, also infected with the spirit of urgency. When Grumman's representative, for example, was told by Colonel Jacquin, a member of the French commission, that its new F4F "Wildcat" fighter, built to take a Pratt & Whitney engine, would have to be redesigned to accommodate Wright engines, he telephoned the Long Island plant immediately and gave the order to begin the redesign. Just one week later, Jacquin watched a Wildcat take its test flight with a Wright engine.

While the aircraft companies were pioneering, getting their most experimental designs into production for the French, Coudert Brothers was on new territory, too, in writing the contracts under these somewhat frenetic conditions. "When we looked at our old contracts from World War I, they were like kindergarten models," says Hughes. "In view of the size and complexity of the orders, and the essentiality of speed, in particular, we might as well have been in a new field." Nonetheless, most of the contracts were nailed into place by early 1940, at which time the French and the British, who had had their own separate aircraft purchasing commission in the States, joined forces, to coordinate planning. Montgomery, thereafter, spent most of his time at the New York offices of the Anglo-French Purchasing Board, while Finletter, Alexis Coudert, and Hughes carried through the work at Coudert Brothers' offices. In March changes in specifications were still being made, and there was still "a lot of work involved" for the Coudert lawyers over the next few months.

The French had hoped to take delivery of their first American aircraft in the spring of 1940, and, despite all the complications, several hundred planes had been delivered when the German offensive began in May 1940. They were too little and too late. Unprotected by adequate air cover, the Allied armies reeled backward before the German blitzkrieg, disintegrating as they retreated. Trapped against the English Channel, a large portion of the armies were lifted off the beaches at Dunkirk between May 28 and June 4. By June 14 the Germans were in Paris, and the French government, which had retreated to Bordeaux, was on the verge of collapse. On June 16 at the Treasury Department in Washington, D.C., the French hastily transferred all their existing U.S. contracts and orders to the British. A few hours later in Bordeaux, Marshal Henri Phillipe Pétain took over the government and immediately sued for an armistice.

Hundreds of the American planes ordered by the French fought in the Battle of Britain in 1940, and they may indeed have tipped the balance in that close-run struggle in the skies for England's survival. But the bulk of the orders came pouring off the assembly lines in late 1940 and in 1941. The major contribution these orders made to the war effort turned out to be the forced growth they had stimulated in the U.S. aircraft industry. All observers agree that, without the seed capital provided by the French and

British orders, the American airplane and air-engine manufacturers would never have been ready to meet the U.S. armed services' own needs when the Japanese bombed Pearl Harbor and America entered the war. Representing the French purchasing commission was "the most important work we had done for the French government since World War I," Hughes has said, expressing himself with a characteristic precision. In view of where the benefit was ultimately felt, however, it may be fairly concluded that this was perhaps the most important work the firm has ever done for the United States as well.

Historian Hippolyte Taine's saying *"Les idées font les passions"* was a favorite of Fred Coudert's. He agreed that ideas create passions, and he liked to add that passions make for war. No matter how much postwar cynics dismissed talk of the "Prussian mentality" as the result of propaganda excesses, Coudert remained convinced that World War I had been an ideological war, and World War II seemed to him simply the second act of the same fight for democracy. Indeed, he began recycling some of his old World War I speeches even before World War II began, particularly the material he had gathered back in 1915 on Houston Chamberlain, Comte Gobineau, and the German enthusiasm for their dogmas of Aryan race supremacy and force. By 1937, when arguing for the need for collective action to check the totalitarian states, Coudert was pointing out that Hitler's *Mein Kampf* was nothing original, merely "the epitome of the old Prussian gospel." Speaking then of "racial purity," Coudert wrote:

> It is evident that such ideas are combative ideas; ideas incompatible with international cooperation and peaceful development. While these ideas dominate a great, powerful and intelligent group of the human race, disarmament and the security of each nation within its own frontier seem quite impossible of attainment. Such security can only be accomplished either through some form of moral disarmament, involving the growth of counter-sentiments more powerful than that of the race and absolute State idea, or by joint action among peoples less dominated by such a gospel and more inclined to the idea of a common humanity and the equal treatment of races and religions upon that common basis.

It was characteristic of Coudert that he should have delivered this statement against the theory of race supremacy in the town of Charlottesville in the then racially segregated state of Virginia.

Coudert was nothing if not intellectually aggressive, and there is a strong pattern in his public speeches and writings of selecting the least sympathetic audiences for his most forceful expositions. The pattern goes back to 1899, when his very first published essay, a scathing indictment of the military's shortcomings in the Spanish-American War, appeared in a military journal, where it was noticed by—and offended—many of his friends from Troop A. Similarly, in the early years of the twentieth century, Coudert's strongest argument for government regulation of corporations had been made to lawyers at the Yale Club, while his most vigorous defense of property rights had been delivered at the East Side Settlement House, a stronghold of European socialist thought. And he won himself no plaudits in the 1930s by repeatedly telling his friends in the League of Nations Association and the American Society of International Law that they were daydreaming in thinking that neutrality and pacifism constituted an adequate foreign policy.

As toastmaster at an American Society of International Law banquet in the spring of 1939, Coudert noted that, in the society's meetings, "We are discussing neutrality so warmly, so cordially, that we have nearly gotten into a civil war over it. So many factions are so neutral that they would like to knock everybody else over the head who does not see neutrality as they see neutrality. . . ." Coudert was himself a fighter at heart. Although he made a real effort to express himself diplomatically, it was never in his nature to back down on his basic theses. Rather, he was inclined to keep hammering away at the same points until public opinion shifted and caught up with him. To Coudert's relief, in 1939 that shift toward a willingness to regard Hitler as a threat to America was beginning.

"There is no more melancholy satisfaction than that of saying 'I told you so,' " Coudert said at a League of Nations Association dinner during the "phoney war." Still, he must have been gratified to find, when invited to address the New York Law School on "International Law and the Present War," that the audience "filled every chair, with standees occupying all available space around the walls." This was the kind of campus audience that would have been predominantly pacifist a few months earlier; now, in November 1939, the students "listened with close attention, punctuating the address with frequent applause," and the long, somewhat dry lecture ended with "prolonged applause" leading to a standing ovation.

Throughout the winter of 1939–40, Coudert was once again—with a strong sense of déjà vu—presiding over "tribute dinners" to France, raising funds for French ambulances, and generally cranking up the old pro-Allied publicity machinery. At age sixty-nine, he was still trim and athletic, thanks largely to his regimen of fencing three afternoons a week at the Fencers Club, figure-skating two other days, and playing golf on Saturdays. Coudert would not neglect his health as he had done in World War I, but his single-minded intensity was still there, and his oratory—deepened by anger at Germany pulling France and Great Britain into war for a second time—had the same hard-hitting, heartfelt emotionalism, as evident in these concluding remarks from a February 1940 speech:

> Today the world stands again at the crossroads. Will it yield to the gospel of blood and iron and forego the hope of peace based upon freedom and human dignity? A quarter of a century ago the great stop battles of the Marne and Verdun halted the onset of this modern scientific barbarism.
>
> When Marchal Pétain uttered the historic words, "They shall not pass!" he referred to the threatening hordes who had reduced to a hideous desert a large surface of the fair land of France. Yet the words had a deeper and a more profound significance in the spiritual sense. The insolence of an assumed racial superiority with its corresponding degradation of man; the Moloch State that can do no wrong and is subject to no moral limitations; that State whose mission is to destroy the small through brutal aggression, and to suppress in the name of biology the mystical craving of the human soul for a better and a higher life—these are the things "that must not pass."

When the German offensive began on May 10, 1940, however, it soon became clear that the Panzer divisions were going to pass— were, in fact, going to crush—the Allied armies, unless those armies could be provided with, among other things, better air cover. It was at this point—on May 19, 1940, to be exact—that the loose group that had campaigned for repeal of the neutrality acts organized itself under William Allen White's leadership into the Committee to Defend America by Aiding the Allies, which Coudert and others, for simplicity's sake, called the White Committee. As one of the organizers of the White Committee, Coudert wrote to Henry Stimson on May 20, urging him to attend a luncheon the next day. It was at this luncheon apparently that the group's first priorities were set, chief among them persuading the Roosevelt administration to transfer immediately U.S. army planes to France and to give the Allies all possible aid in material and finance "short of war."

The White Committee was extraordinarily effective in achieving its aims. Indeed, journalists at the time and later historians have described it as perhaps the most influential lobbying group ever created. This is not particularly surprising, given that Roosevelt, sympathetic to the Allies, was only waiting to be pushed by public sentiment. Yet the speed at which the White Committee moved was amazing. Within a week, it had set up offices, printed stationery, organized regional chapters, established a youth division, and started to circulate petitions destined for the White House and Capitol Hill. Within two weeks, it had placed full-page advertisements in most of the nation's leading newspapers, and its petitions were flooding into Washington, D.C.

In the Coudert Brothers offices, both Coudert and Tom Finletter, another White Committee organizer, were thoroughly caught up in May and June 1940 with the lobbying campaign, while Ferdinand Coudert was busy as one of the initial organizers of the committee's youth division. (David DuVivier, who would join Coudert Frères at a much later date, was also a member of the youth division's first steering committee.) In early June, Ferdinand was drafting the text of the youth division's initial statement of aims, settling the question of what letterhead to use, agreeing to appear on the platform at a rally, firing off telegrams to congressional leaders, and borrowing Hugh Fitzgerald's Columbia Law School yearbook in order to compile a mailing list. It is not clear how much legal work got done at Coudert Brothers' office during those tense weeks of the Battle of France, but the firm, pro-Allied to the last man and woman, added its full share to the hundreds of thousands of petitions sent to Washington.

By June 12, 1940, Roosevelt had gone on the radio to promise, in language picked up directly from the White Committee petition, all aid "short of war" to France. Moreover, Grenville Clark of the White Committee had succeeded in getting Roosevelt to commit himself to appointing two of the committee's most prominent members—Henry Stimson and Frank Knox—as secretary of war and secretary of the navy, respectively. Coudert, who was by then a member of the smaller informal group setting policy for the White Committee, wrote to Stimson on June 12 that "The Committee has been successful beyond its expectations." Anticipating that Stimson, because of his new appointment, would be unable to attend the next meeting, Coudert asked for his views on what the next set of priorities should be: "Is there anything further that we can do to sustain the struggling armies of France and the menaced Empire and Fleet of Great Britain?"

The tragedy of the situation, though, was that, as fast as the

White Committee was moving, events were moving faster. By June 12, the great bulk of French armies was no longer struggling; it was smashed. At least a million British and French soldiers were already prisoners of war, and thousands of French soldiers had been discharged from broken-up units and left to find their own way home. One of these was Maurice Force, a French law expert who had been working at Coudert Brothers' New York office before being called up for service in 1939. Another was the former Coudert Frères associate John Dubé, who had established a successful practice of his own in Nice during the 1930s and who was the correspondent attorney there for both Coudert Brothers and Coudert Frères. Although overage and a Canadian national, Dubé had been serving as commandant of a French volunteer ambulance corps, but by June 12 he had been discharged and was on his way back to Nice.

If Americans like Coudert had no clear idea of how far the military situation had deteriorated, neither, in fact, did Dubé. Returned to his law office in Nice, Dubé learned that the British would be sending ships to Bordeaux to evacuate Commonwealth nationals, but he remembers being fairly optimistic about the chances of the French army regrouping and being uncertain whether to leave or stay. What decided him finally was the fact that he needed to consult with Coudert Brothers in New York anyway in connection with the estate of his longtime client Dr. Bengué, the inventor of Ben Gay ointment. Almost in the mood of taking a short business trip, Dubé packed up, and he reached Bordeaux around June 15. In that city, crammed to the last inch with refugees, Dubé found panic and fear running high in the final hours of the Third Republic. Thousands of the people there—refugees from countries already overrun by Hitler, citizens of nations at war with Germany, Jews of all nationalities—desperately needed to escape France.

"It was a real *sauve qui peut* atmosphere," recalls Dubé. Still, invited to share the champagne and *pâté de foie gras* that three Morgan bankers had brought with them from Paris, Dubé was not surprised to hear one of them say that he planned to retreat to Biarritz to wait for "the war to blow over." It seemed as realistic an attitude as any, though German bombs were even then falling on the port of Bordeaux. Around June 17, Dubé boarded a coal ship bound for a blacked-out London, his first stop on the way to New York. As it happened, if he had lingered six more days, he would have spent the next four years, if he had survived, in an internment camp.

By the time Dubé arrived in New York, Harold Johnson of Coudert Frères was already there, for Hugh Fitzgerald can remember discussing with Johnson on June 10, 1946, the implications of Italy's declaration of war on France. Another Coudert Frères partner, Russell Hare, however, cut his departure fine. Still in Paris after the German occupation, he and his secretary Colette Romonet, made several trips back and forth through the German lines— taking, Madame Romonet said later, considerable risks to attend to some last-minute client affairs—before they finally left Europe by what was by then the only exit route for Americans—the trek through Spain and Portugal to the port of Lisbon, where the twice-weekly Pan Am flying boat service provided the one remaining civilian transport link between Europe and the New World.

John B. Robinson, on the other hand, never gave a thought to leaving France, according to his secretary Yvonne Bazin. As the leading attorney for the British and American communities in Paris, Robinson was responsible for numerous estates and trusts whose beneficiaries had already left France as well as for other property left in his care by absent clients. Moreover, at age sixty-five, he had spent the last forty-one years of his life in France and had few personal ties left to the States, and his wife's health virtually prohibited her traveling, for she suffered from what a French lawyer at Coudert Frères described as "arterial sclerosis of the brain" and was "nearly mad."

As the Germans approached Paris, Robinson's main concern, according to Bazin, was protecting the Coudert Frères client files. "We had a lot of Jewish clients, you see, quite a lot," Madame Bazin recalled in 1990 at age ninety-one. There were also sensitive files relating to the property of prominent individuals in countries at war with Germany. Millions of people were trying to find transport out of Paris after June 10, 1940, but Robinson, for whom money was not a problem, was able to acquire a truck—"a very, very big truck," says Bazin. All the office files were loaded onto the truck, and Robinson and Bazin (whose husband was then in Brittany with the French Army) drove the files and Mrs. Robinson to Robinson's place in the country, "his little château on the Rhône."

Following the armistice on June 17, France was divided into a German-occupied zone and a much smaller unoccupied zone to the south. Robinson's château was within the occupied zone, and in a few days some German troops swept up the driveway and knocked at the door. "Fortunately," Bazin recalls, "the German officer was most interested in the grounds. I took him around the grounds, and he particularly wanted to see the *allée.*" This *allée* was a promenade lined with trees whose branches interlocked overhead. "I think the Germans were interested in that," says Bazin, "because they could not tell from their airplanes what was underneath. When the officer saw there were no shells, no guns placed there, he was satisfied and went away." The files, however, were clearly no safer in the countryside then they would be in Paris. When word came that the Germans in Paris were behaving "correctly," Robinson and Bazin returned to the city and reopened the Coudert Frères office at 52, avenue des Champs-Élysées.

The Coudert Frères employees came back to work, for, war or no war, everyone still had to earn a living. Throughout the war, the only outward change in the office routine was the break that came each morning when German troops marched up the Champs-Élysées. The Germans paraded at the same hour each day, and as soon as the first row of marching soldiers was visible from the tall windows that looked out over the avenue, the Coudert Frères lawyers and secretaries pushed their chairs back from their desks and stood up. Their backs turned ostentatiously to the windows, they stood silently until the Germans had passed. Then they turned around, resumed their seats, and went back to work. It was a very small form of daily defiance, but it was one that did lessen somewhat everyone's feelings of helplessness.

As for the sensitive client files, Robinson turned for help to attorney René de Chambrun, whose office was located on the floor below Coudert Frères at 52, avenue des Champs-Élysées. De Chambrun was a French citizen by birth, a direct descendant of the Marquis de Lafayette; he was also an American citizen by virtue of the automatic citizenship rights conferred, in perpetuity, by a grateful post-revolutionary Congress upon all descendants of Lafayette. The de Chambrun and Coudert families had been friends since the period immediately after the Civil War, when Frederic René Coudert had been attorney to the French consulate in New York City and René de Chambrun's grandfather had been legal counselor to the French legation in Washington, D.C. In the next generation, Fred Coudert and René de Chambrun's father, the World War I hero General Adolphe de Chambrun, had continued the friendship, and Fred Coudert had prepared an affidavit of support of René de Chambrun's admission to the New York State bar in 1932.

De Chambrun arranged for Robinson to hide the Coudert Frères files at the Convent of Picpus (Société Civile de l'Oratoire et du Convent de Picpus), of which his father was a curator. There, a few steps from Lafayette's tomb, they were safely kept by the nuns, until they could be returned to Robinson during the winter of 1945–46.

Meanwhile, although the United States maintained diplomatic relations with both Vichy France and Germany until December

1941, Robinson's position as an American citizen in occupied France became precarious long before that date. Because of his age, he did not initially have to register with the Germans as younger Americans did, but he was often stopped on the streets and asked to show his papers. The American diplomat Robert Murphy, who frequently visited Paris during the first years of the war, once told Hugh Fitzgerald that he had seen Robinson stopped and questioned by a German officer about why he had no papers. Robinson took a self-confident, almost arrogant line with the German, until the officer backed off. "Robinson," Murphy told Fitzgerald admiringly, "knew how to handle the Germans."

On the other hand, because he was well past military age, Robinson was not interned when younger Americans in France were swept up after the U.S. invasion of North Africa. Following D day, however, the Germans rounded up all Americans, regardless of age. At that point, Robinson went into hiding at the home of some French friends, but he would emerge safely a few months later upon the liberation of Paris.

Because postal and telegraphic communication with Paris was totally cut off in May 1940, Robinson made his decision to remain in France and then to reopen the Coudert Frères office entirely on his own, without consultation with his New York partners. Fred Coudert never faulted Robinson for his decision, but, according to Dubé, he was deeply disturbed when he learned that the office had been reopened. For one thing, Coudert had no faith in the "correctness" of the Nazis. "Mr. Coudert, Sr., was not naive about the Nazis," says Dubé. "Of course, none of us would know the full score of what they did until after the war, but I would say that Coudert was a good deal less naive at that point than some. And I don't suppose there's any harm in saying this after all these years, but, as the war went on, Mr. Coudert was afraid that Robinson would be put in a position of collaborating. This was no reflection on Robinson, who was really a wonderful human being and the last person you would think of doing such a thing, of his own free will. It's simply that Coudert knew that when people are sitting on your back with a knife at your throat, there's no telling what you may do. Of course, we know now that nothing of the sort happened, but Mr. Coudert, I know, was very concerned. It was one of the things worrying him all during the war."

By the time Robinson had returned from his château to Paris, communication with New York was theoretically possible again, although conducted under German censorship controls. In July 1940, Hopkins wanted to cable Coudert Frères about an estate matter. If actually sent, that cable would have been a rarity, for in the early summer of 1940 Coudert made it clear to everyone at 2 Rector Street, recalls Jim Hughes, "that we must have no further contact with Coudert Frères or with John Robinson from that time forward." In view of Paris's status as an occupied city, the partners decided there would be no attempt to carry on business as normal. Nonetheless, the U.S. State Department offered Coudert Brothers the courtesy of using the diplomatic pouch to convey letters to Coudert Frères, provided the letters were written in English and related on their face strictly to American interests in France. A thin trickle of correspondence did go out through that pouch until December 1941, but only of the most necessary kind, such as the transmittal of papers that needed to be signed by Americans still in France in order to settle estates. The two offices exchanged no personal or office-related news; Scip Bellinger died during this period, for example, but Robinson was not told of his death. And after Pearl Harbor, even this slight line of communication was severed.

Immediately after the fall of France, during the summer of 1940, the people at Coudert Brothers in New York were worrying not just about Robinson and all the other individual clients and friends caught behind the German advance but about the fate of England, which was now taking the brunt of the German blitz. Coudert, through the White Committee, was pushing that summer for the transfer to Great Britain of fifty overage destroyers, which England said were vital to its ability to keep open its lines of supply. In July, Coudert wrote to Stimson, "The White Committee is striving valiantly along the trails that you aided us to blaze. We are encouraged to believe that Great Britain may by her own efforts save us and civilization besides but we do hope that the U.S.A. may be giving substantial help. They desperately need destroyers." Coudert was taking the optimistic view of Britain's efforts on principle; no one could be truly certain how the Battle of Britain would end. "It was," says Hughes, "a strange, terrible, suspenseful time."

It was against this backdrop of general anxiety that the New York office confronted the horrendous tangle of business and personal problems created for its clients by the fall of France. Some of these problems were beyond Coudert Brothers' ability to resolve. What, for example, could the firm do for an American who wanted to know if his second home in France was intact, if his servants were safe, and if there were any way to arrange to pay the property taxes, which had previously been handled by a British banker at Morgan & Cie. in Paris? The answer was nothing, except to advise him on how to contact Morgan & Cie. himself. Then there was the marquise who wanted to transfer money to her daughter-in-law's account in New York, if the daughter-in-law could arrange to repay her in francs in France. That matter required consultation with the Chase Bank, which handled the daughter-in-law's French accounts. With its ties cut to Coudert Frères, Coudert Brothers had no knowledge itself of what could and could not practically be done in occupied France.

Where Coudert Brothers could help was with the problems French nationals and others had in connection with their property and assets already in the United States. And they had many problems, because the United States government moved immediately at the start of the German offensive in the spring of 1940 to "freeze" property within the United States belonging to nationals of countries conquered by Germany. An executive order, quickly ratified by Congress, prohibited on April 10, 1940, any transactions involving property of Denmark and Norway or their nationals, except under license from the Treasury Department. The "freezing orders" were extended to the Netherlands, Belgium, and Luxembourg on May 10, to France and Monaco on June 17, to Latvia, Estonia, and Lithuania on July 10 (when they were seized by the USSR in accordance with its pact with Germany), and then to other European countries as the war progressed.

The purpose of the freezing orders was to protect nationals of these occupied countries and keep whatever property they had in the United States from falling into the hands of the Germans or their allies. "If this had not been done," Hughes points out, "physical pressure could have been brought on nationals of these friendly countries or their families to transfer assets to unrightful owners. It was a benign act, and, although there was resentment in some quarters, the great majority of our clients realized they were being protected." The freezing orders did not change the title to any assets, but they kept affected foreigners from using their assets without first obtaining a license. Treasury licenses were of two kinds: general licenses, the most common of which permitted persons living in the United States to draw a fixed sum each month from their own blocked funds to meet their living expenses, and special licenses, which were considered on a transaction-by-transaction basis and were more the rule than the exception.

Montgomery, Hughes, and Alexis Coudert handled most of the "frozen assets" matters for Coudert Brothers, although other associates like Hugh Fitzgerald found themselves at various times assigned to this area as well. According to Hughes, the firm was already completing applications for special licenses before the French collapse, but it was, of course, on June 17, 1940, when France was added to the list of blocked countries, that the associates found themselves writing applications fast and furiously. Without a special license, companies like Coty International Corporation and Renault could not use their U.S. funds even to meet their payrolls in the United States or pay their U.S. suppliers. "The Treasury normally granted special licenses to companies so that they could operate their businesses here, with the usual conditions being the filing of regular compliance reports and no foreign transfer of funds," Hughes says. "There were some cases where we had to supply special evidence or even go to Washington to present the case. But the applications were routine in most instances. Still, they were interesting for me as a young associate, since I learned a lot about the affairs of some of our very good clients."

Individual nationals of blocked countries and Americans who had income from those countries or had been resident there before the war also needed licenses. Changing the registration of a security, paying an insurance premium to the U.S. subsidiary of a foreign insurance company, selling or buying any property, spending any money beyond the monthly sum specified in the applicable general license—all of these acts required either a special license or an amendment of the general license. As the Treasury Department got more organized, it developed general rulings for handling estates and trusts, but Coudert Brothers' multijurisdictional estates were a special headache in themselves.

The fall of France produced another type of problem for certain Coudert Brothers' clients. These were American companies like Coty and Durand Ruel, which, because they had had substantial operations in France, had large sums of money on deposit in France. They did not want to leave these funds in France, but U.S. corporate income tax rates were so high, they were hesitant to repatriate the money and see most of it disappear in taxes. Harold Johnson by then was in New York, and one of his clients in Paris had been National City Bank's Paris branch. According to Dubé, "Johnson and Coudert put their heads together and came up with the idea of setting up a City Bank subsidiary and bringing the funds to Havana. But to have the Treasury of the United States accept this as a nontaxable event, a resident of Cuba had to be the head of the corporation holding the funds." Johnson and Coudert asked Dubé, who was sharing offices at 2 Rector Street with Coudert Brothers, if he would head the corporation and go to Cuba for the three to four months needed to establish residency.

"I was quite flattered," says Dubé. "They were giving me, you see, sole signatory power over millions of dollars." Dubé went to Cuba in December 1940 and stayed until April 1941; he would return again for a shorter period later on. As the war went on, however, and it became obvious that France would not be liberated any time soon, the clients decided there was no point continuing to hold their money offshore in Cuba. "After a few years," says Dubé, "they decided to bring it to the U.S. and pay the taxes."

As this anecdote suggests, neither Johnson nor Dubé had much trouble reestablishing active practices in New York. Johnson remained a Coudert Frères partner, while Dubé continued his independent practice, but both were hospitably welcomed by the New York office and worked closely with each other and with the New York partners on many matters, just as they had in France. As for Russell Hare, the third partner in Coudert Frères, he ended up, after not quite a year at 2 Rector Street, going down to Washington, D.C., at Fred Coudert's request, to reestablish a Coudert Brothers office there.

By the spring of 1941, when Hare visited Washington, the nation's capital was already beginning to experience a war-driven leap in population and office space was at a premium. Coudert had hoped for premises in Jackson Place, but the firm had to settle for a rather dingy office that Hare found in the Bond Building—the same building in which Coudert Brothers had been located earlier in the century. There was some discussion, initiated by Hare, that the Washington branch might be set up as a branch of Coudert Frères, but nothing came of the idea. Indeed, Hare practiced in Washington only from May 1941 to February 1942, when he was struck by sudden illness. Percy Shay—rushed down from New York "temporarily"—then became the partner at the Washington, D.C., office and would remain the only partner there for the next twenty-four years.

In the spring of 1941, about the time the Washington, D.C., office was being set up, Coudert Brothers began preparing to defend one of the firm's oldest clients, the Banque de France, against an action brought by the Banque Nationale de Belgique. Involving the central banks of two major European countries, this was, as Fred Coudert would say, an "important litigation," and he gave it his personal attention, which was just as well, for the Banque de France case was to prove the most controversial litigation Coudert Brothers ever handled.

The origins of the case go back to February 1940, when, in anticipation of the German offensive, the Banque Nationale de Belgique sent the Belgian gold reserves, the fourth largest in the world, abroad for safekeeping. Large deposits were made in London and New York, and 228 tons, about a third of the Belgian national funds, were entrusted to the Banque de France. In May, all the gold on deposit with the Banque de France was moved to coastal ports, and, following Dunkirk, the French began hastily shipping it abroad. There was considerable difficulty finding transport, but over 700 tons of French gold were sent, under conditions of great secrecy, to Canada, New York, and Martinique between June 2 and June 12. On June 17, the gold at Lorient, which included the Belgian gold, was loaded onto a French auxiliary cruiser, and at 3:00 in the morning on June 18, after Pétain had taken over the government, the cruiser steamed off to rendezvous with French ships from Brest carrying 736 tons of French gold. This small convoy sailed for Dakar in French West Africa.

The Belgians would later maintain that in mid-June the Belgian cabinet, then in exile in France, had accepted an offer from the British to send a naval vessel to pick up the Belgian gold in France and transport it to New York. On June 18 the Belgian cabinet members arrived in Bordeaux, settled into lodgings, and presumably informed Governor Georges Janssen of the Banque Nationale de Belgique of the transport arrangements. The British ship was then at the port of Bordeaux, and Janssen, who was also in Bordeaux, sent a note requesting the Banque de France to deliver the gold to the British, if feasible ("si les circonstances le comportent"). But the instructions of June 18 came too late, after the Belgian gold was already on the high seas, and the Belgian gold ended up in Dakar.

Following the armistice, the French government was left in control only of the southern unoccupied zone of France and such colonies as remained loyal to the new government, which included French West Africa. With two-thirds of the French living under German rule in the occupied zone and with nearly 2 million soldiers in German prison camps, Pétain's administration was immediately subject to tremendous pressure from the Germans to cooperate with them, one of the first issues raised being that of the Belgian gold. From July 1940 onward, the Vichy French government refused repeated requests to hand over the Belgian gold to German representatives, but on October 30, 1940, they agreed to deliver it to the Banque Nationale de Belgique in Brussels (under German occupation), if so requested by the latter institution. The governor of the Belgian bank, Georges Janssen, however, was the very person who had tried to arrange on June 18 for the Belgian gold to go to New York. Still in France on June 26, he had then tried to salvage the situation by attempting to sell the Belgian gold in Dakar to the U.S. government so that the tangible gold holdings could be "earmarked" as U.S. gold reserves, but the United States refused the request in comformance with its policy of not holding any gold overseas. On October 30, back in Brussels, Janssen remained determined that the Belgian gold should not fall into German hands, and, in one of the lesser known acts of bravery of World War II, he categorically refused to request the return of the gold from Dakar. He would later pay for his resistance with his life, and his courage, which relieved the French of a difficult situation, both shamed and elated Vichy officials.

The relief unfortunately was only temporary. On November 29, 1940, a German official was complaining about the Belgian gold situation to Pierre Laval, who was the second-highest-ranking member of the Vichy cabinet, next to Pétain, and one of those convinced that France's best option was active collaboration with the Germans. Laval picked up the phone, in the presence of the German official, and ordered that the Belgian gold be turned over to the Germans forthwith. This produced a French cabinet crisis, partly because Laval's act constituted a recognition that the German occupation of Belgium was legitimate, which carried with it the implication that the German occupation of most of France was also legal. By mid-December Pétain had dismissed Laval from the cabinet and placed him under arrest, but the old marshal, who was then eighty-four years old, lacked the courage to countermand Laval's order. Afraid of German retaliation upon the French, the Vichy cabinet wobbled and finally decided to order the Belgian gold shipped back to Europe but to deposit it with the Reichsbank in the name of the Banque de France (i.e., to have the Banque de France appoint the Reichsbank as subdepository). Simultaneously, the French Treasury gave an indemnity to the Banque de France that, if the Germans then seized this gold (as they were certain to do), the treasury would place an equal sum at the disposition of the Banque de France for eventual restitution to the Banque Nationale de Belgique. The treasury also quietly notified the Banque Nationale de Belgique in Brussels that it considered itself bound to restore to the Belgians the full 228 tons from the French gold holdings.

The Banque de France, of course, wished to go on record as having nothing to do with the whole deal. Accordingly, in December 1940 the Vichy minister of finance, Yves Bouthillier, and the governor of the Banque de France, Pierre de Boisanger, negotiated the text of a letter of protest. In the final draft, which Bouthillier found acceptable, the Banque de France noted that transferring the gold without instructions from its depositor violated the laws of deposit, that it felt, nonetheless, constrained to accept the government's order to transfer the gold since the government was maintaining that the matter was of *"importance capitale"* to the nation, and that the government had agreed to assume all responsibility for the transfer and its consequences.

Once the decision was made, the French did not rush to execute it. The responsibility for shipping the gold from its depository several hundred miles inland from Dakar rested ultimately on the governor-general of French West Africa, Pierre Boisson, and his superior, General Maxime Weygand, two old soldiers who were loyal to Pétain but strongly anti-German. Not in the least eager to help the Germans, the colonial authorities reported that, because they did not have enough airplane fuel to fly the gold out of French West Africa, every ingot would have to go by truck caravan across the Sahara. There were no Germans in West Africa, not even a consular officer, so no one was in a position to contradict the French authorities, and the first gold apparently did not leave French West Africa until March 1941. To the accompaniment of a string of artful excuses—the trucks have broken down, no spare parts are available, the weather is bad—the French managed to drag the shipments out until June 1942. The Germans repeatedly offered the use of their planes, estimating that they could have all the gold flown out in six weeks at most. But the French shrugged, buying time. Weygand and others of anti-German sentiment in Vichy France were following a policy of *attentisme,* or attentively awaiting the moment when France could make a move against the Germans that would not be suicidal and, in the meantime, meeting German demands with evasion and delay. The French hoped for a change in fortune—the British might defeat Rommel, Hitler might drop dead, the Americans might enter the war, the British might take up their hints that the shipments from Casablanca to Marseilles should be intercepted and turned back—but time was not on their side.

Meanwhile, members of the Belgian cabinet had escaped from Bordeaux and reached London, where they set up a government-in-exile. Since many high Belgian and Vichy officials, not to mention most of the French Deuxième Bureau (Military Intelligence), had already figured out various ways to keep information flowing intermittently but regularly out of their countries, the exiled Belgian government knew by December 1940 that Vichy had agreed to deliver the Belgian gold to the Germans. In Washington, D.C., Belgian ambassador extraordinary Georges Theunis conceived the idea of suing to attach the French gold on deposit in the name of the Banque de France at the Federal Reserve Bank in New York. Alleging that the Banque de France had refused to return the Belgian gold on demand and converted the same, the Banque Nationale de Belgique—not the one in Brussels but one serving the exile government in London—obtained an attachment order against the Banque de France in February 1941, pending a trial on the issues.

A curious and important fact about the Belgian suit was that it was brought in the United States, which was a neutral country, and not in Canada, which as part of the British Commonwealth was at war with Germany. The French had large gold deposits in Canada as well, and one would think that the Belgian government-in-exile would prefer to bring suit in that sympathetic jurisdiction to recover its gold. However, the Belgian government-in-exile, although resident in London and working closely with Britain in the war effort, was concerned about British intentions with respect to the gold. The Belgians were, in fact, under considerable pressure to turn over their gold in London to their British hosts, who were growing more and more desperate for funds with which to purchase arms from the United States—which, it will be recalled, would only sell them to the British on a cash basis.

The quiet tug-of-war between the Belgian government-in-exile and the British over the Belgian gold began late in the summer of 1940, on the eve of a British expedition to seize Dakar and the Belgian gold stored there. An "acrimonious dispute" broke out when the British revealed that they intended to use whatever gold was captured to finance their purchases of war material in the United States. General Charles de Gaulle, whose Free French forces were an integral part of the expedition and were expected to govern French West Africa after it was seized from Vichy, went out of his way to reassure the Belgian representatives in London that he would not permit the British to use the gold as they pleased and would look out for their interests. De Gaulle held firm on this point, even when the British threatened to scrap the expedition, and the British government gave in. The expedition was a military failure, though, and the gold remained in French West Africa under Vichy control.

By December 1940, the British had nearly exhausted their own gold reserves and similar assets, and permanent undersecretary of the Foreign Office Sir Alexander Cadogan wrote in his diary on December 24 that he had conferred with British Treasury officials "about the Dutch and Belgian gold, which we must try to snaffle. We *can* snaffle the Belgian, but I don't want to be harder on them than the Dutch." Cadogan, though, was mistaken about being able to "snaffle" the Belgian gold on deposit at the Bank of England. Camille Gutt, minister of finance, war and commerce in the Belgian refugee government, told a U.S. Treasury official a few months later that "the British had tried very hard to 'bamboozle' the Belgian Government in London into selling their gold to the British against sterling. The Belgians had not agreed to this and have only made an arrangement with the British which involves a loan of gold until after the war."

It was not that the Belgians did not want to help the British. The Belgian exile government, in fact, had a steady and enviable income throughout the war from the Belgian Congo, most of which went directly to help the war effort. But the Belgians had need of money that they could use independently of British control, for they had one objective to which Churchill's government was strongly and vehemently opposed: they wished to provide charitable relief, principally food and medicine, to their own people in Belgium. Between the effects of the British blockade and the rapacity of the Germans, the Belgians were starving in the winter of 1940–41. For that matter, so were the nationals of every other European country except Germany, but the situation in Belgium was especially acute. The daily ration for adults there was only nine hundred calories a day, as opposed to the minimum requirement of twenty-six hundred calories.

"The Belgians must eat," Gutt told the American press, when asked the reason why the Belgian government-in-exile had brought the suit. "Naturally the English blockade is a combat arm and we would not want to weaken it; but we would explore and test what can be done, without weakening it, in the way of feeding our children and our sick." In World War I, America had been generous in providing relief to German-occupied Belgium. The Belgians hoped that America would be generous again and that, in response to American public opinion, Roosevelt would prevail upon Churchill to let relief supplies go through. In that eventuality, the Belgians could use the gold attached in New York to finance their relief shipments, without interference from the British.

The Belgians had specific reason to be hopeful of American help early in 1941, for Roosevelt had successfully insisted in December 1940 that Churchill lift the "hunger blockade" sufficiently to allow a few shiploads of American Red Cross supplies to reach Vichy, and the U.S. State Department in early February concluded a pact with General Weygand to allow some supplies to reach the Vichy colonies in Africa. Dependent on American aid, Churchill resisted the partial lifting of the blockade as stubbornly as he could, warning Roosevelt that "The anxiety we have always felt about this [Red Cross] project is that it would lead to similar demands on behalf of our German-occupied Allies." What the Belgians were not to know was that there was a faction in the U.S. State Department, centered in the Office of the Economic Advisor, which agreed that it was dangerous to lift the blockade even to permit occasional relief shipments and which bitterly opposed any American action that would embarrass England. One of those opposed to the Belgian plans was the head of the Office of the Economic Advisor, Herbert Feis; another was one of Feis's aides, Tom Finletter, who took a leave of absence from Coudert Brothers in 1940 to accept a position as special assistant for international economic affairs in the Office of the Economic Advisor.

Ultimately, Roosevelt was to swing behind the British point of view. Thus, visiting the White House later in 1941, Belgian minister of foreign affairs Paul-Henri Spaak encountered a chilly reception:

> The President was cold and matter-of-fact in what he had to say. I explained to him the food situation in occupied Belgium and exerted all my powers of persuasion to interest him in the fate of my compatriots. He listened to me impassively. When I ended my plea, he declared coldly, without betraying the slightest sign of human warmth or compassion, that nothing could be done. This unfeeling answer was accompanied by comments which angered me, and this anger was all the harder to contain as I was forced to hide it. He declared that the trials through which Belgium was passing were not so tragic. . . . I was dumbfounded, and so was M. Theunis, who was with me. It was he— his English was very much better than mine—who replied pointedly, but to no effect.

Not being able to foresee this future, however, the Belgians selected New York as their venue to attach the French gold, in the hope of being able to use it for relief shipments, and retained John Foster Dulles of Sullivan & Cromwell as their counsel. The Banque de France retained Coudert Brothers, a more or less automatic action since Coudert Brothers had represented the bank since the nineteenth century. The Banque de France, which had no office in New York, had never actually generated much legal work or large fees, but Coudert Brothers had always been glad to have it as a client because of its prestige.

Since it was later alleged that its representation of the Banque de France was proof that the firm had pro-Vichy and fascist sympathies, it is perhaps worthwhile to mention what else was going on in Fred Coudert's life in the spring of 1941 when he took this retainer. He was still extremely active in the affairs of the Committee to Defend America by Aiding the Allies, writing and speaking in favor of lend-lease. White and other key members of the committee would resign that spring over the question of providing U.S. naval

escorts for British supply ships, an action they feared would bring
America into the war. White and those of like mind had wished to
aid the Allies, not to have American soldiers go to war. Coudert,
though, believed that America ought to fight, and on this litmus-
paper issue, he came down firmly in favor of the convoys. In March
he traveled to Havana as a delegate to the Inter-American Bar Association, one of those goodwill gatherings encouraged by the U.S.
State Department in its efforts to build up hemispheric solidarity
against the Axis powers, where he gave a speech extolling the Constitution as "the complete negation of the totalitarian state." And
he was organizing a benefit for Bundles for Britain, a charity sending aid to victims of the blitz.

On the personal side, Coudert was still recovering from the
appalling news that his old friend Henri Bergson, who had bravely
returned voluntarily to occupied Paris and pinned on his yellow
star as a Jew, had died alone in Paris of cold and starvation. He was
corresponding with Stanley Baldwin, who mentioned that their
mutual friend, Oxford classical scholar J. W. Mackail, was homeless
at age eighty-one, his London residence having been destroyed in
a bombing attack. And he appears to have been using his network
of influential friends to gather data on what was happening to the
Jews under Hitler, for in late spring Baldwin wrote to Coudert
thanking him "for all the trouble you have taken in getting me information about the unhappy Austrian Jews."

Coudert never answered the allegations made against him and
his firm, but his actions and words speak for his continued vehe-
ment opposition to Fascism. The allegation that, by contesting the
Belgian lien on Banque of France funds in the United States, the
firm was trying to free up the money that Vichy would surely use
to aid the Nazis was very wide of the truth: the gold in question
was "frozen" in the Federal Reserve Bank in New York City.
Whether the Belgians or French held title to it, it could only be
used under treasury license, and—as every lawyer involved well
knew—there was not the remotest possibility that Secretary
Morgenthau would let the gold, whatever the outcome of the suit,
be used to provide comfort to Hitler. Moreover, on the basis of the
Belgian exile government's statements to press conferences in both
London and New York, Coudert had every reason to believe that
the Belgians would use the gold to finance relief shipments to the
Continent—a proposal that he, Finletter, and others viewed as actively damaging to the British war effort.

World War II was in many ways a simple war, the straightfor-
ward conflict between good and evil that Fred Coudert said it was,
but the people caught up in the war did not always behave in sim-

ple ways or from simple motives. This was evident, for example, when Fred Coudert, Paul Fuller, Jr., and Mahlon Doing began conferring with Jean Martial, special representative of the Banque de France, who arrived in New York on February 21, 1941, two weeks after the Belgians obtained the attachment order. The Belgian case was directed specifically at the Banque de France, not the French government. As Jan-Albert Goris, editorial writer for the official information sheet put out by the exile government, summarized the grievance, "When the Belgian Government ordered the Banque de France to ship her deposits to London, this same bank shipped them to Africa and at the first request of the Nazis handed them over to the enemy." Accordingly, the Banque de France had an obvious defense in the argument of *force majeure:* the French government had done both the shipping and the handing over to the enemy. There were also defenses in the specific facts of what happened on June 18, 1940, and, given the loose wording of the Belgian instructions on June 18, in the law of contracts.

It developed, however, that Martial did not want to employ any of these defenses, unless there was no alternative, because the bank wanted to avoid, if possible, a court decision. If the Banque de France lost in the New York courts, it was concerned that it would have the double liability of having to reimburse both the Brussels and the London Belgian banks for the loss of the Belgian gold. On the other hand, a victory in the U.S. courts would mean that the Banque de France was relieved of responsibility for restoring their gold to the Belgians, and the Banque de France did not wish to be relieved of the responsibility. It maintained that it owed the 228 tons of gold to the Banque Nationale de Belgique, that it was prevented by circumstances beyond its control from returning the gold to its depositor, but that it had a solemn obligation to do so at the first possible opportunity and it would be disgraceful to seek to evade that obligation. The Banque de France was prepared to promise that, even if the French government did not put the necessary funds at its disposal, the bank itself would reimburse the Belgians from its own assets—for, despite its quasi-public role, the Banque de France was a private corporation. There was a question of honor at stake, and surely the Belgians would understand, if it was properly explained to them, that they might have confidence in the Banque de France's fidelity to its trust?

The Belgians didn't understand. They wanted their gold not after the war but immediately to feed their children in German-occupied Belgium. Nonetheless, the Banque de France continued to seek an out-of-court settlement, while pursuing, in the same spirit of *attentisme,* a delay in the trial on the issues. An initial challenge to the competence of the Banque Nationale de Belgique to bring suit in New York was successful, but the Belgian bank overcame this difficulty by assigning its claim to two American citizens resident in New York, Daniel de Gorter and Henri Wild. Next, in July 1941, Coudert Brothers entered a motion to dismiss the suit. The grounds on which a dismissal was sought were (1) that the parties had agreed any dispute arising out of the transaction should be confined to the courts of France; and (2) that assumption of jurisdiction by the New York courts "would constitute an unconstitutional burden on foreign commerce." Both contentions were immediately overruled, but, since the Banque de France still hoped for a settlement, the second argument was kept alive by Coudert Brothers in appeals all the way to the U.S. Supreme Court. When the procedural issues were exhausted, the discovery process began, and the depositions advanced sufficiently to indicate that the Banque de France would predicate its defense on the intervention of the French government and its exercise of *force majeure*.

By the fall of 1942, however, the American representatives and attorneys for both banks had approved a proposed settlement agreement, in which the Banque de France guaranteed the restitution of the gold upon the cessation of hostilities. In Vichy France and England, the directors of the two banks had also agreed to the settlement in principle, and certain minor changes in the text were being negotiated at the same time as the case was being prepared for trial. But the United States invaded North Africa in November 1942, communications with France were suspended, and both trial and settlement negotiations had to be indefinitely postponed because Coudert Brothers could no longer consult with its client. The Belgians did not receive their 228 tons of gold until late in 1944, when the French government was reconstituted under General de Gaulle.

One of the peculiarities of the Banque de France case was the fact that Coudert Brothers' Washington files show Percy Shay raising some matter with Tom Finletter at the State Department in 1942 on behalf of the Free French—the bitter enemies of Vichy France. Furthermore, a confidential report prepared by J. Edgar Hoover of the FBI in April 1942 alleges that Fred Coudert was retained by René Plevin, General de Gaulle's special emissary to the United States, in the fall of 1941, when the Banque de France case was well advanced. The report, which was declassified in 1979, states: "When Mr. Plevin left the United States in 1941, he decided that he would do something big for the Free French Delegation, and as a result he personally hired the Coudert firm of lawyers for

the Free French Delegation, he, Plevin, paying the retainer's fee."
The source of this information is given as the secretary to the Free
French delegation in New York City.

The FBI report contains outright untruths on subjects not related to Coudert Brothers and is generally so shoddy that it is difficult to take any of it seriously. Yet Plevin and Coudert Brothers
had had contact in 1939–40 when Plevin, as one of the senior
members of the French Economic Mission in London, had been
supervising the French aircraft purchases. It is not wholly improbable that he might have consulted Coudert Brothers, at least informally, for some reason in 1941. The FBI report has to give one
pause, as does the fact that Coudert Brothers continued to represent the Banque de France after its Vichyite governors had been
dismissed and Gaullist loyalists placed at its helm.

In fact, Coudert Brothers, acting for the Banque de France,
signed the settlement in late 1944 with the Banque Nationale de
Belgique, and in December 30, 1944, the new governor of the
Banque de France, who had been appointed personally by General
de Gaulle, sent Coudert Brothers a telegram reading,

> Vous exprime mes plus vifs remerciements pour le concours si
> efficace et si éclaire que vous avez bien voulu prêter à la
> Banque de France au cours de cette longue instance et de la
> competence avec laquelle la procedure a été conduité par vous.
> [I extend my warmest thanks for the very effective and enlight-
> ened assistance that you have provided to the Banque de
> France during this extended proceeding and the competent
> way it was handled.]

When Fred Coudert visited France in 1946, at a time when reprisals were being conducted against Vichy sympathizers and the
emotional wounds of the war were still raw, the new Gaullist management of the Banque de France gave a breakfast in his honor.
Moreover, in 1953 the Banque de France, in commemoration of its
150th anniversary, struck a handful of medals for presentation to
persons who had given "extraordinary" services to the bank and
notified the firm that one of those medals would be awarded to
Fred Coudert. All of this tends to suggest that there was more going on beneath the surface of the Banque de France case than at
this late date—with all the protagonists dead many years—can possibly be recaptured.

The most important impact of the Banque de France case on
Coudert Brothers, however, was the excoriation of the firm by the
American press for representing the bank. This flailing was, of

course, rather unusual, for lawyers are seldom attacked in America for accepting clients whose views are unpopular. It is generally understood that the common-law system would founder if lawyers prescreened their clients or their clients' ideas for acceptability. From the Confederate blockade runners of the 1860s to the accused murderers and felons defended by Fritz Coudert in Prohibition days, Coudert Brothers during its long history had represented many a controversial figure without incurring any criticism. Why, then, was the Banque de France case any different? The answer to that lies in the timing of the attacks on the firm, which did not begin until 1942 when Fritz Coudert was running for reelection to the State Senate.

By that year Fritz himself was a highly controversial figure, because he had chaired a Senate committee investigating the alleged subversive activities of the Communist party in the public schools of the city of New York. The investigation began in early 1940, when liberals and democratic socialists in the labor union movement were looking for ways to expose the tactics of the Soviet-controlled Communists and root them out of the unions. They focused on the teachers' unions, and Coudert, who had a good record of support for academic freedom, was approached to head the Senate subcommittee. Coudert agreed, for numerous reasons. His grandfather and father before him had, during their tenures on the Board of Education, worked to protect teachers from holding their positions at the whim of a political party. Back then, the party in question was the Tammany Democrats, not the Communists, but the issue seemed much the same, nonetheless. Fritz, like his father, also had a very strong dislike of Soviet Communism, a dislike based not only on conservatism but also on friendship with many Russian refugees. And finally there was the fact that Stalin had just concluded his nonaggression pact with Hitler. Fritz adhered to the conservative wing of the Republican party in all respects except one: he was no isolationist. In fact, he was anxious to strike a blow against Hitler. Thus, it was no coincidence that the Coudert subcommittee began its inquiries not long after the signing of the Ribbentrop-Molotov Pact and ended them, abruptly, in June 1941 when Germany invaded the USSR.

During its brief duration, the Coudert subcommittee took reams of testimony but, largely because of its sudden termination, apparently accomplished little, except to stir up emotions and confirm both Communists and anti-Communists in their own opinions. Fritz's widow, Paula Coudert, in 1985 published a privately printed biography of her husband, which makes a spirited effort to demonstrate that the Coudert subcommittee was reasonably respectful of witnesses' rights and reputations and was not merely an irresponsible witch-hunt. Still, the inquiry generated more heat than light—and so did the election campaign of 1942, in which Fritz defended his seat against a liberal Democrat, Jerry Finkelstein. As an incumbent, Fritz had the edge, but in the final days of the campaign, as reported by the *New York Times,* Finkelstein charged that Fritz, "through his law firm, Coudert Brothers, had represented 'the Hitler-dominated Vichy government' in this country" in its endeavor " 'to usurp Allied gold for the benefit of the Nazis.' " These were deadly charges, because by the fall of 1942 the United States was at war with Germany. Over the next several days, furthermore, Fritz personally was accused of being a Laval agent, a fascist, and, more mildly, a stooge who was unaware of the dangers of fascism. Those were the published attacks. Simultaneously, it appears almost certain that there was a whispering campaign that the Couderts and their firm were anti-Semitic.

Fritz soon gave up trying to answer the accusations and went on the offensive, alleging that he was being made the subject of a smear campaign by the Communists and trying to cast doubts on Finkelstein's patriotism. The campaign turned, in short, into a classic electoral free-for-all. The accusations against Fritz fell short of their immediate aim, for a considerable number of labor union and Jewish leaders came to his support, and he won the election.

Among those who thought the attacks on Fritz unjust was, interestingly, one of the plaintiffs in the Banque de France case. On a vacation in Maine in August 1943, Mal Doing wrote to Paul Fuller, Jr., that he had encountered one of the Belgian bank's assignees:

> I forgot to tell you on the 'phone the other day that upon my arrival here I found among the guests *"the"* Daniel De Gorter of "De Gorter v. Banque de France." He is here with his family and they are very charming people. Upon being referred by the proprietor to "Mr. Doing of Coudert Brothers" as reference, Mr. De Gorter replied, "If Coudert Brothers like the place, it's good enough for me."
>
> Once or twice we have jokingly referred to each other as "enemies," and upon one occasion De Gorter waxed indignant against [the periodical] "P.M." for its scurrilous attack on Fritz during the campaign, and said that he had been sorely tempted to write Fritz a letter for publication. Only his position as nominal plaintiff in the case stayed his hand. Tell Fritz for me. I'm sure it will please him as it has me.

I went trout fishing with De Gorter yesterday. Everything
was rosy except the weather and the trout. . . .

While the accusations may have been unfair, their effect on
the firm of Coudert Brothers was, nonetheless, long-lasting. Some
forty and fifty years after the fact, in places as far-flung as Beijing
and Johannesburg, people from Coudert Brothers have been
asked, "Aren't you the law firm that represented Vichy France?"
But what Coudert Brothers will never know is how seriously the ru-
mors injured it. How many possible clients or prospective employees never walked through its doors because of the Banque de
France case cannot even be guessed at.

"There was nothing improper about Mr. Coudert representing
the Banque de France," says one retired Jewish partner who has
heard the "pro-Vichy" accusations over and over again. "I might
not have made the same decision, but I have the advantage of
hindsight. I don't think Mr. Coudert did anything wrong. I do
think it caused far more trouble than it was worth."

Coudert Brothers' younger associates and staff members began entering the armed services early in 1941, and after Pearl Harbor the only young men left in the firm were Alexis Coudert and
Jim Hughes, both of whom had such poor eyesight that the military was in no hurry for their services. Hughes, who joined the
State Guard, expected to be called up eventually, but never was.
Alexis, in 1944, was ordered to report for a pre-induction physical,
but flunked the eye exam and was turned away. Meanwhile, as the
only young men in the office, the two of them were extremely
busy—but so were the older lawyers and the staff.

Because the firm was so shorthanded, staff members were
asked to take only two of the four weeks of vacation time to which
they were entitled, but they were offered two weeks' additional pay
in compensation. "There was a lot of work," recalls mailroom clerk
Rudy Reimer, and indeed there was, with alien property cases laid
upon frozen assets matters piled upon all the new problems posed
by wartime economic regulations and controls. "We got the Washington office just in time," says Hughes. "With the wartime priorities and gasoline rationing, it became almost impossible for
ordinary civilians to travel to Washington by air."

The Trusts and Estates Department moved its wills upstate,
where they would be safe from any bombing attacks on Manhattan.
But Fred Coudert was never in any real doubt that America would
win the war. Indeed, he had stopped worrying unduly about the
war's outcome once the Lend-Lease Act passed and the U.S. Navy

began escorting British convoys. Based on his knowledge of what had happened in World War I and his faith in America's economic power, he was certain from then on not only that his country would fight but that it would win.

A few days after Pearl harbor, Fred Coudert went down to Washington and visited his son Ferdinand, who was an officer by then in army intelligence, and Tom Finletter, who was with the State Department. Ferdinand remembers standing in a kitchen with his father, and Finletter telling them in confidence the news that was being kept secret from the public: the Pacific fleet had been all but wiped out at Pearl Harbor and America's western flank was virtually undefended. Even with this knowledge, the senior Coudert remained certain of eventual victory. He would spend the three and a half years of America's war talking and writing not so much about the war as about the peace that was to come and the need for the victors to establish an international organization that would be more effective than the old League of Nations.

Succeeding Secretary of State Cordell Hull, Coudert was elected president of the American Society of International Law in 1942 and was reelected annually until 1945. The organization gave him a perfect medium to urge and support the creation of the United Nations—an idea that was even then in the air. Like Coudert, many older men were anxious to spare the next generation the mistakes that had been made at the peace table in World War I.

In the meantime, however, there was a war yet to be won. A survey of some former and future Coudert Brothers lawyers in the fall of 1944 would have found Lieutenant Hugh Fitzgerald in New Orleans, where his navy landing ship was being commissioned. Fitzgerald took the unwieldy vessel through the Canal to Pearl Harbor, where it joined an invasion group going west to Guam and later became part of the Iwo Jima invasion force. Undergoing aviator's training in the fall of 1944 was a twenty-two-year-old marine officer named Carl Eldridge, who would distinguish himself for bravery at Iwo Jima, but for marine lieutenant Lawrence Brody, the war was already over. Twice wounded lightly in the fighting for the Marianas, he had received a serious wound, necessitating amputation of his leg, in his third beachhead campaign and was undergoing treatment at a stateside naval hospital.

Navy lieutenant Joe McManus was also in the Pacific in the fall of 1944, on board a destroyer escort that was on hunter-killer operations in the China Sea, searching out Japanese submarines. Lieutenant Gene Wadsworth was an air combat instructor at a navy installation in Georgia, and at the U.S. Naval Academy, nineteen-year-old Milo Coerper was expecting the war to last long enough to let him fulfill his hope of becoming a submariner.

In Washington, D.C., was a French lawyer, Lucien Le Lièvre, who had taken his place in the French Army upon the call-up of reserves in August 1939. Le Lièvre's unit had been up in the mountains of the Vosges when they heard the news of France's capitulation on the radio, and a week later they had come down from the mountain to surrender. Moved from a holding area in Colmar to a fortress over the Rhine, Le Lièvre had eventually ended up, with seventeen thousand other French officers, in a prison camp in Nuremberg. Noticing that the latrines were connected by pipes that had manholes outside the compound, Le Lièvre and two other officers laid plans for an escape, which they effected on May 21, 1941. Thus, Le Lièvre had already had an eventful war. To continue the fight, however, he had registered for the U.S. Army draft, which, after some delays because he, too, had problems passing the eye exam, had called him up and assigned him to the Free French forces. By the fall of 1944 Le Lièvre was in a unique situation: he was a U.S. officer on temporary detachment, serving as general counsel to a Free French economic mission in Washington, headed by Jean Monnet.

Also in a powerful position in Washington, D.C., was H. Struve Hensel, general counsel in charge of U.S. Navy contracts, who was being assisted by Ensign Sol Linowitz. At the Pentagon, Captain George Farnham was supervising army personnel assignments, and Lieutenant Dick Wincor was doing Japanese translation work at Arlington Hall, the headquarters of the "Magic" code-breaking and analysis operation. Wincor was vaguely aware that somewhere around the building was a Major "Ferdie" Coudert. As of 1990, the former Major Coudert had not been released from his wartime oath of secrecy, but it seems a reasonable assumption that the army's Signal Intelligence Service was making use in 1944 of his exceptional linguistic abilities. And over at the State Department, Tom Finletter, a civilian, was in charge of all questions relating to the foreign policy aspects of foreign exchange and alien property as executive director of the Office of Foreign Economic Coordination.

In the European Theater, Lieutenant Commander Charles Torem, who had participated in the invasion of southern France, was on Mediterranean patrol off the coast of French North Africa. Lieutenant Commander Bill Shields, Jr., had been in the Pacific but by the fall of 1944 was probably in the Mediterranean as well. And Captain Maurice Force, who was probably then in Italy, had let his wife know, in a guarded way, that he expected to be ordered to Paris soon.

But the first Coudert Brothers lawyer to reach Paris was Gerry Dunworth, who was with army intelligence. Entering the city a few weeks after its liberation, he headed for Coudert Frères at the first opportunity. Arriving about lunchtime, he was warmly greeted by the staff and told that Mr. Robinson was right across the street at The Travellers club. Why didn't Mr. Dunworth join him? Dunworth protested that he couldn't go into The Travellers, which was a very elegant establishment, looking the way he did: he was wearing an Eisenhower jacket, was packing a pistol on his hip, and was not particularly well shaven. But, as the secretary insisted, Dunworth went across the street and found Robinson playing billiards, with a martini glass in his hand.

It was a very happy reunion. "Robinson was so delighted to see someone from New York, and he wanted to hear all the news. I didn't know what was going on in the New York office myself, because I had been in the Army since early 1941, but I could tell him that Mr. Bellinger had died and a few other things." It turned out that, by improbable coincidence, that day—October 5, 1944—was both Robinson's seventieth birthday and Dunworth's thirty-third. They celebrated by having lunch together and then went for a stroll through the streets of Paris. "The U.S. soldiers were everywhere," says Dunworth, "and they kept saluting me." Because he was in intelligence, Dunworth wasn't wearing any insignia, but he wasn't actually an officer. (He would be given a battlefield commission during the Battle of the Bulge later in the year.) Not being an officer, Dunworth couldn't return the salutes, but Robinson had no such inhibitions. "Every time a G.I. saluted us, the old gentleman saluted right back. He was having a wonderful time."

Having a less wonderful time a month later was a young private first class, just turned twenty, named Allen Russell, who was the second scout on a patrol that was wiped out in Holland. Knocked down by two machine-gun bullets that went through his back, Russell lay on the ground for two hours before the medics got to him. As one medic crouched over him to verify that he was dead, a mortar shell landed nearby, breaking Russell's arm at the shoulder and wrist. He was taken to a field hospital and then to the American Hospital in Paris, which happened to have one of the finest orthopedic surgery sections in Europe, largely because of the generosity of one member of its Board of Governors, John B. Robinson. Thus, the charitable interests of Coudert Frères's senior partner helped to save the life of a future partner of Coudert Brothers. It was one of the nicer things to happen in the war.

Chapter Twelve

RECONSTRUCTION
AND RENEWAL

Aside from Robinson's survival, the news reaching Coudert Brothers after the war was mostly grim. So many friends had died. So many were missing. Frenchmen were killing Frenchmen, as old scores from the war were settled. "It was just one piece of horrible news after another," recalls Ferdinand Coudert. Fuller, with his deep-seated kindliness and gentleness, took it all to heart. "One reason for my becoming reclusive (as you call it)," Fuller wrote to Fred Coudert in 1946, "is the difficulty I find in capturing anything resembling a 'happy mood' in the company of more than one or two friends. It seems impossible to escape from the atmosphere of animosity & hate & recrimination that characterizes our times."

Although France was suffering from civil disorders and deepening starvation in 1945, the first order of business for Coudert Brothers was rebuilding the Paris office. The major difficulty was that the two Coudert Frères partners who had left in 1940 would not be returning. Russell Hare had died, and Harold Johnson had left the law to take a limited partnership in a Wall Street brokerage firm, where he was already on the road to earning some of the many millions with which he would later endow Hampshire College. Fuller, therefore, asked John Dubé to join Coudert Frères, but Dubé declined, as his practice in New York was doing very well.

John Robinson through his own efforts, however, soon had the Paris office partially restaffed. He struck an arrangement with

274

Max Shoop, who had been with the OSS in Bern, whereby Shoop joined Coudert Frères as a term partner for a fixed number of years. He hired as an associate Stephen Millet, a young American who had worked with the Resistance in France, and Maurice Force decided to work for Coudert Frères rather than return to New York.

In Robinson, Shoop, and Force, Coudert Frères had a distinguished base on which to reconstruct the practice. Robinson, now seventy-one years old, had the trust and affection of the English-speaking community in France and was already busy rewriting their wills and trusts to take account of all the changes that had come with the war. Shoop had been a partner before the war in the Paris office of Sullivan & Cromwell, which had been one of the few American law firms besides Coudert Frères to continue operating in Paris during the Depression. Shoop joined Coudert Frères because his old firm hesitated to return to France, and he brought with him some of his former clients, including INCO, the international nickel conglomerate; he was soon also helping the *New York Herald Tribune* untangle its affairs.

Like Robinson, Shoop was a bon vivant. Despite his many years in France, Shoop spoke French with a strong American accent, according to Mary Lehovich, who was his secretary immediately after the war, but he had adopted something of the style of a European. An elegant dresser, he wore a flower in his lapel and the laceless type of shoe called "pumps" in the daytime. "The Americans were always taken aback to find a man wearing what they considered evening slippers to the office," says Dubé. "They were always talking about that." Shoop arrived at Coudert Frères each day in a limousine, and from the tall second-floor windows at 52, avenue des Champs-Élysées, his secretary could see his Rolls-Royce sweeping down the avenue and know that within so many minutes, Shoop would be at his desk.

But the most *distingué* of the group was Maurice Force, an eminent French attorney and chevalier of the Legion of Honor. In the postwar period, Force was several times invited to accept a cabinet position, but, since French governments in this period seldom lasted longer than a few months, he refused the invitations. It was Force, however, who introduced to the firm a number of companies owned by the French State or closely connected with it, which resulted, among other things, in Alexis Coudert becoming counsel to the U.S. subsidiaries of a major French reinsurance company, later known as the Unity Group.

With American businessmen wary of returning to France and many Frenchmen suspicious of American military and economic power, Force made it his business to try to improve French-American relations. He saw to it, for example, that various ministers and deputies of his acquaintance who were going to visit the United States had letters of introduction to Coudert Brothers, and at the same time he alerted Fritz Coudert or Tom Finletter that they might care to arrange a luncheon so that the Frenchmen in question could meet prominent Republicans or Democrats, as the case might be. Others whose interests were less political were often directed to Alexis Coudert, with happy results: Force told Alexis that many visitors of distinction had complimented him on "your intelligence, your gracefulness [*gentillesse*], and your great simplicity." All of these introductions were performed with the kind of delicacy and tact that only a Frenchman could achieve, and a not incidental aim was the polishing of the prestige of the Coudert name.

Force was aided and abetted in his efforts by a foreign law expert in the New York office, Dr. Ivan Soubbotitch, the former Yugoslavian ambassador to the Court of St. James's. When Alexis Coudert was made a chevalier of the Legion of Honor in 1952, at a ceremony in which complimentary remarks were made about Coudert Brothers as a whole, the two men could scarcely contain their joy and pride. A busy correspondence went back and forth across the Atlantic, full of elation over the honor given to "our Alexis" and "our firm." Their loyalty and concern for the firm, in which neither was a partner, were indeed remarkable.

The future success of Coudert Frères, however, would ultimately rest not on the shoulders of the older men in Paris but on Charles Torem, who in early 1946 was still in the U.S. Navy, commanding a discharge station in South Boston. A graduate of Harvard Law School who had practiced in New York and Florida before the war, Torem dropped by Harvard's Veteran Placement Bureau in the winter of 1945–46 and ran into Professor Louis Sohn, who had received a cable from Max Shoop stating that Coudert Frères needed as soon as possible a young lawyer who spoke French. Torem, who thought he spoke excellent French until he got to France and learned otherwise, applied to the New York office for the position at Coudert Frères.

Towering in height and erect in bearing, Torem even at age thirty-one, was not a figure to be overlooked. Thus, Hugh Fitzgerald can remember walking down a hallway at 2 Rector Street early in 1946, seeing "this tall fellow in a brown naval uniform," and thinking "Who's that?" It was Torem arriving for his interview with Alexis, which went so well that Alexis invited him home for the weekend. "He came to our house on Long Island, and I can still remember them chatting about whether he'd join the firm," Alexis's son Tracy said years later. "I must have been only about seven years old, but meeting Charlie Torem is something I've never forgotten."

Alexis and his guest spent much of the weekend in rapid-fire conversation. "They had an intellectual style in common," says Tracy, who saw them together many times after 1946. "With their style of debating and reasoning, there was always a quick pace to the discussions. Each knew where the other was going, and they communicated *fast*. There was an incisiveness: they didn't waste any words getting from one point to the next." By the end of the weekend, it was clear that the firm had found not just an associate for the Paris office but John Robinson's probable successor.

Before he left New York, Torem was also interviewed by Fred Coudert, by Finletter, by Fritz, and possibly—Torem can't quite remember—by Fuller. As he made his farewells, Torem asked Finletter what the firm expected of him. "Finletter said in his tight-lipped way, 'Just do a good job,' " recalls Torem. Alexis added that Torem should get ready as quickly as possible to take over in Paris, because Robinson was, after all, in his seventies. "No one ever dreamed that Robinson would go on practicing for nearly another twenty years," says Torem. "Robinson was such a wonderful person, every day I spent with him was a pleasure. He was a great old-fashioned human being—but I can't say the set of instructions I was given was particularly helpful."

Although civilian air transportation to Europe had just been restored, obtaining foreign visas was difficult. The French, for example, would only issue a visa if the U.S. State Department swore out an affidavit that the visit was in the United States' national interest. Jim Hughes made the fourteen-hour flight to England in March 1946 to negotiate an acquisition for Duro-Test Corporation, a New Jersey light bulb manufacturer, and went on to France and Switzerland to reestablish banking relationships for other clients. Alexis and his father would visit Europe in August 1946 so that Fred could attend a meeting of the International Olympic Committee, of which he was a member. But, because of the passport and visa complications, such trips had to be planned well in advance. Torem finessed the problem by arranging to take his discharge in France, which allowed him to get a seat on military air transport, and he reported for work on June 1, 1946.

Despite Coudert Frères's elegant offices and Robinson's benevolent presence, Paris was a hardship post. During the first years after the war, the food rations allowed to the French (and the British and most other Europeans) were actually lower than they had been during the war itself. There was also not enough heating fuel and clothing, and the Communists were agitating, organizing strikes, and threatening a takeover similar to those then going on in Eastern Europe. Torem initially spent much of his time trying to help families discover what had happened to their relatives and assisting them to recover their property. In the course of these assignments, he traveled throughout Europe.

"There was devastation everywhere," he says. "You will understand that the devastation in Germany at that time did not exactly break my heart—we were still under the illusion that every German had been a Nazi—but there was so much that was needed. People needed every kind of consumer goods, they needed machinery, they needed everything. There were tremendous opportunities for American companies, aiding Europe to rebuild itself." Torem wanted to be part of that reconstruction—but the number of American businesses willing to reinvest in Europe could practically be counted on the fingers of one hand. With the foreign exchange restrictions, there was not even much trade. Most of the corporate work in the office was simply property recovery and war claims cases.

By the winter of 1947–48, which was the worst in Europe in modern times, Torem was so disheartened that he was thinking of going back to the States. The top people at Coudert Brothers, however, wouldn't hear of Torem leaving. Fred Coudert shared the vision of a reconstructed Europe, and he was sure American businesses would be returning soon. In June 1948 Tom Finletter arrived in London to take up his post as special ambassador for the Marshall Plan, and he visited Torem, to talk in an encouraging way of the prospects for Europe's economic recovery. More practically, Finletter saw to it that Torem became a partner in Coudert Frères. This was as fast as any associate had ever been made a member of either Coudert partnership, equaling the previous speed record set in the 1890s by Fred Coudert, who had had all the advantages of being the founder's son. Even more practically—since Torem was being made a member of a partnership showing negligible profits—Alexis told Torem that there would always be a place for him in the New York office if things did not work out.

Greatly encouraged, Torem stayed and continued to concentrate his efforts on developing a practice oriented toward trade and investment work for American companies. The wealthy expatriate families who were the traditional mainstay of the Paris practice, however, continued to provide most of Coudert Frères's income, and at times Torem found it necessary to resist being pulled into the gravitational orbit of this side of the practice. In

October 1948, for example, Alexis asked Torem to firm up relations with a wealthy elderly client—perhaps best referred to as "Mrs. S." Torem dutifully complied, but then vented his feelings in this epistle:

Dear Lex:

This is just a happy little note to tell you how I am getting on.

Some time ago Mrs. S. wrote that she wished her maid to get a visitors visa to the United States, in order to bring with her the old blind dog of Mrs. S.

It appears that she is very close to this faithful ancient beast.

This morning, I was advised rather frantically that the Embassy had refused the visa for technical reasons, that Mrs. S. had already purchased a ticket for maid and hound, and that if something were not done, not only would she probably forfeit the fare, but even have to get up at 6 o'clock in the morning to get Fifi ready!

At this point, our smiling young hero, with not a thought on his mind except six contracts, four licensing arrangements, a snarl with the Office des Changes, no money, and a perpetually ringing telephone, dropped all of these trivia, put on his rusty six-shooter, and swang into action!

East Lynne was never more exciting!

As the hands of the clock spun around, the drama here got thicker. I could just see that poor old hound dog having to spend six months in Paris alone with nothing but a seeing eye pooch as its faithful guide.

At the Embassy, I swept aside the horde of poor unfortunates whose families have been massacred in Eastern Europe, in France, in Italy, and who have been patiently waiting in line to get a chance to visit their last surviving relatives in America, and stormed into the Vice-Consul's office. As you can see this matter simply could not wait.

For the Vice-Consul, who, in a cavalier mood of contempt and scorn, could not see either the urgency or importance of this visit, I whistled, sang, danced and recited the first four acts of "Romeo and Juliet." Just before being thrown out of the Embassy, I was handed the visa!

I called Mrs. S. up to tell her the good news and she collapsed with gratitude. Of course, she is taking her French business to the office of Mr. Szalpka. However, I can assure you that any dog cases which she or her friends may have, will be ours.

I wish you would tell your good clients that I am trying to

concentrate on bigger things, and in a completely reckless move, and with the consent of JBR [Robinson] and MS [Shoop], that I am no longer handling canine matters, and am limiting myself to other larger quadrupeds.

I think that any new additions to our office, should first be given a short and intensive course on animal husbandry.

See you at the next Grange meeting.

"I am very happy to learn that you were able to obtain a visa for Mrs. S's beloved hound," was Alexis's bland, tongue-in-cheek reply. "I envy you such interesting cases." Torem continued to have his share of "interesting" cases—and some of them actually were fun. Torem represented Prince Aly Khan, for example, in his divorce from Rita Hayworth and went out to California to confer with the actress. This trip he pointed out to Alexis should not be deducted from his vacation time, assuring him facetiously that the three hours he had spent alone with the world's reigning sex symbol, with the blinds drawn, had not been in the least restful.

After Max Shoop suffered a serious stroke in 1953, Torem was also distracted by the responsibility of running the office. Rumblings and grumblings about the amount of time administration was taking from more important things, like business development, became a regular feature of Torem's letters to Alexis. At the same time, Torem was becoming almost indispensable in the affairs of the American Chamber of Commerce in Paris and serving as the American representative on the Court of Arbitration of the International Chamber of Commerce. "I think Charlie Torem worked about a twenty-four-hour day," says one of the former New York partners. "All his energy went into building up Coudert Frères, and he had tremendous energy." The round-the-clock effort began to pay off in the mid-1950s when the trickle of American investment in France turned into a growing stream. Coudert Frères then was not only, once again, in the right place at the right time, but it had the right man already on the spot.

In sharp contrast to the elegant Paris office was the New York office, which, immediately after the war, was as dingy as ever and overcrowded as well. For lack of space, one of the returned veterans, Gerry Dunworth, sat for a while in the firm's tiny library, surrounded by a lot of commotion, until Alexis came to him with an idea: "Alexis said, 'We have two men's washrooms on this floor, and I don't see why we need them both. Why don't we turn one of them into an office for you?' I said that would be just fine."

The washroom was quickly converted, and Dunworth moved

into his new premises. Shortly thereafter he was at his desk one noontime, talking with a client, when the door opened and in burst Paul Fuller, Jr. Fuller stopped. He looked at Dunworth and the client; his glance slid sideways toward the white tile walls; he looked back at Dunworth—who was not in any doubt that Fuller had believed he was entering the gentlemen's room. "Can I help you, Mr. Fuller?" asked Dunworth, rising from his desk. Fuller pulled himself together, walked over to shake hands with Dunworth, and said ruefully, in his quiet way, "No, Gerry, the only problem I have at the moment is not something you can help me with."

"Gee," exclaimed the client after Fuller had left, "what a nice firm this is, when a senior partner comes in and shakes hands with a young associate before he goes to lunch."

"Well," replied Dunworth, trying to keep a straight face, "that's just the kind of firm it is."

It was a nice firm, and, in Dunworth's opinion, it was also an exciting one. He had spent some time in 1946 helping Percy Shay at the Washington, D.C., office and had been only too glad to get back to "headquarters." "Things were happening in New York," Dunworth recalls. For one thing, despite the impression made by its musty premises, Coudert Brothers was making more money than it had seen since the Depression. Profits distributed to the partners jumped from nearly $146,000 in 1943 to almost $270,000 in 1944. In 1945 the firm distributed approximately $400,000 in profit, which was the kind of money it had been making in the early 1920s. It seemed as if there were reason to hope the hard times were over.

Because of the Depression, some of the older associates— specifically Walter Barry, Lewis Innerarity, and Frank Wells—had had their promotion to partnership long delayed. Even when Colonel Kingsbury had died in 1938 and Scip Bellinger in 1941, no new partners had been made. But during the war, all the remaining associates were allocated shares in the profits and began to be treated as partners. Alexis Coudert, for example, always used 1942 as the date that he became a member of Coudert Brothers, and there is a note from Fred Coudert to Miss Bainbridge that suggests that Barry, Innerarity, Wells, and Jim Hughes were considered partners, at least in Fred Coudert's mind, in 1943. The firm was so informally run, however, that the partnership agreement of 1929 did not get revised immediately. Then, within an eight-month period in 1944–45, first Alexis and Ferdinand Coudert's names were added to the partnership agreement, followed by Barry, Hughes,

Innerarity, and Wells. Thus, Coudert Brothers went from nine partners on Pearl Harbor Day to fifteen partners by V-E Day.

In order to create these wartime partners, the "family" partners reduced their shares to the point that, for the first time in Coudert Brothers' history, more than 50 percent of the profits went to people who were not named Coudert or Fuller. Because of other provisions in the partnership agreement, this did not affect the control of the firm, which still rested firmly in the hands of the older members of the family. Rather, it was an indication that Paul Fuller, Jr.—who would die in 1948—and Fred Coudert were preparing to hand over to the next generation.

By the time the veterans came back, in fact, a good deal of responsibility had already passed to Alexis Coudert. Dunworth and Fitzgerald found, for example, that the "Old Man" wanted to shake their hands and hear all about their wartime experiences, but it was Alexis who told them what salary they would make, where they would sit, and for whom they would be working. "Alexis was pretty much running the place when I got back," says Dunworth, and the firm's correspondence files confirm his statement. Matters as large as approving the allocation of shares in Coudert Frères and as small as deciding which charitable appeals to answer were all directed to Alexis, who would check around informally to get the sense of what the partners wanted to do and then see that it got done. Although he never used the title, he was, in effect, the firm's managing partner from around 1944 on.

Another noticeable change after the war was the fact that both George Montgomery and Tom Finletter, the partners who had been handling most corporate matters in the 1930s, were seldom seen around 2 Rector Street. After his wartime service in the State Department and an assignment helping the U.S. delegation to the San Francisco conference that established the United Nations, Finletter in 1947 chaired the influential Truman Commission on Air Policy, in which he drew on what he had learned as counsel to the French Aircraft Purchasing Commission. As a result of his report, "Survival in the Air Age," America tripled its air power after the war, instead of scaling back, and Finletter applied his expertise in this area again when he served as secretary of the air force from 1950 to 1953 during the Korean War. He returned to Coudert Brothers for the rest of the 1950s, but, following an unsuccessful run for the U.S. Senate at the urging of Eleanor Roosevelt, moved on in 1960 to an appointment by President Kennedy as NATO ambassador. This public service career, of course, made Finletter at times a relative stranger around the office, particularly between 1941 and 1953.

The work for the French Aircraft Purchasing Commission in 1940 also left a lasting effect on George Montgomery. Like Finletter, Montgomery had been profoundly shocked by the information then revealed to the senior members of the firm about America's military unpreparedness. Unlike Finletter, however, Montgomery developed a deep bitterness toward President Roosevelt, who he felt had not only neglected America's defenses but lied to the American public as well. As wartime economic controls went into place, Montgomery began to believe that Roosevelt was serving as a front for a conspiracy to nationalize all industry. "A delightful charming man" is how his former colleagues remember Montgomery, but when he started talking politics, many of them tuned him out. William Buckley, Sr., the head of the Buckley oil companies, though, understood Montgomery's angry suspicion of wartime controls and his passion for the old frontier ethic of self-reliance. The native Dakotan and the oilman son of a Texas sheriff developed a rapport far beyond the usual attorney-client relationship.

Around 1940, Montgomery began spending most of his time at the Buckley headquarters in New York City. Until his death in 1966, in fact, Montgomery was more often at his client's office than his own. "The whole firm knew that if you needed George for any reason, you should call him over at the Buckleys," says an attorney who joined the firm several years after the war. "Wherever Old Man Buckley was, that's where Montgomery would be."

With Finletter disappearing into public service and Montgomery into the Buckley fold, Jim Hughes was taking care of providing advice to most of the firm's corporate clients. This component of the firm's practice was growing rapidly; in billings, it had reached an equal footing with litigation, and it was about to overtake and surpass the estates work for the first time. Nonetheless, Hughes was the only attorney concentrating more or less full time on the corporate/commercial practice, for Alexis Coudert, who had been the other associate under Finletter and Montgomery, was running a general practice. In a letter to a friend at the end of the war, Alexis said he seemed to be doing more litigation than anything else.

In 1946, another attorney who would be important to the development of Coudert Brothers' corporate practice joined the firm as a partner. This was William ("Bill") Shields, Jr., who had been working as in-house counsel for Tiffany & Company. Shields and Alexis Coudert were, as Alexis once said, "brothers-in-law once removed": they had married sisters, whose father in 1946 was chairman of Tiffany & Company and the major stockholder. Thus, when

Shields joined Coudert Brothers, the famous jewelry concern came with him as a client. Even so, Shields was doing real estate work for individuals, drawing wills, and administering estates. The concept of the general practice was very much alive and well at Coudert Brothers in 1946.

Tiffany's, though, was a great client to have—and all over the firm other exciting new work was coming in, including the firm's first major antitrust suit. During the war, because it had been easier for the military to deal with monopolies than with a myriad of small suppliers, the Department of Justice had virtually suspended antitrust prosecutions. Now that the economy was returning to peacetime conditions and a populist Missourian was in the White House, the Department of Justice was cracking down. One of the first prosecutions it revived was directed against three companies, Imperial Chemicals, Ltd. (ICI), Du Pont, and Remington Arms, which had given each other exclusive worldwide patent licenses on inventions that had proven to have critical uses during the war. Coudert Brothers had been representing ICI since 1938, and ICI's chairman was a friend of Fred Coudert. The British company wanted to give Coudert Brothers the case, but it also wanted a "name" attorney representing it in the courtroom arena. Fred— who was well up in his seventies and retired from courtroom practice—turned, therefore, to a younger man whom he much admired: Charles Evans Hughes, Jr., the son of the Supreme Court justice and head of the Hughes, Hubbard firm. It was arranged that Hughes would work with Mahlon Doing of Coudert Brothers on the case—and then Hughes died suddenly, tragically young, leaving Doing as ICI's lead counsel.

Although Doing had argued major cases before the U.S. Supreme Court in the 1920s, when he was only in his early thirties, his real love was the preparation of briefs. He seldom went to court anymore, leaving the actual courtroom presentations mostly to Lewis Innerarity: "I make the spitballs," Doing once said, "and I let Lewis throw them." With his analytical bent, Doing was a master at organizing complex cases: it was he who had steered the Black Tom explosion case successfully for twenty-three years through all its domestic and foreign venues. The ICI antitrust case was even more massive in terms of the documents and evidence to be assembled than Black Tom; it was so big that none of the "major" firms of the 1940s could handle it alone. Just as Coudert Brothers brought in Hughes, Hubbard to help, Du Pont's regular counsel, Covington and Burling, called in Root, Ballantine; and Remington, which was less immediately involved, retained Donovan & Leisure. As the various counsel began to confer, it became evident that Doing had the most experience, and—"name" partner or not—he became the lead trial counsel for all the defendants.

No one was overmuch concerned that Doing and his colleagues from the other firms involved were not antitrust "specialists." To assist Doing, Coudert Brothers hired a new associate named Joseph A. McManus, who had worked on antitrust cases at his previous firm, but the thinking of the time was that a great trial attorney could handle anything. It would be these postwar antitrust prosecutions themselves, in fact, that helped to create a new breed of specialist, for many of these cases were long tunnels, and associates who entered such a tunnel and spent years of their lives on only the one case naturally emerged at the other end as specialists. The ICI case, however, under Doing's direction, was kept moving along fairly expeditiously, and Judge Sylvester Ryan strove for a decision that would settle the matter and not lead to endless appeals. Ryan succeeded: his decision—that the parties should simply swap back all the rights they had given each other, to restore the situation *ante bellum*—seemed so reasonable no one cared to contest it. Pleased with the outcome, ICI gave Doing enough further work in the 1950s that, at one point, he was practically shuttling between London and New York.

Walter Barry was also breaking ground in the postwar years in another field new to Coudert Brothers—libel law. Barry was getting his libel cases thanks to a novel insurance policy that an "old drinking buddy" of his, a broker named Cecil Davis, had dreamed up. At the time Davis devised the policy, the radio networks were all self-insured, and CBS had run into trouble out in California, where juries had awarded some unprecedented six-figure sums in a few libel suits. Massachusetts Bonding and Insurance Company agreed to offer a libel protection policy, and Davis sold it to CBS on the understanding that Barry would represent the insurance company and handle all the cases. By the 1940s the arrangement was not giving Barry such a heavy caseload that he needed his own associate just yet, but the prospects were roseate.

And the Estates and Trusts lawyers were excited by some sophisticated trusts that tax counsel Raymond Goodell had devised for the Schlumberger oil and gas interests. Goodell had joined the firm in "of counsel" status in 1939. "It was Paul Fuller who brought him in," says Ferdinand Coudert. "My father was not convinced we needed a tax specialist." Goodell, though, was an immediate example of the usefulness of specialization. A brilliant man, Goodell lived mentally much of the time in the more rarified levels of the tax code. "It was difficult for him to do his own tax return," says another former Estates and Trusts partner. "At each line, his thoughts would go wandering off into all the possible permutations and ramifications. He was almost too much of a genius to fill in a simple 1040." According to Ferdinand, Goodell "did some interesting things with splitting trusts and setting up trusts in the Netherlands Antilles and all that sort of thing. He came up with quite a few ideas that others borrowed and made commonplace later. Goodell was really *somebody.*"

"We were moving in new directions, trying new things" is the way Hughes summarizes those postwar years. No move was more radical, though, than the decision in 1950 to leave 2 Rector Street for new premises in the midtown section of Manhattan. At the time all firms of any reputation or standing were still clustered in the Wall Street district, and Joe McManus, Doing's young associate, overheard "heated arguments" among the partners about the decision to move. "They were proud of being a downtown firm. They thought it would be a terrible thing to leave downtown." In fact, however, Coudert Brothers was not a "downtown" firm, in that its clients were not Wall Street banks and investment houses. "Many of our best clients came in from Europe to see us," says Hughes. "They would fly into Idlewild, stay at the good hotels in midtown— and they found it a nuisance to have to travel all the way to Rector Street."

The firm finally decided it had no choice in the matter. It was expanding so rapidly it had to have more space, and downtown, where no new buildings had been constructed since the 1920s, no space was available. So Coudert Brothers moved into the brand-new Look Building on Madison Avenue, and soon even the strongest traditionalists were reveling in such unaccustomed luxuries as the central air-conditioning and carpeting. In acquiring more furniture to fill the additional space, however, the firm kept to its parsimonious habits: it bought what it needed secondhand from one of its advertising-agency clients. Still, the ad agency's discards, it was agreed, were a decided improvement. "Everything and everybody seemed to brighten up once we got to Madison Avenue," says McManus. "Even the secretaries, who had been dressing in this spinsterish way, went out shopping at lunchtime and started showing up in new clothes. The whole atmosphere changed. I think it was the best thing that could have happened to us."

As an associate, Joe McManus was on salary and unaware of the firm's profit situation, but, true to Parkinson's Law on the inverse relation between the dignity of the premises and the profitability of the concern, the year after Coudert Brothers moved into its new quarters, its earnings flattened and would refuse to turn up again substantially for another seven years. An associate who joined the firm in 1957, Emilio A. ("Mike") Dominianni, is convinced that the post-1951 doldrums were due largely to the firm's innocence about money. "There were no business controls on any practices," recalls Dominianni. "There was this sense that the lawyer owed a great deal to society, and you should not worry overmuch about billing, and somehow the money and fees would all get provided. That was not everyone's attitude, but that was the general attitude. It was like they were living in an ivory tower. A good client was one that brought in an interesting legal problem, never mind whether he could pay the bills or not."

Dominianni's impression is borne out by Hugh Fitzgerald, who says, "Clients were not supposed to be turned away for economic reasons. That was the attitude that filtered down from the top, from Mr. Coudert himself. And I can't tell you how many times we put hours into looking at a case, determining that the case wasn't strong enough to pursue, and then we didn't send a bill, because it turned out there wasn't a case."

According to Jim Hughes, the firm had begun billing by the hour during World War II for frozen-asset matters and certain other types of work related to government regulation: "You couldn't bill by the results on these things. Billing an hourly rate was the only way that made sense." Fees for much of the Estates and Trust work were set by the courts as they are today, although less emphasis was put on the number of hours involved. Otherwise, billing consisted mostly of a partner staring at a corner of the ceiling, weighing the results achieved and what the work was probably worth to the client, and coming up with a number. The problem with this method of billing was that the attorneys often had no real idea of what their services were worth. Immediately after the war, for example, "Hoppy" Hopkins sent Dunworth out to Idlewild to greet the Countess Niel and her sister, the Countess de la Mettière. American-born, the sisters had lost their American citizenship when they married Frenchmen, and they were now returning to the States in 1946 as widows to try to regain their U.S. nationality. Coudert Brothers had always done the Countess Niel's legal work; the other countess had her own attorney, who was also at the airport to meet the ladies.

After great difficulties, because the U.S. State Department was thoroughly unsympathetic, Dunworth got a U.S. passport for the Countess Niel. Her sister's attorney was successful, too, and he telephoned Hopkins and asked him, "How much are you going to charge Countess Niel?" Hopkins, who had begun practicing law in the 1890s, admitted that he was thinking of extracting a big fee, perhaps $1,500. The other attorney squealed down the wire, "You can't do that! I'm charging her sister $9,000." So Hopkins stared at the ceiling and revised his bill upward to $7,500. Dunworth went over to the hotel, presented the countess with the bill, and she sat down and wrote out a check on the spot. The firm was thrilled: it gave Dunworth, who was earning about $3,000 as an associate, a bonus that year of $1,000. But the incident left unaffected the firm's "by guess and by golly" approach to billing and its underlying diffidence about charging for its services. By the mid-1950s Alexis Coudert, who was the firm's outstanding "name" partner, was charging, in those matters where he had to bill an hourly rate, the sum of $12.50 an hour. Fortunately for the firm's exechequer, he more often charged a flat fee, for that hourly rate was not enough to cover overhead.

In the 1950s very few of the firm's partners had any independent income—the Depression had not given them the chance to amass savings—but they didn't apparently worry much about their relatively static incomes. The typical partner was drawing about twenty thousand dollars in the mid-1950s, which was so much better than the salaries and draws of the 1930s that it seemed no doubt like riches. And, as Dominianni observed, the lawyers were having fun. One of Alexis's managerial problems, in fact, was getting his older partners to ease up. In response to an anxious inquiry from Alexis about seventy-nine-year-old John Robinson, Maurice Force wrote in 1953, "With respect to J.B.R., you should not be unduly alarmed. It's only a question of fatigue. The man is in good health but working as he does at his age[,] it's dangerous. . . . We are all devoted to him, but he is stubborn and handling large estates. He thinks that he alone can do the job. . . ."

In New York, the situation was much the same. Walter Barry loved his practice so much, he refused to take a vacation. Mal Doing was half-blind by the mid-1950s but insisted on doing his own research, which he could, in fact, do faster and more efficiently than anyone else in the firm. The image of Doing that fixed itself on Dominianni's memory is of "the great old lion, sitting in the library, holding a book almost to his nose and flipping the pages steadily, hour after hour." But Frank Wells, everyone agreed, was in a class by himself. Wells kept two shifts of secretaries busy: one secretary worked from 9:00 A.M. to 5:00 P.M., the next from 5:00 P.M. to midnight. Wells himself worked many nights past midnight, until whatever hour Mrs. Wells came in from New Jersey and dragged him away.

In 1952 Alexis hired Allen Russell, who had been clerking for Chief Justice Harold Stevens of the U.S. Court of Appeals in Washington, D.C. The idea was that Russell would be Wells's assistant and get Wells out of the office before midnight. What happened was that Wells was so busy, he didn't say hello to Russell for a week, and it took Wells about six months to give Russell some real work to do. "I think he finally got used to seeing my face," Russell says. "He just didn't know what to do with an associate. Most of the partners were used to doing everything for themselves." What impressed Russell and the other associates, however, was not just how hard Wells worked but how much fun he had doing it.

Russell's first introduction to the law had been Harvard Law School, whose overcrowded lecture halls in the postwar years he had found intellectually stultifying. "Harvard Law operated on a philosophy of fear, which was resented among the veterans group," says Russell. "Many dropped out in disgust. I kept going just on faith that actual practice would be much more interesting." Clerking for Judge Stevens did excite in Russell an interest in the law, and working for Frank Wells proved a joy, particularly since Russell started out as a spear carrier to Wells in a case that was then unfolding like a serial thriller—an estate suit known as the Greer Case.

The Greer Case was an old-fashioned "missing heir" case, revolving around the question of who was the heir to the estate of Mrs. Mabel Greer, a society matron who on her deathbed had confessed that, in her youth, she had had an illegitimate child and had given it up for adoption. What happened in the courtroom in this case was so extraordinary that the New York Supreme Court judge who heard the appeal, Justice David Peck, felt impelled to write it up for the general public. His book, *The Greer Case: A True Court Drama,* turned into a modest best-seller for Simon & Schuster; the Greer Case also went into the Harvard Law School casebooks, and eventually it became the basis of a television show, starring actor Raymond Burr. What made the suit so fascinating was the determination of Wells and the other attorneys to get at the truth and discover what had happened to Mrs. Greer's long-lost son. Several times satisfactory answers seemed to have been reached, but Wells would not accept them. He kept digging further and further into Mrs. Greer's background until finally the truth emerged.

Judge Peck chose to write up the Greer Case because, he said, it was as near-perfect an example as one could find of the adversary system working to produce the truth and because the dedication and creativity of the lawyers gave him so much professional pride. Wells, as attorney for the estate, of course, came in for much praise. This is how Peck described Wells as the case began in 1946:

Though he was still under forty, graying at the temples had started to mark a finely chiseled face with distinction. He had been well schooled in the law and well trained in practice according to the exacting standards of a great firm, which had recognized and rewarded his ability and diligence with a partnership. Pleasant of manner and voice, he eschewed histrionics and relied on meticulous preparation and matter-of-fact presentation. Painstaking study of all the information at hand about Mrs. Greer . . . had left him puzzled and unsatisfied. He wanted to know more.

To satisfy Wells's quest to know more, practically every associate in the firm ended up digging around in Mrs. Greer's past. Hugh Fitzgerald found himself cross-examining aging ex-chorus girls who had once known Mabel, and Allen Russell and Gerry Dunworth were among the team dispatched to New England to hunt for certain vital birth certificates. Happily, the Greer estate was enormous, and the fee was more than enough to justify the expenses. But Coudert Brothers' pride in Frank Wells centered partly in the fact that it knew that Wells would have done the same if Mrs. Greer had died a pauper. "Frank Wells never cared whether there was a nickel in a case or not," says George Farnham, who joined the Estates and Trusts Department in 1948 when the Greer Case was in progress. "He gave his all to every client."

One of the treasured legends of Coudert Brothers is that Wells died from being hit over the head with a spike-heeled shoe brandished by Muriel Reynolds, who was in the midst of a divorce from tobacco magnate Dick Reynolds, Jr. The story is not accurate. Wells did represent Dick Reynolds in that divorce and other matters, but it was in the course of another matrimonial case that the wife became hysterical upon discovering Frank Wells in the couple's apartment and clonked him with her high-heeled shoe. Wells left the apartment, returned to the office, and worked until evening. Then, not feeling well, he left the office at what for him was an early hour and drove himself home to New Jersey. There he collapsed into unconsciousness, and the next day he was under an oxygen tent in critical condition at Montclair Hospital. This happened in 1956. Wells recovered, continued to practice law as sharply as ever (although he kept shorter hours), and then died suddenly in 1959 at age fifty-three. There is no evidence that the shoe incident was related to Wells's death, but Wells's colleagues are convinced, regardless, that there was a direct relationship. They *want* to believe there was, because it seems to them so completely fitting that Wells's cause of death should have been his dedication to his client's interest.

Everything about Coudert Brothers' peculiar ethos in this period—the love of the law, the refusal to turn away an interesting case for economic reasons, the fierce professionalism—traces back eventually, of course, to Fred Coudert. It was under his demanding personality that Mal Doing, Frank Wells, and Walter Barry had been trained, and Joe McManus got a taste of what they had gone through when, in 1947, the Old Man let Doing know that he would like young McManus to research a question in international law. This was, of course, to be the test of whether McManus could be let loose on the ICI case. "Everyone in the office took it so seriously," says McManus. "I couldn't have worked harder if I were preparing to make my debut before the Supreme Court. And then I got in there, my knees shaking, and the Old Man threw all these intense, searching questions at me. Finally, he said curtly, 'That's all.' Doing told me later that the Old Man had been pleased, but it was not what you would call a comfortable experience. I didn't enjoy it." No one ever enjoyed being on the receiving end of Fred's intensity, but there is no question he was the ultimate source of "the exacting standards of a great firm."

In 1948 Fred was diagnosed as having cancer. The cancer proved operable, but the removal of the tumor left Fred, who had always been so physically active, unable to fence or swim or golf again. At age seventy-seven, he fell then at last into an old man's schedule, arriving at the office around 10:00 A.M., taking a long lunch with old friends or occasional dignitaries, and then returning home. Barred from exercise, Fred wrote almost as much as ever, mostly articles for the *American Bar Association Journal* and other legal periodicals. As he passed his eightieth birthday in 1951, he began gathering the articles that Allan Nevins would edit for a collection of his writings and he agreed to be interviewed for the Columbia oral history project.

Coudert had plenty of time for reflection, and as his thoughts ran backward over the years, he began revising some of his previous opinions. He had never liked James Carter, the U.S. counsel at the Bering Sea tribunal in the 1890s, and one of his favorite clubroom stories over the years had featured Carter storming into a meeting of the American delegates and castigating the blankety-blank Papist foreigners on the panel of judges—forgetting that his co-counsel Frederic René Coudert, who sat through this tirade expressionlessly, was Catholic himself. Now, Fred began to see some of Carter's virtues in retrospect, and he wrote a sympathetic and glowing eulogy to the man for the *ABA Journal.* He decided that another man he had very much disliked, President Woodrow Wilson, might have been right after all to try to keep the United States out of a war for which it was not ready. Preparing for the oral history prompted Coudert to ask himself whether he had been right or wrong in things he had done: often he was not sure.

In 1955 Hugh Fitzgerald entered the Old Man's office one day and found him lost in thought. They talked a bit about his health and the acute suffering caused by his illness, and then Coudert told Fitzgerald in a quiet way that Fitzgerald found quite moving, "Once I thought I knew a great deal. Now I don't know anything. I don't know anything anymore," he repeated, "except that you *must* love your fellow man." This was virtually the last conversation that Fitzgerald had with the senior Coudert. On April 1, 1955, Coudert died, at age eighty-four.

Fred Coudert, the young man who had wanted to "do things," had made, through his arguments in the Insular cases and writings on constitutional and international law, as much of an impact on the law as any practicing attorney can achieve. He had also left his mark on public affairs, particularly during World War I. Because of these activities, part of Coudert's legacy to Coudert Brothers was its reputation and high standing in the community of law. Another part of his legacy, as Charles Torem was to say, was the firm's morality. "A great lawyer and a complete gentlemen," Coudert had an acute sense of right and wrong, and—whether he had always been right or not—he had always deeply wished to be so. One of Coudert's greatest services to the firm, though, was the fortitude with which he had met the misfortunes of the Depression and World War II, when international trade dried up and international law was of little interest to practical men. His father and uncles had created America's first international law firm; through some hard times, the second Frederic René Coudert conserved its resources and enhanced its reputation. It would be left to the next generation to expand and build on this foundation.

Chapter Thirteen

ALEXIS TAKES
THE LONG VIEW

Alexis Coudert, who left the strongest mark on Coudert Brothers in his generation, once wrote: "It seems to me that I really never took much interest in anything of an intellectual nature until I went to Law School." The recipient as a prep-school student of comments from his headmaster, Horace Taft, about his "lack of interest," young Alexis was not responsive to methods of instruction emphasizing recitation. It was the "case study" method at Columbia Law School, stressing give-and-take between instructor and student, that brought him alive mentally, and he relied ever after on Socratic dialogue to clarify his own thoughts and to help others focus theirs.

Alexis used the technique on his own children. "We'd be out driving," recalls his son Tracy, "and he'd pick up on a statement and ask: what about this? what about that? He'd get a very rapid back-and-forth dialogue going—to help you, of course, but for fun, too. It was part of his nature." Alexis used the approach more formally in Columbia's classrooms, where he taught comparative law courses several evenings a week from 1946 to 1955. Most of all, he used it on the young lawyers at Coudert Brothers—wave after wave of them for more than thirty years.

"Our father was always happy to see the young men and help them along," says Ferdinand Coudert, "but there was not the intellectual interaction between them that Alexis enjoyed. Alexis was more of a teacher. He was very, very anxious to get extremely intelligent lawyers into the firm, and he loved working with them." The interaction, however, was definitely a two-way street. This was the way Alexis learned, the way he tested and straightened out his own thoughts, and the way he came to decisions. Sensing that this "name" partner was genuinely interested in learning from, as well as teaching, them, the young lawyers did not feel for Alexis the awe that some of their predecessors had felt for Fred Coudert. Rather, they felt flattered—and charmed.

Indeed, everyone at Coudert Brothers felt comfortable with Alexis. Intelligent but not intimidating, occasionally acerbic but essentially good-natured, patrician but not parochial, Alexis had a relaxed, accepting way about him that put others at their ease. Caught up in a conversation with Alexis, elated by the sense that here was a listener who really wanted to know their point of view, people tended to forget momentarily the position he held in the firm. One former secretary can remember carrying on a lively conversation with Alexis one evening and then a few minutes later suddenly realizing, "Here I am, twenty-some years old, a secretary, and I've just been telling the senior partner my opinion of how the firm is run—and he was *interested.*" Similarly, a current partner will never forget the day, as an associate in the 1970s, when, after a long conversation with Alexis about the counterculture, he went back to his cubicle where "it dawned on me that I had as good as told Alexis Coudert that I had smoked pot regularly in college. I thought, how stupid can you get? But he had seemed to be enjoying our conversation so much—appreciating the points I was trying to make—I didn't think about holding back."

Because it was so easy to talk with Alexis, it was always easy, in turn, for Alexis to know what the firm was thinking, to gather its sentiments as in a mirror and reflect them back, to interpret one party's views to another, to build consensus and to sense when the firm was ready for certain moves and when it was not. These are the skills of a political leader, and Alexis had them to such a marked degree that many at Coudert Brothers wondered why Alexis did not, like so many "name" attorneys at other law firms, end up in public service in Washington, D.C. Alexis, however, had no taste for the antagonisms and contentiousness that are the concomitants of public influence. Nor was he in much sympathy with the whole concept of governance.

"I do not particularly like to accept your conclusion that intervention on a governmental level is essential," Alexis told a *Yale Law Journal* editor, Richard Gardner, in 1950. The comment referred to the Point Four program, but it summarized Alexis's attitude toward government in general, with respect to either the nation or

Coudert Brothers. He had little urge to control anyone, disliked the whole concept of people being forced to do things for their own good, was always reluctant to intervene uninvited in someone else's affairs, and, when required to do so, inclined to do the bare minimum consistent with obtaining the desired end. These are not attitudes compatible with "big government"—but they were perfect for managing Coudert Brothers in the postwar years.

As Allen Russell has pointed out, "Coudert Brothers didn't need much management then." The firm was small—there were only about two dozen lawyers—and the staff was mainly composed of long-term employees. They included Tom Moran, the mainstay of the Estates and Trusts Department, who had joined in 1914; Elizabeth Friel, who had become Fred Coudert's secretary during World War I; and mailroom clerk Rudy Reimer. Other important staff members were Bill Ford, who was a general clerk and eventually looked after the library; John Evans, a "beautiful typist" who was Ferdinand Coudert's secretary for many years; filing clerk Helen O'Rourke; secretary Kitty Fallon and her sister Teresa, who ran the switchboard; Tom Burke, who prepared tax returns and helped clients arriving on the ocean liners to clear customs and immigration; and Ken Shields, who was first James Hopkins's secretary and then Miss Bainbridge's assistant.

The lawyers who worked with these staff members have similar things to say about them: that, as a group, they were wonderful workers, whose conscientiousness and integrity made Coudert Brothers a pleasant place to work, and that they were, collectively, intensely loyal to the firm but also personally to the Couderts. Many of the staff, after all, could remember Alexis as a little boy who wanted to be a rabbit-keeper when he grew up and Ferdinand as a mischievous imp who once wreaked havoc on the switchboard when left unattended on a visit to the office. Miss Friel had sent the younger Couderts their allowances when they were in prep school and located their missing tennis rackets for them. And when Fred Coudert died in 1955, the family turned automatically to Tom Moran, leaving all the funeral arrangements in his capable hands. It was these relationships that gave Coudert Brothers the feeling of being an extended family; strong loyalties ran back and forth between the Couderts and the employees, built up over decades.

Under these circumstances, staff supervision gave Miss Bainbridge no trouble at all. She had only to write out and sign the paychecks, approve requests for vacations, and determine raises, leaving her time for her other responsibilities, which included all bookkeeping, all payments, all purchases, all questions of equipment and supplies, all insurance and pension matters, and all banking matters. In short, as their father had done, the Coudert brothers delegated to her everything that could possibly be delegated. "Miss Bainbridge almost ran the firm," says Ferdinand. "She was marvelous." She was also the reason that Alexis could handle a full-time practice, teach part-time at Columbia, head Columbia's Parker School of Foreign and Comparative Law, and serve as de facto managing partner between 1946 and 1955. "Managing" financial matters was not anything Alexis, or his brothers, had to worry about: that was Miss Bainbridge's domain. It was up to the partners to bill their clients and bring in some money; after that, Miss Bainbridge took over.

The Couderts loved Miss Bainbridge, but even they found her formidable at times, and the young lawyers tended in her presence to fall into the manner of meek schoolboys. Those associates who became partners in the early 1960s report a common experience: as was the firm's custom at the time, Miss Bainbridge personally brought each new partner a paper for his signature, and, looking at it, each realized he was seeing only the signature page of the main partnership agreement. "Miss Bainbridge," said Allen Russell or Mike Dominianni or whoever the new partner was, "shouldn't I read the agreement first before I sign this?" Then Miss Bainbridge would fix them with her most schoolmarmish glance and reply austerely, "Do you wish to be a partner in this firm?" "Yes, Miss Bainbridge." Her finger would point toward the signature line: "Then, sign here." To a man, they picked up their pens and signed.

Only years later did these partners discover that Miss Bainbridge had been acting entirely on her own initiative in keeping the partnership agreement secret from them. The Couderts had no idea that she was doing any such thing—but Miss Bainbridge was not arbitrary. She had good reasons for the things she did, and in this case it seems probable that her reason arose from the George Mason *contretemps* of 1959. A well-liked young attorney who became a partner in 1955, Mason found to his dismay that he earned no more money as a partner in 1957 than he had as an associate in 1955. Those were fairly flat years for the firm, and eventually Mason went to see a headhunter and was offered in 1959 a position with W. R. Grace at twice the income, which he accepted.

"The older partners like Mal Doing were shocked," recalls Gerry Dunworth, who had become a partner at the same time as Mason. "No one ever left Coudert Brothers. It was simply unheard of, like a priest leaving the cloth." Doing was even more shocked when he looked at the partnership agreement, which he had written himself, and realized that it provided a payout to any withdrawing partner of one-half his percentage share for four years after his withdrawal. The provision had been meant to apply only to retiring partners, but it had not been phrased in that way. "It just never had occurred to Doing that anyone would leave Coudert Brothers short of retirement," Dunworth explains. "It never crossed his mind."

The incident had a happy ending, in that Mason reassured Doing that he knew the provision was only meant to apply to retirees and he had no intention of standing on his contractual rights. "George Mason was a gentleman about the whole thing," says Dunworth. Doing immediately rewrote the partnership agreement, inserting what has ever after been known in the firm as "the Mason clause." But Miss Bainbridge did not allow new partners over the next several years to read this agreement, and the most likely explanation seems to be that she had temporarily lost faith in Doing's draftsmanship.

Because of incidents like these, there are those who believe that Miss Bainbridge was the true head of Coudert Brothers in the 1950s. But policy was actually set and the major decisions ultimately made by the three Coudert brothers. Fritz Coudert, however, was a congressman in Washington, D.C., far more involved in politics than in the firm. Ferdinand was actively practicing estates law, and, while he was starting to gain in his long-running battle to persuade bank trust officers to accept common stocks as a reasonable investment for trust portfolios, he had not discovered within himself any great enthusiasm for the law per se. And Alexis disliked making decisions without first getting input from everyone affected. Add in the smallness and friendliness of the office, the respect the Couderts felt for senior partners like Doing, Tom Finletter, and Tom Kelly, and the fact that everyone had been working together for some twenty or thirty years and it is apparent why Ferdinand Coudert says decisions were not exactly made: they evolved.

Annual partnership meetings were casual affairs, generally taking the form of a cocktail party at Fritz's apartment, but the partners lunched together every other Tuesday at the University Club, and they were constantly in and out of each other's offices. By the time a decision had to be adopted, most questions had been so thoroughly canvassed in hallways and offices that it was a foregone conclusion what the action would be. And the Couderts were not aloof from all this discussion; they were part of it. "The Couderts all got a lot of advice," one retired partner says drily, "whether they wanted it or not." Mostly, however, they sought it out, particularly

Alexis, who preferred in any case to develop his own ideas through interaction.

Intensifying the tendency to discuss everything ad infinitum was the fact that Coudert Brothers was, as Hugh Fitzgerald points out, "a cautious and conservative firm." With the Depression vivid in everyone's memory and the firm not particularly flush with cash, any decision to spend money entailed anxious, painstaking examination. A decision not to spend money, on the other hand, could be taken in a snap. In 1953, for example, Walter Barry died suddenly at age fifty-three—another litigator cut off in his prime. The day after his death five partners, including Alexis—who were the only five partners who happened to be in the office that day— decided to inform the landlord that the firm would not need to continue its lease on Barry's office space on the fifteenth floor of 488 Madison Avenue. It was an instant decision, based on the assumption that the firm would not be able to hold onto Barry's clients since Coudert Brothers' two surviving star litigators, Frank Wells and Mahlon Doing, were tied up on other matters.

Fortunately, Alexis did not rush to notify the landlord; it bothered him that only five partners had been present, and he wrote to Doing, who was then in London on ICI business, "I would like to hold up any irrevocable decision until your return." In the interim, Barry's most important client, Seaboard Insurance, which had taken over the network libel policies from Massachusetts Bonding, had to decide what it would do about obtaining new counsel. Seven days after Barry's death, Alexis wrote to Doing, "the scramble for the Seaboard business began among the major law firms." Coudert Brothers could offer only the services of an associate, Carleton G. ("Carl") Eldridge, Jr., who had been working with Barry less than two years, but, in a great compliment to the firm and to Eldridge, the Seaboard directors voted (though not without dissent) to leave their business in the hands of this Coudert Brothers associate rather than avail themselves of the talents of a partner at any other firm.

Over the next year, Eldridge and Gerry Dunworth, who was assigned to help Eldridge, would try or settle some one hundred cases for Seaboard alone, and the firm would be glad it had held onto its fifteenth-floor space after all. The quick unanimity of the initial decision not to renew the lease, though, speaks volumes about the firm's attachment to the principle of keeping the overhead down—as does the fact that Alexis kept Doing posted on these important developments by ordinary mail rather than by the more expensive means of an overseas telephone call or cable.

In contrast was the manner in which the firm went about deciding to move from 488 Madison Avenue to the Pan Am Building at 200 Park Avenue in 1963. The building was new, the address excellent, the rent fair for premium office space, but the landlord insisted on a thirty-year lease. This was a major commitment to spend money, and the firm chewed the decision over like a dog worrying a bone. Hugh Fitzgerald reports that "Finally, Tom Finletter said, 'Gentlemen, what it comes down to is this: do we have enough faith in ourselves to think we'll still be here in 30 years?' " That remark tipped the balance, for Coudert Brothers had plenty of confidence in itself. The firm, in fact, was about equally weighted between pride in what the name Coudert Brothers stood for, on the one side, and fiscal prudence, on the other: it was a seesaw, waiting to be tilted in either direction, depending sometimes on just the push of a felicitous phrase.

Ferdinand says that, of the three Coudert brothers, he and Fritz were the most conservative. Their inclination was to go slow and not rush into things, to accept the firm's tried-and-true traditions and examine innovations carefully. Alexis was of a different ilk, partly, it seems, because of his method of tackling problems. "He would test and question everything, reduce everything to its elements and put it back together again," says his son Tracy. "He took a lot of kidding from some friends, because he would give an intellectual response when most people would give an emotional one, but he was naturally a logical person. He enjoyed being logical."

Alexis applied his analytical bent to whatever propositions required his attention. If those were traditional firm practices and principles, he might, by the time he had finished ripping them apart and putting them back together, be firmly on the side of tradition—or he might not. Alexis, for example, was strongly opposed to anything that threatened the long-standing thesis that Coudert Brothers associates should generally have some time to spend with their families. It seemed to him that the firm's opposition to becoming a "sweatshop" had a real utility, in that it made Coudert Brothers a pleasant place to work, attractive to intelligent, able people. On the other hand, it was Alexis who decided in the 1950s to throw out the firm's old files, many of them dating well back into the nineteenth century, which were stored in a warehouse in New Jersey. The rent on the storage space kept spiraling upward, and Alexis could not see that the files would ever be of enough use to anyone to justify the expense of keeping them.

Alexis's fundamentally pragmatic approach is especially evident in a 1946 article, "Direct Foreign Investment in Undeveloped Countries," that he and associate Asher Lans wrote for an issue of

Law and Contemporary Problems. One of the few articles Alexis ever produced as author or co-author, it stands as a remarkable example of the persistence over time of an intellectual outlook, for it embodies the same approach to the law developed by Alexis's father and grandfather, beginning with the brisk avowal in its first paragraph that international law should not be treated as "a body of revealed doctrine" but as a diplomatic convenience among nations. In the second paragraph emerges a second basic principle of the Coudert approach to the law: the assertion that the international lawyer is "remiss in his function as counsellor unless he is prepared to deal with a wide variety of 'non legal' factors in collaboration with specialists in economic, political and psychological problems."

The theme of the article, which the issue's editor described as "enlightened," is simply that "American business interests operating in foreign countries can probably achieve greater protection by means of intelligent collaboration with local governments and people than by reliance upon theoretical doctrines of international law." The article, in fact, is an extended argument for the long-term advantages that American businessmen would derive from treating the peoples of undeveloped countries with respect for their national aspirations and showing a due concern for their fears of economic imperialism. Here is the same championship of the rights of the weak that can be traced back through Fred Coudert's writings on corporate regulation to Frederic René Coudert's concern for Elmira prisoners, women schoolteachers, and religious minorities, and ultimately, indeed, to the chivalric strain and sense of Pauline charity that Charles Coudert, Sr., brought with him from France. The romanticism of a French cavalryman's ethics, however, had been mingling for four generations with the American practical genius for getting things done, and it is noticeable that "Direct Foreign Investment" advocates a line of behavior simultaneously because it is ethically correct and because, pragmatically, no other means can, in the final analysis, deliver the desired end—in this case, that of safeguarding clients' overseas investments.

Most pregnant with implications for Coudert Brothers' future, though, is the article's theme that there is no hope for those who try to beat against the winds of change blowing through the undeveloped countries. American businessmen are urged instead to catch those winds and run before them. "The fundamental problem which now confronts foreign enterprise," the article states, "is that of adapting itself to the new economic nationalism of Latin America and the Near and Far Eastern countries." Rather than fight excess profit taxes in these nations, "it would seem wise for American corporations" to cooperate in their institution. Rather than trying to dodge the regulators, "it would seem to be wise for foreign owned utility companies to take the initiative" in introducing more modern techniques of rate control. The list of things it would be wise for foreign businessmen to do is long, and the message is consistent: adapt to prevailing conditions, or risk a complete shipwreck in the future.

Many of Alexis's traits—the cool rationalism, the charm, the essential tolerance, the liking for harmony, the minimalism— sound reminiscent of an eighteenth-century gentleman, yet, comfortable with flux and believing in accepting the new, rapidly and without undue repining, Alexis was entirely at home in the second half of the twentieth century. In a time of accelerating change in world economies, in the legal profession, and in Coudert Brothers' own practice, he was to put his influence decisively on the side of adaptation.

In early 1946, at about the same time that Alexis was writing "Direct Foreign Investment," he told one of the returning servicemen, "We've always been a small family firm, and I suppose we always will be. Fortunately we have enough clients now, so our prospects look good. I don't ever want this place to turn into a factory firm; no one wants that. But for our size, we'll do all right. We may not make fortunes, but we'll get along."

Within the next decade, however, Alexis had radically altered his thinking. He had decided that the firm was not the right size, that it had to grow much larger. "Alexis had the dissatisfaction, more than anyone else at that time," says his brother Ferdinand. "He thought it was a case of expand or die. We could not continue as a small firm."

Twice in its century-long history Coudert Brothers had been in a good position to grow, but it had not taken advantage of its opportunities. In the age of robber barons, Frederic René Coudert had turned aside from work for the railroads and public utilities, apparently out of distaste for the ethics of those potential clients. In the Roaring Twenties, when corporate work had become entirely respectable, Fred Coudert had been well placed as a director of First National Bank and two major insurance companies to develop Coudert Brothers' domestic corporate business, and the firm, moreover, was then doing considerable international bond business on both sides of the Atlantic for investment banks and securities houses. Fred, though, had not seized the moment to turn Coudert Brothers into a banking and securities law firm like those headed by his friends Paul Cravath, John Davis, and Frank Polk. Why he did not is an open question, but contemporary commentators agree that the work done by the growing armies of associates at those firms in the 1920s was of an almost mind-numbing boredom, and it is likely that securities work as such simply didn't appeal to Fred. His interests lay elsewhere, and by the time he was persuaded to bring in the two former Cravath associates, Tom Finletter and George Montgomery, to develop the corporate practice further, time was running out. The stock market crash of 1929 was just around the corner, and Coudert Brothers entered the Depression without having cemented any strong relationships on Wall Street.

Thus, the Wall Street firms had taken one path, and Coudert Brothers another. In 1955 Coudert Brothers was a general-practice firm, most notable for its elite clientele, which included many foreign individuals and companies, and for its expertise in international law. It had continued to go its own way, sticking to the formula laid down by its founders. Indeed, the basic nature of the firm's practice had changed so little in one hundred years that Frederic René Coudert and his brothers could easily have recognized it. All that might have surprised them was that Coudert Brothers in 1955 had more businesses than individuals as clients and that it was providing general representation, on a regular or retainer basis, not to four or five but to thirty or forty companies. That one distinction, though, made an extraordinary difference to Coudert Brothers' situation. It meant that Coudert Brothers, always an international law firm, had become by 1955 primarily an international business law firm.

This was a virtually unplanned development. The general prosperity of the American economy in the decade following World War II had been such that, as Joe McManus would later say, new corporate clients had simply tumbled in "like Topsy"—that is, no one "rainmaker" had been responsible for bringing them in. Walter Barry and Frank Wells, Jim Hughes and Tom Finletter, Alexis Coudert and Maurice Force, Tom Kelly and Ray Goodell, Bill Shields and George Montgomery had each picked up a handful of new clients during that decade. The cumulative result, though, was that Coudert Brothers could no longer be described as a firm engaged in litigation and estates work, with a small corporate component. It was now a firm doing mostly corporate/commercial work that had a litigation and estates capability.

This shift in the sources of Coudert Brothers' income meant that it was sailing out into the same waters that were already being cruised by such very large ships as White & Case, Shearman & Sterling, the Cravath firm, Sullivan & Cromwell, and numerous others. These Wall Street firms averaged about eighty lawyers in 1955, almost all of them corporate specialists; Coudert Brothers had about twenty-eight lawyers—not all of whom did corporate work even part of the time and few of whom did corporate work all of the time. The Wall Street firms serviced the giants of U.S. industry; Coudert Brothers provided service to small and medium-sized companies, some of which—like Tiffany, Coty, and Bengué—had names that were household words, but more of which—like Michelin, Peugeot, and Thiokol—were scarcely recognizable to the average American, and most of which were utterly obscure. Each Wall Street firm had a relationship with at least one large commercial bank or securities house that ensured a large volume of steady work as well as referrals to new clients; Coudert Brothers had no such close ties to any Wall Street institution.

A latecomer to the ranks of business law firms, Coudert Brothers was clearly at a disadvantage. It was like an elegant steamer yacht going into a shipping business dominated by fleets of large cargo ships that had long since charted the local waters. Looking at Coudert Brothers' size, large potential customers had to hesitate to give the firm all their business—if only for fear that the weight of their cargo would sink the ship. Hence, Alexis's conviction that Coudert Brothers had to "expand or die."

Alexis believed that Coudert Brothers had to grow, however, not just in order to be able to compete for clients but in order to compete for associates. Attracting the right young people to the firm was, Alexis thought, absolutely critical to whether Coudert Brothers would survive and prosper in future years, and he wanted to hire only the highest-ranking Ivy League students. "He was very aggressive about that," recalls Ferdinand Coudert. "He put great stress on the academic record. He wanted only the best students from the best schools." Yet in the 1950s there was a shortage of graduates coming out of American law schools, largely because of the low birthrates during the Depression. For the first time in anyone's memory, top-ranking students at the best schools were getting two or more offers of jobs at good firms, and they could pick and choose where they wanted to go. As a result, starting salaries at major law firms were driven up during the decade from three to eight thousand dollars, and still there were not enough bodies to go around.

Since Alexis was constantly advising young men and women on their career choices, as a courtesy to friends or in his capacity as a Columbia law professor, he was well aware of the sentiments of the fifties generation. He realized that, as children of the Depression, they placed a high value on long-term security and stability, and those who wanted to practice corporate law generally thought exclusively in terms of working with a firm that had a list of solid, established Fortune 500 clients—companies like Philco, American Motors, and the New York Central Railroad that everyone knew were going to last the ages.

Nonetheless, Alexis was able to find the corporate associates he wanted for the New York office, partly because he needed to hire only one such associate every three or four years and partly because Coudert Brothers' reputation in international law attracted approaches from those who had a special interest in this area. Alexis had been corresponding in 1950 about the Point Four program with Yale law student Richard Gardner, for example, because Gardner had sent him an unsolicited copy of an article he had written on the subject. Gardner later sent Alexis another article on an international law topic, more correspondence ensued, and in due course a future U.S. ambassador to Italy arrived to join Coudert Brothers' ranks.

Allen Russell had sought out Coudert Brothers for the same reason: having graduated from Princeton's Woodrow Wilson School of International Affairs and studied at the Sorbonne, he wanted to practice international law. Another member of this age group, Milo G. Coerper, had taken a Ph.D. in international affairs at Georgetown University after completing law school. He had already practiced law in Washington, D.C., for five years when Alexis hired him in 1960 to work with Percy Shay, and Coerper hoped that at Coudert Brothers' Washington office he could expand the expertise he had developed in Foreign Claims Settlement Commission cases and develop a public international law practice. Similarly, John Carey made a lateral transfer to Coudert Brothers as an associate in 1956 because he thought it "would be interesting to work with a firm that had a world perspective." Carey found it so interesting that, encouraged by Dr. Soubbotitch, he went back to school to earn an LL.M. degree in international law.

Although hired by Ferdinand Coudert to work in the trusts and estates area rather than by Alexis to work on corporate matters, Coudert Brothers' first woman associate had the same interest in international law as her male contemporaries. The daughter of a Belgian mother and an American father, who had traveled extensively in Europe as Western Electric's general patent counsel, Katherine V. ("Kay") Woodward had wanted to be an international lawyer like her father, but in her teenage years she picked up the message—most notably from a high school teacher—that this was not a realistic ambition for a female. Therefore, after majoring in foreign languages at Wellesley College, she had gone directly into an overseas job with the U.S. government—nominally as a member of the Foreign Service, but actually as an agent of the Central Intelligence Agency. Only in the late 1950s, when she was approaching thirty, did Woodward decide that she had taken the societal messages of her girlhood too seriously—and that if she wished to be "unrealistic" that was her own business and no one else's. Still working for the CIA in a headquarters job in Washington, D.C., she enrolled in Georgetown University's law school, taking classes at night and receiving her degree in 1961.

Wanting to be not just a lawyer but an international lawyer, Woodward sent her résumé in 1961 only to the American law firms that had overseas offices. There were exactly five such firms, as she recalls, and her credentials were so good that she received invitations to be interviewed at three of them. At two interviews, though, Woodward sensed a real reservation because of her sex. Indeed, one interviewing partner told her outright, "We don't really like to hire women. Women cry." The third interview was with Coudert Brothers, however, where Ferdinand Coudert was not only polite but charming. Called back for an interview with George Farnham, Woodward was offered a job as an associate and within a few years was indeed concentrating on international matters, developing an expertise in ancillary administration.

For people like Gardner, Russell, Coerper, Carey, and Woodward, Coudert Brothers' internationalism was a more important factor than its size. Still, Alexis knew that most of their contemporaries did not feel the same way. Taking the long view—and Alexis was always one to take the long view—he believed that, in order for the firm to be certain of having its choice of the very brightest young lawyers, it would have to be large enough to give young people the sense of security and career opportunities they wanted.

In any event, the changing environment around Coudert Brothers was rewarding size, and Alexis believed strongly that Coudert Brothers had to adapt accordingly. "Alexis felt," says Ferdinand, "that we couldn't very well succeed and stay small. Large firms represented the wave of the future, and we had to go with that wave. We just couldn't continue the way we were."

The years from 1955 to Alexis's death in 1980 are thought of at Coudert Brothers as the "Alexis years," and during this period—stimulated, encouraged, nudged, and led by Alexis Coudert—the firm did grow. From 1955 to 1972, it expanded cautiously, quintupling in revenues but taking only small, manageable risks. In 1972 the pace of change accelerated, the firm grew bolder, and, in the final eight years of Alexis's life, it began spinning off new offices at the rate of nearly one a year. By the time Alexis died, Coudert Brothers extended from Beijing to Brazil to Bahrain, and its older parts were pulling in new business at a rate that would have astonished Fred Coudert.

Not long after Alexis's death, retired mailroom clerk Rudy Reimer visited the New York office, which by then filled three floors of the Pan Am Building. Reimer, who had started working for Coudert Brothers in the 1920s, looked at the telecommunications room, which operated twenty-four hours a day, keeping all parts of the Coudert Brothers network in touch with one another. He looked at the computers, at the thousands of pieces of mail that his successors handled each day, at the clocks set for Tokyo time or London time and, turning to his escort Gerry Dunworth, Reimer exclaimed in honest bewilderment, "Gerry, it's like a different planet! How did we ever get from Miss Bainbridge to all this?"

Dunworth's reply was the same that anyone at Coudert Brothers would have given. The modern Coudert Brothers, Dunworth said, was the product of Alexis Coudert's vision.

Alexis had the broad vision, the firm says—but its transformation was, in fact, a group effort. Ideas fizzed throughout Coudert Brothers during the Alexis years, brought to the surface by Alexis's willingness to listen and learn. Initiative and self-reliance flourished, both released by Alexis's laissez-faire attitude toward governance. And, most of all, people evaluated each other's ideas with a certain measure of charity and accepted each other's idiosyncratic actions with a degree of conscious tolerance. That acceptance, too, was part of the atmosphere created—or, in the opinion of those with the longest memories, continued—by Alexis.

"There was a decency with which people treated each other," says one retired partner who worked for several other law firms before joining Coudert Brothers in the 1960s. "There were tensions and disagreements, of course, and the usual office politics. We were human. But people tried hard to behave well and give another person the benefit of the doubt—even if they really didn't like that person very much. Alexis had a way of getting the best out of people, while inspiring them to behave in a gentlemanly manner."

The Alexis years had their share of frustrations, setbacks, and problems, but, on the whole, those who were at Coudert Brothers then say that they were fun to live through: fun because of the character of the people in the firm and Alexis's style of leadership, and fun because Coudert Brothers was succeeding. The whole period, in fact, has something of the flavor of a Horatio Alger story, as this honorable but relatively small, respectable but far from wealthy law firm strove to succeed in a field that it was entering in a come-from-behind position. The various phases of the story, indeed, seem to deserve the old Alger-style titles: "Slow and Sure," "Try and Trust," "Pluck and Luck," "Brave and Bold"—all leading, everyone hoped, to the ultimate Alger goal, "Fame and Fortune."

Chapter Fourteen

GROWING
WITH THE CLIENTS

Much of Coudert Brothers' growth between 1955 and 1972 could be described as "Slow and Sure," for it was the kind of organic growth that comes to any law firm whose clients are prospering. The corporate clients with which Jim Hughes and Bill Shields worked, for example, were providing an income to Coudert Brothers by 1970 equal to the entire earnings of the whole firm in 1955. These clients had all been rather small companies in 1955, but they had had good names, quality products, and fine management. In the benign economic climate of the 1960s, they grew, and Coudert Brothers grew up with them.

From 1960 forward, Coudert Brothers also took deliberate steps to try to force its pace of growth, most notably by opening two new overseas offices in partnership with Coudert Frères and by inviting into the firm additional partners. Before examining these planned moves, though, it is necessary to look more closely at the corporate practice in New York—for it was really that practice's initial success that gave the partners the courage to try some of the forcing moves that Alexis and others advocated.

Providing a solid center to the corporate practice in New York was Jim Hughes, who had been concentrating on corporate/commercial work since his arrival at the firm in 1935. Made a partner in the midst of World War II at the young age of twenty-eight, Hughes had played an instrumental role in holding Tom Finletter's clients when Finletter went off to Washington, D.C., as well as Paul Fuller, Jr.'s clients when Fuller died. And Hughes's talents had essentially been the base from which the postwar expansion of the firm's corporate practice had been launched.

Unlike so many Coudert Brothers partners of the postwar era, who were general practitioners, Hughes confined himself to business law and business problems, and he exuded a reassuring sense of knowing exactly what he was doing. Thus, John Dubé turned the Bengué Corporation's affairs over to Coudert Brothers, comfortable in the knowledge that Hughes would do the work. Finletter accepted a major bankruptcy case, that of California Eastern Aviation, Inc., despite the fact he didn't have time for it, confident that Hughes, his former associate, would handle it just as well as he could. And when a small Trenton, New Jersey, company named Thiokol Chemical Corporation began asking Ray Goodell for advice beyond his tax expertise, Goodell introduced its president, J. W. Crosby, to—in Crosby's words—"a young lawyer, Mr. James Hughes, who he felt was better suited to our needs." Crosby would preside over Thiokol through its years of greatest growth, as it built the Minuteman missile and the rockets that would send John Glenn into space, and he says, looking back, "It was a lucky day for Thiokol when Jim Hughes became our legal representative and board member. His understanding and sound judgment contributed in no small measure to the growth and development of our company."

By the early 1950s, Finletter, Montgomery, and several other partners were routinely handing over to Hughes any particularly complex corporate matters that came into the office. "Most of the tough problems requiring ongoing expertise or sustained attention ended up in his jurisdiction," says Hugh Fitzgerald, who worked side by side with Hughes for some thirty years. "If the matter was complicated or was going to take time, everyone was quite content to have Jim Hughes do something about it. For practical purposes, he was regarded as the senior corporate person." Allen Russell, who trained under Hughes, says simply, "He was an extraordinary corporate lawyer."

As the senior person in the fastest-growing area of the firm's practice and as the partner who had the highest billings for several years, Hughes naturally had considerable influence in the counsels of the firm. Fred Coudert's three sons held—through the "family control" clauses in the partnership agreement—all the executive authority in the firm, but in the late 1950s they began regularly including Hughes in their deliberations. Hughes says that they did so because "the Couderts, and particularly Alexis, had come to the conclusion that the administration of a growing firm required the participation of more than members of the family."

Beyond that, however, Alexis wanted to include Hughes in the family discussions because Hughes agreed entirely that Coudert Brothers had to grow and that its best chances for growth lay in building on its reputation and expertise in international affairs: Alexis and Hughes had been talking about these subjects since they had been associates together, and on the fundamentals they saw eye-to-eye. Hughes supported Alexis in his more activist view of the firm's future. At the same time, Fritz and Ferdinand appreciated the fact that Hughes was a practical person, given to business-like methods. Hughes's basic approach of "Let's do it—but let's put it in writing and do it right" sat well, on the whole, with all three controlling partners—the more so because Hughes was not one to insist that his own ideas were invariably right. He advanced his opinions in what one former partner describes as "his upright and forthright manner," but if they did not win support, he threw his weight behind whatever course the brothers and other partners did decide upon. Like Alexis, Hughes was greatly concerned to avoid schisms in the firm, and an important clue to his outlook lies in the fact that he eschewed the use of the phrase "my client." Any client with which he worked—even Michelin or Thiokol, on whose boards he sat for three decades—was always scrupulously referred to as "our client" or "a client of the firm's." Hughes was, above all, a team player, and one of his chief hopes was to see the firm pulling together as a team.

Significantly, the firm that Hughes joined in 1935 had not been particularly strong on teamwork, especially at the practice level. Although the lawyers worked together on major projects such as the ICI antitrust case, individualism was really the order of the day. The Old Guard, the men who had become partners in the 1920s, functioned, for the most part, not only as general practitioners but almost as sole practitioners. Thus, Russell says of the early 1950s that "Coudert Brothers struck me as just a pleasant congregation of individuals who happened to like each other enough to want to work in the same office and pool their income to pay the rent. There weren't that many occasions when they actually worked together." In other words, if a Frank Wells or a Walter Barry was doing general corporate work for a client and a lawsuit came up, he handled the litigation himself; if an executive of the company needed a will, he wrote the will; and he asked for help only when so overloaded, he couldn't avoid it.

By concentrating on what he knew best and farming the other pieces out around the firm to people who were more expert in those areas, Hughes set a powerful counterexample to the "general practitioner/sole practitioner" model in the 1950s. Specialization was, of course, the trend throughout the whole profession at the time, but at Coudert Brothers it was Hughes who most encouraged and supported its development, training lawyers who thought of themselves as corporate lawyers not as generalists. "Jim Hughes really organized the Corporate Department as a department," says Russell. "It gave me, at least, the sense of belonging to a group and of there being an organized corporate practice at Coudert Brothers, which frankly I had never had before."

Hughes was also the person who organized and headed transactional teams, which got the younger men accustomed to working together fairly often. These so-called "corporate teams" worked particularly well because of Hughes's approach to dealing with young people. Despite his own youthful appearance, accentuated by his jaunty bow ties, Hughes was a staunch traditionalist in office relations: formal and reserved, but treating even the rawest of recruits with grave professional courtesy. "Hughes would take you to meetings with clients," recalls partner Andrew S. Hedden, Jr., of his early years with the firm, "and after giving his analysis, he would turn to you and ask your opinion. Of course, everyone in the room—including you—knew you were just out of law school and as dumb as they come, but Hughes had this beautiful manner of treating you as a full-fledged colleague." Another partner, Anthony Williams, recalls, "Hughes often sat down and asked the advice of an associate. That was an exciting and heady thing. You felt like you were working *with* him, and he was a good man to work with."

From the corporate teams, there arose the fixture of the "corporate lunch," which became the occasion for partners and associates to get together regularly and keep each other informed on what was going on in the corporate area of the practice. And, unspectacular and mundane as they were, these corporate teams and corporate lunches had their effect: the young men trained in the 1950s and early 1960s were not the lone wolves their predecessors had been. They showed much less reluctance to see the clients for whose affairs they were principally responsible being serviced by others and were more in the habit of cooperation. Coudert Brothers continued to have an exceptionally high proportion of "solo practitioners" well past the 1950s, but it also had developed skills in and habits of coordination that went beyond what had previously prevailed and that were to prove one of the firm's assets as its practice grew more far-flung.

* * *

While Jim Hughes worked with numerous corporate clients, Bill Shields worked with only a few—but two of them, Tiffany and the Buckley oil and gas companies, were prime examples of the kind of growing client that sustained Coudert Brothers between 1955 and 1972. Although small, Tiffany was a very active client, in part because it had a prestigious reputation that needed constant defending—to the joy of the firm's litigators, who loved working with Tiffany chairman, Walter Hoving. There are numerous stories about Hoving still circulating at Coudert Brothers—one of the most charming involving his wish to induce a massage parlor in Washington, D.C., to take down its sign advertising "the Tiffany magic touch." As a born-again Christian, Hoving did not want to sue and give the massage parlor free publicity; attorney's letters threatening suit went unheeded; and finally Hoving arranged to station a photographer on the sidewalk outside the parlor. The photographer took photographs of everyone entering and leaving the premises, and "within two weeks," Milo Coerper recalls, with relish, "the sign came down."

It was also Hoving who got Coudert Brothers involved in a five-year civic battle to protect Central Park, which began in 1960 when Parks Commissioner Robert Moses accepted a gift from Huntington Hartford to build a sidewalk café complex in the park at Fifth Avenue and Fifty-ninth Street. Leading a group of Fifth Avenue merchants, Hoving sued to block what the *New York Times* would describe as this "unwise invasion" of stone, steel, and glass into the park's edge.

A new associate at Coudert Brothers, William Rand, who was a former assistant N.Y. district attorney and assistant general counsel to Governor Nelson Rockefeller, acted as trial counsel for Hoving's group. Coudert Brothers received more newspaper coverage from this case than any other matter it handled in the 1960s, for this was a hotly political controversy, of the sort that Fred Coudert had used to engage in during his heyday. It was a pity, in fact, that Fred had not lived to see it, for he would have known just about everybody involved. (As a Columbia trustee, for example, Coudert had conducted Moses's oral examination for his doctoral degree in 1917.) And the fundamental legal issue—the right of citizens to challenge unwise decisions of government officials—was one that had always been dear to his heart.

As with so many earlier Coudert Brothers' cases of this type, the battle against the "beneficial bulldozer" was won through a combination of legal and publicity skills. Rand orchestrated a slow series of pretrial motions, tried unsuccessfully to postpone the actual trial in the New York Supreme Court, and then—with a brief interruption in 1962 while Rand served out a term as a Supreme Court judge himself—launched a series of appeals. Meanwhile, the bulldozers were blocked, Hoving and the Sulzberger family rallied public opinion, and eventually a new administration was elected that killed the project. "We lost the lawsuit and won the case," as Rand puts it, adding wryly that throughout the long struggle, "We never lost a Republican judge, and we never won a Democratic judge."

The Buckley companies were also what attorneys call "a sustaining client," basically because they were constantly raising capital to fund new oil and gas exploration ventures. Until his retirement in 1966, George Montgomery continued to represent the Buckleys, spending his time at their headquarters, but, as the volume of work grew, he drew Shields into this client's affairs. By the mid-1950s, Shields was spending about 75 percent of his time on Buckley public offerings and related securities work. Then, Shields began to need the help of associates. First John Carey, then Adam Fremantle, and finally E. Timothy McAuliffe were hired, and, thus, as the Buckley companies expanded, so did Coudert Brothers.

Described by Mcauliffe as "a fabulous gentleman, almost larger than life in size and demeanor, fun to be with and easily liked," Shields moved socially among that milieu of old-line New York families to which the Buckleys, the Hovings, and, for that matter, the Couderts also belonged. He had all the right labels—Buckley School, Taft School, Yale, junior-year Phi Beta Kappa, Harvard Law, U.S. Navy, and every city and country club that counted. Shields was proud of his affiliations and got so much enjoyment out of them, it brought pleasure to others. A football tailgate party, for example, was all the more fun because Shields was such a true-blue Yalie, and when he argued that the firm should move to the Pan Am Building, it promoted a lot of good-humored chaff—it being maintained that Shields's interest in the Pan Am Building arose from the Yale Club being just across the street.

As loyal as Shields was to his various institutions, he was equally loyal to friends, associates, and clients. "Shields made a real effort to be helpful," says McAuliffe. "He went out of his way for people. He was a good, strong friend that you could rely on." "He looked after his clients very, very well," adds Fremantle, "and that, after all, is what it's all about."

By around 1960 the Couderts were also drawing Shields into the administration of the firm, and, although he was related to Alexis by marriage, Shields took, says Hughes, "an independent line. He had his own way of looking at things." Shields was, however, another voice for expansion on international lines. His own practice was almost wholly domestic, but his background and thinking were far from provincial. Shields thought in world terms, as America's East Coast patricians almost always have, and he was, in the final analysis, a competitor. He wanted his football team to win, he wanted Coudert Brothers to win, and he thought building on its international reputation was the winning formula.

Although he was with Coudert Brothers for a relatively brief period, George Nebolsine also made his impact on the young men with whom he worked. Nebolsine's background was entirely different from anyone else's at Coudert Brothers, for he was a Russian émigré, born in Sevastopol in 1902. Escaping Russia during the revolution, Nebolsine worked his way through Williams College and, after graduate studies at Princeton and a stint at the Foreign Policy Association, attended Yale Law School. Thereafter, he had spent most of his career at the side of Thurlow Marshall Gordon, who eventually became the name partner in Cahill Gordon.

According to his older brother, Ross Nebolsine, in 1954 when Cahill Gordon was going through some splintering as several groups of partners broke away, Nebolsine decided to make a change and, therefore, he sought an introduction to Fred Coudert. Although Fred had known Nebolsine's father when the latter had served as Russian naval attaché in Washington around 1910, he had never met the son before, and he found himself much impressed. Described by Russell as "a great Russian bear of a man, with an expansive, mercurial temperament," Nebolsine had the kind of cultured interests that appealed to the senior Coudert, including an excellent palate, a love of fine food, considerable ability as an artist, expertise in Romanesque architecture, and a taste for politics. (Nebolsine was a friend and informal advisor of H. J. Heinz, Jr., of the catsup family, who was a power in Pennsylvania Republican politics.) Like Coudert himself, Nebolsine had brilliant conceptual abilities: he saw the law in broad strokes and was cheerfully willing to leave some of the more tedious details to the juniors.

Most importantly, Nebolsine was building a practice that did not really fit in at Cahill Gordon and that generated painfully little income, but which Fred Coudert recognized as meeting his standards of an "important practice." What Nebolsine had done was develop contacts among attorneys in postwar Germany that had led to his representing some major German companies in their first postwar efforts to distribute their products in the United States.

These were companies like Daimler-Benz, Robert Bosch, Thyssen Steel, Krupp, and, in fact, most of the German steel and wire manufacturers. On these companies' efforts was riding the German "economic miracle," which, in turn, was vital to the rebuilding of West Germany as a democratic nation—a transformation that Coudert regarded as essential to the world's future. Nebolsine's thinking was that, if he could be based at Coudert Frères in Europe, he could develop this German practice further and feed the business back to the New York office. The senior Coudert heartily concurred and sent off a letter to John Robinson, informing him of the plans.

Robinson was infuriated, says Charles Torem. "He wrote back that he had never heard of Nebolsine, he wasn't going to have a stranger thrust upon him as a partner, and Fred was completely overstepping his prerogatives." As Torem points out, eighty-year-old Robinson was the only person in the firm at that time who could call the eighty-three-year-old Coudert "Fred" or who could deal with him on such equal terms. Coudert did not push the matter, and Nebolsine joined the New York office instead, as a term partner. Nevertheless, Paris saw a great deal of Nebolsine in following years, for he spent extensive periods of time on the Continent—"cultivating the European garden for us," as Fitzgerald has put it.

Nebolsine had a tough row to hoe, partly because John McCloy, the former U.S. high commissioner for Germany and chairman of the Chase Bank, seemed to be going after the same clients on behalf of his old firm, Milbank Tweed. In 1956, for example, Nebolsine was told by executives of a major German corporation that a Chase Bank officer had recommended that they use Milbank Tweed as co-counsel for their U.S. affairs. "It is not my plan to take this lying down," Nebolsine wrote angrily to Alexis from Germany. "I propose that either you or I, as you prefer, speak to David Rockefeller and ask him point blank whether he is aware and approves of his Treasurer urging a client whom we introduced to the Chase to take other counsel."

Alexis got on the phone immediately and reported back to Nebolsine, "This morning I spoke to David [Rockefeller]. . . . [He] was horrified at the suggestion that the initiative for such a recommendation should have come from Chase Bank. He said he was most pleased to have us in the matter and that it would never have occurred to anyone at the bank to suggest our replacement or even the addition of co-counsel." Nothing more was heard about Milbank Tweed.

Thus energetically overcoming the difficulties posed by the fact that Coudert Brothers was not firmly locked into the Wall

Street "old boy" network, Nebolsine fought to build and hold his client list—but his efforts never produced much money. "It was a great shame," says Ross Nebolsine. "My brother would really have liked to make some big fees." Allen Russell, one of the associates who took care of details for Nebolsine, says that billings were low simply because the U.S. operations of these companies were small: "If I recall correctly, Robert Bosch in the mid-1950s consisted of one loft on Madison Avenue through which it distributed about $100,000 in imports. Today, Bosch has $1 billion in U.S. sales and manufacturing plants all over the country." Nebolsine, though, did not live to see this expansion, for he had diabetes, which he neglected, according to his brother, and he died suddenly of a stroke in Paris in 1963.

While he lived, however, Nebolsine taught the younger men with whom he worked a lasting lesson in the practice of international law: "When representing a subsidiary in the U.S.," he told them, "always make sure you know the people at the foreign parent company as well." After Frank Wells's death in 1959, Russell began working for the U.S. subsidiary of Mannesmann, which had been one of Wells's clients. Mindful of Nebolsine's stricture, Russell went to Alexis and said he'd like to go to Germany to introduce himself to the Mannesmann executives. Although Russell was still only an associate, Alexis approved the trip. Russell was given a very courteous reception by Mannesmann's in-house counsel, taken to lunch, and told, apologetically, in the course of the meal, "You know, we would like to give Coudert Brothers more business, but we aren't the sort of company that gets sued very often." "It was obvious, then," says Russell, "how much I had to learn about the German system and how much explaining I would have to do about what U.S. lawyers are good for."

When Nebolsine himself died, Alexis without prompting, sent Russell to Germany to firm up relations with Robert Bosch. Alexis also told Milo Coerper to pack his bags. An associate in Washington, D.C., Coerper had been working with Nebolsine on a set of major antidumping cases, the "steel wire rod cases," before the U.S. Tariff Commission, representing the German Steel Association and German Specialty Steel Commission. Astonished, because he was only an associate, but more than willing, Coerper took off and visited the various major German steel companies, solidifying the firm's contacts.

That was personally a pivotal trip for Coerper, who would—as one thing led to another—become general counsel for the German-American Chamber of Commerce, attorney for the General Marketing Organization of the German food and beverage industry and for the German Stabilization Fund, a registered foreign agent for German interests, and most recently, a member of the German delegation to the World Intellectual Property Organization. These were all events Coerper had never dreamed of when he elected to study Spanish in school, and, with Alexis's encouragement, Coerper twice enrolled to take crash courses in German and once took a brief leave in Germany to study the language and culture.

Russell and Coerper had to learn through experience what they needed to know about foreign cultures in order to practice international law. For Alexis Coudert, of course, that kind of knowledge was part of his inheritance. Like their father before them, Alexis and his brothers had been raised in a bilingual environment. (Their mother, Alys, who had been partly educated in Germany, was, in fact, rather a better linguist than their father.) Everything in Alexis's upbringing—the continual discussions at the dinner table of world events, the stream of distinguished foreign visitors, the family trips abroad on the great ocean liners—was conducive to an ability to think outside of the bounds of the American legal system and culture.

Recognized as one of America's experts on international and foreign law, Alexis had not only served as acting director of Columbia's Parker School of Foreign and Comparative Law, but he had played an important role in its founding in 1949. As a trustee of the Parker Foundation, Alexis had urged the use of the foundation's funds to establish a school emphasizing the study of foreign legal systems, and the resulting Parker School was more his own creation than, in his modesty, he usually cared to have people know. In the 1950s, Alexis served as American representative to the International Committee of Comparative law, an organization set up under the auspices of UNESCO, as American secretary general of the Union International des Avocats, as member of the U.S. Council Committee on International Commercial Arbitration, and as a member of bar association committees in such areas as international law, admiralty and stateless peoples.

Alexis Coudert was in many respects, like his great-uncle Paul Fuller, Sr., a lawyer's lawyer, whose knowledge was freely at others' disposition. He was so much an authority on the French civil code that Coudert Frères, which had an office full of civil code experts, often referred knottier questions to him, and he was consulted by many lawyers outside the firm—most of whom he never even thought of billing for his time and trouble. Coudert also helped to start the Parker School's publishing program and gave considerable advice and encouragement to such legal academicians as René David, Martin Domke, John Hazard, and Henry P. DeVries. Coudert wrote little himself, but there are numerous books in Coudert Brothers' library—pioneering studies on international law published in the 1950s—in which Alexis's name is mentioned warmly on the acknowledgment pages.

Alexis's own practice was quite varied, and he liked it that way. Bill Rand worked closely with Alexis on litigation matters, and his explanation of how Alexis assigned litigation work in the 1960s gives an idea of the kind of legal work Alexis enjoyed doing. Antitrust matters, Rand says, were automatically assigned by Alexis to Joe McManus. General commercial litigation went to Gerry Dunworth, who also got stuck with the matrimonials. (Dunworth once represented the wife in a divorce and so impressed the husband that he retained Dunworth in a matter that brought in a large fee; and Alexis, according to Rand, was always hopeful that lightning would strike twice.) Libel and intellectual property matters went to Carl Eldridge. "And whatever was left over," Rand says, "especially if it was off-beat or had an international angle—no matter how small it was, if it involved an interesting legal issue—those things he liked to keep for himself."

Although Alexis went on doing litigation and estates work almost to the end of his life, the larger part of his practice by 1960 was corporate work, especially for European corporations. When the firm was small, corporate associates usually started off working full-time for Alexis for at least a few months before being assigned elsewhere. When the firm grew larger, Alexis still found ways to work directly with a considerable number of corporate associates, often by asking their help with one of the nonprofit organizations he represented. Thus, Tony Williams to this day serves as a director of a clinic outside Mexico City because Alexis asked him one morning, "Do you know anything about Mexican Indians? Would you like to know something?" And another associate of the 1970s, Joel Adler, was similarly drawn into the affairs of the Salk Institute and of a charitable foundation that sent medical equipment to Poland.

As a result, most of the associates knew firsthand Alexis's style of practicing law, and it was one that left a lasting impression on them. Alexis, they say, was a careful lawyer, he was a good draftsman—but he was so much more than that. "Alexis Coudert," says one former associate, "was the absolute antithesis of everything narrow and crabbed about the profession." The approach that Alexis suggested in the 1946 article "Direct Foreign Investment" was the one he followed in actuality: like his father and grandfather, he practiced a humanistic sort of law, taking into account more than the letter of the statutes and the case law. The environment of the deal—the culture in which it was taking place, the psychology of its participants, possible political and economic repercussions—were automatically factored in when he gave his advice. Of course, every lawyer does these things to a certain extent, but in talking with associates, Alexis brought such points into the discussion in so natural and easy a way—and his understanding of human nature and of other cultures was so broad—that the younger lawyers felt almost as if a new world were being opened up to them, and they never forgot the lessons Alexis quietly slipped in, every now and then, under the cover of a simple conversation.

The younger—and older—lawyers loved Alexis, however, because his wide perspective could always be expanded just a little bit more to encompass their own way of seeing things. When Alexis started practicing law, for example, it did not initially occur to him—any more than it had to his father—that finance should be a part of a lawyer's repertoire. International economics he understood and appreciated; corporate finance he knew little about.

In the 1950s, though, there was a new breed of lawyer appearing on the scene, a type that Mike Dominianni calls "numerate lawyers," by which he means attorneys equally comfortable analyzing the financial and legal aspects of a business situation and able to relate the one to the other. A numerate lawyer himself—he was a CPA as well as an attorney—Dominianni joined Coudert Brothers as a Trusts and Estates associate in 1957 and spent his first several years in a state of astonishment at how little numbers, balance sheets, and financial reports meant to many of the senior lawyers at the firm.

"In those days, lawyers disdained numbers," Dominianni recalls, with just a little pardonable exaggeration. "When you started talking dollars and balance sheets, even business lawyers turned off. That sort of thing was handled by the accountants. 'What about the taxes in a transaction?' 'Oh, let the accountants worry about that.' That was how lawyers thought."

In 1961 Dominianni finished an advanced degree in tax law at New York University and started concentrating on tax matters, which brought him into increasing contact with Alexis Coudert— and set the stage for some culture shock. "I always talked in Tax Code sections," Dominianni says, "because I had been trained to do that. This was a Section 102 matter, and that was a Section 104. In the beginning, I couldn't understand why Alexis and Jim Hughes used to start laughing when I did that. I thought the way I talked was normal; they thought it was funny. Alexis used to kid me that someday I ought to learn to speak English." Then Dominianni got a blackboard with chalk, and he began to make financial presentations—and Alexis had something else to tease him about. "I'd come down the hallway with a new scheme, and Alexis would groan—in a joking way, you know—and say, 'Oh, no! Here he comes with those pictures again!' "

It was a case of the accountancy-trained lawyer confronting the humanities-trained lawyers, the technocrat trying to convince the classicists—and it was the latter who quickly gave way. "I was really bull-headed in those days," says Dominianni. "I'd bang on the desk if I had to, I'd dig in my heels. Ah, youth!" he adds. "To have that kind of energy and certainty again! But I knew I was right. The tax rates were so high, the tax law considerations had to be treated as more than just a peripheral."

The crux of the matter—what Dominianni was trying to persuade Alexis and Hughes to do—was to plug him in at the beginning, instead of at the end, of a transaction. In a relatively short time—before the end of 1961, in fact—he had succeeded, to the extent that Hughes, practical and business-minded himself, was using his services heavily. Then the Paris office discovered Dominianni's capabilities and began telephoning, and by 1963 Dominianni was one of the busiest associates in the firm. In one instance, in the mid-1960s, a British company was on the verge of making a U.S. acquisition and had arranged its finance with a U.S. insurance company. Congress chose that inauspicious moment to enact the Interest Equalization Tax (IET), placing a 15 percent tax on money borrowed by foreigners. The partner in charge called from London and said, "The tax will kill the deal. How are we going to get rid of it, Mike?" Studying the IET provisions, Dominianni located a section that exempted from the tax a new corporation organized overseas to borrow in the United States, if all the proceeds were invested in the United States or held as cash. A perfect provision for the British client—except that such corporations, although they might be located in the U.K. or anywhere else, were called in the new law "Less Developed Country Corporations."

"The British were a little shocked when they learned they were about to organize an English company that would be considered here, for tax purposes, a Less Developed Country Corporation," Dominianni admits. "But British pride recovered quickly when they realized that status was going to save them about $1.5 million in taxes. They said, 'Right-o, carry on.' " Dominianni obtained an IRS ruling that the new company would qualify, and next came the awkward moment of trying to explain the situation to the U.S. insurance company.

"We had a meeting with the insurance guys, and they kept asking about the IET," says Dominianni. "I kept saying, don't worry about it. I didn't want to tell them that we were qualified under the Less Developed Country Corporation exemption and shake them up. At the end of the meeting, I finally had to break the news to them, and they were shook up all right. But we had the IRS ruling, and we eventually got them satisfied and happy again."

The next and final stage was obtaining approval from the Federal Reserve Bank in Washington, D.C. Alexis and Dominianni went down to Washington on the train together, and, mindful of how Alexis felt about code section numbers, Dominianni said, "Alexis, if we talk about the Less Developed Country Corporation exemption, eyebrows are going to go up. We've got to call this the Section 4915(c) exemption." But the days when Alexis had laughed about code section numbers were in the past. When the proper moment came, Alexis said in his charming, low-key way, "Oh, but this is a Section 4915(c) exemption, of course." Impressed if not enlightened, the bankers nodded their heads wisely, murmured, "Of course," and moved on to other topics. Once again, Alexis had adapted to the wave of the future, and in that moment, tax law—the specialty that Fred Coudert had doubted the firm needed in 1939—may be said to have come of age at Coudert Brothers.

Chapter Fifteen

A FLAG
IN FIVE CITIES

Expanding with its clients' needs was one path to growth, the slow and sure route, but by the late 1950s there was a new mood percolating through the New York office: a desire to force the pace of growth a bit and a corresponding willingness to examine seriously some of the ideas floating around for increasing the firm's client base. This was good news for Charles Torem at Coudert Frères, who for the past decade had been lobbing proposals for overseas officers toward New York, hoping that one or more of them would hit his partners' fancy.

Torem's earliest suggestion for a new office came in 1947, following a trip to Germany, where he had observed that business was brisk for American lawyers in the zone that lay under American military law. Some of the Coudert Brothers partners must then have had some interest in Germany, too, for at about this time Percy Shay in the Washington office sounded out Dr. Ernst C. Stiefel about opening a Coudert office in Frankfurt. A refugee from Hitler's Germany, Stiefel had become a member of the New York bar in 1944 and in 1947 was working for the U.S. War Department's Office of Military Government (Germany). He had recently been readmitted to the German bar, and, therefore, could establish an office in Frankfurt. "I explained to Shay, however," recalls Stiefel, "that under German law it would be impossible to open an office in the name of Coudert Brothers. The office would have to be in my name, and I did not want to return to Germany. I felt there would be not enough business." Indeed, Germany's cities were so scarred by rubble and craters that visiting them was, in Torem's words, like "landing on the moon," and Alexis ultimately concluded that the timing was premature for a German office.

In 1952, with France excited over the prospects for the development of the Saharan oil fields, Torem urged strongly the creation of a Casablanca office, and he even got Max Shoop to fly out to Morocco to examine the possibilities. But on the subject of Casablanca, he got no encouragement from New York. There followed proposals for various Italian cities and for Brussels, because the European Economic Community would be headquartered there; all of these landed in New York with dull thuds, but Torem kept trying.

Torem always had good business reasons why Coudert Brothers should plant its flag in the cities he proposed, but he never had a strong preference for one location over another. Instead, Torem wanted Coudert Brothers to be in all these locations. He longed, he admits, for "offices anywhere and everywhere, as many as possible." Years before the firm started to act on the idea, Torem had dancing in his head the vision of what a later partner was to call "the international network"—the concept of Coudert Brothers as a grid of interlocking offices covering the globe.

The concept of the "international network" was, of course, implicit in Coudert Brothers' history, particularly that period at the turn of the century when Coudert Brothers had stretched from Manila to Paris. Between the world wars, a few other New York firms had established offices in Europe, and in the early 1950s one or two firms were starting or restarting their offices in London and Paris and eyeing additional locations. The "international network" was not an original concept, but, for the enthusiasm with which he took it up and, most of all, the persistence with which he pursued it from 1948 on, Charles Torem stands as the modern father of the idea at Coudert Brothers.

Torem's proposals always went directly to Alexis, and the earliest ones went straight from Alexis to Fred Coudert, which is where they usually died. When one considers that the senior Coudert at age seventy-one mandated the opening of a Washington office, at age seventy-nine endorsed the radical move to a midtown location, and at age eighty-three took a chance on George Nebolsine, it is apparent that he never entirely lost his willingness to gamble. Foreign branch offices, though, were something that Fred had tried in his youth, and he had concluded that they were more trouble than they were worth. And once Fred formed a conclusion, he was not, at any age, likely to change his mind.

For a few years after Fred's death in 1955, Torem's suggestions continued to stir little excitement in New York, partly because of a lingering desire to do things the way the Old Man would have wanted to do them but also, more importantly, because of financial considerations. The peculiarities of partnership taxation being what they were, starting a new office was going to require the partners to provide the initial capital from their own after-tax incomes, and nearly half the partners in the New York office at this time were men in their sixties, on the verge of retirement and, therefore, not anxious to take great risks. Thus, there was a stasis at the New York office, as fiscal prudence and conservatism warred with the partners' pride in the firm and desire to see it expand. By around 1957, however—with Alexis's influence and persuasiveness providing the critical push—the mood had tilted definitely toward investing in Coudert Brothers' future.

Any new venture, it was understood, was going to be a small one. "Some people felt a real fear about the financial consequences to themselves if a new venture should fail," Ferdinand Coudert recalls, so the firm, therefore, was not going to be gambling great sums. Moreover, as Torem points out, "We were anxious to expand on our own. We didn't want a bigger partner, we wanted to keep our own identity. Whatever we did had to be manageable in size." Within these parameters, though, all the partners were generally willing by 1957 to take some sort of risk. The firm, in fact, came very close to opening an Italian office, but the American lawyer in Italy who would have been a partner dropped out in the final stages. Germany was also again considered, but the restraints on the entry of foreign attorneys were considered too inhibiting.

Then, in 1959, Pearl & Sigmon, a two-man London firm of American lawyers, approached Charles Torem about a possible merger with Coudert Brothers. Stuart Pearl was getting on in years, and he and Sigmon thought it best to become part of a larger, stronger entity. Torem referred the suggestion to Alexis. Alexis put it before the New York partners, and they reacted with an enthusiasm that Italy and Germany had never generated.

The timing was exactly right, for 1959 proved a banner year for the firm: the U.S. recession of 1957–58 had ended, and Coudert Brothers' profits jumped 25 percent over the year before, easing the older partners' financial fears and putting everyone in an optimistic mood. The place also seemed right, for London was known territory: Mal Doing had been spending long stretches of time there on ICI business, Tom Finletter had been Marshall Plan ambassador in England, George Nebolsine went through London on practically every trip to Germany. "The question was," recalls Ferdinand, "why we hadn't been there years before."

Bill Shields flew over to London to check the situation out and reported back favorably to New York. Barent Ten Eyck, who had joined Coudert Frères in 1958, indicated that he was willing to transfer to London to give the new office a Coudert coloration. In a short time, a four-party partnership agreement had been signed by Coudert Brothers (the partnership operating the New York and Washington offices), Coudert Frères, Pearl & Sigmon, and Barent Ten Eyck, establishing "Coudert Brothers-London," which opened its doors for business in April 1960.

The founding of "CB-London" marked the start of Coudert Brothers' "Try and Trust" period—a decade during which the firm made a series of comparable small mergers, trying to speed up its own growth. The year after starting CB-London, for example, the New York partnership effectively absorbed the small estates firm of Taylor, Wadsworth, & Burr, when David Taylor and Eugene Wadsworth joined Coudert Brothers. The next year, 1962, Thibaut de Saint Phalle—who, despite his name, was very much an American—became a partner in Coudert Brothers. As de Saint Phalle had once practiced law with Barent Ten Eyck in Paris (in the partnership of Ten Eyck & Saint Phalle), this move, too, had something of the spirit of a friendly merger. And, then, in 1965 CB-Brussels was set up, as a partnership among Coudert Brothers, Coudert Frères, and Robert Gottschalk, an American lawyer already practicing in Belgium. Once again, the Coudert name was on the door in five cities: New York, Paris, Washington, D.C., London, and Brussels.

Despite everyone's hopes, both the London and Brussels offices got off to slow, disappointing starts. During the 1960s, Brussels ended each year with modest losses, while London's results wobbled back and forth between red ink and black. Some years London turned a small profit, producing a spurt of optimism that it had at last turned the corner; the next year, the bottom line would turn out to be a negative figure again.

The partners felt they knew what Brussels' problem was: the office just didn't have enough business. After the signing of the Treaty of Rome in 1958, several American law firms had opened up branches in Brussels, which was to be the center of European Economic Community law practice. As far as the Coudert people could tell, none of them showed much profit in the 1960s, except for Cleary Gottlieb, which had started off with a larger staff and which was reputed to have close ties with Jean Monnet, the father of the EEC. Several other American law offices shut down, but CB-Brussels struggled along. Gottschalk went back and forth between New York and Brussels, and Eric Osterweil, an associate hired from another firm, handled the day-by-day work, most of which came in from the Paris office. Coudert Frères clients had just enough need for assistance with EEC matters to make it worthwhile to continue the office, but not enough to make it financially successful.

Why London did not prosper was more of a puzzle, and many lawyers tried their hand at solving it. After Pearl, Sigmon, and Ten Eyck, disappointed by the initial results, withdrew from CB-London in 1962, they were replaced by Edward A. Gottesman, a young, talented American attorney. A graduate of the University of Chicago's program for the intellectually gifted, Gottesman had taken his degree from Yale Law School at age nineteen. Alexis Coudert had met him while Gottesman, as fellow at the Association of the Bar of the City of New York, was sitting out the two years that had to pass before he would be old enough for admission to the bar. As soon as he was admitted to practice, Gottesman, at age twenty-one, went over to London at Alexis's invitation, and for the next two years he was the sole attorney at CB-London, doing mostly tax work and trying to build a practice in cross-border transactions.

In 1964 Gottesman was joined by one of his law-school classmates, Samuel L. Highleyman. Having had his education interrupted by military service in the late 1940s and, again, during the Korean War, Highleyman had been as much older than most of the students at Yale Law as Gottesman had been younger. Despite the difference in their ages, though, Gottesman and Highleyman had gotten along well, and this was an important factor when Alexis, Torem, and Gottesman began talking about adding a corporate partner to the London office, for Gottesman was not only bright but impatient with minds that worked differently from his. Highleyman, who was then an associate at O'Melveney & Myers specializing in international business transactions, met Gottesman's standards. ("In retrospect," says Highleyman, "I'm still flattered Ed wanted me. The guy was really that brilliant.")

Then in 1965, Lawrence R. ("Larry") Brody, who had been practicing U.S. law in London on his own for the past nine years, joined the office. Gottesman pulled in a big transaction: the purchase by a major British publishing company of a stake in a group of American trade and professional magazines. (This was the deal that the IET tax had placed in jeopardy.) Highleyman came up with several large pieces of work, including a contested takeover on the London Stock Exchange of the British subsidiary of a U.S. Fortune 500 company—probably the first contested takeover any part of the Coudert Brothers ever worked on. Brody brought in a large, profitable estate, and CB-London seemed to be on its way. New associates were hired: E. Timothy McAuliffe and later John van Merkensteijn. Associate Van Kirk Reeves transferred from the Paris office to help out. Even Alexis Coudert himself was in London, for ten months between the summer of 1967 and spring of 1968. (Alexis transferred himself to London for personal reasons—not unconnected with the fact that his daughter Alison had married Gottesman a few years earlier—but the move was perceived within the firm as a strong affirmation of the importance of the foreign branches.)

By the mid-1960s there was no shortage of good lawyers at CB-London, and for every lawyer there, another dozen or so would have been happy to take his place. Indeed, one of McAuliffe's duties as a new London associate was writing the rejection letters to lawyers who had sent their résumés on the off-chance that CB-London might have an opening. Somehow, though, the London office never quite found a steady source of income in the 1960s. McAuliffe recalls periods of "high excitement" in 1965–66 as the office worked on major transactions, alternating with months when the fees came spluttering in for such things as serving divorce papers for another U.S. law firm and preparing tax returns for Americans in the U.K.

The practice that everyone was hoping London would develop was, of course, one like Coudert Frères's, and to understand why London had such trouble doing so, one has to look across the Channel to see what was happening during the same period at Coudert Brothers' oldest overseas office. The 1960s were boom years for Coudert Frères, as its legal staff expanded from about ten lawyers in 1960 to approximately thirty in 1969. "Every year," says Roger J. Goebel, who began working as a Coudert Frères associate in 1963, "we seemed to be adding more space and taking on more people."

The major clients of the Paris office were American companies with operations in France, such as Ford, Alcoa, Procter & Gamble, Ashland Oil, and MCA/Universal, but the office, Charles Torem estimates, spent about 70 percent of its time advising on French law and only about 30 percent on U.S. law. This was possible because historically the French legal profession—the *avocats* and *notaires*—had not been interested in giving advice on business law, and there had grown up a third, unregulated category of persons, known as *conseils juridiques,* who were permitted to draft commercial contracts and provide commercial legal advice. Anyone of any nationality could be a *conseil juridique:* it was essentially a self-proclaimed title, although most *conseils juridiques* had French university degrees in law. Coudert Frères had more *conseils juridiques* on its roster in the 1960s than it did American lawyers, and they included not only Frenchmen (and Frenchwomen) but also Belgians, Africans, and the distinguished Rumanian expert in French civil and EEC law Dr. Lazar Focsaneanu.

Unless they were otherwise qualified, under New York State bar rules the *conseils* could not be partners in Coudert Frères, and this prevented Coudert Frères from making any non-American partners in the 1960s. Nonetheless, Coudert Frères had a dual status. It was an American law firm practicing U.S. law in France, and it was also a French *conseil juridique* firm that happened to be one of the largest, if not the largest, such firm in France. Thus, clients could obtain from Coudert Frères advice on both the U.S. and French legal aspects of a business deal. Moreover, the best of the Coudert Frères lawyers—and Charles Torem, in particular—gave their advice in the context of a thorough understanding of both French and American business practices and cultures.

The Ford/Richier acquisition—although it occurred in 1972—was in many respects typical of the kind of matter handled by Coudert Frères in the 1960s. On the one side of the deal was France's leading tractor manufacturer, Richier, a family concern headed by a self-made man getting on in years, who knew he ought to sell his business but who was by no means certain he wanted to—and who was particularly unsure whether he wished to sell it to Americans. On the other side was Coudert Frères's client, Ford Motor Company, wanting to acquire Richier. And deeply involved in the transaction were the French government, which raised the question of whether as a matter of policy the Americans should be allowed to buy a company that was a national institution, and the French labor unions, which feared that American efficiency methods would jeopardize their workers' jobs.

There were delicate, drawn-out negotiations—with the French government, which, unable to find a better "French solution," eventually agreed to the initial purchase by Ford of a minority stake and then, if Ford proved a good citizen, to a second-stage completion of the deal; with the unions, which settled for clauses committing Ford to compensate for any job losses with certain levels of purchases of French-made goods; and with Mr. Rochier, who expected of Ford Motor Company the same personal style of doing business that prevailed in France. Understanding the French business climate, Henry Ford did conduct the negotiations in person, but the Ford company could not sign the brief, almost cursory type of contract commonly used in France for the sale of a business.

"The toughest part," says Torem, "was getting Mr. Richier to accept the American style of contract, with all the lengthy representations and warranties as to assets and liabilities." Mr. Richier was a man of honor, whose success had been built on the reliability of his word. The draft contract, to his mind, verged on the insulting in its legalistic detail, and the great challenge was bringing him to understand why the Americans insisted on the warranties.

Much of Coudert Frères's success, therefore, lay in the fact that, understanding both the French and American mentalities, it could actively further a deal, rather than inadvertently undermine it. "Charles Torem," Alexis Coudert once said, "doesn't just sell legal skills; he sells wisdom." Roger Goebel spent some thirteen years working with Torem and another several years in New York with Alexis Coudert, and out of this experience he coined the phrase "bridging the cultural gap" to describe what it was that both Torem and Coudert did so well. In a February 1989 *Tulane Law Review* article dedicated to Torem, Coudert, and Henry deVries of the Parker School, Goebel maintained that "at least half the role of the transnational lawyer" lies in assisting clients to overcome the barriers created by different cultural, social, political, and economic systems:

> This assistance covers a wide spectrum: helping clients . . . to convert their normal legal and business methods into those that can be successfully employed in a foreign environment; conducting negotiations and general business dealings between a client and his commercial adversary in such fashion as to help both sides understand the reasons for each other's basic concerns and desires so that a successful business deal can be struck; helping a client properly manage a subsidiary or other foreign investment vehicle in the light of the customary ways of operation in a local environment; and drafting a contract in a manner that can facilitate a practical application . . . that is not basically disruptive of either party's cultural or social traditions.

To conduct its style of transnational practice, Coudert Frères needed, of course, American lawyers who were willing to remain in France long enough to become thoroughly conversant with the French business culture, and finding such Americans was not easy. "Plenty of people thought it would be delightful to live in Paris for three or four years," says Goebel, "but it was hard to find people who would commit their lives to it." Goebel himself had not the slightest intention of devoting any significant portion of his life to Coudert Frères. He told Alexis Coudert that he was looking for about six months' experience practicing law, after which he wanted to find a teaching position—but Alexis sent him to France anyway. There, Goebel received in the fall of 1963 a correspondingly chilly reception from Charles Torem.

According to Goebel's recollection, in their initial interview Torem asked Goebel if he had ever practiced law; Goebel admitted he hadn't. Did Goebel know anything about U.S. taxes? No. How good was Goebel's French? Practically nonexistent, Goebel replied. With a withering gaze, Torem thereupon dismissed Goebel, his final disgusted words being "My God, I don't know how Alexis can do these things to me!" Goebel's reception, however, was standard for new Coudert Frères associates. Whatever their qualifications, new associates were usually greeted with cold suspicion that they would not last, would disrupt the whole overworked office by needing to be trained, or would otherwise prove an intolerable burden. There followed the thawing period during which Torem realized that the associate was actually being useful and—if the associate lasted that long—by Torem becoming as upset at the thought of the person leaving as he had been at his or her arrival.

W. Laurence ("Laurie") Craig and Robin Tait, who came to Coudert Frères in 1964, survived the trial period and remained at the Paris office for the rest of their careers, the one initially helping to build Coudert Frères's international arbitration practice in the 1960s and the other getting a Eurodollar loan/financial market practice off the ground. Edwin Matthews was another who filled Coudert Frères's need for transnational lawyers, arriving as an associate later in the 1960s and becoming a partner in 1972. There were never quite enough such American lawyers in Paris for the size of the practice, though, and Coudert Frères always had the hurried, harried atmosphere of a workplace where people were on deadline and the clock was ticking into the final moments.

Thus, Coudert Frères's situation—plenty of clients, not enough suitable lawyers applying for jobs—was the reverse of CB-London's, where there were plenty of job applicants and not enough clients. A factor in London's slow start was undoubtedly the fact that potential clients did not feel the "cultural gap" in the United Kingdom that they did in France. The United Kingdom, after all, had given the States its language and common-law legal system in the first place; even the differences—such as the distinction between barristers and solicitors—were familiar to most businessmen, if only from murder mysteries and movies. Americans investing in or trading with the U.K. often felt entirely comfortable going directly to an English solicitor.

Moreover, there was no category in England comparable to

the *conseils juridiques;* CB-London could have no solicitors in its own office; and the American lawyers at CB-London had signed written undertakings that they would not advise on questions of British law. "We were very scrupulous in staying within the bounds of our permission from the Law Society," says Brody. As a result, says Goebel, "the role of an American law firm in the United Kingdom had to be a very limited role, compared to its role in France." As the office was constituted, the clients to which CB-London could be most useful were not so much American companies doing business in the U.K. as British-based companies needing help with investments in the States, but until the end of the 1960s, when the dollar weakened, the flow of investment was going east across the Atlantic—and CB-London had a tough time just staying in the black.

In hindsight, another of CB-London's problems appeared to be its location in Mayfair, a fashionable residential district, rather than in or near the City of London. The choice of location reflected the fact that CB-London's original partners expected not only to attract business clients but also to do estates work for wealthy individuals—and that expectation, in turn, is a reflection of how strong Coudert Brothers' trusts and estates practice was in 1960. The corporate/commercial part of the practice was larger and growing more rapidly, but trusts and estates work remained, as Mike Dominianni has said, "a very valuable and lucrative practice."

By its nature, estates work provided occasional great windfalls for the firm. When Wadsworth and Taylor joined Coudert Brothers in 1961, for example, they brought with them some $6 million in fees, principally from the estate of one of Jay Gould's heirs, Howard Gould—and that $6 million made a very pleasant onetime bump in income to a firm then grossing about one-fifth that amount. One of the important aspects of the trusts and estates work, however, was that it gave the firm a sense of security. Any given will drawn by Coudert Brothers might not turn out to be the testator's last will and testament. (With reference to a client who he knew was visiting other law firms and drawing up a new will every few months, Alexis once said drily, "I feel like I'm holding a ticket in a lottery. It's certainly going to be exciting when we all race down to the courthouse and find out which firm she visited last.") The backlog of wills at Coudert Brothers was such, though, that it gave the partners the sense of knowing where their next dollar was coming from.

In the early 1960s, a regular feature of life at Coudert Brothers was the fall meeting at which Miss Bainbridge announced how much cash she had on hand for the Christmas distribution, which was the more important of the two annual distributions of profit to the partners. At that time many partners billed their clients only once a year, at the end of the year. As a result, the figure Miss Bainbridge announced was invariably quite small. "Then," says Allen Russell, "all heads would swivel toward the Trusts and Estates partners and we would wait expectantly to hear how much money they planned to bring in during the last quarter. Trust and Estates was still being perceived as a kind of reservoir for the whole firm."

Trusts and Estates also remained the most cosmopolitan part of the firm. George Farnham, who took over the administration of the department as Tom Kelly slowed down, kept a log of wills probated by Coudert Brothers, and in that log one will find, here, a case requiring expertise in Yugoslav-Jewish rabbinical law; there, a case involving a probate proceeding of some twenty years' duration in the courts of India; and, on another page, a matter that would have gone badly astray had Coudert Brothers not known that the form of affidavits in Egypt varies with the religion of the affiant. In the course of his career at Coudert Brothers, Farnham learned how to open a safety-deposit box in just about any place on the globe that had a banking system, and Ferdinand Coudert says—not immodestly, for this was knowledge handed down from generation to generation—that there was nothing Coudert Brothers did not know (or know how to find out) about lawfully keeping assets out of the hands of tax-gatherers, however remote or obscure the jurisdiction. Islamic law, Chilean law, Chinese law, and virtually every other kind of foreign law came into play in the estates and trusts Coudert Brothers handled—at a time when the corporate practice was primarily dealing with Western Europe.

What one will not find in Farnham's log for the 1960s, however, is a significant number of estates worked on jointly with Coudert Frères. Such estates had once been the heart of Coudert Brothers' estates practice, but after World War II wealthy Americans had not flocked back to France in any great numbers, for living conditions there were too hard and the threat of Communism too real. The habits of those on the Social Register changed entirely in the late 1940s and 1950s, with the retirement to the Riviera villa going the way of the ocean liner, white gloves, and tea dances, and the need for Coudert Brothers' special expertise in French-American estates was also lessened by the Tax Convention of 1946, which eliminated many of the problems of double taxation of estates.

Because of the lagtime between the making of a will and the death of the testator, these developments began to make themselves felt only in the mid- and late 1960s, and one of their effects was to cause Trusts and Estates to seem less central to the firm's practice. Under the "old formula" laid down by the original Coudert brothers nearly one hundred years earlier, estates work had been the glue holding the Paris and New York offices together, making the attorneys on both sides of the Atlantic mutually dependent on each other. Moreover, estates work had permeated the New York office, providing a good share of the litigators' caseload and even bringing in corporate clients. (Coudert Brothers' oldest continuing client in the 1960s, for example, was the Zerega family, who had begun drawing up their wills with the firm in the 1870s and years later began using the firm for the corporate work related to their pasta business.) By the late 1960s, however, the "old formula" was definitely a thing of the past, and from the relatively light amount of business that the firm was able to refer among its parts—not enough, fundamentally, to make London or Brussels profitable—it was evident that no new formula had yet arisen to take its place.

The new offices and new partners of the 1960s gave Coudert Brothers the sense of being a firm on the move, but they had little discernible effect on the way the firm was perceived by outsiders. In 1952 when Allen Russell received a job offer from Coudert Brothers, his uncle in the small upstate town of Auburn, New York, had decided to check this firm out. Calling an acquaintance who was familiar with the major New York firms, Russell's uncle had been told, "Coudert Brothers? Oh, they're the Tiffany's of law firms." Nearly two decades later, in 1969, the father of another prospective associate, Andrew S. Hedden, Jr., telephoned a lawyer friend with the same question and got back, almost word for word, the same answer: "Coudert Brothers? The Tiffany's of law firms."

The epithet was, of course, a compliment, implying that Coudert Brothers was an elite firm, doing quality work for a high caliber of client. There was also the implication, though—at least by 1969—that Coudert Brothers was perhaps a bit staid or old-fashioned. In the 1960s, observers divided the major New York law firms into two lots: the gentlemanly firms and the more dynamic, aggressive firms. Coudert Brothers definitely fell into the former category in just about everyone's opinion—including the firm's colleagues at Coudert Frères. "There are any number of complimentary words I could have used about Coudert Brothers in the 1960s," says Roger Goebel. "I'm sure *aggressive* would not have been one of them."

Yet the firm's reputation overlooked one very important aspect of life at Coudert Brothers: the resourcefulness and initiative that were repeatedly required of its younger lawyers. The firm was so small that it did not have much depth to its lineup, and when a pinch hitter was needed, the person sent out onto the field was as likely to be an associate as a partner.

The stellar example of a Coudert Brothers associate who, when initiative was required, rose to the situation was Carl Eldridge. When the Seaboard Insurance directors had taken the gamble of leaving their libel cases in his hands, Eldridge had been a thirty-one-year-old unknown associate, with less than four years' experience altogether in practice and only eighteen-months' experience in libel work. Yet he had taken hold of Walter Barry's practice so firmly that by 1963 he was being recognized as one of the great trial lawyers of his generation.

He had done it partly on sheer tenacity. Eldridge went about preparing for his cases like a bulldog, mastering every detail and begrudging nothing in time and effort. "He never got surprised in the courtroom," says Philip Silverberg, who as an attorney at CBS worked closely with Eldridge for a number of years. "He had always done his homework."

Eldridge also used what Mike Dominianni has called "his command presence" to full advantage. A tall, heavy-bodied man with beetling brows, Eldridge looked like the former marine officer he was; no one was ever very surprised to learn that he had won the Distinguished Flying Cross and two air medals for his part in the bloody Iwo Jima campaign. "Eldridge," says Silverberg, "could make just about anybody quake in their boots."

Like so many tough guys, Eldridge was also about as soft-hearted as they come. "He was a very kind person," says Congressman Fritz Coudert's son, Frederic René ("Fritz") Coudert III, "but not everyone knew that." Eldridge was generous in sharing his expertise with younger men in seminars, and he did a fair amount of quiet, unobtrusive volunteer work. But in lighting out against his clients' opponents, he was an unrelenting adversary.

Most of all, Eldridge had, as Dominianni says, "superb seat-of-the-pants instincts for where the law was going in a new field." Many still current precedents in libel law, intellectual property, and the First Amendment right of freedom of the press are cases that Eldridge fought and won. To take just one example, the docudramas that became a staple of television fare derive their license to re-create recent historical events with actors and imaginary dialogue, in large part, from a 1963 case, *Youssoupoff v. CBS,* involving a drama about the assassination of the sinister Russian monk Rasputin in 1916. Prince Felix Youssoupoff, who had murdered

Rasputin, objected that he had never said or done some of the things depicted; but Eldridge effectively pressed home the contention that it was sufficient for the broadcast to be "based on fact," if the portrayal was innocuous to Youssoupoff's reputation, personality, and character. In another landmark case, Eldridge successfully defended historian William Manchester when Jacqueline Kennedy sought to stop publication of *Death of a President.* "He was a leader," Dominianni had said, "in fixing the balance between a person's right to privacy and the people's right to know."

As television sets became a fixture of American homes, Eldridge's practice mushroomed, and by the 1960s he was representing insurers that provided libel coverage not only to CBS but also to ABC—and eventually he would be appearing in court for all three major networks, plus Metromedia as well. Whatever the insurance company, the policies always stipulated that only Carl Eldridge should defend the network or networks covered. Indeed, by the late 1960s Lloyd's of London was writing a clause into its policies that coverage would apply only if Eldridge had approved the program before broadcast time. Thus, by the time American households in the 1960s sat down to watch one of their favorite shows, the chances were that Carl Eldridge had already screened the episode and determined its content to be nonlibelous. He was the unquestioned leader and authority in this field of litigation.

Carl Eldridge's was the spectacular case, but there was not one of his contemporaries who had not been thrown into situations for which they, too, were not entirely prepared. The first time Allen Russell, for example, was ever in a room with investment bankers, he walked in alone; there was no senior man beside him whose lead he could follow. Following family tradition, Alexis had Fritz III meeting alone with clients before he was even out of law school. Down at the Washington, D.C., office, Milo Coerper was completely on his own; whatever came in, however unfamiliar, he had to handle as he thought best. And John Carey got a fair warning of what a young Coudert Brothers lawyer's life was like on the day he reported for work, when Bill Shields filled him in quickly on the major matters in hand—and took off for a vacation in the wilds of Maine, saying "Don't try to call me. Just use your own judgment." ("I thought that was an invigorating approach," says Carey.)

Talking among themselves in the 1960s, the senior associates and junior partners agreed that they had probably had to develop more self-reliance and agility than they would have at any other firm. The senior partners must have had nerves of steel to trust them so much, but, anyway, life at Coudert Brothers had certainly never been boring.

In 1963 Carey went to Alexis with an idea: "Shouldn't we be recruiting on law-school campuses?" he asked. "Every other law firm seems to be doing that." Alexis talked it over with some other partners, and, as the firm needed one new associate from the Class of 1964 anyway, Carey was given authority to go on a recruiting trip. Carey's recollection is that he went to Harvard Law School, which was his own alma mater; to Yale, because he had taken his undergraduate degree there; and to Columbia, because of its ties to the Coudert family.

As a recruiter, Carey had Coudert Brothers' strength in international affairs to play on, but there were two other things that he particularly wanted to get across to the students. "I tried to tell them," he says, "that they would find that the relationship between partners and associates at Coudert Brothers was unlike that at any other firm. And I told them that, if they came to Coudert Brothers, they would have an interesting life."

Mark Lebow, a Harvard Law School student, became the first associate ever recruited on campus by Coudert Brothers. Because he had to complete his military service after graduation, Lebow actually started working at Coudert Brothers in 1965. Three years later he was handling all the smaller pieces of commercial litigation, with only minimal supervision from Gerry Dunworth, and the firm was casting around for an associate to work for him.

In the fall of 1964 Coudert Brothers again recruited one student directly from the Harvard campus: W. Preston Tollinger, Jr., who, while still an associate, would establish not one, but two, overseas offices for Coudert Brothers. In the fall of 1965 the single associate recruited was Charles R. Stevens, who five years later led the firm's entry into the Far East—an event that was to prove one of the most pivotal in Coudert Brothers' history.

Thus, through the recruitment process, Coudert Brothers' image of itself in the 1960s as a dynamic firm became self-reinforcing. To use a phrase not yet current, it was the "entrepreneurial types," the people who liked the idea of early responsibility, who showed the most interest in Coudert Brothers; and there is no record that those who joined the firm in the expectation that they would have a chance to show initiative were in any way disappointed.

Chapter Sixteen

1969:
AVANT LE DÉLUGE

By 1969 Coudert Brothers was not only recruiting two or three associates a year from law-school campuses but had a program for "summer associates," who worked at the firm during the summer before their last year of law school. One of the three summer associates who reported for work in May 1969, George Shenk, knew a fair amount about Coudert Brothers before he arrived. He had taken graduate courses from Dick Gardner at Columbia's School of International Affairs, and one of his friends, Philippe Schreiber, was already working for the firm. Aware of Coudert Brothers' reputation as the preeminent international law firm, Shenk arrived prepared to be impressed by its size—and so he was. "I thought it was a very large firm," Shenk recalls. "Fifty lawyers in one office seemed like a lot to me. I didn't know any better."

The partners in New York did know better. While Coudert Brothers had almost doubled in size over the past decade, the Wall Street firms had grown just as fast or faster. The burgeoning new issues market on Wall Street had created great opportunities for securities lawyers, and firms with over one hundred attorneys had become a commonplace. It seemed distinctly possible that a few downtown firms would soon have two hundred lawyers or more.

Nonetheless, in late May 1969 a visitor to the thirteenth floor of the Pan Am Building would have noticed numerous signs that the bull market of the 1960s was affecting Coudert Brothers as well. On the south side of the building, for example, this hypothetical visitor would have found Bill Shields and associates Adam Fremantle and Tim McAuliffe gathered in Shields's large office (it had its own private washroom) planning public offerings in British Columbia, Ontario, and Quebec of shares of Magellan Petroleum, one of the Buckley companies. At the same time, associate Preston Tollinger, laboring in his office on the north side of the floor, was cleaning up the prospectus for the first public offering of a company, jointly owned by a Dutchman and a German, that manufactured mechanical control systems.

Walking around to the east side of the building, the visitor would go past the office of H. Struve Hensel, a distinguished practitioner who had joined Coudert Brothers in 1966 at Shields's suggestion. By the 1960s Hensel's name was already in the history books, for in 1940 Under Secretary of the Navy James Forrestal had asked Hensel to leave his partnership at Milbank Tweed and help him reorganize the Navy Department. As head of the Legal Procurement Division, general counsel to the navy, and, in 1945–46, assistant secretary of the navy, Hensel, according to historians of World War II, had played a vital role in the navy's rapid material buildup, and he had also served in the Eisenhower administration as assistant secretary of defense. When engaged in private practice, Hensel was primarily a securities lawyer, and in this last week of May one of the summer associates, Thomas Ragan, was learning from Hensel how to draft a prospectus and finding him "a marvelous teacher."

And over on the west side of the building was the office of Fritz Coudert III, a thirty-six-year-old partner who had put together one of the fastest-growing practices in the firm by building up contacts on Wall Street. Among his clients were four investment companies—J. M. Hartwell & Company, J. M. Hartwell & Company, Inc., Hartwell and Associates, and Park Westlake Associates—that in May 1969 were among fourteen respondents defending themselves against charges of insider trading in connection with their sale of Douglas Aircraft stock, allegedly on the basis of information received from Merrill Lynch. The SEC charges rested on what was then an unprecedented definition of an "insider," for it had never previously been suggested that a brokerage house, much less its clients, could be at fault in receiving and acting on information to which the public at large was not privy. The *Wall Street Journal* headline on the story read ACTION STUNS WALL STREET, and the *New York Times* reported that the charges had "touched off an uproar in the brokerage community." In May 1969 Merrill Lynch had already settled with the SEC, but its customers, certain they had done nothing wrong, were ready to fight on; and, as trial counsel for Coudert Brothers' clients, Joe McManus was preparing to present their defense.

In Fritz III's opinion at this time, what Coudert Brothers really needed to do in order to grow faster was to take the same path followed by the Wall Street firms: develop a steady relationship, if it could, with one or two banks or major corporations like IBM and focus on a domestic practice. "The international practice was exciting," recalls Fritz III, "but it was less profitable and not as steady. It seemed to me that if our objective was to grow, we were doing things the hard way. We could always have international law as a specialty, but other firms were bigger for a reason: they were concentrating on lower cost/higher profit banking and securities work. My viewpoint was that we were just banging our heads on the wall by not making a serious effort to act like a normal New York City law firm."

By May 1969, however, outside events were signaling that Fritz III's hopes for a "normal" development of the firm would be disappointed. American hegemony, both moral and financial, was being fractured under the pressures of the Vietnam War. International investment and trade were about to open up, with Europeans and Japanese challenging Americans in a much more competitive market. "The floodgates were opening," says Fritz III, "and Coudert Brothers was going to be swept along with the tide."

There were many scattered signs of the Vietnam War around the firm in May 1969. Not far from Carl Eldridge's office, for example, an associate had put up an antiwar poster. Eldridge, the ex-marine, glowered at it every time he walked by, but the poster stayed up. One attorney was writing a letter to a client, gently explaining that, regardless of the fact that the Students for a Democratic Society had advocated violent sabotage of U.S. industry, it would not be advisable from a civil rights viewpoint for the client's personnel department to ask job applicants if they were SDS members. And the summer associates, George Shenk recalls, were being very well treated: "There was a war on; young men were at a premium." Indeed, John Carey and Mark Lebow were actually planning social activities for this year's crop of summer "guests"— activities that Carey and Lebow would pay for out of their own pockets. (The firm's frugality was so well established, it never occurred to either of them to ask for reimbursement.)

The world economic changes that the war was hastening were somewhat less visible. If one dropped by Jim Hughes's office in the last week of May 1969, however, Mike Dominianni would be found there, seated in a leather chair with brass studs. Dominianni had spent so much time in that particular chair over the past eight years talking with Hughes that he had long since worked one of the studs on the armrest loose, and he was probably playing with that stud again as he and Hughes conferred about the latest stage of Thiokol's acquisition of the fibers business of W. R. Grace. The previous year, Thiokol had bought Grace's U.S. fibers business, and Hugh Fitzgerald and associate John Wyser-Pratte had just returned from the closing in Ontario for the sale of the shares of Grace Fibres (Canada) Ltd. Now the last stage, the purchase of Grace's related manufacturing business in Scotland, was being worked on. Ed Gottesman at CB-London would be retaining and working with a firm of British solicitors, McManus would be needed to answer some antitrust questions, and the client was talking about possibly doing a Eurodollar financing. If that came to pass, then Robin Tait's expertise at Coudert Frères would be required as well. Coudert Brothers had been pulling together multinational teams like this for nearly a decade now, and the mechanics had become fairly routine. What was unusual was the discussion of a financing in the Eurodollar market. As a result of the United States' trade deficits of the late 1960s, Eurodollar deposits were reaching unprecedented high levels. In May 1969 almost every acquisition Coudert Brothers had in hand was still a matter of a U.S. company acquiring foreign assets; in five years' time, the routine Coudert Brothers acquisition would be a case of a European client buying the depressed stock of a U.S. company, with the acquisition often being funded in the Eurodollar market.

Coudert Brothers was, of course, not fully prepared for the radical changes that were coming in the patterns of international business, but it was a great deal better prepared than most. For one thing, it was already well-accustomed to working in an international context. In the last week of May 1969, for example, only Fritz III, estates partner Eugene Wadsworth, and the Entertainment Litigation Department, composed of Eldridge, Eugene Girden, and associates Gordon King and Tim Hart (who had come to Coudert Brothers from CBS's legal staff), were working on purely domestic matters. The other forty-some lawyers were all handling at least one matter that had an international angle, however many domestic matters they were also attending to.

Over in the Trusts and Estates Department, for instance, Kay Woodward was getting ready for the upcoming Rolling Stones' tour of the United States, for the financial backer of the tour, Prince Rupert Loewenstein, was a client of CB-London and it had been arranged that Woodward would cosign checks with the tour manager to maintain the backer's control over the expenses. Gerry

Dunworth and Mark Lebow were waiting for the verdict to come down in *Watts v. Swiss Bank,* one of those classic Coudert Brothers cases revolving around the issue of whether French or American testamentary laws should take precedence. This particular case also involved the question of whether Swiss Bank was a bank or an agency in the United States, and the verdict, when it was announced on June 2, was everything Coudert Brothers wanted. ("WE WON!" Lebow entered jubilantly in his desk diary.)

Diagonally opposite Dunworth's southwest corner office, McManus in his northeast corner office had his feet on his desk. Reclining with a lit cigar in his hand, he was proofreading the response to the Federal Trade Commission's New York field office, which was conducting an informal investigation of a German client's pricing practices. (The firm's antitrust litigation expert, McManus was also this week sending to the warehouse his files in the Electrical Equipment antitrust cases, which were the civil suits that followed the criminal conviction of General Electric and other manufacturers of heavy electrical equipment on price-fixing conspiracy charges. Representing the public utilities clients of Reed & Priest, which had no litigation department, McManus had served on the steering committee of lawyers that organized, prepared for trial, and finally settled [on terms generous to their clients] the eighteen hundred civil suits that had been filed nationwide.)

Roughly in the same area of the office Allen Russell was writing a letter to alert a German client to a possible customs problem that might arise in connection with the new Fair Packaging and Labeling Act. At Russell's request, associate Van Kirk Reeves (who had worked in Paris and London and was now in New York) was conferring with tax attorney John E. ("Jack") McDermott, Jr., on a workman's compensation question for the U.S. subsidiary of yet another German client. And associate Charles R. Stevens was drafting the new Liberian aircraft-registration law, which it was hoped, by at least one client, would make Liberia a center for aircraft registration as it already was for ship registration. (The law went on the books, but aircraft owners failed to respond to the opportunity.)

Around the corner, on the east side of the office, sat Bob Gottschalk of CB-Brussels and former partner Thibaut de Saint Phalle, who was now "of counsel" to the firm. De Saint Phalle had brought with him to Coudert Brothers work for Becton-Dickinson, and associate Blake Franklin was researching the laws on lotteries in Puerto Rico, Germany, and Mexico for the medical supply company, which was apparently considering offering some sales prizes in those jurisdictions. Also on this side of the building was the office of Ernst Zeisel, who had come to Coudert Brothers from Czechoslovakia as a Jewish refugee from Nazism. "The sweetest guy imaginable," in the words of one current partner, Zeisel was on salary but kept a portion of the fees he brought in, and many of his clients were émigrés and refugees themselves.

Next to Zeisel was the partner for whom Roger Goebel, Philippe Schreiber, and George Shenk were all working this month: Lucien Le Lièvre. Qualified to practice law in both France and the United States, Le Lièvre had become well-known in the French business community through his role as legal advisor not only to the 1944 Gaullist economic mission to Washington, D.C., but to the Ministry of National Economy in the first postwar French government. As French counsel between 1946 and 1966 to the law firm that became known as Dewey, Ballantine, Le Lièvre had mounted a strong challenge to Coudert Brothers' traditional monopoly on French-American business. In 1966 Le Lièvre had joined Coudert Brothers as a partner, thus bringing under one roof the two largest French practices in the United States, and this move was proving by 1969, says Le Lièvre, "a happy and successful marriage."

Le Lièvre's roster of clients included Compagnie Général d'Électricité, Creusot-Loire, Dassault, Dior Couture, Elf-Acquitaine, Roussell-Uclaf, Schneider, and Skis Rossignol. The day was coming when many of these companies would be beginning to buy U.S. companies, but in May 1969 Le Lièvre's practice was heavily oriented toward problems of distribution and sales in the United States. He was just wrapping up, for example, a major project in connection with Richier's introduction to the United States of the tower crane, which had the advantage over the standard U.S. boom crane of being able to place loads where they were to be used. The introduction of the tower crane had required first the amendment of regulations and codes in all the states, which had been written for boom cranes only, and then—since U.S. construction companies lease rather than buy cranes—the organization of a new U.S. company to import and rent Richier's novel handling equipment.

As these random examples from one week in May 1969 indicate, Coudert Brothers had a stockpile, like no other firm, of experience in international legal problems, of lawyers fluent in foreign languages, and of people who wanted to work and liked working with foreigners.

In 1966, after Ferdinand Coudert retired, the partnership agreement had been amended to transfer executive control of the firm from the Couderts themselves to a five-man committee composed of Alexis Coudert, former congressman Fritz Coudert, Jr., Jim Hughes, Bill Shields, and estates partner Gene Wadsworth. The new face in this group was Wadsworth—although he was hardly a stranger to Alexis, since their acquaintance went back to their undergraduate days at Yale. The other four were the same "kitchen cabinet" who had been setting policy and making day-to-day decisions together for almost a decade. The change in the partnership agreement had simply formalized the existing situation.

Since the nonfamily members of this executive committee, which was known as ExCom, outnumbered the family members, it could be said that in 1966 Coudert Brothers ceased to be a family firm. Alexis's influence on Coudert Brothers was so great by 1966, however, that such a statement would be fundamentally misleading. The creation of ExCom is better viewed as a moment of passage in the gradual, graceful relaxation of the Couderts' control, which had been going on for some years. This was a natural process, reflecting the firm's growth and Alexis's own preference, but until the day Alexis Coudert died, Coudert Brothers would be led by a Coudert.

In May 1969, of the five members of ExCom, both Shields and Fritz Coudert, Jr., had health problems. Shields would retire in 1970, and Fritz—whose doctors suspected that he had been suffering undiagnosed strokes since as early as 1959—would die in 1972. Thus, Alexis Coudert, Jim Hughes, and Gene Wadsworth would be presiding over the firm during the years when its growth rate turned upward at an acute angle. They were the "benevolent oligarchy," but they saw themselves from the beginning in 1966 as a transitional form of governance. It was Alexis's intention that the partnership should become entirely self-governing, and one of ExCom's running preoccupations would be what Hughes calls the "question of succession"—or, arriving at a formula that all the partners could agree on for selecting a different kind of ExCom, one not appointed by the Couderts.

In late May 1969, however, ExCom was preoccupied by two other major concerns. One was the imminent arrival of Sol Linowitz as a partner based at the Washington, D.C., office. Former general counsel for Xerox and a director of the Marine Midland Bank, Linowitz had just completed a term of service as ambassador to the Organization of American States. It was Struve Hensel who had introduced Ambassador Linowitz to Alexis Coudert, and Linowitz's acceptance of the firm's partnership offer was widely regarded, both inside and outside the firm, as a coup for Coudert Brothers. Linowitz had not yet moved into his office, but he was already writing memos about the possibilities of a Mexican or Brazilian branch of Coudert Brothers. It appeared that Ambassador Linowitz, too, was going to be a voice for international expansion.

The other main concern was getting everyone's signature on the new Paris partnership agreement, the text of which had been under negotiation with the Coudert Frères partners—Charles Torem, Laurie Craig, and Robin Tait—for a full two years. This agreement included a new provision to merge Coudert Frères and Coudert Brothers at some future time, when Torem should have died or withdrawn from Coudert Frères. Despite the wording, with its implication that such a merger would take place only over Torem's dead body, this provision actually represented a step forward toward a unification that had been discussed periodically for several decades.

Jim Hughes was the person who had kept bringing the topic up. Back in the 1930s, Hughes as a young associate had been an interested observer of the aftermath of John Robinson's push to have the share of fees allocated to Coudert Frères, on matters that both offices worked on jointly, increased from one-third to one-half. Fred Coudert had agreed to the new division in 1933, but with the reservation that the fees on the large estates would be separately negotiated. That provision led from the 1930s onward, in Hughes's opinion, to "continuing friction, misunderstanding, and lack of collegiality." Actually, from the office files, it is clear that the fee arrangements quickly got so tangled that only Miss Bainbridge knew who was due what on which matter. There is a somewhat plaintive 1939 note from Fred Coudert, for example, asking Miss Bainbridge to refresh his memory on the fee division in a particular estate, and her reply was that the probate fees were to be split with two-thirds going to Paris, trustee fees for one inter vivos trust were to be split 50/50, the testamentary trusts were on a 60/40 basis, except for a trust for the widower, which was a 50/50 split, and one other trust, which had apparently yet to be negotiated because she had no record of what the arrangement was. It is no wonder that Fred needed his memory refreshed, for the firm was working on up to twenty-five such matters at a time.

Thus, Hughes had decided "early in the game" that the "historical arrangement of the two firms being deemed to be separate, with New York having only a financial interest in Paris, was impractical" and that, if continued, it was bound to encourage a sense of the firm being composed of "separate fiefdoms." The period after the war seemed like a good time to change the structure, but Hughes found that "the Couderts really didn't want to do anything about it. They'd lived with this for such a long time, it seemed natural to them." The Coudert Frères partners most definitely disliked the idea of unification. John Robinson cherished the independence of the Paris firm and thought that a merger of the partnership could lead only to the Paris office being dictated to by the larger New York office. Accordingly, having received no support from the controlling partners on either side of the Atlantic, the subject was dropped.

Then, the London office was set up as a separate partnership, which Hughes agreed was, under the circumstances, the only feasible course. "Using the Coudert Frères model," he notes, "was the easy way to start off. The pattern was at hand, and Pearl & Sigmon didn't want to simply be absorbed. There were many practical reasons for doing it that way." But when CB-Brussels was started as the fourth separate partnership in the Coudert organization, Hughes began raising the question of unification again with Alexis and other members of ExCom. Although Hughes could cite various misunderstandings and inconveniences attendant on having four separate partnerships, the strength of his feeling seems to have arisen from a gut-level, or aesthetic, sense for form and structure: "I thought we had a false form of organization. We should be one united firm. But it seemed you either recognized that immediately and instinctively, or you didn't."

By the mid-1960s, however, Alexis had begun to agree that it would be better to have the firm united. "Paris and New York had such different corporate cultures, Alexis was not sure a merger would actually be feasible, but that was his only reservation," says Hughes. "Generally, he was in favor of the principle, if it could be worked out."

From that point on, the fate of the unification proposal rested in Charles Torem's hands. Would he support it or not? Following Robinson's lead, Torem had always upheld the autonomy and prestige of Coudert Frères, never letting anyone forget Paris's importance in the order of things. And Torem's view of Coudert Frères's world position was not unlike Charles de Gaulle's view of France. The story is told that one day Torem and a large group of New York partners were riding in an elevator together at the Pan Am Building. From the front of the elevator, Jack McDermott asked half-seriously, "Is anyone else worrying, like me, about what would happen to Coudert Brothers if this elevator crashed?" From the back of the elevator came Torem's voice. "I," he announced with stately emphasis, "worry about that whenever I'm *alone* in an elevator."

Torem's great physical height, his jealousy of Coudert Frères's independence, the wonderfully imperious manner that he could assume, and the fact that he had restored Coudert Frères to glory combined to present a temptation that few could resist. "Le Grand Charles" was his nickname on both sides of the Atlantic. As when applied to de Gaulle, the epithet was used sometimes with exasperation, sometimes with affection—always with respect. Naturally, it was assumed that Torem would not be in favor of unification, but that was not the case. What weighed heavily with Torem was that the new younger partners in the Paris office, Laurie Craig and Robin Tait, were for the idea, as were associates Edwin Matthews and Roger Goebel, who were about to become partners. And Alexis was saying that unification would be good for the younger people, giving them greater security. Thus, the 1969 Paris partnership agreement signified an agreement in principle with the concept of a unified firm. "It was just a question," says Torem, "of how to do it, so that the French would not be swallowed up."

While that was being thought out, the partners in 1970 decided to begin the process of unification with CB-London. "There was then an overall plan," says Mike Dominianni. "We were setting out to form a single multinational firm, not merely a confederation." Dominianni was chosen as chief negotiator on behalf of the New York partnership, and the whole matter was approached in high spirits, with much joking about "treaty negotiations" and "foreign diplomacy." Ed Gottesman in London, however, did not want to become part of a unified firm and decided instead to go into practice on his own. Larry Brody opted to stay with Coudert Brothers, as did Alfred Crotti, who had recently joined the London office. British-born Adam Fremantle and Van Kirk Reeves transferred from New York, and Richard Wincor, a copyright and literary property rights expert, signed on in an "of counsel" capacity, and these five became the nucleus of what was by 1971 a virtually new London operation, which took up quarters in the City of London.

The focus of negotiations then shifted to Paris. Ed Matthews there proposed the creation of an interoffice policy committee (known as Interpol) to give the smaller offices greater say in the affairs of the partnership—an idea quickly accepted as an answer to the other offices' fears of being overwhelmed by New York. There were complicated tax questions to be ironed out, and CB-Brussels required another set of negotiations—but by 1972 the deed was done. Coudert Brothers was now one firm, with a Paris office known as Coudert Frères, and it entered its years of dramatic growth with the members united into one partnership and prepared to share each other's fortunes.

* * *

If there was one way in which Coudert Brothers was clearly not prepared in late May 1969 for the growth it was about to undergo, it was administratively. In that month ExCom was making plans for a party to celebrate Miss Bainbridge's sixtieth anniversary with the firm. Almost seventy-eight years old, Miss Bainbridge still provided virtually all the administration the firm received and was still keeping the accounts by making pen-and-ink entries in hundreds of separate ledger books.

She had tried to retire in 1967, but Alexis had not permitted it. She was indispensable, Alexis told her then; she must not even think of retiring, for the firm could not do without her. So, grandmotherly and a bit stout, Miss Bainbridge soldiered on in her large outside office, two doors from Alexis's.

There were good reasons why Alexis valued Miss Bainbridge so highly. The most important was the fact that client funds and firm funds were completely safe in Miss Bainbridge's hands. With Miss Bainbridge controlling all bank accounts and signing all checks, the partners could have peace of mind, for her integrity was unshakable. In addition, the force of her character was such that the staff felt for her every bit of the same respect that the partners did. "You would never dream of talking back to Miss Bainbridge," says former secretary Mary Lehovich. "It would never occur to you to do such a thing—and really there was no reason to. She was always absolutely fair to everyone."

Moreover, although the accounting and payment system was archaic, it did have the strong advantages of being simple and fast. When Andy Hedden, a brand-new associate in May 1969, needed to have a check drawn for a client disbursement, he simply walked down the hall and knocked politely on Miss Bainbridge's door. She called him in, listened to what he wanted, satisfied herself that the purpose was legitimate, and handwrote the check on the spot. Hedden was back at his desk in two minutes, having formed the impression that "Miss Bainbridge had to have been one of the most competent people I've ever met."

This speed was what Alexis and most of the rest of the firm were accustomed to and wanted. In any area where he did not feel the consent of all the partners was required, Alexis liked to move fast and informally. When law-school students were interviewed for jobs, for example, Alexis preferred to make the job offer immediately and orally—not in writing a day or a week later. He had no interest in creating bureaucratic procedures and systems, and a firm as small as Coudert Brothers, of course, didn't feel the need for them.

Struve Hensel, however, found himself frustrated by the lack of information that came out of Miss Bainbridge's domain. The situation was a familiar one to anyone who has worked in a small office: Miss Bainbridge had just enough time to do the work; she had no time to make elaborate reports on what she was doing. The partners were given gross figures on outgo and income, and that was all the information they got. With his extensive experience in managing the Navy and Defense departments, Hensel was incredulous that he could not obtain figures on accounts payable, the aging of accounts, monthly operations, or even what capital investments the firm had. "How can we justify our lack of knowledge about our business," Hensel wrote in 1969, "our lack of planning and our lack of controls?"

The absence of financial information to be used for short-term and long-term planning was indeed a drawback, but the firm's more serious administrative shortcoming lay perhaps in the area of timekeeping and billing. Miss Bainbridge considered how and when partners billed their clients to be none of her concern; billing fell into the realm of what she had been trained to view as the almost sacred relationship between attorney and client. The partners were on their own here, and, on the whole, they were operating in 1969 not much differently than they had been in 1949.

When Mike Dominianni had come to Coudert Brothers in 1957, he had been shocked by the fact that no one ever asked him to account for how he spent his time: "I kept asking myself how are they going to know what I'm doing? How are they going to bill for my time?" Dominianni thought there should be a timekeeping system for the firm's attorneys, such as the one used by accounting firms. Carl Eldridge agreed entirely, as did Jim Hughes. "Alexis was a little saddened by the idea," Dominianni recalls, "but he supported it." Although Dominianni was only an associate, Alexis gave him opportunities to present his suggestion to all the partners, but the idea did not go over well.

"The older men found it very distasteful," Dominianni says. Indeed, the concept of timekeeping struck at the heart of the Old Guard's value system. To keep track of one's hours as if one were a factory worker punching a time clock, to account to someone else for how one spent one's day as if one were not a gentlemen whose word was to be trusted—these things were more than distasteful: they struck the Old Guard as fundamentally unprofessional. Most of the older partners, however, retired in a wave between 1964 and 1966, and then it became possible for Dominianni to design a monthly timekeeping sheet, which was passed out to the partners and associates with ExCom's blessing.

In the late 1960s Coudert Brothers had about twenty-five partners. About seven—not surprisingly, the seven who had the largest billings—filled out their timekeeping forms faithfully and turned them in punctually each month. There was nothing that could be done about the partners who took time reports more casually, except keep trying to persuade them that there was a connection between the timekeeping and the profit distributed at the end of the year. "All I remember about partnership meetings in the 1960s," says Bill Rand, "is Mike Dominianni going on about time reports and how we could all improve our billings, and most of the rest of the partners around the conference table more or less falling asleep."

The partners could yawn with impunity, but the associates could be leaned upon. If the visitor to Coudert Brothers in May 1969 saw an obviously nervous associate standing outside Carl Eldridge's open door, taking deep breaths in order to pump up his courage, the young lawyer was probably one who had just been told by Miss Bainbridge that she could not release his paycheck until he explained to Mr. Eldridge why his time report was late. Eldridge, it will be recalled, was the litigator who "could make anybody quake in his boots," and most associates preferred not to have to present such explanations more than once.

As for the partners, many continued to show a lack of enthusiasm about businesslike billing and timekeeping habits, and a good few chronically underbilled, omitted to bill, or failed to follow up on past-due bills. Coudert Brothers, in fact, did not really begin carefully billing for all its time until the clients themselves—or, rather, the clients' accounting departments—began demanding detailed statements.

"We are a business," Hensel wrote emphatically to ExCom in 1969. ExCom knew that, but the feeling was pervasive on ExCom and throughout the firm that Coudert Brothers was not *just* a business. As an associate, Tom Ragan would learn from his encounters with ExCom that "Alexis, Hughes, and Wadsworth were good bean counters, but they did not want bean-counting to control. They had a real concern for the old-fashioned values. When you went to see them, they wanted to know: Are you a good lawyer? Are you serving the clients well? Are you upholding the prestige of Coudert Brothers? Are you having fun?"

How to reconcile those values with a firm that was growing larger every year was a challenge that Coudert Brothers did not begin to address until after Miss Bainbridge retired in 1970. It turned to that problem late—almost too late, in some people's opinion—but that was not Miss Bainbridge's fault, and when she retired, she received all the honor and dignity that were her due. Tony Williams can remember a day in 1973, not long after he began work at Coudert Brothers, when Miss Bainbridge came back to visit the firm: "Suddenly, all these office doors were swinging open and senior partners were popping out into the corridor, practically bowing as this little elderly lady went by." Miss Bainbridge had been one of the great personages of Coudert Brothers, and when she left, an era had ended. Another era—what one might call the "pluck and luck" chapter of Coudert Brothers' history—was about to begin.

Chapter Seventeen

THE ASIAN ADVENTURE

In October 1970, a few months after Miss Bainbridge's retirement, twenty-eight-year-old Charles R. Stevens buckled himself into an economy-class seat on a jet bound for Tokyo. Having been given an expense account of twelve thousand dollars and a mandate to build a Japanese practice, Charlie Stevens was setting off to become the firm's pathfinder in the Far East. Coudert Brothers' great Asian adventure had begun.

Stevens had been preparing himself for this moment for some ten years, for Japan had been his fascination since he had started taking Japanese history and art courses as a Princeton undergraduate. The Princeton-in-Asia exchange program had given him the opportunity to spend the summer of 1962 in Japan, and a National Defense Fellowship for the study of strategic languages had provided the chance to begin learning to speak and write Japanese. By his last year at Harvard Law School, Stevens was taking advanced Japanese, and he was determined to find a way to combine his interest in Japan with the practice of law. In the corridor outside Harvard's International Legal Studies offices, Professor Toshio Sawada, who was doing graduate work at Harvard, mentioned that Coudert Brothers was looking for people like him, and Stevens went over to the placement office and signed up for an interview with John Carey.

By the fall of 1965, as Stevens was registering for his interview, Coudert Brothers had already been trying for several years to find

351

a way to develop a Japan practice. American law firms were not then allowed in Japan, with the exception of a few firms that had started practice during the Occupation and had been "grandfathered" when Japan had closed the door to foreign attorneys in 1955. In the early 1960s Carl Eldridge had flown to Tokyo to talk with one of these Occupation law firms, Anderson, Mori & Rabinowitz, about the possibilities of a joint venture but had returned discouraged by the Japanese restrictions. Next, Coudert Brothers had made a partnership offer to a Japanese-American lawyer, who would have been based at the New York office, but he had been seriously injured in an automobile accident before arrangements had been firmed up. "There were a number of us interested in Japan," Carey recalls, "but doing anything depended on finding the right people."

Accordingly, when they talked at Harvard in 1965, Carey encouraged Stevens to come down to New York for further interviews. Stevens visited several Wall Street firms before arriving at Coudert Brothers, and those firms, he found, "viewed this interest in Japan as a curiosity. It was all very well for the halcyon days of youth, but now I would want to get serious, of course, and become a bond lawyer." By contrast, as Stevens was passed from office to office at Coudert Brothers, he found that everyone wanted to talk about Japan, and then he was taken around and introduced to Alexis Coudert.

"It was an amazing experience," recalls Stevens. "I was amazed I was being interviewed by the senior partner, in the first place. I was further amazed that he was interested in Tokyo. And then he offered me a position then and there, saying that if I proved myself as a domestic lawyer, after a few years the firm would like me to start a Japan practice." Cancelling all other interviews, Stevens arranged to report for work at Coudert Brothers in July 1966.

Stevens was at Coudert Brothers for only six months when, by prearrangement, he left on a Fulbright Fellowship to take courses in commercial law for a year at the University of Tokyo. There he studied under Professor Makoto Yazawa, whom Stevens describes as "the academic father" of the Coudert Brothers' Japan practice, for Yazawa provided the insights into the Japanese legal system that would be vital to building a transnational practice. Stevens also resumed an acquaintance with Japanese attorney Kazuhiko Tanaka and obtained a part-time job at the firm headed by Kazuhiko's father, Judge Haruhiko Tanaka, who was a former High Court judge and former solicitor general of Japan. The Tanaka firm represented Japan Air Lines and the Sumitomo group of companies, among other clients, and its practice, reflecting its clients' needs, was orienting itself toward international commercial work, led by Michio Nishi, a cousin who had studied law at the University of London in the 1950s and had joined the family firm after a distinguished career on the bench.

While Stevens sat in Judge Tanaka's office as a foreign legal trainee, working on one or two matters referred by Coudert Brothers, he arranged for the younger Tanaka, in turn, to visit Coudert Brothers' New York office for a month. The groundwork was being laid during this year for a correspondent relationship—and the idea was glimmering for a closer tie. Just as Japan would not allow a firm like Coudert Brothers to open an office in Tokyo to give advice on American law, New York State after 1957 would not permit firms like Judge Tanaka's to have a New York office, advising on Japanese law. But young Americans could get visas to work for Japanese firms as "trainee" foreign legal consultants, and young Japanese lawyers could also work as trainees—or *stagiaires,* as they were usually called—for law firms in New York. Coudert Brothers, in fact, had had a steady stream of foreign *stagiaires* visiting its offices since at least the end of World War II, most of them young attorneys from Latin America and Europe.

Upon his return to Coudert Brothers in February 1968, Stevens promptly wrote a memo suggesting a formal relationship with Judge Tanaka's firm, based perhaps on the exchange of trainees, but ExCom felt that before any further steps were taken, Stevens—who was obviously going to be the key person in such a relationship—had to get some actual U.S. practice experience under his belt. For two years, Stevens did securities work for Fritz III, wrote the Liberian aircraft-registration act for Mike Dominianni, did corporate work for Jim Hughes—and grew restive. All he really wanted to do was work on Japanese matters. "Asia," he said once, "has been the obsession of my generation"—a sweeping and dubious generalization, but one reflecting accurately his own frame of mind. Between 1968 and 1970, in his spare time, Stevens was writing letters to Coudert Brothers' clients, trying to drum up some Japan business; he was making connections with overseas Japanese executives, working with Ambassador Linowitz and John Carey; he was teaching a comparative law course based on Japanese law at Columbia—and he felt as if none of this amounted to very much. He wanted to get back to Japan and get a practice started. "Ever self-sure," says Stevens, "in 1970 I decided I was ready to get going."

A job offer from the law school of University of Washington in Seattle forced the issue. "Alexis learned that I was thinking of leaving," Stevens said, "and he mobilized ExCom." Bill Shields, accompanied by Stevens, flew to Tokyo to talk with Judge Tanaka in 1970, and Sol Linowitz made a follow-up trip. The two firms reached an understanding for mutual cooperation—which went as far as it could go, given the restraints on foreign lawyers in both New York and Japan. And in October 1970, Stevens flew to Japan.

This was not the start of a Coudert Brothers office in Tokyo: this was the beginning of a commute. For the next twelve years, Stevens would spend on average one week a month in Japan—constantly going back and forth between New York and Tokyo—and other points in the Far East. While in Tokyo, the tall, blond, Japanese-speaking Caucasian sat in the Tanaka offices, working with the Tanaka lawyers and meeting their Japanese clients. Then he would make the fourteen-hour flight back to New York, where the U.S. legal work was done for the Japanese clients.

In 1971 the Japan practice produced nearly enough fees to cover expenses, and in 1972 it showed a small profit. "The first two years," says Stevens, "were really quite a success." Coudert Brothers began hiring young Japanese-speaking American attorneys, mostly located and recruited by Stevens himself, to provide backup in the New York office, either before or after putting in their stints as trainees in Tokyo. Eugene Danaher, Susan Goldberg, Robert McIlroy, Arthur M. Mitchell, and Toby Myerson were among the early Japan practice associates, and simultaneously most of Judge Tanaka's young attorneys came to the United States to study and then do practical training at Coudert Brothers. The Tanaka name went on Coudert Brothers' letterhead, and the practice connections steadily tightened as personal ties grew between the young Japanese and American attorneys.

Shortly after Stevens made his first business trip to Japan as a Coudert Brothers lawyer, he had published in *The Business Lawyer* (July 1972) an article on "Japanese Law and the Japanese Legal System," in which he noted that corporate advice "is still not recognized as a lawyer function by most of Japanese business society. . . . Introduction of a lawyer into a business conference is thought to be an unfriendly act, an act equal to an explicit threat of litigation." He also commented that, while Japanese companies were using American law firms for their U.S. activities, "these contacts are viewed by most Japanese businesses at best as a concession to a necessary evil." The customary methods of resolving business disputes in Japan were extralegal, which meant, among other things, that the fewer than nine thousand private practitioners serving Japan's some 100 million people concentrated largely on personal liability suits, real-estate-related suits, and criminal work.

In the context of the Japanese legal system, the Tanaka partners were as unusual in their way as Stevens was in his, for the firm was one of only a handful doing commercial work at all, much less international commercial work. Thus, Coudert Brothers was extraordinarily fortunate in being able to effect personnel exchanges with the Tanaka firm. But the initial modest success of the Japan practice only whetted Coudert Brothers' desire to become a permanent resident in East Asia, not just a transitory business visitor. The firm needed a home base in Asia, a city where it could have a listing in the phone book and an office with its name on the door.

In 1972, following President Nixon's historic trip to China, the Montreal law firm of Phillips & Vineberg suggested that Coudert Brothers join it in a Hong Kong joint venture. The Canadian firm had opened a one-man Hong Kong office in 1971 to work on Canadian-China trade matters, and it was interested in having an American partner to share expenses, particularly since it appeared that U.S.-China trade was about to open up.

Hong Kong was yet another locale that prohibited the entry of American lawyers, but Neil Phillips's proposal gave Coudert Brothers a reason to investigate whether the ban could be overcome. Alexis Coudert and Charles Stevens had been talking with Professor Jerome A. ("Jerry") Cohen of Harvard Law School about the prospects for developing a practice in Asian countries other than Japan, and, when Cohen was consulted about the Phillips & Vineberg proposal, he thought it was possible that Hong Kong might be persuaded to remove its bar against non-Commonwealth attorneys. Cohen, who had once lived in Hong Kong, had known the attorney-general of Hong Kong, Denys Roberts, for a number of years and was willing to sound him out on Coudert Brothers' behalf. Cohen's contacts in Singapore were even better; there, he knew not only the attorney-general Tan Boon Teik but also Prime Minister Lee Kuan Yew, who had visited Harvard more than once.

Cohen said, in effect, to Alexis: "While you're at it, why don't you look into opening a Singapore office, too?" Alexis thought that sounded fine, and Cohen, accompanied by Charlie Stevens, flew into Hong Kong and Singapore. In both locales, they found the attorneys-general receptive to the idea that admission of foreign lawyers could be helpful to the development of their city-states. They returned with tentative agreements, subject to the approval of the local law societies, and began drafting a memo to ExCom laying out the arguments for opening CB offices in both Hong Kong and Singapore. ExCom found itself convinced. Mike

Dominianni was asked to prepare budgets for two Far East offices, and the proposal was put on the agenda for a partnership meeting.

It was all that simple. "Other American firms at the same time were making systematic studies and finding out why they couldn't make a go of a Hong Kong or Singapore office," notes Robert Hornick, who would later be based in the Singapore office. "Coudert Brothers had no systematic study. It just did it. And since they couldn't make up their mind whether they'd rather have a Hong Kong or Singapore office, they opened in both places at the same time."

The twin proposals, Tim McAuliffe recalls, raised scarcely any discussion at the partnership meeting: "I'd say the general attitude was 'Sure, why not?' Actually, it was almost as if ExCom simply announced we were going to do this, and everyone said, 'Fine.'" Dominianni's budgets projected that CB-Hong Kong and CB-Singapore would lose about $250,000 before they went into the black—a sum exceeding two-thirds of the entire profit of the firm back in 1955. Coudert Brothers, however, had come a long way both in income and in spirit between 1955 and 1972. It was more profitable and less cautious, and it also had faith in its leadership.

"When Alexis, Hughes and Wadsworth suggested something," Joe McManus says, "consulting the partners was almost *pro forma*, because we had confidence in their judgment and we knew they had the welfare of the whole firm in mind. It was Alexis who had the idea of pointing the firm toward international expansion. He was taking the long view, and we were glad he was." McAuliffe adds, "Alexis's personality was such that, if you could see your way clear at all, you wanted to do things his way. It was a pleasure to give him support."

Aside from their trust in Alexis's vision, a goodly number of partners were stirred by the thought that their law firm was about to pioneer into territory where no American law firm had gone before. If London had been chosen as a location for a Coudert Brothers office in 1960 partly because it was comfortable and familiar, Hong Kong and Singapore were endorsed in 1972 partly because they were so exotic. "Some people were immune to the thrill," recalls one current partner. "But I think, in general, there was a current of excitement about the new offices, a kind of psychological lift. After our experience with London and Brussels, no one expected Hong Kong and Singapore to make any real money—but they did seem like the kind of places where a law firm like Coudert Brothers ought to be. Europe was on our doorstep, but going to Asia was a truly international move."

Any pioneering venture has an aura of romance to it, and, not surprisingly, when members of the firm talk about Coudert Brothers' early years in the Orient, it is often the romantic images that first come to mind. They talk, for example, about the colonial-style wooden bungalow that Coudert Brothers leased from the government of Singapore to house its young lawyers; of its wide verandas and the sitting room on the second floor, where the view through the open shutters of the tropical bush gave one the feeling of living in a Somerset Maugham novel; and of the stands of bamboo and frangipani trees. They talk about the beauty of the Hong Kong harbor; about calling up the boat boy in Hong Kong and instructing him to put some beer on ice and bring the pleasure junk around to the mooring nearest the office; and about entertaining clients on the gently swaying junk, watching the lights come on at twilight in the hills around the bay.

They talk, too, about the youth of the Coudert Brothers lawyers who manned these offices, and the spirit of adventure—lighthearted and youthful in tone—that they brought to their assignment. George Shenk, for example, tells about the day the typhoon warning flags went up in Hong Kong, and Preston Tollinger went on working. The wind began shaking and battering the office windows, and Preston Tollinger kept working. Finally a retreat was made to Tollinger's penthouse apartment, which had huge glass windows on all sides. "There were no shutters up; nothing was taped," recalls Shenk, who had arrived in Hong Kong only that morning. "I was pulling my mattress into the hallway to escape the shredding glass I was sure was going to be flying around the guest room at any moment. Tollinger and company were in the kitchen, checking on the supplies of Sara Lee brownies and vodka: that was their idea of preparing for a typhoon."

The adventures, though, were sometimes more serious, as when Gage McAfee, senior associate and head of the Singapore office, withdrew in cash the ten thousand dollars that represented his life savings, placed it in a briefcase, and on Thursday, April 24, 1975, as the Viet Cong drew near the outskirts of Saigon, flew into the beleaguered city. For several weeks McAfee, who had once worked for the U.S. government in Vietnam, and one or two clients and friends had been devising increasingly desperate plans to evacuate Vietnamese friends from Saigon. The last plan had involved the purchase of a U.S. Navy surplus air-sea rescue plane, which was to land on the Saigon River and pick up people assembled in small boats for evacuation. The disappearance of the American pilot who had gone to Saigon to make the preliminary arrangements, however, had doomed that hope, and McAfee had no idea at all of how he could help when he took off for Saigon on April 24. Against the advice of other clients and colleagues in the firm, he went in on a scheduled Singapore Airlines flight simply "as a gesture, to see what I could do."

The young lawyer's last-minute effort, however, proved "phenomenally lucky." Dodging past the distracted marine guards at the U.S. embassy, McAfee found his way to the upper floors and, through the kindness of the ambassador's executive secretary, Eva Kim, was able to secure emergency parole documents for the people on his list of names and the address of a safe house. Then, taking taxis and buses, riding on the backs of taxi-motorcycles, clutching his cash-stuffed briefcase, McAfee crisscrossed the city in the suffocating heat, collecting his people and bringing them to the safe house. There and at a staging area near the airport, a handful of young Foreign Service officers were surrounded by such chaos and confusion that McAfee found himself volunteering to stay and help with the general embassy evacuation effort.

Thursday night and all day Friday, McAfee alternated completing paperwork and signing personal sponsorship documents for Vietnamese, with driving busloads of refugees to the airport, bluffing his way through checkpoints at times by waving his long-expired official ID cards. On Friday night, as McAfee labored on, the rocketing of Saigon began. On Saturday, the Singapore Airlines flight on which McAfee held a ticket was cancelled, but the twenty-five Vietnamese friends he had originally rounded up made it out on a military flight; and on Sunday, April 27, the last day planes could still land or take off at the city's airport, McAfee departed on Air Vietnam.

There was even a sense of adventure and romance back at the New York office, where associates worked all night to field inquiries from the Far East offices and prepare replies before the close of business on the other side of the Pacific. For Bob Hornick, much of the romance centered on the telex machine, which stood in a three-by-three-foot room like an idol in a temple. The machine was temperamental and antiquated: it punched out tape as it transmitted, and another former associate can remember one night the tape flowing halfway around the thirteenth floor and feeling, as he picked it up, like a bridesmaid gathering the bride's train. But Hornick, who had never dealt with such a machine before, approached the telex "in awe," convinced he was standing "at the forefront of modern communications." None of the fancier equipment that came later gave him the same *frisson* of excitement he got from standing watch in the lonely New York office at night, as the messages started coming in by telex from points halfway around the globe, where the next day had already begun.

* * *

Before the two offices ever opened, however, they were very nearly stillborn. In the summer of 1972, while Coudert Brothers was still drafting the joint venture agreement with Phillips & Vineberg, Stevens received a call from Hong Kong informing him that the local law society had problems with the wording of the undertaking in which Coudert Brothers was to promise it would not practice local law. Stevens went down to Hong Kong, worked that out and returned to Tokyo, where he got the word that the Singapore law society was also raising objections. He wheeled around and went down to Singapore, to reiterate that Coudert Brothers was seeking permission to advise on only American and international law.

It seemed a good idea, though, to get the offices established as fast as possible, before anyone else had second thoughts. Stevens had already lined up his best friend in the firm, Preston Tollinger, to go to Hong Kong, but he had not yet succeeded in persuading anyone to commit himself to Singapore. As it seemed urgent to get going, Tollinger took off in October 1972 to man both new offices.

The official game plan—the memo prepared by Cohen and Stevens for ExCom—stated that the Hong Kong office, working with Phillips & Vineberg, would concentrate on representing small to medium-sized American and Canadian manufacturers in Hong Kong and develop some China work. The Singapore office, on the other hand, was supposed to reach profitability on the strength of the securities market that Prime Minister Yew was going to create there. The first thing Tollinger learned was that the game plan was constructed of chimeras. With the Cultural Revolution in full sway, there was not going to be any volume of China–U.S. trade anytime soon, and the Singapore securities market existed only on paper—in the columns of the local newspapers controlled by the government.

The idea of having one person commute between Hong Kong and Singapore, Tollinger also found out, was not as practical as it had seemed when he had looked at a map in New York. By the time the airlines detoured to avoid flying over Vietnam, the flight between the two cities chewed up the better part of the working day. "It was not exactly like the New York shuttle to Washington," recalls Tollinger, who decided to give nominal attention to Singapore and concentrate on Hong Kong, where he at least had the company of Edward Rubin, the Phillips & Vineberg attorney with whom he was sharing offices.

So there was Tollinger, with the CB shingle hung out in Hong Kong and Singapore—and nary a client in sight. But luck—

"wonderful, blind, dumb luck," as Tollinger once put it—was about to come to his rescue. At an American Chamber of Commerce lunch, Tollinger found himself seated near the Wells Fargo Bank representative, who expressed his delight at finding there was an American lawyer based in Hong Kong. "We have to send all our promissory notes back to New York, and it takes forever," said the Wells Fargo man. "Please, will you do one for us?" "Sure," said Tollinger. "Why not?" Then Morgan Guaranty sent around some work; then a trickle came in from Chase Manhattan and Bank America and Manufacturers Hanover; and eventually a flood from Citibank—and CB-Hong Kong had found its niche.

Because the New York office did no work for the large U.S. banks, servicing them had never figured into the East Asia game plan at all. The economic development of Asia, however, had turned Hong Kong into a regional banking center, with large American banks leading the march in major financings and loan agreements. There were any number of Hong Kong solicitor firms that could have served those banks, but New York head-office legal departments were uncomfortable at the thought of writing multimillion U.S. dollar agreements under Hong Kong/English law. At the same time, the solicitor firms gave the impression that they much preferred to deal with the British banks. "The American bankers felt they were running into colonial snobbery," says Owen Nee, who went to Hong Kong as a Coudert Brothers associate in 1973. "There were mutterings that the Hong Kong solicitors were trying to be more British than the British and treating the American banks as if they were second-class."

The result was that the Hong Kong offices of American banks were having their documentation done in New York, entailing slow turnaround times, cumbersome communications, and a loss of control by the local branches. As the first American law firm in Hong Kong, Coudert Brothers found itself filling a need it hadn't even known existed. "It turned out we were in the right place at the right time," one of the later Far East partners, Barry Metzger, would say. "We had just come for all the wrong reasons."

Tollinger's background was almost entirely in general corporate and securities work, but—by another piece of luck—he had done a little banking work, helping Alexis with the affairs of the French-American Banking Corporation. Among other matters, he had worked on one—precisely one—Eurodollar loan in New York, which, it developed, was one more Eurodollar financing than any other lawyer in Hong Kong had ever handled. "In the kingdom of the blind," Tollinger has remarked, "the one-eyed man is king," and in Hong Kong, Tollinger—slight as his experience was in New

York terms—was the international banking expert. By early spring 1973, business was flowing in so fast that Tollinger was hollering frantically for help. "Tollinger, Rubin and bananas are all growing on trees," he telexed to Stevens, urging him to get permission from ExCom to send an associate out to Hong Kong and to hire a senior associate to anchor the East Asian practice in New York—preferably his old friend from Harvard days, Jonathan D. ("Jan") DuBois, who was then at Cravath.

DuBois reported for duty on April 1, 1973, in time to work on CB-Hong Kong's first ship financing, a $15 million multicurrency transaction involving a vessel auspiciously named *The Happy Venture*. DuBois went looking for the precedent file, and Robin Tait was asked to mine Coudert Frères precedents, but nothing turned up that the younger lawyers could use as a guide in writing the multicurrency provisions. So Tollinger drafted, DuBois revised, and they argued the multicurrency risk concepts endlessly by telex and telephone. The two spent so much time polishing the document that ultimately they billed for only about a quarter of the hours put in—and, still, when they looked at the agreement later through more experienced eyes, they noticed that they had the same clause appearing in several places. But the client bank was satisfied, and *The Happy Venture* led on to a large amount of ship financing work.

Meanwhile, Stevens was looking for associates willing to go out to Hong Kong and Singapore and give Tollinger help on the spot. While he was seeking suitable candidates, warm bodies from Coudert Brothers' existing ranks were kept shuttling out to Hong Kong—Japan practice associate Susan Goldberg, George Shenk, and Stevens himself—to cover the holes until the more permanent people went into place. But the backup would never have been required without Tollinger's ability to bring in clients and his virtuoso performance in a one-man office.

"Tollinger," says Adam Fremantle, who worked in the Hong Kong office for a few years, "could turn his hand to anything." The speed at which he transformed himself into an expert on banking in Asia was astounding." Tollinger talked at high speed, learned at a frenetic pace, and went through work as if he were wired to a private energy source. "And every now and then," recalls Owen Nee, "there'd come this extra volt through the circuits, and he'd really take off."

Tollinger, at age thirty-two, carried off his role as Coudert Brothers' representative in Hong Kong and Singapore with insouciance, and his memos to New York—couched in a breezy style the firm quickly began calling "Tollingesque"—rivaled Charles Torem's for collectibility. The memo on rental subsidies referring to the "Greater Southeast Asia Co-Prosperity Sphere Housing Allowances" did not find great favor with some of the World War II veterans, but many of Tollinger's more hilarious reports from the Hong Kong front got passed around the Pan Am Building so often, they were dog-eared before they went into the files.

Taking a cheerful line, Tollinger turned all kinds of minidisasters and problems into profit. The Hong Kong office, for instance, was furnished in the traditional low-budget Coudert Brothers style, and, there being nothing cheaper than bottom-of-the-line Hong Kong furniture, the chairs had a marked tendency to tip over or collapse beneath their occupants. One of these tippy chairs gave way under a dignified, elderly Chinese manufacturer on his first visit to the office. Tollinger picked him up from the floor, blithely dusted him off—and helped him to buy a shopping center in Daly City, California. "Anyone else would have been sued," says one of the former Hong Kong associates. "Tollinger emerged from that debacle with one of the best clients we had."

Also in these early days, an American came around to see Tollinger with a tax problem: his auditors had told him that if he sold a company he owned in Hong Kong, much of the gain was going to be treated as ordinary income. Tollinger asked the New York tax partners if they could see any solution to his problem. "New York said, no, there was no way around it," Tollinger recalls. "Then, as an afterthought, they threw in the comment that if the stock went into his estate, it could be treated on a stepped-up basis. So, of course, the first thing I told the client was: 'Your only hope is to die.'" The client calmly replied, "No problem." It turned out the man had incurable cancer and less than a year to live—which is why he had wanted to sell his company in the first place. An arrangement was made for Jardine's, the Hong Kong merchant bank, to purchase an option to buy the company after the client's demise. The client died, satisfied that his business affairs were in order, and Jardine's was so impressed with Coudert Brothers' tax "planning," it, too, became a CB-Hong Kong client. Luck was plainly rolling with CB-Hong Kong in these early years, tugging it from one unexpected success to the next.

Meanwhile, from time to time, Tollinger took Cathay Pacific's early morning "rubber omelet" flight to Singapore, mainly just to show his face at the office and around town. CB-Singapore had no business, and, asked what had kept the office alive, Tollinger once explained brightly, "It wasn't alive as far as I could tell." The office's only clients were the noted photojournalist Carl Mydans and his wife, writer Shelley Mydans, who had been referred to CB-

Singapore by Jim Hughes's son, Jay Hughes, an estates and trusts associate in New York. Tollinger went to lunch with the Mydans, he went to dinner with the Mydans—never were there clients more treasured by their attorney.

It was the need to staff Singapore as well as to expand Hong Kong that kept Charlie Stevens hunting for recruits. Stevens wanted people who felt about Asia as he did, people who knew the languages and something of the cultures and who already had experience in the Far East. The number of such people who also happened to be well-qualified American lawyers was almost infinitesimally small in the early 1970s, and when Stevens found such a person, he was apt to go after him or her with concentrated determination and persuasiveness. CB-Singapore and CB-Hong Kong were, in a real sense, Stevens's own offspring, and he worked for their welfare unrelentingly.

Some of Stevens's recruits were only too happy for the chance to return to East Asia. Gage McAfee, for example, had arrived in Vietnam in 1969 in the wake of the My Lai incident and had been put to work trying to remedy some of the worst excesses of the Phoenix Pacification Program. As chief legal advisor, it was McAfee's job both to investigate reports of war crimes and abuses by Phoenix personnel and to prevent such incidents, and for the two years he was in Vietnam (with side trips to Cambodia and Laos), he was given a great deal of responsibility and leeway by his immediate boss, William Colby.

After that experience, it had been hard to come back to New York in 1971 and fit into the Wall Street groove for which he had been groomed from Andover to Harvard to Columbia Law School. McAfee began working for Davis, Polk, but a year later he was approached by Stevens, who was offering the lure of a chance to build the Singapore office. "It was the attraction of doing your own thing, as in Vietnam, that I couldn't resist," says McAfee. "That, and the adventure of doing something different where you could make a contribution. I loved Davis, Polk, but at that time they were weighing the idea of opening a mid-Manhattan branch and worrying about things like whether having another office a mile uptown might divide the firm. The attitude was so cautious compared to Coudert Brothers'." McAfee's father and uncle—both partners in large Wall Street firms—told McAfee he was crazy to go someplace so far away from where the action was. "They had the Wall Street view of the world," says McAfee. "I thought Asia was where things were really happening, and I wanted to be in the action."

Another of Stevens's recruits, Owen Nee, had a similar family background. His father, too, was a partner in a large New York law firm, and Nee says, "From the time I was a small boy, I had expected to be a New York corporate lawyer." Under the pressure of the Vietnam War draft, Nee's life had taken some detours after graduation from Princeton in 1965—to Hong Kong, where he taught English at the Chinese University for two years as a Princeton-in-Asia fellow, and to Vietnam, where he had earned a Bronze Star as a paratrooper in Army Intelligence—but nothing had changed his childhood resolution. By the time Nee graduated from Columbia Law School in 1973 and joined Coudert Brothers as an associate, he wished only to put the war behind him and get on with his life. Unlike McAfee, Nee was not looking for any more action or adventure.

Nonetheless, Stevens, who had known Nee back at Princeton, was determined to get him out to Hong Kong in 1973. After all, the Welsh-descended younger lawyer spoke two Asian languages with fair fluency, had already lived in Hong Kong, and even had family there, through his wife, Amber Nee, whom he had met at the Chinese University and courted on his R and R leaves from the army. For Stevens's purposes, Nee was a natural for the Hong Kong office, and he kept up a steady pursuit. "Although I had lived in Hong Kong and spent time in Vietnam," Nee says, "I thought, in both cases, once was enough. More than enough, actually. But it was impossible to get Charlie to appreciate that."

Stevens brought pressure to bear, and Nee finally reluctantly agreed to become CB-Hong Kong's first associate. "I don't know why I agreed," says Nee. "It had something to do with the fact that, after all, I liked Charlie, and I liked Preston a lot, too. But Charlie really just talked me into it, countering every objection I raised. He was so single-minded—and that really has been the reason why the East Asia practice grew. Back of everything that the rest of us did, you'll find Charlie acting as the dynamo. He didn't just begin the practice: he saw it through."

Behind Stevens, however, was Alexis Coudert. When Stevens was recruiting outside the firm, his chief hurdle was simply getting prospective candidates to New York for an interview. Once a candidate had met Alexis Coudert, that candidate could be counted as practically "signed up." "Alexis did make you feel special," says Nee, "every time you sat down with him. He was a true leader, and he had that ability to make you see in him the leader you want."

Several of Stevens's most important early recruits were lawyers who came from the world of legal scholarship and nonprofit foundations, and it was an important asset to the recruitment effort that they could recognize in Alexis Coudert, the former Columbia Law School professor, an intellect that was at home in the world of ideas and ideals. One such young lawyer was Barry Metzger, who had spent five years with the Ford Foundation's International Legal Center, first in Sri Lanka and India and then as director of Asian programs based in New York. Impressed by Coudert's vision, Metzger went out to CB-Hong Kong, which he headed by the late 1970s; later he would establish a Coudert Brothers office in Sydney, Australia, and then move on to take charge of CB-London.

Another was Bob Hornick, who had spent two years in Indonesia after graduating from Harvard Law School on a fellowship from the International Legal Center. In 1973, still on the fellowship, Hornick was back at Harvard, teaching and writing what was to become the basic English-language treatise on Indonesian law, when Harvard professor Jerry Cohen introduced him to Charlie Stevens. Hired as an associate, Hornick was "amazed at the free range I was given. I had an open ticket to visit Indonesia. In effect, Alexis said, 'Go to Indonesia whenever you want, as often as you want. Keep in touch with the people you know there, keep up your expertise.' The willingness to let associates play the role they did was unique."

When, at the end of Hornick's first year as a practicing lawyer, he was asked to cover the Singapore office for a month so that McAfee could take a vacation, Hornick found the request "exhilarating—and very scary." On his own in Singapore, Hornick got a phone call on a Saturday morning from a client who needed a loan agreement for a transaction in Sabah. "He said he would pick up the documentation at 5:45 A.M. Sunday on his way out of town. I called Preston Tollinger in Hong Kong and asked him, 'What do I do now?' Tollinger said not to worry; he would grab the late afternoon plane to Singapore and come help me." By 9:30 that Saturday night, Tollinger was sitting cross-legged on McAfee's bed in the old wooden bungalow, with a typewriter on his lap, banging out a loan agreement that got wrapped up at 5:00 A.M. "That was how I learned to draft a Eurodollar loan agreement," says Hornick. "I never learned so much in so short a time as I did on that occasion."

Although Hornick was conscious in 1974 of how much he had yet to learn about American law, he was far ahead of all other non-Indonesians in what he knew of Indonesia's legal system, which he once described as "a fascinating and complex mixture of Islamic commandments, Dutch legislation and uniquely indigenous institutions." That unusual knowledge was to become eventually one of CB-Singapore's great strengths, for the city-state of Singapore in 1971 had revamped its bank regulatory system to encourage use by foreign banks of Singapore as a base for "offshore" loans to development projects in such nearby countries as Malaysia, Brunei, and Indonesia. Of these, Indonesia, which was undergoing an oil boom, was the most important to international investors, but Indonesia barred American attorneys from practicing there. Thus, a good deal of the international legal business generated by Indonesian projects gravitated toward nearby Singapore, and CB-Singapore happened to have access to virtually the only Western international lawyer who was familiar with Indonesian law.

Like the Coudert Frères attorneys in France, Hornick became an expert at guiding Western businessmen through the cultural as well as legal intricacies of a foreign environment. It fell to Hornick to explain to eager investors why, for example, they must be prepared to accept delay and ambiguities. In a speech in New York in 1974, he noted:

> ... delay, postponement and indecision are time-honored ways in Indonesia of telling someone that what he is doing is important. In Indonesia, you don't rush into things which have important consequences; you demonstrate something is important by taking your time, and I think many Indonesians instinctively do this in the case of foreign investments. Someone who is going to spend $500 million dollars couldn't possible want to do so right away. Delay is thought to be appropriate.
>
> [Moreover], Indonesians didn't like to say no. If they don't like something, they say yes—and then postpone taking any action on it. Sometimes, therefore, a delay means you'd better rethink your proposal because it isn't liked.

Gradually the ranks of Coudert Brothers' Far East practice was to fill with lawyers, like Hornick, who were country or regional experts: in Singapore, former Peace Corps volunteer Stuart Rubin and a former advisor to Indonesia's Legal Documentation Center, Douglas Aden; in Hong Kong, Barry Metzger and David Halperin, who had worked under Henry Kissinger at the National Security Council; and in a Korea-oriented practice in New York, Timothy J. O'Brien, another former Peace Corps volunteer. In effect, Coudert Brothers was to benefit from the complex of public and private programs—National Defense language programs and fellowships, Ford Foundation studies, university-level international studies—that had arisen in the postwar years to address the United States' lack of preparedness for the international involvements it had assumed. As late as 1946, when Charles Torem had arrived in Paris, he had had no more academic preparation or training for an international assignment than John B. Robinson had had when he arrived in Paris in 1899. The situation of most of the Coudert Brothers lawyers who were sent to the Far East in the 1970s, however, was much different—and they could apply themselves to "bridging the cultural gaps" perhaps a little sooner.

Nonetheless, there is nothing like a foreign assignment to bring home to an American lawyer how unusual his own legal system is. In Hornick's and Stevens's observations as neophyte lawyers of the Indonesian or Japanese legal systems in the early 1970s, there are definite echoes of Charles Torem's reactions upon his first exposure to the French legal system in the late 1940s. It was not that Indonesian or Japanese law were particularly similar to French law—but that all three were so very different from the legal system that had evolved in the United States.

As a young lawyer in Paris going to hear the great *avocats* argue in court, for example, Torem had been impressed by their "eloquence and polished oratory" but "puzzled by the lack of deadly legal research without which American lawyers do not move from A to B," until he realized that "the importance of 'precedent' was not the same as at home. In France, earlier court decisions were taken casually as a possible guideline which do not necessarily have to be followed." In Japan, Stevens learned that case law played an even less important role, but for a different reason: the cultural prejudice against litigation was so strong that relatively few important commercial issues had ever been the subject of a written judicial opinion.

In his early years in France, Torem also soon realized that French businessmen "did not have much use for commercial lawyers" and that executives and engineers did all the negotiation. Attending one significant closing, involving Westinghouse and Framatone on atomic energy facilities, Torem noted "there were 200 men in the room, of which 198 appeared to be engineers." In Japan, the percentage would most likely have been more absolute; no lawyer might have been allowed in the room at all.

France's governmental structure immediately after the war made it difficult to obtain permission to invest in France. "Negotiating," Torem wrote, "with the many 'competent' administrations (Finances, Industrie, Trésor, Affaires Économiques), le Plan, and the Offices des Changes, was incredibly complex, of Kafka dimensions." Attempting to obtain authorization for an American-owned company to make ballpoint pens from the aluminum fuselage of planes shot down over France, Torem was unable to report success after six months of frustrating negotiations. When the client rejected Torem's interim bill as "ridiculous" for the results shown, the Coudert Frères lawyer replied that he had been "very, very busy with numerous French ministries." The client snorted: "Well, maybe you have been very, very busy, but so is a waltzing mouse, and I won't pay law fees to waltzing mice." Three months later, when the investment license had been finally secured, Torem presented it and the bill, commenting, "In order to get anything done in France these days, as you now can see, one has to be a waltzing mouse."

Yet the number of checkpoints on investment in France in the 1940s was smaller than that in Indonesia in the 1970s, where a mouse would have had to waltz with six to ten governmental bodies to get provisional approval, apply to another three to get foreign personnel into Indonesia, and obtain, in one case, thirty-seven signatures just to clear a piece of equipment through customs. Part of the problem was that Indonesia at this time was relatively inexperienced in dealing with foreign investors and was wary of being taken advantage of. France after the war, on the other hand, was more straightforwardly trying to discourage foreign investment, which it felt it could not afford because of its shortage of foreign exchange. For different reasons, the same multiplicity of jurisdictions arose, and in both cases a more centralized, simplified procedure would evolve as attitudes toward American investment became more favorable.

With a more relaxed attitude toward international commerce and its consequent expansion, there also came, in France at least, a greater acceptance of international commercial lawyers. A milestone for practitioners of transnational law was the enactment of France's *Conseils Juridiques* Law of December 30, 1971, which raised these commercial law advisors to a regulated—and, therefore, more prestigious and recognized—status, like that of the *avocats* and *notaires,* and which simultaneously created a procedure by which foreign individuals could secure the status of *conseil juridique.* Lobbying to protect Coudert Frères interests in this 1971 law was E. Ernest Goldstein, a former University of Texas law professor and expert in antitrust law and industrial property rights who came to work for Coudert Frères on a sabbatical in the 1960s and simply stayed on—with one interruption to work for President Lyndon Johnson in the Executive Office. Savvy in the ways of politics, Goldstein as a Coudert Frères partner occasionally did some lobbying, to good effect, on U.S. tax law revisions that would affect the Paris office or its clients. His lobbying efforts with respect to the 1971 law were also effective, although considerably aided by the fact that, as one of his partners noted in another context, "the French government had a generally benevolent view toward these [foreign] firms, which were seen as enhancing the role of Paris as a center of international commerce."

Some of the beneficial provisions of the 1971 law, however, were not available to foreign lawyers in France unless their home countries extended equal courtesies to French lawyers. As a result, the New York law firms in Paris, including Coudert Frères, sought the help of the Association of the Bar of the City of New York in enacting an amendment to the state's judiciary law, which created in 1974 a licensed status for foreign lawyers, that of "foreign legal consultant," so that they could advise in New York on the law of their own countries and international law.

These changes in the regulation of lawyers reflected the fact that as American investment money moved outward through the world in the postwar decades, American lawyers followed in its wake. By 1974, how those lawyers were received differed greatly from country to country, depending largely on official attitudes toward foreign investment itself. At one extreme was France's generally welcoming attitude, and at the other were countries like Indonesia, which barred foreign attorneys absolutely. In between were countries like Singapore, which displayed considerable ambivalence, wanting investment from the West but sometimes not the culture and ideas that went with it.

In 1974 three American law firms that had followed Coudert Brothers to Singapore were unceremoniously notified that their work permits, which were about to expire, would not be renewed. The three firms were forced to shut down their offices, which they had only just opened the year before, and depart. Coudert Brothers' work permit, however, happened to be valid for another six months, and Gage McAfee, feeling as if his career was on the line, set to work to try to persuade the government and the law society that Coudert Brothers should be allowed to stay.

McAfee's chief argument was that an international law firm like Coudert Brothers was pragmatically necessary to Singapore's development as an international financial center: international law firms were as much a part of the infrastructure of multinational business transactions as overseas phone lines. McAfee believes, however, that his argument would have fallen on deaf ears had not several clients come forward to affirm that CB-Singapore's presence was indeed one reason why they were doing deals in Singapore and not in Hong Kong or New York. In any event, the government relented, and the work permits were renewed.

Throughout the 1970s, though, CB-Singapore lived from year to year, never quite sure how long it would be allowed to remain. The Coudert Brothers attorneys themselves were accepted on a personal level—McAfee became the first foreigner to head the local Community Chest drive—and it appears that eventually it simply became accepted that Coudert Brothers, as it hung on year after year, was not in Singapore to make a few quick, exploitative dollars but to be part of a long-term movement in economic history. The verandas and frangipani trees were indeed charming and memorable, but, once familiarity turned the romantic into the commonplace, the real excitement for the Coudert Brothers attorneys involved in the Far East practice was the sense of being on the leading edge of history, as the Pacific Basin countries, gaining confidence with experience, took their place as full participants in the world of international trade and investment.

Chapter Eighteen

RIDING THE WAVES OF FOREIGN INVESTMENT

I n 1879 Coudert Brothers had obliquely announced the opening in Paris of its first overseas office, through the publication
of a slim volume, *Marques de Fabrique: Leur Protection aux Etats-Unis
et en France,* addressed to French lawyers and businessmen interested in recent treaty developments affecting French and American trademark protection. On the first page of this work, Frederic
René Coudert commented on the technological revolution of his
era and the manner in which it had changed concepts of speed
and distance. Writing in French, Coudert noted, "The extraordinary development of commerce, due in large part to steam and
electricity, has created increasingly close relations among civilized
nations." Alluding to the introduction of the telephone three years
earlier at the Philadelphia Exposition but anticipating by nearly
fifty years the feasibility of transatlantic telephone service, Coudert
added, "When the voice of the French trader can arrive at the ear
of a businessman in New York within minutes it must be recognized that the old limits have disappeared."

Coudert wrote in 1879 in a tone of rejoicing about the disappearance of those *"anciennes limites,"* and it is understandable that
he did. Aside from stimulating more international trade and investment, the new technology made it possible for Coudert to do such
things as attend international conferences abroad and visit Europe
to meet with clients there. Moreover, the operation of a foreign of-

fice like Coudert Frères would have been inconceivable without the steamship, the railroad, and the telegraph.

In a comparable fashion, the firm's East Asian practice was inextricably linked to the new technology of the 1970s. Just as *Marques de Fabrique* had marked the opening of Coudert Frères nearly one hundred years earlier, a 1974 article in *The Banking Lawyer,* written by several Coudert Brothers attorneys but signed at their insistence by Alexis Coudert, served as an indirect announcement of Coudert Brothers' presence in the Far East. The article's title— "The Regulation of Foreign Banking in Japan, Singapore, and Hong Kong"—signaled the growing interest of international banks in the services provided by the new Far East offices and the firm's ambition to foster this development and become a prominent international banking law firm. The opening of branches of New York commercial banks in the Far East, however, was fundamentally underlaid by advances in computer and telecommunications technology.

Coudert Brothers arrived in Hong Kong and Singapore in 1972 just as international lending began to be stimulated by easier communications between head offices and far-flung branches, more rapid location of capital, faster transmittal of funds, and a general lowering of the barriers posed by physical distances to financial dealings. Coudert Brothers, eschewing the practice of local law, had no role to play in loans of Hong Kong dollars to Hong Kong businessmen, but it came into its own when the Hong Kong branch of an American bank led a syndicate of European, Japanese, and American banks to lend U.S. dollars to a joint venture of multinational partners doing business in Indonesia. Then, the firm's knowledge of American and international law became an important attraction to clients.

In 1972 the international syndicated loan was still a relatively new idea, but such loans would expand exponentially in volume after 1973 when the OPEC oil-price increases created the dilemma for New York and London banks of how to recycle the tremendous dollar deposits in the accounts of the Middle Eastern oil producers. Much of this money had to be channeled into foreign loans, for lack of domestic borrowers, and the size of the transactions created the need to spread the risks and syndicate the loan. Thus, the international syndicated loan—a product of both electronic and economic developments—became commonplace in the financial community, and the firm's Far East offices began generating a much greater income than anyone had really expected.

The success of the firm's offices in Asia, however, put great pressure on traditional office practices in New York. Suddenly, there was a vast increase in demand for communications and for capacity and speed in origination and reproduction of documents. The international banks could move and had to move fast: two weeks was about the maximum for putting together a syndicated loan. But the New York office had only its one cranky telex, no dictating equipment, few photocopiers and a mere handful of early vintage word processors.

Jan DuBois, newly arrived at Coudert Brothers as a senior associate, volunteered, without invitation, to crusade for an across-the-board upgrading in office equipment. DuBois's concern was natural, for he was closely involved with the burgeoning international banking practice. He had arrived at the firm to "play traffic cop," for the lawyers in Hong Kong, Singapore, and Tokyo, funnelling their questions and requests to other partners or associates who could help. In corporate securities or tax matters, DuBois had a choice of lawyers to turn to, but no one at the New York office knew much about international banking. DuBois's own background was largely in antitrust, via the Justice Department and Cravath, but out of necessity he began a learning-by-doing course to become competent in the documentation of international loans. Within a few years, his colleagues were regarding him as the firm's leading international banking specialist.

Thus, Coudert Brothers' files from the mid-1970s contain memos from DuBois concerning multimillion-dollar loan transactions lying incongruously near contemporaneous memos carefully analyzing the advantages of buying a $150 piece of office equipment. But many other partners and associates were at the same time doing similar nitty-gritty administrative chores, because the firm had not quite learned how to live without Miss Bainbridge or figured out when and to whom to delegate. "We had committees of partners for every conceivable task," says Allen Russell. "Doing things ourselves was going to save us from building a bureaucracy. We all," he adds ruefully, "had a lot to learn about management."

DuBois's equipment memos were directed mostly to the Finance Committee (FinCom), composed of Mike Dominianni, Carl Eldridge, and Struve Hensel. "They were very careful about spending money," says DuBois. "Eldridge, in particular, believed that making it easy to produce documents would just lead to a proliferation of paper. The more photocopiers and word processors you had, the more drafts people would turn out, when they should be putting in the thought and analysis to do it right the first time." This was a sensible viewpoint in the context of Eldridge's entertainment litigation practice, but it overlooked where the expenses really lay in the new electronic age. Secretaries were having to be paid overtime because they were obliged to stay late, waiting in line outside the telex booth for a chance to send off their bosses' messages. The firm was paying for "on-line" time to transmit at the rate of 14.5 characters per second by telex, when equipment was available to transmit at 2,400 characters per second. And to save the one hundred dollars a month rental cost of a second telex, the young and promising banking practice was being placed in jeopardy of failing to meet the clients' expectations with respect to speed.

As usually happened at Coudert Brothers, Alexis came to the rescue, appreciating what DuBois was trying to say and gently intimating to FinCom that they should think again about loosening the purse strings. A typical compromise occurred in 1976 when the fax machine was first coming on the market. DuBois ardently wanted the fax capability, FinCom still fervently wanted to hold expenses down: it was agreed that Coudert Brothers' first fax machine would be Exxon's super-cheap Qwip, which cost only one-tenth as much as other brands. The machine had barely been installed when Eldridge found himself one night with an urgent need to transmit a brief over one hundred pages long to Providence, Rhode Island. The usual courier services wouldn't do, because there was a heavy snowstorm over the East Coast and no assurances that trains or airplanes could get through. To DuBois's intense gratification, the fax machine—albeit releasing a smog bank of putrid smoke and emitting an odor of burning zinc over the whole thirteenth floor—took Eldridge's brief and zipped it off to Providence, proving, DuBois hoped, the advantages of foresighted investments in technology.

Speed was a constant necessity in the international banking practice, but Coudert Brothers' success in East Asia was not built on speed alone. Although it had the initial advantage of being closer to the source of Hong Kong banking business than any other American firm, the lawyers that represented the big banks in New York were quick to set up Hong Kong offices of their own. As early as the summer of 1973 Preston Tollinger was writing memos about the "threatening hordes" of American competitors, and by the end of 1973 other firms had begun to follow Coudert Brothers to Hong Kong. CB-Hong Kong, however, still kept growing and doing the biggest international deals. The young Coudert Brothers lawyers had been fearful of what would happen when older practitioners arrived in Hong Kong, and when they realized that their office was booming nonetheless, the reaction was the euphoria that follows a release from tension. They were quick to tell each other and the world, "We are great. We are the premier international financial law firm in Asia." "We were arrogant," says Barry Metzger, "young and arrogant. Everyone kept telling us that, so I guess it was true. But we really did have something to be proud of." "The esprit in the East Asia Group," says DuBois, "was right off the scale."

What Coudert Brothers became known for in Hong Kong was originality. When banks must put a deal together within ten days, the temptation for their lawyers, of course, is to lean heavily on form files, using the documents from the last similar deal with the necessary changes of names and amounts. Perhaps it was because Coudert Brothers didn't have much in the way of a precedent file, but recycling was not its style. The East Asia banking lawyers prided themselves on producing "thinking" documents, on being more than scribes. They had a reputation for writing customized agreements that closely conformed to what the bankers really wanted to achieve and that were realistic in relation to actual banking practices, so that Coudert Brothers attracted the difficult and unique transactions.

Putting extra thought into a document that has to be done within a compressed period of time leads to long hours and hard work. Everyone in the East Asia Group, however, was young, and most were either single or (whether *pro* or *post hoc*) divorced. They had energy to burn—and they worried Alexis Coudert considerably. He fretted about the health of Owen Nee, who was working long hours as Tollinger's associate in Hong Kong; about George Shenk, who lived out of a suitcase in borrowed apartments in Hong Kong for two years before going to Tokyo to build up the banking practice there; about McAfee, Metzger, Stu Rubin, and DuBois. Most of all, he was anxious about Tollinger and Stevens.

"My father," says Alexis's son, Tracy, "didn't worry about what decisions the young guys made or whether they would succeed. He chose people he had confidence in, gave them full support and didn't ask or want them to call him every day. But on his one trip to the Far East, when he saw how hard Preston Tollinger was working, he came back saying he didn't think Preston could keep it up. And Charlie Stevens was doing that crazy flying schedule—that worried him. He was afraid those guys were going to kill themselves for Coudert Brothers, which was the last thing on earth my father wanted. He was concerned about the prosperity of the firm, but not at the expense of the well-being of its people."

In 1975 Jan DuBois was out in Singapore, getting its banking practice under way. Late in the year, traveling on business from Singapore through Seattle and New York to Switzerland, he was not feeling up to par but assumed that he was simply tired. On his third night of round-the-clock negotiations in Switzerland, however, DuBois lost his ability to speak and swallow—which he found extremely inconvenient since the firm's client was not present in Switzerland and was controlling the negotiation only by telephone calls with DuBois. Fortunately—for it turned out that DuBois had an exotic neurological disorder—Alexis took alarm.

The trustee of the New York Eye and Ear Infirmary and several other New York nonprofit medical organizations, Alexis wanted DuBois back in New York City getting proper medical attention. "Struve Hensel had almost died in Switzerland a few months before," DuBois recalls, "and Alexis was in no mood to take any chances on Swiss hospitals or to accept my self-diagnosis that I was just a little tired!" Alexis dispatched two Coudert Brothers partners to Switzerland to convey an order that DuBois must return to New York and check himself into a hospital, rather than travel on as he intended through Bombay to get back to work in Singapore.

DuBois's collapse at age thirty-four was the realization of Alexis's worst fears, but DuBois's affliction turned out to be controllable, and he did not linger in his hospital bed. Despite Alexis's misgivings, he soon got back onto his feet to work on a Japanese bank's problems with a loan that had gone sour. It seemed that nothing Alexis said could slow these young lawyers down. "Many times he told us to look out for our health, to take time for our families and—although he would never have used such a cliché—to stop and smell the roses," says one current partner. "I think it was only when I turned forty-five that I remotely began to appreciate what he was trying to say."

In any event, the energy kept flowing, and ten years after the Hong Kong office got its first client, one banker was saying that she preferred working with Coudert Brothers because "they are receptive and ingeniously creative. We often approach them before making a bid . . . they'll often come up with novel ways to approach the deal." She made this statement in response to a survey by the *International Financial Law Review* asking bankers which firms they preferred to use when doing syndicated Euromarket loans. Coudert Brothers, which had had virtually no banking practice a decade earlier, was ranked as one of the "top ten" law firms, and Jan DuBois was among the four individuals cited as "outstanding performers," being singled out for his "ability to train his associates and to reduce documents to their most concise form, avoiding the 'boilerplate' that is often used."

* * *

Because of the youth of the lawyers who opened Coudert Brothers' Asian offices, the firm's expansion across the Pacific was sometimes referred to as the "Children's Crusade." Those who were knowledgeable about the mores of other law firms, where client contact was carefully rationed out to even senior associates, marveled that Coudert Brothers would let such young people represent it overseas or build their own practices in New York. The Coudert Brothers associates were amazed at times themselves. "I never heard," says Jan DuBois, "of another major New York firm that was so generous in underwriting the dreams of youth."

The responsibility given certain associates in the 1970s, however, was just the outgrowth—in perhaps more dramatic form—of the attitudes and practices that had characterized Coudert Brothers since at least the 1950s. But what had been born in necessity, by virtue of the smallness of the firm, had become by the early 1970s a tradition, almost a philosophy. "Giving the young fellows their chance" was how the older men talked about this aspect of their role as trainers and mentors, and it meshed well with a firm culture that valued individual initiative, decentralization, and enjoyment of the practice of law. The idea was that the law should be fun, and what could be more fun for a young attorney than the opportunity to advise a real client or negotiate with opposition counsel?

Most of the associates of the 1970s who became partners have a "war story" about the first time—invariably at a startling young age—that they entered legal combat on their own. When Andy Hedden, for example, was about six months out of law school, he was assigned by Jim Hughes to help a senior associate, John Kennedy, with a public offering. Kennedy left to take another job, and Hughes told Hedden simply to continue on his own and let him know if any problems arose. "Fortunately," says Hedden, "the lawyers on the other side were kind to me."

Joel Adler, again less than one year out of law school, was working with Alexis on the acquisition of a company in Massachusetts by a consortium composed of the French Atomic Energy Commission, the Belgian Atomic Energy Commission, and a subsidiary of Fiat. Alexis one day told Adler that he should make plans to go to the closing in Massachusetts and explained the when, where, and how of getting to the closing. "We were sitting side-by-side on the sofa in his office, and I said, 'But, Mr. Coudert, who is the partner who will be going with me?' " Alexis tilted his head, lifted an eyebrow, and began to smile. "Oh, you can do it yourself," he said encouragingly. "I was hysterically nervous," states Adler, who recalls being desperately concerned that he didn't know how to greet the Fiat executive in Italian. "I went rushing around to find someone who would write out for me how to say 'Pleased to meet you' in Italian. And I went to the firm's library and found this primer on acquisitions, which I was still trying to finish reading on the Boston shuttle."

A year later Adler was working with Allen Russell on a ship-financing transaction, which had the interesting feature of not involving a single American party. Coudert Brothers' client, an Italian shipowner, was acquiring an oil tanker under construction in Japan, which had been originally commissioned by an overseas Chinese through a Bermuda-based company. The financing was being provided by two Swiss-based banks, the insurance was arranged in London through Lloyd's, and the vessel was to operate on a ten-year time charter with a British-based company. It was a fairly complex deal, but Russell was a careful trainer and Adler felt well-primed when he was sent to the meeting where he would walk through the draft of the ship mortgage with the banks' counsel. Moreover, Adler was now wiser and more experienced—he was all of two years out of law school—and he knew that the session would be routine. The tough issues had already been negotiated and agreed to, and it only remained to ensure that the text conformed to everyone's understanding.

Therefore, Adler was not nervous when he entered the meeting, and indeed everything went well until the conferees reached the standard clause giving the mortgage-holder the right to enter upon the vessel to ensure that it was "tight, taut, and shipworthy." The *commandante* of the Italian shipowner's fleet, who was sitting at the table and had previously shown no signs of life, came awake then and said, "No! No one will come aboard my ship unless I, the captain, invite them to do so." Adler, taken aback by this unexpected objection, explained that it was customary for the mortgage-holder to have that right, but the *commandante* was unmoved. The banks' counsel gave Adler a stare and a shrug that said clearly, "He's your client. You handle it." Thinking frantically, Adler devised some alternative wording the *commandante* would accept, and, as a result, that particular ship's mortgage ended up with a clause mentioning nothing about rights but instead reading, "The owner *may* from time to time invite the mortgagee to come upon the vessel and *shall* so invite the mortgagee if requested to do so."

George Shenk has another classic story of this type, about being swept up by Lucien Le Lièvre one evening and taken to a meeting at another law firm's offices. The Coudert Brothers client, a French distributor of men's suits, was seated at a table being offered the chance to purchase a minority stake in a publicly listed garment-manufacturing company. He wanted to move the deal along that evening, so Le Lièvre and Shenk went through a mound of paper sitting on the table, with Le Lièvre identifying the issues. Then Le Lièvre departed for a prior appointment, leaving young Shenk to conduct the negotiations. "It was a wild situation," Shenk recalls. "The attorney for the seller had been a classmate of Alexis's. The lawyer for the company was the president of the Chicago bar association. And I was less than two years out of law school!"

Around 11:00 P.M., Shenk realized that he wasn't sure what provisions should be made in case of bankruptcy, and he tried to call Mark Lebow. Lebow wasn't home. Le Lièvre, Shenk knew, was unreachable, so Shenk next dialed Alexis Coudert's number. "I'd never worked with Alexis, but it seemed to me that calling the senior partner late at night was a normal thing to do. And Alexis acted as if it were perfectly natural—for me to be in that situation and for me to be calling him." Shenk returned to the conference table, the negotiations were concluded around 1:30 A.M., and Coudert Brothers' client pulled out his checkbook.

Shenk said, in some alarm, "No, you can't sign now. The sales contract is supposed to be tied into a supply contract. Tomorrow, Mr. Le Lièvre will wrap this all up for you." The client, however, didn't want the negotiations to cool off, even overnight, and Shenk found himself negotiating a provision to cover the supply angle. At 5:00 A.M., never having had any supper, Shenk staggered home and fell into bed. Minutes later he was on his feet again, having remembered that he had to move his car to the other side of the street because of the parking regulations in Manhattan. After a few ragged hours of sleep, Shenk was at the office, telling LeLièvre, "Well, we signed last night." Le Lièvre said, "You did *what?*" But when Le Lièvre looked over the documents, he was pleased, and years later he was still telling people how young Shenk had "pulled the laboring oar" in this French client's first significant U.S. acquisition.

Coudert Brothers, says Ernst Stiefel, was "exceptional in the encouragement given to young people," and it is unanimously agreed, by retired and current partners alike, that Alexis Coudert set the tone of the firm in this respect. "He trusted all of us, no matter how young," says Charlie Stevens, and it is often said that Alexis had a "special relationship" with the young lawyers in the firm. Yet, Alexis, in truth, had a special relationship with almost every attorney at Coudert Brothers. He was completely open-minded, responding to intellectual ability where he found it, regardless of gender, nationality, or age. For this reason, Alexis and the sixties generation, which often acted as if they had discovered civil rights all on their own, seemed made for each other, and they did have a wonderful rapport. But it must be noted that Alexis was age-blind at both ends of the scale.

If Coudert Brothers was the law firm that was sending twenty-six-year-olds out to negotiate deals and creating thirty-year-old partners, it was also the firm that invited into partnership in 1969 J. Arthur Leve, who was then eighty-one years old. Shortly before his death in 1975, *The New Yorker* prepared a profile of Leve that began, "We've just called on Mr. J. Arthur Leve, who will be eighty-seven this June and *thinks* he is the oldest practicing lawyer in New York, if not in the U.S.A. In any event, he is *sure* that he was admitted to the bar—in March, 1912—before all but one of his fifty-odd partners in Coudert Brothers were born." Leve's career began with representation of the International Ladies Garment Workers Union, visiting one of the firetrap factories in 1912: "One toilet for two hundred people. Piecework by girls of ten or twelve, for a mere pittance. Windows were closed. The air was suffocating." In the 1920s he traveled across country in a private railroad car, playing bridge with silent-movie stars Marie Dressler, Lillian Gish, whom he was dating at the time, and Marilyn Miller. *The New Yorker* reporter, reading old newspaper accounts of Leve's career, mentioned these highlights: "Goulds and Gould estates galore! Sir Joseph Duveen! Oscar Hammerstein! Baron James Henri de Rothschild! Winston Churchill! The Hotel Pierre! Mrs. James Stillman!"

Like Alexis's great-grandfather Benjamin Tracy, who had still been going strong in his eighties on the eve of World War I, Leve did not come to Coudert Brothers to rest on his laurels. He was writing briefs, preparing court cases, and enjoying his practice right up to his death. He was fairly deaf, but sharp, and those in the firm who didn't know his actual age placed him as somewhere in his late sixties when he was actually nearly twenty years older than that. Alexis appointed Leve the chairman of the firm's retirement committee. "It was thought," explains Russell, "that he would be impartial because of his age." The move was actually Alexis's tongue-in-cheek way of saying that retirement should be linked to productivity, not a fixed calendar age.

In the late 1960s, Alexis became convinced that there was bound to be a great step-up in foreign investment in the United States, and he began to get Coudert Brothers ready for that development. His sense of where the world economy was moving was one reason he suggested that Le Lièvre "marry" his French practice to Coudert Brothers. Le Lièvre, with his dual qualifications in French and American law, was obviously going to be in a unique position to provide integrated advice to French investors in the United States. It was also a reason Alexis was glad in 1971 to welcome back Sam Highleyman, who had wandered off from CB-London in 1967 to work for Technicolor and the Walter Reade organization, for Highleyman had always been primarily a mergers and acquisitions lawyer, oriented toward British and European transactions.

In the process of preparing for the investment wave, Alexis also approached Ernst Stiefel with a well-thought-out proposal. Back in 1947, after returning a negative reply to Coudert Brothers' inquiry about setting up a Frankfurt office, Stiefel had settled down as a foreign law consultant at the New York firm of Cleary, Gottlieb. From time to time during the years that U.S. investment was pouring into Germany, Alexis and later Milo Coerper had repeated the question of whether Stiefel would care to set up a German office, but Stiefel, happy at Cleary, Gottlieb, remained uninterested in leaving New York. In 1971 Alexis changed the question. Now he asked if Stiefel would care to move to Coudert Brothers' New York office in the position of counsel to the firm, Alexis's thinking being that Steifel would be an asset working with the German corporations that were and would be investing in the United States.

Stiefel was then sixty-five years old, a fact that fazed Alexis, who was fifty-seven, not in the least. Given the situation of the international economy, Alexis was confident that the best part of Stiefel's career was still ahead of him. Alexis realized that the German legal profession put more emphasis on academic reputation than Americans do, and Stiefel had impressive academic credentials. The holder of degrees from the Universities of Heidelberg, Strasbourg, and Paris, he was not only a member of the New York bar and a German *Rechtsanwalt* but also a French *licencié en droit* and a British barrister. Indeed, Stiefel had been the first and was still the only lawyer in the world qualified in four countries, and he had published prolifically in both German and American legal journals. From the German point of view, however, Stiefel lacked the "correct" title. "Working with American companies for Cleary, Gottlieb, it didn't matter what my position was," Stiefel notes. "But the German business here was becoming more important, and to attract German clients, it was necessary for me to have a proper title. Alexis was very foresighted in this and in the ideas he presented to me about what we could do together."

Stiefel was also impressed by the fact that Alexis and Milo

Coerper came downtown in person to present their ideas to him. Stiefel had an excellent reputation, but, having had to start a practice from scratch relatively late in life in a newly adopted country, he felt he was not yet so distinguished that Alexis Coudert should call upon him. "I was honored by the visit," says Stiefel. "I know of no other personality of Alexis's standing who would have done that." So Stiefel, not without "great regret" at leaving Cleary, Gottlieb and trepidation for the future, allowed himself to be persuaded to come to Coudert Brothers and start trying to build, in effect, an entirely new practice at the age of sixty-five.

It is a measure of the confidence that Alexis was able to instill in people, of whatever age, that Stiefel took this gamble, and the results were beyond anything Stiefel had expected. Stiefel's client list became loaded with giant German corporations, he was retained as advisor to the German consulate, he was elected a director of the German-American Chamber of Commerce, and he became sought after as a lecturer and speaker at important international legal seminars. The association was and remains some twenty years later greatly and mutually productive in terms of reputation, prestige, and money. "This was all the product of Alexis's vision," says Stiefel. "I did not expect what did happen. It arose from *his* vision, not mine."

As expected, U.S. mergers and acquisition work on behalf of European investors mounted steadily in 1972 and 1973. The money was being drawn to the United States by the favorable exchange rates, the relatively low interest rates on Eurodollar loans, and, in the case of the Germans particularly, the haven of security the United States seemed to offer in a time of Cold War tensions, regardless of all the evident weaknesses in the American economy.

Around 1973 Allen Russell sent Joel Adler to visit the headquarters of a German client that was then in the midst of acquiring a manufacturing concern located outside Detroit. "Why are you making this acquisition?" Adler asked a director of the German company. The German, a distinguished gentleman with silver hair, gestured to the east, commenting that he was sitting a few kilometers from the border with East Germany. Then he gestured toward the west, noting that in that direction lay Switzerland, then the Low Countries, then the whole expanse of the Atlantic Ocean and, finally, a thousand miles of American territory before one reached the state of Michigan. "He was telling me indirectly," says Adler, "that when the Soviet tanks rolled into West Germany, they wanted assets parked as far away as possible."

Thus, there was a satisfactory surge in Coudert Brothers' transatlantic business in the early 1970s—and then came the unexpected event: the plummeting of the Dow Jones industrial average in the aftermath of the Arab "oil shock" to 570 points in 1974. At that moment the wave of European investment erupted as if an underwater volcano had gone off. German private companies, for example, invested in the United States in 1975 a sum as large as they had invested in the previous twenty years put together. The effect on Coudert Brothers was dramatic. "The practice exploded," says one former associate of the 1970s. "The firm exploded," says another. "Everything exploded," says a third. "We were never the same again."

Confirming Alexis's vision, the three relative newcomers—Le Lièvre working with the French, Highleyman with the British, Stiefel with the Germans—were among those squarely in the New York front line, taking the impact of the tidal wave, along with Alexis himself, Mike Dominianni, Allen Russell, and a few others. This was no Children's Crusade: the partners involved were all older men who could well remember when an acquisition costing a foreign client several hundred thousand dollars had counted as a major investment. But now they were advising on deals involving tens or hundreds of millions of dollars. One of Highleyman's British clients, for instance, pumped over a billion dollars into U.S. acquisitions, sold the weaker companies off, bought some more and ended up with a $4 billion U.S. base. The numbers were mind-boggling compared to 1960s figures—but with the exchange rates favoring them and inflation on the rise in the United States, the prices seemed bargains to the Europeans.

As with international banking, most of the foreign investment work came in on a transactional basis. Coudert Brothers had a steady relationship with some clients that were undertaking ambitious, sustained acquisition programs, including Robert Bosch, Reed Publishing, and L'Air Liquide. Larry Brody had such a client in London, a medical publishing company, which contributed greatly to putting CB-London on a solid footing. For clients like these, Coudert Brothers felt a deep thanksgiving. But corporate acquisition work in the 1970s had the same basic irregularity to it that litigation had always had: as one deal was winding up, another might be starting for a different client, or there might be a lull. In the late 1970s, though, there were few lulls. "We lived from hand to mouth," says Stiefel, "but our mouths were always very full."

When Coudert Brothers corporate lawyers remember the 1970s, therefore, they think of discrete glamorous or interesting deals, just as litigators talk about their most significant cases. In the opinion of many associates of that period, Le Lièvre handled perhaps the most glittering and varied string of transactions. He represented, for example, Compagnie de St. Gobain-Pont-a-Mousson, the famous French glass manufacturer, when it exchanged its interest in a joint venture with Certain-Teed for a 35 percent share in Certain-Teed itself, and represented St. Gobain again in 1976–77, when it decided to take control of the troubled building-products company and launched a successful tender offer. Le Lièvre was retained also by the Agache-Willot textile and chain-store group, headed by the Willot brothers, when it moved to acquire the bankrupt Korvette's chain in 1979. "This was a difficult negotiation," Le Lièvre recalls, "because the Willots did not want to disburse any moneys." They wanted the creditor banks to accept the guarantee of one of the Agache-Willot subsidiaries in lieu of cash, and Le Lièvre praises his then-associate George Yates for successfully conducting most of the negotiations.

Le Lièvre also served as counsel in Moët-Hennessey's acquisition of Dior perfume, the French government's sale of its Bull computer business, and Elf-Acquitaine's purchase of M&T Chemicals. The list of notable transactions goes on, but these examples suffice to give the flavor of the period. "Bigger names, larger deals, higher stakes—that was the story of the seventies," summarizes Adler.

Hired away from a larger New York law firm to help Le Lièvre in 1973, Anthony C. ("Tony") Kahn noticed that the French clients followed a "classic pattern" as they expanded in the United States. Initially, Kahn points out, the French company would find a U.S. distributor. All going well, it would then set up a representative office. Next came the search for an American partner that could help either in expanding the distribution network or in setting up a manufacturing capability in the States. And ultimately the French company would begin acquiring U.S. companies, until its U.S. holding company had become a major entity in its own right. This was indeed a classic pattern: starting back in the 1870s, for example, Coudert Brothers had assisted Coty perfume as it progressed through each of those distinct stages of expansions. It had taken Coty, however, more than sixty years, stretching from the 1870s through the 1930s, to complete the process. In the speeded-up atmosphere of the 1970s, some of Le Lièvre's clients went from the first to the final stage within the decade.

Throughout the profession the switch to a "transactional" practice was distressing to many older lawyers, but Coudert Brothers, because of its international orientation and its litigation strength, had historically had more "one-shot" clients than was typical of the old-line banking and securities law firms. In an interview in 1980, Alexis chose to treat this characteristic of Coudert Brothers' practice as an advantage, stating that a client base in which no one client accounted for more than 5 percent of the firm's billings not only assured the firm's health but also "helps us attract and keep the best people. By doing special work for lots and lots of clients, our lawyers are always doing something different, which is much more fun than taking the same old bond issue or debenture offering and marking it up again."

"At Coudert Brothers you never knew exactly what would come across your desk," says Brian E. McGunigle, recalling his years as an associate. Working with Allen Russell in the 1970s, he did the things all corporate associates do, assisting with general corporate and commercial projects, drafting contracts, working on acquisitions, and advising on issues about to ripen into litigation. But he also stayed awake nights worrying about how to retrieve a group of Man Ray's surrealist paintings from a dock in Italy, for he was helping Russell with the administrative details of shutting down the New York Cultural Center. Because Coudert Brothers did not have a real estate or employee benefits department, he did real estate contracts and closings and wrote "laborious, tortured memos attempting to explain ERISA to pension plan trustees." And he worked on some litigation. "Commercial litigation was short-handed," McGunigle explains, "so there was a tacit assumption that corporate associates would pitch in." One suit over a finder's fee, alleged to be owed by Robert Bosch, was won by Joe McManus at the trial level, but the verdict was reversed by the Delaware Supreme Court. "And that," McGunigle says, "is how I came to have my name on a petition for *certiorari* to the U.S. Supreme Court. It's the sort of thing I never imagined would happen to me as a corporate lawyer."

Tony Kahn found himself actually in a courtroom one day in 1975, contesting the imposition of a temporary restraining order on the opening of Régine's nightclub. "The major problem was the temperature of the dishwasher water," Kahn recalls. Kahn, who had been doing trademark licensing work for Régine's brother, a French industrialist, had never argued in front of a judge before, but he was able to convince the judge to allow Régine's to open on time, on condition that the dishes would be stacked on trolleys and wheeled to a nearby hotel for washing. "The judge made me personally responsible for seeing that the plan was carried out," says Kahn. "So I spent the night of the opening party, until 4:00 A.M., supervising the dishwashing. It was certainly one of the most unusual legal duties I can imagine."

Kahn, having come from another law firm that specialized in

corporate work, had a clear idea of what was unusual and what was not about the Coudert Brothers' style of practice. Marvin Milbauer, having arrived at Coudert Brothers straight out of law school at age twenty-two, learned that his work was less specialized than it might have been at other firms by the way others reacted to him. At a bar association meeting, for example, Milbauer was asked by a tax associate at another firm what he was working on. "Well," said Milbauer, "we've been qualifying a 501(c) charitable organization, and we've been amending a pension plan and getting it approved by the IRS." The tax associate did a double take. "Are you *sure* you're a corporate associate?" he asked.

No one thought that the broad training given Coudert Brothers' corporate associates was in all aspects ideal. "Part of the reason," says Sam Highleyman, "that we went out and hired senior-level associates from Wall Street firms, like Tony Kahn and Jan DuBois, was that they had received that Wall Street style of specialized training. And as the workload increased, they were a godsend." On the other hand, the senior-level associates wanted to come to Coudert Brothers because, as Kahn says, "we could play a more significant role. At another firm, if you were a few years out of law school, you might be the low man on a team of five to eight lawyers. At Coudert Brothers, you were likely to be number two or number three on the totem pole, or even on your own. The challenges were greater, the experiences broader, and the relationships with clients more satisfying." Adds McGunigle, unconsciously echoing virtually every other corporate lawyer of the 1970s, "Coudert Brothers was a fun place to be."

This was the attitude—the emphasis on having fun—that had probably kept Coudert Brothers out of the mainstream of banking and corporate work in the 1920s. But now banking and corporate law were jumping into a different course, and it felt almost as if the rest of the legal profession was arriving where Coudert Brothers had always been. In any event, the increase in foreign investment did fantastic things to Coudert Brothers' statistics. In 1974 the number of lawyers in the worldwide firm went over the hundred mark, and by 1980 Coudert Brothers had well over two hundred attorneys, with most of the growth in the latter part of the decade coming in the New York office, which began to sprawl over several floors of the Pan Am Building. At the same time, the average partner earnings more than tripled between 1972 and 1980. In 1972 any partner individually billing around $150,000 had been considered a "heavy hitter," a stalwart of the firm. In 1974 a few partners billed $500,000 each, and a year or two after that the $1 million level was reached, according to Highleyman, who was keeping a close eye on these numbers because he was in contention for leading the list.

At the same time as foreign investment work was increasing, the entertainment litigation practice, led by Carl Eldridge, was undergoing its own considerable expansion. "There was an influx of major cases," recalls Michael C. ("Mike") Calvey, who became a litigation associate in 1973, "partly because of the growth in investigative reporting and, in particular, the introduction of the television "newsmagazines" like *60 Minutes* and *20/20.*" Representative of these major cases were *Anthony Hebert v. CBS,* which was prompted by *60 Minutes'* questioning of the accuracy of Hebert's allegation concerning American war crimes in Vietnam, and *American Family Life Assurance Co. ("AFLAC") v. ABC,* which arose from a series of evening news reports questioning the value of "cancer insurance" and similar kinds of supplemental health care insurance. Both were representative not only because of the First Amendment issues they raised but also because they both were prolonged and expensive pieces of litigation. "Perhaps it had something to do with there being more publicity about First Amendment cases or the fact that lawyers were better educated on how to prepare these cases," says Calvey, "but people were more willing to pursue suits of this type, even though they were extensive or expensive."

In any event, there were more claims hitting the networks in the 1970s and larger claims, involving substantial sums. As a direct result, the Entertainment Litigation Department at Coudert Brothers—which represented the insurers of all three networks—doubled in size between 1972 and 1980 (when Eldridge led a section of two other partners and nine associates). Always one to worry over the smallest detail of a case, Eldridge had earlier been the despair of many associates for his reluctance to delegate; therefore, a telling indication of how much the practice had grown by the late 1970s was the fact that Eldridge decided then to turn over real responsibility for ABC and CBS matters, respectively, to two senior associates, Mike Calvey and Pamela Ostrager. Thus, it was Ostrager who handled the later stages of the Hebert suit and Calvey who conducted the AFLAC litigation. (The networks eventually obtained summary judgments in their favor in both cases.) In any event, the volume of entertainment litigation was reaching a new peak by the late 1970s, and the "Eldridge Group," as it was often called within the firm, was bringing a million or two a year into the firm's coffers.

Making big money was fun, but that was not the sense in

which Alexis Coudert used the word. To Alexis, "fun" was synonymous with "intellectually challenging," and another statistic that took off in the 1970s was the firm's publication rate, which may be taken as a reasonably reliable sign that the Coudert Brothers lawyers were enjoying what they were doing. A listing of some of the articles that Coudert Brothers attorneys wrote in the 1970s provides a convenient guide, too, to other matters the firm was then working on—for syndicated loans, U.S. acquisitions, and entertainment litigation were only part of the excitement of the decade.

The flow of capital from Europe to the United States was dramatic because it was a new development, but U.S. capital continued to move into Europe, actually at a larger volume than it had in the 1960s. Coudert Frères's representation of multinational corporations in Europe remained one of the most interesting parts of the firm's activity, reflected in such articles as "Developments in the Control of Foreign Investment in France" by Charles Torem and Laurie Craig (*Michigan Law Review,* 1971), "Denigration and Disparagement—a Franco-American Comparative Analysis" by Torem and E. Ernest Goldstein (*Texas International Law Journal,* 1972), and "Subsidiary in France: Problems of Control under French Law" by Torem and Albert Rau (*Texas International Law Journal,* 1973).

Coudert Frères also was handling major matters for some Western and African governments, particularly with respect to oil, gas, and mineral development contracts between those governments and private companies and with regard to the problems of government-owned industries or state monopolies. Coudert's special counsel, Jean-Claude Petilon, qualified as a lawyer both in France and in America, was conducting negotiations for a number of major projects all over Africa, while long-standing relationships of Robin Tait with legal staff at the World Bank opened opportunities for Coudert's lawyers to be chosen as counsel on a number of World Bank and IFC projects for Madagascar, Chad, and Guinea, among others. This aspect of the practice is represented by Jan-Anders Paulsson's article "Sovereign Immunity from Execution in France" (*International Lawyer,* 1977).

Torem was also greatly interested in the prospects for East/West trade, which turned out to be one of those developments perennially hoped for but never quite materializing in the 1970s. Henry Z. Horbaczewski's article "Profitable Coexistence: The Legal Foundation for Joint Enterprises with U.S. Participation in Poland" (*The Business Lawyer,* 1975) took a positive attitude toward Poland's potential, but his description of some of the difficulties state enterprises had in dealing with foreigners ("The consequences of a bad deal for the [Polish] manager may be imprison-ment") provides vivid insight into why U.S. businessmen were not rushing into East/West ventures.

The firm was also organizing complicated litigations and arbi-trations. The presentation of large, complex international arbitra-tions was, in fact, one of Coudert Frères's specialties, accounting for nearly a third of the Paris workload. In the early 1950s, when Charles Torem had been one of the few American lawyers with ex-pertise in private international commercial arbitrations, this method of dispute resolution had been relatively novel; but by 1970 it had become greatly favored by international businessmen who appreciated the opportunities it offered to select the language in which the case would be heard and to pick one of the three judges who would decide the dispute. "There was always the expec-tation, too," says Torem, "that arbitration would be faster and sim-pler."

Private arbitration generally was faster, but in the 1970s Coudert Frères handled an increasing number of public interna-tional arbitrations, many of them involving issues arising from na-tionalization of private property, and some of these absorbed the office's attention for considerable periods of time. The decade opened, for example, with the *Liamco* arbitration, a celebrated case often cited for setting standards for just compensation, in which Torem, Laurie Craig, and Paulsson represented Atlantic Richfield in its suit against Libya for compensation for the nationalization of the oil company's Libyan subsidiary. And the decade closed with the start of the complex, long-running *Pyramids Oasis* case, orga-nized by Laurie Craig, in which Coudert Frères represented the Canadian owners of a Hong Kong company that had entered a joint venture with a state-owned Egyptian company for a tourist de-velopment project that was first approved by the government and then cancelled.

In between, Craig succeeded to Torem's position as the U.S. member of the International Court of Arbitration (as Paulsson would later succeed him), and he, Paulsson, and William W. Park, a former Coudert Frères lawyer turned law-school professor, began literally writing the book on international commercial arbitration. "Our idea," says Craig, "was that all the little secrets of arbitration that we had gained by experience—secrets that no one knew or that had been buried in obscure articles—should be available to other practitioners." The result was a volume, *International Commer-cial Arbitration*, that has gone into several editions.

Meanwhile, the much smaller Washington, D.C., office spent three years living with an important antitrust case. This was the

Consumers Union suit against all the American, German, and Japanese steel companies and the U.S. government, challenging the voluntary restraining agreement that had been blessed by the U.S. State Department. Milo Coerper represented the German steel interests in this major case, particularly Krupp, which was chosen in an agreement between the Consumers Union and the European steel producers to serve as the test case, or "representative guinea pig." There was also antidumping work for the Japanese, and a host of other trade problems, some very large, some fairly small, handled by not only CB-Washington but many of the other Coudert Brothers offices. Thus, the decade found Coerper chairing a panel on "Sovereign Compulsion Defence in Antitrust Litigation" (American Society of International Law *Proceedings,* 1978), Toby S. Myerson providing "A Review of Current Antidumping Procedures: United States Law and the Case of Japan" (*Columbia Journal of Transnational Law,* 1976), and George Yates writing on "Substantive Law Aspects of Enforcement of Foreign Judgments between Foreigners in France" (*International Lawyer,* 1976).

The Brussels office continued to concentrate on European Economic Community antitrust problems, as suggested by Stephen O. Spinks's "Contemporary Antitrust Regulation of Joint Ventures in the European Economic Community" (*Vanderbilt Journal of Transnational Law,* 1978) and Frederick Lukoff's chapter on "Distribution Agreements" in *EEC Competition Law* (1978). And Roger Goebel's article on "Professional Responsibility Issues in International Law Practice" (*American Journal of Comparative Law,* 1981)—although written after the decade had closed—serves as a reminder that the 1970s witnessed the Arab boycott and the Foreign Corrupt Practices Act, with all the fascinating issues they raised for international business lawyers.

It is in the nature of legal articles that they age rapidly: laws, cases, and techniques soon lose currency. One piece of writing by a Coudert Brothers attorney in the 1970s that is likely to last, however, is Dick Wincor's book *Contracts in Plain English* (McGraw-Hill, 1976). A charming, often hilarious, and none-too-reverent explanation of what it is American lawyers do and how their thought processes work, *Contracts* was intended for the foreign businessman or international lawyer, but it has proved a favorite with young lawyers entering the profession. The author of a volume on chess openings, Wincor compares the American legal style of negotiation to the playing of chess in a throwaway line in his preface, and the ensuing text is structured not unlike a chess analysis—although nowhere near as stolid. Rather, it sparkles with the sense of fun and intellectual joy that Alexis hoped all the young people in the firm would come to feel about the law.

The decade of the 1970s brought to Coudert Brothers not only technological and economic change but also social change. The French *Conseils Juridiques* Law of the early 1970s, making *conseils juridiques* members of a regulated profession, cleared the way for the New York partnership to admit French lawyers as members of the firm, and in 1974 the newly unified firm elected its first non-American partner, Hubert de Mahuet, who had been with Coudert Frères since 1965. In nominating de Mahuet, Charles Torem noted that no other American law firm in Europe had yet created a European partner. If Torem's information was correct, than de Mahuet was almost certainly the first foreign citizen since the mid-nineteenth century to become a partner in any American law firm, as well as the first in Coudert Brothers' history.

Laurie Craig and Robin Tait, who had introduced a new emphasis at Coudert Frères on recruiting and training young American lawyers in the 1960s, also began in the wake of the *Conseils Juridiques* Law to recruit young French attorneys in a more systematic way. Among the French lawyers they hired in the 1970s were such future partners of the unified firm as Jacques Buhart, Jean-François Carreras, and Nicholas Sokolow. All together, the *Conseils Juridiques* Law, for which Coudert Frères had lobbied, was to prove a key step in Coudert Brothers' becoming a firm of truly international composition—and one that would look increasingly momentous as more non-Americans became members of the firm throughout the 1970s and 1980s.

Domestically, particularly in the large New York office, there were very visible changes in the area of female and minority hiring. In 1974, as head of the Personnel Committee, John Carey prepared the firm's first Equal Employment Opportunity status report, and he labeled Coudert Brothers as "inadequate" in the categories of minority (i.e., nonwhite and Hispanic) and female lawyers as well as minority office and clerical workers.

The statistics reported by Carey were worse than one would expect of a firm that had always been as cosmopolitan, polyglot, and slightly maverick as Coudert Brothers. But throughout its history Coudert Brothers had merely practiced "passive nondiscrimination," and the results were, by 1974, rather embarrassing. Personnel agencies in New York City had begun sending black and Hispanic secretaries for interviews at large law firms around 1963, but the agencies used by Miss Bainbridge were evidently not among the most progressive in this regard. In any event, it was not until Miss Bainbridge's last years at Coudert Brothers that she finally hired a black office worker.

Alice Shanahan, Miss Bainbridge's successor as office personnel manager, moved the process along fairly briskly, and the facts that 19 percent of Coudert Brothers' one hundred office and clerical workers in its New York office were minority members in 1974 and that one of its five managerial slots was filled by a member of a minority—although Carey deemed those numbers "inadequate"—actually represented a considerable improvement over a very short period. Nonetheless, John Carey, who was at this time U.S. member of the Geneva-based United Nations Subcommittee on Protection of Minorities, took one look at the 1974 figures and told ExCom that "I would strongly urge that we embark on some 'affirmative action,' as federal law puts it." In the same 1974 memo, he informed ExCom that he had already "gotten in touch with a secretarial agency in Newark, recommended by the personnel department of a major corporation where I have a good entrée," in the hope that it would supply more nonwhite job applicants than Coudert Brothers' existing agencies were doing.

As for Coudert Brothers' record in hiring nonwhite lawyers, it reflected faithfully the firm's practice of not recruiting at all prior to 1964 and of recruiting after 1964 only at the elite law schools, none of which was noted for its numbers of minority students. Of the approximately thirty associates in the New York office in 1974, one Chinese American and one black American could be counted in the "minority" column. During the rest of the 1970s, the number of "minority professionals" did increase, however, largely because of the firm's special appeal to young Asian-American lawyers.

Coudert Brothers' basic attitude toward women lawyers had also been traditionally one of "passive nondiscrimination," which is to say that its hiring patterns reflected fairly closely the society, or societies, in which it operated. France, which had lost so many young men in World War I, had many women entering the professions between the wars, and John Dubé is reasonably certain that as early as 1928 one of the women at Coudert Frères was a lawyer—but unfortunately he cannot remember her name, nor does he recall whether she was a member of the French bar or an unlicensed *conseil.* Coudert Frères, though, definitely had a number of female *conseils* by the 1930s, including, most notably, Madame Suzanne Tripier, who retired from the Paris office in 1959.

The situation at the New York office was much different, partly because so few American women went into law. In fact, the firm records suggest that the first woman attorney hired by the

New York office, Kay Woodward in 1961, was probably also the first who ever applied to the firm, at least in the post–World War II era. (There are no surviving records for the prewar era.)

As a pioneer, Woodward found that her presence at the New York office was welcome and acceptable, insofar as she didn't expect any special treatment. For example, during her first week on the job, she was asked, like any other new associate, to attend the partners' luncheon at the University Club. The day after her invitation was issued, however, it was cancelled: a check of the club's policies had revealed that women were not allowed to enter the dining room. "This was not Coudert Brothers' fault in any way," says Woodward. "They did ask me to lunch, but society was like that then, and we accepted it. Obviously, it never occurred to the partners that they should change their venue, and it never occurred to me either that they should." Woodward understood that she had entered a man's world, and it behooved her not to ask for favors.

Woodward ran into difficulty only when she did have to ask for a dispensation peculiar to her sex: an unpaid maternity leave. One survey of women lawyers working for large firms in the early 1980s found that women even then ranked the issue of maternity leave as the most difficult they had to face, the one where they were most likely to encounter a lack of sympathy and even overt hostility. Woodward, as a pioneer in the 1960s, found herself on perilous ground when she became pregnant. "There were partners who said I ought to be fired, the job should not be kept open for me even for five months. Some made a point of telling me so directly; they were quite frank about it."

Although there was apparently a strong push by some partners to create a formal policy making military and government service the only acceptable bases for a leave, ExCom decided to continue to handle these situations on its usual *ad hoc* basis. Woodward was allowed to take a leave not only when her first child was born but again when she had a second child. Yet she suffered a slippage in seniority, salary, and, she thinks, reputation, and she found having to ask for leaves in the face of opposition an unpleasant experience. One well-meaning partner told Woodward in an effort to help her get a perspective on the situation, "You can't expect the firm to give you raises when you have children and your first loyalty will obviously be to your family, not the firm." "Listening to comments like that," says Woodward, "is like having cold water tossed in your face. It definitely cools your ardor."

"I had loved the firm almost blindly," says Woodward. "Afterwards, I still liked working there, and I particularly liked working with George Farnham, but I had lost that starry-eyed feeling." When women associates began coming into the firm in significant numbers in the 1970s, therefore, Woodward was feeling that she was an objective observer. No longer strongly prejudiced in Coudert Brothers' favor, she concluded, nonetheless, that the younger women were treated "very fairly and very well." Opportunities for promotion were limited for both sexes in Trusts and Estates, Woodward says, but the women who had the chance to go into corporate or litigation work were, in her opinion, judged solely on their merits.

Susan Goldberg, who became an associate in 1972 and would become Coudert Brothers' first woman partner in 1979, once wrote, "I never felt I was discriminated against in job assignments or in more subtle ways. . . . As one of the first members of the East Asian Group, I can also state that the prejudices of some Asian clients were never a barrier to women being employed in that group or given the same opportunities as male associates." Judy Mann, who became an associate in 1969, adds that "Coudert Brothers was maybe a little better than some other firms. It had a few male chauvinists around, but it had also had men who worked very well with women, who were really just marvelous, and I enjoyed my time there."

In late 1974 four of the twenty-six associates in the New York office were women—not a large percentage but large enough to make themselves felt when they decided to express their resentment at the fact that the firm held many functions in the Sky Club, a male-only club located on the top floor of the Pan Am Building. Once the women spoke up, Susan Goldberg says, the club's membership policy "was changed in late 1974 or early 1975, at the instigation of Alexis Coudert himself, who was a member of the club's board. Women were thereafter permitted to use all club facilities." There was less than a fourteen-year span between 1961, when Kay Woodward and the Coudert Brothers partners accepted a club's discriminatory policy as an immutable, if regrettable, fact of life, and 1974–75, when a small group of Coudert Brothers women insisted upon the alteration of the Sky Club's policy. The radical revolution in attitude during that brief time span is a revealing measure of how fast the firm was changing on all fronts in the 1970s.

Chapter Nineteen

A SPECIAL GRACE

For all that happened in the 1970s, Coudert Brothers veterans best remember the decade as the one in which the firm planted new offices in far-flung parts of the globe. Located in five cities in 1970, the firm was established in thirteen by the end of the decade. A large portion of the firm's resources went into planning, staffing, and nurturing these new offices, and an even larger share of energy into investigating the several dozen sites that were eventually ruled out. A constant running topic of discussion at Interpol meetings was: Where shall we go next?

At the December 1973 meeting of Interpol, for example, Gene Wadsworth raised the idea of having an office in Monaco or Nice. Charlie Stevens and Preston Tollinger made a presentation about Indonesia's possibilities—and, although he did not bring them forward at this particular meeting, Stevens had some ideas about a Manila office, too. Charles Torem was pushing strongly for a branch office in the Ivory Coast, and Jim Hughes put on the table a suggestion for an office in Madrid.

That Coudert Brothers would be creating more offices was taken for granted, but there was a consensus at this meeting, in Goebel's words, that "the expansion should be structured." "Mr. Dominianni," read the minutes, "stressed that there should be no casual planning of offices and Mr. Hughes urged that there should be a careful selection of spots in the world that would be of interest." In practice, however, orderly planning took a subordinate role to individual initiative in determining the direction of the firm's growth in the late 1970s.

"The way these things worked," says Wadsworth, "is that someone would get an idea for a new office. He'd work up a formal proposal and, first thing, he'd try to sell it to Alexis. If Alexis was persuaded, then there was a good chance that the rest of the firm would say, 'Well, maybe the idea has merit.' But Alexis did not initiate these things. The pressure to grow in the foreign field always came, in the first instance, from some individual who had a strong interest in some particular part of the world."

The Rio de Janeiro office established in 1976 was the brainchild of Sol Linowitz, who had been talking up the idea of venturing into Latin America ever since he had left his ambassadorship to the Organization of American States and joined Coudert Brothers in 1969. The "backers" of the San Francisco office, set up in 1977, were Mike Dominianni, who was working with a French client that was undertaking an ambitious acquisition program in the West, and Charlie Stevens, who wanted a base to serve Japanese companies investing and doing business in California. And the idea for the pair of Near Eastern offices founded in the winter of 1978–79—in Riyadh, Saudi Arabia, and Manama, Bahrain—originated with John Wyser-Pratte, who found an enthusiastic co-planner in Adam Fremantle.

The four new offices of the late 1970s met with widely varying degree of success. With a clientele already somewhat assured, CB-San Francisco got off to a smooth start, and within four years it had already grown to approximately the same size as CB-Washington. CB-Rio showed a profit—but on a very small base. And CB-Riyadh and CB-Bahrain were on shaky grounds right from the start. Coudert Brothers began to discuss the idea of setting up a Near Eastern office in 1973, but by the time it committed itself to the two offices, the oil boom was ending. Tom Ragan, who was sent to found the outpost in Bahrain, set foot in the island sheikdom on the very day that the shah fled Iran. "The nearly three years that I was there," Ragan recalls, "were a tense, unsettled period. You had the constant sense that Americans were not very welcome. Besides, we had been expecting to do work for American contractors in Iran, and there went a large chunk of the planning all to pieces."

Three years earlier, Ragan had been the first Coudert Brothers lawyer in Brazil. In Rio, he was the "guest" of the Ulhoa Canto firm, gracious hosts who made him feel welcome in the warm Brazilian manner. In Bahrain, he was initially under the "sponsorship" of a member of the local bar who seemed anything but eager to have the arrangement succeed. Ragan found himself becoming distrustful of his sponsor; worse, he had the uneasy impression that the sponsor himself was under heavy security-police scrutiny. "I don't know that anything was wrong," says Ragan, "but the atmosphere of the place was devious and difficult for me to deal with." The Carioca culture was easygoing and vibrant; the desert sheikdom was puritanical and, for Westerners, constricted. Ragan went almost directly from the one to the other, with less than a year between the two assignments, experiencing all the contrasts at full strength.

Yet Ragan emphasizes that the four small satellite offices that Coudert Brothers set up in the late 1970s seemed to him to have more similarities than differences—similarities enforced by size. Rio, San Francisco, Riyadh, and Manama were all one-man offices at their conception, and that single lawyer always needed to be in two places at once, trying both to circulate in the community in order to develop contacts and to sit behind the desk and get the work done. "You felt like you had to get out and market," says Ragan, "and at the same time you needed to do some billable work so that the office could break even on the books." And the work that came in tended to be eclectic, forcing the Coudert Brothers' attorney into a "generalist" mode.

In 1981 CB-Bahrain acquired the services of a second attorney, Jeanne Cassin. One of her first questions was "Where is the form file?" "I told her there was no form file," Ragan recalls. "Whatever came in, we just had to do it. And there was no point sending things to New York, because it was going to take two days by courier each day. We couldn't run down the hall and ask a more senior person to look over our drafts. We were it. The Lone Rangers."

Another point of similarity was that the Lone Rangers were young. Only in Riyadh was Coudert Brothers represented by a partner, Adam Fremantle, but Fremantle was himself a fairly young partner. ("Adam's hair turned gray before he was thirty," Ragan recalls, "and he got a lot of respect from the expatriate bankers. They thought he was older than he was.") For the most part, Coudert Brothers was relying once again, as in Hong Kong, Singapore, and Tokyo, on the energy of associates in building these new practices, and the firm delegated responsibility to them liberally. Tony Williams, for instance, at age thirty was asked by ExCom to fly to California and come back with a recommendation as to whether the California office should be in Los Angeles or San Francisco. "These were cities with two-hundred-man law firms," Williams notes. "I was astounded they were asking me to make the choice."

But ExCom felt that, as Williams would be heading the office, he should make the recommendation. ExCom also had Ragan negotiate the joint-venture agreement with the Brazilian law firm of Ulhoa Canto; again, the thinking was that, since he would be living with the results, he should play a major role in setting the terms.

It is the common lament of representatives far from their home offices that management doesn't listen and doesn't care. Coudert Brothers' attorneys were never much tempted to join in such complaints during the Alexis years. On the contrary, listening to others' horror stories, they felt lucky in their management. "Even though you were three thousand miles away from headquarters, you never had to watch your back," says Larry Brody, who headed CB-London. Ragan particularly appreciated the fact that he could rely on ExCom's word: "Alexis, Hughes and Wadsworth made decisions, and they kept them. You could appeal, but they were not wobbling all over, changing their minds from one day to the next, second-guessing you or themselves."

And management was considerate. Owen Nee and his wife had at one point packed up to move to Hong Kong, when Charlie Stevens realized he had enough bodies already in Hong Kong and decided to cancel the plans. "Alexis said, 'No,' " Nee recalls. "He said, 'We can't do that to him. We've led him into making all the arrangements. He's going to go.' " "Alexis," Ragan says, "recognized the personal decisions that were involved in going abroad. He understood the human dimensions of these things, what your hopes and anxieties were." Rio, San Francisco, Riyadh, and Manama were brave, lonely, little outposts, but the attorneys always knew that back at the home office someone appreciated the common experiences they were going through.

The last overseas venture on which Coudert Brothers embarked during the Alexis years, the enterprise known in the firm as CB-Beijing, was an uncommon experience for all concerned. To begin with, CB-Beijing was physically different. In China, Coudert Brothers did not have an office with standard furnishings and a secretary. Rather, CB-Beijing operated out of room 1009 on the tenth floor of the East Wing of the Beijing Hotel, which constituted the only quarters available to foreign visitors at the time the United States and the People's Republic of China resumed diplomatic relations in 1979. The Coudert Brothers' attorneys on China duty slept in room 1009, worked there, met with clients, with someone inevitably sitting on the beds, and took most of their meals in the big, noisy hotel dining room.

There were numerous other American and European lawyers

in that dining room, adding their voices to the babel effect. Those lawyers, however, were transients, visiting China for a few weeks in order to represent their clients in specific negotiations. Only Coudert Brothers' attorneys had visas that enabled them to remain in China year-round and to maintain a permanent lock on a Beijing Hotel room—visas that they were given initially as guests of and consultants to the Beijing municipal government group that was in charge of foreign trade development for the city. Formally, CB-Beijing began as an educational, goodwill, cultural-exchange endeavor. Five days a week, for two years running between 1979 and 1981, Jerry Cohen, Owen Nee, and Steve Orlins took turns teaching, at Coudert Brothers' expense, a course on international law, foreign investment, and foreign trade for Beijing public officials.

Because the course was the rationale for CB-Beijing's existence, the firm did not describe CB-Beijing to the outside world as a law office. Yet Coudert Brothers could represent foreign clients in China, and it didn't want to give the impression that it couldn't. This led to semantic caution, as displayed in this exchange at a Parisian conference on China trade in November 1979:

MODERATOR: I did not get this straight; do you have, or do you intend to set up, an office in Peking?

OWEN NEE: We have a presence in Peking at the moment.

MODERATOR: I see, yes.

Whether CB-Beijing was called an office or a presence, however, Coudert Brothers was the first foreign law firm in the People's Republic of China. Its position was unique, for CB-Beijing had been called into existence not just to meet the needs of Coudert Brothers' clients but also to meet the needs of the Chinese government, which in 1979 was beginning a crash effort to create the legal framework needed to do business with the West.

"People often said back then that China had no laws," comments Nee. "Actually China had the same multitude of laws found in any state-planned economy. How much freight a railroad should carry, when and where, was a law. How to carry eggs, how to pack chickens—every small aspect of life was regulated pursuant to law." What China, as a Communist country, did not have was provision in its laws for the concepts of private ownership, profit, or return on investment. Unlike the Eastern European countries, moreover, China did not recognize international law or have any mechanism whereby international law could overlay domestic law.

In addition, China had turned itself into a totally closed society, one cut off not only from foreign investment and trade but from foreign thinking. Other countries have periodically withdrawn from the international economy since World War II, but when they reentered, they have had the cultural and intellectual resources to make a quick readjustment. Indonesia, for example, had actively discouraged foreign investment between 1957 and 1967, but when it decided to reverse policy in 1967, there were Indonesian economists trained at Berkeley and MIT available to recreate the legal framework and policies needed to attract investment. China, on the other hand, had sent its educated cadres to the communes to do manual labor, destroyed its libraries, and made it so dangerous to display any familiarity with Western ideas that it had eradicated virtually all knowledge of what was going on in business, economics, and law in the rest of the world.

Thus, when China changed course in the late 1970s, it lacked investment law, company law, patent law, trademark law, tax laws for foreign investment and trade, a civil code, a criminal procedure code, commercial law, environmental law, contract law, trade treaties, acceptance of international arbitration, and international law of any kind. Moreover, in the absence of such formal, written law, there were neither customary practices nor remembered traditions to fall back on. From the perspective of international business law, China was, as Torem told that conference in Paris, "a vacuum."

This aspect of China's intention to modernize is what caught the imagination of lawyers around the world—that the Chinese, in Torem's words, "start with zero." In the world's largest country, there was a legal tabula rasa, and what the Chinese would write upon it was of importance not just to China's economic development but to the global balance of power. China's rapprochement to the West was an extraordinary moment in history, and no one was more aware of that than Jerry Cohen, the director of the East Asian Legal Studies Program at Harvard Law School and the outstanding Western expert on Chinese law. As a consultant and later counsel to Coudert Brothers, Cohen was to play, in the words of British author Jan Morris, "an almost unique role in the opening of the People's Republic to American business."

Until 1972, Cohen's direct contacts with the People's Republic had been, like those of all Americans, nonexistent. He had had to use Hong Kong as his vantage point for research into the Chinese legal system; the newspapers in which refugees from mainland China wrapped their personal belongings were among the sources he utilized for his academic studies. With the advent of "ping-pong diplomacy" between the United States and China, however, Cohen was able to pay four visits to China between 1972 and 1978, meeting with senior officials, not always in an atmosphere of perfect cordiality. Direct and occasionally blunt, Cohen was frank in his opinion of Chinese Communist ideology and of the efforts of his hosts to confine his travel schedule to certain "show places." Some high-ranking Chinese were equally blunt in expressing their low opinion of law and lawyers. Part of this scorn arose from the general Eastern dislike of legal advocacy, once tersely summarized by Charles Torem as "the theory that only bad people need courts and lawyers." Another part of it, though, was ideological: that all American international lawyers were "the running dogs of Wall Street imperialism" was the kind of thing Cohen was told during the "Gang of Four" era.

Yet Cohen, because of his frankness as well as his stature as a scholar, earned the respect of Chinese officials. When the government determined it would need laws to encourage Western investment, it was to Cohen that it turned for information on international law. In February 1979, one month after the restoration of diplomatic relations with the United States, Cohen and a group of Coudert Brothers attorneys—Charles Stevens, Charles Torem, Gage McAfee, Owen Nee, and Alice Kung—arrived in Beijing at the invitation of the Ministry of Finance to engage in a week of "intensive discussions" on international tax problems. In March a similar Coudert Brothers delegation, led by Torem, at the invitation of the China Council for the Promotion of International Trade, organized a series of lectures that was attended by one hundred mid- to high-level officials.

"The Chinese," Torem noted later that year, "wanted to hear about Western and U.S. experience in attracting and controlling foreign investment, the laws relating to joint ventures in Socialist countries like Yugoslavia and Rumania. They wanted to know about various Asian laws on joint ventures and foreign investment, about U.S. tax laws and international accounting principles." The Chinese, as it turned out, were gathering background information for a law on joint ventures, which appeared in July 1979.

By July, Coudert Brothers had committed itself to teaching the two-year course for the Beijing foreign trade group, and in August the firm organized its first tax conference for the Ministry of Finance. Coudert Brothers was to conduct such conferences for the Ministry of Finance biennially throughout the 1980s, issuing the invitations to American professors and tax experts, paying their expenses and providing the translations into Chinese of the extensive papers prepared for these conferences, which would then be published by the ministry.

From the initial seminars through the continuing tax conferences, Coudert Brothers played a remarkable role for a private law firm. One would normally expect a not-for-profit academic foundation to undertake these kinds of endeavors. But Coudert Brothers had the resources that had been assembled over the years by Charles Stevens—the Chinese-speaking attorneys, the translators, the staff personnel in its Hong Kong office; it had the confidence of the Ministry of Finance; and its partners had the willingness to invest in this sort of "cultural exchange."

In the initial flurry of legislation written in 1979–80 to encourage foreign investment, the Chinese used information and advice gathered from many sources. The new Chinese patent law owed much to the Japanese patent-registry system, for example, and laws dealing with real estate tended to be modeled on the Hong Kong British system. But there was an overall American slant in many of the new laws affecting foreign trade and investment, especially in the area of taxation, where Coudert Brothers was working closely with the Ministry of Finance to develop the terminology and principles. "Can you imagine," says Nee, "trying to translate into Chinese such terms as 'foreign tax credit' or 'arm's-length transaction'? It was quite difficult working out these concepts, and I think Coudert Brothers, without question, was helpful to the Ministry of Finance in developing the tax terms used today."

At the same time as Coudert Brothers was trying to satisfy the Chinese curiosity about American and international law, it was also, of course, representing clients in negotiations with Chinese governmental agencies. In July 1979, when the three Coudert Brothers attorneys settled into room 1009 of the Beijing Hotel, a routine developed whereby one would teach the course, while the other two attorneys did business from their hotel room or went back to Hong Kong to meet with clients and oversee the drafting there of contracts and proposals. Every two weeks, they would rotate responsibility, with one of the others taking over the course.

Of the three, Cohen was, of course, a professor by vocation; Orlins was a young lawyer who had recently spent three years with the U.S. State Department, specializing in Chinese legal affairs; and Nee was the member of the trio who had actual experience practicing law. "Jim Hughes," Nee explains, "wanted someone representing clients who had more than an academic knowledge of law, and I was designated."

After working at CB-Hong Kong between 1973 and 1976, Nee had happily returned to New York and settled down, as he had long planned, to becoming a New York corporate lawyer. For more than two years, Nee never went near East Asian matters, and then

Barry Metzger at CB-Hong Kong decided that he was needed back in Hong Kong again. "I didn't want to go," says Nee. "Amber didn't want to go. But once again Charlie talked us into doing things we really didn't want to do." Nee was, in Stevens's opinion, "one of the best young technical lawyers in the firm and one of the best business-getters." Stevens had no intention of letting Nee slip away, so back the Nees went to Hong Kong again, where Nee in late 1978 drafted the basic game plan for Coudert Brothers' China practice.

Americans were interested in investing in China from the moment diplomatic relations were restored, but not until China published its joint-venture law in the summer of 1979 did the interest turn serious. The first matters that the CB-Beijing attorneys negotiated were hotel deals, including the Great Wall Hotel, a $90-million joint-venture project. Then China began putting offshore tracts up for bidding by oil exploration companies, and work flowed in from many oil industry giants. Coudert Brothers also prepared the contracts for the first visit of the Peking Opera troupe to New York and for several movies and educational television programs.

Charles Torem at Coudert Frères was the most effective publicist for CB-Beijing in its early years. "Torem was just great," says Nee. "He would write and write, push and push, to get word of the China office out. Large American companies that he was representing in Europe became some of our best clients in China in those early years." Torem was also interested enough in China to visit that country several times after his first trip in 1979, making the long arduous journey again in 1981, 1983, and 1985.

There were special difficulties, however, in practicing law in China. One was sorting out the opportunists from those who were representing legitimate investors. "Situations like that attract fraudsmen of various types," says Nee. "We had a few of those as clients, too. There were some people with very big names, putting up great fronts, who turned out to be all front. You wondered how they got their reputation."

Originally, it had been expected that the attorneys in Beijing would negotiate contracts, while the drafting was done in Hong Kong. It soon became apparent, however, that CB-Beijing could not confer with CB-Hong Kong and maintain the confidentiality of its clients' affairs. The long-distance lines to Hong Kong were monitored by the government, and the one telex available to foreigners was a communal machine in the Beijing Hotel. "You could go down at night," recalls Nee, "and read everyone's telexes and find out what terms the people you were bidding against were offering."

In the interest of speed and privacy, CB-Beijing needed office equipment in order to make revisions to contracts under negotiation, and Nee brought a typewriter in from CB-Hong Kong in his personal luggage. The typewriter having lost a screw somewhere en route, Nee made a foray to the local department store to buy screws and a screwdriver, and he found himself surrounded at the counter by a small crowd who thought his purchases might reveal something about Western technical expertise. There was nothing technologically advanced, however, about Nee's typewriter or any of the other equipment he subsequently carried in from Hong Kong. Under U.S. export control laws, sophisticated equipment could not be brought to China, and room 1009 gradually filled up with balky antiques. CB-Beijing's word-processing capability, for instance, initially consisted of a temperamental old mag-card machine. Nee took it apart for repairs and put it together innumerable times—all part, he joked, of being "a full-service law firm."

The one overriding problem in China, though, was simply finding out what China's laws were. A client interested in establishing a textile factory needed to know the labor laws in order to calculate their impact on the joint venture's profitability, but the labor laws were not published. When a client firm was developing a proposal for a coal mine in the middle of China, it had to know the cost of railroad shipment to the coast, but the railroad regulations were not obtainable. And China's tax rates were initially guarded as if they were a national defense secret.

The "lack of information about where to go, whom to talk to, what to do" was not peculiar to China. It was a common problem for lawyers in all non-Western countries, as Bob Hornick told an audience at the Association of the Bar of the City of New York in 1974. Using Indonesia as an example because he knew it best, Hornick recounted the difficulties he had encountered in finding out what its laws were: the State Gazette was often a year or two behind in printing new statutes, no library had a complete set of old gazettes, and most of Indonesia's laws weren't published in the gazettes or anywhere else.

> Ultimately, [Hornick said] the solution is to visit the various ministries and inquire about what regulations exist, though this is an unsatisfactory way of keeping up with new law—both because of the effort required, and also the unreliability of such a network of personal contracts. Also, one finds a curious reluctance on the part of some officials to share regulations. If you are friendly with an official he may give them to you. Under no

circumstances will he sell them. Even the State Gazette is not available by subscription. . . . you cannot put yourself on a list to subscribe to things and you cannot buy them.

In China the difficulty in obtaining statutes and regulations was compounded, of course, by the closed nature of the People's Republic, and the CB-Beijing attorneys spent hours visiting ministries, explaining why copies of the laws were needed, building contracts and making friends. To obtain the text of a previously unpublished law or regulation was a triumph. As fast as Coudert Brothers got its hands on such materials, it translated and published them so that other firms and lawyers could have access to them. Translation was such an important part of what Coudert Brothers was doing in China—from English to Chinese for seminars, course materials, contracts and correspondence and from Chinese to English for laws and other documents—that a translation section grew up at CB-Hong Kong, guided by Amber Nee.

Under an arrangement with a commercial publisher, Owen Nee provided English texts of laws and commentary for what became a multivolume series on Chinese law. Jerry Cohen, Charles Stevens, and Gage McAfee also took the time to publish information on the laws and practices of the People's Republic, and the East Asia Group and Torem were indefatigable in participating in continuing legal education seminars and conferences during the first few years of CB-Beijing's existence. Between seminars and courses for the Chinese on American and international law and articles and seminars for Americans and Europeans on Chinese law, disseminating information took up a major share of everyone's time and energy during the period between 1979 and 1983 when Coudert Brothers was the only law firm with a "presence" in China.

All this unremunerated work was very much in the spirit of Alexis Coudert, who had written back in 1946 of the need to cooperate with the peoples of developing countries in the creation of equitable laws governing foreign direct investment and to make long-term commitments that could produce goodwill. "I wouldn't want anyone to overemphasize our ideals," Nee has said. "We were just trying to do our best to represent our clients and our profession in a difficult environment." But that mixture of idealism and pragmatism so evident in Alexis's article on "Foreign Direct Investment," written in his own youth, was also at work in the China practice. Perhaps overriding both idealism and pragmatic concern for Coudert Brothers' prestige, however, was the intellectual excitement of the situation. "When we started this, we were so excited about it," says Nee, "we didn't spend much time thinking about moral reasons we should or shouldn't do it." For that matter, the reports setting out the financial justifications have a decidedly perfunctory ring to them. The opportunity to break new ground in the development of international law was irresistible in and of itself to the kind of law firm Coudert Brothers was and the kind of people Alexis had surrounded himself with.

The first letter sent out by CB-Beijing in 1979 was addressed to Alexis Coudert—as a self-consciously symbolic act, acknowledging that CB-Beijing would never have existed without CB-Hong Kong and the rest of the East Asia practice, and that the East Asia practice would not have come into being without Alexis's vision of what Coudert Brothers should be. Alexis himself would never visit CB-Beijing, and the attorneys there knew he would not. For the previous three years, it had been known that Alexis had a fatal, incurable form of cancer, and by 1979 it was clear that his time was running out.

Those who joined Coudert Brothers in Alexis's later years noticed immediately that the firm had a distinctive atmosphere. In 1975 James B. Sitrick, an international tax lawyer, moving from another large New York firm to a partnership at Coudert Brothers, observed that Coudert Brothers was more decentralized, largely because it had so many more offices. "The atmosphere was also more internationalist," Sitrick recalls, "pleasingly so, from my point of view. I was coming from a firm where, as an international specialist, I sometimes felt like the odd man out. Many firms then were going into international law for its glamour, but at Coudert Brothers you felt there was a real expertise and interest and depth of commitment."

Sitrick, though, was especially struck by "the standard of civility that had been set by Alexis. I know it sounds odd, but people dealt with each other on a higher plane. And in a dog-eat-dog world, Coudert Brothers preferred not to make profitability its only standard. People were sending out bills when they got the chance, whether that was six months, nine months, or twelve months after the fact. There was this attitude that 'We are not here to send out bills.'"

Most of all, Sitrick liked the people. "I suspect Alexis orchestrated my welcome to a certain extent, but everyone was very friendly and cordial. They were inviting me to dinner parties and asking me to represent the firm at conferences almost from the first week I arrived." His new fellow partners, Sitrick observed, "had a wide range of interests, spoke a great variety of languages, and were very well read. There were fascinating public figures like Sol Linowitz and Struve Hensel, who was a font of conviction and ideas; Alexis Coudert, who was the quintessential gentleman; Charles Torem, who was simply *sui generis*. It was a cosmopolitan, sophisticated group of people."

From the most lowly possible perspective—that of a first-year associate—Tony Williams in 1972 also noticed that the people at Coudert Brothers were distinctive. "I can still remember everyone who interviewed me," said Williams in 1990. "Each was a different personality and a little different from what I expected to find. They weren't all cut from the same mold."

Williams, who interviewed at nineteen law firms and ultimately received nineteen offers, came to Coudert Brothers because Alexis offered him a job on the day of his interview. "I thought, 'This is the kind of place that reacts quickly,' " Williams recalls. " 'They know what they want, and they go after it.' " As impressed as Williams was, however, he had a definite suspicion that, when he had showed up earlier in the day to be interviewed, no one had been expecting his arrival. "I think John Carey forgot to tell anyone I was coming. I've thought many times since, how, on that first day, I saw the best of Coudert Brothers' traits and the worst—the great entrepreneurial spirit, mixed with that administrative disorganization."

Stiefel, coming to the firm as counsel in 1971, also noticed the disorganization. "It was a form of democracy by chaos," he says. "I'm sure that if Alexis had chosen to be a dictator, the firm would have been richer much sooner and had a more even, consistent quality. But it wouldn't have had that free spirit that was so charming."

The characteristics that Sitrick, Williams, and Stiefel—and many others—noted are those that recur in history in descriptions of other small organizations going through a creative flowering, ranging from the merchant venture companies of Elizabethan England through the computer enterprises of Silicon Valley. Coudert Brothers' atmosphere, however, was not imitative of anything: it was simply the natural outgrowth of Alexis's preference for consensus, his informal manner, his distaste for bureaucracy, and his willingness both to trust and to delegate.

The sudden, dramatic growth of the firm in the late 1970s, however, turned some of the qualities that had always been assets into liabilities. "There were people going after the same clients, bodies bumping into each other, partners charging off in all directions without consulting anyone else. The firm was a *sukh*, a street bazaar," Jan DuBois recalls. Concurrently, Jim Hughes says, "There was a real demand for ExCom to make rules, where no one had ever felt the need for them before, and to establish more formal mechanisms." In the mid-1970s, according to the minutes, ExCom was being asked for rulings on dozens of subjects, from whether the firm would pay tuition for bar-preparation courses to what transfer allowances lawyers should get when moving from office to office.

On important matters, though, Alexis and ExCom had always waited for a consensus to emerge. Forcing decisions upon his partners was not Alexis's style, but by the mid-1970s consensus was becoming very hard to achieve. "There had always been the feeling that we were one team, pulling in one direction," McAuliffe recalls. "There were so many more people in the late 1970s that we lost that feeling. The group was too large not to have divisions."

Sitrick tells the story of how Charles de Gaulle was once alleged to have exclaimed, in exasperation, "How can you govern a country like France that has three hundred different kinds of cheeses!" "That was Coudert Brothers in the late 1970s," says Sitrick. "Two hundred and fifteen lawyers, 215 different types of cheeses." Coudert Brothers, like France, was so full of strong-willed individuals pulling in different directions that it was essentially ungovernable—except by Alexis Coudert.

"I have seen," says Larry Brody, "the partners vote against a proposal by a proportion of ten to three. And Alexis would stand up and say, 'I would like you to vote for this proposal, as a personal favor to me.' And on the next vote the proposal would pass unanimously." The younger lawyers in the 1970s often talked about Alexis's charisma—a very apt term, for in the original Greek it referred to that special grace that enabled the early Christian martyrs to walk through an arena of lions and come out unscathed. Coudert Brothers was full of great lions, for successful lawyers tend to have strong egos, but behind Alexis, the pride was always willing to close ranks.

Even so, reaching consensus on major issues was extremely difficult. Eugene Wadsworth and the retirement committee wrestled with many different versions of a retirement plan before one finally received unanimous approval in the 1970s. And every suggestion for solving the "question of succession" failed in a straw vote or informal survey between 1966 and 1976. In 1976, though, Alexis was told by his doctor that he had only four years to live, and the "question of succession" could no longer be postponed. In 1978, on Sol Linowitz's suggestion, two more members were elected to the three-man ExCom, and provision made for an election of all five members every two years.

In the summer of 1979 the firm celebrated the one hundredth anniversary of Coudert Frères. At a dinner party on a boat cruising down the Seine, Alexis stood up to make some informal remarks on Coudert Brothers and its place in history. He was in especially good form that night, Gerry Dunworth would recall. "We applauded and applauded. We all felt we could have gone on listening to him for hours." Alexis made no secret of his illness, but he was stoical about it. Only his family—and Charles Torem, to whom he had always been so close—realized that on that glorious night the French cuisine and wines had no taste or aroma for Alexis, Paris itself had no sparkle.

In his final year, Alexis was fully aware that the firm had to adapt once again—this time not to grow, but to adjust to its own success. "I think he felt he knew what the solutions were," says his son, Tracy, "but he couldn't make the problems go away." "There were things," says Jim Hughes, "that Alexis was too ill by then to deal with. But he wanted very much to leave behind him a healthy, prosperous firm, and I think he certainly did."

Hughes made that assertion in 1990 in full knowledge of all that happened in the decade following Alexis's death. The history of the post-Alexis years will have to include the story of how a group of East Asia Group partners nearly broke away from the firm, of how a new emphasis on productivity, proper billing procedures, and computerization took for many older partners the fun out of practicing law at Coudert Brothers, of how the firm went through as many different experimental forms of governance as the French had during the French Revolution, and of how the firm experienced for a while a truly alarming rate of turnover.

But the firm Alexis left turned out to be healthy—healthy enough to survive all the dissension and confusion of its rough transition to self-governance, to develop procedures that worked for a larger organization yet were still democratic, and to use the money flowing from its improved productivity to take risks and do exciting things that Alexis would have enjoyed. Charles Torem in the 1980s, for example, was to be the moving force behind Coudert Brothers' becoming the first American law firm in Moscow; Lucien Le Lièvre at age sixty-eight moved to Belgium and brought new life and spirit to CB-Brussels; Sam Highleyman and David Jacobs created a prosperous branch in Los Angeles; Barry Metzger set up a Sydney office that became staffed entirely by Australians; CB-Beijing acquired a satellite in Shanghai; Japan allowed individual American lawyers to open offices, and Coudert Brothers in Tokyo assumed the name of the Charles R. Stevens foreign law consultancy; Robert S. Franklin and Edmund S. Cohen built a large tax department; and Gordon Spivack and a group of other new partners gave the firm a sophisticated antitrust capability.

In the 1980s Coudert Brothers survived fire (in Rio de Janeiro), earthquake (in San Francisco), and revolution (in Beijing and Shanghai). It even survived its own excesses and self-created dramas. "Our only problems at the time of Alexis's death," says Allen Russell, who as managing partner in 1979–81 took the brunt of those problems, "were those of success." Russell kept firm hold of his sense of humor and, battered as he got at times as one crisis followed another, he was able to say he felt fortunate that, at least, he was not having to deal with the problems of failure. Alexis's legacy was a firm that was brave and bold, colorful and successful.

Alexis worked to within ten days of his death on November 2, 1980. At a memorial service for him, Henry deVries of Columbia's Parker School, Charles Torem, and Sol Linowitz delivered the principal addresses. Over the years that followed, Jim Sitrick remembered from time to time a portion of Linowitz's speech, never without feeling a shiver at the power of the ambassador's words. Linowitz kept no text of his remarks, but in 1990 Sitrick, who was then chairman of ExCom, recounted the passage that had so affected him in these words:

> Linowitz said at the service, "There was a time when I discovered by accident something quite admirable that Alexis had done for the firm, and I told him that I thought our partners ought to know about this. Alexis asked me, please, not to tell them. I knew that for someone of Alexis's modesty, what I proposed would make him uncomfortable. I told Alexis, though, that I thought the partnership had the right to know what he had done for them, and I was going to bring it up. Alexis said then, "Well, if you must, will you at least please wait until I've left the room?"
>
> Then Linowitz paused, and he looked out over the gathering of mourners and he said, "Now we can at last talk freely about the greatness of the man, for . . . Alexis has left the room."

Twenty

EPILOGUE

A few years back, as a free-lance writer researching this history, I was wandering the corridors of Coudert Brothers after hours when a young tax partner stopped me and asked, "What are you finding out? Were we *ever* a good gray law firm?"

"Never," I said. "In fact, right now I'm writing a World War I section where the senior partner is coming to fisticuffs in a courtroom with an angry German naval captain. The same partner's cousin, who was Rodin's mistress, is nursing French soldiers—and I feel like I'm teetering on the verge of sounding like an E. Phillips Oppenheim suspense thriller."

The partner's eyes lit up. "Oh, that's wonderful" he said. "I knew our history had to be like that. It just *had* to be!"

It was possible to write this book only because members of the present-day firm, having a presentiment that their history might turn out to be interesting, actively enouraged the research. They opened the firm's records and sat willingly for hours of interviews. "If anyone is a little difficult or diffident, let me know," James B. Sitrick, the Chairman of ExCom, told me early on, but the one person I had trouble interviewing was Charlie Torem, and that was owing solely to the countless interruptions as Torem took phone call after phone call from clients. "Where were we?" Torem would say abruptly, hanging up the phone. "1953," I'd barely have a chance to reply—and then the telephone would ring again. But, bit by bit, we finally worked our way through even his enormous storehouse of memories.

Coudert Brothers is a conglomeration of bright people, who in the late 1980s knew little of their institution's history beyond a cluster of tantalizing "campfire" anecdotes that had been handed down from senior attorneys to junior attorneys over the years. Was it really true that the father of the first Coudert brothers had escaped from the Bastille? Did a later partner get killed by a blow to the head from a high-heeled shoe? Was there a partner who turned down a U.S. Supreme Court seat? Plain curiosity had much to do with Coudert Brothers' receptivity to the idea of a "firm history."

Beyond curiosity, however, there existed, some seven years after Alexis Coudert's death, a deep-seated wish to pay tribute to him. Only shortly before I began work on this history, the firm had established the Alexis C. Coudert Memorial Lectures at the Association of the Bar of the City of New York, but the urge to honor Alexis's memory was far from satisfied. And I believe that one reason why the partners I interviewed were open and confiding (to a degree that at times left me astounded) was that they so fervently hoped that somehow I was going to be able to pin down on paper what had made Alexis special.

Speaking of leadership, Eric Larrabee has written that it "is instantly recognizable in the present yet arduous to reconstruct when the present has faded into the past." I never knew Alexis Coudert, and writing about him proved arduous indeed. I was continually told that Alexis had "transformed the firm," yet I could not trace back to him a single concrete proposal or action precipitating that transformation. He originated nothing, claimed no responsibility as an originator—and still he is credited within the firm with every success of his era and as rigorously shielded from blame for any of its failures or shortcomings. "In his presence men behaved differently," Larrabee writes of another leader, and so it was with Alexis Coudert. His leadership was not one of action, but of influence.

Certainly after Alexis died, men and women behaved differently. As fleetingly alluded to in the last chapter, barely two months after Alexis's funeral the firm came close to splitting apart. Rancors, restlessness, and discontents, suppressed in Alexis's presence, rose to the surface, and it appeared that, if the firm of Coudert Brothers were to survive, it would be as a truncated version of itself.

It was interesting to me, as an observer come late to the scene, to note how irresistibly many partners who went through that unhappy, factious period kept returning to the subject. For the younger partners, in particular, it seemed to linger in their memories, years after the fact, as an epic moment. The '60s generation has a way of imbuing drama into every situation, and listening to their recollections, I came to think of the internecine struggles of 1981 as akin to chapters from the *Iliad*. I could vividly see Mike Dominianni and Charlie Stevens squaring off like staunch Hector and rash Achilles and sense the atomsphere at the 1981 partnership meeting when Hugh Fitzgerald rose to invoke so movingly the Olympain shade of Alexis and laurel-wreathed Sol Linowitz pled for peace.

Coudert Brothers did not, in fact, plunge into a Trojan War in 1981. But it hovered for a few months on the eve of battle. And the contemplation of the possible carnage and bloodshed made everyone concerned well aware that even a great law firm is mortal. It can lose limbs and vital organs. It can die.

So this history was researched and written at a time when a number of Coudert Brothers partners were interested in the continuity of the firm. Their interest could hardly be described, by the late 1980s, as urgent. They had already addressed the problems that had surfaced so tumultuously in 1980 and 1981 and were, by and large, satisfied with the results. By then, the immediate post-Alexis period was just close enough in time that, as partners talked of those years, their voices tensed with remembered angers and discontents—but far enough away that, without exception, they would break off in the middle of describing some past tense confrontation and begin to laugh at themselves. "Ah, well," they'd say in some variant or another, "it did have its funny moments, too. The fact that we were so serious about the problems was almost funny in itself—but, I can tell you, it took me a long time to see the humor in it all."

Two things seemed to have restored the firm to its sense of humor by the late 1980s, and one of these was a growing confidence in the institutional processes it had created in 1981 and 1982. The East Asian practice partners who had threatened to break away in early 1981 had been anticipating that, without Alexis, they would have no voice, no friend, no protector at the center of power in New York. To answer their concerns, Interpol, the committee representing all offices worldwide, was given the power to make the vital decisions of how the partnership income would be distributed among the partners, where and when new offices would be opened, and who would become a partner. To assist Interpol, an Associate Review Committee was formed to carry out procedures intended to provide early, objective evaluations of associates' partnership potential. Meanwhile, to ExCom in New York

City was left the day-to-day management of the firm, and James Sitrick, elected Chairman of ExCom in 1982, helped ease the situation by a selective approach to the issue of centralization versus decentralization: successful offices were to run on a loose rein; financially wobbly offices were to receive help from "headquarters"—not a barrage of criticism, but courteously, if firmly offered help. "Sitrick poured civility on troubled waters by the barrelful," recalls Allen Russell. "And to good result."

Few would have guessed at the beginning of the decade, however, that the new system of governance would be essentially unchanged and that ExCom would have the same chairman ten years later. Back then every step taken seemed tentative, the accord fragile—a thin rope bridge thrown across the chasm of discontent. Still, the strands of the bridge held, clients came in, lawyers went about their business—and people began to trust the firm's governmental system and decide there was a "life after Alexis."

Even more important than the perception that the systems were reasonably fair and were working, though, was the sharp increase in the firm's profitability. The concerns long raised by Dominianni—that costs had to be gotten under control and billing practices improved—were also attended to at last. The amount of revenue falling to the bottom line and thus into partners' pockets increased dramatically—a situation certain to promote good humor among the beneficiaries.

Moreover, as mentioned earlier, Coudert Brothers elected to use some of its newfound profits to take risks. After a half-decade of relative dormancy, the spirit of adventure broke loose in the mid-1980s. In quick succession, six new offices opened: Sydney (December 1984), Los Angeles (1986), San Jose, California (1986), Shanghai (1986), Tokyo (1987), and Moscow (1988). And the speed with which they were established was matched, in most cases, by the rapidity with which they turned a profit. In Los Angeles, for example, Coudert Brothers' own Japan-related work gave the new office a jump start, while the absorption of five attorneys from DeBroeck & Rachlin, a firm specializing in representing high-tech companies put it into first gear within about six months. The nucleus in San Jose comprised four DeBroeck & Rachlin litigators, who made San Jose as well a success from the start. Shanghai neatly fed the "China practice," while Moscow, originally a one-man office staffed by an associate, Richard N. Dean, quickly began advising a host of large multinationals.

Moscow, though, was as important to the firm for its psychological effect. Like Beijing before it, Moscow was a major groundbreaking move, conducted by Coudert Brothers with panache and delight in the idea of being "the first." From Torem's, Sitrick's, and Dean's initial visit to Red Square (which included a state dinner with Gorbachev and his officials in the Kremlin), to Sitrick's break-fast meeting in Paris with Henry Kissinger, to Sol Linowitz's diplo-matic base-touching in Washington, D.C., Moscow symbolized to the firm an affirmation that its spirit of adventure was as lively as ever.

In addition to new offices, however, Coudert Brothers in the same short span of years acquired or strengthened whole specialty areas in the U.S. domestic practice. The same year that the "high-tech" specialty was added out in California, one of the nation's out-standing antitrust groups joined Coudert Brothers *en masse:* fourteen new partners led by Gordon Spivack, who would a few years later win one of the most important U.S. Supreme Court vic-tories in the firm's history, the *Kodak* antitrust case. Real estate came back to the fore with the addition of Peter Britell, and a bankruptcy capability was added in 1988.

As a result of its expansion, Coudert Brothers practically dou-bled in size, growing from 189 lawyers in eleven cities in 1980 to 350 lawyers in eighteen cities by the early 1990s. Its revenues quad-rupled, and net income improved still more. The "blossoming" of the late 1980s, in fact, dwarfed in magnitude all other expansion-ary periods in the firm's history.

It was also true to the Coudert Brothers' tradition in being somewhat accidental and unplanned. James Sitrick, who presided over the 1980s expansion, had believed back in 1982 (and earlier) that the firm was big enough and perhaps too big. "I can remem-ber handing Alexis a copy of E. F. Schumacher's *Small Is Beautiful,* urging him to read it," Sitrick recalls. "A few days later Alexis handed it back, saying 'Very nice, Jim, but—I'm afraid it's too late for us.' " Nonetheless, Sitrick cherished the idea that a relatively small size would help to preserve the firm's "warm, personal, civ-ilized, entrepreneurial, innovative qualities" as well as its "intellec-tual tone."

"But what do you do when you have the chance to invite the Spivack group into your firm?" Sitrick says. "Or to be the first American law firm in Moscow? You don't say no to opportunities like that. So we've been opportunistic. We've grown. But," he adds, with a humorous shrug, "at least we've grown in interesting ways."

Thus, with the firm enjoying so much success, its continuance was not an urgent subject in the late 1980s. Yet, there was a con-cern, lingering from the aftermath of Alexis's death, about what was holding Coudert Brothers together and what would hold it to-gether in the future. The institutions of its governance were functional but young, put together in a sensible way but not the subject of any enthusiasm. And, if material good fortune was the only glue, then Coudert Brothers could evidently dissolve in the first economic downturn.

Lest future generations forget, the 1980s were a period when there was much talk of "corporate culture," and this book happened to be begun at a time when Coudert Brothers, in a mild way, was interested in identifying the strands in its culture. The firm's values and approach were looked to to inspire the loyalty that had previously attached to the Couderts themselves. The firm knew what these values were. For one thing, well aware of the centrifugal forces inherent in an eleven-office or an eighteen-office firm, Sitrick never missed a chance at any annual meeting to reaffirm the value of innovation, a sense of adventure and fun, civility, tolerance for differences and even eccentricity, and above all, the commitment of the firm to international law. What the firm did not know, until this book was started, was that those values could be traced straight back to the day when Frederic René Coudert hung out his shingle in 1853. It was a discovery that pleased them very much, and I can only hope that my knowledge of their pleasure did not taint my objectivity.

Flipping through these pages now that they are set in type, however, I think that, if anything, I reacted in the other direction and underplayed the true colorfulness of Coudert Brothers' past. I see, for example, that, for all the research I did on the incident, in the end I barely mentioned Fred Coudert's fistfight with the German captain, and I left out entirely the pay-off of the British spy that took place in Coudert Brothers' offices in World War I. I must have been thinking that, if I put in every plum, the cake would be too rich to be digestible.

In any event, my chief aim was to write an "old-fashioned" narrative history of the sort that, combined with histories of other firms, could form the basis for a more analytical work someday. I did not begin with the idea of developing a thesis as to why Coudert Brothers survived when other did not, partly because I don't see the least use in the exercise. I don't believe there are lessons to be learned from history, because circumstances and personalities never repeat exactly.

Nonetheless, I see an argument lurking in these pages, gently hiding itself as a recurring theme. I keep repeating that the Couderts were gentlemen in their professional dealings and that they were first-rate international lawyers. I think perhaps it is high time that I drew the explicit connection and stated that, as far as

I can tell, the Couderts became preeminent in international law because they were gentlemen.

Gentleman (and *lady*) are terms in need of replacement; they carry too strong a Victorian scent. But the concept underlying both terms is a person easily able to comprehend another's point of view, to sense another's feelings, and to exercise the self-restraint that will avoid bruising those feelings. Dealing constantly, as they did, with people of different cultures, the Couderts, I believe, could hardly have succeeded if they had not been gentlemen.

In some areas of life, nice guys finish last. In international law, nice guys may actually have the edge.

In a recent speech to his partners, James Sitrick quoted Sir Isaiah Berlin's comment that America is "the only successful multicultural society in the world" and went on to comment himself that what has made its success possible is "at the core the decency, the sensitivity, and the courtesy displayed toward those who disagree with us." And it may not be unlikely that Americans like the Couderts took the lead in developing multinational law practices not only because of their country's economic strength but because Americans, when they are operating at their best, have a generous attitude toward differences. They are a friendly, open people, as such things go. Natural gentlemen, as Frederic René Coudert once said.

Sitrick, however, was making his point as a way station en route to the conclusion that "Coudert Brothers, like America, is not yet perfect, and it is my sad task to announce that perfection is unlikely to be achieved by the week after next." Yet, notwithstanding the "unprecedented competitiveness in the legal profession, and the worldwide economic recession, CB is superbly well positioned to continue its success of the past decade—if we continue to show courtesy, good will, and a little sense of humor."

If the past history of Coudert Brothers is a guide, he is surely right. Given my skepticism about the uses of history as a guide, I cannot be sure that he is, but, now that the book is done and I can be heedless of objectivity, I will say unabashedly that I am rooting for the continued success of courtesy, good will, and a sense of humor.

There may be no lessons to be learned from history. But there is a great deal of inspiration to be drawn there.

Sources and Notes

Abbreviations

CB papers—Coudert Brothers files. These include two nineteenth-century ledgers; scrapbooks on public activities of both Frederic René Couderts, father and son, including copies of unpublished speeches and articles, as well as notes for some oral arguments and the exchange of letters with Taft on the Philippine Customs cases; scrapbooks of letters from friends in France during World War I; a brief but useful memorandum on the firm's history dictated by Frederic René Coudert in 1949; the Banque de France and Black Tom files, but otherwise few client files prior to 1946.

CF papers—Coudert Family files. These include results of genealogical researches by family members and professional genealogists; Charles Coudert's farewell letters from prison and Lafayette's 1824 letter to him; hundreds of letters to Elizabeth ("Lizzie") Coudert, principally from her husband; several dozen other pieces of nineteenth-century family correspondence; newspaper clippings from a clipping service employed by the first Frederic René Coudert, (but in some cases torn or with dateline information missing); letters from Fritz Coudert to his father during World War I and law school days; a collection of letters from dignitaries to the second Frederic René Coudert from World War I onward; and numerous nineteenth-century photographs of the family.

FRC oral—"Reminiscences of Frederic René Coudert," Columbia Oral History Project.

Author's note: All quotations in text that are not attributed in the following notes are from the CB or CF papers.

Père et Fils

Lafayette ceremony: *New York Daily Tribune, New York Herald, New York Times,* and *The World,* September 7, 1876. * "To listen to him": Theron G. Strong, *Landmarks of a Lawyer's Lifetime* (New York, 1914). * "spectacular inauguration": Janet Headley, "Bartholdi's Second American Visit," in the New York Public Library, et al., *Liberty: The French-American Statue in Art and History* (Cambridge, 1986). Relocated in 1913, *Lafayette* no longer faces the statue of Washington.

Charles Coudert in France: Saumur conspiracy: Louis Desire Veron, *Memoires d'un Bourgeois de Paris,* vol. 2 (Paris, 1853). * Récamier's efforts: Duchesse d'Abrantes, *Memoires sur la Restauration,* vol. 5 (Paris, 1856). * Montmorency's reaction: Duc de Broglie, *Souvenirs: 1785–1870,* vol. 2 (Paris, 1887). * Constant, brain of opposition: Jacques Droz, *Europe Between the Revolutions, 1815–1845* (New York, 1967). * Chateaubriand: de Broglie, op. cit.; *Souvenirs et Correspondence tires des papiers de Madame Récamier,* vol. 1 (Paris, 5th ed., 1879). * Constant to Récamier: *Lettres de Benjamin Constant a Madame Récamier, 1807–1830* (Paris, 2nd ed., 1882). * Du Cayla influential; Edouard Herriot, *Madame Récamier et ses Amis* (Paris, 1904). * Escape: B. Appert, *Dix Ans à la Cour du Roi Louis Philippe et Souvenirs du Temps de l'Empire et de la Restauration,* vol. 1 (Paris, 1846); *New York Times,* Jan. 3 and 6, 1880; *Evening Post,* Jan. 2, 1880.

In New York: Frances Trollope, *Domestic Manners of the Americans,* vol. 1 (London, 1832), * Coudert as teacher: Paul Fuller, "Charles Coudert, Jr.," Bar Assn. Memorial. Longworth's Directory, 1828 forward. U.S. Census, 1850 (NYS, vol. 55, 17th ward NYC, p. 362). T. Wood Clarke, *Émigrés in the Wilderness* (New York, 1971). * "Mr. Coudert started life": *Sun,* April 23, 1892, quoted in Henry Watterson, *History of the Manhattan Club* (New York, 1916). * "leading and influential": Lyman Horace Weeks, *Prominent Families of New York* (New York, 1897). * "culture and refinement": *Ibid.* * "The prominent feature": Strong, op. cit. * Bayard: F. R. Coudert, "Attorney and Client" and "The Lawyer's Responsibilities," in *Addresses* (New York, 1905).

Brothers in Law

Education: Columbia and classics: Thomas Bender, *New York Intellect* (Baltimore, 1988). Frederick Rudolph, *The American College and University: A History* (New York, 1965). * Bar admission: David McAdam, ed., *History of Bench and Bar of New York* (New York, 1897–9); analysis of seventy-eight biographical sketches in this work of lawyers born between 1827 and 1837 yielded percentages attending high school and college. * "was stung": Paul Fuller, "Introductory Note," to F. R. Coudert, *Addresses* (New York, 1905). * Graduation address: Ibid; Sketch of FRC in McAdam, op. cit. * "very eminent": Sketch of Sanford in McAdam, op. cit. * "great reader": Fuller, op. cit.

Early practice: Notaire/avocat: Edward Patterson, "Frederic René Coudert," Bar Assn. Memorial. * "You may have an office": F. R. Coudert, "Attorney and Client," in *Addresses.* * "through his influence": *New York Times,* Sept. 15, 1882. * Gaillardet: *New York Times,* May 28 and 29, 1858. * "very early": Paul Fuller, "Charles Coudert, Jr." Bar Assn. Memorial. * Blatchford: Robert T. Swaine, *The Cravath Firm and Its Predecessors, 1819–1948,* vol. 1 (New York, 1946); Lawrence

Friedman, *A History of American Law* (New York, 2nd ed., 1985). * Hoffman/ Brady/O'Conor: F. R. Coudert, "The Bar of New York from 1792 to 1892," in *Addresses;* Coudert, "Charles O'Conor," Bar Assn. Memorial. * Fuller: Robert I. Gannon. S.J., *Up to the Present: The Story of Fordham* (Garden City, 1967); Evening Post, Aug. 14, 1915; F. R. Coudert, "Paul Fuller," Bar Assn. Memorial. * "young fellows": Elihu Root in Association of the Bar of the City of New York, *Addresses delivered February 17th 1920* . . . (New York, 1920?). * Edmonds: Charles Edwards, *Pleasantries about Courts and Lawyers of the State of New York* (New York, 1867); Arthur Schlesinger, Jr., *Age of Jackson* (Boston, 1975).

Civil War and later: "born into": *New York Times,* Jan. 2, 1896. * Johnson: Bernard C. Steiner, *Life of Reverdy Johnson* (Baltimore, 1914). * Bar Assn: George Martin, *Causes and Conflicts* (New York, 1970). * Seton Hall and Corrigan: Correspondence of the Couderts with Archbishop Corrigan, Archdiocese of New York archives. William F. Marshall, *A Sketch of Seton Hall College* (South Orange, 1895); N.Y. Catholic Historical Records Commission, *The Bishops of Newark, 1853–1978* (South Orange, 1978). Coudert Street in South Orange runs today through the former Coudert property. * Eugene Kelly: Henry Hall, ed., *America's Successful Men of Affairs,* vol. 1 (New York, 1895); *New York Times,* April 4, 1887, July 21, 1892, Dec. 20, 1894.

À Paris

1870s cases and causes: Remington Arms: *New York Herald, New York Times,* and *World,* Feb. 14, 1872 forward. Moorfield Storey, *Charles Sumner* (Boston, 1900). * Boileau: Pamela Herr, *Jessie Benton Fremont* (New York, 1987); *New York Times,* Aug. 3–4, 11–12, 1869; March 4, 15, and 28, 1873; April 10, 1873. *La France,* March 6, 1873. *Le Figaro,* March 6, 1873. * General Average: "eight rules virtually"; *The New York Maritime Register,* Dec. 18, 1878. * Statue of Liberty: "angling to steal"; *New York Times,* Oct. 6, 1876. New York Public Library, et al., *Liberty: The French-American Statue in Art and History* (Cambridge, 1986), esp. essays by Janet Headley and June Hargrove.

Paris office and family: "knowledge, acumen": Paul Fuller, "Edmond Kelly," Bar Assn. Memorial. * Fuller's "self-effacement"; F. R. Coudert, "Paul Fuller," Bar Assn. Memorial. * Charles Coudert, Sr.: *Herald,* Jan. 6, 1880; *New York Evening Post,* Jan. 2, 1880; *New York Times,* Jan. 3 and 6, 1880. * "one of the leading French lawyers": *New York Evening Post,* Sept. 15, 1882. *New York Times,* Sept. 15, 1882.

New York practice: Fuller's "kindly friendship": Coudert; op. cit. * 1882 directories: Wayne K. Hobson, "Symbol of the New Profession: Emergence of the Large Law Firm, 1870–1915," in Gerard W. Gewalt, ed. *The New High Priests; Lawyers in Post-Civil-War America* (1984). * Office atmosphere: *New York Times,* June 16, 1895. * Holden's "exhaustless patience": Paul Fuller, "Daniel J. Holden," Bar Assn. Memorial. * "graceful and incisive": Coudert; op. cit. * U.S. Electric Light: Robert Corot, *A Streak of Luck: The Life and Legend of Thomas Alva Edison* (New York, 1979). * "things which were perverse": *Philadelphia Press,* undated clipping in CF papers. * "attorneys are human"; F. R. Coudert, "Attorney and Client," in *Addresses* (New York, 1905). * "always at the disposition": F. R. Coudert, "Paul Fuller," Bar Assn. Memorial.

Championship of the Right

Women's rights; Barnard: "friendly and active:" Alice Duer Miller and Susan Myers, *Barnard College: The First Fifty Years* (New York, 1939); Horace Coon, *Columbia: Colossus on the Hudson* (New York, 1947); *New York Times,* April 17, 1895; *Proceedings at the Installation of Seth Low LL.D.* . . . (New York, 1890). * "is as stupid": *Evening Telegram,* May 5, 1894. * "are quite competent": *New York Times,* June 10, 1895.

Education commissioner: "championship" *New York Times,* Dec. 5, 1888. * Grace's campaign: Allan Nevins, *Grover Cleveland: A Study in Courage* (New York, 1932); Henry Hall, ed., *America's Successful Men of Affairs.* * "unusual zeal": Paul Fuller, "Frederic René Coudert," in U.S. Catholic Historical Society, *Historical Records and Studies,* vol. 3, (New York, 1904).

Catholicism: "contempt": address at 1890 banquet, ms. in Corrigan papers (mistakenly attributed to "James" Coudert). * "quasi-petrified" letter of March 25, 1896, in Corrigan papers. * APA: Thomas J. Curran, *Xenophobia and Immigration, 1820–1930* (Boston, 1975). * "most brilliant": *New York Times,* June 21, 1894, and Jan. 2, 1895.

Speaking ability: "noise and tumult": *New York Times,* Jan. 2, 1896. * "caused his hearers": *New York Times,* Oct. 16, 1892. * Columbia: *New York Times,* April 14, 1887; "face gleamed" *New York Graphic,* April 14, 1887. * Clubs: *Club Men of New York, 1895–97* (New York, 1896) * Billiards: Theron Strong, *Landmarks of a Lawyer's Lifetime* (New York, 1914). * "There were few": "Frederic René Coudert," Bar Assn. Memorial. * "blithesome": *New York Daily Tribune,* Dec. 21, 1903. * "personal favorite": *Herald,* Dec. 21, 1903. * "cheer after cheer": *New York Times,* Oct, 27, 1893. * "remarkable popularity": *New York Times,* Jan. 2, 1896. * "Socially": quoted in William J. C. Berry, *The Association of the Bar of the City of New York: The First Quarter-Century of Its Library* (New York, n.d.). * "quick sympathy": Paul Fuller, "Introductory Note" to F. R. Coudert, *Addresses* (New York, 1905).

Bar reforms: Field controversy: George Martin, *Causes and Conflicts* (New York, 1970). * "I have never": *New York Times,* Nov. 9, 1897. * Robinson: Mark D. Hirsch, *William C. Whitney: Modern Warwick* (New York, 1948). * "fairness, courtesy": David McAdams, ed. *History of Bench and Bar in New York,* vol. 1 (New York, 1897–9), p. 103; John L. Strong, ed., *The Arguments of the Honorable William D. Shipman and Frederic R. Coudert, Esquire.* . . . (Worcester, 1881). * "On the whole": Martin, op. cit. * Presidency: Associaton's *Minutes* vol. 3 (1885–Jan. 1895). * Maynard: Martin, op. cit.; Nevins, op. cit.; Frank Thompson, *Review of the Association of the Bar of the City of New York* (New York, 1900); Assn.'s *Yearbook,* 1892. * "Notwithstanding": *New York Times,* Oct. 27, 1892. * "hampered": Fuller, op. cit. * "have not given": *New York Times,* Nov. 1, 1894.

Reform politics: Clubs: Henry Watterson, *History of the Manhattan Club* (New York, 1916?); *Herald,* Jan. 6, 1880. * Offices refused: *Herald,* Dec. 21, 1903; *New York Times,* Dec. 28, 1892; *Commercial Advertiser,* Dec. 27, 1892; *Mail & Express,* Dec. 27, 1892; other clippings in CF papers. * Office-holding: F. R. Coudert, "Young Men in Politics," in *Addresses.* * "At the close": *New York Times,* June 21, 1894, and

Jan. 2, 1895, * "Reason must triumph": "The Anglo-American Arbitration Treaty, *Forum,* March 1897.

Coudert and Cleveland: Nevins, op. cit. * "Toledo blade": *Assn. of the Bar of the City of New York, Addresses delivered February 17th, 1920 . . .* (New York, 1920?). * Union Pacific: Letters from Coudert, April 4, 1885, and Nov. 17, 1888, Cleveland papers, Library of Congress. * Statue of Liberty: Letter from Coudert, Sept. 28, 1886, Cleveland papers; Cleveland's reply in Allan Nevins, ed., *Letters of Grover Cleveland, 1850–1908* (Boston, 1933). * "The suggestion was made": *Philadelphia Press,* undated clipping in CF papers. * "purity": April 5, 1888, Corrigan papers. * Mrs. Cleveland: *Herald* and similar articles in CF papers. * "he was fairly lifted": *New York Times,* Sept, 24, 1888. * Manhattan Club dues: FRC Oral History; Cleveland papers, Library of Congress. * 1892 campaign: *New York Times,* April 13, 1890, Oct. 9, 1891, Feb. 1 and 12, 1892; Oct. 16, 1892; *Herald,* Feb. 12, 1892. * Aimee's wedding: *Herald,* Nov. 26, 1890. * Virginia's wedding: *New York Times,* Nov. 11, 1892. * "grievously disappointed": Nevins, *Grover Cleveland: A Study in Courage.* * 1893 Court Appt.: Nevins, op. cit.; Robert McElroy, *Grover Cleveland: The Man and the Statesman* (New York, 1923); Cleveland papers.

In the Cause of Peace

Young Fred: "closest and dearest": F. R. Coudert, "Paul Fuller," Bar Assn. Memorial. * Columbia: FRC Oral History. * "Young Men in Politics": *New York Times,* Jan. 12, 1890, reprinted in F. R. Coudert, *Addresses* (New York, 1905). * "passed such a brilliant": *Freeman's Journal,* undated clipping in CF papers. * Gymnasiums: James W. Gerard, *My First Eighty-Three Years in America* (Garden City, 1951).

Bering Sea: General: William Williams, "Reminiscences of the Bering Sea Arbitration," *The American Journal of International Law;* B. F. Tracy, "The Bering Sea Question," *North-American Review* (May 1893); *Fur Seal Arbitration: Proceedings of the Tribunal of Arbitration . . .* (Washington, 1895). * Foster's objection: Patterson, "Frederic René Coudert," Bar Assn. Memorial. * Carter: Joseph S. Auerbach, *The Bar of the Other Days* (New York, 1940); F. R. Coudert, "Some Reminiscences of James C. Carter," *ABA Journal* (Nov. 1946). * "highly socialistic": FRC Oral. * Headlines: Chicago *Herald,* May 4, 1893; also *New York World, Evening Post.*

Venezuela: General: Allan Nevins, *Grover Cleveland: A Study in Courage* (New York, 1932); Andrew D. White, *Autobiography of Andrew Dickson White,* vol. 2, (New York, 1905). * Fish: Festus P. Summers, ed., *The Cabinet Diary of William L. Wilson, 1896–97* (Chapel Hill, 1957). * "Everybody here": Edward Sandford Martin, *The Life of Joseph Hodges Choate,* vol. 2 (New York, 1920). * "I make no apology": Corrigan papers. * "clear, thorough": *New York Times,* Oct. 5, 1896. * "very much the same boundary": FRC Oral.

Supreme Court cases: "brilliant" presentation: Lloyd Paul Stryker, "Frederic R. Coudert," Bar Assn. Memorial. * All other quotes from FRC Oral.

Will contest: Corrigan papers; *New York Times,* July 22 and 29, Aug. 19, Sept. 10, Oct. 3, Nov. 9, 10, and 16, Dec. 8, 1897, Jan 5, 1898.

The Torch Passes

Practice in 1899: Biographical information on CB lawyers drawn from entries in *National Cyclopaedia of American Biography, Who Was Who,* Bar Assn. Memorials, and *Evening Post* profile of Paul Fuller. Description of Brez estate provided to author by Eric Cafritz. * FRC in Spanish-American War: FRC Oral.

Insular Cases: General: FRC Oral. * "eat its cake": *The Oxford History of the American People.* * Dooley: "The Supreme Court's Decisions," in Edward J. Bander, comp., *Mr. Dooley on the Choice of Law* (Charlottesville, 1963). * "reserved the right": Loren P. Beth, *The Development of the American Constitution: 1877–1917* (New York, 1971). "judges' own feelings": Ibid. * Not logical: *History of the United States,* vol. 4 (New York, 1933).

Of Aliens and Automobiles

Frederic Renè's death: Dec 21, 1903, issues of *New York Daily Tribune, New York Herald* ("splendid constitution"), *New York Times,* and *Sun.*

Insular Cases: "He saw the waterworks": "Practical Legal Difficulties Incident to a Transfer of Sovereignty Following the Spanish War" (1902), printed in F. R. Coudert, *A Half Century of International Problems: A Lawyer's Views* (New York, 1954). * Philippines Customs: memo dictated by FRC in 1949 and copies of correspondence with Taft in CB papers. * Taft on Chinese: Champ Clark, *My Quarter Century of American Politics,* vol. 2 (New York, 1920). * Ponce: FRC Oral. * Gonzales: FRC Oral; F. R. Coudert, "Our New Peoples: Citizens, Subjects, Nationals, or Aliens," *Columbia Law Review* (Jan. 1903), reprinted in *A Half Century of International Problems.* * "Our expansion": Letter from Coudert, July 2, 1901, Theodore Roosevelt papers, Library of Congress.

Practice: Fuller: Robert I. Gannon, *Up to the Present: The Story of Fordham* (Garden City, 1967); Fordham University School of Law, 75th anniversary commemorative booklet, 1980; F. R. Coudert, "Paul Fuller," Bar Assn. Memorial. * Two types of women: Elihu Root in Association of the Bar of the City of New York, *Addresses delivered February 17th 1920 . . .* (New York, 1920?). * Selden Case: Allan Nevins and Frank Ernest Hill, *Ford: The Times, the Man, the Company* (New York, 1954); Carol Gelderman, *Henry Ford: The Wayward Capitalist* (New York, 1981); Robert Lacey, *Ford: The Men and the Machine* (New York, 1986); FRC Oral. * Highway regulation: *New York Times,* Dec. 1, 1912, Feb. 19, March 13, May 5, Oct. 25, 1913; entry for John B. Murray in *National Cyclopaedia of American Biography,* vol. 24 (New York, 1935).

War for Democracy

Legal philosophy: General: F. R. Coudert, *Certainty and Justice* (New York, 1913); F. R. Coudert, *A Half Century of International Problems: A Lawyer's Views* (New York, 1954); FRC Oral; letters to *Evening Post,* Oct. 6 and 20, 1904. * "I am a believer": *Proceedings* of the American Society of International Law (1923). * Corporation Counsel: *New York Times,* Jan. 3, 7, and 9, 1914; FRC Oral. * scandalous": *New York Herald,* March 22, 1914. * "Our whole industrial structure": oral argument, *U.S.* v. *Delaware, Lackawanna & Western Railroad Co.*, et al. * "questions of expediency": "Constitutional Limitations on the Regulation of Corporations," *Columbia Law Review* (Nov. 1906). * "watertight compartments": address to Century Club in Hartford, Feb. 12, 1904, printed in revised form in *Certainty and Justice*. * "fetiches"; unpublished speech, Feb. 2, 1911, to Phi Delta Phi law fraternity. * "Riparian Rights": *Columbia Law Review* (March 1909); *Coudert* v. *Underhill*, 107 N.Y. App. Div. 335 (1905). * "The regulation movement": "Address on Regulation of Corporations," *Journal* of American Social Science Assn. (no. 44, 1906), reprinted in *A Half Century of International Problems*. * "It is impossible": address to Century Club, Hartford, Feb. 12, 1904. * Ruggles chair: FRC Oral. * "would have seemed to them": *Proceedings* of American Society of International Law (1944).

Outbreak of war: General: FRC Oral. * FRC in France: *New York Times*, Aug. 14, and 17, Sept. 13, 1914; address in Buffalo, Feb. 7, 1915, printed in *Why Europe Is at War* (New York, 1915). * "The questions raised": "Is Neutrality Consistent with International Cooperation?" *Proceedings* of the Academy of Political Science (Jan. 1935). * "to be a buffer": letter to Frank L. Polk, Sept. 28, 1915, printed in *A Half Century of International Problems*. * *Dacia:* Frederic L. Paxon, *American Democracy and the World War* (New York, 1966).

Mexican mission: General: Clarence E. Clendenan, *The United States and Pancho Villa: A Study in Unconventional Diplomacy* (Ithaca, 1961); Howard F. Cline, *The United States and Mexico* (New York, 1963); Larry D. Hill, *Emissaries to a Revolution: Woodrow Wilson's Executive Agents in Mexico* (Baton Rouge, 1973); Arthur S. Link, *Woodrow Wilson and the Progressive Era, 1910–1917* (New York, 1954); Robert E. Quirk, *The Mexican Revolution, 1914–15* (Bloomington, 1960); Woodrow Wilson papers, Library of Congress. * "He is a Democrat": quoted in Hill, op. cit. * Dominican Republic: see Link, op. cit. * "Justice is the perfect adjustment": "Leonce Fuller," Bar Assn. Memorial. * Carrancista sympathizers: see Clendenan, op. cit. * Coudert disagrees: *Evening Post*, Feb. 13, 1913; *New York Herald*, Oct. 17, 1913 and March 8, 1914; *Evening Sun*, April 21, 22, and 27, 1914; *New York American*, April 27, 1914. * "You may be sure": quoted in entry for Fuller in *National Cyclopaedia of American Biography*, vol. 16 (1918). * "a scholar": Ibid.

Pro-Allied activities: General: FRC Oral. * Claire (Duchesse du Choiseul): Robert Descharnes and Jean-François Chabrun, *Auguste Rodin* (Secaucus, 1967); *New York Times*, March 14, 1919. * Viereck's: "Peace as a Permanent Investment," *Monthly Journal* of the British Empire Chamber of Commerce in the United States of America (April 1929). * *Appam:* "The *Appam* Case," *American Journal of International Law* (April 1917), reprinted in *A Half Century of International Problems*.

Prosperity in the Twenties
Faith During the Thirties

Estates practice: "A is an American": "Some Considerations in the Law of Domicil," *Yale Law Journal* (1927). * Lebaudy: *New York Times*, Jan. 12, Feb. 2, June 3, Dec. 23 and 25, 1919. * Gould suit: Alexander Schlosser, *Lawyers Must Eat* (New York, 1933); Kate Simon, *Fifth Avenue: A Very Social History* (New York, 1978).

Fraser: Matthew Josephson, "The Hat on the Rolltop Desk," *New Yorker,* Feb. 14 and 21, 1942; Richard Hofstedter, *The Progressive Historians* (New York, 1968): FRC Oral. * "Martyrs I suspect": quoted in Michael E. Parrish, *Felix Frankfurter and His Times: The Reform Years* (New York, 1982).

Miscellaneous: Rocca case: F. R. Coudert, "Rights of Consular Officers to Letters of Administration under Treaties with Foreign Nations," *Columbia Law Review* (March 1913). * "attitude adopted": ms. copy of F. R. Coudert's review of General F. V. Greene's *The Present Military Situation in North America* for *North American Review* (1915). "When another lawyer says": quoted in Introduction to F.R. Coudert, *A Half Century of International Problems: A Lawyer's Views* (New York 1954). * "It is always delightful": "Migratory Bird Refuges and Public Shooting Grounds," Hearings before Committee on Agriculture, House of Representatives, 67th Congress, 2nd Sess., Feb. 16 and 17, 1922; Coudert was appearing without fee for the American Game Protective Assn. * 1920s Supreme Court cases: untitled essay in Francis L. Wellman, ed., *Success in Court* (New York, 1941). "I congratulate": FRC Oral.

Baldwin (ch. 10): Description of Baldwin's views based on Keith Middlemas and John Barnes, *Baldwin: A Biography* (London, 1969).

War Again

French aircraft: Jean Monnet, *Memoirs* (Garden City, 1978); John Morton Blum, *From the Morgenthau Diaries: Years of Urgency, 1938–1941,* vol. 2 (Boston, 1965). * American people would not tolerate: unpublished speeches, esp. July 7, 1937, and Feb. 24, 1938. * "exceptional ability": letter to *New York Times,* Aug. 11, 1940. * Wildcat: Richard Thruelsen, *The Grumman Story* (New York, 1976). * Transfer of contracts: CB attorneys were not present June 16; Montgomery issued opinion letter upholding validity of transfer a few weeks later. * Effect of French orders: Monnet, op. cit., Blum, op. cit., Forrest Pouge, *George Marshall: Ordeal and Hope, 1939–1942* (New York, 1966).

Aid to Allies: "filled every chair": *New York Law Journal,* Nov. 30, 1939. * White Committees: article by Charles G. Ross, *St. Louis Post-Dispatch,* Sept. 22, 1940. * Coudert letters to Stimson: Henry L. Stimson papers, Yale University Library.

Banque de France: "important litigation": Report of the Committee on International Law," New York State Bar Assn., for presentation Jan. 23–24, 1942, represents Coudert's only public discussion of the case. He chaired the committee, and this segment of the report has his unmistakable stamp. * Movements of French and Belgian gold: Yves Bouthillier, *Le Drame de Vichy* (Paris, 1951); Robert Aron with Georgette Elgoy, *The Vichy Regime: 1940–44* (New York, 1958); Geoffrey Warner, *Pierre Laval and the Eclipse of France: 1931–1945* (New York, 1969). * Belgian cabinet's migrations: Paul-Henri Spaak, *The Continuing Battle: Memoirs of a European, 1938–1966* (Boston, 1972). * British efforts to remove gold from France: P. M. H. Bell, *A Certain Eventuality: Britain and the Fall of France* (Westmead, 1974). * Janssen: Bouthillier, op. cit.; July 1, 1940, cable conveying Federal Reserve Bank's refusal, State Dept. files, National Archives. * In Dakar: Thomas C.

Wasson, "The Mystery of Dakar: An Enigma Resolved," *The American Foreign Service Journal* (April 1943); Maxime Weygand, *Recalled to Service* (Garden City, 1952); Robert Murphy, *Diplomat among Warriors* (Garden City, 1964); Robert Mengin, *No Laurels for de Gaulle* (New York, 1966). * Slow-down tactics: Cables from U.S. Embassy in Vichy, March 6, 1941, and April 21, 1941, State Dept. files, National Archives; reports from Murphy in Algiers, Feb. 1942, State Dept. files, National Archives; Murphy, op. cit. * Britain's need for gold: Bell, op. cit.: Brian Crozier, *De Gaulle* (New York, 1973) ("acrimonious dispute"); François Kersaudy, *Churchill and de Gaulle* (New York, 1982); Martin Gilbert, *Winston S. Churchill*, vol. 6 (Boston, 1983); Warren F. Kimball, ed., *Churchill and Roosevelt: The Complete Correspondence*, vol. 1 (Princeton, 1984); David Dilks, ed., *The Diaries of Sir Alexander Cadogan, 1938–1945* (New York, 1942) ("must try to snaffle"). * "the British had tried": memo from Cochran to Morgenthau, April 11, 1940, Morgenthau papers, FDR Library. * Belgian hunger: summary by Howard Dexter White of Treasury, April 10, 1941, in preparation for Gutt's meeting with Morgenthau, National Archives; Gutt press conference, *New York Times*, April 8, 1941. * "The Belgians must eat": *New York Times*, April, 18, 1941; also April 6, 1941. * "The anxiety": Kimball, op. cit. * Hunger blockade generally: Gilbert, op. cit., Murphy, op. cit., William L. Langer, *Our Vichy Gamble* (New York, 1947). * Feis for blockade: Joseph P. Lash, *Roosevelt and Churchill, 1939–1941* (New York, 1976); Langer, op. cit. * "The President was cold": Spaak, op. cit, * White Committee division over Lend-Lease: William Allen White, *The Autobiography of William Allen White* (New York, 1946). * Coudert for Lend-Lease: unpublished Feb. 6, 1941 address to Long Island chapter of White Committee; *Christian Science Monitor*, April 23, 1941; *New York Times*, March 18, 1941. * Bundles for Britain: *New York World-Telegram*, May 3, 1941. * "When the Belgian government": Jan-Albert Goris, *Belgium in Bondage* (New York, 1943). * Dulles/cartels: allegation seems to have orginated with I. F. Stone in *PM* article of June 4, 1944; Nancy Lisagor and Frank Lipsius, *A Law Unto Itself* (New York, 1988). * FBI report: April 25, 1942, in National Archives file. * Banque de France medal: letter from Maurice Force to Alexis Coudert, Jan. 8, 1953, CB files; medal was probably not awarded, but it has not been possible to confirm either way. * Campaign charges: *New York Times*, Sept. 29, Oct. 20, 27, 28, 30, and 31, 1942.

Author's note on Banque de France case: Tom Finletter went to Washington, D.C., to work under Feis sometime in 1940; this was supposed to be a temporary position but was made formal in March 1941. Coudert Brothers was first consulted by the Banque de France's special representative around February 21, 1941; in late February or early March 1941, Fred Coudert visited Washington prior to leaving for Cuba to attend the Inter-American Bar Assn. meeting organized by the State Dept. Knowing how careful Coudert had been during World War I to clear all his activities as U.S. counsel to the Allies with the U.S. State Department, how closely he had worked with Stimson in World War I and on White Committee matters, and how ardently Coudert wanted a British victory, this author believes that in Washington Coudert discussed the proffered Banque de France retainer with Stimson, Feis, or possibly Cordell Hull (whom he also knew). It would have been most extraordinary if Coudert, who had been close to so many secretaries of state and done so many unofficial errands for them; had not sought some kind of unofficial clearance before entering into a case that was, in truth, a matter of state. This author believes that Coudert did leave Washington with an indication that certain highly placed persons would prefer, in the interest of Britain's successful prosecution of the war, that Belgium's suit be blocked. This belief is based strictly on the author's knowledge of Coudert's character, opinions, and habitual methods of operation; such conversation, if indeed they ever took place, was certainly not recorded.

Reconstruction and Renewal

Greer Case: David W. Peck, *The Greer Case* (New York, 1955).

Growing with the Clients

Central Park: "unwise invasion," *New York Times*, Aug. 28, 1963.

1969: Avant le déluge

Hensel's navy service: see, for example, Eric Larrabee, *Commander in Chief* (New York, 1988).

Riding the Waves of Foreign Investment

1970s practice: Banking survey: *International Financial Law Review*, March 1983. * Arthur Leve profile: written by Geoffrey Hellman but not published owing to Leve's death. * "much more fun," *The American Lawyer*, June 1980. * Susan Goldberg, letter to editor, *The American Lawyer*, July/Aug. 1983.

A Special Grace

Cohen and China: Jan Morris, *Hong Kong* (New York, 1989).

Acknowledgments

I am profoundly grateful to Ferdinand W. Coudert, whose generosity of spirit, concern for the scholarly integrity of this project, and many kindnesses greatly facilitated my researches. Because of his help, his father and grandfather are alive in my mind and, I hope, on these pages.

Frederic R. Coudert, III, Tracy Coudert, Paula Coudert Rand, and William Rand also provided much kind assistance. On the Fuller side of the family, I am indebted to Paul Fuller, Jr.'s daughter, Mrs. Louis K. Timolat, his son-in-law John Hurd, and especially his grandson Michael Hurd, who made available to me the fruits of his own many years of genealogical research.

At Coudert Brothers, it was Jonathan D. DuBois who opened doors for me, and throughout the four years of research and writing, his interest and support were invaluable. My good friend of thirty years, Jane C. Rubens, a Coudert Brothers attorney, first introduced me to the firm. It was Jane who suggested I write this book, provided encouragement and the benefit of her long experience with Coudert Brothers, and in many ways, small and large, facilitated the project.

I am also grateful to the numerous current and former partners and employees of Coudert Brothers who submitted to interviews. A special thanks, however, is due to four retired partners, whose length of memory made them particularly valuable sources of information and who, as a result, were heavily taxed with re-

429

quests for further detail and enlightenment. Gerald Dunworth (who unfortunately did not live to see the final publication), Hugh F. Fitzgerald, James S. Hughes, Sr., and Allen Russell responded to my requests with unflagging courtesy, good humor, and sympathy.

I benefitted from an essay on Coudert Brothers' history that Eric Cafritz had earlier prepared and made available to me. Arless Leve kindly gave me a copy of the *New Yorker*'s proofs of Geoffrey Hellman's unpublished article about her father. I gratefully acknowledge permission from the Archdiocese of New York to use the Coudert letters in the papers of Archbishop Michael A. Corrigan.

Laura Seitz generously shared with me information she had collected on James Richards, and W. Graham Matthews made available the valuable fruits of his researches into the Panama Canal purchase. Count René du Chambrun gave me copies of letters written by John B. Robinson and other information.

I am indebted for assistance in research to Nancy Alderman, Margo Biberman, Milinda Cody, Charles L. Creesy, Vija Doks, John Franklin, Laura W. Haywood, Kay Long, and Rebecca Wright. Milo Coerper, partner in the Washington office, saved me much labor and expense by arranging for the locating and photocopying of documents needed from Washington, D.C., depositories.

And a special debt is owed to my mother Virginia S. Kays, the late Gladys Walterhouse, and my very patient husband Willem Veenswijk.

INDEX